RADICAL VISIONS
AND AMERICAN DREAMS

RADICAL VISIONS
AND AMERICAN DREAMS

CULTURE AND SOCIAL THOUGHT
IN THE DEPRESSION YEARS

Richard H. Pells

HARPER & ROW, PUBLISHERS

NEW YORK, EVANSTON, SAN FRANCISCO, LONDON

1817

To Warren Susman

CONTENTS

INTRODUCTION

If the writing of history is not only a means of understanding the past but also a form of communication to the present, then few historical episodes better illuminate the strengths and weaknesses of modern American life than the experience of the Great Depression. The 1930s was a time in which many of the tensions that still afflict our culture and society were most dramatically revealed. The ability of American political institutions to respond to a crisis of unprecedented proportions, the effort to find effective remedies for a sick economy, the fervent desire to experiment with new types of artistic expression, the growing importance of the mass media and popular culture, the very capacity of ordinary men and women to adapt to change while still preserving intact some of their basic ideals, all these were central issues with which Americans wrestled throughout the decade. More important, the way in which such dilemmas were resolved (or ultimately evaded) continue to have important consequences for the kind of society we live in today. Thus any effort to re-examine the conflicts and passions of the 1930s becomes, inevitably, a commentary on contemporary problems as well.

The present study attempts to explore the impact of the depression on American culture and social thought. More specifically, it focuses on the efforts of a number of leading American intellectuals to discover alternatives to those political beliefs, economic institutions, social values, and artistic preoccupations that had dominated the nation prior to 1929. In this enterprise, many writers and artists hoped to persuade their fellow citizens that the American people could never be adequately fed or clothed or housed or employed as long as they continued to rely on a capitalist economy, that the United States must break at last with the liberal tradition both politically and philosophically, that an individualistic and competitive value system had become not only obsolete but inherently destructive to the nation's social and psychic stability, and that the country desperately needed a new literature, a new theater, and a new cinema in order to bring all of these changes about. These ideas led in turn to an intensification of the intellectual's desire to overcome his historic isolation from public affairs, to make his essays and novels and plays and films more meaningful in the lives of ordinary people, to devise a realistic program and strategy for democratic socialism, to create a new spirit of community and cooperation throughout the land, and to help inspire a genuine political and cultural revolution that would transform the lives of every American.

Nevertheless, though their intentions were innovative and radical, it is possible to see (particularly in the years after 1935) an underlying conservatism in their outlook as well as in the implications of their ideas. Many of the positions developed in the early 1930s could be used either to change or to reinforce the existing culture and social structure; the latter tendency became more pronounced during the closing years of the decade. It is my contention, then, that intellectuals in the 1930s were both radical and conservative, ideologically sophisticated and hostile to social theory, artistically experimental but also hungry for popular acceptance, at once critical and supportive of traditional American ideals. In the end, however, these contradictions were by no means unique to the depression experience; they are at the very center of the American intellectual's continuing ambivalence toward his native land.

Every author brings to his subject certain controlling questions and concerns, and these frequently determine what material will be used and which ideas will be emphasized. In my own case, I wished to investigate the depression experience not only as a crisis for American culture and society but also as an opportunity to discuss some more general issues that have plagued intellectual life in the twentieth century. If I could offer no solutions, I wanted at least to deal with the continuing problems of the role of the writer in American society, the relationship of art to politics and ideology, the connections between reform and revolution, the effort to build a democratic mass movement which could still remember its radical objectives, the inevitable tensions between cultural rebellion and social change. At the same time I felt it necessary to explore not only the programs and ideas of literary critics and media theorists but also to find out what themes and values were actually being portrayed in the novels, plays, and films of the period. Finally, I wanted to examine the 1930s as a test case for the strengths and weaknesses, the contributions and failures of American radicalism in the modern world.

As a result of these preoccupations, I decided to deal primarily with the ideas of writers and artists who were generally associated with the Left. It was not my purpose, however, to discuss once again the factional intrigues of various radical groups, nor to engage in another debate about the influence of the Communist party on intellectuals; this has been done elsewhere and perhaps at excessive length. Moreover, because I was more interested in what was actually written during the period (rather than in the second thoughts of the decade's survivors) and because I believe that what intellectuals write for public consumption is more important than what movements they join or what petitions they sign, the work pays less attention to organizational activities, private correspondence, and subsequent memoirs than to those sources which appeared in the decade itself: journal articles, books, novels, plays, and films. Above all, I wished to avoid as much as possible the traditional categories of analysis, to ask new questions about the nature of the decade's political and cultural commitments, to assess the significance of issues like planning, the search for community, the fascination with symbols and myths, the desire for a counter-culture and a counter-morality different from those of the middle class, the strain of existentialism that seemed to underly the period's radical façade.

Given the assumptions and purposes of the book, certain principles of selection followed. For the most part, I would concentrate on those writers and artists who most effectively presented the ideas or advanced the arguments with which I was especially concerned. At the same time, I tried to remain faithful to what seemed the major preoccupations of the intellectual community itself during the 1930s, and so I focused on those themes and issues that continually reappeared in the works of art and the social criticism of the decade. In sum, I sought to analyze statements that were representative or influential, as well as those that best revealed the central values of the period. Thus I traced the debate over concepts like planning and the changing attitudes toward the New Deal and the Soviet Union as they emerged in the magazines and books of the 1930s. But I also dealt at length with certain works which, while they were not necessarily widely read or discussed at the time, still served as characteristic expressions of the decade's intellectual mood: Robert Lynd's *Knowledge for What?*, Mordecai

Gorelik's *New Theatres For Old,* the novels of Daniel Fuchs, James Agee's *Let Us Now Praise Famous Men.*

But no matter how inclusive I attempted to be, there remained several important but unavoidable omissions. Some intellectual tendencies were excluded because they did not seem to reflect or have an impact on the ideas of those writers under consideration. Thus there is little mention of Keynesian theory, nor any discussion of the European emigrés who fled from fascism to the United States in the 1930s; both these movements exerted a more visible effect on American thought during and after World War II. Similarly, though I analyzed the extent to which the Southern Agrarians and the New Critics shared certain assumptions in common with their antagonists on the left, I did not deal with conservative social critics such as Walter Lippmann and Lawrence Dennis, whom radicals largely ignored. For the same reasons, I chose to neglect trends within the academic community. Most of the writers and artists whom I studied had no official relationship to the universities, and their ideas developed outside the formal disciplines of history, economics, or sociology. Finally, some figures simply did not fit into any category on which I was relying. Hence playwrights such as Eugene O'Neill as well as novelists such as John O'Hara, F. Scott Fitzgerald, and Thomas Wolfe are briefly cited but not extensively evaluated; for these omissions I have only regret.

Behind the author's methodology, however, lies his basic attitude toward the subject. My own feeling is that the 1930s raised crucial questions which we have not yet satisfactorily answered, that many of its economic ideas and works of art were genuinely creative, and that the ultimate failure to construct an alternative culture and social philosophy has left tragic consequences for the intellectual and political life of the country in the years after 1945. As a result, we are left to grapple not only with the meaning of the depression experience but also with its legacy to our own time.

There are several people who have been extremely important in influencing the organization and conception of the book, and I should like to thank them here. Donald Fleming of Harvard University provided invaluable advice on matters of style and structure from the very beginning of the enterprise. John Higham of the University of Michigan offered both encouragement and shrewd criticism. Mark Solomon of Simmons College gave me the benefit of his own ideas, his experience, and his friendship. Patricia Wismer read the entire manuscript, and her response, as a non-expert, was sometimes more significant than that of the professional historian. My wife, Betty, displayed superhuman understanding, sympathy, and patience from beginning to end. Needless to say, their aid has strengthened the book, but for its weaknesses I alone am responsible.

I should also like to express my gratitude to Harvard University, the University of Texas, and the Charles Warren Center for Studies in American History, whose research grants afforded me the time and resources to complete the manuscript.

Finally, I must acknowledge the man to whom this book is dedicated. Many of his suggestions are incorporated in the work; many of his ideas are reflected in the argument; many of his objections have forced me to revise my own point of view. But more important, Warren Susman has served as a model of what a teacher, a historian, and an intellectual ought to be. I am more grateful for that than anything else.

—RICHARD H. PELLS

RADICAL VISIONS
AND AMERICAN DREAMS

CHAPTER I

PROLOGUE—PROGRESSIVISM
AND THE 1920s

One of the more compelling myths about American history is its susceptibility to categorization by decades. Especially in the twentieth century, when successive crises seem to produce a new generation every ten years, Americans are peculiarly addicted to the notion that monumental changes occur with the taking of the census. Thus we tend to think of the Progressive era as having ended conveniently around 1919; the 1920s as a self-contained entity closes appropriately in 1929 with the stock-market crash; the depression dutifully lasts ten years and is followed by the postwar decades, each of which assumes a singular personality usually drawn from the party in power.

While this way of visualizing the past does correspond to reality in important respects, it nevertheless obscures the continuity of movements, issues, and ideas over a longer period of time. It may be more accurate to consider the social and cultural experience of America as an ongoing series of tensions and conflicts, none of which is ever more than temporarily resolved. In this view, certain events become somewhat less cataclysmic than they originally appear, and a legendary crisis does not usher in a "new era" nearly so much as it passes on the problems of the old.

Yet the sense of living in a totally new situation is not entirely imaginary. For those who have been wounded by some massive social upheaval, the psychological scars remain to shape the way they see and act in the world. The issues they confront may be part of the nation's heritage, but their mental set, the words they use to describe their perceptions, the special urgency with which they search for solutions, the mood of a society coping with what it thinks is unprecedented, all combine to form a distinctive state of mind which becomes *in fact* something genuinely new. The feeling of hovering uncertainly between past and future, traditional and revolution-ary, makes every emergency seem apocalyptic, but at the same time it forces people to deal with reality and with themselves in ways that are often truly creative. In this mixture of old and new, a decade can be seen both as a transmitter of historic controversies and as a unique period of time in its own right.

It has been customary to proclaim October 1929 as the month that symbolized the death not only of the 1920s but of a simpler, more pristine America. With the collapse of the Wall Street boom, a new age presumably was born—one which would alter the institutions and character of the country beyond recognition. Indeed we instinctively respond to the 1930s as the beginning of our own time; it is somehow "modern" and contempo-rary in contrast to the earlier, more remote decades of the twentieth cen-tury. As we watch old films on television or in revivals, as fashion designers return to the depression for stylistic ideas, as politicians debate the legacy of the New Deal, it is easy to conceive of the decade as a social and cultural watershed between "our" world and "theirs." But many of those who lived through the 1930s revealed, however unconsciously, a far greater sense of their relation to and dependence on the past than we now acknowledge. On a variety of levels—political, economic, social, intellectual—the principles and programs of these years had their roots in the Progressive era and the 1920s. It is in the beliefs and experiences which preceded the depression that we find an initial understanding of what the depression itself meant.

1. *The Dynamics of Prewar Reform*

The opening years of the twentieth century were crucial in molding the outlook, expectations, and assumptions of the intellectual community as well as those of ordinary men and women. During the height of Progressiv-ism a number of social and cultural ideas coalesced briefly around the movement for immediate political reform. The seeds of the Progressive spirit had germinated slowly in the years following the Civil War, fertilized by the often disparate values and aspirations of free-lance intellectuals and university professors imbued with the ideal of public service, novelists and journalists suddenly conscious of their "social" obligations, agrarian radi-cals and urban labor leaders, declassed professionals, socialists of all tem-peraments and doctrines, men of old wealth disturbed by the brutalities of industrial capitalism and uneasy about their own status in modern society, an increasingly anxious middle class frightened by monopolization on the one hand and by the potentially revolutionary "lower classes" on the other, and an emerging generation of politicians sensitive to the new moods. Traumatized by the depression of the 1890s and the wave of Populist agitation threatening to engulf the land, searching for "new frontiers" to replace the one Frederick Jackson Turner announced was now closed, these groups merged by the turn of the century into a loose and occasionally incompatible alliance of reformers bent on testing their ideas, hopes, and fears in the laboratory of state and national politics.

From the outset, Progressivism as a model for social change meant different things to different men. For some among the older middle class, the Progressive movement promised a restoration of competitive capitalism, the resurrection of laissez faire, the dismantling of monopolies and trusts, a decentralized economic order, and the revival of personal opportunities somehow diminished by the rise of industry and the city.[1] For others, the heyday of Jeffersonian individualism was already passed, if it had ever really existed. To the new professionals, technicians, and managers—themselves creations and servants of corporate America—Progressivism involved what Robert Wiebe has called a search for "order": an effort to grapple with the inherent anarchy of economic life by introducing further elements of organ-ization and stability to industrial capitalism. Together with some business-men (and many socialists), they shared the desire for a rationalized economy, the urge for a more efficient system of production and distribu-tion, a growing reliance on executive and administrative decision-making, an acceptance of bureaucracy, and a longing for reforms that might elimi-nate the danger of widespread social chaos. Though great concentrations of wealth and power still bothered them, they were averse neither to monopoly nor to regulation.[2]

Yet whether they followed the "New Freedom" of Woodrow Wilson or the "New Nationalism" of Theodore Roosevelt, the men of the Progressive generation were seeking some way of coming to terms with and retaining control over the new institutions of twentieth-century America. Living at the dawn of an era extraordinarily complex and increasingly interdepen-dent, forced to adapt to conditions for which neither agrarianism nor nine-teenth-century liberalism had adequate explanations, they strove to make sense out of the modern world with ideologies and forms of political action that blended old and new. Ironically, they became radical innovators with profoundly conservative goals.

It was probably the intellectuals who saw more clearly than anyone else the need for a different set of concepts and attitudes with which to understand and act upon social conditions. For nearly a century they had felt themselves out of touch with American life—isolated from the centers of power, repelled by the dominant ethic of greed and acquisitiveness, yet largely unable to bring the values of the mind into harmony with daily experience. Rarely were they comfortable in the role of critic or artist. When Progressivism appeared, with its emphasis on rational persuasion and social change through education, many writers eagerly enlisted in the army of reformers. Since the Progressives assumed that America might be remodeled through the application of intelligence to social problems, and since they had an abiding faith in the capacity of ideas to awaken public virtue, the movement was in its turn perfectly suited to the skills and ambitions of the intellectual community.

For these reasons, the cultural mood of Progressivism seemed peculiarly utilitarian. The yearning to experience "reality" no matter how sordid, to influence politics no matter how corrupting, to be of "service" no matter what compromises were involved led a number of writers to forgo detached inquiry and speculation—indeed to abandon the very belief that such speculation could ever be truly disinterested. The age of a priori truths and timeless values was dead. In its place, men grew more sensitive to the ways in which thought was determined by history, culture, and class. Theory, they discovered, must henceforth be related to the surrounding environment. Thus Pragmatism emerged as an experimental philosophy for human action. The law was seen as an accumulation of judicial decisions rather than as a set of fixed constitutional principles. Historians shifted their preoccupation with the past to a conscious concern for the present. Social scientists studied the personality and behavior of men against the background of existing institutions. Educators rejected formal pedagogy and sought instead the adjustment of the child to contemporary social needs. Journalists and novelists adopted naturalistic techniques to expose the underside of American life in the hope of stimulating reform. Intellectuals began to visualize themselves as advisers to statesmen, and in 1912 one of their own finally captured the Presidency for them all.[3]

Perhaps their creed was most eloquently expressed in Herbert Croly's The Promise of American Life, where the impulse toward a democratic collectivism was elevated to a cultural as well as an economic ideal. Croly published his book in 1909. It rapidly became the bible not only of the Roosevelt wing of Progressivism but also of that group of liberal intellectuals whose voice became the New Republic after 1914—among them John Dewey, Walter Lippmann, Walter Weyl, George Soule, and Bruce Bliven.

While many of Croly's ideas were later substantially modified and expanded, they served as the point of departure for an entire generation of writers who believed that America could be fundamentally transformed without having to endure a violent revolution. As such, *The Promise of American Life* was both an influential summary of the prewar reform spirit and a classic illustration of how the liberal mind evolved during the first three decades of the twentieth century.

Essentially, Croly argued that the United States desperately needed a thoroughly new ideology, political order, and value system which might correspond to changes in the structure of social and economic life. The tradition of individual opportunity, small-scale enterprise, and unlimited personal freedom had been supplanted by an age of corporate consolidation, the growth of specialization in business and politics, and the rise of labor unions designed to protect the interests of employees as a group. Yet in Croly's estimation, Americans still viewed the world with the archaic conceptions of the nineteenth century. This conflict between outmoded mental habits and new social conditions was a major cause of their present predicament. "The existing concentration of wealth and financial power in the hands of a few irresponsible men," Croly asserted, was itself "the inevitable outcome of the chaotic individualism of our political and economic organization."[4] Where the nation had once thrived on the ethic of competition and private gain, it could now neither tolerate nor return to a society based on these principles. Instead, the "promise of American life" was to be fulfilled "not merely by the maximum amount of economic freedom, but by a certain measure of discipline; not merely by the abundant satisfaction of individual desires, but by a large measure of individual subordination and self-denial."[5]

Specifically, Croly recommended an acceptance of economic and political centralization as the most efficient means of organizing a modern society. This meant the development of a strong national government capable of regulating giant corporations in the public interest, the use of taxation to redistribute wealth, the elevation of labor unions to parity with government and industry, and a general faith in leadership and expertise as the guiding instruments of reform. At no point, however, did he advocate socialism. Seeking to protect as much as possible the areas of "individual self-expression," but recognizing that new forms of liberty depended on basic changes in the economic order, he nevertheless insisted that "the institution of private property in some form" be preserved.[6] At bottom, Croly was groping toward the idea of a mixed economy as the best way of making personal initiative compatible with social welfare.

Yet Croly's outlook was never exclusively economic or political; indeed, his paramount concerns were always psychological and moral. A combined form of private capitalism and state ownership might resolve some of the contradictions in American life, he conceded, but the "unity" of such a society "must lie deeper than any bond established by obedience to a single political authority, or by the acceptance of common precedents and ideas. It must be based . . . upon an instinctive familiarity of association, upon a quick communicability of sympathy, upon the easy and effortless sense of companionship."[7] In short, Croly's stance was fundamentally cultural; he envisioned an almost mystical community in which men made their own distinctive contributions to a country of shared goals and values. Nationalism to Croly was more than the sum of America's political and economic institutions; it represented an "organic" society in which individuals and groups harmoniously interacted. "The individual becomes a nation in miniature," he proclaimed, "but devoted to the loyal realization of a purpose peculiar to himself. The nation becomes an enlarged individual whose special purpose is that of human amelioration, and in whose life every individual should find some particular but essential function."[8] In this way, personal freedom and social responsibility could both be served.

The attractiveness of Croly's book to his generation lay in its implicit glorification of middle-class virtues, as well as in its ability to propose radical reforms without departing too far from the present social order. By justifying the trend toward economic and political consolidation as generally "progressive," and by re-emphasizing the merits of individual effort and leadership as important elements in his philosophy, Croly permitted men to adjust more easily to the new world while retaining at least some of the values of the old. Moreover, his reliance on technicians and experts, his positive nods to efficiency and organization, his rejection of a labor movement committed to socialism suited well the skills and self-image of the rising managerial class. Finally his nationalism, no matter how democratic or organic, seemed particularly appropriate to a country entering the world arena as a major power. Thus Croly had given to the Progressives at precisely the right time a unified and coherent social theory which allowed them, temporarily, to see some order in an otherwise bewildering experience.

If *The Promise of American Life* contained the substance of Progressive thought at its most refined, the essays of Van Wyck Brooks announced the specific role writers wished to play in implementing these ideas. Between 1915 and 1917 Brooks published a series of provocative articles which attempted to explain why the nation's intellectuals had led such a marginal existence during the nineteenth century and to set forth the sort of tasks they could reasonably undertake at present. Although Brooks's subject was somewhat narrower than Croly's, he was equally preoccupied with the problems of culture and community. Like Croly, he hoped to discover some point of unity, some organic interrelation between self and society that could help reshape American life along more satisfying lines. And like Croly, he offered both his own generation and its successors a compelling terminology with which they could better understand their world.

"America's Coming-of-Age," his most famous essay, appeared in 1915. It contained Brooks's seminal ideas and provided a new way of discussing the nature and role of American art. Writers, Brooks contended, had been historically alienated from an environment which was itself divided between ideals and reality, piety and opportunism, culture and finance. These strains he labeled "Highbrow" and "Lowbrow," both of which he dismissed as equally undesirable.[9] Nevertheless the conflict between those dedicated exclusively to thought and those engaged solely in material acquisition left the writer in an intellectual and emotional vacuum. "The theoretical atmosphere in which he has lived," Brooks declared, "is one that bears no relation to society, the practical atmosphere in which he has lived bears no relation to ideals. Theory has become for him permanently a world in itself; practice has become simply a world of dollars."[10] Consequently American writers remained suspended between the world of intellect and the world of action, never able to see how one might reinforce the other.

What Brooks proposed was the creation of a "middle tradition, a tradition which effectively combines theory and action," the roots of which he found in the career of Walt Whitman.[11] To Brooks, the significance of Whitman was that he gave Americans for the first time a sense of something "organic" in their lives. Although the word as Brooks originally used it was intentionally vague, organicism became the central metaphor in his mind for an alternative culture and society.

In "America's Coming-of-Age" as well as in the *Seven Arts*—the celebrated journal he edited with James Oppenheim, Waldo Frank, Randolph Bourne, and Paul Rosenfeld between 1916 and 1917—Brooks diagnosed the central disease of American civilization as an insane individualism. This historic obsession with self-reliance and personal achievement not only distorted economic practice but made it impossible for the nation to develop the spiritual and emotional resources necessary for a truly healthy society. Even American artists had been seduced by the ethic of individualism, Brooks suspected. Retreating either into an alienated solitude like Nathaniel Hawthorne or totally absorbing the values of the surrounding environment like Mark Twain, they had failed to produce a national culture in which the entire society could participate fully. "Our ancestral faith in the individual and what he is able to accomplish . . . as the measure of all things," Brooks declared, "has despoiled us of that instinctive human reverence for those divine reservoirs of collective experience, religion, science, art, philosophy, the self-subordinating service of which is almost the measure of highest happiness."[12] Lacking a tradition in which "art and thought and science organically share in the vital essential program of life," American society was intolerably fragmented, chaotic, anarchistic.[13] If the culture was divided between thought and action, art and reality, these were only symptoms of a cancerous incoherence that afflicted every cell of the nation's life.

For Brooks, like Croly, the formation of a genuinely organic social and cultural experience depended on the substitution of self-fulfillment for self-assertion. This implied the adoption of a completely new value system as well as new economic institutions. Americans had to recognize that their identity and freedom were fundamentally "social," that their psychic health demanded cooperation and mutual responsibility, that the ideals of competence and craftsmanship in a collective enterprise were ultimately more satisfying than personal aggrandizement. Thus the individual "personality," like the solitary artist, must discover a "middle plane between vaporous idealism and self-interested practicality" in order to establish an "organic" interrelationship with other men.[14] In sum, Brooks was calling for the creation of a new community—one which he sometimes described as "socialist"—that would fuse man's private desires and his social instincts. As with Croly, his philosophy rested on the elemental conviction that "the more deeply and urgently and organically you feel the pressure of society the more deeply and consciously and fruitfully you feel and you become yourself."[15]

Articulated most clearly by Croly and Brooks, this effort to synthesize theory and practice, liberty and community, self and society lay at the heart of the Progressive movement—and it would continue to attract the imagination of radical intellectuals and activists in the following decades. The prewar writers were hoping to forge a unique alliance between culture and politics, and their concept of reform embraced every facet of the nation's experience. As Christopher Lasch has shown, they were offering "political solutions for cultural problems and cultural solutions for political problems. On the one hand, they proposed to improve the quality of American life by means of public administration. On the other hand, they proposed to attack such public problems as the conflict between capital and labor by eliminating the psychological sources of conflict, by 'educating' capitalists and laborers to a more altruistic and social point of view—in other words, by improving the quality of men's private lives."[16] When the Progressive generation spoke of corruption and exploitation, they meant these words to have an ethical as well as an economic meaning. When they called for the development of a national culture, they envisioned not only an artistic renaissance but also a revolution in values and behavior that would extend beyond the elite and the avant-garde to affect the life of the average citizen. When they urged the creation of a new sense of community, they intended not only the further democratization of social and political institutions but also, in Brooks's phrase, "a kind of spiritual teamwork" that could heal the psychological divisions in American life.[17] At times, writers came dangerously close to investing the reform movement with burdens it could not possibly bear. By giving politics a function which was largely moral, and by demanding that art undertake the salvation of society, the tenuous balance between social and cultural concerns was always threatening to collapse—as after 1917 it did.

In sum, Progressivism represented the first response of the twentieth century to those transformations in industry, technology, labor, communications, and urban living which threatened to obliterate nineteenth-century America. No longer would unlimited expansion, competition, and production of goods bring automatic progress; instead, men had to rely increasingly on planning, efficiency, and expertise in controlling the rate and direction of change. Because Croly and Brooks were among the few to codify these sentiments into a clear philosophy, and since much of the earlier frontier mentality lingered on to shape political rhetoric, the Progressive movement adapted most uneasily to the new conditions. Constantly hovering between the desire to break up the monopolies and restore laissez faire on the one hand, and the need to make corporate capitalism function more effectively on the other, the Progressives remained ambivalent in their analyses and contradictory in their legislation.

Nevertheless, in many areas they provided a symbolic union of thought and action whose example the 1930s would try to duplicate in form if not in substance. For the generation of intellectuals who came to maturity during these years, the Progressive crusade offered a unique opportunity to influence policy, develop and publicize programs appropriate for the new society, and help generate a revolution in literary as well as in political life. Whether one sought in the *New Republic* to modernize liberalism by tendering careful advice to the Wilson Administration, or called in the *Seven Arts* for a national aesthetic which would rejuvenate the American spirit, or proclaimed in the *Masses* that the time was ripe for both socialism and personal liberation, writers again enjoyed the heady experience of participating actively in the nation's daily affairs. The specific doctrines mattered less than the general feeling that art and politics, consciousness and society could indeed be joined. Whether they marched with Roosevelt, Wilson, or Debs—whether their ideas carried conservative and even anti-intellectual implications not to surface until much later in the century—the Progressives invented the language and set forth the goals that future movements for social change would naturally inherit.

As long as these impulses could be translated into concrete legislative proposals, particularly on the state level, Progressivism flourished. While they could concentrate on specific reform measures, writers and politicians were able to overlook the tensions and inconsistencies that underlay their activities. Yet in the name of anti-bossism and citizen participation they devised the long ballot, complex referendums and non-partisan city elections, all of which made it virtually impossible for "democracy" of any sort to function without the aid of political machines. Valuing the administrative skills of neutral experts and bureaucrats, they created commissions to regulate industry and transportation and thereby helped to diminish competition even more by encouraging only the most efficient and centralized enterprises to survive. Trusting in the informed individual to promote and direct social action, they often mistook exposure of a problem for its solution, while neglecting the possibilities of group and class conflict as additional incentives for change. Seeking to represent the "public" as a whole, the Progressives ignored the extent to which they spoke only for the bourgeoisie. Largely excluded from the Progressive consensus were the immigrants, the workers, and the blacks—all of whom provided dynamite for the social explosions of the 1930s. Thus the Progressive movement inevitably foundered on the more fundamental questions involving the structure and future course of American society, the basic redistribution of wealth and power, and the ultimate purposes of social innovation in an increasingly illiberal age. Eventually the coalition of reformers, politicians, and intellectuals began to dissolve as the issues of war and revolution replaced those of urban corruption and trust-busting.

2. The Political Mood of the 1920s

For many Progressives, America's entrance into World War I, the failure to produce a peace consonant with Wilsonian ideals, and the inexplicable intervention in Russia's revolution were mortal wounds from which the entire movement could hardly recover. Looking back on the experience in the 1920s, one of the *New Republic* editors lamented: "The war did no good to anybody. Those of its generation whom it did not kill, it crippled, wasted, or used up."[18] For those who witnessed the slaughter first hand, as well as for those who stayed home to brood on the collapse of Wilsonian idealism or to follow the ideological confusion within the Socialist party over its stand on the war and Bolshevism, the years between 1917 and 1920 were profoundly disillusioning. Some, agreeing with Randolph Bourne that liberalism had been irrevocably shattered by its support of the war and Versailles, renounced political action altogether (though not necessarily the zeal to renovate America which had brought them into reform politics in the first place). Others continued to cultivate their liberal principles but in the far less fertile soil of the 1920s. And still others, disheartened by their failure to merge art and revolution, and appalled by the decline of the Socialists as a mass party embracing different groups and regions throughout the country, found themselves politically and culturally adrift in the era of Harding and Coolidge. It was not that Progressivism as a program or ideology suddenly died in 1919, but rather that it disintegrated into its component parts. No longer a workable coalition, the Progressive example nevertheless remained as a memory from the past and a model for the future.

The intellectual community found itself after 1919 in a world that seemed only to magnify many of the problems with which the Progressives had desperately struggled. The war had accelerated the trend toward economic consolidation. Wartime planning had momentarily stabilized industrial production and the distribution of goods, reorganized the chaotic transportation system, allocated priorities along more rational lines, expanded the discretionary power of the President, and generally served as a prototype for an ordered and efficient economy. Though government controls were rapidly withdrawn after the armistice, the indirect effects of the war experience could be seen throughout the 1920s in the increasing standardization of products and processes, the emphasis on scientific management and technical expertise, the growing reliance on large-scale manufacturing and finance, and the emergence of trade associations to reduce competition further. Corporate capitalism was in full bloom, nourished by rising prices, the expansion of credit and installment buying, the spectacular performance of the automobile and service industries, the revival of residential construction, the highly publicized exploits of real-estate speculators, and the apparently inexhaustible profits to be made in the stock market.[19]

In the wake of these developments American society began to take on the look of a white-collar paradise, complete with chain stores, suburban housing booms, the dependence on recreation as an escape from work and on advertising as a guide to life, and the dual appearance of the radio in the living room and the movie theater in the neighborhood. Largely hidden from view were the more unpleasant realities of life in the 1920s, particularly the rise in technological unemployment as machines replaced men in the factory, together with the decade-long depression in agriculture, mining, and textiles. For most Americans the 1920s was a period not so much of prosperity as of sheer survival, with little money left over after the bills were paid to enjoy the party others seemed to be throwing. And as the years wore on, it became increasingly difficult for the average man to consume what the economy could produce—an ominous sign which the pitchmen of the "new era" chose to ignore.

On the surface at least, the 1920s seemed an unpropitious time for reform or radical activities. The fervent hopes and pervasive optimism of the Progressive era were both casualties of the war. The carnage on the battlefield and the intrigues at Versailles exposed the liberal faith in social reconstruction through education, reason, and intelligence as naïve and even dangerous illusions. Moreover, domestic politics after Harding's triumph in 1920 offered little to sustain the imagination or energies of those dedicated to remodeling society. The Progressive coalition was badly splintered. Though it managed to come together briefly in 1924 under the banner of Robert La Follette, the entire Presidential campaign exuded the feeling of a last fling, a one-shot performance that could not survive the defeat and death of its most charismatic star. Throughout the decade, Progressivism existed more as a cluster of ideas and unrelated programs than as a serious political movement on a national scale.

The Left fared even worse. The Socialist party was in appalling disarray, riddled with internal divisions, weakened by defections to the infant Communist sects, unable to regain its prewar prestige or strength.[20] The legendary IWW, victimized by governmental repression and a failure to sink permanent roots in the trade unions, with its leading figures in jail or in exile, virtually disappeared as an effective radical organization. Yet neither the AFL, having lost a series of major postwar strikes and now growing more conservative in an age hostile to labor, nor the new Communist party, with its factional struggles and sectarian posture, could realistically speak for radical alternatives.

Despite these formidable obstacles, the reform spirit managed to remain alive after 1920. Though many artists and literary critics proclaimed their disenchantment with politics and decided to concentrate exclusively on cultural affairs, an important group within the intellectual community retained some interest in political action even if its members could not agree among themselves on programs or ideology. Because the prospects for change appeared so much more limited in the 1920s, however, the mutual tolerance which marked the prewar debate between liberals and socialists had vanished. Instead their mood was now characterized by internecine bickering and apocalyptic visions. A sense of confusion surrounded these writers and affected the magazines to which they contributed. All felt isolated from American political life and frustrated by their inability to influence its direction. Yet to abandon politics altogether seemed to them only an admission of one's impotence. Throughout the decade they felt it necessary to define their own position in relation to the rest of America; this constant search for a suitable role was woven into every program they advanced. Marginality bred a crisis of identity.

Four publications spoke for and enlarged upon their dilemma. The leading heir to the Progressive synthesis was the *New Republic*. Its editors had encountered a series of shattering blows to their hopes for liberal reform, beginning with the failure of the Versailles peace conference to implement the lofty goals of a war they had originally supported, and culminating in the La Follette defeat, which symbolized for them the official burial of the Progressive movement as a political force. Nevertheless, the presence of Herbert Croly's name on the masthead represented their link to the past, even though he was no longer an active participant after 1928. The *New Republic* carried on under the slightly tarnished banner of liberalism throughout the 1920s, remaining influential largely because it was able to attract some of the leading writers of its time. From 1923 on, daily control passed to experienced journalists such as Bruce Bliven and George Soule. Book reviews, always a crucial part of the magazine, were edited by T.S. Matthews, Robert Morss Lovett, Edmund Wilson, and, in the following decade, Malcolm Cowley. An impressive cast of regular contributors included John Dewey, Stuart Chase, Lewis Mumford, and Charles Beard.

The *Nation* took even more pride in its reputation as the historic voice of liberalism in America. But the magazine reflected the personal idiosyncrasies of its leader, Oswald Garrison Villard, and it regularly found space for more peripheral issues than its sister journal, the *New Republic*. The tone and point of view were entirely Villard's; sympathy for Britain, insistence on free trade, and campaigns for the public ownership of natural resources dominated its pages. Only in the literary department, under the guidance of Mark Van Doren, Joseph Wood Krutch, Henry Hazlitt, and Freda Kirchwey, did the magazine express a unified outlook or exert a substantial influence on contemporary thought.

If the liberal periodicals frequently wandered about an issue in search of a consistent philosophy, their radical colleagues possessed definite programs but few opportunities to apply them to specific problems. The 1920s, if often indifferent to reformist proposals, were even less hospitable to socialist ideas. While a number of European countries appeared ripe for revolution in the war's aftermath, America emerged from the conflict as the world's leading creditor nation and strongest capitalist power. War had not fulfilled the Marxist prophecy so far as the United States was concerned; rather than eroding the foundations of America's economy, it had reinforced them immeasurably. The resulting sense of prosperity and complacency led radicals to feel despair at the present while dreaming of revenge in the future.

On the whole, the *New Masses* maintained a commitment to positive thinking. When it began publication in 1926, its masthead boasted a glittering array of artists, literary and social critics, novelists, poets, reporters, and anyone who could vaguely classify himself as socialist. In theory the journal was attempting to resurrect the non-partisan vigor and experimentation of its illustrious ancestors, the *Masses* and the *Liberator.* But the tone and style of the *New Masses* in the late 1920s were largely the work of Michael Gold, and those less dedicated to radical politics or a particular form of art gradually withdrew. Meanwhile, the Communist party emerged as the guiding ideological force in the magazine's development.

Yet to be a "communist" or "socialist" in these years meant very little. One was simply a "radical," more or less influenced by Marx. No periodical better expressed this eclecticism than the *Modern Quarterly.* Born in 1923 as the private organ of its editor, V.F. Calverton, the magazine published almost anyone who would write for it. Calverton himself demonstrated a remarkable capacity for absorbing diverse and contradictory ideas. He operated his journal as a clearinghouse for whatever seemed to him "modern" in the world of culture and politics, psychology and socialism, sex and revolution. Although its most frequent contributors by the end of decade were confirmed Marxists like Max Eastman and Sidney Hook, the *Modern Quarterly* attracted intellectuals from both the liberal and radical camps.

Each of these publications hoped in some way to influence both the intellectual community and, if possible, the larger society. None acquiesced in powerlessness; all of them scorned the expatriate example as an escape from social responsibilities. The immediate tasks therefore were to arrive at a definition of their own function, clarify their relation to America in the absence of a mass movement for either reform or socialism, and discover an effective political strategy they could reasonably follow.

For radicals none of this was easy to do. Severely disappointed by the failure to save Sacco and Vanzetti in 1927, aware of the structural weaknesses in the façade of Coolidge prosperity but unable to convince or even reach the average citizen, and exhausted by a decade of factional controversy and political defeats, writers assaulted one another in lieu of an enemy who would not respond. In the pages of the *Modern Quarterly,* Calverton summarized the mood of futility which harried left-wing intellectuals during the 1920s: "With the dominant parties there are no significant issues at stake, and with the minor parties what issues there are have either been weakened by compromise or obscured by an unfortunate, although courageous, denial and defiance of reality. Nowhere is there light or hope. The radical movements of Europe have little meaning or application on American soil. American radicals are isolated from the American scene."[21]

The failure of the radical parties to develop realistic and concrete programs for America was duplicated in the eyes of the *Modern Quarterly* and the *New Masses* by the liberals' refusal even to think in ideological or broadly conceptual terms. If radicals sounded too European and doctrinaire, the liberals seemed entirely too pragmatic and restrained in their analysis. Throughout the decade, the contributors to both journals vigorously attacked their liberal counterparts for an unwillingness to pursue a problem to its ultimate roots, for a fragmented view of society that focused on its discrete parts at the expense of the whole, for a naïve trust in education and parliamentary institutions while ignoring the virtues of class struggle, for an inability to see that the governing elite would never voluntarily relinquish or modify its power but must instead be fought by revolutionary means, and for an all too simple faith in the goodness of human nature to stimulate change without appreciating the extent to which capitalism had imprisoned man's intellect and warped his emotional life.[22]

Not wishing to appear excessively dogmatic, however, the *Modern Quarterly* and the *New Masses* insisted that they were as empirical and "scientific" as the liberals. Indeed they claimed that their version of science revealed a greater sensitivity to the laws of historical development and the interrelatedness of social conditions than the Pragmatists, who conceived of science solely as technique and experimentation devoid of values or goals. Convinced that Marxism provided a comprehensive view of the world and a political strategy far superior to the liberals' timid dependence on democratic processes and piecemeal solutions, the radicals contended that only socialism could liberate modern industry from the fetters of private profit, poverty, and exploitation.

Yet their appeals frequently met with monumental indifference. For most socialist writers the 1920s was, in the somber words of Michael Gold, "a decade of betrayals . . . dominated by Ramsay MacDonald, Mussolini, and other Judases."[23] It was a period they tried to endure stoically, consoling themselves that an apocalyptic upheaval would soon clear away the economic and cultural debris of a sick and decadent society. The revolution of which radicals spoke was not merely a form of political action but a cleansing force. Secretly yearning for a catastrophe that would topple the madhouse they were certain America had become, the radicals looked forward to a time of purification in which the United States could begin anew as Russia seemed to be doing. Living in and for the future, always the future, they believed with Gold that "this depression, this cowardice, this callousness and spiritual death will not last forever among the youth of America. This mean decade of ours will pass on."[24]

There was some truth in the radical accusation that liberal journalists failed to extend their analysis to its ultimate conclusions. Throughout the decade the *New Republic* and the *Nation* tended to assume the permanence of capitalism, and thus advised their readers to work through existing political institutions. Moreover, they often approached issues in a partial way, examining them as specific difficulties to be solved through the proper legislation proposed by individual progressives within the two major parties. Both magazines conducted an unceasing crusade against private power monopolies and prohibition, dutifully supported the organization of labor unions and urged more income for the farmer, advocated a reduction in armaments and the recognition of Russia, criticized Versailles and warned against America's entrance into the League of Nations. The *Nation* carried on its own personal war against the protective tariff. Yet much of their discussion lacked the kind of sustained economic and social criticism with which radicals hoped to expose the system as a whole.

Nevertheless this concentration on particular details did not stem, as the radicals would have it, from a congenital evasiveness on the part of liberal intellectuals. For one thing, it reflected the prewar belief that the solution of immediate problems was a necessary first step on the road to more fundamental change. For another, it resulted from the liberal denial of a "system" as such. It was absurd, argued the *New Republic* editors, to be either "for" or "against" capitalism because the economy was "not a well defined and static 'order.' It is itself changing, a very disorderly and uncertain condition of flux." One had to weigh separately both its good and bad features. "Capitalism," Bruce Bliven and George Soule reminded their readers, did provide improved standards of food consumption and housing, an expansion of education, and new commodities like the automobile. It had produced more goods, generated a spectacular rise in national income after the war, stabilized prices, validated the theory of high wages, reduced working hours, and moderated the historic cycle of boom and bust. But each of these contributions, they felt, should be measured against the disadvantages inherent in the economy: the nagging depression in agriculture as well as in coal and textiles, real wage rates that remained static or declined even as production continually climbed, the persistent failure of collective bargaining, the implacable survival of unemployment, serious inequities in the distribution of wealth, the limitation of prosperity to the industrial states, rigid tariff barriers, and the inflation of speculative credit.[25]

To deal with these matters, the *New Republic* called through most of the 1920s for more information, greater expertise, and stronger regulatory commissions. Minimizing the effectiveness of mass pressures and class conflict, the editors chose instead to rely on short-term reforms, open-ended experimentation, and knowledgeable administrators. They warned that would-be revolutionaries must first pay attention to "concrete struggles, which may seem individually of slight import or dull to those who have their eyes fixed on a broad regeneration of society."[26] But specific programs designed for particular problems seemed to them the only rational way to alter institutions, especially in a decade so hostile to social innovation of any sort.

Therefore it was predictable that many liberals would endorse Al Smith in the election of 1928. Their reasons were interesting because they revealed the state of mind and set of values most politically oriented writers held at the time. The *New Republic,* still hoping to influence public policy and taking seriously its responsibility to provide political direction to the intellectual community, carefully studied the available options before announcing its support for Smith. Its editors were prepared to agree that only a radical party would truly reorganize American life, but radicalism had "for the time being" failed. Writers and artists could not by themselves transform society, and the working class with whom they might be allied was presently apathetic and inert. The liberal, in their view, should thus acknowledge the intrinsic limitations of political activity, recognize that voting for a minor party was just a "negative intellectual assertion," and concentrate on the immediate task of finding an effective alternative to those Republicans who had become the spokesmen for plutocracy. Realistic political action, not theoretical debate and agitation, was the principal requirement at the moment.[27]

This argument was not merely a concession to expediency. Hoover reminded the *New Republic* editors of an eighteenth-century philosopher rather than the engineer or scientist he was supposed to be. He seemed unable to deal with problems in a precise or experimental manner, they complained; instead he resorted to abstractions about the merits of an eternal laissez-faire world.[28] It did not matter that Hoover in his actual policies may have been much closer to the *New Republic*'s attitudes than its editors ever admitted. Certainly he understood the degree to which the American economy was no longer competitive, and his vision of a tightly integrated, corporate commonwealth was not so very different from Herbert Croly's. Nevertheless Hoover's unforgivable sin, in the eyes of the *New Republic*, was that he sounded too much like an ideologue, too much the theoretician, too much the intellectual.

For similar reasons the *New Republic* rejected the Socialist party—not so much because Socialists were radical but because, like Hoover, they too were impossibly doctrinaire and wedded to untested generalizations. "The failure of industry and government," the journal observed, "is too complex to be laid out in pretty, logical lines according to any preconception, whether radical or conservative." Therefore, the editors threw their support to Al Smith because he symbolized to them the type of hardheaded, practical politician who would handle issues in an empirical, concrete way. The attack on national problems, they proclaimed, "is bound to be piecemeal, realistic, and experimental, in so far as it makes any headway at all in solving those problems. This sort of thing is what we understand by progressivism—not a magnificently loyal adherence to some ready-made set of comprehensive principles."[29]

On one level, this was simply a shrewd reading of the contemporary scene. Since they foresaw no social upheaval in the near future, since Hoover's victory itself ratified the "sense of well-being in a successful capitalist order" that most people seemed to feel, the editors were trimming their sails to the prevailing political winds.[30] But on another level, these ideas expressed a certain anti-intellectualism, a discomfort with theory and abstract social analysis that sometimes verged on self-hate. In a strange way, many liberals rejected Hoover because he was too much like themselves. Their disdain for ideology, their attraction to whatever appeared useful and practical, their obsession with being "realistic," all reflected a gradual retreat from the values of the mind—at least on the part of those writers still concerned with politics—which may have been the decade's most damaging legacy to the 1930s.

Nevertheless, it would be a mistake to assume that this tendency toward anti-intellectualism was the only or even the most important strain in liberal thought during the 1920s. No flurry of detailed recommendations could satisfy the desire for a broader perspective on social problems. To many liberals, the primary lesson of the Progressive experience was the need for less moral exhortation and a more sophisticated attitude toward questions of class and power. They were not nearly so oblivious to the underlying structural defects of American capitalism as the radicals imagined. Where they differed was in the search for some way of making their programs directly relevant to present circumstances. On the one hand, as an antidote to what they considered the misty idealism of the Progressive era, contributors to the *New Republic* and *Nation* argued for concrete legislation which could pass Congress and be effectively enforced. On the other hand, they were still entranced by the dream of a totally new society. Thus they longed to find a middle ground between abstract theory and practical politics, combining for themselves the role of social critic and influential adviser to those in power, just as Herbert Croly had tried to do. For liberal writers in the 1920s, the Progressive example was not so much forgotten as simply in need of redefinition and reapplication to contemporary issues.

This was especially true after the brief recession of 1927. Many liberals realized that the "new era" in economics had not exorcised the specter of a full-scale depression. Consequently, the need for an effective set of ideas and tactics was even more acute. While radicals eagerly seized on every sign of economic weakness as a confirmation of their belief that revolution must inevitably follow the next social disaster, less apocalyptic observers confined themselves to probing beneath the prosperous surface of American life in an effort to uncover the roots of ultimate collapse.

George Soule, who had become an editor of the *New Republic* in 1923 and served thereafter as the journal's most authoritative voice on economic affairs, continually pointed out the danger signals of depression. Prosperity in the 1920s, Soule maintained, had depended from the outset on a rapid expansion in auto sales and the rise of new service industries. Moreover, demand had been conveniently buttressed by installment buying and easy credit. But now the boom was vulnerable. For the first time since 1921, he suggested, people were spending less, the purchase of automobiles was slowing down, and housing construction had begun to decline. Meanwhile, the trend toward monopoly that had infected the economy since the Civil War made it unusually difficult for business to adjust its rigid price structure to these new conditions. In a more general way, America was feeling the impact of its decade-long tendency to overproduce goods, at the very time foreign and domestic markets were shrinking.[31] At this juncture the only force that kept the economy afloat was the hypnotic ticker tape on Wall Street. With all eyes on the stock market, Soule commented, "a whole nation is speculating in a sense in which a nation never speculated before."[32]

Yet ironically the market and the boom it continued to fuel were both generating inflationary pressures beyond actual demand, and thus helping to dig prosperity's grave.

To Soule, the fundamental problem was the failure either of real income to rise or of prices to fall. Corporate profits increased enormously during the decade but were never adequately rechanneled into private investment, higher wages, or fuller employment. This in turn led to a serious maldistribution of wealth and purchasing power. The vast majority of Americans simply could not consume what they produced. At some point in the future, warehouses and retail stores would be choking with goods, but there would be no one to buy. Then the speculation would end, and the gaudy monuments of the "new era" would come tumbling down.

But Soule and the *New Republic* were unwilling to interpret these difficulties as necessarily intrinsic to capitalism. Instead they preferred to focus on the problems of purchasing power and overproduction as flaws in an otherwise acceptable economic system. Given this perspective, however, they were certainly capable of calling for far-ranging reforms to deal with such questions. Occasionally the *New Republic* came very close to advocating some form of nationalization, some means of moving beyond capitalism, even before the 1930s. In the late 1920s the editors were already contending that a depression could not be prevented by sporadic public works projects. What America really needed was an "agency of social control" which could direct national development, regulate capital investment, organize the country's credit resources, and expand purchasing power. Yet this still might not be enough. "Depression and unemployment undoubtedly arise," they concluded, "from a lack of plan and from the spasmodic and haphazard activities of private enterprise."[33] Throughout the decade they rebuked business for its essential chaos and anarchy. The evils of competition and individualism were just as vivid in their minds as they had been in Herbert Croly's. Words like "planning" and "control" consistently flavored their language, though their search for solutions almost always stopped short of socialism.

Yet no matter what sorts of criticism they leveled at private enterprise during the years before the stock-market crash, most liberal intellectuals saw reform as a way of strengthening capitalism. The main obstacle, in the *New Republic*'s view, seemed to be the obtuseness of businessmen who did not recognize that social and economic change could help them in the long run. Why were industrialists and bankers unable to understand, complained the editors, that a strong labor movement would result in more efficient production, that a fairer distribution of wealth would increase purchasing power for their goods, that lower tariffs would open up foreign markets for American surpluses, that the private planning they used inside their own corporations could have its analogy in public planning for natural resources and urban development?[34] If only the capitalists themselves could be converted, the cooperative commonwealth of government, labor, and business envisioned by the Progressives might still become a reality. Armed with the proper analyses, programs, and arguments, the editors assumed that they could help accomplish this conversion.

In any event, the *New Republic* remained convinced that radical ideologies were simply irrelevant to the problems of American life. Whatever the weaknesses and fantasies of liberal thought, "to believe that a proletarian philosophy may be brought into being in this country where the germs of class-consciousness are scarcely discernible is to submit to a self-delusion."[35] Thus the editors were left in a curious position, denying the possibility of socialism on the one hand but acknowledging the need for substantial modifications in capitalism on the other.

Ultimately they chose to rest their case with Veblen and Croly rather than Marx. Admitting the growing collectivization of American society, they placed their faith in technicians, engineers, and professional groups, instead of in the working class. Even the labor movement was advised to depend on experimentation, not dialectics. "It is . . . entirely possible," they declared, "that the point of departure for American collectivism may be function, rather than class consciousness. This may be the unique aspect of our culture."[36] Therefore they urged the adoption of new techniques and strategies that would closely fit those conditions peculiar to America. The idea of a *functional* collectivism based largely on middle-class organizations and a pragmatic labor movement permitted them to advocate reforms which sounded radical, while at the same time they were able to draw back from the threat of revolution. In short, the *New Republic*, as the representative voice of many liberal intellectuals, was trying desperately to keep its feet in both the capitalist and the socialist camps, though committing itself firmly to neither.

3. *Values, Morals, and Life-Styles*

Whatever the ambiguities of the liberal or radical stance during the 1920s, there were many intellectuals who no longer believed in political activity of any kind. Nor did they assume that economic reforms would automatically lead to improvements in the quality of American life, a greater appreciation for works of the mind, or a stronger sensitivity to relations among men. For them, the Progressive effort to forge an alliance between culture and politics appeared increasingly futile.

The prewar generation had managed to combine, however briefly, an interest in psychology, education, literature, and social change. No reform movement seemed complete unless it included a program for the liberation of the spirit as well as for the reorganization of institutions. The men who wrote for the *Masses,* the *New Republic,* the *Nation,* or the *Seven Arts* during these years all shared the dream of a new society transcending bourgeois values, Puritan codes, and genteel standards of art. Moreover, they saw the intellectual's role as crucial in posing alternatives both to the existing social order and to the repressive cultural climate that prevented America from achieving its full potential.

Yet even before the war there was some skepticism about the relationship between cultural and political revolution. Writing in the *Seven Arts* in 1917, Van Wyck Brooks criticized Pragmatism for emphasizing intelligence and practicality at the expense of imagination as the supreme "value-creating entity." In Brooks's opinion, the followers of John Dewey were afflicted with a "complacent, mechanistic view of life" and had thereby "sanctioned the type of mind whose emotional needs are so limited that the efficient pursuit of some special object is all that it demands of life."[37] Randolph Bourne extended this attack much further when he accused liberals generally of elevating technique above ideals, a position that led them in turn to sacrifice their independence and integrity in the service of Woodrow Wilson's war. Both Brooks and Bourne were already questioning whether programs for social and economic change should be so closely entangled with the desire for a renaissance in art and philosophy.

It was not until the 1920s, however, that the union between culture and politics began visibly to disintegrate. To some readers, the economic discussions which dominated the lead editorials and articles in the *New Republic* and *Nation* seemed peripheral to the main problems of the decade. Politics appeared a dreary business, best left to the administrators and bureaucrats. Those who tried to restore the influence of Progressivism or to create a viable radical movement in the United States were wasting their talents and energy. No one was listening. Thus at a time when it had become much harder to sustain a faith in the possibilities of reform on any level, a number of intellectuals tried to redefine their roles on a somewhat narrower basis. In so doing, they hoped to confine themselves to areas in which they could truly be effective.

Waldo Frank, a colleague of Brooks on the *Seven Arts* and a man who had always considered himself something of a socialist, spoke for many in the following decade when he observed that institutional changes were presently impossible "until we have . . . a previous revolution in the attitude and vision of the American people." Given the confusion and lack of purpose which seemed to characterize modern society, "no mere effort for economic reform can effect American rebirth." In Frank's judgment, "a creative reconstruction of American life is only feasible by means of groups of men devoted to the causal task of spiritual re-education, of the creating of values. . . ." Here he was insisting on the need for a fundamental transformation in outlook and consciousness, together with a new conception of life's potentialities. "The essence of the issue at this stage is moral —is spiritual," he declared.[38] And the primary task of the writer, the way in which he might make a genuine contribution, was to focus principally on cultural problems. For only when the nature and quality of American civilization were fully explored—only when men knew precisely what psychological and metaphysical forces accounted for their present malaise— could they again think rationally about forms of political action.

Thus the intelligentsia in the 1920s launched an extensive critique of American society which stressed not so much its political corruption or economic inequities as its stupidity, aimlessness, and vulgarity. Writers who were themselves children of the middle class eagerly repudiated bourgeois habits, assumptions, and prejudices.

The most exhaustive analysis of this kind occurred in a symposium edited in 1922 by Harold Stearns, called *Civilization in the United States.* The title was deliberately ironic since the participants concluded that America in fact had no civilization worth mentioning. Many of the contributors' ideas were clearly drawn from those Van Wyck Brooks had first articulated in 1915. Throughout the essays there ran a persistent complaint that American life was irrevocably divided between theory and practice, ideals and experience, culture and the market place. Lewis Mumford castigated the modern city for its devotion to commerce and industry at the expense of human living; there could be no shared purpose or sense of community among the skyscrapers, factories, and thoroughfares designed for people to spend money rather than time. The physical growth of the nation had brought forth a populace that was emotionally impoverished: "The highest achievements of our material civilization—and at their best our hotels, our department stores, and our Woolworth towers are achievements—count as so many symptoms of its spiritual failure." Ultimately, Mumford declared, "the industrial city did not represent the creative values in civilization; it stood for a new form of human barbarism"[39] Elsewhere in the volume Van Wyck Brooks lamented the absence of a genuine national culture, H.L. Mencken chortled over the idiocies of the average American politician, George Jean Nathan chronicled the decline of the theater, and George Soule offered a post-mortem on the death of radical politics. Others exposed the national deficiencies in education, advertising, art, business, the small town, and family life. Stearns himself delivered the symposium's central message when he traced the typical American "contempt for mere intellectual values" to the "native pioneer suspicion of all thought that does not issue immediately in successful action."[40] This traditional hostility to culture and the affairs of the mind accounted for the country's addiction to pragmatism, its obsession with practicality, its insane race for wealth and success. The basic trouble, in Stearns's view, was that "we still *think* in pioneer terms, whatever the material and economic facts of a day that has already outgrown their applicability."[41]

The assumption that nineteenth-century values had lingered on into the modern world, thereby freezing America in attitudes totally inappropriate to twentieth-century conditions, was particularly appealing to intellectuals in the 1920s. Over and over again writers reproached the pioneer for destroying the wilderness but substituting nothing in its place, exalting the principles of individualism and competition while ignoring the benefits of cooperation and community, and sacrificing art to the hard demands of daily survival. Where Frederick Jackson Turner had identified the frontier as the cradle of American democracy, Lewis Mumford in *The Golden Day* charged it with betraying all that was valuable in human civilization. The difference between the two interpretations itself demonstrated how the issues had changed. While Turner in 1893 was primarily concerned with political and economic problems, and thus sought to explore the frontier past as a way of posing structural alternatives for the present, Mumford in 1926 focused largely on the cultural and literary legacy of the pioneer—and found it responsible for the mental sterility of American life. Where Turner could envision new forms of democracy through political action and governmental intervention, Mumford's more cosmic perspective made reform of any kind seem trivial and hopeless.

Nevertheless the emphasis on values and life-styles, as opposed to questions of state and finance, permitted intellectuals to deal with matters over which they might exert some influence. By arguing that the central dilemma of American life was its outmoded ideas and attitudes, writers could then point to a change in consciousness as the only legitimate means of transforming society. And who was better suited to offer new ideals and values than the intellectual himself?

Hence when William Ogburn offered his conception of "cultural lag" in

Social Change, a book published in 1922, the term quickly became an important part of the intellectuals' vocabulary. Drawing on the insights of both sociology and anthropology, Ogburn speculated that nations or groups resisted innovation because their customs, mores, and mental habits did not correspond to changes in material conditions. For various reasons their "culture" lagged behind developments in science, technology, and industry. At certain crucial points, the tension became so acute as to cause serious physical and psychological breakdowns in a given society. Not until new forms of mental and social behavior were invented could balance be restored. To many writers in the 1920s, this sounded like a perfect description of America's own predicament.

Ogburn had provided a tool of analysis that others found easy to use. Perhaps the most celebrated application of his ideas occurred at the end of the decade. In 1929 Robert and Helen Lynd published *Middletown,* their now classic examination of Muncie, Indiana, which bore the revealing subtitle "A Study in Modern American Culture." The book was not only a superb sociological investigation of middle America during the 1920s, but it also illuminated brilliantly the uncertainties, frustrations, and pain which ordinary men and women had suffered in trying to adapt to a new world.

From the beginning the Lynds wanted to explore the effects of economic and technological developments on attitudes toward work, leisure time, education, religion, and the family. Although they were careful to distinguish between the middle and working class in terms of the way each adjusted to the twentieth century, they assumed that all the citizens of Middletown were faced with certain common experiences and problems. Using 1890 as the symbolic year in which the nineteenth-century pioneer spirit finally gave way to the industrial revolution, the Lynds recorded the impact of mass production, electricity, the telephone and telegraph, advertising, the automobile, the radio, and films in transforming every aspect of human life in Middletown.

What they chose to emphasize was not so much the economic consequences of industrialization as its destruction of traditional neighborhoods and communities, the isolation of men from one another, and the individual's sense of being at the mercy of external forces over which he had little control. The average worker, they found, no longer took any satisfaction or pride of craftsmanship in a job that demanded the subordination of his personality to the routine of the assembly line. Large offices and factories located far from the homes of the employees made the entire work process seem strikingly impersonal. For both classes, only the weekly paycheck invested the job with any real meaning or purpose. The ability to earn and spend money had become the main compensation for an otherwise pointless life.

Moreover, the Lynds discovered that the use of leisure time, the retreat into family affairs, the perpetual urge to consume could all be just as unrewarding as work itself. None of these provided an escape from the problems of the twentieth century. The people of Middletown were being subjected to conflicting pressures. On the one hand, the automobile, the radio, and the movies contributed to the disintegration of family and class solidarity by making leisure largely an individual pursuit. On the other hand, the mass media tended to standardize habits, attitudes, and values, absorbing the city into an increasingly homogeneous nation. In neither case could men any longer feel themselves a part of some identifiable local or regional community. As the church and schools ceased to be effective transmitters of moral ideals, as the sense of shared expectations declined among groups and within the home, the individual was either thrown back on himself or became more and more dependent on prepackaged and stereo-typed images for whatever emotional sustenance he could find.

In the areas of both work and play, the Lynds concluded, Middletown clearly exemplified the problem of cultural lag. Change was occurring on different levels at different times, and men could not easily synchronize their ideas or behavior to the new environment. "A citizen," they observed, "has one foot on the relatively solid ground of established institutional habits and the other fast to an escalator erratically moving in several directions at a bewildering variety of speeds. Living under such circumstances consists first of all in maintaining some sort of equilibrium."[42] In an effort to overcome this maladjustment, at least temporarily, the people of Middletown had engaged during the 1920s in an orgy of civic boosterism, club-joining, and a general insistence on conformity to the accepted mores and values of the city. Desperately and somewhat pathetically, Middletown was trying to "link its emotional loyalties together, to vote the good-fellow ticket straight" in response to "its increasing sense of strain and perplexity in [a] rapidly changing world that can be made to hang together and make sense in no other way."[43] To the Lynds, this eruption of conformity and organized group activity represented a tenuous balance between old and new, between the individualism of the nineteenth century and the isolation of the twentieth, between the standardizing influence of the mass media and the search for a genuine sense of community.

The authors tended to sympathize with Middletown's attempts to impro-vise group experiences because they realized that these were symptoms of a profound cultural crisis. The outburst of "school spirit," the Babbitt-like camaraderie of the Rotary Club, the transformation of religion from a set of beliefs to a social occasion, the hostility to criticism of any kind, all testified to the need for shared values and purposes which modern American civilization seemed unable to provide. The plight of Middletown was a microcosm of what had been happening throughout the country since 1890. That the Lynds decided to focus on the collapse of ideals and behavior patterns when confronted by a revolution in economic life only reflected the particular perspective of the 1920s. But the recurring desire for some sort of group ethos, the insistence on new forms of cultural adjustment, the assumption that social change in America had to mean more than political reform would all become major themes in the following decade as well.

Middletown was as exhaustive an analysis of American society as the 1920s produced. Yet there were other problems that disturbed writers beyond those the Lynds raised. Much of the decade's concern with the impact of science and technology on human behavior expressed a widespread feeling that life in the United States was becoming increasingly mechanized and bewildering. Ever since the late nineteenth century, writers had been ambivalent about the advance of science, never certain whether it promised a new millennium or a menace to man's very survival. Throughout the Progressive era, these doubts were submerged beneath the liberal conviction that scientific methods could be effectively applied to the solution of social problems. But when the war demonstrated the destructive uses to which technology could easily be put, and when the Pragmatists came under attack for their unquestioning faith in intelligence and technique despite mounting evidence of human irrationality, the lingering reservations about science were revived. It was not surprising that a book like *The Education of Henry Adams*—with its somber warning that civilization was mortally threatened by the new scientific discoveries—became a bible for many intellectuals in the 1920s.

Many of the decade's efforts to understand and deal with science centered around the symbol of the machine. Unable to decide whether it represented the most sophisticated achievement of the modern mind or a supreme expression of evil, writers sought to assess the machine's impact on the economy, on literature, and on man's capacity to sustain a rational life. But in all these areas, the analysis invariably centered on science and technology as metaphors for an abstract and soulless universe rather than as concrete tools for use in daily affairs.

One of the more characteristic appraisals in this vein appeared in the *New Republic* during 1929 under the title "Men and Machines." Written by Stuart Chase, the series attempted to chart the direction in which American society seemed to be moving under the navigation of modern science. His conclusions were far from comforting. Chase focused explicitly on the danger of automated unemployment and argued that inventions no longer served mankind. In the past technological discoveries had opened up new opportunities for employment while contributing to the general progress of civilization. But since 1921 this process appeared to have ended. "A new job," Chase observed, "can no longer be created as fast as the machine tips a man out of an old one. Adjustments which used to have the freedom of years must now be made in months."[44] Even the middle class was suffering a kind of proletarianization as their jobs became mechanized. With production growing more efficient, purchasing power remained stagnant and surpluses piled up. Technology, in Chase's view, was now introducing the specter of mass unemployment, and no one seemed able to control the course of automation or avert an inevitable collapse.

Chase was appalled by the paradox of a situation in which technological improvements meant human catastrophe. Production was no longer socially useful. America had arrived at a stage where "the better we are able to produce, the worse off we shall be. This is the economy of a mad-house. The machine, God knows, is willing enough; but we lack the directing intelligence to make it function."[45] In short, the liberal reliance on knowledge and expertise stood helpless before the unharnessed power of science.

If this description of the present was bleak, the lack of alternatives was positively terrifying. For Chase envisioned no way out. Recognizing that "only a profound readjustment in the whole financial structure . . . [could] bring this vicious process to an end," he rejected both reform and radicalism as possible solutions.[46] The liberal formula of specific legislative proposals was far too limited in the face of what was truly an all-encompassing crisis. But the Marxist faith in a massive social upheaval, ending in the abolition of production-for-profit, was much too dangerous. Machines had created such an interdependent and complex civilization that to tamper with the mechanism at any one point might trigger a breakdown of the entire apparatus. To Chase, the problems inherent in modern technology resembled a disease of the central nervous system; revolution could not cure but only paralyze.[47] Having scorned partial reforms and drawn back in horror from the abyss of revolution, Chase was left with nothing to do but trace the progress of the disease as it slowly consumed the American people. His position was a perfect example of the decade-long tendency to portray a problem in such cosmic terms that political or economic solutions seemed painfully irrelevant.

Where Chase was disturbed by the effects of technology on the social order, the poet Babette Deutsch feared its impact on the whole modern sensibility. As society grew more dependent on scientific abstractions, she feared that opportunities for direct personal knowledge and feeling would diminish. Since these were the roots on which art thrived, the machine threatened to strangle literature at its source. Men, she complained, were no longer familiar with the processes that ruled their lives. The relation between the individual and the things he used had become starkly impersonal. A technological civilization could be understood, if at all, only by highly trained specialists. Moreover, science forced rapid and perpetual changes in the society so that standards were continually in flux. All of these factors contributed to the general sense of dehumanization that pervaded American life. Art suffered because men had no access to "experience passionately grasped," nor could the "discovery of permanent values" which was the poet's traditional task be sustained in an era of constant turmoil.[48] Though she hoped that the machine could eventually be assimilated into man's consciousness, she considered the day of reconciliation between poetry and science to be extremely remote.

This presumption of an inhuman civilization glorifying machine processes and calculating success in terms of material acquisitions, a conveyor-belt society preaching individualism while reducing everyone to a cog in the wheel of industrialism, caught the imagination of many writers in the 1920s. It was a compelling image both because it described America in words literary intellectuals could appreciate and because it provided a justification for uncompromising hostility to the society as a whole. But it also reflected their conviction that no amount of technological progress would make life aesthetically or emotionally satisfying. If mechanical improvements could not bring with them meaningful values, if science shattered old myths without creating any new ideals, then "civilization" was merely an incoherent jumble of physical objects none of which could compensate for the essential emptiness of modern life.

Perhaps no book more fully embraced this vision than Joseph Wood Krutch's *The Modern Temper,* published in 1929. Here was a mordant examination not only of America but of the human predicament in general. The very sweep of its subject and the melancholy tone of its conclusions summarized the attitudes of a generation of writers weaned on Henry Adams, T. S. Eliot, and Oswald Spengler. As such, it represented a cultural and moral indictment far beyond anything Stearns or the Lynds had conceived.

Krutch portrayed a world in which the classic liberal and Marxist faith in the power of science to control nature for human needs had turned out to be a betrayal. Science, especially biology, which saw life as a random product of evolution, and psychology, which emphasized the non-rational sources of social behavior, had only undermined man's trust in reason and his ability to make free moral choices. Under the impact of scientific discoveries, Krutch pointed out, men had begun to accept the fact that they were living in a universe without purpose or meaning, so that they could not take solace in any of their traditional beliefs. A crisis of values resulted in which the individual had no intimate connection with his environment or his community. He lived in the twentieth century in an anguished state of disharmony, ambiguity, and isolation. Art, religion, and philosophy all stood exposed as the charming illusions of mankind's childhood—now forever lost. And included in the catalogue of dead faiths was the notion that society might be perfected by reforming its institutions. Both liberalism and socialism, Krutch asserted, were based on the false assumption "that the only maladjustments from which mankind suffers are social in character." In truth, the fundamental conflict was not between man and society but "between the human spirit and the natural universe."[49]

To put the issue in these terms was to underscore the essential futility of political and social action. People might commit themselves to a cause, but this simply revealed an ignorance of their present plight. The effort to develop effective social programs was a pleasant exercise, a way for well-intentioned human beings to pass the time. But the modern man had learned too much; he realized that "this world in which an unresolvable discord is the fundamental fact is the world in which we must continue to live, and for us wisdom must consist, not in searching for a means of escape which does not exist, but in making such peace with it as we may."[50] Krutch advised an existential acceptance of despair as the first sign of maturity: "If we no longer believe in either our infinite capacities or our importance to the universe, we know at least that we have discovered the trick which has been played upon us and that whatever else we may be we are no longer dupes."[51] Like a Hemingway hero, Krutch had discovered that nature was indifferent, that political slogans had no significance for life, that a man was eventually broken by the world and could hope only to survive "strong at the broken places." To many in the 1920s, this was a chilling yet persuasive message.

But not everyone was convinced. There were some writers who retained the prewar belief in the essential beneficence of science and technology. For them the machine was not something to be feared or hated; it was instead a neutral instrument which could be used for good or evil. Two of the leading proponents for this point of view were Lewis Mumford and John

Dewey. Though they found little else to agree on in the 1920s, Mumford having censured Pragmatism for its lack of imagination and its acquiescence in American materialism in *The Golden Day,* they shared the conviction that technology could be made an integral part of social progress and human culture. Rather than describe the world in terms of static opposites —nature versus man, science versus poetry, the machine versus the spirit —they argued that these dualisms were merely the inheritance of nineteenth-century thought, all of which bore very little relation to twentieth-century needs.

Mumford in particular denied Krutch's contention that science had displaced men from the center of the universe. In Mumford's view, *The Modern Temper* abandoned all hope of reconciling men to their environment. By assuming an eternal conflict between science and human freedom, Krutch had made it impossible for individuals to function in or act on the modern world. Mumford, on the contrary, wanted to stress the ways in which society could absorb technological discoveries without losing sight of larger cultural values. "We would not destroy the rigorous method of science or the resourceful technology of the engineer," he explained. "We would merely limit their application to intelligible and humane purposes. Nor would we remove altogether the mechanical world-picture, with its austere symbolism; we would rather expand it and supplement it with a vision of life which drew upon other needs of the personality than the crude will-to-power."[52] Brute fact and human creativity could be joined. Man was not simply a passive victim of nature but might, at least partially, control and refashion his environment. Mumford saw no sense in grieving over a universe which partly responded to men; neither was there any reason to surrender faith in science and politics. "If Man belongs to the system of Nature," he declared, "Nature as disclosed by science is still a part of the system of Man. Science exists and develops in a human and social medium."[53] Thus only by concentrating on the points of interrelationship between science and culture, the process by which each molded the other, would America's material and spiritual needs both be served.

John Dewey was even more explicit. "It is not true that machinery is the source of our troubles," he asserted in the *New Republic* during 1929. "It opens opportunities for planning and extends the ability to realize such ends as men propose. If we do not plan, if we do not use machinery intelligently on behalf of things we value, the fault lies with us, not with the machine." For Dewey, the major obstacle to the creative use of science was not the "machine age but the survival of a pecuniary age." American technology was harnessed to a system of private profit, a "money culture" that emphasized power, commercialism, and success to the exclusion of a genuinely "integrated life."[54] Like the Lynds, Dewey was suggesting that America's central problem was one of cultural lag—a conflict between industrialism and potential abundance on the one hand and a rigid adherence to capitalist values on the other. Only when men finally renounced the ideological heritage of the nineteenth century, the commitment to individual competition and a trust in unlimited economic accumulation as ends in themselves, could science be devoted to improving the quality of American life.

Both Mumford and Dewey wanted to overcome the cleavage in American civilization to which Van Wyck Brooks had first called attention in 1915. They were trying to establish a balance between the practical and the ideal, between social and economic affairs on the one hand and the realm of the mind and spirit on the other. Recognizing that an important segment of the intellectual community was sickened by the overwhelming ugliness of modern industrialism, they nevertheless hoped to demonstrate that art and technology, humanism and science, men and machines could in fact live together. If these notions seemed unpersuasive to the majority of writers during the 1920s, they would prove more compelling in the years following the stock-market crash.

Their perspective was most systematically expressed in a symposium edited by Charles Beard in 1928, entitled *Whither Mankind*. The contributors included some of the most influential writers in the 1920s: Bertrand Russell, Sidney and Beatrice Webb, Havelock Ellis, James Harvey Robinson, Stuart Chase, Carl Van Doren, Mumford, and Dewey. An air of intense urgency hung over the essays in response to a feeling that the time for man to achieve some psychological and moral stability was running out. As Beard remarked in his summary, the "old rules of politics and law, religion and sex, art and letters—the whole domain of culture—must yield or break before the inexorable pressure of science and the machine." Yet throughout all the articles there ran a common theme: "that by understanding more clearly the processes of science and the machine mankind may subject the scattered and perplexing things of this world to a more ordered dominion of the spirit." Thus "nowhere in these pages," Beard concluded, "is there a signal for surrender or retreat."[55]

But neither was there an exceptionally stirring call to action. Although a number of intellectuals in the 1920s longed to reconcile the obvious advantages of American industry and technology with the equally obvious need for a more humane way of life, though they still occasionally yearned for a reunification of culture and politics, they were unable to suggest a coherent program by which any of this might be accomplished. Much of the debate remained on the level of abstraction and exhortation because the issues they chose to emphasize remained almost entirely moral and psychological. This in itself reflected the outlook of writers who felt cut off from the levers of political power and whose skills were not being effectively used by the general public or its leaders. Their insistence that thought and action, art and science, morality and mechanization were in constant battle was not just a passing commentary on a peculiar national problem. It revealed a deeper fear on the part of intellectuals that they themselves were isolated from and irrelevant to the social order. Most of the time, therefore, they identified their own difficulties with the plight of culture in modern America, seeking to expand its importance as a means of strengthening their influence in the larger society.

4. *The Artist in Exile*

Any discussion in the 1920s about the standardization of mass production, the superficiality of middle-class culture, the fraudulence of advertising, or the menace of technology eventually returned to the issue of the intellectual's relation to his fellow citizens. In order to escape the debilitating sense of alienation and impotence, many writers were forced to confront the question of how they might function in an environment that provided them with no stable role. American intellectuals, unlike their European counterparts, had no traditional ties either to class or to political movements. There existed no natural constituency for whom they could automatically speak, no ongoing community that would translate their ideas into social or cultural policy. Writers and artists lacked an adequate definition of their place and responsibilities; hence the self-conscious tendency of each generation to begin anew, to ransack the past in search of usable models for present action, to *create* values that might possibly capture the allegiance of the entire nation. But precisely because their obligations were so unclear, they often found it excruciatingly hard to agree among themselves on a solution to their dilemma.

With the appeal of social activism seriously muted during the decade, a number of writers turned their attention to art and literature, both as a refuge from what they believed to be the oppressive complacency of American society and as a means by which they could establish their unique identity as intellectuals. Disgusted by the uses to which ideological abstractions could be put, indifferent to all the liberal slogans that had been invoked to justify World War I, many literary critics and creative artists tried to build a sanctuary for pure ideas and feelings which would be invulnerable to political manipulation.

In a fashion typical of the 1920s, a majority of book reviewers for the *New Republic* and *Nation* either unconsciously assumed or explicitly insisted on a separation of art from all external pressures. Thus William Troy, a frequent contributor to both journals, observed in 1929 that "what is most characteristic of our younger critics today, as it is most pertinent to the fresh reinterpretation of our literature, is the impulse to approach works of the past as *literature* and not as something else—not as moral tracts, or psychological reports, or social documents." In Troy's opinion, what art needed now was an even "more rigorous esthetic discipline" than presently existed.[56] Almost as if in response to this plea, *Hound and Horn,* a literary journal born in 1927 and edited through the remainder of the decade by R. P. Blackmur and Lincoln Kirstein, summarized its credo: "Criticism has no meaning and no value until a work of art has first justified itself esthetically, until it is accepted as a work of art. A sound philosophy will not produce a great work of art and a great work of art is no guarantee that the ideas of the artist are sound. Consequently our standard for judging the arts is technical. We demand only that the given work should be well done. . . ."[57] Like most of the decade's little magazines, *Hound and Horn* offered its readers complex and sophisticated essays on fiction and poetry, hoping thereby to maintain some literary standards in a period otherwise marked by shoddy thinking and cultural confusion.

This tendency to assess works of art primarily in aesthetic terms was part of a general revolt against ideology. Both Stark Young and Joseph Wood Krutch, drama critics for the *New Republic* and *Nation* respectively, displayed no inclination to praise or condemn a play on the basis of its social purpose (or lack of one). Their reviews emphasized the internal structure of the work and their personal response to the evening's performance. Similarly Gilbert Seldes, the *New Republic*'s movie reviewer and author of an influential study of popular culture, *The Seven Lively Arts,* rejected the notion that a work's content might determine its quality. Chiefly concerned with the technical skill of the director and the film's impact on an audience, Seldes argued that even the blatantly propagandistic Russian films should be judged without reference to their point of view. Given genius, fascism or any other political sentiment could inspire a great work of art which one might appreciate regardless of its subject matter. The crucial element for Seldes was not a film's "ideas" but how they were presented. "It is the passion itself, not the object of passion, which counts."[58]

These attitudes were not limited to liberal or resolutely apolitical journals. In the *New Masses,* the poet Kenneth Fearing vigorously objected to the Marxist habit of equating good art with successful propaganda. "Revolutionary propaganda, to be effective, must be one-sided and dishonest and sentimental," he asserted, "and any play that is sentimental, no matter how effective it may be, is perishable and intrinsically not good." In Fearing's estimation, the radicals were trying to have it both ways. They praised the new Soviet cinema and the burgeoning proletarian dramas of the New Playwrights Theatre in America for presumably uniting modernist technique and revolutionary content, avant-garde experimentation and social uplift. This allowed them to maintain a connection between art and politics and to evaluate one in terms of the other. Fearing denied the relationship and warned that radical dramatists and critics would have to choose between their cultural interests and their political commitments.[59]

Behind the desire to discuss art apart from its social consequences lurked the belief that, in America at least, conditions were relatively stable. Ideology was therefore unnecessary. "Propaganda" seemed not only harmful to culture but irrelevant to society. Yet this may have been less an objective appraisal of contemporary possibilities than a reflection of the intellectual community's own state of mind during the 1920s. For much of their approach toward art was shaped by the experiences they had undergone since 1917.

The most common characteristic of the generation that grew up before and after World War I was its origins in rural and small-town America. These were classic young men from the provinces: Kenneth Burke and Malcolm Cowley from Pennsylvania, Sherwood Anderson and Hart Crane from Ohio, Theodore Dreiser from Indiana, Ernest Hemingway from Illinois, Glenway Wescott from Wisconsin, Sinclair Lewis and F. Scott Fitzgerald from Minnesota, Ezra Pound from Idaho. More often than not they found the village or farm claustrophobic, unsympathetic to any form of personal eccentricity, too constricting for individual creativity and self-expression. Yet the prospects offered by the larger society were equally unappealing. America needed brain power but only of a certain type. The corporations could use men with managerial or financial training but not those who were disturbed by the way people lived in the cities or on the land. Industry had openings for technicians and engineers but not for those who were skeptical about the capacity of science to build a humane civilization. Advertising agencies welcomed experts in the art of manipulating language, but they showed little interest in those for whom words and communication were methods of transforming man's imagination. The government recruited men who could efficiently administer the growing bureaucracy, but those who cared about politics as a means of changing class relationships were never encouraged to apply. Consequently many sensitive middle-class men and women found themselves on the margins of society, with talents and ambitions for which there was no institutional outlet.

So they migrated by the hundreds to places and occupations that appeared more congenial. They formed bohemian communities of like-minded souls—starting out very often in Chicago, then in New York, and finally in Paris. They deliberately isolated themselves from the Babbitts and the Philistines who seemed to have overrun America during the 1920s. They opened salons, formed little magazines, started a novel, or exchanged their poems with one another. Safe from the bourgeoisie, they experimented with psychology, with sex, with art, and with their lives.

Through all of these adventures there ran the unstated assumption that the surrounding environment could not really be altered, that literary interests and skills would never be served by social reform, that the only practical task for the emancipated and rootless intellectual was the creation of an alternative life-style and culture beyond the grasp of bourgeois America. Given the increasing standardization of consumer goods, the growing interdependence of social institutions, and the national faith in bigness as a sign of quality, there seemed no political program—whether liberal or radical —that would free the inner spirit from the stifling conformity of middle-class life.

It was not surprising, therefore, that the central criticism of American society during the 1920s was its indifference to the value of personal vision, its failure to let the individual grow at his own pace and think in his own way. Politics represented an intrusion on one's privacy; society blocked one's access to direct experience. In reaction to this, the writer often turned to moral, psychological, and aesthetic issues in an effort to recover a sense of his own identity and independence apart from the pressures of social responsiblitity. For as Alfred Kazin has pointed out, "what remained to the artist, who was always the special victim of this world, was the pride of individual self-knowledge and the skill that went beyond all the revolutionary and sentimental illusions of a possible fraternity among men and gave all its devotion to the integrity of art."[60]

If writers could not exercise any control over history or the social structure, if they could not influence external events, they might at least devote their talents effectively to matters of technique, style, and craftsmanship. In art, the world of imagination supplanted the world of time and place. Pure fiction and poetry were seen as ends in themselves, beyond the need for any extraliterary justification—beyond the need even to communicate with an uninitiated and insensitive public. The most extreme manifestation of this tendency was Dada, where what Malcolm Cowley called the "religion of art" became a denial of "any psychic basis common to all humanity," an intensely individualistic attempt to transcend the bounds of logic, language, and conventional morality in order to reach a higher plateau of personal freedom and insight.[61] The economic prosperity of the 1920s fueled this artistic renaissance, liberating bourgeois intellectuals from the narrow perspective of nation or class, permitting them to pursue their aesthetic principles and private rebellions in relative isolation from the daily business of earning a living.

Yet most American writers did not intend either to preach or to glorify escapism. Instead they understood the extent to which artistic improvisation could contribute to the creation of new values, new kinds of social behavior, new ways of seeing the world. The artists of the 1920s, according to Frederick Hoffman, took seriously the need to invent "new forms of expressing the human drama. They were not aided by any secure ordering of social or religious systems." The greatest victim of the war had been language because it no longer bore any relation to personal experience. The accuracy of words, therefore, became a "major necessity." In essence, artists were calling for a "formal revolution that was also a moral revolution. The concern with form was basically a concern over the need to provide an esthetic order for moral revisions."[62] Man's survival depended on his capacity to restate and reinterpret his experience at a time when the conventional explanations about society and politics seemed obsolete. Thus the gravest criticism Fitzgerald could level at the upper class was that it was "careless," insensitive, vulgar, *culturally* inept. In response, Hemingway and Cummings experimented with new literary styles just as their characters experimented with new forms of conduct. Ezra Pound and Gertrude Stein demanded precise communication as a crucial first step in redefining moral principles. The individual, in the fiction and poetry of the decade, was learning once more how to speak before he could learn how to live. Far from encouraging a separation of art and life, American writers were arguing for their mutual reinforcement. While they rejected the notion that literature should be socially uplifting or morally didactic, they believed firmly that it could refine an individual's sensibility, reawaken his imagination, intensify his awareness of the world, and thereby alter him in a way that ordinary institutional reforms might never achieve.

Moreover, their expectations of what art could accomplish were not limited solely to the individual. To have abandoned social action in the traditional sense did not mean that they were surrendering all hope for a genuine transformation of American life. Many writers saw artistic experimentation and cultural analysis as preludes to a more fundamental change in the social order. Magazines like the *Dial* and *Hound and Horn* insisted on the intellectuals' almost messianic responsibility to save civilization, to stimulate in their readers a moment of mystical conversion in which each man became a part of an "organic" society, to nourish a prophetic vision of the new commonwealth based not on political intelligence but on art and the moral imagination.[63] From this perspective, the world of culture was itself a model community of men sharing the same values, the same feelings of comradeship, the same dedication to the rejuvenation of America through painting, poetry, and prose. As each person who came in contact with culture was inspired to make over his own life, so the society as a whole might eventually be recast. The place to begin was with the individual, but no one knew where it all would end. For the moment, at least, many agreed with Waldo Frank when he declared on the eve of the stock-market crash that the "true radical" was not the social activist or ideologue but the "man who gets at the roots of himself, whence must issue all his understanding of the world and all his creative actions upon it. Radicalism must begin at home" with one's own "self-search." Hence Frank would "continue to deem it my duty, as a radical, to accept my solitude, to strive to better myself as an instrument of truth, and to produce . . . organic literary works which may possibly nurture the revolutionary action of tomorrow."[64]

Nevertheless, there were some who found this kind of cultural radicalism vaguely dissatisfying. Granted the need for introspection, for the purification of language, for an avant-garde community of artists, for a future revolution in values, none of these worthy goals seemed to answer the question of how one functioned in the present, steadfastly opposing but not losing contact with the larger society. To Edmund Wilson—a contributor to the *Dial* and an associate editor of the *New Republic,* a man who could discuss cultural and social problems with equal facility—art was neither a world in itself nor a substitute for political action. Toward the end of the decade, Wilson attacked the expatriates as well as those who stayed home to proselytize for an organic society. Both groups, he complained, were indulging in fantasies about what they could actually accomplish. They were posing as secular priests for the new culture, but they had no clear program for relating art to social change, and therefore no coherent idea of the role intellectuals could truly play in transforming America. In the meantime, they were "evading the realities of national life."[65] No matter how appalling the United States might appear, with its Chamber of Commerce banalities, its worship of business, and its political corruption, "it is up to the young American writers to make some sense of their American world." For America had in fact become a symbol of modern life everywhere; there was no escape into Bohemia or the religion of art or the myth of the coming millennium. In Wilson's judgment, the "new social and moral ideals" would depend not so much on artistic experimentation and personal conversion experiences as on a "resolute study of contemporary reality."[66]

Similarly, a number of former expatriates themselves began to urge a reconciliation between the artist and America. In truth, the migration from New York to Paris had always been fitful throughout the 1920s; there were often as many writers returning to the United States as fleeing from its shores. Moreover, the journey to Europe usually served to enhance the writer's understanding of home as much as it exposed him to trends in international culture. Whether in Germany or France, Italy or Spain, the American artist's most characteristic theme was the difficulty of adjusting to the postwar world—a dilemma he shared with the residents of Middletown. In the end the expatriate tended to write about the things he knew best, and by the closing years of the decade he began to leave Europe for good in order to gain a better view of his subject.

His arrival did not go unannounced. By the late 1920s the veterans of the expatriate movement were calculating its successes and failures. In 1929, Malcolm Cowley began submitting essays to *Hound and Horn* and the *New Republic* which would ultimately comprise the bulk of *Exile's Return*. His close friend and colleague, Matthew Josephson, was at work on a study of the national literature to be published in 1930 under the title *Portrait of the Artist as American*. Josephson's experience was hardly typical; as a co-editor of *Broom* in 1924, he had displayed a serious interest in adapting the rhythms of art to the beat of the machine age—a position not universally admired by other writers. In addition Josephson, like Edmund Wilson, had always been concerned with social issues; in 1928 he presented his *Life of Emile Zola*, which sought in part to demonstrate how an intellectual could also be a man of action.

In *Portrait*, Josephson acknowledged that the two roles were not particularly compatible. He discovered in the great nineteenth-century novelists— Nathaniel Hawthorne, Herman Melville, Henry James—such an elitist "hatred and suspicion of democracy," such a consuming fear of the masses, that their resulting physical or spiritual exile raised a fundamental question of whether the artist and the "people" could ever coexist.[67] The problem was even more disturbing when Josephson was forced to admit that, precisely by isolating themselves from America, writers like James could thereby create the "finest literature" the world had ever seen. Their work did not suffer because they were uprooted from their native soil, as Van Wyck Brooks had charged; on the contrary, what American writers "might have lost by living only vicariously was richly redeemed through [their] life in art."[68]

But for some in Josephson's generation, this rigid separation of society and art was no longer possible. Echoing Wilson, Josephson recognized that postwar Europe had become more and more like America. Exile itself was ceasing to be a practical option at a time when every new bohemian community and every new experimental magazine were rapidly absorbed by the advertising industry and the commercial press. There was nothing left to do but come to terms with America. "The salvation and the strength of artists," Josephson declared, lay "in their ability, hereafter, to incorporate themselves within the actual milieu." Consequently, he concluded his analysis of American literature by calling for the development of a *popular* culture, a "rapprochement" with the "rhythms of the cinema, the music of towers, the architecture of motor cars and shop windows, the magnificent new machines."[69] In Josephson's case, the intellectual had truly come home. And in the next few years the positions he and Wilson advocated would seem increasingly appealing to a new generation of writers seeking to rediscover their native land.

By the end of the 1920s, the expatriate generation was beginning to feel more comfortable in America, more willing to publish in established journals like the *New Yorker,* more anxious to communicate with a larger audience than could be found in Bohemia. New York itself seemed more congenial to cultural affairs, with the new "cubist" architecture of its buildings, the "little theaters" moving from Greenwich Village to Broadway, the Guggenheim subsidies to deserving young writers, and publishers increasingly sympathetic to experimental literature.[70] Still, the basic questions remained. Could the intellectual reintegrate himself with America and yet survive as a moral force? At what point did his hunger for acceptance, respectability, and influence threaten his original talents and commitments? What in fact was the relationship between art and society? How, precisely, should politics and culture be reconciled, if at all? And what contribution might the writer make to the reconstruction of American life? These were the underlying problems with which Herbert Croly and Van Wyck Brooks struggled at the beginning; no one had offered satisfactory answers during the 1920s.

Nevertheless, in the spring of 1929—while the economic indicators continued to rise and a prosperous nation celebrated the "new era," when the department stores were stocked full with goods and the mortgages on the house were almost paid, when Hollywood began to add sound to its epics and radio had become the most important piece of furniture in the living room, when all the signs pointed to the overwhelming success and stability of the social system—Edmund Wilson paused to describe what life in America was like for the alienated man. Writing in the *New Republic,* Wilson used the career of the literary critic John Jay Chapman to dramatize the dilemma of an individual suspended between a desire to affect the destiny of the United States and the fear that his integrity might be corrupted in the process. It was clear throughout the article that Wilson meant to illustrate the difficulty of determining his own role—and that of his fellow intellectuals—in a country generally hostile to ideas of any kind.

Wilson was quick to underline the similarities between Chapman's era and the present. Like the generation of writers who had matured during the 1920s, Chapman by the turn of the century had "ceased to believe in the possibility of organized political reform." But he was still confronted with the task of gaining an "intellectual foothold," of establishing a "vital relation with the society about him." Chapman's predicament symbolized for Wilson "the peculiar position in America of the man of high moral and intellectual standards who is unable to compromise with American life." On the one hand, Chapman was too principled to become either a popular writer or a successful politician. He could not sacrifice his honor or his intense dislike of industrialism on the altar of power and prestige. On the other hand, by maintaining his purity he ran the risk of irrelevance. Forgoing power, he was "thrown back and in upon himself."[71]

In Wilson's view, Chapman resolved this crisis by adopting the role of intellectual-as-critic. He became a "protestant" in the root sense of the word; he would commit himself to various causes but in his own way and according to his own standards. "Practical agitation" was to be dependent not on social movements or political parties but on "individual action" itself dictated by a "moral attitude." Faced with the horrors of modern capitalism and the rampant vulgarity of American life, one could "look to nothing but the individual conscience." Thus Chapman represented the very model of an effective cultural radical; he concentrated on the "moral [rather than economic] issue of business and industrialism," and he thereby maintained "the point of view of the humanist in a world preoccupied with trade."[72] To Wilson, Chapman's stance demonstrated the only method of survival in a society indifferent to taste, courage, and faith. The intellectual, Wilson concluded, should remain an individualist, a solitary man of principle, but as such he could raise and debate the ultimate problems confronting civilization more cogently than any political activist. In this way he might preserve his personal independence, critical intelligence, and ethical vision, while at the same time discharging his social responsibilities.

For most writers in the 1920s, this was as far as they could go. Following Wilson and Josephson, they might tentatively re-enter American life, agitating for moral, cultural, and social changes, but not really believing that any of these were immediately possible. The tensions between men and their institutions, art and politics, personal values and social action, the intellectual and America, still existed. The effort to revamp the country's institutions and culture, first envisioned by the Progressives, remained at best a utopian dream. Perhaps the time was not yet ripe for anything more. The 1920s had been a period of transition in which men drifted from one experiment to another, re-evaluating the past and seeking to orient themselves more effectively in the present. The future—the real future that would be born in October of 1929—was undisclosed and unimagined.

Yet there was one brief moment in the 1920s when men received a premonition of the world to come. In Boston during 1927 people were marching: immigrants, workers, liberals, radicals, intellectuals. Funds were raised, committees were formed, meetings were held, petitions were drawn up, picket lines appeared, men were clubbed and arrested. On the night that Sacco and Vanzetti were executed the temporary united front collapsed, another attempt at collective action had failed, and each man returned to his private life. "For a time," Malcolm Cowley later recalled, "it seemed that Sacco and Vanzetti would be forgotten, in the midst of the stock-market boom and the exhilaration of easy money. Yet the effects of the case continued to operate, in a subterranean way, and after a few years they would once more appear on the surface."[73] And when they did, the future had officially arrived.

CHAPTER II

POLITICAL AND ECONOMIC
THOUGHT, 1929–1935

1. *Responses to the Crash*

On October 24, 1929, the bottom began falling out of an already shaky stock market. For the next several weeks the news became progressively worse. The symbol of American capitalism was collapsing, and no one from bankers to politicians appeared able to halt the slide. The market had been acting strangely for months, and since the beginning of the year there were ominous signs that prices were dangerously inflated. But few anticipated such an overwhelming disaster or recognized its implications for the rest of the economy. In effect, Wall Street was suffering a series of mysterious convulsions, for the moment beyond diagnosis or cure.

Initially, the most striking consequence of the stock-market crash was not that it forced people to re-evaluate their assumptions about the prosperity of the 1920s but that it had so little impact on American attitudes or behavior for almost a year. When the official explanations of a "temporary readjustment" began to issue forth from Wall Street and Washington, these seemed reasonable and persuasive. The essential soundness of the economy went unquestioned, and not only by spokesmen for industry or government. Within a month the financial bulletins retreated from the front page to their accustomed place in the back of the newspapers, production and sales maintained their steady pace, and most stores found the Christmas season surprisingly prosperous. To all appearances, the boom would continue, and perhaps even swell, during 1930.

If the country as a whole remained unaffected by Wall Street's confusion, this was also true of the intellectual community. The liberal and radical press, though alert to the economy's shortcomings throughout the 1920s, reacted to the stock market's gyrations with as much equanimity as the White House. The *New Masses,* whose readers had grown accustomed to its annual predictions of capitalism's collapse, seemed oblivious to the possibility that such an event might actually be happening. Since 1928, under Michael Gold's management, the magazine had become a vehicle for proletarian short stories of the most primitive kind. Little space was devoted to systematic economic or political analysis. Gold's worker-writers recorded their oppression and demanded revolution without much reference to what took place in the larger society. Moreover, the Communists and their opponents on the left were generally preoccupied with doctrinal and factional disputes, many of which originated in the Soviet Union. Consequently both the *New Masses* and its radical counterparts practically ignored the crash and gave little notice to the ensuing depression until late in 1930. For most of this time, American Marxists displayed a remarkable talent for disregarding the country in which they were living.

The performance of the liberal journals was not much better. At first the *New Republic* and the *Nation* echoed President Hoover in denying the existence of a fundamental crisis. The *Nation* attributed the crash to a "speculative mania" which had puffed up prices far beyond their true value, but it declined to search for any underlying structural weaknesses in the economy. America, the editors assured their readers, was still enjoying "normal prosperity."[1] Like Hoover, they predicted that any possible period of stagnation could be overcome by a "restoration of confidence."[2]

The *New Republic* also denounced the evils of speculation in stock prices but took an even more sanguine view: "The ultimate result will, of course, be extremely good for business and the country; it will make available more credit and more energy for legitimate productive enterprise."[3] Both journals had carefully assessed the state of the economy throughout the 1920s, both were aware of imbalances in purchasing power and the specter of inventories outgrowing domestic and foreign markets, yet neither was initially willing or able to relate the troubles on Wall Street to more basic problems. The dire warnings of an imminent economic disaster had become a normal part of liberal rhetoric, but no one, including the liberals themselves, actually imagined that these omens might some day be confirmed. It was as if the liberals had cried wolf too often without really believing in its existence; when the beast finally appeared, they were looking the other way.

Even as the momentum of production gradually slowed during the winter of 1930, and as cold statistics began to reveal a rise in unemployment, the liberal press retained its composure. By March the *New Republic* admitted the presence of a "genuine industrial depression" in the United States but hastily added that a business revival was "sure to come" by summer. Far from having abandoned hope in either Hoover's leadership or the economy's essential strength, the editors believed the crisis might actually "call forth the utmost promise of industrial capitalism." They encouraged the President to form an alliance with the "more progressive forces of business, engineering, and management" because it was "highly important that enlightened capitalist industrialism be given its chance."[4] In good pragmatic fashion, the *New Republic* insisted that free enterprise receive the opportunity to save itself before any other experiments were considered. The stock-market crash had come as a "test" of the system, and the editors were quite willing to wait until all the results were in. Furthermore, their mood in the early months of 1930 reflected a basic inability to foresee how desperate the situation would become. In this they were not alone.

Yet the expected revival never occurred. Instead, economic conditions during the spring and summer of 1930 continued to deteriorate. President Hoover had extracted agreements from key industrialists to stabilize prices and wages, but these pacts were entirely voluntary, unenforceable, and generally powerless to prevent individual businessmen from cutting back production and employment in a panicky effort to salvage profits. Slowly, inexorably, America's industrial plant was shutting down. People stopped buying what they did not absolutely need. Goods piled up in warehouses. Factories went on half shifts and laid off an increasing number of men. Local relief agencies found it harder to keep up with the demand for their services. A dull pallor settled over the cities that would somehow stubbornly endure throughout the decade.

And now all the weaknesses which had lain hidden beneath the prosperity of the 1920s rose to the surface, thereby intensifying the crisis. The wheat, corn, and cotton crops were bountiful—too bountiful for the available markets either at home or abroad. At the same time the smaller farmers, the tenants and sharecroppers, whose hold on the land had always been painfully tenuous, came to know the meaning of extreme rural poverty. The soil they tilled would not yield as it had ten or twenty years before, and even when the harvest was decent prices remained so low that a season's labor served only to push the farmer still further in debt. But he could not escape from this vicious cycle by leaving the land. There was no work in the mines, in the textile mills, at the steel furnaces, or on the assembly lines. No new products, such as the radio or automobile, burst forth to reawaken the economy, and there was no longer enough credit with which to buy such luxuries anyway. Men, women, and children hit the road, thumbed rides, rode the freights, all in search of jobs that were nonexistent. After a while, the destination became unimportant; the point was simply to keep moving. With winter approaching, the relief lines grew longer, and shanty towns built out of a civilization's refuse began to spring up on the outskirts of the larger cities. Someone called them "Hoovervilles," and the name stuck.

The plight of the nation was visible everywhere. By the winter of 1930–1931, the middle class started feeling the depression: the weekly paychecks were smaller, the corner stores had fewer customers and their survival became questionable, there was less need for lawyers and the doctor bills went unpaid, young men graduated from college and roamed the streets unemployed, public school teachers and civil servants were not always certain when or if they would be paid, the smell of money was no longer in the air. Broadway plays began to close prematurely, the movies found it harder to attract audiences despite the recent conversion to sound (on the other hand, public libraries—with free books and warm rooms—reported a surprising increase in the use of their facilities), publishers stopped advancing large sums for unwritten manuscripts, and writers clogged the outer offices of magazines hoping for an occasional assignment or book review in order to pay the rent and buy a meal. A year after the stock-market crash, there were few in America for whom the depression was not a direct and daily reality.

Yet the collapse of the economy did not immediately force people to re-examine their assumptions about the basic endurance of American capitalism, nor to search for totally new strategies and programs with which to rebuild the society. Quite the contrary, the depression—at least during its first year—seemed for some an unprecedented opportunity to realize long-cherished projects and goals. This was particularly true for those who had been involved in liberal politics since the Progressive era and who continued to champion reformist ideas throughout the 1920s.

Many of their attitudes were clearly reflected in the pages of the *New Republic.* Enjoying a larger circulation than any other magazine of its type, able to attract a wide variety of contributors who saved their most important statements for its columns, the *New Republic* entered the 1930s as an extremely influential spokesman for the liberal point of view as it had evolved since Croly's *Promise of American Life.* Croly himself died in 1930, but his intellectual legacy was well preserved by Bruce Bliven and George Soule. They in turn opened the magazine to writers like John Dewey, Stuart Chase, Charles Beard, Felix Frankfurter, Rexford Tugwell, Lewis Mumford, and Leo Wolman, all of whom had developed coherent positions on social problems long before the stock-market crash. These men belonged to the Progressive generation, where their ideas first took shape. They were slower to revise their original commitments than a slightly younger group of contributors whose interests were primarily literary and whose formative experiences had occurred during the war and the 1920s: Edmund Wilson, Malcolm Cowley, Matthew Josephson. But despite the differences in mood and opinion that began to emerge in the magazine near the end of 1930 and that signaled a growing radicalization of the intellectual community over the next several years, the *New Republic* remained "an excellent vantage point from which to look out at a world in crisis."[5]

The man most responsible for the *New Republic*'s economic posture was George Soule. During 1930 he analyzed the depression in terms that were fairly familiar to anyone who had followed the journal since World War I. As the nation's economic indicators spiraled downward without interruption, the *New Republic* abandoned its earlier hope for a swift recovery. Now Soule returned to the argument he had set forth in the 1920s: the fundamental problem of American capitalism was the failure of consumer purchasing power to keep pace with production.

In Soule's view, the roots of the crash could be traced to the peculiar "prosperity" of the previous decade. In the 1920s technological progress had stimulated industrial production to a point where it simply overwhelmed the capacity of domestic and foreign markets to buy American goods. Moreover, since 1923 the income of wage earners failed to rise rapidly enough to absorb the surplus, nor did retail prices fall sufficiently to enlarge mass purchasing power. The "New Era" was itself artificial, according to Soule; it had been kept alive by expansion in the auto and service industries, a temporary construction boom, installment buying, and exports financed by loans and the complicated reparations structure. A collapse was therefore inevitable once all the markets became glutted. This in turn generated an unending cycle of declining production and mounting unemployment. Soule was gloomy about the future; in the absence of any increase in farm incomes, wages, and salaries, he foresaw only a gradual decrease in prices and a long depression unprecedented in American history.[6]

Meanwhile the *New Republic* editors were growing disenchanted with Hoover's tactics in meeting the crisis. In their estimation, the Administration appeared too timid and indecisive, too ready to rely on the voluntary cooperation of businessmen, too addicted to the rhetoric of individualism and laissez faire. They doubted that industry could really discipline itself to carry out necessary reforms because the impulse toward competition and maximization of profits was all too irresistible. Hence both the *New Republic* and the *Nation* by the fall of 1930 began calling their readers again to battle, dusting off the old demands and slogans which made up the liberal agenda of the 1920s. The time now seemed ripe, as it had not been since 1917, for all their favorite programs: reduced tariff barriers, national unemployment insurance, government regulation or partial ownership of utilities, the creation of a federally run railroad system, a broad housing program subsidized by the government, reform of the coal and oil industries, a national program for conservation, a more tolerant attitude toward the organization of trade unions, and the start of comprehensive economic planning. In addition they advocated immediate federal relief to the hungry and unemployed, a policy of controlled inflation, the expansion of credit, and a public works scheme, all as emergency measures to stem the depression.[7] As before, the magazines continued to support individual progressives in Congress while hoping that one of the major parties would somehow convert itself into an instrument for full-scale social change. None of these ideas was new or revolutionary, but at this juncture they sounded sufficient.

Occasionally, the *New Republic* would wonder "whether capitalism can survive as we know it, or must be at least modified greatly in the direction of a socialized order."[8] But despite their random speculations about socialism, the editors did not during 1930 really expect or desire any drastic transformations. By choosing to concentrate solely on the problems of technology, overproduction, and purchasing power, George Soule was still suggesting that these were flaws in an otherwise perfectible economy. Though he recognized the extreme disparities of wealth and poverty in America, the absurd contrast between swollen warehouses and desperate human need, he did not see these issues as either inevitable or inherent in a profit-oriented system. The pressures of technology and the capacity to consume had simply gotten out of balance. This was causing serious maladjustments in other parts of the economy, but equilibrium could be restored through wise political leadership, shrewd legislation, and intelligent planning. Thus the *New Republic* placed its faith in a series of concrete measures passed by liberal Congressmen, a strong labor movement, a flexible partnership between government and business, and an "authoritative body of impartial experts," all of whom might collaborate to produce a "genuine modification of capitalism from within."[9] Throughout the first year of the depression, the journal held fast to the Progressive ideal of an alliance between the state, labor, industry, and the intellectuals, which could rise above narrow class interests and dedicate itself to the use of modern scientific methods in serving the "general welfare."

2. The Challenge to Liberalism

The position of the *Nation* and *New Republic* depended on a sharing of power and a strength of purpose which had little basis in reality. As the depression entered its second winter, it was becoming increasingly evident to liberals that their prospective coalition would not be realized. Herbert Hoover seemed sadly incapable of providing the necessary leadership, while the Democrats represented a weird mélange of Southern conservatives, agrarian reformers, and urban disciples of Al Smith. The labor movement, still controlled by AFL veterans, had abandoned any concerted efforts at industrial organizing after the celebrated but futile steel strike of 1919; they displayed no great inclination to resume their activities now. The intellectuals remained isolated, just as they had been during the darkest days of the 1920s. Only the Communists and Socialists appeared to be interested in writers, and then largely for their names rather than their ideas. Finally, business itself seemed unwilling to surrender any of its power or prerogatives on behalf of a planned society. Trying to maintain price levels while mercilessly slashing production, wages, and employment, each corporation was engaged in a frantic struggle for its own survival. In the meantime more factories closed, small businessmen failed, local relief agencies and private charities exhausted their funds, and the shadow of the depression lengthened.

Faced with a bleak and unpromising situation, many writers grew impatient with the old solutions and tactics. Over the next two years a major debate took place among intellectuals of widely differing backgrounds, interests, and loyalties. The discussion centered on two basic questions: what sorts of institutional changes were needed in order to revive the American economy, and what political strategy could best bring these about?

In the process, some who had devoted their attention primarily to cultural affairs in the 1920s would find it necessary to turn again to social and economic issues and to assume political obligations they had considered unimportant during the previous decade. Others would feel compelled to revise or renounce their liberalism in an effort to understand and deal more effectively with the crisis. Still others would seize on the depression as an opportunity to create a radically new society, to solve at last the problems that had been plaguing the nation since the dawn of the twentieth century, to build a political movement and a social philosophy which might fundamentally transform American life. What the Progressive generation had failed to accomplish in a period of relative prosperity and optimism would be attempted once more—but this time against the background of profound social collapse. By the beginning of 1931 most writers could agree with the *New Republic* that "the morale of business itself is shaken; the old recipes of 'rugged individualism' and uncontrolled competition are seen on every hand to be insufficient. Our mechanized civilization has advanced to a point where it cries out for planning and control in the interests of all—a sort of planning and control which cannot possibly be executed without encroaching on vested interests and traditional property rights." Thus the depression, for all its attendant suffering, pushed "the door wide open to those of us in America who have the wit and the character to pass through it."[10] The argument now centered on how to move past the door, and what men might find on the other side.

For liberals, the most pressing issue in the opening months of 1931 was the need to organize a new political party. Given the dramatic failure of the major parties to cope with the pain and turmoil of the depression, the *Nation* reluctantly concluded that there was no essential difference between Republicans and Democrats. The Republican leadership, the journal observed, had faithfully represented the interests of big business throughout the postwar years, but the Democrats aspired only to substitute themselves as the trustworthy agents of capitalism. Neither party was addressing itself to the problems of farmers, labor, small businessmen, white-collar workers, or middle-class professionals. These groups, the magazine went on, must soon recognize that their primary needs collided directly with those of bankers and industrialists. As they became increasingly conscious of their plight, it would be the task of liberals to begin building an "independent" political movement which could give direction to their demands and frustrations. But the *Nation* stopped short of formulating radical objectives for this movement; it advocated only that the "people" be given a voice in government "at least equal" to that of big business.[11] The *New Republic* advanced a bit further. Admitting the similarities between the two established parties, it proposed a "realignment which puts the conservatives in one camp and the progressives in another."[12]

The effort to construct such a party received substantial and well-publicized discussion at a Conference for Independent Political Action, held in Washington during March of 1931 and attended by some of nation's foremost liberals: John Dewey, Stuart Chase, Oswald Garrison Villard, Paul Douglas, George Norris, Sidney Hillman, Leo Wolman, Alfred Bingham, Robert La Follette, Jr., Bronson Cutting. There was considerable disagreement among the participants over both immediate reforms and long-range goals, so that the results of the conference were discouraging. But this did not deter Dewey from continuing to campaign for a new politics—however much it sometimes resembled the old.

In a series of articles for the *New Republic,* Dewey offered a program that tried to sound both traditional and innovative, "Progressive" and radical. He rejected the classic liberal urge either to reform one of the major parties or to launch a third party which might wield the balance of power but could never revolutionize American life on its own. Both of these tactics were susceptible to the charge of opportunism and did not provide any coherent political direction over a long period of time. However, he was equally critical of the existing radical alternatives. The Communists, in his opinion, were preoccupied with events in Russia, spoke a language Americans could barely comprehend, and appeared too doctrinaire. He considered the Socialist party more attractive because many of its specific proposals embodied liberal goals, but socialism as an ideology had little appeal for people at this point.[13] Thus neither course held out a realistic hope of altering American society.

Instead, Dewey suggested a strategy he thought might have some chance of success in circumstances peculiar to the United States. In the first place, he contended, any new party would have to court the middle class, although it should of course pay close attention to the labor movement as well. The American bourgeoisie was still fluid, according to Dewey, still sympathetic to the problems of the lower classes, and just as vulnerable to the depression. No blueprint for social change could ignore its power or reject its participation.[14] Secondly, he insisted that the objectives of the party be framed in liberal terms. This was not simply a matter of expediency; Dewey himself tended to speak of social conflict in the Progressive idiom of special interests versus the "people," private gain versus the public welfare. He sometimes reduced the issues of the depression to one central question: "Are the people of the United States to control the government and to use it on behalf of the peace and welfare of society; or is control to continue to pass into the hands of small, powerful economic groups which use the machinery of administration and legislation for their own purposes?"[15] Woodrow Wilson or Louis Brandeis could not have phrased it better. Finally, Dewey wanted the movement to remain flexible and pragmatic: "No commitment to dogma or fixed doctrine is necessary."[16] No positions should be taken that could not be translated into immediate legislation, at least as a first step toward more fundamental change.

In effect, this was a program for those who had always believed it possible to merge concrete reforms with a thorough restructuring of American society and who wished to experiment with radical politics while preserving their ties to the kind of Progressivism first outlined by Herbert Croly and further refined by the *New Republic* during the 1920s. Dewey's position marked the point to which many intellectuals and activists of the prewar generation had moved by the spring of 1931, but to some it was not nearly far enough. Given the intensity of the crisis, the devastating conditions in which more and more American were forced to live, these goals began to appear sadly inadequate to a number of younger writers who did not share Dewey's residual faith in liberalism, who wanted greater ideological clarity in their political organizations and a more inspiring vision of the good society. The ideas and suggestions that flowed from the pages of the *Nation* and the *New Republic* seemed somehow too cautious, too committed to conventional political action and piecemeal solutions, too much concerned with "national" unity at the expense of creative social conflict. In the eyes of James Rorty, an aspiring poet who had once devoted his literary talents to composing copy for advertising agencies in the 1920s but who now felt the pressure for more serious intellectual activities, the only way out of the depression rested not with traditional Progressive reforms but with the radical Left. To satisfy men like Rorty, the discussion would have to advance beyond its concern with discrete economic problems to embrace every facet of human life. "For the issue," Rorty declared, "is the profit system and it is a revolutionary issue inescapable whether one is talking about the law, education, industry, the arts, or race relations."[17]

In all of these areas capitalism loomed as an omnipresent social evil, responsible for the never-ending cycles of boom and collapse, the irrational extremes of wealth and poverty, the imperialist thirst for foreign markets which could be sated only through war. For those writers who had turned to Marxism in the 1920s—men like Michael Gold, Joseph Freeman, V. F. Calverton—these were not new discoveries but simply a verification of their original predictions. Nevertheless they welcomed the depression because they saw in it an opportunity to escape from the political wilderness to which they had been consigned throughout the previous decade. The time had come for radicals to claim the leadership of the intellectual community. Now they were gaining an audience willing to question capitalism as an economic system in a way that had not been done before. "Whatever comes of it," Gold observed, "it marks a great turning point in the consciousness of the American nation. It is the first time that America has ever examined itself."[18] He, for one, was confident that neither capitalism nor the United States could possibly emerge from the experience unchanged.

To many radicals during the spring and summer of 1931, liberals constituted the principal opposition as well as the most fertile supply of potential recruits. On the one hand, they constantly berated the efforts of bourgeois intellectuals to save capitalism by reforming its methods. The *Nation* and the *New Republic,* Michael Gold snorted, never explained who would reorganize the society or in the interest of which class. The liberal journals always celebrated expertise, planning, and efficiency, but without total nationalization carried out under the guidance of the working class these ideas might easily lead to fascism. In Gold's view, the liberal refusal to attack the heart of the system—its dependence on competition and profit—made all reformist proposals suspect and even dangerous. On the other hand, he urged liberals to recognize that the future social and political battles in America must be fought between conservatives and radicals. No longer could intellectuals practice the "art of straddling." The problems of American society had lost their "beautiful prewar vagueness. One must decide now between two worlds—cooperative or competitive, proletarian or capitalist."[19] Those who, like John Dewey, wished to follow a middle road would find themselves increasingly doomed to irrelevance.

Yet the insistence on choosing sides in a world starkly divided between two eternally hostile camps, on either committing oneself irrevocably to the revolution or suffering a slow intellectual death, was by no means limited to Marxists. Influenced to some extent by the radical indictment of capitalism, but even more by the daily evidence of social dislocation, a massive assault on liberalism was well under way among writers of all political persuasions. Concepts like individual liberty and parliamentary democracy, the Progressive reliance on reason and education, the middle-class trust in legislative reforms and neutral social planning were all being called into question. In their place, many intellectuals displayed a growing sensitivity to political action and policy decisions based on power rather than rational persuasion, an easier acceptance of social and economic conflict as a positive force in human life, and a greater willingness to explore more radical theories and movements. Underlying this ferment was a mood of disillusion with conventional habits of mind so widespread that a classic prewar reformer like Lincoln Steffens could almost too eagerly proclaim, ". . . we liberals, the world over, have had our day, we and our liberal principles, practices, and promises."[20]

The desire to break with the liberal tradition in America, to develop programs and ideologies that might prove more effective in the context of the depression, was dramatically reflected in two books published in the early 1930s. Both John Chamberlain's *Farewell to Reform* and Lincoln Steffens's celebrated *Autobiography* exerted a substantial influence on the intellectual community because they summarized the case against Progressivism in such a way as to make their own political alternatives seem new and revolutionary. Though the origins of their attack could be traced to Croly's *Promise of American Life,* though some of the battles they were fighting had already been decided fifteen years before, Chamberlain and Steffens were consciously rephrasing the arguments to fit the present economic debacle. Thus their books represented both a continuation of and a departure from standard liberal thought as it had evolved during the past three decades.

When *Farewell to Reform* appeared in 1932, John Chamberlain was a daily book reviewer for *The New York Times.* He therefore concentrated most of his attention on the mental world of the Progressives rather than on their political behavior or legislative successes. As his title implied, Chamberlain wished to show that "in the United States 'reform' has always had a 'return' connotation," that the historic purpose of the liberal movement in America had been to restore the "methods and possibilities of a more primitive capitalism," that it was now necessary to renounce this heritage if the nation should survive.[21] His chief villains were the Wilsonians; he castigated them mercilessly for their failure to recognize the inevitability of industrial growth and economic consolidation, for their futile crusades against the trusts and monopolies, for their paranoid fear of bigness and centralization, and for their addiction to obsolete Jeffersonian ideals. In his view, the New Freedom "was looking both backward and forward, hoping somehow to restore the age of competition in an age whose technological discoveries worked irresistibly toward mass action, mass marketing, mass bargaining at the factory door."[22]

Like many of his contemporaries, Chamberlain was particularly sensitive to these retrogressive strains in liberalism since—whatever the intentions of the Progressives—their philosophy now seemed fatally intertwined with the rhetoric and policies of Herbert Hoover. In its present incarnation liberalism had come to mean rugged individualism, free enterprise, strict reliance on the "laws" of the market place, and voluntary agreements among industrialists rather than government regulation. To those who saw the practical effect of these ideals in the daily lives of the hungry and unemployed, it seemed increasingly obvious that individuals did not now exercise any personal control over their environment, that economic problems had become too complex to be solved by conferences of businessmen, that equality of opportunity was a myth in an era of centralized wealth, and that the glorification of individualism had failed to develop a sense of community or social control. Thus Chamberlain, writing with one eye on the present and one on the past, blamed the prewar generation for not seeing in the emergence of corporate capitalism an invaluable opportunity for further collectivization.

So far, Herbert Croly would have found little in these propositions with which to disagree. But Chamberlain was not content simply to rehearse the arguments against both Hoover and the New Freedom. He went on to accuse the New Nationalists and their spiritual descendants—Croly, Veblen, Dewey, Soule, Chase, Beard—of deliberately ignoring the problem of power, of relying exclusively on technicians and experts to rationalize the economy without reference to how they "may be expected to oust the high priests of the price and profit system."[23] These liberals had plans but no organization; they wanted order but shunned politics; they talked vaguely of the "nation as a whole" but declined to work "with men, with blocs, with groups, with classes," who made up the reality of American society.[24] Croly's nationalism, Veblen's instinct of workmanship, Soule's mixed economy, Dewey's emphasis on the middle class, the *New Republic*'s insistence on experimentation and pragmatic reform, all drew back from a fundamental challenge to capitalism.

By 1932, this was no longer satisfactory to men like Chamberlain. They now regarded the government not as an impartial instrument for dispensing social justice but as an arena in which power might be transferred from one group to another. They did not look on enlightened businessmen as potential allies but as a ruling class unwilling to surrender its wealth and privileges without a fight. Increasingly, they were identifying liberalism with moral exhortation, laissez faire, and a stubborn defense of the status quo. Thus, when they turned to collectivist solutions, they began to investigate the ideas not of Croly but of Marx.

Chamberlain spoke for a new generation of writers whose values and expectations had been formed either in the 1920s or under the impact of the depression, but when a charter member of the Progressive club such as Lincoln Steffens recorded his disenchantment with liberalism this carried even greater weight with intellectuals. Steffens's best-selling autobiography received considerable credit for converting its readers to a radical perspective, though many of the book's arguments were familiar to anyone who had suffered through Versailles and the death of Wilsonian idealism. Indeed, Steffens's experiences—as he recounted them in 1931—closely resembled those Frederic Howe had chronicled in his own memoir of 1925, *The Confessions of a Reformer*. Both men carefully cultivated the pose of disillusion with liberal values, both found their inherited attitudes and career aspirations substantially removed from "real life," and both felt cut off by their middle-class backgrounds from the political and social conflicts that dominated the twentieth century.

Steffens recalled that as a young man he could never distinguish between appearances and reality, between slogans and facts, between official lies and the truth that somehow always lay buried beneath the sanctimonious clichés of liberal reformers.[25] While the masses paid rapt attention to the drama of Progressivism, the "real" decisions were being made offstage, behind the scenes, in the back rooms of bosses and businessmen. Consequently Steffens, like Howe, decided that he must "unlearn" all the sophisticated theories and blueprints; he would see "not what thinkers thought, but what practical men did and why."[26] Only by a systematic absorption of social facts, a prolonged exposure to the way men actually behaved under pressure could he begin to understand how to deal effectively with modern life.

So, having abandoned all social philosophies and misty idealisms, Steffens became a voracious if somewhat amoral observer of American politics and finance. A man dedicated to viewing society without illusions, Steffens sought experience wherever he could find it—almost as a means of shocking his own middle-class gentility. He wanted to know how the United States was really ruled; in the process he delivered his famous dictum that the system, rather than bad men, was chiefly responsible for corruption, oppression, and injustice. Traditional reform was useless because it spoke in the language of high principle and social uplift, placing its faith in the election or appointment of impeccable individuals, whereas the true "politicial problem is an economic, an engineering . . . not a moral problem."[27] Presumably, capitalism was at fault and must in some way be altered.

To this point, Steffens was largely repeating the lessons many liberals had learned after World War I. But where writers like Frederic Howe and George Soule might seek in the 1920s to translate their disappointments with Progressivism into a more limited but no less sophisticated theory of social change, Steffens in the 1930s remained curiously anti-intellectual and unideological. Despite his emphasis on institutions, he still displayed more interest in superior individuals than in the abolition of capitalism. No longer capable of believing in political abstractions, he was left like Chamberlain with an attraction to sheer power and technique. Steffens could admire the bosses, the crooks, and the financial manipulators, not only because they flouted bourgeois morality but because they possessed a certain existential integrity—a commitment to their craft that constituted a higher form of professional ethics. In their own way they were more honest and less hypocritical than the reformers; they settled for unadorned facts and did not try to justify their behavior with noble rhetoric.[28]

This fascination with the men who got things done also moved Steffens to praise the Bolshevik revolution—not for its philosophy or values but for its results. He saw the future in Russia, and it was good because it "worked." Thus he did not especially mind the Soviet dictatorship, and he sympathized with its efforts to emulate American expertise, large-scale manufacturing, and industrial efficiency. The Communists "coveted not our reformers and good men, but our big, bad captains of industry . . . not our Constitution, laws, and customs, not our justice, liberty and democracy, not our respectability, good intentions, and law-abiding morality—none of our ideals, not even our business ideals, but only our machinery, our big business production, our chain stores and other beginnings of mass distribution."[29] To Steffens, this was the perfect approach to life in the twentieth century: economic, scientific, activist, but by no means moral or doctrinaire. For him, the retreat from liberal reform led to a strange kind of radicalism, a worship of personal strength and charisma that found Lenin, Mussolini, and Henry Ford equally appealing. Yet these attitudes were not unique to Steffens; they became an important element in political thought throughout the 1930s.

Inevitably, the assault on liberalism penetrated the fortress of its staunchest defender, the *New Republic*. During 1931 the journal had been questioning its own political position, but the editorial staff was seriously divided over how far this re-examination should go. Bruce Bliven and George Soule, although advocating basic changes in the economic structure, often stopped short of calling for a revolutionary transformation of American society. They couched their arguments in radical language, but the substance was sufficiently ambiguous to disturb others on the magazine who desired more systematic direction. Finally Edmund Wilson, the journal's literary editor since the late 1920s but now increasingly concerned about the nation's drift and decay, launched a frontal attack on the *New Republic*'s timidity and reserve. Like Chamberlain and Steffens, Wilson was disenchanted not only with liberal politics but also with the American intellectual's characteristic refusal to commit himself, to plunge into action, to experience life directly without relying on fancy abstractions and arid formulas.

In a lengthy article entitled "An Appeal to Progressives" Wilson chose not to pummel the dead horse of laissez faire or nineteenth-century individualism but rather to focus on the assumptions behind the *New Republic*'s historic celebration of planning in order to show that even this ideal was not truly radical. In Wilson's eyes, Herbert Croly and his successors had displayed a more mature understanding of modern America than most of their contemporaries, but they continued to believe in the efficacy of tradi-

tional politics and law to stimulate social change, and they expressly rejected the idea of an international working-class movement using all possible weapons to revolutionize human life. Hence, all of their programs
concealed a faith in the ability of capitalism to restrain and reform itself.[30]

To Wilson, the depression had permanently shattered this form of liberalism. It seemed to him impossible that intellectuals could any longer trust
in capitalism's gradual metamorphosis into something called a planned
society. Private enterprise had never provided social justice; now it could
not even guarantee security and order. But this was not all. As many of his
colleagues were to do in the next few years, Wilson defined the crisis in
moral and psychological as well as economic terms. The buoyant optimism
and expansiveness which marked the country's youth was disappearing; the
outlets for mobility and success were closing; there was no new enterprise
or political leader to capture the national imagination; the future was blank.
With the collapse of prosperity, a "dreadful apathy, unsureness, and dis-
couragement" had settled over American life. "What we have lost is . . .
not merely our way in the economic labyrinth but our conviction of the
value of what [we] were doing. Money-making and the kind of advantages
which a money-making society provides for money to buy are not enough
to satisfy humanity—neither is a social system like our own where everyone
is out for himself and the devil take the hindmost, with no common purpose
and little common culture to give life stability and sense."[31] The ideals of
nineteenth-century middle-class democracy had ended in an orgy of selfishness, mindless commercialism, and a blighted environment. A society so
rotten at its core, suffering from cultural as well as political diseases, could
not in Wilson's estimation be expected to reform itself.

In the face of this devastation, Wilson believed that the liberals who had
been "betting on capitalism" while hoping to mitigate its more obvious
injuries to the human spirit must now dissociate themselves completely
from all the old shibboleths and loyalties. Among other things this meant
that writers would have to enter into genuine and concerted opposition. No
longer could they be fearful of violence, of disturbing the existing class
relationships, or of ceasing to influence those in power. Wilson urged them
to surrender the comforting if illusive vocabulary of democratic reform and
speak out clearly: "We have always talked about the desirability of a
planned society—the phrase 'social control' has been our blessed
Mesopotamian word. But if this means anything, does it not mean socialism? And should we not do well to make this perfectly plain?"[32] Only when
they asserted emphatically that their goal was the "ownership of the means
of production by the government" would people begin to listen again.[33] In

Wilson's view Progressivism as a meaningful ideology and guide to political action was dead. For intellectuals to become effective, they would have to transfer their allegiance to a new economic and philosophical system. In essence, Wilson was calling for a conversion to Marxism.

Yet for all his bitterness at liberals, Wilson himself was unable at this point to make the ultimate commitment. Nowhere in the article did he take seriously the claims of the Communist party. Instead he hoped to prove that there was "still some virtue in American democracy." At most, Wilson encouraged his fellow writers to "take Communism away from the Communists" by adapting Marx to American conditions.[34] But he offered few suggestions on how this was to be done, or how a true socialist revolution could be carried through in the United States. For the moment, his attitudes and motivations were similar to those of Steffens: anti-bourgeois, unideological, concerned more with style than with political doctrines or strategy. It was only as the depression wore on that Wilson would attempt to support his radicalism with a systematic examination of Marxist thought.

Confronted with all these attacks, George Soule sallied forth to explain again the *New Republic*'s position. But the critics had made an impact, for he was now unwilling to brandish the liberal emblem as such. Instead he tried to demonstrate that his journal's point of view had been misunderstood, that it was indeed calling for a fundamental change in the social order.

Throughout 1931, Soule's essays reflected the degree to which his own generation was beginning to adopt a more radical posture. Like Chamberlain, he identified liberalism with the doctrine of natural rights and laissez faire; this freed him to argue that the *New Republic*'s brand of reform had always been directed toward creating "a genuine economic liberty by planning and organizing industry for the general welfare." Moreover, the fact that the magazine's values were primarily "experimental and scientific," that it entrusted its faith to no "exclusive orthodoxy or group of absolutes," seemed to him quite in keeping with the general revolt against Wilsonian idealism following World War I.[35] These attitudes had persisted into the 1930s, despite the growing attraction to Marxism. Finally, Soule denied that the *New Republic* depended on the ability of capitalism to reform itself. It had simply been more realistic to say that "the chief fault of the existing disorder was lack of planning and control" rather than blame "the profit motive or the lack of public ownership of the means of production."[36]

In Soule's mind, planning did not conceal a desire to save the system; on the contrary, it represented a chance to move step by step toward a fully socialized society. The *New Republic*, he argued, did not expect capitalists to submit voluntarily to regulation; they would surrender power only under the strong pressure of government and labor. Businessmen might initially be given an opportunity to cooperate, but if they proved unwilling, then "we should want to go as far as necessary in substituting the power of the public for the power of private owners."[37] The editors merely conceived of planning as an experiment which ought to be tried, especially now that the economy was so sick. The point was not to abandon hastily a program that in any case had little in common with conventional liberalism but to discover whether events had not made the *New Republic*'s program even more relevant in dealing with the present crisis.[38]

Where Soule differed from Gold, Chamberlain, Steffens, and Wilson was in his refusal to believe that capitalism was really on the verge of imminent collapse. Consequently he disapproved of the growing tendency to discuss social questions in apocalyptic terms, and he regarded the easy use of ultra-revolutionary language by some writers as dangerously utopian. It permitted them to satisfy their private longing for a different order by imagining a dream world and indulging in highly emotional rhetoric; meanwhile they were absolved of all responsibility for clarifying their methods and goals.[39] "Many talk as if 'capitalism' were one complete system and 'socialism' were another," Soule remarked, "and as if there were no possibility of change except to jump from the pure conceptual form of the one to the pure conceptual form of the other."[40] This state of mind provided no realistic political mechanisms by which men moved from the present into the future; it worshipped power and revolution but left the existing institutions intact. For his part, Soule believed that it was possible to initiate partial planning without having complete socialization, that capitalism would gradually disappear without violent class warfare, and that change in America could come only in piecemeal fashion. In effect, he envisioned radical ends achieved through liberal means—a position that would prove enormously difficult to sustain in the 1930s.

Ironically, Soule's perspective was unpopular not because it seemed inadequate or impractical but because it sounded painfully unimaginative. The cool precision of the *New Republic*'s outlook might appeal to economists and social scientists steeped in the tradition of Dewey and Veblen, but it demanded no personal sacrifice, no sense of danger and discipline in a heroic battle against a visible enemy. It was these feelings that excited men like Steffens and Wilson—as well as the new generation of writers growing up without jobs, without faith in long-term political action, and without any nostalgia for the prewar reform movement. By the early 1930s young intellectuals, particularly those attracted to literature and the arts, were searching for values and commitments more suitable to their sense of moral outrage at the chaos and brutality of the capitalist system. Soule's conception of planning promised an ordered and harmonious community of men in control of rather than victimized by their environment, but it did not offer the experience of direct personal engagement and struggle along the way. The *New Republic* might be realistic about how much social change one could reasonably expect in the United States, but it rarely appreciated the intense desire on the part of many writers to participate actively in a compelling cause—almost as a way out of the depression's malaise. Those who rejected liberalism did so in the final analysis because, beyond its political and ideological defects, it no longer seemed an emotionally satisfying guide to life.

3. *The Attraction to Russia*

The disenchantment with traditional reform was heightened by the existence of a concrete alternative against which American institutions and ideals could be measured. Behind the debate over liberalism and planning loomed the specter of the Soviet Union. No discussion about the nature of social change, no programs for political action could possibly avoid considering the Russian "experiment." From the moment the Bolsheviks seized power the course of radical thought was influenced by their policies, rhetoric, and symbolism. For better or worse, the American intellectual's ability to devise a new social philosophy and value system in the 1930s depended to a great extent on what he thought about Russia.

Ever since the day in 1917 when John Reed departed for Moscow to view the revolutionary turmoil at first hand, American newspapers and magazines had dispatched a steady stream of observers to report on the construction of socialism. Throughout the 1920s Marxist journalists, liberal social scientists, novelists and poets made the journey, although not in anything like the numbers that were to visit Russia in the following decade. Their motivations were often ambiguous. Some went with a mixture of antagonism and envy; others, with a genuine interest in the progress of the experiment or with a residual loyalty to the intellectuals' dream of social democracy. The latter sentiment was particularly true of Jewish writers, many of whom were refugees from Czarist oppression and who cared deeply about the transformation of their original homeland. But whether they were old-stock Progressives who had voted for Wilson believing he was a more refined version of Debs, or immigrant radicals with their roots in the working class and instinctively Marxist in outlook, many saw the Bolshevik revolution as a natural continuation of the socialist tradition which was the special hope and dream of Western intellectuals. Even those who firmly rejected Marxism could not ignore the land in which socialism was actually being tried. So they traveled to the Soviet Union to see for themselves whether another way of living and ordering reality could work.

Nevertheless, the prosperity of the 1920s fostered the illusion that America had sufficient time to await the final results of the experiment. With the collapse of the stock market and the onset of the depression, however, interest in Russia took on a new note of urgency. Now the descriptions of Soviet life were clearly designed to evoke comparison with events in the United States. The U.S.S.R., with its shining five-year plans and its sure sense of direction, seemed somehow a reproach to confused, tired, chaotic America.

The Russians were building a society whose political, economic, and cultural values tested the most cherished of American assumptions. Moreover, the pilgrims to Moscow felt a sensation of being present at the dawn of a new age; as the old world died, another was being born before their very eyes. All of this invested the Soviet Union with a moral and psychological superiority which the United States appeared unable to match. "For Russians," Stuart Chase exclaimed in 1931, "the world is exciting, stimulating, challenging, calling forth their interest and enthusiasm. The world for most Americans is dull and uninspiring, wracked with frightful economic insecurity."[41] While the West struggled helplessly with the depression, its people at the mercy of economic forces over which they had no control, the U.S.S.R. strode purposefully into the future—bidding the rest of mankind to follow if they dared. This alone was enough to inspire many writers who knew and cared little about fine points of doctrine. But even for those who were ideologically sophisticated and seriously concerned with the details of social reconstruction, Russian communism was a powerful magnetic field. As George Soule admitted:

> If it goes on in the course of time to produce at least as high a standard of living as ours without our insecurity, to demonstrate the possibility of planning and control over a complex industrial system and to offer a full measure of the more intangible satisfactions, the effect will be as momentous in history as was the discovery of America at the end of the Middle Ages. Not only shall we know that capitalism as we have experienced it is undesirable, but that a different and better order is actually possible.[42]

For a growing number of writers in the early 1930s, the Soviet example provided not only an alternative to democratic capitalism but a plausible replacement for the dying American Dream. Thus its appeal rested as much in its symbolic suggestion of a new way of life as in its more prosaic social and economic programs.

Yet the effort to learn from the communist experience was complicated by the extraordinary difficulty of finding out precisely what was going on in Russia. This was not so much because of Soviet propaganda or the carefully arranged tours of model factories and collective farms as because Americans generally saw what they wanted to see. It was impossible to report objectively about the U.S.S.R.; a visitor's judgment was often filtered through the lens of his own values and expectations. Whether hostile or sympathetic, the traveler arrived with so many preconceptions that Russia became not a nation in the throes of social revolution but an image in the observer's mind. The "truth" about the Soviet Union frequently depended on whatever issues and problems seemed uppermost in the United States; thus writers tended to emphasize the literacy campaigns and the explosion of mass culture in the 1920s while concentrating on the complexities of economic planning after 1930.[43] But regardless of one's special interest, almost every visitor had an emotional stake in the success or failure of socialism so that they were rarely able to offer detached appraisals of a backward land struggling to enter the twentieth century.

Some did not even try. For the American Communists, a posture of non-partisanship and objectivity was considered immoral and irresponsible. The New Masses did not feel neutral about Russia or socialism. Instead it conducted an unceasing crusade against the critics of the U.S.S.R., charging that they either misunderstood or deliberately distorted the struggles within the Politburo, the decision to industrialize rapidly, the policy toward kulaks, and the continuing rumors of famine. All of these crises had to be placed in the context of Marxist analysis, but, even more important, the Soviet Union had to be defended as the fatherland of socialism. The New Masses eagerly assumed both tasks for its readers. In the early years of the decade, when the Communists feared an imminent invasion of the U.S.S.R. either from Japan or the West, the magazine portrayed the advance of socialist construction in glowing language—constantly contrasting the harmony and order of Soviet life with the disintegration of American society, seeking always to persuade the world that socialism had made Russia strong enough to resist attack.[44] No distinction was made between the goals of Russian foreign policy, the pressures of modernization, or the needs of the working class. Each of these elements was bound up with all the others; one either accepted or rejected the whole package. To the New Masses, the Bolshevik program was no longer an "experiment"; it had been proved a total success beyond doubt.

Though non-Communist writers did not share the unshakable faith of the *New Masses*, they were often just as enthusiastic over developments in Russia. But they usually translated their praise into peculiarly American terms. For many liberals, the idea of the Soviet Union as an "experiment" was especially appealing because it made the entire experience seem scientific and pragmatic—an unfinished test where final judgment could be suspended until all the results were in. This eliminated the need to evaluate or criticize the more unpleasant aspects of the dictatorship, since the system was still being perfected.[45] Moreover, Russian propaganda often emphasized achievements that sounded typically American. Both countries valued the material rewards of mass production, both respected the machine and its power to transform life, both celebrated industrialism and technology, both worshipped bigness as a sign of quality and progress, both preached the virtues of efficiency and physical growth.

In addition, the fascination with industrial statistics, the awe at modern factories and brand-new towns, the spectacle of natural resources being harnessed for man's use, all served to underscore the priority granted to economic development over parliamentary democracy and civil liberties in the 1930s. The dictatorship could be excused because formal political freedom seemed a bit of a luxury in times of economic crisis and revolution. When writers considered the issue of repression at all, they frequently thought not of Stalinism but of fascism, whose rising menace tended to reinforce and expand Russian prestige throughout the decade.[46]

Most important of all, the Soviets appeared to be accomplishing under socialism what American liberals had never won under capitalism. While the United States suffered under the anarchy of the market place, while it failed to make its enormous productive potential serve human needs, while its citizens became disoriented in an apparently unmanageable environment, the Russians were building a rational and ordered society. To a man like Frederick Schuman, a liberal political scientist and frequent contributor to the *New Republic*, the Soviet Union was fulfilling not Marxist but Progressive ideals. "For the first time," he pointed out, "a great people has embarked upon a consciously organized effort to plan its entire economic life." In Schuman's view, the Stalinist regime was merely an administrative agency through which economic chaos and exploitation would be replaced by "intelligently directed planning and cooperation."[47] Schuman approved of the decision to collectivize agriculture and eliminate the kulaks at whatever cost because this meant a further step toward the planned society—just as liberals urged government regulation of business as another blow at free enterprise.

In essence, the Bolsheviks were pictured as rather like the *New Republic*'s consummate technicians—committed to experimentation, concerned with economic efficiency and expert social control, men who got results without worrying too much over morality or doctrine. Indeed many liberals preferred the flexible, pragmatic, practical Stalin to Trotsky, whom they regarded as an ideologue, a utopian, an ineffective intellectual in a world that demanded action more than ideas. If Soviet society seemed excessively regimented, this was due not to Stalin's policies but to the whole nature of modern life. The factory whistle, the assembly line, the bureaucracy, all diminished man's freedom; the Russians were only trying to humanize these institutions as much as possible. Since American liberals could not yet perform this service for their own society, they might at least sympathize with the Soviet effort.

Yet whether Russia was seen as an alternative to or fulfillment of liberal programs, its ultimate appeal lay in what it stood for psychologically and culturally. The image of death and rebirth, of the old world decaying as the new emerged in all its youthful strength, ran through most descriptions of Soviet life. Even the hardships in Russia imparted a sense of spirit and energy to writers whose own country was floundering without purpose or direction. For Louis Fischer, the *Nation*'s correspondent in Moscow, the Soviet Union became a symbol of everything America had once been and was no longer. Revolution and nation-building extracted a heavy price from the Russian people, but Fischer believed that pain inevitably accompanied any human battle to build a new order:

> The truth about Russia is Janus-faced. Everyday life is hard and black. People suffer. . . . But there is another, a bright and encouraging side: the birth of new "Socialist" cities, the erection of giant factories and farms, the thrill of a whole continent tapping new sources of creative energy and marching toward economic independence and a better standard of living. . . . The hardships of today sometimes impress and depress me, but more often the light of the future blurs them out of sight, and the focus of my mind's eye shifts to the positive, the constructive, the creative. The difficulties are those concomitant with growth and youth.[48]

With the rest of the world appearing so rotten and senile, with so little to be hopeful about amid the wreckage of the depression, Fischer preferred to associate himself with any signs of optimism and progress he could find. Like the foreign traveler in Jacksonian America, he marveled at the dynamism and potential of the Soviet Union. And like the United States a century before, Russia was struggling to possess the future. More than anything else, Fischer was overwhelmed by the conviction that the Soviet Union and history were moving along the same course.

John Dewey, otherwise skeptical of Marxism, was also taken with Russia's remarkable resemblance to nineteenth-century America. The Soviet Union intrigued Dewey as a frontier land "inhabited by a strangely young folk, with the buoyancy, energy, naïveté and immaturity of youth and inexperience. . . . Freed from the load of subjection to the past, it seems charged with the ardor of creating a new world."[49] Here was the legend of the second chance, another Puritan city on a hill. It was easy—perhaps too easy—to see in the Moscow of Stalin the Concord of Emerson and Thoreau. It was even easier to transform the Soviet Union into an image of one's own hopes for America.

But what really attracted Dewey was not so much the pioneer spirit of Russia as its cultural promise. The chief task of the Soviet leaders, as he interpreted it, was not simply to build new economic institutions but to create a totally new state of mind. They were attempting to substitute "a collectivist mentality for the individualistic psychology" inherited from the past.[50] To Dewey, this revolution in attitudes was a more permanent achievement than any political or social program the regime might undertake. Far from trusting to the inexorable operation of Marxist "laws," the Soviets—like good instrumentalists—were actively trying to liberate man's consciousness and will so that he could control his own life and environment.

In this context, Dewey was transfixed by the "release of human powers," the denial of economic determinism, the insistence on the importance of ideas which he found in Russia.[51] Moreover, in developing institutions that emphasized cooperation and social responsibility, the Soviet Union was relying heavily on "education" in its broadest sense. There was no longer a separation of school and society because men were being systematically trained in the classroom and in daily life to serve the needs of one another.[52] Nor were Russian intellectuals isolated from their countrymen. Since the Bolsheviks placed so much weight on education, the position of the intelligentsia in the U.S.S.R. was clearly more appealing to Dewey than the frustration writers endured in the West. " 'Intellectuals' in other countries," he pointed out, "have a task that is, if they are sincere, chiefly critical; those who have identified themselves in Russia with the new order have a task that is total and constructive. They are organic members of an organic going movement."[53] Dewey never embraced the romantic ideal of the artist-in-exile. Like Fischer and many other writers in the 1930s, he tended to favor whatever forces seemed positive, "progressive," and powerful. By helping to build a new society and a new culture, intellectuals in the Soviet Union appeared to be making history in a way that American writers had conspicuously failed to do since World War I. For this reason, Dewey was both admiring and slightly envious of his Russian counterparts.

Thus Dewey's Russia resembled a model Progressive school, committed to experimentation and cultural conditioning, devoted to communal and collectivist values, interested in "socializing" every person in the land. Though Dewey disliked the rampant dogmatizing, the propaganda about class war and world revolution, he came away basically sympathetic to the "scientific" spirit he discovered in the Soviet Union, as well as to its belief that individualism was dead. Yet the visit did not convert him to Marxism largely because he viewed the whole enterprise through typically American eyes. Ultimately Dewey described communism as an effort to find out whether *democracy* (liberty, equality, brotherhood) could be achieved more completely in a collectivist rather than capitalist society. Since the outcome was still in doubt, he admitted that he preferred "seeing it tried in Russia rather than my own country."[54] But by concentrating on the revolution in ideas instead of the economic changes taking place in the U.S.S.R., by extolling Russia's open-ended pragmatism over its Marxist faith in historical destiny, by adhering to liberal sentiments while trying to separate them from their roots in capitalism, Dewey remained philosophically at home. What he thought he saw in Russia was the combination of thought and action, theory and practice, which constituted the very core of his own Progressivism.

In sum, the Soviet Union symbolized in the minds of many American writers both an extension of and a replacement for their traditional political commitments and values. They used it as a metaphor, in much the same way as the Agrarians used the South, to suggest a desirable cultural alternative. Russia and communism were attractive not necessarily for ideological reasons but because the Bolsheviks claimed that they were using human intelligence in the interests of social control. The Soviet experiment called on men to transcend their backgrounds and inherited assumptions, to enter into a painful struggle with the blind forces of nature, to participate actively in the creation of a new world. No other philosophy in the 1930s, certainly not liberalism, demanded or promised as much. A large number of American intellectuals, if they did not always accept or even fully understand the substance of Marxism, nevertheless believed that socialism in its Russian form represented a compelling substitute for their own decaying society.

Yet it was precisely this equation of socialism with Russia that helped to paralyze radical thought in the 1930s. Among other things, it often led to an obsession with the Soviet Union on the part of both sympathizers and critics, rather than to a sustained exploration of Marxist ideas. Indeed the strength of one's socialist values and loyalties frequently depended solely on the course of events in Russia. The very notion that the Soviet Union was an unfinished experiment in socialism could force Max Eastman—a man not noted for his praise of Stalin—to warn that "if the Soviet culture as it developed did not bear out in essential ways the hopes predicated upon it, I should be ready to abandon the idea of improving human society by guiding a revolution toward socialism."[55] This attitude provided the writer with a convenient excuse for rejecting his radicalism altogether should he grow disenchanted with the U.S.S.R.

The trouble was that in the Soviet Union the good and the bad were visibly juxtaposed. Since many facets of the old Russia had survived into the post-revolutionary era, an observer could never be certain which elements were due to the nation's peculiar history and which were the products of Marxist doctrine. Was the Stalinist regime a throwback to the days of the Czar, or was it inherent in socialism? No American seemed able to answer this question satisfactorily. As Edmund Wilson recognized, "the opponents of socialism can always put down to socialism anything they find objectionable in Russia. The advocates of socialism are betrayed into defending things which are really distasteful to them and which they have no business defending."[56] In his opinion, the existence of the Stalinist dictatorship lay at the "core of the whole Russian question"; it had to be faced candidly by any advocate of socialism in the United States.[57] Unfortunately, few writers in the 1930s possessed the candor or courage to admit these unpleasant facts. Because so many hopes were invested in the success of the Soviet experiment, and because Stalinism represented the only concrete model of a socialist society, it became psychologically impossible to achieve a balanced perspective on Russia. Intellectuals either defended the U.S.S.R. with an emotional intensity that crippled rational judgment, or they implacably condemned every policy and program the regime advanced. Whichever position one adopted, the capacity to offer *critical* support—to analyze the Russian adventure dispassionately while sympathizing with its announced objectives—was almost always absent.

As a result, the attack on liberalism and the parallel attraction to the Soviet Union often ended not in a conversion to radical theory but rather in a commitment to special forms of culture and myth. Men like Chamberlain, Steffens, Wilson, Fischer, and even Dewey were indeed searching for an alternative social philosophy, but their positions tended to emphasize matters of technique, style, and spirit more than doctrinal nuance. Opposed to capitalism, disillusioned with Progressivism, they chose to concentrate almost exclusively on action, expertise, and power—none of which had much to do with programmatic solutions to the nation's problems. Though they talked a good deal about the merits of community and collectivism, though they appreciated the need to create a new set of values for the American people, intellectuals were not as yet prepared to define the goals the country should seek. They knew what they were against, but they had only symbols and images to suggest what they were for. Abandoning liberalism, they were not truly socialists. Ironically, in a period that was supposed to be heavily influenced by Marx, most American writers during the early 1930s lacked the rudiments of any effective ideology.

4. *Alternatives to Capitalism*

For all the weaknesses in their outlook, however, a number of intellectuals were beginning to reach certain fundamental conclusions by 1932. It was in this year, at the very bottom of the depression, that some writers attempted to describe more systematically what could be done to build a new society. Over the past twenty years, the concept of planning had been a major weapon in the liberal arsenal; now three books appeared within months of one another, each of which sought to translate that idea into a comprehensive program for social change. Their arguments were particularly important because they mirrored the desire of most intellectuals to break with the reform tradition, yet find an alternative that still corresponded to American conditions. None of these books was especially dramatic, nor did they hold much appeal for those who eagerly awaited the revolution; they were sober, detailed, clinical examinations of the existing social order and the ways in which it might be slowly remodeled. Nevertheless, they represented the farthest point to which writers had moved in a time of increasing desperation and despair, when the nation's political and economic institutions had clearly failed to cope with the crisis of capitalism.

Perhaps the most influential—and the least radical—of the three books was *The Modern Corporation and Private Property.* Its authors were both established academicians. Adolph Berle taught law at Columbia, while Gardiner Means was a professional economist; their study had been financed by the prestigious Social Science Research Council. The work was designed more as an objective analysis of changes in America's corporate structure than as a call to political action. But neither its technical prose nor its monographic format prevented the book from exerting a profound effect on liberals and radicals alike in the years following its publication. Whatever the authors' original intent, their ideas were continually cited as evidence that capitalism had to be replaced by a more collectivist economic system.

One reason for the extraordinary impact of the book was that, despite the difficulty of its style and subject matter, it contained a relatively simple thesis which many writers in the 1930s could understand and accept. Essentially, Berle and Means argued that the familiar assumptions about property and capitalism were obsolete, that those who were stockholders in or owners of the modern corporation no longer exercised control over its daily activities, that real power was passing to a new class of managers whose ultimate motives and interests had little in common with the traditional quest for profit. They were more concerned with efficiency, consolidation, planning, and stability than with the old entrepreneurial values of expansion and risk. All of this meant that the notion of "private" enterprise—in which individual owners of property were directly responsible for their particular businesses and in which the resulting competition presumably contributed to the general progress of society as a whole—had nothing to do with how the modern economy actually operated.[58]

Moreover, Berle and Means believed that the divorce of ownership from control had challenged two of the most cherished American ideals: individual initiative and the opportunity to rise through ability and hard work. With the emergence of a bureaucratic mentality that pervaded corporate life at every level, loyalty to the organization became more important than personal originality or creativity. "To the dozen or so men in control," the authors declared, "there is room for such initiative. For the tens and even hundreds of workers and of owners in a single enterprise, individual initiative no longer exists. Their activity is group activity on a scale so large that the individual, except he be in a position of control, has dropped into relative insignificance."[59] Thus the world was closing in on the average American. Absorbed into mass society, wedded to an impersonal organization, indistinguishable from his fellow citizens, he could hardly keep from appearing less ambitious and less heroic than the nineteenth-century pioneer. In the twentieth century, security and survival were considered more compelling than freedom and success. With no particular pride in their work and no feeling that they were striving to build a better society, both the white-collar and working classes grew resigned to the presence of large institutions which defined their identities and shaped their lives.

Since economic and social behavior had become thoroughly collectivized, there seemed little reason to preserve the antiquated forms of private property or the individualistic values on which they were based. But Berle and Means stopped short of advocating measures either to dismantle the corporation or to socialize the economy. Instead they were willing to retain the corporate structure, but they wanted it somehow to serve the needs of the entire country. "Neither the claims of ownership nor those of control can stand against the paramount interests of the community," they asserted. Once the classic prerogatives of private ownership had disappeared, neither the stockholders nor the managers could claim the right to have the corporations run in their behalf. In effect, the authors were proposing the idea of a "neutral technocracy" in which business activities would be regulated by the state for the welfare of the whole nation.[60] In a mood typical of the 1930s, they were less concerned with the issues of bigness and monopoly than with the problem of power. Given the economic changes that had taken place in the twentieth century, who would now control the new giant organizations? Their answer was a strong government presiding over a mixed economy halfway between capitalism and socialism. It was not surprising, therefore, that they should soon find their talents better used in Washington than on Morningside Heights.

If Berle and Means chose to call for a kind of welfare capitalism under liberal direction, others decided at this point to abandon private enterprise altogether. By 1932 the heirs of the Progressive tradition were searching for an "American"-style socialism, and nowhere was this better expressed than in Stuart Chase's *A New Deal* and George Soule's *A Planned Society*. Both writers now agreed with their critics on the left that planning alone could neither end the depression nor provide a decent human life in the United States. Consequently they tried in their books to suggest a coherent political strategy and economic program that was at once democratic and radical, that linked immediate reforms to a full-scale social revolution, that would convert Herbert Croly's collectivist ideals into a daily reality for every American. Yet behind their explicit desire to move beyond liberal capitalism lay some curiously conservative notions and conclusions—and these were perhaps as characteristic of the decade's state of mind as its burgeoning romance with Marxism.

Significantly, Chase and Soule rejected capitalism not because it was exploitative or oppressive but because it appeared wasteful and inefficient. For them the main evil of a marketplace economy was that it fostered competition, anarchy, and chaos. Individual businessmen fought with one another over the available markets, expanded or cut back production solely according to calculations of profit and loss, and distributed goods largely on the basis of whoever could pay. All of these traits contributed to the general irrationality of American life and accounted for the terrible spectacle of human want amid potential plenty. Capitalism never offered any sense of social purpose or direction even in the best of times; now the depression literally shattered the system into its component parts. In their view, the country was afflicted with a crisis of mismanagement and disintegration. Any effort to deal with these problems either through legislative reform or marginal readjustments only generated more confusion because capitalism itself was inherently unstable.[61]

This sense of total collapse, of a society in various stages of decomposition, had a profound effect on most Americans—intellectuals as well as ordinary citizens. The depression meant more than simply the failure of business; it was to many people an overwhelming natural catastrophe, much like an earthquake that uprooted and destroyed whatever lay in its path. Men became preoccupied with floods, dust storms, and soil erosion not only because these constituted real problems but also because they were perfect metaphors for a breakdown that appeared more physical than social or economic. It gave Americans the feeling that their whole world was literally falling apart, that their traditional expectations and beliefs were absolutely meaningless, that there was no personal escape from the common disaster. It propelled the individual into a void of bewilderment and terror. Thus the crisis seemed to require a response that promised peace and safety more than further uncertainty. What men wanted very often was not revolution but recovery.

For these reasons, Chase and Soule tended to stress the virtues of order, discipline, and social control in their proposals for a new America. Concerned less with the elimination of the profit motive as such than with the re-creation of equilibrium and security in economic affairs, they called for a tightly integrated system of production, distribution, and consumption, managed by the state in the interests of general social need. In essence, they were demanding a complete reallocation of wealth and resources, a well-regulated adjustment of prices to purchasing power, a balanced relationship between industry and agriculture, and a forced march into the economy of abundance.[62] Since capitalism was already half collectivized, with partial government supervision of banking and tariffs, private trade associations and cartels, corporate monopolies, consumer cooperatives, and labor unions, it seemed a simple matter to advance toward a fully socialized economy.[63]

What stood in the way was not so much class divisions as the old nemesis of cultural lag: Americans still adhered to an outmoded individualism, a refusal to see that personal freedom was impossible without social coercion, an unwillingness to surrender the dream of success for the more enduring vision of a harmonious and stable commonwealth.[64] Once these preconceptions and inherited attitudes were erased, the nation itself could be reconstructed. By concentrating on the influence of "obsolete" values, Chase and Soule made the period of transition seem less dangerous and disruptive than it might otherwise appear. They continued to stress the importance of rational debate, education, and non-violence, precisely because they recognized the country's strong desire to avoid—rather than intensify—social conflict. Thus they were trying ingeniously to use America's conservative impulses and traditions for radical ends. Their brand of socialism was still "scientific," pragmatic, and gradualist; it depended for its success on disinterested technicians and engineers, not on partisan ideologies.

Sometimes the result of all this could seem disturbingly elitist. "The drive of collectivism leads toward control from the top," Chase exclaimed with equanimity. He for one was quite attracted to the idea of a "board of managers" who would transact the nation's social and economic business with a minimum of interference from the "people."[65] In his scheme of priorities, skill and efficiency were simply more important than popular participation; control should be vested in those who knew most about how to run a complex society. It was not surprising that both he and Soule, given their view of the depression as the product of anarchy and chaos, should refer to the example of planning during World War I or talk at length about a "general staff" to cope with the emergency. Their rhetoric frequently sounded martial, and their solutions pointed to an extremely centralized, highly structured, and potentially repressive social order.

But these possibilities remained latent in their thought. However conservative their approach to social change, however fearful of a massive upheaval that might further destroy rather than rebuild the country, Chase and Soule were nevertheless committed to socialist alternatives within the framework of democratic procedures, constitutional rights, and electoral action. They rejected the concept of a Leninist-style revolution in the United States, not so much on moral or ideological grounds but because they did not believe that the American working class would at present accept the doctrines of class struggle. Consequently, they focused on immediate practical reforms as a step-by-step progression away from private enterprise and toward collectivism. For political leadership they looked to an alliance among workers, farmers, and a rising middle class of engineers, technicians, industrial managers, teachers, and disaffected professionals.[66] Here Chase and Soule were speaking for the majority of their contemporaries. It was in this coalition, dedicated to the general goals of central planning and democratic socialism, that most writers placed their faith for the rest of the decade.

Ultimately, the aims of the movement were as much psychological as economic. On the one hand, Chase and Soule envisioned a system in which the government operated the nation's industrial and agricultural plant in the public's behalf. On the other hand, they sought to overcome the problems of chaos and disintegration by developing a new spirit of mutual help and social responsibility. Hence Soule chose to emphasize man's "organizing" instincts, his natural inclination for sharing and cooperation, his fervent desire to escape the remorseless competition and acquisitiveness of capitalism.[67] Socialism therefore promised not only to make modern life more rational and coherent; it would also end one's feeling of "being individually at war with society, of being baffled and burdened by an irrelevant environment." For Soule, planning meant the creation of a "warm and active bond with our fellows," a sense of comradeship that would solve America's spiritual as well as social crisis.[68]

This kind of analysis was not unique to Chase or Soule; others were thinking along similar lines. Toward the close of 1932, a new magazine called *Common Sense* appeared. Edited by Alfred Bingham and Selden Rodman, it regularly published articles by John Dewey, Lewis Mumford, Max Eastman, Roger Baldwin, Theodore Dreiser, John Dos Passos, Scott Nearing, John Chamberlain, James Rorty, and A. J. Muste. Yet despite the wide spectrum of political beliefs among its contributors, the journal had a consistent philosophy for which Bingham was largely responsible. In an early essay entitled "Looking Forward" he sketched his view of the "good society" America might become in the year 2000—and in many ways it captured what writers truly had in mind when they thought about social alternatives.

Bingham's America was remarkably ordered, clean, and symmetrical. Parks were nicely balanced with thoroughfares, cities were well integrated with the countryside, traffic congestion and air polution were nonexistent, industrial and agricultural production were almost totally automated, the people appeared vigorous and healthy, work and leisure perfectly complemented one another, and men were equal without being absorbed into a faceless mob. No longer plagued by advertising, commercialism, competition, or greed, human life had become simple, direct, and functional.[69] This happy state of affairs—so obviously in contrast to the misery and ugliness of the 1930s—was accomplished through the formation of a new political party which gained the allegiance of the majority of Americans, wrested power from the Republicans and Democrats, gradually abolished the system of private profit, and brought forth "not a new tyranny under a bureaucratic machine, but a democratic republic of industry and a decentralized representative government . . . dedicated to the ownership and control of the country by the people."[70] The lesson of this, for Bingham, was that men "can now produce in plenty, and that they need only work together with a larger community loyalty in distributing what they produce, to reach an unheard-of standard of living, a new moral health, and a new beauty," all of which would come with the elimination of poverty, exploitation, and selfishness.[71] When the struggle for personal survival had ended, when men no longer detested their present jobs or worried about their future security, when economic activity served the common welfare, then genuine freedom for the individual was possible.

This was an eminently sensible utopia, of the sort usually associated with Scandinavia or Russia or later with the TVA. If it lacked much emotional appeal, if it seemed a bit too clinical and efficient, this was because Bingham saw the depression as a complex disease which had to be cured by intelligence, rational analysis, and expert skill. In a situation as desperate as the 1930s, restrained language seemed more appropriate to *Common Sense* than anticipations of the apocalypse.

The approach of men like Chase, Soule, Bingham, Berle, and Means, all reflected the yearning of most American intellectuals in 1932 that the nation should pass from an era of expansion and progress to one of consolidation and repose. After three centuries of uninterrupted growth the country was no longer young, but in their judgment it appeared to be drifting into maturity without any purpose or direction. The future ceased to hold out infinite possibilities; instead, the frontier was closed, the birth rate seemed to be declining, machine production had outstripped its markets, and men were becoming more aware of their own limitations. Thus writers began to focus on the need for a stable, well-regulated, responsible society—one that did not threaten to fly apart at any moment. "Coherence" was more than a metaphor; it literally meant a social order in which every element was organically interrelated, in which the past had been assimilated naturally into the present, in which man had regained *control* over his environment and his destiny. This was at once a profoundly radical and conservative vision. It promised to fashion a society different from anything Americans had ever known, yet at the same time restore to them a sense of rationality and community they had somehow lost in the massive upheavals of the nineteenth and twentieth centuries. In addition, it represented both a continuation of and a break with the Progressive tradition: liberal in strategy, socialist in ultimate aims. After three years of bitter controversy and debate over how most effectively to deal with the depression, some writers were able to suggest at least a tentative program for political and economic recovery. What they needed now were constituents beyond the intellectual community—and this was to prove a more difficult problem than the depression itself.

5. *The Election of 1932*

Throughout the early 1930s the American people appeared remarkably passive and resigned, waiting for something to happen that might alleviate their suffering but unable to act positively in coping with the crisis. Despite well-publicized hunger marches and demonstrations of the unemployed, the years between 1930 and 1932 bred not anger but apathy, not militance but hopelessness, not determination but confusion and panic. Only writers and certain groups within the middle class seem to have been thoroughly radicalized by the depression, and their dissatisfaction with American life often preceded the stock-market crash. Already estranged from the prevailing culture and values of the 1920s, feeling themselves to be outsiders because they were intellectuals in a society which had no place for their talents, they were psychologically predisposed to move to the left in the 1930s. For them, this was a time of hope and expectation; the worse conditions grew, the more they became impatient for a revolution of some kind.[72] But no one—neither writers nor ordinary citizens—had been confronted with real political choices since the depression began. Now the period of bewilderment and speculation came to an end with the Presidential campaign of 1932.

For a number of prominent intellectuals, disgusted with the inertia of the major parties and put off by the Socialists' timidity, the only way of calling attention to the seriousness of the crisis was by voting Communist. This was a gratifying gesture not so much because writers agreed with the party's programs but because it served as a moral challenge to a decaying system. Edmund Wilson, observing the performance of William Z. Foster before a typically obtuse Congressional committee, declared that the American Communists appeared emotionally healthier than anyone else. They at least knew exactly what they wanted and had adopted an "uncompromising policy to get it." Whatever their faults—"their pedantry, their conspiratorial leanings, their dependence on an alien tradition and their consequent partial incomprehensibility to the people they have set out to convert" —the Communists possessed an inner strength and resolve no other group could match. "They are people," Wilson concluded, "who are willing to die for a religion," and in a nation bereft of any sustaining beliefs or values this was an invaluable commodity.[73] Wilson admired their faith in themselves, their sense of solidarity and purpose, their unwavering commitment to the future. Amid the social and economic debris of the depression, the Communists alone seemed durable.

To Wilson and many of his colleagues, these were precisely the qualities Hoover, Roosevelt, and Norman Thomas all lacked. Thus in September of 1932 fifty-two intellectuals endorsed an open letter announcing their intention to vote for the Communist candidates, Foster and Ford. Their reasoning was incorporated into a pamphlet entitled "Culture and the Crisis," written primarily by Malcolm Cowley, Matthew Josephson, and James Rorty; its co-signers included Sherwood Anderson, Newton Arvin, Erskine Caldwell, Robert Cantwell, Lewis Corey, John Dos Passos, Waldo Frank, Granville Hicks, Sidney Hook, Langston Hughes, Frederick Schuman, Lincoln Steffens, and Edmund Wilson. In it they asserted that the Republicans and Democrats merely wished to patch up capitalism, that the Socialists were more interested in maintaining their respectability and winning elections than in the daily struggles of the working class, and that only the Communists were committed to a total social and cultural revolution. There was no longer any middle ground; the intellectuals had to choose between a world that was slowly dying and one that was about to be born. By supporting Foster and Ford, the pamphlet argued, writers could help wring concessions from the major parties, expand the Communists' influence among the masses, and prepare the country for a genuine socialist transformation.[74]

Others were less certain that supporting the Communists would have these results. In George Soule's view, the American people were simply not in a revolutionary mood. In the absence of a strong labor movement and the emergence of a widespread socialist consciousness, one could either vote for Franklin Roosevelt as a lesser evil or for one of the minor parties as a symbolic protest.[75] Faced with this bleak estimate of the political situation, the *Nation* and the *New Republic* reluctantly settled on Norman Thomas as the best of a bad lot. They acknowledged that Roosevelt occasionally spoke as if he had some insight into the causes of the depression, but his remedies promised "no change whatever in the basic characteristics of the American economic system."[76] The Socialists, on the other hand, had no organization, no mass support, and no hope of winning any election in the near future. Nevertheless, the journals urged support for Thomas because he came closest to their ideal of democratic socialism and because a large Socialist vote represented a first step toward the construction of a new party that might conceivably take power in 1936.[77]

While the intellectuals were debating the relative merits of Foster or Thomas, most people took the only practical alternative offered them and swept the Democrats into office. No one was quite certain what the election results really meant beyond a negative desire to defeat Hoover, nor what to expect from the new Administration except possibly more of the same.

But in comparison with the ominous news coming from Germany, mused the *New Republic,* "the reaction of the American people to the calamities that have befallen them is astonishingly mild."[78] Yet how long the United States would retain its composure was an open question.

6. *The New Deal and Its Critics*

Economically the winter of 1932–1933 was the worst in American history. After three years of depression the nation's industry, agriculture, and banking system lay mortally wounded. Funds for relief of the poor and the hungry had been completely exhausted on the city and state levels. No longer did anyone dare to predict the return of prosperity. The Republicans were a defeated party, but their successors offered little evidence that they could deal with the country's problems more capably. On the eve of a new President's inauguration the political leadership of the United States seemed as bankrupt as its economy.

The *Nation* reflected the mood of many when it described the present situation as more desperate than at any time since 1861. "The country faces the gravest crisis in its peace-time history," brooded the journal. "The life of the country is at low ebb." Since the old formulas had visibly failed, the *Nation*'s editors pleaded with Franklin Roosevelt to "try new leaders and new ideas, and to venture boldly into untrodden paths."[79] The *Nation,* the *New Republic,* and *Common Sense* all had a set of specific recommendations to greet the incoming President: firm government control of production and prices, the restoration of consumer purchasing power, massive public works projects, recognition of labor unions, nationalization of banks and transportation, and a general attack on the system of private profit.[80] Yet even these would not be enough. "Our civilization is extremely sick," declared the *New Republic,* "and the most important cause of its sickness is the maldistribution of income." What America really required "was a drastic transfer of wealth from the Haves to the Have-nots."[81] As yet no one knew whether the Haves would surrender their power and possessions without a struggle, or whether Roosevelt was prepared to battle them if they refused. The magazines were deeply pessimistic, however, about his desire or capacity to undertake this sort of cure.

Their skepticism was to some extent unwarranted. Whatever its campaign rhetoric, the new Administration seemed to share many of the same attitudes and aims as the intellectual community. The speechwriters, lawyers, and economists who came to Washington with Roosevelt were by no means innocent of ideology; on the contrary, they had a relatively coherent and sophisticated sense of what needed to be done. Unlike those Progressives whose view of reform stressed good government and moral uplift, many of Roosevelt's advisers had some experience with social work among the urban lower classes; they understood that morality was less important than the problems of housing, health, unemployment, and poverty. Moreover, they were quite willing to make special adjustments for groups which had been left outside the Progressive consensus; immigrants, workers, and Negroes were all offered at least token recognition, if not open admission into the middle class.[82]

In addition, most of the early recruits to the New Deal traced their intellectual lineage not to Woodrow Wilson's New Freedom but to the tradition of Herbert Croly, Simon Patten, John Dewey, and Thorstein Veblen. Men like Rexford Tugwell, Raymond Moley, and Henry Wallace accepted the inevitability of bigness in industry and government; they were more interested in the regulation and control of monopoly than in restoring competition. They tended to emphasize the importance not so much of individual freedom but of economic equality and social security for the nation as a whole.[83].

Moreover, the key word in the vocabulary of the Roosevelt Administration was "balance." Like the radical intellectuals, the New Dealers were especially disturbed by the *chaos* of private capitalism; in their view, American life needed a greater sense of order and control if the nation was to survive the depression. Where they differed with the radicals, however, was in their desire to create a harmony of interests among all classes without destroying the profit system at the same time. To them, national unity was more compelling than class struggle. In an emergency very much like war, they believed that government, business, and labor should all subordinate their internal differences to the common welfare. Opposed equally to laissez faire, trust-busting, and socialism, the architects of the New Deal sought an economy that was efficient, stable, and well regulated. They thought this could still be achieved while leaving industrial and corporate capitalism intact.[84]

Perhaps these attitudes were best expressed in Henry Wallace's *New Frontiers,* published in 1934. The title of his book was itself significant, since Wallace was trying to explain how America might preserve her most cherished traditions while adapting to an environment with no more room for unlimited expansion and opportunity. Like Chase and Soule, Wallace was bothered by the problem of cultural lag; in order to govern effectively, his generation had to face both ways. "The great difficulty in designing social machinery," he pointed out, "is that it must be so fashioned as to operate in two worlds: it must utilize the habits and beliefs of our old individualistic pioneer world; simultaneously it must operate in a new world where power-ful economic forces have made mincemeat of many established habits and beliefs."[85] With the disappearance of the frontier and free land, when the continent had filled up and there were no longer any safety valves to siphon off discontent, the United States was growing more like Europe. The days in which America could enjoy its youthful freedom and irresponsibility were over. Now the nation needed to take on the duties and obligations of maturity, or suffer a revolution that would destroy everything it held dear. For Wallace, this meant that unrestricted competition had to give way to a "balance among all our major producing groups . . . in such a way as does not build up a small, inordinately wealthy class."[86] He therefore conceived of the state as an equal "partner" with businessmen, farmers, workers, and consumers—all of whom would cooperate to stabilize production and make the economy function in a more disciplined manner.[87]

Yet even beyond this, Wallace had a vision of what the future society might look like. Disavowing both planning and socialism, he conceived of a "modern democracy as essentially a graded hierarchy of New England town meetings with responsible, democratically selected people dealing with the hard facts of just quotas at every step."[88] In his mind, America's new frontier would retain the pioneer respect for the individual but re-nounce its preoccupation with thrift, production, and acquisitiveness. "The need henceforth," he proclaimed, "is not to learn how to compete with each other for enough of this world's goods, but to learn how to live with each other in abundance." It therefore became government's duty "to make individual and group interest coincide."[89] Ultimately, Wallace concluded, if "power and wealth were worshiped in the old days, beauty and justice and joy of spirit must be worshiped in the new."[90]

None of these goals posed a direct challenge to capitalism; instead, Wal-lace wanted to adapt the profit system to the demands of a more integrated and complex social order. But in the process he and his New Deal col-leagues used much of the same rhetoric as the Left. They all seemed hostile to individualism and competition; they all spoke favorably of community, social responsibility, balance, centralization, cooperation, and control. Thus it became very difficult in the next several years to keep clear the ideological lines between the Roosevelt Administration and its radical critics—a prob-lem that was compounded by the intellectuals' own tortured ambivalence toward the New Deal. Unable to decide whether the new President was truly friend or foe, the Left tended to revise its attitude with nearly every shift in policy.

One immediate effect of the change in Administrations was to rivet the intellectuals' attention on Washington. For a while, they were less interested in what was happening in Moscow or even in the American countryside; newspapers and magazines were filled with discussions of the 100 Days. This in turn made writers seem somewhat more passive; they spent most of their time simply reacting to the legislative proposals of the New Deal rather than presenting new ideas of their own as they had before 1933. The broad search for social alternatives gave way increasingly to an evaluation of concrete programs emanating from the White House. Throughout 1933 and 1934, it was Roosevelt who dominated their thought.

At first, most observers responded favorably to the New Deal. During the spring of 1933, the Roosevelt Administration appeared to be committing America to a genuine social revolution. The Democrats, as William Leuchtenburg has argued, submitted an "unprecedented program of government-industry cooperation; promised to distribute stupendous sums to millions of staple farmers; accepted responsibility for the welfare of millions of unemployed; agreed to engage in far-reaching experimentation in regional planning; pledged billions of dollars to save homes and farms from foreclosure; [undertook] huge public works spending; guaranteed the small bank deposits of the country; and . . . for the first time, established federal regulation of Wall Street."[91] But writers were particularly impressed with the Industrial Recovery Bill and the potential of the National Recovery Administration. The codes imposed on industry, the agreements on wage and hours, the procedures to recognize labor unions, all seemed to introduce an element of order into the economy. The *Nation* characterized the NRA as a promising first step toward a "collectivized society," with a strong labor movement and a fundamental redistribution of wealth. The *New Republic* saw it as an instrument to expand purchasing power while controlling wages and prices in the interests of workers and consumers. Moreover, it encouraged political conflict within government agencies rather than between classes, which seemed the only way a struggle for power could take place in an advanced technological society. *Common Sense* hailed it as the official end of laissez faire and nineteenth-century individualism.[92] Each of these magazines assumed that the NRA reflected at least some of their ideas about planning; now the question became how far it would go, what objectives it should seek, which groups might exercise control. For the moment, however they were pleasantly surprised.

Yet the initial euphoria could not last. Throughout the spectacle of the 100 Days writers were never certain whether they were witnessing the birth of a planned society or the creation of a corporate state bearing an uncomfortable resemblance to Italy and Germany. As 1933 wore on and the economy remained stagnant, their enthusiasm for the New Deal's experimentation began to wane. The Roosevelt Administration's efforts to follow a middle road, to reform American capitalism without disturbing the basic class relationships, seemed to be having exactly the opposite results. Prices were rising but wages were not; competition declined, but so did production and purchasing power; labor unions received the right to organize, but there were no jobs for their new members; marginal and inefficient enterprises were driven to the wall, but monopolies and cartels flourished; crops were plowed under while men went hungry; the nation flew the blue eagle but prosperity did not return.

By the winter, George Soule declared that the NRA could not even stem the depression, much less introduce a form of democratic socialism. As long as business refused to resume production until its rate of profit was assured, and as long as government failed to pump enough money into the hands of consumers to provide people with a decent standard of living, America would sink into a condition of "stabilized poverty."[93] The economy was caught in a vicious cycle: recovery depended on the revival of business activity and a reduction in unemployment; this in turn depended on consumer demand, which was nonexistent so long as men were out of work and incomes stayed perilously low. All the old panaceas—the state as an impartial broker between business and labor, federal control of production and prices, a public works program—were proving futile in breaking this cycle. Unless income rose faster than prices, or unless some new stimulus (such as military spending) reawakened the entire economy, the depression seemed likely to continue indefinitely.

For magazines like the *Nation* and *New Republic,* the failures of the New Deal further confirmed their disenchantment with liberal reform. In the *Nation*'s view, the crucial weakness of the Roosevelt Administration was its preoccupation with reviving industry; any benefit to the workers, small farmers, or ruined middle class had to "trickle down from the top, which is no profound change from what we have had." The editors were convinced that the NRA represented only another indirect subsidy to the bankers and manufacturers; the cost of the depression was still being paid primarily by labor and the poor. They were increasingly disappointed with Roosevelt's unwillingness to move to the left—to use the crisis as an opportunity for taxing corporate profits, nationalizing the banks, assuming control over transportation and public utilities, and reallocating the country's wealth more equitably.[94] As far as the *New Republic* was concerned, the New Deal would soon have to decide whether to fight or surrender to the capitalists. The Roosevelt Administration, argued Bliven and Soule, was trying to create an impossible equilibrium between capital and labor; in effect, it was seeking revolutionary changes without offending anyone. The very survival of the New Deal now depended on its ability to abandon the illusion that it could establish some vague harmony among all classes and pressure groups. Instead, the President must determine clearly what he wanted, identify his opponents, and mobilize the support of those whose interests he was attempting to serve. The *New Republic* exhorted Roosevelt to "choose sides and struggle loyally for the side [he] has chosen."[95]

Despite these criticisms, however, neither journal was yet ready to relinquish all faith in the ultimate success of the New Deal. By the close of 1933, they had arrived at a position of mingled encouragement and skepticism. Though they felt deceived by the early promise of the 100 Days, they stopped short of outright repudiation. They believed that the New Deal could at least alleviate some of the suffering Americans presently endured, even if it would not challenge the basic arrangements of capitalism. In the meantime, the task of those who desired "complete social control of industry" was clear to the *Nation*: they should analyze each piece of New Deal legislation in minute detail while keeping the whole picture in view, support all its leftward impulses and expose any lapse in the direction of reaction, work for a militant labor movement as the only "ultimate counterbalance" to corporate capitalism, and demand on every occasion that government take over the country's basic industrial and financial institutions.[96] For all its failures, the New Deal was "educational" in their estimation. It taught people that planning could not be achieved under capitalism, and it showed men what they must do if they sincerely wanted a socialist America in the future.

Not everyone was as equivocal about the new Administration or as content to weigh its specific assets and liabilities. After the flush of the 100 Days had paled, a number of writers became increasingly hostile both to the New Deal's style and its objectives. It was not only that the flood of alphabetical agencies seemed unable to solve the central problem of want amid plenty, or that the President tended to postpone urgent social reforms while he concentrated on a revival of business activity. It was not even that the NRA and the AAA, the jewels of Roosevelt's recovery program, were dominated by the large industrialists and planters—while labor's right to organize was unenforced, small businessmen went bankrupt, and sharecroppers were driven off the land. Behind these issues lay a general feeling that the New Deal was as chaotic as capitalism itself. Far from appreciating Roosevelt's pragmatism, writers continually complained of the confusion and incoherence that pervaded Washington. Men who were still committed to the value of ideas (despite their frequent admiration for technique and power) remained deeply suspicious of the New Deal's mental sloppiness and its lack of a clear social philosophy. The Administration appeared to them not only inconsistent but genuinely anti-intellectual. In a typical indictment, Lewis Mumford saw the New Deal as nothing but "aimless experiment, sporadic patchwork, a total indifference to guiding principles or definitive goals, and hence an uncritical drift along the lines of least resistance, namely the restoration of capitalism."[97] Consequently, the Roosevelt Administration seemed to mirror the worst aspects of American culture: action without theory, "realism" without imagination, movement without vision. Though some had earlier objected to the abstract moralism of the Progressives, they were not prepared to embrace a politics completely devoid of ideology or ultimate values.

For others, the New Deal represented the last gasp of liberalism in a world that had become polarized between fascist reaction and socialist revolution. Indeed, the very effort of the Democrats to "civilize" capitalism was seen as hastening the day of reckoning. To James Burnham, at this time an editor of the little magazine *Symposium,* the New Deal was now moving perilously close to dictatorship. Its yearning to be an impartial broker was itself an ominous sign: "The illusory belief that the state is autonomous, independent of classes, and therefore able to balance their claims, which is Roosevelt's belief, is fundamental to fascism."[98] The Administration could not remain neutral much longer in the struggle between opposing social systems, and Burnham was fairly certain which side Roosevelt would choose.

The Communists were convinced that the choice had already been made. For them, the period between 1929 and 1935 was one of ultra-militance, sectarian politics, and revolutionary rhetoric. As a result they tended to regard all the New Deal legislation as a deliberate scheme to salvage the capitalist system by moving America toward fascism. In their judgment, Roosevelt's weakness was not that he lacked a consistent social philosophy; on the contrary, he quite consciously intended to set up a corporate state with the government in command. To this end, the NRA seemed designed to further monopoly control of the economy, the AAA restricted production in the interest of higher prices and profits for the large landowners, Section 7a of the Industrial Recovery Bill prepared the way for company- and government-sponsored labor unions, the CCC represented a form of military training for the young, and the Art and Writers' Projects meant that the state would now regiment American culture.[99]

If some felt this analysis was a bit extreme, Earl Browder, the Communist party's chairman, offered a more sophisticated version in the pages of the *New Masses*. Essentially, Browder contended that there was no significant difference between Hoover and Roosevelt. Both defined "recovery" as a revival of profits, both used reform to strengthen corporate capitalism, and both saw their duty as primarily to protect private enterprise against all threats from within and without. They disagreed over only the methods to reach these goals. Ironically, Browder seemed to prefer the Republicans. They at least were open and "honest" in their reactionary designs. Roosevelt, however, was devious; he hoped to deflect revolt by concealing the true class alignments from the masses. Thus, Browder argued, the New Deal pursued a policy of inflation which appeared to raise wages but actually diminished the workers' share of the national income. It encouraged shorter hours, but this had the effect of distributing the burden of unemployment among a larger number of people. The Democrats made a great show of protecting small business while speeding the trustification of industry as a whole. Their welfare measures formally expanded social services, but neither the amount of money appropriated nor its method of dispensation enhanced the dignity and self-respect of the poor. Browder was willing to admit that all of these policies "choked and disintegrated" mass discontent "for a time" by "abandoning a clear posing of issues." But in his rather optimistic estimation, this only intensified the inherent contradictions of capitalism and postponed the inevitable struggle for power and a new social system.[100]

The striking aspect of the Communists' point of view was how plausible it sounded to many intellectuals in the mid-1930s. Liberal reform was increasingly seen not only as an instrument of corporate capitalism but as an enemy even more insidious than Wall Street and the Republicans. The ideas and analyses of the Hoover years were being confirmed by the New Deal's disappointing performance. In the eyes of writers moving rapidly to the left, liberalism could neither solve the depression nor lead the way toward a better society; instead it simply reinforced the worst features of the existing order.

There was little the Roosevelt Administration could do by 1935 to shake this conviction. The *New Masses, New Republic,* and *Nation* all greeted the "second 100 Days" with considerable suspicion and disapproval. Despite the renewed outburst of social legislation, the Communists remained unimpressed. They opposed the five-billion-dollar WPA program, arguing that it would reduce wages below the already inadequate limits set under the NRA codes and provide business with a convenient source of cheap labor. They feared that the Wagner Act might open the door to government-controlled unions. Finally they attacked the Social Security Bill because it furnished nothing in the immediate future for the aged and unemployed, excluded a large number of occupations from its benefits, and shifted the burden of payment to those least able to bear its cost.[101]

Similarly, both the *New Republic* and the *Nation* saw the WPA as just another emergency measure, underfinanced and severely restricted from competing with private enterprise, while Social Security appeared only a feeble beginning at a nationwide system of unemployment insurance and old-age pensions. Meanwhile production continued to lag, twelve million workers were still without jobs, government housing remained little more than a promise, and prices were rising much faster than income. The basic trouble with the New Deal, in their opinion, was its inability or unwillingness to undertake "genuine social-economic planning." Apart from TVA, they considered most of Roosevelt's measures as stopgaps which would probably be eliminated once capitalism recovered from the crisis. The emerging welfare state seemed to them merely an indirect subsidy to business—making it even less responsive to poverty and unemployment, accelerating the trend toward monopoly, stimulating demand for privately produced goods, and preserving an economic system based on scarcity rather than abundance. Roosevelt, they concluded, had created a situation in which industrialists and bankers were learning for the first time how to earn profits in a depression.[102]

7. *Waiting for the Revolution*

While the New Deal was driving intellectuals closer to radicalism, it was having exactly the opposite effect on most other Americans. Whatever the imperfections of its political and economic programs, the Roosevelt Administration had succeeded in reducing the tension and fear which plagued the country in the early years of the depression. Through an expert use of the mass media, through the reliance on a rhetoric that was very traditional even as it introduced unprecedented reforms, through the insistence on national unity and cooperation in a time of extreme emergency, through an emphasis on order and security rather than social upheaval, the New Deal gave people the sense that their problems were at last being recognized if not yet solved. Thus America no longer seemed on the brink of collapse, and the predictions of an imminent revolution began to sound increasingly unrealistic. This did not necessarily mean that the Democrats had won the allegiance of all the disinherited groups within society but rather that many radicals did not really understand what kinds of circumstances could produce and sustain a movement for basic social change.

A number of writers and activists assumed that working-class uprisings would most likely occur when conditions reached bottom. There was an irresistible temptation to believe that men moved toward revolutionary action only when no other alternatives existed; revolt was seen as a product of hopelessness. According to this view, the depression should have been the perfect catalyst for a major social transformation. As times grew worse, people were inevitably "radicalized."

Yet many observers, touring the country between 1933 and 1935, found that suffering produced only frustration, apathy, and a sense of defeat. Bruce Bliven, investigating New England and the Midwest, was amazed by the absence of either enthusiasm for or opposition to the New Deal; nowhere did he discover a mood of drastic impatience or a visible desire for militant action. Americans of all classes seemed to regard the depression as a natural calamity, beyond human control and probably beyond human rectification. Consequently, they displayed none of the resentment and bitterness which led in other countries to fascism or revolution.[103] Others were astounded that capitalism still possessed inexhaustible resources for smothering discontent. "The tragedy of justified revolt," lamented Roger Baldwin in 1935, "is that it can be bought off so cheap" by farm subsidies, relief payments, WPA projects, and rural electrification. The wave of strikes that periodically engulfed the country, he pointed out, did not represent an assault on the New Deal but rather an effort to enforce its promises.[104] And if liberal reform were to succeed in reviving the economy, this would further deflate the radical movement. As one writer warned in the *New Republic,* "those who feel that revolution and not prosperity is just around the corner, should keep in mind that if capitalism shows any signs of giving the workers even illusory security—in other words, a job—the revolutionary spirit will burn even lower and more fitfully than it does at present."[105]

Because the country seemed so indifferent to radical appeals—and since few suspected that men might more readily act when conditions began to improve, rather than in a period of total despair—some writers tried to locate the causes of America's political "backwardness." The nature and values of the working class were obvious problems for any radical. It was not accidental, V. F. Calverton noted in the *Modern Quarterly,* that farmers were undertaking more militant forms of action than the workers during the depression. Agrarianism was the dominant political sentiment for much of the nation's history. But the farmer, according to Calverton, had never been forced to adopt European social categories. Lacking the experience of a feudal past, confronted with an enormous expanse of free land, his chief task was to subdue a hostile environment, not a landlord class. Moreover, the pioneer spirit and the habit of perpetual migration tended to magnify individual effort; the sense of shared needs, collective action, and class consciousness seemed irrelevant to agrarian life. And because the United States was for so long an agricultural country, these traits had infected every other group within the society. The result, in Calverton's view, was that the agrarian perspective tended to retard contemporary social movements. Although the farmer opposed corporate capitalism and baited Wall Street, he never wished to abolish private property or the profit system. His individualist and competitive ideals were closer to those of the lower middle-class shopowner and independent producer than to the working class. Should he continue to dominate American radicalism and should the workers fail to develop a truly socialist ideology, Calverton feared the rise of an American-style fascism catering to the anxieties and aspirations of the petit-bourgeoisie, but controlled by the very industrialists and bankers who were the real enemies of both farmers and workers.[106]

Yet the workers themselves appeared woefully unprepared in composition and experience to lead a mass revolt. As Malcolm Cowley pessimistically observed, the American "proletariat" was not homogeneous; instead it was splintered into black and white, native- and foreign-born, skilled and unskilled. Moreover, it was thoroughly disheartened by past defeats. In addition, there was no institution (like the soviets in Russia) by which the workers could seize power, nor any unified party of the Left that might function as the brains and strategists of the revolution. Yet the major impediment, in Cowley's as well as Calverton's estimation, was not the weakness of the working class but the incredible endurance of bourgeois values and habits of thought among all Americans.[107] Until these could be eradicated there seemed very little prospect in the immediate future for a social revolution in the United States.

What had happened was that many radical intellectuals were depending on the economic crisis alone to provoke an uprising. Throughout the early 1930s they scanned the horizon for signs of the final conflict. But it never appeared because the political and ideological groundwork had not been laid in the years preceding the depression. Thus most Americans, confronted with a disaster they could neither prevent nor explain, devoted their energies to survival rather than revolution. The New Deal, with its offer of economic recovery, social security, and an ordered society, understood these impulses far better than the Left. If the Roosevelt Administration could not address itself adequately to the nation's material problems, it could at least respond shrewdly to America's psychological needs—and in a crisis like the depression this may have been initially more important.

8. *Toward a Social Democracy*

As long as domestic political and economic issues remained uppermost in the minds of intellectuals, their commitment to radical alternatives did endure. Only now, having abandoned hope of an imminent revolt, they began to think more seriously about what kind of movement was necessary to engage in a long-term struggle for social change. Throughout 1934 and 1935 numerous books and articles appeared calling for a broad coalition of groups and classes dedicated to moving the country beyond the New Deal toward an indigenous form of socialism. As such they reflected whatever political consensus writers had achieved by mid-decade.

George Soule, in a less speculative frame of mind than two years earlier, offered a candid appraisal of the political situation in *The Coming American Revolution*, published during 1934. The book attempted to show where America stood on the revolutionary spectrum, and his conclusions were not particularly encouraging. Soule acknowledged that most of the recent converts to radicalism had been middle-class writers and professionals rather than workers. Even worse, the Left was looking for the wrong kind of upheaval: rioting mobs, violent class struggle, dramatic assaults on the government, a convulsive overthrow of capitalism. In Soule's judgment, this was a Leninist fantasy that had no basis in American realities.[108] Instead, "a true revolution" in the United States would take "many years, even generations in the making." It involved fundamental changes in technology and economic institutions, the disintegration of the old regime in the face of crises it could not solve, a gradual realignment of social classes and the rise of new groups to power, the growth of new political organizations that gave coherence to the popular longing for action, the disaffection of intellectuals and skilled technicians from obsolete customs and thought patterns, the emergence of alternative values stressing cooperation and sharing rather than individualism and competition, and finally the fusion of all these disparate elements into a new social order.[109] Much of this had already begun to happen in America, according to Soule. The country was indeed in the midst of a profound social revolution—though different from anything the Left had expected. But some crucial components were missing, and thus the old forms of authority managed to survive despite the hold of the depression.

Economically, Soule argued, conditions were presently ripe. Technology and machine production made possible a higher standard of living for every person; they also promised a more equitable distribution of goods and wealth. Yet monopoly capitalism had become so rigid, so centralized, so wedded to the profit motive that it could neither fulfill the country's needs nor respond flexibly to an economic crisis. Soule believed the depression demanded a sophisticated control of production, prices, wages, investment, and purchasing power, but these all threatened the prerogatives of business; as a result, the capitalists refused to surrender their power, and the nation plunged further into poverty.[110] The New Deal, in Soule's opinion, had postponed a total collapse by frantically pumping money into the economy. But as long as business would not resume production until its rate of profit was assured, government spending could be only a temporary expedient.[111] In the long run, he was convinced that Keynesian economics would not keep capitalism afloat.

Moreover, groups had begun to appear in America, especially at the technical and managerial level, whose interests were fundamentally different from those of the traditional bourgeoisie. Soule was much impressed with the growing importance of industrial unions, white-collar professionals, service occupations, even the movement of economists and lawyers into government; to his mind, these changes in social composition heralded the emergence of a more collectivist life-style.[112]

They also led to a search for alternative values and goals. The classic ideals of competition, laissez faire, private profit-seeking, and individual opportunity were slowly being replaced by concepts like planning, economic security, and social control—all of which Soule felt were "by nature antagonistic to the basic requirements of capitalism."[113] This intellectual ferment was still in its early stages; most people seemed more concerned with reforming the existing system than advancing toward a completely new ideology. The old order, Soule realized, was threatened more by its own stupidity and failures than by a revolutionary opposition. At the moment there was no disciplined mass movement with a coordinated program to provide effective leadership, nor were Americans "mentally" prepared to take over their economic institutions.[114] But in his estimation, it must only be a matter of time before a political party emerged which could unite these new classes and ideas into an organization capable of seizing power. Soule was confident of the outcome: "Just as feudalism was compelled in the end to give way to the rise of the middle classes and capitalism, so capitalism must in the end give way to the rise of the working classes and socialism." The revolution would come gradually, almost imperceptibly, "by peaceful and constitutional methods."[115] Eventually, new political and social institutions would formalize what had already taken place beneath the surface. For Soule, this was the only way social change could occur in the United States.

Essentially, *The Coming American Revolution* was an effort to fashion a political strategy that took into account the lack of class consciousness among the workers, the persistence of bourgeois values among all segments of the population, the tenacity of capitalism even in the most unfavorable circumstances, and the ability of liberal reform to undercut native radical movements. Soule recognized that all the present agitation, strikes, labor organizing, and talk of third parties were just a beginning; any serious plans to transform the country would require the kind of lifetime commitment writers and activists had never displayed in the past. Furthermore, the struggle must proceed on all fronts: political, economic, social, and ideological. Finally, a true revolution had to be based on the traditions, experiences, and culture indigenous to the United States; neither Russian communism nor European social democracy could provide an adequate model for American radicals. If all of these conditions were met, Soule believed there was still a chance to erect a new society on the foundations of the old.

Others shared his restrained optimism. From the Marxist Left came a more orthodox analysis of the social situation which tended to reinforce Soule's assessment—Lewis Corey's *The Crisis of the Middle Class,* published in 1935. Under the name of Louis Fraina, Corey had been one of the founders of the American Communist party in 1919. Unable to withstand the factional disputes of the 1920s, he left the movement and turned his attention increasingly to economic theory, maintaining his commitment to radicalism but without any party affiliation. By the 1930s, Corey had become preoccupied with those factors that made the United States unique; it was hardly accidental that his major work should focus on the role of the bourgeoisie in any future revolution. In the book, Corey tried to adapt Marxism to the peculiarities of American society and to show that an alliance of the middle and working classes could eventually lead to socialism.

Like his predecessors—Croly, Steffens, Dewey, Berle and Means, Chamberlain, Chase, Soule—Corey insisted that the growth of monopoly capitalism, the centralization of wealth and power, the emergence of collectivist institutions like the corporation and the labor union had all destroyed the old middle class of small property owners and independent entrepreneurs. In its place there arose a new group of salaried employees, government bureaucrats, industrial managers, clerks, salesmen, technicians, and professionals, who were now dependent on the organization for which they worked, who desired steady employment and economic security more than personal advancement, whose jobs were essentially "social" in nature, and who found themselves "wavering between the proletariat and the bourgeoisie."[116] Corey went on to argue that the traditional liberal ideals of freedom, equality, and democracy could no longer be achieved under capitalism. America was moving in the direction of either fascism or socialism, and the white-collar class would have to choose.

But the decision was not entirely theirs to make. The heart of Corey's book was his assertion that the "new" middle class was being rapidly "proletarianized," that their economic and psychological problems were no different from those of the workers, that even in America the suffering and alienation of the masses were growing to the point of revolution—just as Marx had predicted. Anticipating C. Wright Mills by twenty years, Corey reminded his readers that salaried employees held no property, could never hope to own the means of production, and had to sell their labor power on an open market unprotected by unions.[117] Moreover, they were just as vulnerable to the terrors of the depression as the working class. Competition became more savage as sales and jobs declined, the small businessman could not survive when his customers remained out of work, machines replaced clerical employees in an effort to cut costs, technicians felt a "degradation of their craft function" as businessmen deliberately sabotaged production and equipment lay idle, professionals found less demand for their services, and intellectuals discovered that the crisis of capitalism also involved a "crisis of culture."[118]

Most important of all, the very nature of bourgeois work was becoming indistinguishable from the assembly line. The typical middle-class job, in Corey's view, was specialized, monotonous, and impersonal—a mechanical routine that transformed offices into white-collar factories, made "confidential relations with the employer" impossible, and destroyed any sense of pride in one's skills.[119] Ultimately the salaried employee felt life to be as dangerous and dispiriting as his blue-collar counterpart, and he could no longer be consoled by the differences in income since both groups were equally victimized by the depression. For Corey, America had ceased to be "exceptional"; the class struggle had come home.

In effect, Corey was contending that "objectively" the white-collar class was already part of the proletariat, that it could solve its problems only by becoming conscious of where it stood and by committing itself with the workers to a socialist society.[120] The one obstacle to this coalition was the nagging survival of bourgeois attitudes. "It is only by the exploitation of their prejudices and passions, of their inherited allegiance to a system now wholly against their own interests," he complained, "that the propertiless can still be rallied to a defense of property."[121] At this point, in his judgment, America needed an ideological as well as a social revolution. Corey wanted not only a radical party which could win immediate reforms while challenging the capitalists' control of the state but also a vision of what the future might actually be like. And he was prepared to suggest its outlines: "Liberty of property must become the liberty of labor. An unrealizable equality of ownership must become the equal right to share in the social property of the community. The democracy of independent small producers must become the socialist democracy of free, creative workers. . . ."[122] Under this new dispensation the job would become a form of "productive social labor," distinctions between manual and mental work would disappear, the industrial plant would be decentralized and men would therefore feel more personal responsibility for its operation, and all of this could lead to a liberation of the human personality beyond anything capitalist individualism had conceived. [123]

Nevertheless, Corey was very unclear about how the middle class was to recognize where its true interests lay. He seemed to assume that the problem of cultural lag might be overcome in the normal course of events, that the workers themselves were engaged in a struggle to overthrow capitalism, and that a socialist majority would naturally emerge once the white-collar groups joined the proletariat. But if the working class was not in fact radical, and if the bourgeoisie did not abandon its traditional faith in the American Dream, then the type of coalition he envisioned could have far different results. Up to a point Corey's analysis of what the two classes held in common was accurate, but their shared interests might not necessarily lead to a radical politics or a socialist ideology. Other more formidable movements were competing for their loyalty. The weakest point in Corey's argument—and indeed in the perspective of many intellectuals during this time—was the conviction that socialism in some form must eventually triumph in the United States and that the main obstruction to its victory was the bourgeois consciousness of the American people. Whether or not this was true, it permitted radicals to refrain from examining their own preconceptions and to trust the forces of history without asking hard questions about what either class really wanted or needed.

Yet given their faith in socialism's inevitability, a number of writers were otherwise fairly sophisticated about the intermediate steps America must take to alter her political and economic institutions. By the middle of the decade, they acknowledged that the working class alone was incapable of mounting a serious challenge to capitalism, that any radical movement would have to speak a reformist and pragmatic language if it wished to be understood by the average citizen, and that native socialists could not model their strategy on the European experience. Furthermore, they realized that the existing parties of the Left might never attract mass support; the Communists were too sectarian and doctrinaire in their approach to other groups, the Socialists were too opportunistic and oriented toward winning elections, and the splinter organizations were too obsessed with events in Russia. Consequently, contributors to the *Nation,* the *New Republic, Common Sense,* and the *Modern Quarterly* all began to call for a new political party "of the broadest possible scope, uniting all the forces which can be made to see their interest in the abolition of capitalism"—a party that would "Americanize" Marx by emphasizing not proletarian dictatorship but the greater democracy and freedom people could enjoy under socialism, that would work for short-term reforms at the same time it raised the radical consciousness of its constituency, that would take advantage of the New Deal's failures by educating Americans to their true social needs, that would minimize class divisions so as not to alienate potential allies within the bourgeoisie, and that would direct its appeal to "all the 'people' against all the capitalists."[124]

Specifically, they believed this movement should include workers, farmers, Negroes, clerks, salesmen, small businessmen, teachers, engineers, white-collar professionals, managers, intellectuals, and any other disaffected elements within the population for whom private enterprise no longer provided a secure and rewarding life. To some extent, this sounded very much like the sort of Popular Front that was to emerge after 1935. More ominously, it described the coalition already being fashioned by the New Deal. In effect, radicals and Democrats were contending for the support of exactly the same groups, and the contestants were by no means evenly matched. Yet as *Common Sense* continually pointed out, the new party should not be content with a negative or reformist program merely in order to win votes. "Unity" was necessary to prevent the middle class from going fascist, but ultimately such a party must dedicate itself to "a planned cooperative commonwealth, with public ownership of the basic means of production" if it hoped to succeed.[125] It was possible that no left-wing party —however imaginative and resourceful—could compete with the magnetism of the Roosevelt Administration, but this was at least a strategy that corresponded to current political conditions within the United States.

Thus by 1935 many intellectuals had arrived at a program that was both radical and fairly realistic. Drawing on ideas whose roots lay in the Progressive era, men like John Dewey, Lincoln Steffens, George Soule, Bruce Bliven, Stuart Chase, John Chamberlain, Edmund Wilson, Alfred Bingham, Lewis Corey, and V. F. Calverton had all renounced the tactics and objectives of traditional reform. They were convinced that the liberal approach to political and economic problems must be transcended, that the

New Deal despite its good intentions hastened the trend toward monopoly and fascism without ending the depression, and that the system of private profit must therefore give way to some form of democratic socialism. In particular they were demanding a fundamental reallocation of wealth and power, a planned economy in which prices and income were carefully balanced to provide a decent standard of living, an elimination of hunger and poverty when industry and agriculture were able to produce enough for all, and a new set of priorities based on the needs of the community rather than individual advancement. Most of these proposals were revolutionary in the context of existing institutions; combined with a broad mass movement, they held out a reasonable hope of transforming American life.

But the desire for order and stability, the dependence on a coalition which was not itself inherently radical, the haunting fear that fascism might follow the New Deal unless an alliance was forged with the middle class, the continued insistence on pragmatism and action at the expense of ideology, and the faith in technical expertise to solve social problems, all could have quite conservative consequences in the later years of the decade. For the moment many intellectuals were committed to what they considered a socialist perspective. Any other strains in their thought would stay buried until the political situation itself began to change.

CHAPTER III

THE SEARCH FOR COMMUNITY

1. *Cultural Radicalism*

The attention of American writers was by no means limited in the 1930s to questions of political strategy and economic reform. Essentially, the depression afforded them an opportunity to experiment with a set of values and a social philosophy which diverged at many points from what the nation had previously accepted. Although these efforts, like those in politics, had their roots in the prewar era, the very nature of the crisis itself gave the Progressive concepts of community and collectivism new meaning. In effect, intellectuals were trying to expand the ideas of Herbert Croly and Van Wyck Brooks into a coherent synthesis of self and society, culture and technology, thought and action. Their notions were often rudimentary and crude, but the decade produced in the work of five writers—John Dewey, Lewis Mumford, Robert Lynd, Sidney Hook, and Reinhold Niebuhr—the beginning of an ideology that seemed appropriate to the new conditions of American life.

None of this group could be considered a product of the depression alone, yet each of them felt compelled to adapt his thought to its pressures. Dewey, for example, was the leading spokesman of the Progressive generation, but he devoted much of his later years to making liberalism an effective instrument for building a socialist America. Mumford began as an archetypal cultural and literary critic after World War I, but he too extended his interests to a broad range of social issues in the following decade. Lynd won fame for his dispassionate study of Middletown in the 1920s, yet he looked increasingly to social science as a tool for action under the impact of the depression. Hook and Niebuhr both started to write before the stock-market crash but saw their work profoundly shaped by the concerns of the 1930s: the problems of man in society, freedom and order, morality and politics, Marxism and America. In each case, these five took the half-formed attitudes and assumptions of other intellectuals and fashioned them into a more comprehensive cultural and social theory. It was in their books and articles that the most creative ideas of the decade might be found.

That social thought of any sophistication could emerge from an experience as shattering as the depression was itself surprising. No period of crisis is especially conducive to calm analysis or new concepts; men are much more prone to fall back on inherited and instinctive values in an effort to cope with a totally unprecedented situation. Perhaps this was why writers who came to intellectual maturity after 1929 seemed less able to engage in systematic political and economic debate than those who had already begun before the crash to search for alternatives to liberal capitalism. In any event, the image of the depression as a cosmic catastrophe which few could satisfactorily explain, of a society literally falling apart, of a world grown suddenly irrational and absurd made the decade considerably less congenial to ideologies than its subsequent reputation might imply. Far from being susceptible to communism, socialism, liberalism, or fascism, many intellectuals were attracted to ideas that often had little political content. One of the most striking features of the period was the way in which social criticism dissolved into moral indictments, cultural rebellion, and visions of the apocalypse.

This resulted in part from the fact that the depression was frequently seen as something more than an economic problem. Institutions had ceased to function. Men lived with a continuing feeling of fatigue, despair, and failure. The disaster appeared the work of an impersonal and indifferent God, and no one knew who might be His next victim or why. The causes of the crisis seemed inherent in the nature of the universe, and they were irremediable.

Yet the notion of a collapse beyond human control, of an end to everything men had known or anticipated, did not lead only to hopelessness. In the midst of tragedy there was for some a kind of euphoria—a mood of utopian optimism that was as unideological as the opposite sense of impending doom. If the old order was dying, the new was being born. Paradoxically, where men believed they could do nothing to save their present way of life, they still expected to have some impact on the future, to influence the course of history, to enter the millennium unscathed. In this view, one's capacity to act—to commit oneself to a cause quite apart from its philosophy or program—became a form of personal and collective salvation.[1]

Thus Edmund Wilson might describe Marxism in 1932 as the only vital political and cultural movement in the West—not so much because he agreed with its social ideas but because it represented a new vision of human life "just coming to maturity" with its "immense creative work" yet to be done (in dramatic contrast to the world of capitalism "dying at the end of its blind alley").[2] And Stuart Chase, otherwise opposed to the destructive force of revolution, could admit that "a better economic order is worth a little bloodshed" because it promised not only new institutions but a "new religion" at a time when "Western mankind is thirsty for something in which to believe again."[3] Indeed violence, like childbirth, might even be an exalting and purifying initiation into new life, for which Americans, long cut off from their pioneer days, were sorely in need. "Why," Chase wondered, "should Russians have all the fun of remaking a world?"[4] This persistent evocation of death and rebirth, the messianic feeling of being present at the dawn of a revolutionary age, served to compensate emotionally for the confusion and terror of the depression. But such apocalyptic sentiments did not lend themselves easily to logical plans or rational thinking.

Instead, they led to an analysis of American problems that was primarily moral, psychological, and cultural—in many ways an elaboration of attitudes that had flourished in the 1920s. Rather than foreclosing on the intellectual heritage of Bohemia, Greenwich Village, and Paris, the stock-market crash tended to reinforce the criticisms of the previous decade. If anything, the sorts of issues that concerned writers before 1929—questions of behavior, life-styles, and values—grew even more important in the 1930s. The shocking breakdown of the nation's industrial machinery seemed only a symptom of some deeper spiritual malaise to which intellectuals had been particularly sensitive since the war. The depression confirmed their belief that American ideals were dangerously distorted and unreal, that competition and acquisitiveness were eroding the country's social foundations, that the quality of human life under capitalism offered men no sense of community or common experience. Writers continued to focus on the intrinsic *anarchy* of private enterprise—not only its inability to produce and distribute goods efficiently but its more basic failure to endow the country with any coherent purpose or mission beyond the making of money. This was a land, one observer wrote, "which has everything needed for comfortable survival except a definition of human life, an objective for 'progress,' and an intelligible and tolerable pattern for the social contract."[5] The chaos of capitalism thus became a metaphor for the fragmentation, disunity, and dissolution that afflicted all of American society, an indictment as cosmic as anything Joseph Wood Krutch had advanced in *The Modern Temper.*

Even the political and economic suggestions of intellectuals involved ethical imperatives. Describing a strike in Virginia during 1931, the novelist Sherwood Anderson was moved by what he took to be "the struggle of all men against the control of all life by the machine." And in this view, conflict could be resolved not by a union or a set of social reforms but by "some leader, some poet who is to come and make what they want understood to their bosses, to all bosses."[6] Here was the most primitive definition of the problem—man enslaved to a job that gave him no pleasure or satisfaction, unable to determine the destiny of his own life, and helpless to articulate his frustration without the aid of a charismatic but possibly apolitical interpreter. Yet the more sophisticated ideas of planning also carried a burden that went beyond the reorganization of industry. The arguments for a planned society invariably concluded with a peroration on the virtues of "cooperative achievement" (Henry Wallace), on the abolition of the profit motive as a "cleansing, wholesome innovation" (Stuart Chase), on the need for moral as well as economic order, on the creation of what George Soule called a "warm and active bond with our fellows."[7] For many writers in the 1930s, the movement to the left was as much a cultural as an ideological phenomenon.

At bottom, this urge to do more than merely restructure institutions reflected a profound loss of faith in the American Dream and an effort by intellectuals to discover some new value system that might fill the void. The United States appeared to be suffering from a decline of energy and morale, a fall from grace more severe than writers in the 1920s had foreseen. Even the liberal worship of expertise and efficiency, or the communist trust in ideology and class struggle, seemed curiously ineffective when the crisis was seen in this light. There was, warned James Rorty, a "great wall facing America," a "rather sudden and terrifying apparition of limits." The nation, once so adventurous and expansive, was no longer living in a world of infinite possibilities. Biologically, economically, psychologically, it was running down. Free land had disappeared, natural resources were diminishing, population was falling, foreign markets were closing, technological progress had factored out the "human dimension." Individually and collectively, Rorty declared, Americans were "exhausted." Those who did escape this "crazy" civilization were fleeing from the "death of meaning which pursues every individual who surrenders himself to the mechanical compulsions of a dehumanized social order." The rest were "face to face with the wall. . . ."[8]

Any such analysis of capitalism which emphasized cultural decay, moral atrophy, the futility and meaninglessness of daily life was not readily susceptible to political redress.

If the crisis of the 1930s was spiritual as well as economic, then it required measures that would not only end the depression and repair a fractured society but also deal with the psychological disturbances of each citizen. There must be, proclaimed Waldo Frank, "a revolution of the inward man" even before the nation's social problems could be solved. Hence he was attracted to Marxism because, beyond its substantive doctrines, it seemed to him an "intuition" that "history is some sort of organism; that thought, event, and fact are integral and continuous." Under its aegis, therefore, the individual could regain a sense of inner "wholeness" he presently lacked under liberalism.[9] That Frank should discover in socialism a hint of Spinoza and Bergson was not at all unusual, given the special intellectual needs of the period.

Others had their own version of what radicalism meant. To Samuel Schmalhausen, an associate editor of Calverton's *Modern Quarterly* who liked to dabble in Freud as well as Marx, America's economic system had produced a truly "sick" civilization. It made a "fetish of individualism," tortured men with inferiority complexes and an overwhelming horror of failure, and generated the sort of pressures which could only result in "psychoneurotic malaise and misery." In an age of "irreconcilable contradictions, conflicts, and cleavages," Schmalhausen conceived of revolution as a form of social therapy that would eliminate the "dominance of the ego in the affairs of men" and replace it with the principles of "cooperation" and "integration."[10] Similarly, the young literary critic Lionel Trilling complained of man's mental and emotional disintegration as his work became more mechanical, specialized, and abstract. The individual was losing a "sense of the self"; he was no longer a complete human being.[11] In essence men like Frank, Schmalhausen, and Trilling chose to concentrate not on capitalism's exploitation or oppression but its inhumanity. In their eyes, the American was a victim of private as well as public dislocations. Living in an insecure and unpredictable world, he had internalized all its divisions and frustrations. To deal with this dilemma the country seemed to need both a controlled economy and a psychological climate where one could find some inner peace. Thus these writers were calling for a change in institutions that might also bring with it a transformation of identity. They wished to introduce a new social order as a prelude to the creation of a new, healthier human being.

In the process, intellectuals rarely despaired of finding life on the other side of Rorty's wall. But they were understandably vague about what the future might actually look like, either for the society or the individual. Therefore it was often easier for them to describe those aspects of American civilization they despised than to set forth structural alternatives. Hopefully a moral rejection of bourgeois traditions might by implication suggest the values writers had in mind when they talked about a different social order. If capitalism not only produced poverty and unemployment but also prevented men from leading a sane existence, if it promoted chaos among institutions as well as between men, if it made both an economy of abundance and a harmonious society impossible, then many writers felt more justified in offering a symbolic reproach to American materialism and greed than in outlining programmatic solutions to the depression.

This state of mind accounted for an extraordinary interest in folk cultures, agrarian communities, and peasant life that sprang up in the early 1930s. Just as intellectuals had been drawn to Europe in the previous decade, or to the image of the Soviet Union after 1929, so they undertook pilgrimages to Mexican villages in search of some mystical experience unavailable in the United States. In each case, they were attracted to societies that seemed outside the pale of capitalist civilization. Commenting on this phenomenon, Waldo Frank speculated that writers sensed in Mexico an organicism, a feeling of order and direction, which was missing in the fragmentation and confusion of twentieth-century America. Thus their books about Mexico took on religious overtones as they romanticized the peasant's intimate connection between "self and soil"—a relationship men in the cities and factories north of the border could no longer enjoy.[12]

Yet their central purpose was not to study life in preindustrial arcadias but instead to launch a serious cultural critique of existing conditions in the United States. One of the best examples of this was Stuart Chase's series of articles in the *New Republic* during 1931, which later formed the core of his best-seller *Mexico, A Study of Two Americas*. Chase had traveled south to examine the mores and outlook of "men without machines." His objective was to contrast Mexican with American life by using Robert Redfield's *Tepoztlan* and the Lynds' *Middletown* as appropriate symbols of the two societies. Feeling like the "rawest immigrant" in a totally new environment, Chase was impressed with the village's handicraft economy, its self-subsistence and full employment, its natural integration of work and play, and the people's sense of partnership in a common enterprise. The village was a perfectly balanced community—in obvious contrast to America's mechanized production-for-profit, urban-industrial blight, anarchic individualism, and neurotic accumulation of wealth at the expense of every other normal human impulse. The United States might be the more practical and "advanced" country, but Mexicans had a "happiness and peace of mind" entirely unknown to frenzied America. The peasant knew what life was really for, and he had a value system which gave his days meaning. In Chase's view, the only other nation in the world that promised similar psychological and spiritual satisfactions was the Soviet Union.[13]

Above all, Mexico attracted the attention of writers like Frank and Chase because it represented the idea of an "organic" community that seemed somehow more cohesive and fulfilling than a contractual society bound together by laws, institutions, legislation, and the state. Once the person found "his true place in the collective group," Frank declared, he became a "social integer"—a state of being "which we must achieve in North America, before we can think of overcoming the false individualism that is the essence of our capitalistic order."[14] It was this vision of human beings as capable of total assimilation with their environment and fellow men, no longer suffering from the isolation and loneliness with which Americans lived, that most appealed to intellectuals in the 1930s. Where private enterprise seemed to separate people from one another, reducing every relationship to a function of the market place, peasant (and by implication socialist) societies exalted communal responsibility over personal aggrandizement. Again, the creation of such a community was essentially a cultural rather than a political aspiration; it depended more on man's innate social impulses than on his commitment to any ideology.

Indeed for some, the key problem of modern life was defined not in terms of capitalism versus socialism or the workers versus the middle class but as culture versus civilization. This was true both for writers on the left and those who were quite self-conscious about their conservatism, since each camp shared many of the same objections to capitalism. Not surprisingly, those most anxious to defend the superiority of rural societies against the intrusions of the assembly line and the profit motive found themselves especially attracted to this kind of analysis. "Super-civilization," argued the Southern sociologist Howard Odum, "stands in many bold contrasts to culture: superstate over . . . the folk and learning; organization over people, mass over individual, power over freedom, machines over men, quantity over quality, artificial over natural, technological over human, production over reproduction. The verdict is one for too much civilization and too little culture."[15] Similarly Herbert Agar, writing the introductory essay in the newly formed *Southern Review* in 1935, pointed to the inherent conflict between culture (as represented by small towns, agrarian communities, "instinctive" democracy, and faith in nature) and civilization (symbolized by cities, industrialization, politics, impersonal human relationships, and an exclusive reliance on abstract intellect).[16]

To critics like Odum and Agar, the United States was strangling on its own technological achievements, scientific expertise, and material success. They sought instead a communal form of living that existed apart from formal institutions and the pressures of industrial capitalism. And the place to find it was not in the doctrines of Veblen or Marx but in the regional experience where, as Lewis Mumford believed, people were naturally "united by a common feeling for their landscape, their literature and language, their local ways."[17] In this view, "culture" was a means of tying men to one another through shared tasks, emotions, and daily behavior—bonds more enduring than any social system or ideology could weave.

Perhaps the most eloquent statement of these ideas came from a group of conservative intellectuals as alienated from American attitudes as their socialist counterparts. In 1930, at the very dawn of the depression, they gathered their revolt against liberal capitalism into a symposium under the militant title *I'll Take My Stand.* Using the metaphor of the South and the values associated with agrarianism in much the same fashion as other writers invoked the Soviet Union or Mexico, they announced their secession from the dominant assumptions of industrial America. The group had originally been organized in the 1920s at Vanderbilt University under the leadership of John Crowe Ransom, Allen Tate, Robert Penn Warren, and Donald Davidson. Later they were joined by Stark Young, John Gould Fletcher, and Frank Owsley, among others. Together they included poets, novelists, literary critics, historians, and journalists. All were committed to preserving a way of life increasingly threatened by the modern worship of science, machinery, urbanization, and economic achievement as an end in itself.

Each writer contributed an essay to the symposium exploring various facets of American society while extolling the Southern alternative. Yet apart from the specific conclusions they advanced, their arguments often echoed the radical denunciation of capitalism as too acquisitive, too profit-oriented, and too individualistic. Free enterprise stood in their minds for chaos, fragmentation, atomism, division, specialization, maladjustment among groups and individuals. Agrarianism, on the other hand, was regularly identified with unity, wholeness, harmony, balance, integrated personalities. These were the primary words in their vocabulary, and they were used to summarize the case against "civilization" more consistently than any systematic social theory.

Like other intellectuals in the 1930s, the Southerners were not so much concerned with the particular economic evils that flowed from capitalism as they were with its psychological costs. The excessive reliance on industrial production, they complained, had isolated man from nature, destroyed his capacity for leisure and cultivated enjoyment, shattered his feeling for local customs and traditions, uprooted him from his inherited environment, and intensified the division between work and play. The result was a "floating" populace cut off from the land and concentrated in large cities, who felt a growing sense of "personal isolation and a fractionation of life functions into an ever-expanding and differentiating system of formalized institutions."[18]

"We cannot separate our being into contradictory halves," warned Donald Davidson, "without a certain amount of spiritual damage."[19] Culture—not only the arts, but customs, habits, and an intimate knowledge of one's region—would surely die in a country where the organic connection between self and social role tended to disintegrate under the impact of technological "progress." It could survive only in a society that satisfied man's emotional needs, provided a stable environment with common values, and defined labor in terms of human fulfillment rather than by the accumulation of wealth. The Southerners longed for a social system in which the individual experienced a "face-to-face interaction" with and an instinctive responsibility for other men. Presently in America, human relationships were "casual, fleeting," haphazard; the alternative was a country which permitted "great personal autonomy" at the same time it encouraged a "mutuality of interests" and an "innate code of obligations" among all inhabitants.[20] Attempting to overcome the anonymity of mass society, they saw in those groups rooted in and familiar with regional traditions the instrument for mediating between private and public life. They loathed capitalism as competitive and selfish, they rejected socialism as only a further extension of the industrial mystique, and they offered the agrarian South as a symbol of how the individual and society might be perfectly integrated. The United States had followed private enterprise to the brink of economic disaster and moral ruin; now was the time to imagine a completely different kind of life.

Despite the symposium's rural utopianism and its reactionary economics, *I'll Take My Stand* struck a peculiarly responsive chord in writers otherwise unsympathetic to the vision of a Southern paradise. This was largely because the argument was couched in essentially apolitical language; its critique of capitalism might apply to any position regardless of ideology. Thus Edmund Wilson, though considering himself a socialist in 1931, could still admit that slavery (as described by the Agrarians) possessed certain advantages over the contemporary exploitation of factory labor. The planta-

tion owner, unlike the modern industrialist, at least accepted moral responsibility for his acts. The planter knew his workers intimately, Wilson asserted; he understood that they toiled for his benefit and he refused to bury
this truth under the weight of liberal rationalizations. But today capitalism
had developed into a highly complex and impersonal system. The refine-
ment of mechanical technique, the importance of engineers and technicians,
and the growth of bureaucracies shut men off from any knowledge of one
another. "The processes," Wilson contended, "which divorce so completely
the people who live on dividends from the people whose labor makes
dividends possible are only one feature of the vast system of abstraction
which dominates the industrial world." The absence of personal contact
between people, and the inability to hold individuals directly accountable
for the consequences of their behavior, all contributed to the "deadening of
feeling, the social insulation, which improverishes life in industrial communities."[21]

Although Wilson rejected the Southerners' specific program as anachronistic, the fact that he should adopt much of their rhetoric reflected the ease
with which many writers mistook a moral condemnation of capitalism for
hard-headed social analysis. To some, the South or Mexico or Russia could
all be appreciated equally as symbols of order, fellowship, and sanity. In this
sense, both agrarianism and socialism often seemed more compelling as
myths than as political alternatives. But if carried too far, what began as
a perceptive critique of modern life could end as a complacent celebration
of provincialism, small-town neighborliness, and the common man—while
the capitalist structure remained intact.

Yet there were sophisticated efforts to shape this form of cultural criticism into an effective social theory. For a few writers, the point was never
to retreat into peasant villages or pre-Civil War romances, but to achieve
a new "equilibrium between man and nature," between the urban "civilization of the state and the machines on the one hand, and the culture of the
folk and of learning on the other."[22] If life under industrial capitalism was
arid and harsh, this did not mean that the factories should be torn down;
rather, the very institutions to which intellectuals now objected might be
used under another dispensation for truly human ends. Where many continued to focus on the conflict of men and machines, merely enlarging on
a theme of the 1920s, several tried to explore their potential compatibility.

By far the most thoughtful and elaborate effort was Lewis Mumford's
Technics and Civilization, published in 1934. This monumental work and
its sequel, *The Culture of Cities*, which appeared in 1938, represented the
culmination of ideas Mumford had been developing since the 1920s. Always

concerned with the relationship between man and nature, art and science, inner feelings and the outer world, he had studied the ways in which Americans drove them apart in *Sticks and Stones* (1924), *The Golden Day* (1926), *Herman Melville* (1929), and *The Brown Decades* (1931). But these books dealt primarily with literature, painting, and architecture. Very much in the tradition of Van Wyck Brooks, they argued that the country had sacrificed its aesthetic and spiritual heritage to the pressures of manufacturing and money-making—with the result that the artist could never find his proper audience, "culture" became synonymous with a middle-class hunger for status, and most people remained content to worship at the altar of power and success. This was the standard indictment of the 1920s: the sensitive intellectual cast as hero, with the Puritan, the Pioneer, and the Philistine as the supreme villains. The depression made these categories sound manichean and simplistic, however; the problems of American society appeared greater than a Brooksian analysis could encompass. Thus in *Technics and Civilization* Mumford sought to adapt the essentially cultural preoccupations of men like Krutch, Frank, Chase, Wilson, and the Southern Agrarians to broader social and economic questions—in effect, to fuse the insights of the 1920s with those of the following decade.

He began to examine the breakdown of medieval society under the impact of science, capitalism, and technology. Before the introduction of clocks (which replaced the sun and climate as an indication of time), the rise of cities (which, like monasteries, demanded an "orderly routine") and the new awareness of perspective in space (which required an accurate observation of nature and human anatomy), men lived in a world of magic, myth, ritual, and ceremony.[23] Now their symbolic patterns of thought gave way to a dependence on reason, experimentation, and facts. The new scientific mind, according to Mumford, was transfixed by anything that could be "weighed, measured, or counted." It reduced the complex to the simple, fragmented life into sequences that could be controlled and repeated, and exalted objectivity at the expense of intuition and feeling. Ultimately, "the method of science and technology" implied a "sterilization of the self, an elimination . . . of the human bias and preference, including the human pleasure in man's own image, and the instinctive belief in the immediate presentation of his fantasies."[24] In essence, Mumford was identifying pastoral and medieval virtues with an "organic" social experience—one in which men, whatever their economic deprivation, enjoyed a sense of harmony within themselves, with nature, and with their fellow men. Science and the machine had destroyed this happy equilibrium and so was fundamentally hostile to all the values associated with culture.

Even worse in his eyes, science and capitalism drew on the same sources of power: "abstraction, measurement, quantification."[25] Both required conscious discipline; both relied on empirical demonstration rather than image-making; both encouraged the invention of bigger and better machines; both led to standardized products and the regimentation of social life under the direction of the soldier, the bookkeeper, the engineer, and the bureaucrat.[26] In its turn, capitalism was responsible for the monstrous uses to which technology was put. Dividing the period between the Renaissance and the twentieth century into what he called the "eotechnic" and "paleotechnic" ages (thereby rejecting the conventional historical categories of Marx), Mumford traced the gradual triumph of mechanization over organicism, the production of goods over human sensibility.

The eotechnic economy, which lasted roughly from the demise of feudalism until the beginning of the industrial revolution, had important advantages over its successor, he believed. This phase depended primarily on the power of wind and water; its major inventions were the clock, the printing press, and the blast furnace. Though it introduced the factory system, though it made work more specialized and impersonal, though it allowed profit rather than craftsmanship to become the ultimate objective, the eotechnic era still retained many of Mumford's favorite attributes. It transformed forests and swamps into villages and gardens; it built hundreds of new cities that were spacious, orderly, and beautiful; its products directly enriched and improved the lives of ordinary people; it tempered "intellectual abstractionism" with a spirit of play. "In every department of activity," he concluded, "there was equilibrium between the static and the dynamic, between the rural and the urban, between the vital and the mechanical."[27] Combining the best of medieval culture with necessary advances in the standard of living, the eotechnic period was a kind of model for the truly balanced civilization Mumford had in mind.

By contrast, the paleotechnic economy epitomized all the worst features of industrial capitalism. Sounding much like Henry Adams in his more sardonic moments, Mumford dissected an age in thrall to coal, iron, and steam. Here the values of life were replaced by those of money, size, and efficiency; work was no longer an extension of human experience but an end in itself; progress was reckoned by the amount of goods a society could produce. The countryside was being plundered to serve the towns, which themselves seemed increasingly "monotonous, sordid, barbarous to the last degree." People grew incapable of appreciating art, amusement, or leisure. Wealth and power became the only realities of a competitive and warlike world.[28] But the most disturbing aspect of paleotechnic society, for Mumford, was the rise of individualism. The earlier feeling of membership in an ongoing community had completely disappeared. Men now became preoccupied with their own separate personalities, having lost all sense of social responsibility or contact with the surrounding environment. Consequently the "private individual" was forced to "compensate by egocentric getting and spending for the absence of collective institutions and a collective aim."[29]

To this point, Mumford was simply recasting the standard complaints of many American intellectuals into a theory of historical development. They all despised modern capitalism because it degraded the workers as well as the middle class, because it harnessed science and technology to a system of private profit, and because it prevented men from achieving personal fulfillment within a stable society. But Mumford wished to do more than lament the passing of the Middle Ages, or extol the virtues of some mythic community that existed solely in a given writer's imagination. Indeed, he hoped to show that the benefits of pre-machine "culture" could be merged with post-capitalist "civilization," that the social and economic conditions of the twentieth century contained in themselves the elements of an entirely new synthesis. The retreat into primitivism, he declared, the celebration of emotion at the expense of the rational intellect, the dogmatic refusal to incorporate the lessons of technology into social behavior were hysterical and reactionary responses to the problems of American life.[30] Mumford sought instead to reintegrate the values he identified with organicism and those he associated with technics. In the process, he wished to give his contemporaries a glimpse of how a program for both culture and politics might be integrated.

In the first place, Mumford contended that technology itself had reached the stage where "the organic has become visible again . . . within the mechanical complex." The new inventions of what he labeled the "neotechnic" age—the telegraph, the telephone, the phonograph, the radio, the motion picture—were restoring the human eye, ear, and voice to the world of machines. Electric power had made it possible for people to communicate and to react instantaneously; as a result, their sense of personal isolation diminished. Moreover, the worker need no longer be a slave to the assembly line. Neotechnic machinery required alertness, responsiveness, a grasp of all the operative parts—in short, a total rather than a specialized knowledge of industrial production and a capacity for intelligent supervision instead of mindless labor.[31] Like Alfred Bingham, Mumford envisioned neotechnic civilization as clean, decentralized, functional, and automated. It thereby released men's energies for leisure and self-expression.

Secondly, Mumford insisted that science and mechanization were never inherently opposed to human culture. On the contrary, they encouraged a new mode of living that was superior to anything Americans had previously imagined. Technics, if properly used, meant a liberation from prejudice and intellectual confusion. It emphasized not only the factual and the practical but also "relatively new esthetic terms: precision, calculation, flawlessness, simplicity, economy . . . elimination of the non-essential." Most important of all, it provided a model for collective and cooperative effort, both in the production of goods and in the organization of society. Thus men needed technology precisely in order to create a new culture. "Our capacity to go beyond the machine," Mumford argued, "rests upon our power to assimilate the machine. Until we have absorbed the lessons of objectivity, impersonality, neutrality, the lessons of the mechanical realm, we cannot go further in our development toward the more richly organic, the more profoundly human."[32]

What stood in the way of this millennium was the system of private profit. Here Mumford traced an essentially cultural analysis to its economic roots. The horrors of mechanization, he pointed out, had nothing to do with technical processes or forms of work. The machine was an impartial instrument whose potential for improving life had been strangled by capitalist enterprise. Now Mumford was insisting that the historic link between capitalism and technics be broken, that order and stability could come only with a "wholesale devaluation of . . . bourgeois civilization upon which our present system of production is based," that the machine be used for truly social purposes by building a "collective economy."[33] He was quite explicit about what sort of society this implied: "Rationalization, standardization, and above all, rationed production and consumption, on the scale necessary to bring up to a vital norm the consumptive level of the whole community —these things are impossible on a sufficient scale without a socialized political control of the entire process."[34] This involved the organization of consumers into effective pressure groups, the beginning of comprehensive regional planning, public ownership of the industrial plant, and production-for-use.

Yet Mumford's version of socialism, like those of other writers in the 1930s, included more than an economic program. A planned society would introduce not only new institutions but, even more significant, new *values*. In his view, socialism promised to emphasize the ideal of integration, shared activities, common allegiances, collective responsibility, and human fellowship—all the impulses that capitalism had presumably destroyed.[35] Furthermore, it permitted men to abandon the myths of infinite progress and expansion, to accept their own maturity and sense of limitations. The period of chaotic advance and haphazard growth was giving way to a new age of "consolidation and systematic assimilation." Instead of fleeing from the present, as James Rorty had feared, America must now be willing to "settle down and make the most of what it has." But the future was far from bleak. Indeed Mumford described it with all the words his generation cherished: discipline, planning, order, control, balance, equilibrium, conservation of resources, a "gearing together of the various parts" that made up social life.[36] Internal coherence had become far more desirable than external growth.

Ultimately, Mumford was investing socialism with a mission that went beyond reform or revolution; he fervently believed it would bring about a fusion of culture and technology, organicism and the machine, human needs and economic well-being. No longer would the body be deformed, the mind cramped, the spirit suffocated. A socialist transformation was going to affect man's consciousness as well as his political arrangements. "With a change in ideals from material conquest, wealth, and power to life, culture, and expression," he concluded, "the machine . . . will fall back into its proper place: our servant, not our tyrant."[37]

This was a vision that combined detailed social and economic observations with a set of strikingly utopian assumptions. As such, it reflected the dominant mood among many of the decade's intellectuals, especially their conviction that the principal objective of politics was to create a new value system. Mumford had undertaken to resolve some of the more disturbing tensions in the thought of the 1930s. Yet his ideas had a curiously static quality. At bottom the book was characteristically weak in matters of strategy and tactics—not a minor flaw in a period interested in moving from the present into the future. Significantly, Mumford avoided all ideological categories, both liberal and Marxist. Resting his case on a kind of technological determinism, he never really located the specific engines of change. Nor were classes, parties, or programs given a prominent role in bringing socialism to America. For all his efforts to unite cultural criticism and social analysis, to extend the moral complaints against capitalism into a comprehensive theory of historical development, he was unable to show how men might actually take over their own destinies. Thus *Technics and Civilization* ended on an ambiguous note of hope and passivity; Mumford's readers were offered a picture of the promised land but not a map for getting there.

2. *The Appeal of Collectivism*

No matter how mystical the concept of an "organic" community might sometimes sound, no matter how many writers displayed more interest in spiritual regeneration than in questions of power and politics, they were nevertheless searching in the 1930s for a view of the world that might correspond to existing social and economic conditions. It was not that intellectuals were ignorant of or hostile to ideology; rather, political theory alone appeared inadequate to solve the enormous problems confronting America. Beyond the material suffering and poverty that flowed from the depression, beyond the obvious need to restructure the nation's economy, most writers felt that the society itself was disintegrating into its component parts. There no longer seemed to be any unifying purpose in which men could believe. What distinguished the depression from earlier crises was this sense of decomposition at every level of public and private life. Where both the Civil War and the battle of Progressivism could be waged with conventional liberal weapons, and where economic development might be expected to heal all wounds, the total collapse of capitalism in the 1930s demanded revolutionary perspectives and programs for which few intellectuals were fully prepared. Because they were inexperienced in matters of theory, because they lacked a political movement that would translate their ideas into action, and because they instinctively suspected that no new philosophy could satisfactorily explain and master the upheavals of depression America, they often lapsed into apocalyptic language and cultural prophecy.

Moreover, American intellectuals had rarely found themselves in a situation that required ideological sophistication. As Edmund Wilson shrewdly observed in 1932, "we Americans have lived and breathed and had our whole national being in the world of the triumphant bourgeoisie." Unlike Europe, he asserted, the United States had never known any other social system; its entire history was confined within the mental horizons of the middle class. In the absence of a pre-capitalist tradition, writers had great difficulty envisioning a non-capitalist way of life. Instead they tended to indulge in moral condemnations of American materialism and individualism, while failing to provide an alternative set of ideals. But now Wilson was convinced that "capitalism has run its course and we have got to imagine something better."[38] In his view, the depression offered an unusual opportunity to break with the bourgeois past, to fashion a philosophy that would deal effectively with what Lewis Mumford described as the future world of "associations and societies, in which the fact of interrelation [will be] as primordial as the parts that are related."[39]

Thus while life in America presently seemed unmanageable and pointless, many detected an embryonic sense of order beneath the surface. Among writers, the depression dramatized not only the failure of the old ideals but also the necessity of redefining basic concepts to summon forth a new understanding of the national experience. By the mid-1930s, "collectivism" had become a key word in their vocabulary. They used it to express a variety of ideas: the desire to transcend the liberal tradition, the recognition that society had grown steadily corporate and interdependent while its state of mind remained individualistic, the notion that men were inherently social beings, the insistence that the needs of the group took priority over those of the private person. At worst, collectivism stood as a vague and hortatory symbol embracing every kind of revolutionary sentiment; at best, it gave intellectuals for the first time since the Progressive era an effective way of talking about the problems of culture and politics in the United States.

For some, the 1930s was a period in which liberalism was to be rejected not only as a political tactic but also as a social philosophy and guide to life. No longer were writers content simply to draw on the ideas of Herbert Croly or Thorstein Veblen; instead they wished to substitute for liberal capitalism both a socialist economy and a radically new value system. In their minds, "collectivism" was a moral as well as an ideological goal.

This was particularly evident among those who were themselves products of the Progressive generation. When the *New Republic* observed its twentieth birthday in January of 1935, the editors published a credo which tried to differentiate their present position from the one that shaped the magazine in its early years. Like America, the *New Republic* had been conceived under liberal auspices. "But nothing is more obvious," declared Bruce Bliven and George Soule, "than that the economic and social order to which a liberal philosophy gave birth and in which it flourished is rapidly degenerating and must in the course of time give way to some other." Specifically this meant that intellectuals would have to end not only their toleration of "individual business enterprise" which was clearly anachronistic in an age of corporate consolidation but also the notion that men were free to do whatever they pleased regardless of the social consequences. Where Croly had advocated a semi-planned economy regulated by the government but still capitalist in its basic character, Bliven and Soule were calling for a fully socialized America. Moreover, where the Progressives had always assumed that the ultimate objective of reform was to expand individual freedom, the *New Republic* now considered economic security to be of greater importance than political or civil liberties. Indeed freedom itself, the editors argued, was often a meaningless abstraction serving merely as a rationale under which one class or group achieved its purposes at the expense of another. "True liberty," however, was "relative and . . . restricted at many points"—depending on who had power and how it was used. In sum, the New Republic in the 1930s wished to redefine the concept of freedom entirely so that it would be seen as a product of conscious social choices rather than as a strictly personal privilege. Precisely in order to salvage historic ideals—"a belief in the brotherhood and inherent value of man, a belief in equality, a belief in objective reason and science, a belief in material welfare"—the journal exhorted its readers to adopt a "collectivist" perspective.[40]

Similarly John Dewey, the father confessor of American liberals, insisted that questions of private rights were directly tied to the type of society in which one lived. For him the issue was never freedom versus restraint but which forms of coercion might be more effective in redistributing power among the contending classes.[41] "The only hope for liberalism," he declared in 1936, "is to surrender, in theory and practice, the doctrine that liberty is a full-fledged ready-made possession of individuals independent of social institutions and arrangements, and to realize that social control, especially of economic forces, is necessary in order to render secure the liberties of the individual, including civil liberties."[42]

George Soule went even further. Objecting vehemently to the "erroneous conception" of "abstract, complete and atomistic liberty," he maintained that true personal fullfillment could come only when public and private needs were no longer antithetical—when the individual had gone so far as to internalize the "external compulsions" of his environment. The ultimate purpose in changing institutions, he asserted, was to build a harmonious and unified community in which freedom was the result of "intricate social discipline."[43]

With their idea of freedom-in-society, Dewey and Soule were reflecting the decade's extreme sensitivity to the "social" aspects of men's lives. Along these lines, many anthropologists and psychologists in the 1930s seemed to be insisting that the emotions and attitudes of individuals were irrevocably conditioned by the norms and institutions of their society. One of the most widely read and influential books of the period, Ruth Benedict's Patterns of Culture, argued explicitly that the "life-history of the individual is first and foremost an accommodation to the patterns and standards traditionally handed down in his community. From the moment of his birth the customs into which he is born shape his experience and behavior." Thus the nineteenth-century notion of an "antagonism between the role of society and that of the individual" had become in her view not only obsolete but dangerous; it prevented modern men from seeing the essential interrelationships between themselves and their cultural milieu, and it created a set of false social and psychic tensions which interfered with the effective functioning of a healthy society. Throughout the book, Benedict wished to point out the radical implications of cultural relativism, the extent to which no social order could be considered permanently good or immune to alteration. She firmly believed that change was necessary whenever the process of disorientation and maladjustment reached a level where large numbers of people in a given society could no longer live by its rules without suffering serious forms of frustration and alienation. But her emphasis on the need for balance and harmony in social life, her feeling that deviant behavior was an illness to be treated rather than an understandable (and possibly creative) response to an intolerable situation, her implicit fear of institutional breakdown and cultural disorder were all indications of how often writers in the 1930s translated the desire for change into an urge for stability.[44]

Similarly, a number of professional psychologists—particularly Karen Horney and Harry Stack Sullivan—had begun to revise what they took to be Sigmund Freud's excessive preoccupation with the inner and hidden self, arguing instead that the focus of concern should be shifted from the introspective individual to the larger society, from the problems of the unconscious to the problems that were socially inspired. Like Ruth Benedict, the neo-Freudians wanted to make clear that a neurotic society created neurotic personalities, that a transformation of public values and institutions might be more therapeutic than extended psychoanalysis. Nevertheless, in the absence of social change, they tended to admire the virtues of social control; they concentrated on the techniques by which the individual might better adapt to his environment, the channels through which eccentric or abnormal behavior could flow into more manageable patterns of behavior.[45] Even if the consequences of their point of view might serve not the needs of the troubled individual but the needs of a bureaucratic society (by illuminating the ways in which some of the tensions within the office or plant could be reduced through better personnel studies, improved industrial relations, and more effective "orientation" procedures), many psychologists in the 1930s preferred behavior that was socially acceptable to whatever seemed personally disruptive.

The depression itself encouraged the conviction that human problems would never be solved by the individual alone—indeed that an emphasis on personal liberation and self-expression might be positively harmful in the context of a national disaster. People could no longer be permitted to pursue their separate interests, warned the apostle of Progressive education, George Counts. Not only was the government to stabilize conditions through a "highly socialized, coordinated, and planned economy," but the schools should undertake to inculcate new norms of behavior in the young. Education, he argued, must stop "striving to equip each individual to surpass his neighbor"; instead, it should teach citizens that the "welfare of the ordinary individual can be advanced only by making paramount the general good." In Counts's opinion, students ought to learn that "intimate cooperation" was more important than competition for grades and approbation, that getting along with others was more virtuous than the urge to succeed.[46] The classroom was supposed to be a model for the new society; its principal lesson would be, in Charles Beard's words, the "subordination of personal ambition and greed to common plans and purposes."[47]

Divorced from their radical aims, many of these propositions often sounded ominously manipulative and repressive. The collective search for knowledge might give way to intellectual conformity, altruism could turn into obedience, the socialization of the individual might end in his smoother adjustment to the status quo. By teaching men to suppress their egos for the betterment of society, education for the future could also be a way of reconciling people to the present—especially if the revolution never came. Paradoxically, these writers were equating freedom with order, human aspiration with social control, liberation of the self with security for everyone. They hoped to show that democratic liberties did not necessarily depend on private property and profit, that attention to the general welfare would also serve the interests of the individual. But they were treading a dangerously thin line between the recognition of social priorities and a desire to lose oneself in the mass. Trying to fashion a distinctive set of values for socialism, they ran the risk of making personal concerns seem less important than the sentiments of the "group"—any group, regardless of program or ideology.

If men like Dewey, Soule, Counts, and Beard found conventional liberalism too individualistic, those who called themselves Marxists were even more dogmatic about the social nature of human experience. But at the same time, they articulated in a heightened way the decade's dominant assumption that one could overcome inner turmoil by becoming part of a stable community, that private problems could be solved through collective outlets. In their eyes, liberalism was not only an outmoded philosophy; far worse, it prevented men from seeing how society actually functioned, and thereby made it impossible to develop the strategies and ideals necessary to abolish capitalist enterprise.

One of the most unrelenting foes of liberalism and individualism—concepts he always tended to equate—was V.F. Calverton. Drawing on ideas he discovered both in Marxism and cultural anthropology, Calverton repeatedly called for a new understanding of the relationship between man and society. Liberals, he argued, had traditionally overemphasized the importance and autonomy of the individual, which led to the false impression that society was nothing more than the sum of its disparate parts. But few realized how rapidly the self was being reduced to cog in some vast social machine, or how irrelevant the notion of a perpetual conflict between men and institutions had suddenly become. In contrast, Calverton asserted that "society constitutes the center of things with the individual nothing more than its by-product. The individual derives his meaning . . . in relation to society and not through himself. An individual . . . cannot live isolated from society, for all [his] tools of operation, language, ideas, concepts, beliefs, convictions, have meaning only in connection with society."[48] Since personal identity and behavior seemed so dependent on what Ruth Benedict had called the "patterns of culture," since individuality was possible only within a specific social context, Calverton stressed the need for men to find freedom through perfect accord with the surrounding environment. And like so many of his contemporaries, he believed this could be accomplished when socialist cooperation replaced capitalist competition.[49]

Similarly Newton Arvin, increasingly attracted to the humanistic aspects of Marxism in the early 1930s, was much taken with the conception of society as corporate and organic. In his view liberal individualism had to be renounced, not just for political and economic reasons, but for one's own psychological survival. The notion of society as composed of "simple, separate, persons" was no longer tenable, he maintained. In the future, men must learn to merge themselves with the group if they hoped both to change their institutions and to become integrated personalities.[50] For both Calverton and Arvin, Marxism provided a convincing description of modern society largely because it seemed to favor precisely those values intellectuals wished to champion in the 1930s: social commitment over personal independence, cohesiveness over fragmentation, the community over the individual. In this sense, they were using Marxism in part as a tool of social analysis but more frequently as a confirmation of their own moral judgments about how life in America should be organized.

Perhaps the best expression of these attitudes appeared in a *New Masses* essay of 1934 by a Marxist poet and philosopher named Rebecca Pitts. The article bore the revealing title "Something to Believe In," and it caught the mood of many writers who found traditional liberalism wanting both ideologically and emotionally. According to Miss Pitts, the fundamental dilemma of the 1930s was how to become part of a social group or class while retaining one's "personal integrity," how the "confused and divided personality" could gain a sense of satisfaction in a collective cause without at the same time sacrificing his "individuality and self-awareness."[51] This was complicated by the recognition that all previous ideals, including the classic American faith in progress, had collapsed under the weight of the depression. Yet if modern man were to escape the "pain of his isolation," she pointed out, if he were to establish an effective relationship with other men, then he must find some new doctrine that deserved his commitment and loyalty.[52] Essentially, Miss Pitts was suggesting that both the external world and man's inner life would remain chaotic and absurd until Americans rediscovered a coherent social philosophy.

Yet she too was less interested in the formal content of such a philosophy than in how it affected daily behavior. Moreover, she did not seem nearly so worried about the preservation of personal idiosyncrasies as she was in discovering a movement one could join. In the first place, she declared, "mere intellectual assent" to a given ideology was not enough; any new belief must address the country's spiritual needs as well as its social problems. Secondly, this meant that the individual would have to undergo a "psychological change" so that he "looks at his world with new eyes and sees himself in a new and *functionally subordinate* relationship to it."[53] Here she imagined an almost mystical transformation of identity in which "a new self emerges—with a new awareness and new purposes [that] are integrated because they are relative to ends and values beyond the individual." Like others in the period, she insisted that personality was a product of cultural conditioning, and that people should therefore learn to adjust their private ambitions to the demands of society. Finally, a true sense of community in the United States awaited men's ability to achieve a "genuine, incorruptible wholeness . . . within themselves in just that degree with which they really can surrender their lives to a reality greater than themselves." Once one was able to regard the "collective 'we' as more significant than the separate 'I,' " he could regain a feeling of unity and fulfillment within an "organic social whole."[54]

All of these writers—those who contributed to the *New Republic* as well as those who appeared in the *Modern Quarterly* or *New Masses*—stressed collectivist ideals as a way of dissociating themselves from liberal politics, bourgeois prejudices, and a laissez-faire economy. They clearly intended their emphasis on man as a social animal to have radical connotations, to suggest both an ideology and value system that would prepare people mentally for socialism. But their ideas also had quite conservative implications, which went largely unnoticed in the early 1930s. The yearning to share and participate in some larger social cause, to subordinate oneself to the needs of the group, might lead not to revolution but to a ratification of existing cultural mores. Rarely was the desire for self-expression considered a necessary ingredient for political action. Indeed individualism was always the chief symbolic villain for most intellectuals in the decade—a trait to be suppressed rather than used as a stimulant in transforming American life. While denouncing capitalism as intrinsically competitive and selfish, many writers were swinging to the other extreme: preferring cooperation and stability to anything they believed divisive or eccentric. In the process they overlooked the extent to which collectivism could become authoritarian, social discipline could inhibit personal development, the urge to belong could result in the pressure to conform, and acceptance of community values could reinforce the status quo. So concerned with combating the disruptive effects of the depression, with making all parts of public and private life cohere, they tended to minimize the areas of conflict and tension that might otherwise be expected to provoke revolutionary changes in the United States.

3. *The Individual and Society*

Not everyone remained oblivious to these dangers. There were at least three books written in the 1930s that tried to make use of "collectivism" both as an instrument for serious social analysis and as a guide to radical action. Each book attempted to treat the country's problems from an ideological but realistic perspective; each recognized that man's desire for privacy and introspection should be protected whatever form the new society might take; each sought to combine liberal values with the task of socialist reconstruction. As such, they gathered the fragmentary ideas of other writers into a fairly sophisticated theory of how Americans could better adapt to life in the twentieth century. Together with Mumford's *Technics and Civilization,* they continued the work begun by the Progressives of helping men understand, function in, and possibly transform their world—politically, economically, and culturally.

Two of the books were written by John Dewey: *Individualism Old and New,* which appeared in 1930 after serialization in the *New Republic,* and *Liberalism and Social Action,* published in 1935. The titles themselves suggested that Dewey was attempting to reconcile certain strains in American thought that had previously been considered antagonistic. Up to a point, he shared with many of his contemporaries the conviction that America's traditional concerns—especially its preoccupation with individual freedom at the expense of rational economic planning—were hopelessly antiquated in an era of large-scale production, corporate mergers, and expanding bureaucracies. The United States, according to Dewey, was suffering from an advanced case of cultural lag: a collision between new needs and pressures generated by industrialization on the one hand and a continuing loyalty to outmoded creeds and habits on the other. Though the daily experience of most people had been profoundly altered by the scientific and technological revolutions of the twentieth century, "their conscious ideas and standards are inherited from an age that has passed away; their minds . . . are at odds with actual conditions." This in turn led to an "acute maladjustment" between men and institutions, a "pathological" situation in which citizens were bewildered by and fearful of the very inventions that promised to improve their lives. Only when their "ideas and ideals" were "brought into harmony with the realities of the age in which they act," only when they fashioned a new ideology to fit the modern world, might Americans become the masters rather than the victims of social change.[55]

In particular, Dewey wanted very much to demonstrate that liberalism, despite its original alliance with the system of private property and unlimited competition, could no longer realize its ideals in a capitalist society. The major reason for this, he submitted, was that the basic mechanisms of production and distribution had themselves become collectivized, thereby circumscribing the opportunities for personal initiative and success. Yet even though "concentration and corporate organization are the rule," they were still "controlled in their operation by ideas that were institutionalized in eons of separate individual effort." Nevertheless Dewey rejected the Marxists' assumption that the only way to overcome this gap between theory and practice was through class struggle; he was not ready to abandon the liberal belief that if men's thought patterns and attitudes were changed, society would eventually be transformed. He therefore proposed that Americans become fully *conscious* of how their industrial process really worked, recognize that "freedom from social control" was a prescription for economic chaos, and begin deliberately to create "cooperative" institutions which might channel the country's wealth and power into public hands.[56] In this sense, reform for Dewey was as much a product of human will and action as a result of historical development.

His central purpose was to show precisely what kind of social philosophy the nation needed to accomplish this mission. Here he parted company with those who wished merely to replace a solicitude for the individual with a worship of community. Dewey agreed that the problem of redefining the relationship between self and society was a crucial task for the 1930s, without which socialism was impossible. Moreover, he admitted that Americans first had to conquer their sense of internal turmoil and confusion before they could construct a truly stable society. The "machine and its technology" might have prepared the way for a form of collectivism in economic affairs, he pointed out, but the "inner man" remained a "jungle" of private frustrations and disoriented activity. Thus he endorsed the decade's characteristic demand that collectivist values be mirrored both in the structure of institutions and in the human personality. Only when the "forces of organization at work in externals are reflected in corresponding patterns of thought, imagination, and emotion," he insisted, could men recover a feeling of "wholeness within themselves." Like others in the 1930s, Dewey was not interested simply in the material benefits of socialism but in the development of a life-style that integrated the individual with the community and offered each person the experience of active participation in a "shared culture."[57]

On the other hand, he was by no means urging a passive conformity to group norms. Instead he looked forward to a release of individuality for genuinely creative work. Dewey assumed that the ideal of collectivism would nurture rather than suppress "originality and uniqueness," that the ultimate objective of social change was to bring forth a "new type" of man whose freedom and self-awareness would flourish precisely because he felt emotionally and economically secure. And this aspiration led him to conclude that certain liberal values were worth preserving after all; they included "liberty, the development of the inherent capacities of individuals made possible through liberty, and the central role of free intelligence in inquiry, discussion, and expression." Where once these principles had been tied inextricably to capitalism, they now could be transferred intact to a "socialized economy."[58] The end result, he predicted, would be an expansion of cultural possibilities, in which the enormous resources of industrial civilization permitted each American to unshackle his mind and enrich his imagination.[59]

In essence, Dewey was hoping to make the liberal concern for intelligence, freedom, and personal identity relevant to the new collectivist conditions of modern life. His conception of socialism was both political and aesthetic; it embraced the principles of planning and the spirit of cooperation in a common enterprise. But unlike Counts or Calverton, Soule or

Arvin, Dewey was capable of threading his way between two opposing ideas without committing himself exclusively to either. Neither an orthodox liberal nor a doctrinaire socialist, neither a confirmed individualist nor a celebrant of collectivism, he wanted to draw equally on both traditions. He was as much interested in retaining the virtues of personal independence as in emphasizing the cultural determinants of human behavior; he wanted as much to liberate people as to give them orderly institutions; he cared as much about self-realization as social control. Ultimately the communitarian ideal was important to him not because it was morally superior to individualism and capitalist greed but precisely because it freed men to pursue their most private ambitions and desires. In Dewey's eyes, collectivism was only a twentieth-century name for the oldest of American dreams.

If Dewey suggested the general outlines of a new social philosophy, Robert Lynd's *Knowledge for What?* filled in some of the details. Published in 1939, the book summarized in theoretical fashion many of the conclusions Lynd had reached in fifteen years of studying American society. In part, *Knowledge for What?* was designed as a polemic against the kinds of questions social scientists in the United States normally asked. Lynd wanted to approach the classic problem of men and institutions from a different vantage point than liberalism customarily permitted. Moreover, he refused to divorce his speculative ideas from what he believed to be their obvious radical implications. Like Dewey, he was eager to formulate a theory of cultural behavior that would at the same time offer practical guidance in transforming America.

Lynd began by charging that his fellow sociologists, economists, psychologists, and historians had become too specialized within their own disciplines, too narrow in the issues they chose to explore, and too hesitant about translating their work into concrete political programs. Usually, he observed, they broke society down into its atomic elements, rarely considering the ways in which different levels of social experience were organically interrelated. As a result, they failed to connect their "analysis of parts to the analysis of the whole." Here Lynd was urging American social scientists to adopt a collectivist perspective, to deal with problems not as discrete phenomena but as segments of an "inclusive totality."[60]

Significantly, the most appropriate method Lynd could recommend for examining these issues was to view them not in the context of institutions or classes but in terms of "culture." Like Chase, Frank, Mumford, and the Southern Agrarians, Lynd possessed a basically anthropological rather than an aesthetic notion of what culture meant. Far from implying a "refined sense of *belles lettres* and sophisticated learning," it referred instead to "all the things that a group of people inhabiting a common geographical area do, the ways they do things and the ways they think and feel about things, their material tools and their values and symbols."[61] Thus he too shared the decade's special interest in the lives of ordinary men, the extent to which their perceptions and behavior were shaped by a specific social setting, the role that myths and rituals played in influencing human thought and action. Indeed, this emphasis on cultural conditioning led many writers in the 1930s to treat ideologies as if they were essentially weapons for winning mass support rather than as instruments of rational political debate. It was not surprising, therefore, that the sorts of questions Lynd considered important involved the emotional as well as the economic effects of capitalism: the feeling of individual powerlessness in the face of large and impersonal institutions, the perception of work as a source of frustration and anomie, the psychology of saving and investment, the moral costs of competition, the disintegration of the family in an industrial society, the subordination of life to money-making.

But Lynd was not advocating a theory of pure cultural determinism, in which institutions were regarded as an independent force existing somehow apart from the people whom they affected. Nor did he think it possible to study the individual as a separate entity in perpetual conflict with society. Together with Dewey, he hoped to avoid the two extremes—to see whether the liberal concern for personal freedom and the Marxist sensitivity to social conditions might be mutually compatible. To test this proposition, Lynd pointed out that "culture and individuals interact," that institutions were the channels through which human beings learned to express their habits and impulses, that society patterned behavior at the same time men were reshaping society. Individuals internalized the demands of their environment, but they also forced the environment to respond to certain "basic processes" within themselves. Consequently, Lynd adopted the phrase "culture *in* personality and personality *in* culture" to describe the ways in which social forces and private instincts actually reinforced one another.[62]

In addition, Lynd believed that beyond the goals and norms a particular culture sanctioned, there were fundamental desires common to all men in every society. These seemed intrinsic to the very experience of being alive and were in effect universal. As such, they contributed further to the relative autonomy of individuals. But more important, they gave Lynd a frame of reference with which to attack his colleagues' "ethical neutrality" in times of crisis. The social scientist, he insisted, must enter the arena and take "as his guiding values, in *selecting and defining his problems,* these deep, more widely based, cravings which living personalities seek to realize." The central issue for Lynd was how to make a given social system fulfill its human responsibilities more effectively. He thus suggested that "wherever our current culture is found to cramp or to distort the quest of considerable numbers of persons for satisfaction" of their basic needs, there lay a fertile field for analysis and action.[63]

This was precisely the standard of judgment he used in his critique of modern American life. Armed with a theory that addressed both cultural and economic questions and that emphasized the distinctiveness of individuals while portraying their problems as fundamentally social in nature, Lynd focused on those areas where institutions failed dramatically to serve the interests of people. To a degree, he shared the decade's characteristic fear of disorder and disunity; a country already in the throes of fragmentation did not look on additional sources of conflict with much enthusiasm. Hence Lynd cited the *lack* of pattern in American culture as the principal dilemma of the depression years. In his opinion, men's aspirations were thwarted "by disjunctions and contradictions among institutions, and even within single institutions; by the disproportionate structuring of power among institutions and within single institutions; and by the erratic reliance upon planning and control at some few points and upon laissez faire, or casual, adjustments at most others." The gears of American society simply did not mesh. Change was sometimes greeted with hospitality but more often with confusion and resistance. Whatever sense of direction the United States exhibited came largely as a matter of chance. The result, he declared, was chaos for the nation and extreme insecurity for the individual.[64]

Yet unlike a number of liberals and Marxists, Lynd did not take refuge in an uncritical worship of stability at any price. On the contrary, it was precisely when a country neared the point of collapse that a revolution seemed to him both necessary and desirable. He acknowledged that men functioned better when public and private tensions were resolved, when America itself had recovered its equilibrium. "But the human personality," he reminded his contemporaries, "also craves a sense of freedom and diversity that gives expression to its many areas of spontaneity. . . ."[65] As much as people longed for social harmony and coherence, they needed a measure of risk and uncertainty in their lives. Once again Lynd was trying to find a middle ground between the values of individualism and collectivity, seeking to expand opportunities for personal inventiveness and self-realization within the framework of a rationally organized society.

To accomplish this, Lynd advanced a set of "hypotheses" by which changes in the social order could be seen not as disruptive but as beneficial. In the first place, given man's tendency to behave irrationally, Lynd recom-

mended that American institutions be structured in such a way as to provide outlets both for intelligence and spontaneous emotion.[66] Though he did
not state the issue in quite these terms, his desire to balance thought and
feeling in daily life represented another effort to reconcile the demands of
"civilization" with those of "culture."

Secondly, Lynd understood that America's traditional encouragement of
competition, mobility, and personal achievement weakened the individual's
commitment to a craft, city, region, or community. He therefore suggested
that any effective reform movement should have a double mission; it must
seek not only to end the depression but also to give people a new sense of
partnership, mutuality, and common purpose in their daily work.[67]

Thirdly, he asserted that the concept of democracy was by no means
limited to parliamentary institutions and electoral processes, that its values
should be extended to every sphere of life in the United States. Specifically
this meant that an economy based on private profit, which no longer served
the needs of the vast majority of Americans, must be abandoned.[68] As an
alternative Lynd envisioned a form of socialism that would be both efficient
in its mastery of modern technology and democratic in its openness to mass
participation.

Finally, he argued that such a society need not lead to conformity and
regimentation. Instead he was convinced that "planning and control [could]
be used to enhance freedom at points critically important to human personality, by eliminating current wastes and insecurities that operate to curtail
freedom."[69] Like Dewey, Lynd regarded socialism as presently the best tool
with which to liberate the individual from the bonds of economic exploitation and cultural anarchy, social injustice and moral paralysis.

In sum, Dewey and Lynd were intensely critical of the liberal tradition,
but they could not entirely repudiate its ideals. At heart, their view of the
world remained pragmatic, pluralistic, and open-ended. Despite their sensitivity to the connection between human needs and cultural resources, they
still believed that the ultimate purpose of reform was to preserve the sanctity of the individual. To them, "collectivism" was always a means to an
end. The 1930s could not lay claim to the discovery of man as a social being;
Progressive intellectuals like Simon Patten, Charles Horton Cooley, George
Herbert Mead, and Herbert Croly had all stressed the necessary interaction
between self and society. But the depression forced writers to concentrate
on the role of groups, classes, and organized movements to the virtual
exclusion of individual effort. Dewey and Lynd were only trying to rein-
troduce a sense of equality in the relationship. If they could no longer accept
liberalism as the handmaiden of capitalist enterprise, they continued to

hope that its more enduring principles—freedom, experimentation, intelligence, rationality, and opportunities for personal growth—might enjoy a new life under socialism.

4. Marx in America

In each of their books, Mumford, Dewey, and Lynd were attempting to provide Americans with a more unified understanding of their world than either the Progressive era or the 1920s had supplied. But the search for a modern and effective social philosophy was not confined to those who saw in cultural criticism or remodeled liberalism a key to the solution of contemporary problems. Insofar as intellectuals did consider ideology to be important in the 1930s, they felt compelled at some point to deal seriously with the ideas of Karl Marx. While many writers (among them Stuart Chase, Newton Arvin, Waldo Frank, and Edmund Wilson) adopted Marxist language to express their sense of moral outrage at capitalism's inefficiency and indifference to human life, thereby welcoming revolution as an instrument of almost religious purification, there were some who saw in socialism the finest embodiment of rational and scientific thinking in the twentieth century. To them, Marxism represented neither a convenient symbol for the disaffection with traditional values nor a mystical vision of the apocalypse. It offered instead a logical, coherent, and realistic appraisal of what America was like and how it might be changed.

In the early years of the depression Marxism won converts not only because it appeared to be working miracles in the Soviet Union, or because the Socialist and Communist parties in the United States defended their political strategies in its name, or even because it became fashionable among certain members of the educated middle class to quote occasionally from the Communist Manifesto. More important, Marxism seemed to explain more convincingly than its competitors the plight in which Americans presently found themselves. To the editors of "liberal" journals such as the New Republic or Nation, to radical intellectuals increasingly obsessed with doctrinal controversy and factional intrigue, to young men just coming of age in the 1930s but without a job or hope of getting one in the near future, Marxist concepts were becoming an indispensable part of their common vocabulary. For one thing, Marxism had accurately predicted the disaster they were now experiencing. It therefore persuaded them that the recurring cycles of boom and bust were not minor flaws in, but intrinsic to, the capitalist system. Marx, writers discovered, had analyzed better than anyone else the impact of technology, the emergence of monopoly capital, the phenomenon of overproduction, the centralization of wealth and power, and the extent to which private ownership retarded the development of a humane society.

In addition, Marxism seemed an appropriate antidote to the traditional goals of liberal reform. By stressing the inevitability of industrial growth and corporate consolidation, it portrayed the Populist crusade against Wall Street and the Wilsonian campaign against the trusts as futile efforts to restore the competitive conditions of nineteenth-century America. Monopolies might hurt the farmer and the small businessman, a Marxist could admit, but they also laid the foundations for socialism. Seen in this light, the duty of modern reformers was not to denounce "bigness" but to seize the opportunity it presented for further collectivization. Moreover, Marxism rejected the liberal assumption that every person was participating equally in the democratic process as long as he exercised the right to vote and had access to the legal protections guaranteed by the Constitution. On this point, liberalism appeared painfully naïve about how power was actually distributed in the United States and how little parliamentary procedures could really accomplish in the face of entrenched privilege. Finally, the liberal effort to expand individual opportunity was attacked by Marxists as hopelessly outdated in an age of mass communication, chain stores, and organization men. Thus as an opponent of agrarian and middle-class dreams, Marxism insisted on the irreversibility of history; as a corrective to exclusively political definitions of democracy, it emphasized economic forces and social classes; as a rival of individualistic values, it preached the virtues of a communitarian ethic.

Yet ironically, the most attractive feature of Marxism to intellectuals in the 1930s was not its understanding of social crises but its recognition of the need for personal action and commitment. What writers tended to focus on in their discussions of Marxist doctrine was the problem of how men could liberate themselves from an oppressive culture in order to change the course of history. Far from accepting socialism as predetermined, they were continually stressing the impact of human consciousness and will in transforming institutions. And it was here that radical intellectuals sought a philosophic rapprochement with the liberal values of their countrymen, in much the same way that they championed the principle of social democracy in political and economic affairs. On both levels they wanted somehow to "Americanize" Marx.

At times it seemed as though liberals and radicals had exchanged roles, each invoking ideals usually associated with the other. In reality, the more sophisticated American writers were hoping to salvage the best elements in both traditions. If liberalism had normally overestimated the capacity of intelligence and education to affect otherwise recalcitrant social forces, orthodox Marxism too often suggested that a person's ideas and ambitions were merely reflections of his position in society. Now men like Dewey and Lynd acknowledged the importance of economic processes and class relationships, while some socialists began to modify their excessive environmentalism by denying that man was *completely* a product of culture and history. Where liberals were becoming increasingly sensitive to the social context of human behavior, radical intellectuals were exploring the possibility that people remained relatively free to control their own destinies. In essence, these Marxists (like their liberal counterparts) were trying to find a common ground midway between the extremes of "individualism" on the one hand and "collectivism" on the other.

Generally, the most creative socialist intellectuals in America were those who could never find a permanent home in any of the established parties on the left. In the early 1930s these included V.F. Calverton, Lewis Corey, James Burnham, Theodore Brameld, Dwight Macdonald, Philip Rahv, and William Phillips, among others—men who consistently displayed their appreciation of ideological categories whether they were discussing politics or literature. In their dedication to Marxism as a social and cultural philosophy they differed from writers like George Soule and Stuart Chase (whose interest in planning was stimulated by their disillusion with liberal capitalism), or Lewis Mumford and Edmund Wilson (whose attraction to socialism seemed primarily aesthetic), or Waldo Frank and Granville Hicks (who saw in the Communist party a vehicle for their own moral salvation). Although they occasionally attended conferences, signed petitions, and formulated programs, their typical means of expression was the magazine article or book review. While occasionally writing for the *Nation,* the *New Republic,* or the *New Masses,* they usually appeared as editors of and contributors to the more theoretical journals: the *Modern Quarterly, Symposium, Miscellany, Science and Society,* the *Marxist Quarterly,* and *Partisan Review.* In many of their essays they maintained a level of analysis that was at times doctrinaire, frequently polemical, but always learned. As such, they were responsible for whatever degree to which the 1930s could be considered Marxist in thought as well as spirit.

One of the most representative members of this group was Max Eastman. His credentials as a radical philosopher were both impressive and long-standing. A product of the Progressive generation who never entertained its faith in liberal reform, Eastman had been chief editor and guiding light of the old *Masses.* His interests, like the period in which he grew up, were thoroughly eclectic. During a time when experimental art and class struggle still seemed mutually compatible, the *Masses* mirrored Eastman's persistent desire to unite poetry and politics, intellectuals and workers, ideas and action. While conceiving of himself as both a socialist and a passionate disciple of John Dewey, he was also among the earliest American defenders of the Bolshevik revolution. Eastman traveled to Russia in the early 1920s and initially responded to the communist experiment with great enthusiasm. But he became increasingly disenchanted with its economic and cultural policies following Lenin's death. His confidence was further shaken by the political defeat of Leon Trotsky with whom he had closely identified, the gradual suppression of all opposition within the party, and the growing power of Josef Stalin. By 1927 Eastman had launched a series of attacks on Soviet life, the ferocity of which steadily escalated in the 1930s. In effect, he was becoming one of the first American casualties of the Bolshevik crusade, and he would spend the rest of his life assessing where it all went wrong. He contributed to numerous journals on returning to the United States, but his temperament and independence drew him naturally to Calverton's *Modern Quarterly,* where he served as an associate editor. Meanwhile, his reputation as an unorthodox Marxist was enhanced by a stream of articles and books, most of which were designed to carve out an ideological position neither communist nor liberal.

Eastman's major complaint against both classical Marxism and its Stalinist mutation was that it tended to read its own goals into the course of historical development. While proclaiming itself an objective analysis of social forces, Marxism seemed in fact a form of prayer or wish-fulfillment. Unable to cast off his Hegelian heritage, Eastman argued, Marx had invented the concept of dialectical materialism to persuade his converts that the world was inevitably moving in the direction they wanted it to go. Since history was naturally evolving by means of class conflict toward a proletarian dictatorship and ultimately a communist utopia, the individual had only to fall in with the rhythm of the universe. This, Eastman repeatedly asserted, was a disguised religion in which every event was predestined. What was worse, the Soviet Union had elevated the dialectic to the status of a catechism, the Communist party had become the new Curia, and Stalin himself was Pope.[70] History, like God, was now on the side of the Left.

Throughout the 1920s and 1930s, dialectical materialism was Eastman's supreme villain, not only because it sounded mystical or because the Russians were distorting it for their own purposes but because he thought it essentially "fatalistic." By endowing the material world with a facility for traveling toward ends which radicals had already chosen, Marxism encouraged men to remain passive while awaiting the outcome of history's work. Marx was not proposing a practical strategy for revolution, Eastman contended; rather, he was simply trying to assure his followers that their ideals and aspirations would some day succeed. Hence the dialectic was merely a convenient way of making changes in social conditions seem to coincide with the communist program. But regardless of what radicals thought or did, regardless of whether or not the real world ever validated their theories, they could always predict the future because Marx taught them that the "general course of history is determined not by the nature of man, but by the nature of things."[71]

Here was the core of Eastman's objection. Conventional Marxism, with its emphasis on the external environment and its faith in the triumph of socialism, left no room for human inventiveness; it deliberately minimized the role of ideas and action in transforming society. Eastman admitted that the notion of historical inevitability had certain psychological advantages. It guaranteed that no matter how impotent those on the left might presently feel, history would eventually make their tribulations worthwhile. Moreover, it permitted intellectuals to identify with the proletariat without worrying about their own class origins or personal motives; as socialists they were all participating in a common destiny.[72] Eastman, however, remained unconvinced. He continued to regard dialectical materialism as a mixture of fact and myth, sophisticated economic analysis and adolescent fantasy, shrewd predictions and messianic dreams.

Up to a point, this was an interpretation shared by many liberal critics of Marx.[73] But Eastman's perspective was not entirely negative. While denying that socialism as presently constituted was a true science of revolution, he believed it did contain elements that could be useful in constructing such a science. In the early 1930s Eastman was moving toward a synthesis of Pragmatism and Marxism that favored an experimental method, a reliance on empirical evidence rather than *a priori* formulas, and an insistence that the truth of ideas be established through human activity. Opposing all theories of causal determinism as well as fixed and final views about reality, Eastman hoped to disentangle Marxism from the Hegelian dialectic and convert it into a series of tentative proposals the effectiveness of which could be tested in daily life. Socialism would appeal to America, he declared, only when it became a scientific hypothesis instead of a fatalistic theology.[74]

Until Stalin destroyed its promise, the Bolshevik revolution was a shining example of what Eastman had in mind. Like Lincoln Steffens, he was enchanted by the Communists' political ingenuity and capacity for social "engineering." In his eyes, Lenin was the perfect pragmatist, conscious of the individual's ability to intervene in history and willing to experiment with various devices until he discovered a workable policy. All Marxists, Eastman proclaimed, could emulate Lenin's flexibility and freedom once they restated the concepts of class struggle and socialist democracy "in the form of a plan-of-action for achieving a desired goal that is not inevitable but *possible.*"[75] With the proper scientific frame of mind, he was suggesting, Americans might themselves make a revolution. Since nothing was preordained, a religious faith in the power of history contributed precious little to the success of any radical movement. All men really needed was a practical program and the will to act.

Eastman was not alone in this effort to "pragmatize" Marxism. Theodore Brameld, an accomplished philosopher in his own right, offered a similar prescription for America's recovery. There was, he acknowledged in a *Modern Quarterly* essay of 1935, a deterministic side to Marx which relied so heavily on economic necessity and historical inevitability that "the responsibility for thoroughgoing change in social forms lies primarily, if not wholly, outside conscious, willful, and aggressive action by that group which would profit by the change." If taken too far, he warned, this could lead to a total acquiescence in the drift of history. But Brameld preferred to underline the other facets of Marxism—its resemblance to instrumentalism, its encouragement of experimentation, its openness to new data. In Brameld's opinion, the United States might accept a version of socialist thought which discarded the absolutist and metaphysical trappings of dialectical materialism. Thus he proposed that Marxism be regarded as "primarily a methodology of dynamic social action against the vicious environment of capitalism." With this approach, history would seem "less a preconceived pattern than a process of social trial-and-error." Determinism could be "subordinated . . . to the conviction that men's plans and their experimental attack upon problematic situations play a major part in settling what the future is to be like." Like Eastman, Brameld was portraying communism as a combination of economic insights, political strategy, and personal activism. As such, it demonstrated that people "are not merely conditioned by, but help to condition, the events of life."[76]

In part, Eastman and Brameld were trying to do for Marxism what Dewey and Lynd had attempted for liberalism: emphasize the natural interaction between self and society, theory and practice, freedom and necessity, the individual and social groups. But Eastman, especially, had reacted with such hostility to what he considered the fatalistic implications in orthodox Marxism that he was in danger of rejecting all social philosophy as inherently confining, mystical, and unscientific. Like many other writers in the 1930s, liberal as well as socialist, Eastman often sounded as though he would like to dispense with theory altogether—preferring instead to concentrate solely on the spontaneous activities of charismatic leaders. His initial criticism of the dialectic as a relic of German romanticism ultimately led him to underestimate badly the impact of environmental forces in restricting human will and behavior. By worshipping the methods of the scientist and the engineer, by minimizing the need to analyze when and how change might take place, by assuming that men were free to experiment with an infinite variety of tactics and programs, by regarding socialism purely as a hypothesis to be tested along with any number of other possibilities, by placing his faith in the unlimited power of individuals to accomplish whatever they wished, Eastman was inadvertently reinforcing some of the most anti-intellectual strains in American thought. Ironically, at the same time as he was calling for a new and more imaginative understanding of the world, his own emphasis on action for action's sake threatened to draw men even further away from the demands of ideology.

Essentially, Eastman and Brameld were attempting to sell socialism to their countrymen by making its methods seem as liberal and pragmatic as possible. This may have been a shrewd concession to traditional American values, but it hardly constituted the kind of full-fledged social philosophy intellectuals said they considered necessary if the depression were to be ended and capitalism overthrown.

There was at least one writer in the 1930s, however, who believed that such a philosophy could emerge from a synthesis of Dewey and Marx without sacrificing or distorting the ideas of either man. Few were better equipped for this task than Sidney Hook. A philosopher by training and a radical by temperament, Hook was also a founding father of what Norman Podhoretz later called the "family" of young Jewish intellectuals just beginning their careers as the depression dawned, whose style and commitments were profoundly shaped by its political pressures and cultural disputes. Included in this group were Philip Rahv, Meyer Shapiro, Lionel Trilling, Harold Rosenberg, Clement Greenberg, and Lionel Abel.[77] As immigrants themselves or the children of immigrants, as products of the New York ghetto who rarely felt at home in America, as men for whom criticism and debate became a way of life as well as a means of upward mobility, they differed in background and outlook from those writers who had grown up during the Progressive era or the 1920s. They did not suffer through the betrayal at Versailles, nor the loss of faith in liberal ideals, nor the expatriate adventure; they were never liberals to begin with, and they did not need Paris to make them feel like exiles from their native land. Often unable to find jobs in universities because they were Jews (though Hook taught philosophy at NYU), more severely victimized by the depression than their predecessors because they had no reputations or contacts on which to fall back, they awaited the revolution at least in part as an answer to their personal and professional anxieties.

Thus they were initially attracted to the Communist party (Hook signed the open letter for Foster and Ford in the 1932 Presidential campaign, while Rahv contributed frequently to the *New Masses*). But they grew rapidly disillusioned with the party's obeisance to Stalin, its bureaucratic rigidity, and its hostility to avant-garde culture. To intellectuals for whom ideas were more interesting than political organizations, essays more important than strikes, personal brilliance more compelling than mass movements, the only real alternative was to follow an independent course. For some this led to a brief flirtation with Trotskyism, but for most it meant a systematic reevaluation of how Marx might be applied to America. And in this enterprise, no one could match Hook's diligence, sophistication, and scholarship. He alone was willing to read all the manuscripts, reinterpret all the texts, and return to the present with a coherent explanation of what Marx really said.

For Hook the years between 1928 and 1936 were taken up with innumerable magazine articles, polemics, manifestoes, reviews, and symposiums, culminating in two difficult but creative summaries of socialist thought: *Towards the Understanding of Karl Marx* (1933) and *From Hegel to Marx* (1936). At first glance, these books were characteristic of the group of radical intellectuals to which Hook belonged: acerbic in style, overwhelming in their display of knowledge, frequently doctrinaire, and heavily influenced by the ideological battles of the European Left. But for all his apparent preoccupation with the Hegelian antecedents of Marxism, the heresies of Lassalle and Bakunin, the reformism of Bernstein, the more revolutionary impulses of Kautsky and Rosa Luxemburg, and the heritage of Lenin, Hook was really writing about issues closer to home. Despite the fact that his ethnic and generational background was different from men like Mumford, Dewey, and Lynd, Hook shared their tendency to combine cultural criticism with political analysis, the "social" insights of Marx with the individualistic values of liberalism. In the end his reading of Marx was clearly marked by the same pressures and concerns that affected the rest of the intellectual community in depression America.

Pehaps this was best revealed in the bitter debate between Hook and Max Eastman which enlivened the pages of the *Modern Quarterly* during the early years of the decade. On the surface, they remained poles apart on the issue of whether dialectical materialism was still a useful theory for modern radicals. But the details of their argument were less significant than the typically American ideas which they held in common. Both men regarded themselves as disciples of John Dewey; consequently each preferred a social philosophy that left considerable room for human innovation and experiment. The point on which they could never agree was whether Marxism satisfied this desire. Where Eastman urged an abandonment of the dialectic in order to maximize the pragmatic and activist strains in Marx, Hook believed that dialectical materialism already gave men sufficient freedom to change their lives. Where Eastman assumed that Marxism was incurably deterministic, Hook underlined its similarity to Dewey's instrumentalism. Indeed for Hook, dialectical materialism was only another way of talking about the interaction between man and his environment, consciousness and social conditions, free will and historical development. In his eyes, Marxism could be seen as both an alternative to and a fulfillment of conventional liberal ideals—the very sort of ideology for which American writers seemed to be searching in the 1930s.

Through all his articles and books during this period, Hook acknowledged the presence in Marxism of certain ideas which some readers might indeed consider fatalistic. Marx had believed that every facet of man's culture was interrelated and interdependent, Hook noted. This implied that each event must be understood in terms of the total social and historical situation, that an individual's needs and aspirations necessarily reflected the class from which he came, that human activity was irrevocably conditioned by the surrounding environment.[78]

Moreover, Hook conceded that for Marx the historical process was irreversible. Hence the problems of industrialization would never be solved by returning to a handicraft economy, as the Southern Agrarians or those who romanticized peasant villages seemed to want. "It is not the machine which oppresses men," Hook explained in a voice that sounded as much like Mumford as Marx, "but the social relations within which machine production is carried on. Consequently it is the social relations of production that must be changed." And history, as Marx divined it, was dramatizing this lesson by moving inexorably toward a transformation of the entire capitalist system. Since society was an organic whole, Hook went on, one could not hope to preserve the "good" features of free enterprise (its encouragement of technological efficiency and personal initiative) while eliminating only the "bad" (its vulnerability to overproduction and cyclical depressions). The Marxist view of history, together with its emphasis on the collective nature of modern life, would eventually force men to adopt a program of

complete socializaton as the sole practical alternative to corporate capitalism.[79] For Hook, these were conclusions which no amount of agrarian
rhetoric or piecemeal reform would ever contradict. To this extent, history
could not be diverted from its chosen course.

Nevertheless, Hook firmly denied Max Eastman's charge that these ideas
permitted men to remain passive while socialism was automatically delivered to them. On the contrary, social change never took place according to
Marx without the intervention of people *acting,* individually and collectively. In Hook's view, Marxism held that there were concrete laws of
economic and technological development which did in fact restrict the
number of options open to mankind at any given moment. At present, these
laws were making life in America more and more collectivized. But this did
not mean that a socialist future was somehow inevitable or predestined. In
the Marxist vision, history was ultimately made by men. Granted a degree
of determinism, Hook reminded his readers that for Marx "human effort
[was] the mode by which the historically determined comes to pass."[80]

At bottom, Hook wished to demonstrate that Marxism encouraged neither complete spontaneity nor a fatalistic reliance on impersonal forces, that
it was "neither a science nor a myth, but a realistic method of social
action."[81] In his opinion, the great strength of Marxism lay in its recognition
that human beings operated within a specific environmental setting—each
mutually dependent on the other. Because men possessed the freedom to
choose between different economic systems which themselves contained
objective laws, they did have some room to select and maneuver. Thus
Hook could say that for Marx there were no "musts" in history, only
"conditioned probabilities."[82] In this sense, Marxism was both more pragmatic and less theological than Eastman or Brameld had imagined. While
strongly voluntaristic in its emphasis on class struggle, Marxism still realized that there were historical limits beyond which men could not expect
to go. As such, it was both an accurate theory of social behavior and a
dramatic call for revolutionary activism.

Yet despite its pragmatic overtones, Hook considered Marxism superior
to modern liberalism because it focused more effectively on those points at
which self and society, private desires and community pressures, personal
consciousness and social background invariably interacted. Although
Mumford, Dewey, and Lynd had also stressed these connections in the
1930s, their analyses were essentially static in Hook's judgment because
they never explained how change actually occurred. Instead, each of these
writers took comfort in the notion that intelligent human control over
existing institutions might eventually solve all of America's problems, with-

out giving men the necessary ideological tools to accomplish this feat. No matter how sensitive they were to the need for collectivist programs and values, their ideas did not seem to include a mechanism by which people could move from the present into the future.

For Hook, the concept of dialectical materialism filled this void admirably. It incorporated and improved on the best insights of Pragmatism while avoiding the messianic and utopian impulses which Eastman decried. As Hook interpreted it, the dialectic was Marx's method of showing how the material world affected man's thought and behavior, yet how human activity in turn altered the world. The relationship was perfectly reciprocal; though people were indeed influenced by their culture, they retained the power to reshape its institutions in truly remarkable ways.[83]

To begin with, Hook pointed out that an individual's hopes and ideals were not simply "passive" reflections of his economic position in society; rather they often played an active role in promoting social change. Once the unconscious attitudes and aspirations of a given class matured into a "systematic ideology," they could either reinforce or modify the "objective conditions" out of which they sprang. While sophisticated technology and large-scale industrialization were the fundamental components of modern capitalism, Hook acknowledged, the human mind was sufficiently free to conceive of other institutional arrangements which might better serve the interests of the populace as a whole.[84] In short, Hook believed that the dialectic provided for the relative autonomy of ideas, values, and culture— all the products of man's consciousness. Though economic factors remained basic to the structure of any society, "ideology" was nevertheless a dynamic element in its own right. To this extent Dewey and Marx presumably agreed on the importance of skill and intelligence in bringing about a social revolution.

Yet if men were able to imagine an infinite variety of alternatives, their present circumstances severely restricted what they could actually achieve. Here Hook was criticizing both the liberal assumption that Americans had the power to accomplish anything they chose and Max Eastman's desire for a philosophy of unlimited freedom. In Hook's version of Marxism people might take control over their lives not by placing their hopes in a mythic past or utopian future, nor by experimenting with many hypotheses in a social vacuum, but by maximizing the possibilities already inherent in a given situation. Specifically, this meant that a pre-capitalist society could not create a socialist economy, any more than an advanced industrial state could expect to restore the nineteenth-century ground rules of competition and laissez faire. Each stage of historical development generated its own unique problems, pressures, and solutions. Because of this, Hook warned, men should want what they could reasonably get. Social change must be willed by human beings, he submitted, but "*what* is willed" and "*when* it is willed" had to depend on the "objective" conditions in which they presently found themselves. At the moment, socialism was a practical alternative for the United States, not because it was intrinsically good for all time but because modern productive techniques and the emergence of a stable working class made possible its realization. Socialism was not preordained, but it would *probably* come if individuals adopted their aspirations to what the occasion currently demanded.[85] As far as Hook was concerned, people were free to direct their strategies and programs toward goals they were actually able to obtain. Anything else would either fail or produce chaos.

Hook therefore recommended dialectical materialism to his contemporaries because he believed that it combined history, technology, economic growth, class relations, and human intelligence more completely than any other philosophy with which he was familiar. It showed precisely how men and social institutions interacted over a long period of time—something liberalism, whatever its modern refinements, had never managed to do. "Conditioned as they are by their environment," he asserted, "human beings can change that environment" through the mechanism of the dialectic. As Hook understood Marx's theory, each stage in nature and history (the thesis) produced a set of particular needs and desires in men (the antithesis); they in turn assessed the possibilities for political and economic change, decided which alternatives would be most effective, and embarked on a course of action designed to translate this potential into a new social order (the synthesis). "The concrete needs of men," Hook declared, "are the true middle term for Marx between nature and history."[86] They enabled human beings to act freely and purposefully, making the most out of the current situation no matter how confining or oppressive the economic system otherwise appeared. In Hook's view, the dialectic was not a religious surrogate nor a vague model for liberal reform. It was instead a realistic way of understanding—and acting on—the natural interrelationship between man's consciousness and his social experience, subjective values and objective conditions, personal will and the movement of history, inner freedom and external necessity.[87]

Even beyond the advantages of the dialectic over other ideologies, what attracted Hook to Marxism was its vision of the universe as forever indeterminate, problematical, and open-ended. Here he came closest to interpreting Marx as a forerunner of Dewey, and he made socialism sound respectably flexible and pragmatic in the eyes of his fellow Americans. In the first place, Hook contended that the dialectical process continued indefinitely; it harbored no fixed or final goals. Each historical epoch demanded a different set of political responses, and the very act of "gratifying *old* needs gave rise to *new* needs—technological, psychological, and spiritual."[88] Hook took this to mean that there were no transcendent rules of morality or justice beyond what a given society enshrined in its laws and customs. Like other writers in the 1930s, he denied that men had absolute rights and liberties independent of a particular class or social group. The traditional ideals of freedom and individuality were all dependent on a specific period and place—a lesson that both liberals and radicals had been repeating since the Progressive era but which they proclaimed with even greater urgency during the depression. "The only thing eternal about morality," Hook concluded, "is man's desire for the better. But what the 'better' is, time and circumstances redetermine from situation to situation."[89] Thus while Marx emphasized the essential relativity of human values and aspirations, according to Hook, he also promised to liberate men from their inherited habits and prejudices—thereby permitting them freely to explore new cultural and social possibilities.

Moreover, Hook argued that Marxism was instinctively pragmatic because it shared Dewey's insistence on the unavoidable connection between thought and practice, ideas and their consequences. Every view of the world affected human behavior in some way, Hook declared. Therefore no one could ignore the fact that any given set of beliefs led men either to change or further strengthen their current institutions. At the very least, he pointed out, "to theorize about the nature of the good society without trying to make the existing society good is in effect to accept the existing society." The explicit purpose behind Marx's own philosophy "was to provide that knowledge of social tendencies which would most effectively liberate action." As a faithful instrumentalist, Hook assumed that action itself would adequately test an idea's validity—especially whether it was capable of achieving the goals it had predicted.[90] Ultimately, Hook was not asking Marxism to be accepted on faith. Like any other scientific hypothesis, he wanted it proved or disproved in the laboratory of political and social conflict. But once all the results were in, he seemed confident that the "truth" of Marx's insights would be verified through experience—a notion that was in the end classically pragmatic and American.

Since he believed that every ideology was a guide to action, to be judged on the basis of its success or failure in gaining the objectives men desired during a particular period, Hook was perfectly willing to recommend socialism as the most practical way of solving America's present problems. It would triumph not because it was inevitable or eternally appealing but because it just happened to answer twentieth-century needs. Indeed Hook criticized Dewey not because they disagreed over basic goals but because Dewey failed to "appreciate the instrumental value of *class struggle* rather than class collaboration in effecting the transition from corporate America to collective America."[91] In Hook's estimation, Marxism corresponded more accurately than liberalism to the current crisis in the United States both as an immediate strategy and as a long-range view of the world. It provided the most coherent explanation of the nature and causes of the depression, it recognized that economic institutions had become permanently collectivized, it formulated a set of ideals geared to the political realities of American life, it possessed in the concept of dialectical materialism a persuasive theory of social change, it showed men the one alternative that would relieve their suffering, and it therefore freed people to seize control over their own destinies.[92] If one wished to be a true pragmatist in the 1930s, Hook was suggesting, if one wanted to choose the most effective course of action, then one should naturally become a Marxist.

Finally, beyond Marxism's contributions to philosophy and politics, Hook was drawn to the ways in which it satisfied man's spiritual needs. Like other intellectuals in the decade, he too wanted both a new economy and a new culture, a new ideology and a new value system. Thus he fervently agreed with Marxism's *moral* condemnation of the middle class. "Bourgeois society," he claimed, was too individualistic, too insensitive to the role of groups and classes, too careless about reducing the "relations or bonds between men . . . to bare terms-elements-atoms. Man becomes the basis of society, not social man—but egoistic man." This in turn led to a psychic confusion within each individual. People never knew, Hook observed, whether they were citizens or economic tools, whether their connection to others was based on a feeling of common humanity and mutual responsibility or on an endless rivalry for wealth and status.[93] Yet social obligations were inescapable; no one was self-sufficient in modern America. The virtue of Marxism as a cultural alternative for Hook (as well as for writers like Edmund Wilson, V.F. Calverton, and Rebecca Pitts) was its refusal to splinter human activity into "innumerable, tiny fragments," or to exalt personal ambition at the expense of communal welfare. Instead it insisted that a man's hopes and ideals were meaningless outside the context of society. Sounding much like Waldo Frank or Lewis Mumford, Hook argued that the psychological and moral conflicts within human beings could never be resolved until the nation itself became an organic community rather than merely a set of laws and institutions. For once men were able to feel themselves equal participants in a common culture, they might then begin to reconcile their private dreams with their public roles.[94]

Nevertheless, Hook made sure that his longing for community did not appear antagonistic to certain well-established liberal beliefs with which he himself sympathized. On the contrary, he shared Dewey's and Lynd's conviction that the classic goals of liberalism would best be realized in a socialist society. Hook vigorously rejected all efforts to elevate the "collective man" into a dogma because this seemed to him both totalitarian and antithetical to the true purposes of socialism. In his opinion, Marxists should attack liberalism only when it functioned as an ideological apology for laissez-faire. Otherwise, they ought to admire its commitment to free thought and personal creativity. Marxism, he maintained, "is hostile to individualism as a social theory, [but] not to individuality as a social value." Like other radicals, Hook emphasized the need for economic security and social responsibility in the 1930s precisely so that the personality of every man might be liberated and enriched beyond anything capitalism had promised. Both liberals and socialists considered the unshackling of the human mind their ultimate objective, he pointed out. And both now recognized that America's institutions must be fully collectivized before individual freedom was genuinely possible.[95] Thus he described Marxism as a natural extension of ideals that had their roots firmly in the liberal tradition.

In the end, Hook's interest in the moral consequences of Marxism, together with his stress on human action as a crucial historical force, reflected the decade's central assumption that the purpose of social revolution was to create a new man as well as new institutions. Marx was a magnificent psychologist, in Hook's judgment, because he understood that men could not change the world "without changing themselves." This meant that once human beings mastered their environment, they might begin consciously to transform their own lives "in accordance with a morally free will."[96] Hook refused to speculate on the precise configurations of a post-revolutionary society, but he never envisioned a utopia in which all difficulties were miraculously eliminated. Instead he was certain that the need for struggle and commitment would persist, although "on a more elevated plane." In the future, man might be expected to wrestle "not with the problem of social existence, but with the deeper problems of personal development."[97] Hence the virtue of socialism for Hook—and for most of his generation—was its continuation of the Progressive belief that politics and culture must remain inseparable.

There was one additional element in his thought, however, that seemed unique to the 1930s. Hook saw in Marxism a message that, for all its revolutionary passion, was fundamentally existential and pessimistic. In his view, Marx had denounced capitalism "not because it makes people unhappy but because it makes them *inhuman,* deprives them of their essential dignity, degrades all ideals by setting a cash value on them, and inflicts *meaningless* suffering." Yet Hook assumed that disappointment and failure were permanent features of man's experience, a fact which socialism would never erase. At most, one could only anticipate a social order where discontent had moral rather than economic causes. "Under Communism," he predicted, "man ceases to suffer as an animal and suffers as human. He, therewith, moves from the plane of the pitiful to the plane of the tragic." The only thing inevitable about revolution, according to Hook, was that conflict would remain after the barricades had been taken down. Nevertheless, he concluded, while Marxism "does not sanction the naive belief that a perfect society, a perfect man, will ever be realized," neither "does it justify the opposite error that since perfection is unattainable, it is . . . immaterial what kind of men or societies exist."[98] He therefore urged people to commit themselves to social change despite their awareness that many problems were ultimately insoluble. For Hook, the psychological strength of Marxism lay precisely in its call to action at the same time it acknowledged the essential tragedy of human life. In this sense it contained the proper balance of optimism and irony, fantasy and realism, innocence and wisdom, appropriate to the mood of the decade. Since America seemed to have lost its youth and expansiveness by the 1930s, since its dreams were more limited and less romantic, the country now required a different view of the world than the Progressives had offered. So Hook stepped forward with what appeared to be a mature philosophy for a society entering middle age.

5. *The Existential Strain*

Sidney Hook's theory combined a Marxist sensitivity to social and cultural conditioning, a Pragmatic emphasis on individual consciousness and will, and an existential perception of the ways in which man's activities gave meaning to an otherwise absurd world. The resulting blend was marvelously unorthodox. For this he was attacked by liberals and communists alike. But he had come closer than anyone else to fashioning an ideology that corresponded to the needs of depression America. Yet even as Hook tried to pull together the scattered attitudes and assumptions of other writers into a fairly coherent social philosophy, some of the decade's most characteristic ideas were being challenged and refined by a man who was neither a liberal nor a Marxist but a Protestant theologian. For all the desire to fuse the values of "culture" with the material benefits of "civilization," for all the efforts to combine personal freedom and social cooperation, it was left to Reinhold Niebuhr to suggest that these ideals might be permanently irreconcilable after all. Without abandoning his own commitment to a social revolution, Niebuhr managed both to summarize and transcend the hopes of his generation.

Niebuhr's background was somewhat more specialized than other intellectuals in the 1930s, but he shared their outlook and experiences to a remarkable degree. Just as they found conventional liberalism increasingly irrelevant to the problems of poverty, unemployment, and industrial collapse, so Niebuhr found himself rejecting the Social Gospel tradition in the Protestant churches. Indeed "progressive" Christianity and liberal reform came to stand for the same things in his eyes—and he began to assail both in the late 1920s.

Having worked among the immigrants and the working class in Detroit before moving to Union Theological Seminary in New York in 1928, Niebuhr understood at first hand their terrible deprivation and helplessness. At the same time, as Donald Meyer has shown, he despaired of reaching them through settlement houses, missions, and periodic appeals to the comfortable bourgeosie. Somehow the Social Gospel did not recognize the overwhelming indifference and intransigence of America's rulers, nor was it responding effectively to the specter of economic disintegration and urban chaos. Where liberal ministers from Walter Rauschenbusch on had sought to convert both capital and labor to the values of their own middle-class constituency, where they had tried to minimize the potential for alienation and disorder among the poor, where they had hoped to reform the American people by instilling in them a greater sense of decency and social concern, Niebuhr regarded all of these objectives as naïve and out of date. Modern civilization still needed religion, he believed, but not one that appeared vague about questions of power, blind to the cruelty of life in its cities, and isolated from the new waves of radical thought that were sweeping the nation in the 1930s.[99]

The conditions he observed in Detroit seemed bad enough; they were catastrophic when applied to the nation as a whole during the depression. Even before the stock-market crash, Niebuhr became thoroughly disillusioned with the Social Gospel movement, just as his more secular colleagues had begun to reject their own liberal heritage. Now, in the wake of economic disaster, he intensified his search for a new theology in the same way that other intellectuals were heeding Edmund Wilson's advice to create a social theory more appropriate to contemporary problems. Not surprisingly, Niebuhr's thought developed along lines that were strikingly similar to those of most writers in the 1930s. His work echoed their concern for the relation between individuals and groups, spiritual values and material welfare, personal identity and social revolution. Yet in his most important and influential book of these years, *Moral Man and Immoral Society* (1932), Niebuhr gave each of these issues an interpretation which at times agreed with and at times differed from the analysis to be found in Mumford, Dewey, Lynd, or Hook. Indeed he cast light on the decade's leading ideas at just the points where he decided to follow his own path. As such, *Moral Man and Immoral Society* both confirmed and criticized the central beliefs of the 1930s.

Niebuhr began by attacking liberalism on grounds that had become fairly familiar among radicals, whatever their doctrinal persuasion. In the first place, drawing on his experience with the Social Gospel, he objected to liberalism's "sentimentality," its "evolutionary optimism," its "romantic overestimates of human virtue," and its faith in progress.[100] As far as he could see, the problems of highly developed and complex countries like the United States were no longer susceptible to moral persuasion, rational argument, education, and the leadership of enlightened reformers. In the future, Niebuhr was certain, men would have to abandon their trust in the automatic improvement of life through science and technology. Like Hook, Niebuhr believed that people needed to act in a positive way if social institutions were to be changed.

Secondly, he argued that liberalism conveniently overlooked the extent to which man's imagination and intelligence were inevitably frustrated by economic interests, class biases, political conflict, an inveterate desire for power, and the inherent "limitations of human nature." From the Progressive era on, he pointed out, liberals had assumed that the evils of capitalism could be eliminated through the intervention of impartial experts and a benevolent government. But they never realized that disinterested reason was always subordinate to social forces and psychological pressures, or that programs designed for the "general" welfare of America were forever being undermined by competing groups and parties. If anything, as the number of movements contesting for wealth and power increased, so did their capacity for irrational behavior.[101] Armed with these bitter observations, for which both World War I and the depression provided ample evidence, Niebuhr concluded that the liberal reliance on personal conscience and "social goodwill" were now obsolete. In the future, he predicted, reform movements must include a "measure of coercion" and force if they hoped to succeed.[102]

To this point, Niebuhr's disenchantment with liberalism resembled that of other intellectuals in the 1930s. And like them, he found himself irresistibly attracted to Marxism—though for reasons that were not particularly ideological. Instead, Marxism seemed the perfect antidote to the liberal virus because it offered a more realistic—and a more religious—understanding of man and his society. For Niebuhr, the strength of socialism lay not so much in its analysis of capitalism or in its use of the dialectic but rather in its emphasis on the role of classes, on the necessity for struggle, and on the importance of power in all human relationships.[103] The true socialist, in Niebuhr's eyes, entertained no illusions about man's rationality or altruism; he knew that noble intentions and moral appeals would never bring change as effectively as the day-to-day conflict among interest groups.

Moreover, Niebuhr regarded Marx as less a revolutionary theorist than an Old Testament prophet and seer. In contrast to Eastman and Hook, he admired Marxism precisely because it contained a messianic and apocalyptic view of history. It gave men faith that their suffering would be avenged, it assured them that a new society was going to arise from the ashes of the old, and it encouraged them to act as a means of achieving personal and social salvation. Paradoxically, Niebuhr noted, it challenged men to assert their will against an "impersonal fate" and an inscrutable God. Like early Christianity, Marxism was not tainted with a belief in evolutionary progress (which Niebuhr considered the traditional hope of "comfortable and privileged classes"). On the contrary, it expressed a vision of the world that was both catastrophic and hopeful, absolutist and activist, despairing and millennial—a perfect philosophy for the poor and the disinherited. Thus Niebuhr portrayed Marxism as a modern version of the "classic religious dream," its psychological and mythic insights far more compelling than its formal doctrine.[104] In this sense, he shared the decade's tendency to glide over the content of socialist theory, while stressing its moral and emotional implications for human behavior.

Essentially, Niebuhr was converting Marxism into an Augustinian critique of liberal reform. But unlike most of his contemporaries, he was too orthodox, theologically, and too pessimistic, temperamentally, to accept all of Marx. He feared that socialism was dangerously utopian in its expectation of perfect justice and equality at the end of history. Niebuhr simply did not believe that an ideal society could ever be achieved on earth, no matter whether liberals or radicals were leading the way. Instead he suspected that, as the promise of paradise went unfulfilled, revolutionaries would increasingly resort to fanaticism and tyranny. For all its Christian insights, Niebuhr felt, Marxism had elevated politics into a religion, thereby making exactly the same mistake as the Social Gospel movement. Both sought to abolish evil by changing man's institutions; both assumed that human nature was infinitely malleable; neither recognized the possibility that religion and morality might have to be separated from ideology and history.[105]

On the other hand, Niebuhr objected to the current worship of collectivism, which he found latent in Marxist thought. Here he broke dramatically with the prevailing values of his generation. In his judgment, Marxism's most serious weakness was its insistence that men led fuller and more satisfying lives when they felt thoroughly a part of some larger community. Niebuhr could accept none of the assumptions behind this idea. Arguing that a "sharp distinction must be drawn between the moral . . . behavior of individuals and of social groups," he proceeded to characterize all organizations, movements, and nations as intrinsically abstract, impersonal, selfish, egotistic, irrational, and anti-social. These attributes were not unique to capitalist societies, as others in the decade believed. Niebuhr was convinced that they applied to all countries at all times. "The larger the group," he asserted, "the more difficult it is to achieve a common mind and purpose. . . ." Because contacts between men in groups were distant and indirect, there was less opportunity for shared loyalties and daily cooperation. Thus collections of people had to depend on artificial symbols, slogans, and myths for whatever unity they could attain. In contrast, it was individuals who seemed more sensitive to the needs of others, more willing to check their private impulses in the interests of reason, more capable of "self-transcendence" in their personal relationships. These traits could never be automatically extended to the society as a whole, he declared. Instead, as individuals were absorbed into the mass, they simply took on its worst vices, a process which culminated in the evils of nationalism and class intolerance.[106]

Throughout this period, Niebuhr continued to favor personal experience over communal ideals. In effect, he was reversing all the standard equations of the 1930s. Where radicals insisted that private problems could be solved through collective action, Niebuhr believed that groups only exacerbated man's feeling of alienation and inner turmoil. Where Dewey and Lynd emphasized the natural interconnection between self and society, Niebuhr pointed out their basic incompatibility. Where Mumford hoped for a synthesis of culture and civilization, Niebuhr suggested that morality and politics might be eternally irreconcilable. In his view, liberals and Marxists both mistakenly assumed that individuals had the same goals and aspirations as classes or countries, when in fact their interests were fundamentally opposed. Personal relations (being more intimate) were marked by love, unselfishness, and an instinctive desire for human brotherhood—all of which were essentially religious impulses. Conversely, social relationships (being more complex) were influenced by considerations of power, longings for justice, and an urge for order; they were therefore dependent on tactics, strategy, and rational calculation. As far as Niebuhr was concerned, love and justice, private morality and public welfare, inner wholeness and economic security could never be fused. Men must therefore begin to recognize that the values associated with culture and those identified with revolution were forever in conflict. If people wished to build a better world, he suggested, they would have to choose between matters of conscience and the pressures of politics, subordinating their own spiritual needs to the demands of social reform.[107]

Nevertheless, Niebuhr was not entirely out of step with his contemporaries. What he really wished to do was show that the connection between man and society was more tenuous than the 1930s supposed. But he never discounted its importance as an issue or ideal. Thus he acknowledged that individuals must act politically and that collective action must be infused with a moral vision. Even within communities men might still preserve a measure of personal integrity at the same time they worked for greater justice and equality. While the conflict between religious values and social programs would always remain, he hoped that each could be used to comment on, criticize, and clarify the goals of the other. "Politics," he predicted, "will, to the end of history, be an area where conscience and power meet, where the ethical and coercive factors of human life will interpenetrate and work out their tentative and uneasy compromises."[108] Niebuhr was disturbingly vague about how men could in fact achieve a balance between culture and politics, but he insisted that both must be embraced despite their contradictory objectives. Ultimately his analysis differed from other writers in the 1930s, not in its desire to harmonize individuals and social groups but rather in its realization that the relationship was essentially paradoxical and full of tension. Like Dewey, Lynd, and Hook, Niebuhr tried to maneuver between the extremes of individualism and collectivism—but where they were optimistic about the degree to which human life could be improved through social theory and economic planning, he was far less certain that man's moral and psychological problems might be so easily solved in the political arena.

At bottom, Niebuhr shared his colleagues' eagerness to overthrow capitalism, but he did not permit himself to imagine that socialist institutions would automatically abolish privilege, selfishness, competition, or injustice.[109] Yet his pessimism seemed appropriate to a generation that looked on revolution as the only possible response to disaster rather than as a final step in the glorious march of social progress. Like Hook, Niebuhr believed that conflict among men was permanent and inevitable, regardless of the economic system under which they lived. Any other view appeared to him romantic, naïve, and blind to the human capacity for violence and jealousy.[110] At this point, Niebuhr was unsure about whether the causes of evil lay in the environment or in man, though he would later decide that the latter was the case. In any event, he argued that a balance of contending forces was the highest political ideal to which people could reasonably aspire. If "greed, the will-to-power, and other forms of self-assertion" could never be fully eradicated or controlled, if indeed coercion and struggle were seen as "necessary instruments of social redemption," they might be partially moderated by intelligence and morality. Again, Niebuhr was unable to say precisely what sorts of institutions he preferred; at best he could only suggest that "equal justice is the most rational ultimate objective for society."[111] But what "equal justice" meant in practice, and how it might be established, remained agonizingly obscure. In the end, Niebuhr was more interested in the *methods* by which a society dealt with its problems than in its substantive goals or ideology. As long as man's ethical impulse could play a role in minimizing the more destructive kinds of social conflict, as long as the "disinherited" received a fairer share of America's wealth and advantages, Niebuhr was satisfied.[112] To this extent, he agreed with Dewey that human reason could be a positive tool in contructing a society that was, if not perfect, at least tolerable.

Niebuhr's deliberate unwillingness to define more clearly what he considered an acceptable alternative to capitalism reflected his underlying skepticism about all social programs, however sophisticated their rationale. In part, his somber view of the world stemmed from the Christian precept that man's salvation would come not through the creation of a just and humane society but rather through the recognition that perpetual peace and brotherhood were impossible without the intervention of God. Throughout the 1930s, Niebuhr reminded his contemporaries that the symbol of Christ stood forever in opposition to nature and history, that the pure religious spirit inevitably transcended politics, that the experience of grace was always an other-worldly phenomenon, that moral ideals were both eternal and absolute while human beings remained victims of time and change.[113] Yet these attitudes did not lead him to advocate resignation and withdrawal. He was severely critical of those religions that used the concept of sin as an excuse to retreat from the problems of men on earth. Rather than morbidly lamenting the stark contrast between "divine holiness" and man's imperfection, Niebuhr preferred to concentrate on the points at which they necessarily met and served one another.[114]

Thus he asked that Americans continue to act in the world, even though they knew that their work was doomed to frustration. They must commit themselves to social reform despite (or perhaps because of) the knowledge that they would eventually fail; this for Niebuhr was the only path to true maturity and salvation. Yet his paradoxical demand did not appeal just to the religiously inclined; it was also expressed by more secular intellectuals in the 1930s. Few believed in utopia; like Hook, most writers expected merely to raise the level of suffering to a higher plane. As a result they displayed a greater faith in the efficacy of human action than in the explicit purposes to which it might be directed. Often they were urging a commitment to commitment rather than to a specific economic system or social philosophy. They therefore agreed with Niebuhr that the individual could at most make moral choices "according to whatever judgments of good and evil he is able to form"; the authenticity of his motives and the preservation of his integrity seemed ultimately more important than his concrete achievements.[115]

This emphasis on personal commitment was probably the decade's great strength and great weakness. On the one hand, it permitted men to retain their flexibility, freedom, and individuality in the face of dogmas, organizations, mass movements, bureaucracies, and centralized power. On the other hand, it tended to distract attention from the difficult tasks of social analysis and political strategy. During the early years of the decade many were able to keep their socialist objectives in sight. Later on, as commitment and action became ends in themselves, the vision of an alternative society began to fade from view. In its place, Niebuhr and his colleagues could only suggest that if men were willing to be content with the modest goal of preventing further catastrophes, if they accepted the notion that the "conscience and insight of individual man" was "incapable of fulfillment by collective man," if they did not take on the impossible burden of creating an "ideal society" but merely sought to improve life within the conditions set by fate and their own limitations, "a progressively higher justice and more stable peace [might] be achieved."[116] If anything, such a mixture of hope and pessimism mirrored the decade's prevailing mood more accurately than any set of principles or policies. The era of liberal optimism was dying; the age of radical existentialism was being born.

6. *Toward a New Ideology*

Taken together, the ideas of Mumford, Dewey, Lynd, Hook, and Niebuhr constituted a remarkable philosophic achievement in a period plagued by intellectual confusion, emotional exhortation and apocalyptic pronouncements. Where some viewed the revolution primarily as a deliverance from moral and psychological chaos, they recognized the necessity of translating cultural criticism into an effective social theory. Where others sought an "organic" community in which men could escape the endless terrors of competition and loneliness, they accepted the collectivization of American life without losing their respect for the solitary individual. Though none of the five was entirely successful in fashioning a new ideology for the 1930s, they did at least lay down the philosophic foundations on which their contemporaries might later build.

Essentially, they were responding to a dilemma no previous generation had faced. If power had become centered in large political and economic units, if personal independence was no longer possible in a corporate civilization, if the United States was now truly a mass society, then the American Dream would have to be either abandoned or redefined. They chose the latter. By combining traditional liberal values, new socialist insights, and a profound moral passion, they hoped to give their fellow citizens a means of understanding and solving the crisis in which everyone found himself.

On the one hand, Marxism (by way of Brooks, Croly, Veblen, and other members of the Progressive generation) taught each of these writers to appreciate the potential of science and technology in serving human needs, the importance of groups and classes in promoting social change, the extent to which the individual was conditioned by history and his environment, the sense of society as a unified whole, the close interrelationship between men and institutions, and the need for further collectivization in both economic and cultural affairs. In effect, the radical view of the world emphasized man's natural harmony with and dependence on other people. "Community" came to mean not only planning and socialism but also a spirit of mutuality, sharing, cooperation, brotherhood, and inner peace. Because they considered free enterprise both economically inefficient and psychologically unhealthy, because they regarded the depression as a sign of the country's moral illness as well as its political bankruptcy, they joined with other intellectuals in the 1930s in wishing to break with capitalism more firmly than their predecessors in the Progressive era or the 1920s. Henceforth they believed that America's industrial plant and its social philosophy must enhance the public welfare rather than private privilege. In this way, people would begin to enjoy not only material well-being but, even more important, a feeling of personal fulfillment within the context of a sane society.

On the other hand, they continued to accept liberalism's concern for rational debate, its reliance on experimentation and scientific hypotheses, its rejection of absolute dogmas and fixed goals, its assumption that the future was undetermined and open-ended, its insistence on human intelligence and the role of consciousness in transforming institutions, its regard for individual freedom and self-expression, its emphasis on the need for action in a revolutionary crisis, its conviction that men made history through the force of their own will power and commitment, and its willingness to test all programs and theories in the laboratory of social experience.

At bottom, they were trying to take from both the liberal and socialist traditions those ideas that seemed most appropriate for a post-capitalist civilization. Thus they focused on the points at which men and machines, culture and politics, private dreams and social responsibilities reinforced one another. If man was a product of his class and environment, they argued, he was also marvelously unique; if he was shaped by historical forces, he still could control his own future; if there were times when the needs of the community took precedence over those of the individual, there were parts of a man's conscience and identity which society could never touch.

Finally, they remained convinced that the central purpose of revolution was to release man from the ancient fear of poverty and unemployment so that he might begin to explore his full potential, unchain his imagination, and discover his humanity. America needed more orderly institutions precisely so that its citizens could find room for spontaneity and freedom. Social control was necessary so that private eccentricity might flourish. Economic security was a prelude to cultural liberation. A transformation of the environment was a first step in the creation of a new person. And if people could never achieve complete happiness or perfection, they might at least know that their pain and suffering were moral rather than physical, that life was ultimately tragic because men were human rather than because capitalism made them animals or automatons.

In sum, Mumford, Dewey, Lynd, Hook, and Niebuhr had managed momentarily to join ideas that seemed otherwise contradictory. They succeeded in preserving a tenuous balance between liberalism and Marxism, morality and politics, private thought and collective action, individual freedom and the search for community, a cultural critique of industrialism and an ideological analysis of capitalism, the desire for psychologically satisfying myths and the need for a coherent social theory. But it would prove increasingly difficult to sustain this equilibrium in the later years of the decade. What they were asking Americans to do was hold two opposing ideals in their minds at the same time. In the context of depression and war, this became a burden that neither the average man nor the intellectual himself could long sustain.

CHAPTER IV

LITERARY THEORY AND
THE ROLE OF THE INTELLECTUAL

1. *The Writer and Society*

It was probably inevitable that the desire to forge a new politics, a new economy, and a new philosophy should be accompanied by an effort to create a new form of art and a new conception of the intellectual's place in American life. Given the principle that any revolution in the United States must be cultural as well as social, novels, plays, and poems all appeared to have a special role in transforming human thought and behavior.

In some respects, that was not an idea unique to the 1930s. Throughout the first three decades of the twentieth century the intellectual community had never abandoned its faith in the power of words to change institutions or surrendered its missionary impulse to save America by means of a literary renaissance. The Progressive generation, speaking through the voices of Van Wyck Brooks and Randolph Bourne, had always stressed the social importance of art. This ideal was kept alive during the darkest years of the 1920s in little magazines ranging from the *Dial* to the *New Masses,* in the essays of men like Edmund Wilson and Matthew Josephson, in the stylistic and moral preoccupations of the expatriate movement, and in the work of creative artists themselves. At no time did writers lose a sense of their own worth even when their experiments were ignored and their books went unread by the vast majority of their fellow citizens. If they felt unappreciated in an era devoted to the frantic accumulation of money and possessions, they took comfort in the belief that the country might yet have need of their services. And with the collapse of the stock market, the moment for which they had been waiting seemed finally at hand. Now the intellectual and the artist could reassume a position of leadership, though they would be asked to think and act in ways they had not previously anticipated.

The 1930s was a period in which writers retained their traditional sense of mission even as they tried to modify its specific demands in an unprecedented situation. Essentially, they were groping toward an understanding of where they had once been as well as where they now stood. Many intellectuals, remembering the excitement of Progressivism, saw the depression as another opportunity to apply their skills and experience to the solution of social problems—and thereby regain some of the power they had lost in the wreckage of World War I. Others turned to Marxism largely because it appeared the only effective guide to action—and a vehicle by which they could as intellectuals again feel relevant and influential. In both instances, the motives were similar. Whether they accepted Roosevelt's invitation to climb aboard the New Deal as advisers and administrators, whether they joined radical movements as ideologues and tacticians, or whether they remained content to criticize and counsel without party affiliation, their perpetual longing to be at the center of events drove them naturally to intervene in public life. If Henry Adams or John Jay Chapman had been unhappy symbols of the intellectual-as-outsider to the 1920s, Felix Frankfurter and John Reed became more appealing models of the intellectual-as-activist to the 1930s.

Yet where earlier reformers and revolutionaries had assumed an automatic connection between ideas and social policy, the depression forced writers to redefine more precisely their relationship to the larger society. This was especially true for those in the arts. Here the need to justify the uses of poetry, fiction, and literary criticism was particularly acute, since none of these could possibly claim to affect daily life as directly as the social sciences. What, after all, were the proper functions of literature and the obligations of the artist in a nation undergoing an economic earthquake? Did they differ fundamentally from the stances adopted by writers in earlier decades? What did "commitment" mean for men who had previously supposed that the articulation of ideas and the perfection of technique were sufficient in discharging one's political and moral responsibilities? All of these questions plagued literary men in the early 1930s because they had always felt more isolated and powerless than their counterparts in other disciplines, because their radicalism was often intensely emotional and therefore highly unstable, and because their urge to create new values and ideals seemed somewhat premature in a country whose energies were devoted—now more than ever—to matters of immediate practical concern. Nevertheless, their dilemma was ultimately shared by economists, sociologists, political theorists, and philosophers as well. Behind the sometimes arcane and parochial debate over proletarian literature lay issues that were to shape not only the course of cultural revolution in the United States but also the self-image of the American intellectual in whatever field he found himself.

The enormous pressure on writers to clarify their role in the crisis led many to denounce their pre-depression attitudes and activities. There was a uniform sense that the 1920s, as a distinct cultural entity, had died with the stock-market crash—and few lamented its passing. For a number of artists and critics, eager to forget or repudiate what they had espoused in the *Seven Arts,* Greenwich Village, or in Paris, the depression was a time of penance for past sins and declarations of future rectitude. The apparent aimlessness and "decadence" of the preceding decade was held up as a terrible warning of what could happen when intellectuals neglected social problems, when form and style became more important than content, when the complexity of a given novel or poem was taken as an indispensable mark of excellence despite its incomprehensibility to ordinary readers.

Thus Joseph Freeman, who enjoyed with Michael Gold a reputation as the leading Communist "authority" on American literature, castigated Theodore Dreiser, Sinclair Lewis, and Sherwood Anderson for concentrating on the inner thoughts and feelings of sensitive individuals who were alienated from a Philistine society but could not imagine any satisfactory alternatives to capitalism. The novelists of the 1920s were unable to think in social or political terms, Freeman charged, so they reflected instead "the utter helplessness of the intelligentsia in the face of modern industrial civilization."[1] And Dwight Macdonald, a young literary and film critic still innocent of Marxist theory in 1930, managed to dismiss Robinson Jeffers and James Joyce as "portents of dissolution," representatives of a cultural era that now lay moribund while a new period of letters was being born.[2] For them and for numerous other writers who welcomed the depression as a liberation from frivolity and commercialism, the early 1930s was a time for settling accounts and bidding farewells. However much they might secretly owe to the work of their predecessors, however much their present opinions distorted the real accomplishments of the past, intellectuals felt it necessary to attack the 1920s as a way of preparing themselves for their new tasks and responsibilities.

Much of the assault was crude and intolerant. Attention to craftsmanship, reliance on autobiographical subjects, hostility to political abstractions were often submitted as conclusive evidence that a certain artist must be indifferent to mass suffering. But two books—Edmund Wilson's *Axel's Castle* (1931) and Malcolm Cowley's *Exile's Return* (1934)—argued the case against the literary past with considerable insight and compassion. Both men had participated in the various artistic movements of the 1920s, both had joined the *New Republic* as literary editors (Cowley succeeding Wilson in 1931), and both had always been disturbed by the intellectual's traditional sense of isolation from American life. But though they had once sympathized with the position of the solitary writer who managed to preserve his personal honor and independence in the face of a corrupt society, the depression made this ideal sound peculiarly antique. Individual moral gestures suddenly appeared out of place when men desperately needed collective solutions to their problems. To bury oneself in one's art at a time of massive social disintegration seemed a selfish luxury which neither the writer nor the country could any longer afford. As a result, Wilson and Cowley began to cast about for a more satisfactory definition of the writer's relation to his work, to politics, and to the people. In effect, their books captured the mood of an intelligentsia which felt itself in transition between one cultural era and another.

On the surface, *Axel's Castle* was a series of interpretative essays on Yeats, Valéry, Eliot, Proust, Joyce, and Gertrude Stein; underneath it contained a devastating critique of the methods and themes that had characterized the literature of the past half century. Running through these years Wilson discovered a connecting thread of attitudes and assumptions which he called Symbolism—and which he held responsible for most of the best and worst traits in modern art. In his view, the Symbolist movement arose in the nineteenth century as a reaction not only to classicism and naturalism in literature but to the ascendancy of the middle class in the West. Believing that it was futile to defy the power of the bourgeoisie, many novelists and poets preferred to detach themselves from all social commitments, withdrawing into a world of private sensibility uncontaminated by the forces of science, technology, and profit. In the process, they came to regard writing as the only form of meaningful activity, art as the sole key to the universe, pure consciousness as the single subject worthy of contemplation, and reality as synonymous with whatever the author chose to see and feel.[3] Within the superior realm of the imagination, they sought a kind of freedom society itself could never deliver.

For the Symbolists, Wilson observed, the purpose of literature was not to reproduce the texture of social life nor to offer moral guidance but rather to disclose the unique personality of a given artist. This led to a revolution in style and imagery, since they found it increasingly difficult to render their experiences and sensations in conventional language. Each writer tried instead to invent a special vocabulary which might adequately express his own particular truth. To Wilson, these experiments could enlarge a man's knowledge of himself, but they also made poetry "so much a private concern of the poet's that it turned out to be incommunicable to the reader."[4] Moreover, Symbolism's preoccupation with personal feelings and inner states of being reinforced the individualistic premises on which bourgeois culture was founded. Far from rebelling against their environment, Wilson was suggesting, the members of the avant-garde had unconsciously absorbed its most destructive features.

Thus what really bothered Wilson about the Symbolists was not their stylistic innovations but their unwillingness to speak plainly about social issues, their haughty refusal to participate in daily affairs, their elitist disdain for politics and economics, their lack of sympathy for "ordinary" men, their preoccupation with solitude and introspection, their celebration of the "isolated or ideal human mind, brooding on its own contradictions or admiring its own flights." As a result they created a literature "indifferent to action and unconcerned with the group"—two of the gravest crimes the 1930s could conceive.[5]

In the name of expanding poetic vision, Wilson asserted, the Symbolists had carried the Romantic revolt against society to its farthest and most dangerous point, exalting subjectivity, disregarding their audience, and purposely divorcing themselves from any contact with the life of their time. Finally, this retreat into the sanctuary of art led to a general cultural exhaustion. One could either follow the path of Axel, shutting oneself up "in one's own private world, cultivating one's private fantasies, encouraging one's private manias, ultimately preferring one's absurdest chimeras to the most astonishing contemporary realities," or one could escape with Rimbaud to a "more primitive civilization" where the simple pressures of survival replaced the need for art of any kind.[6]

Fortunately, Wilson concluded, these two options were rapidly being foreclosed by events in the real world. The depression and the experiment with socialism in Russia were again obliging intellectuals to inquire whether it might be possible "to make a practical success of human society." The Symbolists, despite their occasional masterpieces, could no longer serve as literary models for writers becoming increasingly concerned with questions of power and politics. Nevertheless Wilson was far less certain than his contemporaries that the demise of modernist art would automatically lead to something better. For all their social passivity and their tendency to "overemphasize the importance of the individual," the Symbolists had given man a perception of life more imaginative and liberating than he had ever known. They understood that fantasy and dreams, illogic and irrationality, spontaneous thought and inner emotions were as important as machines, property, and class relationships. At bottom, Wilson did not wish to dispense with the culture of the past but to incorporate its best insights and values into the present age. He looked forward to a form of art that combined symbolism and naturalism, artistic excellence and social consciousness, private feelings and public action. The Symbolists had charted the reality of the self, he acknowledged; now a new generation of writers must draw on their discoveries in exploring the reality of the world.[7] If Wilson was vague about what this literature might actually look like, if he could name no American writer who exemplified his ideal, he was nevertheless proposing that art follow economics and philosophy in reconciling the individual with society.

Where Wilson hoped to preserve the technical contributions and personal viewpoint of the Symbolists, Malcolm Cowley was less sure that these virtues were needed in the current crisis. In this sense *Exile's Return* more accurately mirrored the intellectual consensus of the early 1930s.

Ostensibly, Cowley had undertaken to write an autobiographical account of his experiences in the expatriate movement and thereby to assess objectively the cultural ferment of the 1920s. On this level the book often succeeded brilliantly in capturing the plight of an entire generation of young men who had grown up in an older America of land, farms, villages, and small towns—only to discover that their skills and interests were strikingly unsuited to a nation of big cities, giant industries, and streamlined corporations. Cowley used his own life as a symbol for those children of the middle class who now felt unwanted by and superfluous to modern civilization, who huddled together to form a new class of intellectuals searching in all the bohemias of the world for anything that promised to end their alienation and give them at least a modicum of power in their native societies. Cowley described with great nostalgia their artistic experiments, their magazines and manifestoes, their efforts to influence the attitudes and life-styles of their countrymen. But he also meant to sit in judgment on the 1920s, to summarize its adolescent flaws and failings from the more "mature" perspective of the depression. *Exile's Return* sought to teach the 1930s the double lesson that cultural rebellion was futile when it bore no relation to politics and that writers were impotent as long as they remained apart from society. Here Cowley struck a sympathetic chord in his readers. Whatever the future variations, this became the dominant theme of radical critics throughout the decade.

In many ways Cowley's story drew on the ancient myths of exile and reintegration, odyssey and homecoming, loss of innocence and adjustment to life. It also paralleled the classic experience of every immigrant trying desperately to assimilate himself in a new environment. Cowley's friends believed they were truly strangers in the land during the 1920s. Their education in the universities had trained them to disparage their own national culture and to favor instead any work of art that rose above "localities, nations, or classes." They went to war not as participants but as spectators. In the trenches they learned to observe and record the furious activities of others while remaining curiously passive themselves. Finally, like "homeless citizens of the world," they roamed New York, Europe, the Connecticut farms and New England artist colonies, seeking to recapture some sense of common purpose, some functional connection to the soil and to other men, some feeling of loyalty to their region or their jobs, which they vaguely recalled from an earlier time. Through it all, Cowley pointed out, they had lost their attachment to any social or cultural "tradition"; neither the past nor the future offered a set of values they could easily trust; they had seceded "from the old and yet could adhere to nothing new." Ultimately, he concluded, they "had been uprooted from something more than a birthplace, a country or a town. Their real exile was from society itself, from any society to which they could honestly contribute and from which they could draw the strength that lies in shared convictions."[8] Like his colleagues on the right and the left in the 1930s, like those who looked to the South or the Soviet Union, Cowley was picturing himself as an alien in search of community.

Paradoxically, the intelligentsia had responded to these difficulties by adopting positions that only accentuated their marginality. In Cowley's view, the 1920s was an age of "escape." The intellectuals seemed to him a lonesome band of refugees, mistakenly fleeing from machines, from mass production, from vulgarity, from greed, from "Puritanism," from the stupidity of the Philistines and Babbitts, from a system that fed the body at the same time it starved the spirit. Since writers could find no haven for their souls in the tawdry realm of politics and social reform, they experimented instead with various styles of life and thought that momentarily satisfied their own moral and psychological needs. Their attitude toward problems, Cowley explained, was always personal; their solutions, always private. Literary men yearned to throw off the hypocrisies and constraints of middle-class America, to follow the path of creativity and self-expression wherever it might lead. Thus they became expatriates, not only from the United States but from all groups and classes that threatened to crush their precious individuality.[9]

But there was no escape, especially through what Cowley called the "religion of art." Even more than Wilson, he reserved his greatest scorn for the avant-garde—for writers like Eliot, who ransacked the past while deploring the present; for Joyce and Proust, who shut themselves up in airless rooms to create great works of art which few people read; for Valéry and Pound, who became obsessed with problems of technique while their audience dwindled away. The most famous novelists and poets of his generation, Cowley complained, were frighteningly inhuman and lifeless. Cut off from the world around them, they could never help redefine the intellectual's relation to the larger society.[10] Down their road lay a dead end.

So Cowley greeted the stock-market crash with visible relief. As far as he was concerned, the depression promised to clear away the hysteria, madness, and decay that ran through the 1920s, as symbolized by the twin suicides of Harry Crosby and Hart Crane at the very end of the decade.[11] Moreover, the crisis effectively closed off the avenues of flight so popular in the 1920s; it showed that the individual was helpless against the impersonal pressures of the environment. Even before 1929, Cowley argued, the cult of individualism had deserted both Bohemia and the market place. As the economy grew more collectivized, artists found their aesthetic principles and private rebellions becoming increasingly stereotyped and ritualistic when they were not completely out of touch with contemporary issues. Now as assembly lines stopped moving and incomes plummeted, the middle-class migrants were forced to come home. What they discovered on re-entering America, he suggested, was that they could ally with other groups in the society after all—particularly those who were struggling for a new culture as well as a new economy.[12]

Here was the moral of the tale. The years of banishment were finally over and reconciliation had begun. The search for personal freedom and an abstract international culture was giving way to a spirit of commitment and a willingness to write about "America." Literature would now be tied to a specific time and place; novels and poems would again have explicit social consequences. "A new conception of art," Cowley proclaimed, "was replacing the idea that it was something purposeless, useless, wholly individual and forever opposed to a stupid world. The artist and his art had once more become a part of the world, produced by and perhaps affecting it. . . ." The intellectual was now being asked "to deal in one way or another with the problems of the day."[13] No longer must the writer be a pariah in his native land. The depression gave him a chance to re-establish communication, sink roots, find an outlet for his talents, join a movement larger than himself. Above all, he might gain a sense of belonging—the greatest gift the 1930s could bestow. In essence, Cowley was predicting that art would help transform a nation of separate individuals into a true community of men. How this was to be accomplished he was no more certain than Wilson. But it hardly mattered. The central point had been made; the intellectual could recover his humanity by plunging headlong into strikes, demonstrations, politics, "life." This was Cowley's principal message to his colleagues, and in the depths of the depression few saw any reason to question its validity.

Both *Axel's Castle* and *Exile's Return* displayed a degree of sophistication and subtlety that quickly disappeared as the decade wore on and the claims on the intellectual's loyalties grew more intense. However much Wilson and Cowley took the present crisis into account, they still sympathized to some extent with those artistic values that had influenced their own work in the 1920s. Moreover, their appraisal of modern literature owed a considerable debt to the ideas of Van Wyck Brooks. Fifteen years earlier Brooks had pointed out the heavy price a writer paid for his continuing isolation from the American experience: the awesome waste of talent, the inexorable decline of imaginative powers, the enormous feeling of futility at being totally ignored. But Brooks believed that the artist could discharge his social obligations by bringing forth a truly *national* culture in which all might share. Now his ideals (and those of Wilson and Cowley as well) were being remodeled and greatly simplified to fit the special demands of the depression.

Where all three men were suspicious of anything avant-garde because it did not seem to address the needs of the country as a whole, later critics resented the giants of American art because they had never served the needs of a specific class or party. Where Brooks, Wilson, and Cowley tried to explain why a Melville or a Pound felt ill at ease in the United States, those who came of age in the 1930s displayed much less patience with their famous literary ancestors. Nor was this simply a matter of new converts seeking to polish their radical credentials by tossing off militant pronouncements about novels and poems they barely understood. A professional scholar like F. O. Matthiessen might concede in 1930 that the "sensitive man" had no choice but to withdraw from the "ruthless individualism" and "lifeless standardization" that characterized American capitalism, but he still accused Nathaniel Hawthorne of turning his back on society and either denying or eluding the problems of his contemporaries. Whatever the extenuating circumstances, Hawthorne had "failed to meet life squarely"; for this there was no excuse.[14] Similarly, Newton Arvin indicted Willa Cather for refusing to confront the "real life of her time," and he found her guilty of seeing every conflict as a "personal triumph or personal defeat" for the individual against the group. In Arvin's estimation, she represented a whole generation of novelists who had a "holy horror of taking sides" when it came to the larger questions of politics and social change.[15]

Even certified conservatives began to disapprove of the writer's traditional disengagement from public issues. Donald Davidson, a prominent member of the Southern Agrarians, complained in *I'll Take My Stand* that the poet was singing "less for the crowd" and more for his own amusement since he rarely felt himself to be an "integral part" of any stable community. But in the process his intellectual growth was stunted while the country could never make full use of its vast cultural resources. This historic dissociation between art and society would end, Davidson insisted, only when the writer finally chose to "step into the ranks and bear the brunt of the battle" to transform the "conditions of life." Momentarily literature might suffer, he admitted but the artist was a "person first of all. He must enter the common arena and become a citizen."[16]

In sum, a growing number of writers were eagerly lining up to repent their prodigal past and swear allegiance to the new gospel of social commitment. The tentative speculations of Wilson and Cowley were hardening into dogma. No group appeared more pleased at this development than those on the left. Unlike Davidson, they were not at all worried about a temporary artistic decline. On the contrary, Michael Gold prophesied confidently, "neither art, nor science, nor philosophy, nor genius, will lose on that great day when [intellectuals] decide to stand [their] ground in America, not run away."[17] And Edwin Seaver, himself a rather recent refugee from Babylon, congratulated his generation on abandoning its "aloofness and disillusion," its "cynicism and disdain." The "lethargy" of the 1920s was being shaken off, he declared. Where writers had once been preoccupied with "self-discovery and self-expression," they were now turning to forms of "social discovery and social expression." Even better, Seaver exclaimed, they seemed willing to "take time out from their books" altogether and "put their convictions into action rather than into words."[18] The intellectual was at last becoming a participant instead of a spectator, so the bells chimed. Whether deserting their studies for the picket lines and trips to Harlan County really represented a revolutionary step forward, whether indeed writers might have contributed more to radicalism had they remained disillusioned outsiders instead of rushing to embrace the "realities" of

American life, all this was for the moment unclear. But whatever one's present political or literary faith, the sermon of the early 1930s seemed increasingly plain: American intellectuals "must accept responsibilities; the time of experimentation, of playing, is ended."[19]

2. The Nature of Commitment

Before the depression progressed very far, the ideal of a "cultural" revolution began to mean something quite specific as it affected the role of the writer in America. However much he had always contributed to political debate and social criticism, however much he might presently theorize about freedom in a planned society and individuality in an organic community, the intellectual was being asked to undertake certain tasks few of his predecessors ever contemplated. And this did not apply just to literary men, though here the pressures were greatest. In every area of thought, however, capitalism was identified as a threat to creativity and an implacable opponent of cultural innovation, while socialism was seen as the sole protector of art and science in the twentieth century. Consequently the writer was told that he should not only become socially engaged but more explicitly that he must join the workers in their struggle against the bourgeoisie. Intellectuals were constantly reminded that they did not constitute an "independent economic class"; therefore they could not assume a "neutral" stance above the battle.[20] The lines were being drawn, the barricades were up, the enemy had been sighted, and writers would be forced to choose sides. The artist, the philosopher, the journalist, the teacher, all were informed that they could best serve the "common good" by deciding to promote a "class good."[21] Concern for the "general welfare" now implied the adoption of a working-class consciousness. In effect, writers were being called on to act in their own self-interest, to recognize that the survival of Western culture depended on the victory of the proletariat, and to commit their minds and their bodies to a socialist future.

Yet these propositions raised some excruciatingly difficult questions. How were bourgeois intellectuals to convert themselves into loyal allies of the laboring man? What form of participation was appropriate for those who had never operated a lathe, fed a blast furnace, or endured the monotony of an assembly line? If writers were not by necessity members of the working class, how could they possibly pretend to share its oppression, absorb its outlook, and speak in its name? Might they realize any benefits in return? What did "action" really mean for men who had rarely been authentic partisans of any political cause?

The only group that seemed ready with answers were the Marxists—particularly those in charge of literature for the Communist party. Throughout the opening years of the decade they assured their fellow writers that all of these problems could be easily overcome. Moreover, they described with great enthusiasm the rewards available to anyone who took his place in the front ranks of the movement. Even prior to the stock-market crash, Michael Gold was dangling the figure of John Reed before the eyes of his contemporaries as a symbol of how they too might conquer their private confusion through participation in the revolution. Reed was an archetypal radical, clearly superior to the "pale" and "careful" liberals for whom social change remained an abstraction rather than a daily struggle. In Gold's opinion, Reed enjoyed "the fullest and grandest life of any young man in America" precisely because he was never afraid to associate himself wholeheartedly with the working class. Although Gold acknowledged a tradition of proletarian suspicion and hostility toward intellectuals, Reed had so successfully combined theory and practice that his own identity was totally transformed. Thus there was "no gap between Jack Reed and the workers any longer." This did not mean, Gold hastily added, that Reed ceased to care about art or ideas; only that he had put both at the service of socialism. To Gold, Reed's career was a perfect model which every other intellectual would do well to follow.[22]

The kind of commitment Gold and his colleagues on the left were demanding involved more than a transfer of political sympathies from one class to another. What they basically asked was that a writer adopt the perspective of the workers not only by articulating their grievances but by changing himself as well. Hence Robert Gorham Davis, a budding literary critic and frequent contributor to the *Modern Quarterly* in the early 1930s, recommended that revolution be seen as a form of therapy in which the intellectual took on an entirely new personality. Like others in the decade, Davis assumed that radicalism was both an economic and an existential phenomenon. "In what is roughly parallel to the method of Freudian analysis," he suggested, the writer should make his subconscious values and fetishes "intelligible," understand how his inner conflicts and disorders had their origins in a capitalist society, and thereby free his "social will" to function more effectively in the modern world.[23] In the same vein Meridel Le Sueur, a poet and journalist for the *New Masses*, announced that she wished to be rid of her middle-class neuroses. "I do not care for the bourgeois 'individual' that I am," she declared. Having surmounted her former anxiety about joining groups, she now hoped "to 'belong' to a communal society, to be a cellular part of that society and able to grow and function with others in a living whole." Toward this end, she was willing to "walk blind," without hesitation and with "full belief," into the "dark, chaotic, passional world of . . . the proletariat."[24] Acording to both Davis and Miss Le Sueur, one could not leave the past in gradual stages, subjecting every step to rational consideration. Instead, the writer had to surrender all his inherited attitudes and assumptions before he could be admitted as a full-fledged member of the working class. Ultimately, they were insisting that intellectuals undergo a profound personal reorientation, a conversion experience so complete that it amounted to a moral and psychological rebirth.

Whether it was really desirable or even possible for the writer to undergo such a metamorphosis appeared somewhat doubtful. Nevertheless one man attempted to show that, quite apart from any benefits to the proletariat, the intellectual could not solve his own problems until he broke irrevocably with the middle class. In 1936, after nearly ten years of effort, Joseph Freeman finally published his massive autobiography, *An American Testament*. The book was a study in contrasts. On the one hand, it presented an extraordinarily moving account of what it meant to be an immigrant, a Jew, an esthete, and a radical, all at the same time. On the other hand, it was so weighted down with political dogma that, especially in the latter pages, the narrative stopped entirely and a communist morality play began. But throughout the book Freeman showed that he could be an astute cultural critic, sensitive to both the interests of the workers and the special needs of the intelligentsia. Like *Exile's Return, An American Testament* was clearly more than an autobiography. Freeman wanted to demonstrate in the story of his own life how socialism might eventually reconcile the historic conflict between poetry and politics. Thus his book was intended as a testimonial to the triumph of order over confusion, unity over disparity, collective feeling over personal ambition.

Freeman's background was significantly different from Cowley's. The soil from which he originally sprang was Russian, not American; he spent his early years in the ghettos of New York, not the small towns of the South or Midwest; he considered himself more truly an outsider than any of the young men who suddenly became alienated after Versailles. He numbered no Yankee patriarchs or Protestant clerics among his ancestors; he inherited instead the traditional Zionism of his relatives and the instinctive socialism of his neighbors. Freeman was an intensely political man from the beginning. He campaigned for Wilson, fought ideological battles on street corners, refused to countenance the Socialist party's ambiguous policy toward World War I, and ultimately welcomed the Bolsheviks as the only true revolutionaries. During the 1920s he wrote for the *Liberator* rather than the

Dial or *Hound and Horn,* traveled to the Soviet Union, where he fully embraced its experiment in communism, and supported Stalin against Trotsky (though not without some misgivings which occasionally surfaced in the autobiography and later drove him from the party). Finally, he entered the depression as a senior editor of the *New Masses* and a relatively undoctrinaire defender of proletarian culture.

Yet through it all, Freeman suffered the same agonies and contradictions that disturbed the rest of his generation. Like Cowley, he felt uprooted from the ancient certainties of rural life. In the "vanished village," Freeman recalled, "you knew what was right and what was wrong. Now nobody knew. You had to make up your own right and wrong, you had to decide everything for yourself."[25] In modern civilization there was neither security nor fixed truths; in a time of transition, all men were immigrants. Hence the sense of exile was universal, and the search for order seemed in part a longing to recapture the past.

This of course was impossible. Instead Freeman and his contemporaries tried painfully to adapt to an environment "utterly different from the one we had been trained to expect." In this effort, he observed, they found themselves caught between the prewar assumptions of liberalism and the postwar theories of Einstein, Freud, and Lenin.[26] To make matters more complicated, they could not help admiring the cultural accomplishments of the bourgeoisie even as they listened with growing sympathy to the political and moral appeal of socialism. In Freeman's view, most of the intellectuals' difficulties stemmed from the fact that they were essentially "declassed." American writers hated capitalism but still respected its art; they wanted to serve the labor movement but continue to write poems and novels; they entertained radical hopes but feared for their own survival as an educated elite. Cut off emotionally and economically from the middle class, they were not yet ready to join the workers. "Isolated on the campus," Freeman conceded, "lacking that sense of comradeship which one gets in a mass organization, we were breaking from an old world without having [discovered] a new one. We felt like pioneers and outcasts."[27]

As a way out of this dilemma, many became what Freeman called "romatic rebels" against the bourgeoisie, challenging its life-style while leaving its institutions intact, seeking personal solutions to problems that were fundamentally social. Yet even here they could not disavow their middle-class origins. Their very concern for "self-expression," Freeman pointed out, mirrored America's traditional "cult of rugged individualism."[28] Moreover, he agreed with Cowley that writers could never resolve the tensions in their lives by fleeing to Bohemia. If Freeman's own experience offered any proof, the intellectual would remain a man of divided allegiances so long as he was faced with a stark choice between art and power, literature and revolution, free thought and "active participation in the work of the world."[29]

But the whole motive behind Freeman's autobiography was to show that this discord need not last forever. He himself had found in Marxism a "clear philosophy which could explain and integrate these contradictory ideas, which could bring order and indicate purpose in the apparent chaos surrounding us."[30] In the first place, Freeman assured his readers that only socialism promised to satisfy their twin longings for "justice" and "beauty." This had a very practical meaning in his mind. Having embraced the Communist party, he was pleased to report that revolutionaries did indeed have some use for the skills of the intellectual. Granted that art was less important at the moment than political organizing, granted even that one might be forced temporarily to give up the luxuries of poetry and fiction, the writer could still engage in journalism, reportage, and public speaking as a way of exhorting the masses to action and thereby help to transform society.[31] If Freeman had not in his youth envisioned this kind of solution to the problem of literature and politics, he was willing nonetheless to adjust his ideals to the demands of the movement rather than ask the movement to fulfill his ideals.

For Freeman had learned a second and more important lesson from his conversion to the cause of the working class. The Communists, both in Russia and the United States, had taught him the supreme value of "discipline." Under their auspices he was able to escape from the "whirlpool of murky subjective puzzles" that paralyzed bourgeois writers in the 1920s; with their guidance he could channel his private problems toward positive social ends; inside their organizations he felt wanted, needed, "at home" in the "real" world, no longer an exile.[32] In a moment of almost mystical revelation, Freeman recognized that through socialism "we replaced I, and to speak of your own life . . . was to speak of the life of mankind in whose development you found your whole undivided being." Armed with this insight, the once bewildered and adolescent rebel emerged now as a clear-headed, mature revolutionary.[33]

In essence, An American Testament touched on all the ideals that flourished among writers in the 1930s—the desire to re-enter American life, the attraction to the proletariat, the eagerness to accept a new role and a new identity, the insistence that men of thought must also be men of action. Moreover, in transmuting his own experience into a parable of how the intellectual might find a sense of order and certainty through social commitment, Freeman confirmed the decade's central axiom that an individual was helpless until he became part of some larger group, class, movement, or community. In the process, he gave voice to the longing of many writers for the personal and professional satisfaction that presumably came from pursuing a collective ideal. At heart, Freeman and his contemporaries no longer agreed with their predecessors that art and thought by themselves could save America. Henceforth, they believed, the values of culture would have to depend on the shape of society, not the other way around.

Yet these ideas contained certain implications which often went unnoticed during the early years of the depression. For example, the demand that writers adopt a new personality better suited to their social role imposed an unnecessary psychological burden which frequently obstructed the other aims they were seeking to achieve. As a result, many intellectuals found themselves paying more attention to the signs of their own salvation than to the needs of their proletarian allies. Rather than discovering what the workers might really want, they spent an inordinate amount of time worrying about whether they had completely suppressed their bourgeois attitudes, whether they had truly been converted to the revolution, whether they were permanently immune to the temptations of the old world. In part, this crisis of identity accounted for the wide use of pseudonyms among those who had moved to the left. Thus Irwin Granich became Michael Gold, George Goetz became V. F. Calverton, Louis Fraina became Lewis Corey, Robert Gorham Davis became Obed Brooks, and Kyle Crichton became Robert Forsythe. More seriously, it reflected the extent to which radicalism for some writers was less a political conviction than an enormous emotional investment in the triumph of the working class—and in any organization that tried to serve as its spokesman.

Such an overwhelming fascination with the proletariat probably revealed more about the intelligentsia's own state of mind than about the realities of American life in the 1930s. Indeed the workers often functioned as a convenient symbol for all the political and cultural goals to which writers aspired during the period. It was not surprising that men who had always felt isolated from the main body of society should now be attracted to other outsiders like the unemployed and the dispossessed. Although most intellectuals had little personal contact with the working class, they could still hope to share its point of view. In their eyes, both groups were economically weak yet morally superior, both rejected the values of the bourgeoisie, and both sought power through radical changes in the social order. For these reasons, there appeared a natural harmony of interest between the intellectuals and the disinherited.

But the effort among writers to end their historic separation from the masses could be carried to dangerous extremes. Somehow the life of the workers seemed richer, more human, less narrow than the life of the intellectual. Thus it became easy to romanticize the intuitive knowledge of the "people," to decide that the common man was really wiser and closer to "reality" than those with formal education. Accordingly, Sherwood Anderson announced that he preferred the natural simplicity of the proletariat to the artificial sophistication of the learned. "Always the workers speak better, more directly, than the intellectuals," he mused. "There is a kind of force, a strength that shakes the nerves. There is something alive here, glowingly alive."[34] And this perception inspired him to call for a form of group suicide. "Down with us," he shouted in 1932. "If it be necessary, in order to bring about the end of a money civilization and set up something new, healthy and strong, we of the so-called artist class have to be submerged, let us be submerged."[35]

Not everyone was quite so eager to celebrate the virtues of the poor, but Anderson's feverish rhetoric did reflect a hidden anti-intellectualism which periodically surfaced throughout the decade. Apart from the recurring tendency to contrast the diseased old order with the physical (and perhaps sexual) vitality of the new, writers revealed considerable feelings of shame and self-hatred at not having suffered like the workers. So they compensated for this apparent deficiency by dismissing their own skills, however useful these might possibly be to the radical movement. In their yearning to serve society as a whole, some overlooked the power of independent analysis and debate; in their desire to participate in the daily experiences of the people, others abandoned the tasks of disinterested inquiry and speculation; in their revolt against middle-class culture, many questioned the value of intellect itself.[36] In their emphasis on a kind of existential commitment to the working class, men like Freeman and Gold were demanding not consciousness but action, not philosophy but faith, not reason but passionate involvement. Ultimately, the intellectual was being asked to desert the very tools of his trade, to become a "new man" by ceasing to think critically. For a generation which required all its mental capacities to transform America's social and cultural institutions, these attitudes could effectively undercut such an effort from the start.

Yet ironically, the urge to break off relations with the bourgeoisie did not really bring writers nearer to the working class. If anything, the gap between the long-range ambitions of the intelligentsia and the immediate needs of the average man remained just as great, largely because a revolutionary situation had not developed in the early 1930s. What happened instead was that middle-class writers and artists became considerably more radical than the rest of the population. In the absence of a militant proletariat, they were forced to turn to surrogates—and here the Communist party played its most important role.

At the outset the party offered precisely the sort of power and organized strength for which many intellectuals had been searching. If the workers were momentarily passive, then the Communists would have to provide writers with an adequate taste of "life" outside the ivory tower. And in this the Communists appeared to succeed admirably. In their presence, Granville Hicks recalled, one felt close to the "real thing"; men could actually imagine that they were "touching history at its vital center."[37] Similarly, Newton Arvin seemed quite willing to entrust his fate if not to the proletariat, then at least to their political representatives. "I believe," he wrote Hicks, "we can spare ourselves a great deal of pain and disappointment . . . if we can discipline ourselves to accept . . . revolutionary leaders . . . for what they must be: grim fighters in about the most dreadful and desperate struggle . . . in all history—not reasonable and 'critically-minded' and forbearing and infinitely far-seeing men." Like Freeman and Anderson, Arvin insisted that "everything gives way before the terrible social conflict itself." Hence the "kinds of questions" in which intellectuals were normally interested "must take their place where they belong, out of the thickest dust and along the rim of the arena." In his view, writers should suspend their judgment and bury their reservations for the duration of the war: "Let's realize that there are far more basic and primitive things that have to be taken care of first . . . and do absolutely nothing, at any moment, to impede the work of the men who are fighting what is really our battle *for us.* "[38] Thus it made no difference to Arvin whether one was talking about the workers or the party; the intellectual remained a subordinate figure in either case.

Nonetheless, commitment brought special rewards that often outweighed any feeling of compromise the intellectual might occasionally experience. To many writers the Communist party was much more than a political movement; its psychological and cultural advantages usually had greater appeal than its ideology. The Communists boasted an array of activities no other radical organization could match. With its magazines, lectures, schools, conferences, and clubs, the party rivaled the New Deal in giving intellectuals a sense of importance, as well as numerous things to do. Moreover, it offered writers a chance to participate in a purposeful, forward-looking, positive enterprise—in stark contrast to the years they had spent as isolated and negative critics of American life.[39] At times the Communists seemed the only alternative to further alienation and impotence—

so writers followed their daily adventures with sympathy even if they did not always join the party.

But for all their attraction to the workers and the Communists, most intellectuals were only reflecting a more basic concern of the decade. What they really wanted was an opportunity to become part of a cause larger than themselves, to merge their separate lives in a movement that promised both comradeship and an end of loneliness, to feel as though they had become significant actors on the stage of history. The 1930s was pre-eminently a period in which men tended to identify their personal problems with social solutions, to see their private experiences in terms of public events. This was particularly true for the striking number of writers who were themselves in their thirties during the depression; the close correspondence of their age to the decade gave them a special sensitivity to the relationship between the individual and history. Having literally grown up with the century, they felt an additional obligation to help shape the country's future course. Consequently they adopted a radical stance as a way of expressing this general desire for community and social responsibility. Their romance with the workers became a symbol of how every individual could hurdle the barriers of race, nation, and class.[40] In the idea of socialism they found an affirmation of universal brotherhood and cultural solidarity that the American people had never previously known.

On the surface these were noble and revolutionary sentiments, but they could lead to extraordinarily conservative results, however unforeseen. In condemning the bohemian irresponsibility of the 1920s, writers sometimes seemed to prefer conventional behavior to any form of spontaneous protest; in assuming that the revolution would succeed only through collective action, they often ignored the benefits of personal rebellion; in seeking community, they frequently appeared willing to settle for order and security. Thus what began as an escape from solitude might easily end as conformity to the group.

3. Toward a Proletarian Culture

The majority of intellectuals managed to avoid these dangers during the early 1930s. Despite their persistent habit of regarding art and thought as vaguely inferior to social and economic issues, most writers really had no choice but to continue the work for which they had been trained. This was especially the case for literary men. Unable to become either workers or political organizers, some chose instead to serve the revolution by creating a genuinely proletarian culture. In the process they hoped to preserve the experimental impulse of modern art by making it intelligible to ordinary people—indeed to salvage the contributions of the avant-garde by giving them a radical social purpose. But essentially they saw their principal role as the creation of an entirely new literature to fit the needs of a socialist society.

First, however, they had to convince their fellow writers that such a form of art was both possible and necessary—not an easy task given the increasingly bitter and rancorous debates among novelists, poets, and critics during these years. It was surely a sign of the times that literary discussions could no longer be conducted in a relatively polite and dispassionate manner. Although there had been many angry quarrels among various groups throughout the 1920s, the issues at stake never seemed fraught with the social and political overtones they now contained. In the wake of the depression, opinions about art became indistinguishable from attitudes toward life. Indeed any effort to keep the two realms separate appeared positively immoral.

Not surprisingly, the most ardent defenders of proletarian literature were Marxists—especially those who were either members of or close to the Communist party. In the pages of the *Modern Quarterly* and the *New Masses* one could find elaborate explanations of why America needed a new aesthetic, together with a sustained assault on the position of "liberal" critics who rejected the merger of politics and art.

V. F. Calverton, for example, rarely missed an opportunity to denounce the "myth" that literature and criticism could be treated as ends in themselves. Throughout the early 1930s he maintained that art was not a form of personal expression; rather it revealed, however unconsciously, the outlook of a particular group or class. In his view, all writing reflected a set of social assumptions and encouraged or discouraged specific kinds of action in the reader. Consequently there was no way in which a critic could arrive at an independent and objective judgment about any poem or novel; the attempt to do so was itself a political act, usually in support of the bourgeoisie. Ultimately those who functioned as "free-agents" were implicitly accepting the status quo. For Calverton, every literary argument was really an ideological manifestation of class conflict. He therefore urged both critics and creative artists to become aware of their social ties and the goals they wished their work to serve. Far from avoiding the political implications of literature, he believed in exploiting them to the fullest.[41]

While Calverton denied that art could ever be neutral, others asserted that this was not even desirable. When writers evaded their social obligations, Granville Hicks suggested, literature itself began to suffer. He agreed that art should always try to capture the whole of human experience, but the posture of nonpartisanship no longer seemed conducive to this ideal. On the contrary, he declared in 1934, "the attempt to remain aloof weakens and sometimes paralyzes the creative faculties. Understanding comes through participation." Artists who cherished their impartiality and detachment did not really comprehend life, according to Hicks, because they could not write about man with any genuine insight. Only when they became passionately committed to one side or the other of a social conflict might they expect their work to flourish.[42] As far as Hicks was concerned, artistic excellence now depended on active involvement in the events of one's age; true understanding flowed from firsthand knowledge of contemporary events.

To those who still thought of literature as dealing with eternal truths, Joseph Freeman responded that no aspect of man's life should be considered "changeless and universal." In his opinion, different groups had different experiences at different times in history. Everything was relative—art as well as human behavior. Only after the revolution, he submitted, could people take seriously the notion of "pure" fiction and "pure" poetry. Until then, "art cannot help being, consciously or unconsciously, class art."[43]

Whether or not the Marxists were successful in persuading others that literature could be an important instrument in transforming society, they themselves had taken on a very special burden. For one thing, they could no longer react to a work of art on the basis of whim or private taste. They were not writing to enlarge their own understanding, nor was their primary purpose to aid creative artists. Instead they conceived of their role as emissaries to a mass audience (or at least to its more "advanced" segments) on behalf of proletarian culture. In addition they sought to proselytize and instruct the uninitiated in much the same fashion as the early Puritans. When James Farrell complained that left-wing critics too often behaved like priests or public-relations men, the *New Masses* replied that this was precisely their purpose. "After all," the editors pointed out, "revolutionary criticism, quite as much as revolutionary fiction, is a weapon in the class struggle." In analyzing a book, they contended, every critic should keep in mind the "effect his review is to make on readers of the *New Masses*. He is speaking for a class and in the interests of a class, and there is no place in his work for irresponsible individualism."[44] Hence the critic was to suppress every trait that might be regarded as excessively personal, undisciplined, or eccentric. In matters of art, the Communists had become a new Elect, and the *New Masses* was to serve as their pulpit.

In the sermons of the fundamentalists, this approach to culture often seemed crude and simplistic. Thus Michael Gold greeted the first novel of a young radical author not as literature at all but as a "significant class portent." To Gold the book, despite its weaknesses, represented one more "victory against capitalism."[45] But in the hands of more learned preachers, Marxist criticism could treat works of art with both seriousness and occasional perception.

Perhaps the most authoritative spokesman for proletarian art was the *New Masses* literary editor, Granville Hicks. In the early years of the decade he effectively performed the dual role of missionary and press agent to the heathen and the doubters. It was hardly accidental that Hicks should be drawn to the image of the intellectual-as-cleric, for he had originally planned to enter the Unitarian minstry in the 1920s. But his interest in more secular matters and his horror at the depression led him eventually to Marxism—though he always seemed less committed to its specific doctrines than to its use as a text in converting an otherwise corrupt world. Through it all, his evangelical temperament persisted. For him, literature remained chiefly a moral rather than an aesthetic experience.

In 1933 Hicks published his *magnum opus*—an extensive appraisal of American fiction entitled *The Great Tradition*. Predictably the work sounded like a jeremiad on the sins of the artist, with Hicks disclosing the only path to atonement and salvation. But his larger purpose was to reassess the country's literary past in order to argue for a special type of novel in the present. From the beginning, Hicks disavowed any pretense of objectivity. He frankly admitted the book's polemical overtones because he saw "no reason to disguise the nature of the conflict in which I am engaged or the side that I have chosen."[46] For Hicks, the function of criticism was not only to explain and evaluate previous works of art but also to steer authors toward a more "acceptable" form of expression in the future. In particular, he intended to show that writers could no longer solve either their literary or personal difficulties "within the framework of bourgeois thought and feeling."[47] Henceforth they would have to transcend the cultural horizons of the middle class if they wished to survive as artists—and Hicks was quite prepared to lead the way.

Invested with this mission, he proceeded in a fashion typical of the 1930s to condemn those who had for one reason or another either deserted the country or tried to avoid its problems by withdrawing inward. Included in this group were such luminaries as Poe, Hawthorne, Melville, Twain, James, Faulkner, and most of the writers of the 1920s—all of whom seemed to Hicks more interested in their novels than in understanding or changing society. In his judgment, their refusal to confront the "central issues" of American life was ultimately disastrous both for art and society. By refusing to write "simply and realistically" about the events of their time, he declared, they were evading their cultural as well as their political responsibilities.[48]

Yet Hicks was not much happier with the results of that other literary tradition he labeled "Realism." Although he granted that the "future" course of fiction lay in the hands of men like Howells, Dreiser, Sinclair, Herrick, Anderson, and Lewis, their novels left him equally dissatisfied. Unlike the Romantics and the expatriates, the Realists at least had "carefully examined and faithfully recorded the life about them."[49] But these qualities alone did not necessarily lead to great works of art, Hicks admitted. For that one needed something more than the simple powers of observation; one needed a coherent philosophy and a systematic point of view, neither of which the Realists possessed. Despite their good intentions, they could not really understand the significance of what they described. They were unable to perceive a "hidden pattern" beneath the obvious chaos of American society. Instead they seemed bewildered and overwhelmed by the complexity of their subject matter; hence, their novels remained peculiarly formless and incomplete. Lacking an organizing idea with which to comprehend and master the upheavals of their age, the Realists did not fulfill their artistic promise or provide the moral guidance America desperately needed.[50]

This was Hicks's major theme, and he kept repeating it at every opportunity. In many ways his greatest objection to the literature of the nineteenth and early twentieth century was not so much that it failed to deal with social problems but that it did so in a muddled and disorderly fashion. As a result, he considered stylistic experimentation much less important than thematic clarity. Like many intellectuals in the 1930s, Hicks could not tolerate inconsistency, fragmentation, disunity, anything that resisted categorization or sounded potentially anarchic—perhaps because these appeared the very forces that had caused the depression in the first place. Thus he was calling for an end to confusion in art just as others were demanding an end to confusion in political and economic affairs.

Fortunately, the generation of novelists just reaching maturity in the 1930s seemed to be answering this appeal. Hicks was delighted to find that the current crop of writers—led by John Dos Passos—displayed in their work precisely the sort of unified outlook he regarded as indispensable. With the help of Marxism, they had discovered that "American life is a battleground, and that arrayed on one side are the exploiters and on the other the exploited." Whatever qualifications this insight might eventually require, it offered a "key to the labyrinth," as far as Hicks was concerned.

"If there is any other working interpretation of the apparent chaos than that which presents itself in terms of the class struggle, it has not been revealed."[51]

Here Hicks was really speaking of his own conversion. Having lost his faith in Protestantism, he had found a new sense of order in the revelations of Marx—an explanation of the world that satisfied both his aesthetic and psychological yearning for absolutes. Although *The Great Tradition* received frequent citations as a model for radical literary criticism, it was really a quite personal document in which Hicks summarized his inner journey from turmoil to certainty, skepticism to belief. Beyond its explicit ideological message, beyond its defense of proletarian fiction, the book provided a quasi-religious lesson in how artists and critics alike might be saved through the revolution.

In other ways, however, *The Great Tradition* was a classic example of how Communist critics frequently treated art and ideas during the 1930s. Whether one read Gold, Freeman, Seaver, or Hicks, certain attitudes and assumptions kept reappearing. As Malcolm Cowley pointed out in his review of *The Great Tradition,* the Communists adopted a curiously moralistic stance when discussing literature. They tended to use Marxism more as an instrument for meting out praise and damnation than as a tool of general cultural analysis. Instead of bringing the insights of history and economics to the study of art, they seemed to evaluate a work solely on the basis of whether or not it adopted the "correct" position on contemporary issues. Rather than interpreting a novel in relation to its own time, they usually judged it "from the viewpoint of a revolutionary critic of the year 1933." And in the process they rarely forgave those who failed to measure up. Consequently their assessments were strikingly ahistorical (a major weakness in men who presumed to follow Marx), while their tone of voice was often harsh and dogmatic.[52]

Furthermore, despite their radicalism, many contributors to the *New Masses* could sound intolerably complacent and smug. Hence Kyle Crichton, who presided over the magazine's humor column when not concerned with more serious duties, announced in 1934 that it was indeed a "great treat being a Communist." While others still clung pathetically to the "lost cause" of democracy and capitalism, he could feel superior because "from the mere standpoint of being on the inside of history, a Marxist has an immeasurable advantage over everybody else."[53] This kind of arrogance flowed from the conviction that the Left could not possibly lose, that the victory of socialism was already assured by its success in the Soviet Union, that Communists everywhere possessed a special wisdom since they were active participants in the struggles of their time. Having identified with a socialist future, men like Crichton found it easy to dismiss the culture of the past as hopelessly naïve, limited, and superficial.

At bottom, these traits were a symptom of how the Communists viewed their own role as critics and polemicists. Unlike their more "liberal" colleagues, those who wrote regularly for the *New Masses* rarely regarded the discovery of new ideas or the encouragement of original thinking as their primary task. It was not that they refused to ask questions or explore issues; only that Marxism provided what they believed were the necessary answers to most problems. Thus the purpose of their work was not to indulge in an unceasing search for truth but to expand and enrich the truths already known. The outlines of the new world were perfectly clear; they had only to fill in the details.

Moreover, most Communist writers had a very different set of vaues and priorities from their counterparts on the *New Republic* or *Nation*. For the latter, intellectual inquiry was considered an end in itself; for the *New Masses,* it existed to serve the "higher" cause of socialism—even if this became confused with the national interests of the Soviet Union. The ultimate responsibility of the Communists was not to unlimited discussion and analysis but to an ideology which in their view made greater *moral* demands than those normally asked of the "independent" intellectual in America. They saw their function primarily as one of publicizing and clarifying the programs of a political party and social class rather than debating theories and re-examining first principles regardless of the consequences. Their essays and books were consciously designed to persuade the doubters, convert the unaffiliated, and exemplify commitment to the uncommitted. Thus they tended to "use" ideas not so much as rational explanations of empirical phenomena but more often as convenient weapons in a battle for the emotions and loyalties of the masses, emphasizing whatever arguments and concepts might sound convincing at the moment. The inherent truth or falsity of a position mattered less than its effectiveness in advancing socialist aims. Yet in an age of frightening uncertainty, when the virtues of detachment and skepticism appeared both anachronistic and dangerous, when the very autonomy of culture and thought was being severely challenged, the Communists' willingness to subordinate the life of the mind to the pressures of politics and society seemed somehow appropriate.

As a result, they became the acknowledged leaders of the movement toward a proletarian aesthetic. They were the ones who defined its objectives and outlined the form it should take. Though Hicks, Freeman, and Gold spent much of their time enumerating the flaws in bourgeois literature, they also paid some attention to what a radical work of art might actually look like. And here their demands on the novelist and poet grew quite precise.

No one expected more from the artist than Michael Gold. On October 22, 1930, in a literary supplement which the *New Republic* attached to its regular edition, he mounted a vigorous (and celebrated) assault on the work of Thornton Wilder. Though his shrill tone offended many subscribers, Gold was trying to explain as clearly as possible why the Communists would no longer tolerate the culture of the middle class, of which Wilder seemed a perfect if somewhat innocent symbol. Gold dismissed Wilder's work as genteel and escapist; it did little more than help capitalists forget "the barbaric sources of their income, the billions wrung from American workers and foreign peasants and coolies." Since Wilder knew that his readers wanted no "lessons" which might disturb their comfortable lives, he obliged them by retreating into the past, by writing about a "museum, not a world," by failing even to use history "as a weapon to affect the present or future." But Wilder's worst sin, according to Gold, was a "rootless cosmopolitanism" which never dared capture the authentic speech and spirit of his native land. Where, Gold thundered, were the cotton mills, sweatshops, coal mines, breadlines, and strikes—all the "blood and horror and hope" of the country's experience? What really seemed to bother Gold was not so much Wilder's lack of radicalism but his failure to confront contemporary realities, his inability to "write a book about America."[54] Thus if Gold had his way, one of the most important features of the "new" literature would be its emphasis on a distinctive *national* style and outlook —an ideal which, ironically, sounded closer to Emerson or Brooks than to Marx.

Elsewhere, Gold offered some general rules by which one might distinguish proletarian from bourgeois art. Gold announced that he for one could no longer "stomach" the kind of novels which concentrated on personal problems or indulged in verbal acrobatics. These qualities merely confused and discouraged the masses. Instead he demanded an aesthetic that was "simple," "realistic," precise, and socially "useful." In his opinion, "facts" had become the "new poetry" of the modern world; the ability to describe life in almost documentary fashion seemed of far greater value than the traditional reliance on imagination, introspection, and stylistic complexity. Gold therefore urged writers to employ as few words as possible and to utilize clear plots and swift action (here, he reluctantly conceded, that arch-bohemian Hemingway could be of some help). Moreover, since Gold found the external conflicts of men and women more interesting than their private anxieties, he argued that "individual tremors, lyricisms, emotions, [and] eccentricities" would have to be merged into some "large objective pattern." Above all, Gold declared, the author should avoid pessimism by infusing his work with a definite "revolutionary elan." Because all literature contained political implications, he believed that proletarian art must consciously incite its readers to radical action.[55]

Gold assumed that the majority of readers would be workers themselves; this was why he insisted on a rigorous simplicity in form and content. If people were presently hypnotized by movies, radio, and pulp fiction, if they had neither the time nor inclination to read at all, they would pay attention to serious literature only if it dealt with the problems of their lives in a way they could easily understand. He had little patience with the Brechtian notion that revolutionary art required new forms of expression as well as new ideas; he wanted to win as wide an audience as possible by using familiar and conventional language to communicate left-wing ideals. In effect, Gold was asking writers to compete with popular culture and the mass media by adapting its techniques to socialist ends—a most awesome task for those who had rarely enjoyed a following outside the avant-garde.

Others were less dogmatic than Gold about what proletarian literature should do, or how it must be written. For one thing, men like V. F. Calverton and Joseph Freeman realized that the largest audience for such an art form would probably come from sections of the disaffected middle class—especially those who were already moving left in the wake of the depression. Indeed Calverton doubted whether a purely proletarian aesthetic was presently possible in a country so unaccustomed to thinking in terms of class or ideology. So both he and Freeman preferred to talk about "revolutionary" fiction and poetry whose message was more subtle and less propagandistic. From this perspective, a proletarian novel need not be written by or addressed to workers, nor must it include a worker as hero; it could be considered revolutionary as long as it reflected the viewpoint of the working class and prepared its readers for basic social changes in the future. To them, what mattered most was not the immediate usefulness of radical art—no one should be expected to move directly from a poem to a picket line—but rather its ultimate success in converting men to a socialist value system.[56]

Yet for all the theories about how best to influence the people, the real significance of proletarian literature seemed to lie in its effect on the artist himself. This theme was stressed repeatedly at the first Congress of American Writers held in New York during April 1935. The meeting was organized by the Communists, but it attracted many well-known intellectuals (among them Malcolm Cowley, Matthew Josephson, Waldo Frank, Kenneth Burke, John Dos Passos, James Farrell, Edward Dahlberg, and Langston Hughes) who sympathized in varying degrees with the revolutionary cause. For the most part, their speeches and papers summarized ideas which had become increasingly fashionable among literary radicals in the early 1930s: They attacked the "irresponsibility" of the previous decade, declared that capitalism was now a menace to Western culture, affirmed the need for social commitment, and demanded an alliance with the working class. But they were particularly interested in the advantages to be gained from having a stable and appreciative audience for whom they could write and whose aspirations they could articulate. Thus Malcolm Cowley asserted that proletarian literature offered the artist a way out of alienation, a growing number of consumers for his work, and the assurance that his private sentiments were also shared by a rising new class firmly rooted in the "real world."[57] Similarly, Matthew Josephson pointed enthusiastically to the position of the intellectual in Russia as a model for how American novelists and poets could find in their art a feeling of solidarity with the masses.[58] Throughout the Congress, it was assumed that the proletarian aesthetic might permit writers to participate once again in the social and political life of their country—a goal which almost everyone believed would liberate, rather than inhibit, artistic originality and insight.

Beyond its benefits to author or reader, however, proletarian literature seemed a way of developing a counter-culture and a counter-morality in a country that until now had known only capitalist and liberal values. For Michael Gold, this was the most important function of the new art. Radicals could not rely simply on strikes, demonstrations, and political organizing, he warned. "You cannot build Communism with masses whose emotions are still of the capitalist world, who have not been penetrated in every fibre with the emotional habits of Communism." It was therefore necessary, in his view, "to form a workers' culture to offset the poisons of the capitalist culture." In addition to revolutionary fiction and poetry, Gold called for theaters, film groups, newspapers and magazines, neighborhood clubs, community activities—anything that might give people an alternative to the life-style and attitudes of the middle class. Ultimately he was urging writers literally to invent a different set of ideals for Americans, to create in their art an image of the "new Communist man."[59] If one believed that a revolution in culture could facilitate the revolution in politics and society, then it was natural to see proletarian literature as a crucial weapon in the arsenal of the Left.

In sum, the concept of an indigenous working-class culture seemed a way of serving both the needs of the masses and those of the intelligentsia. On the one hand, by showing through art that competition and money-making were not the only goals of human activity, that one could imagine institutional arrangements other than those offered by the bourgeoisie, the Communists hoped to radicalize men and prepare them for socialism. On the other hand, by insisting that a cultural transformation must coincide with (or even precede) changes in the social and economic order, they invested writers with a new sense of importance and purpose. Henceforth, art would no longer be relegated to the essentially passive role of portraying and commenting on the conditions of American life; instead it could become a positive instrument in shaping ideas, influencing behavior, and altering the environment. Writers were now not only observers but creators, not only thinkers but activists. Moreover, proletarian literature became a device by which the novelist, the poet, and the critic would all be reunited with the community, sharing its emotions and values, receiving its support and encouragement. Finally, the revolutionary movement permitted writers to feel they were continuing and improving on the work of the avant-garde by producing a form of art which was neither personal nor universal but *social* in style and content. Thus the proletarian author could build on the foundations laid down by the Romantics, the Symbolists, the Realists, the Bohemians, and the Expatriates, while avoiding their philosophical confusion and political isolation.

Yet throughout the early 1930s, the theory behind proletarian literature always seemed more appealing than its actual results. Because of pressure from Moscow as well as their own impatience with anything that did not immediately relate to the social crisis, the Communists tended to simplify and vulgarize what might otherwise have been an interesting cultural experiment. Marxist critics set up some imaginary ideal to which young authors should aspire, but in practice they were willing to settle for much less. They usually assumed that the value of a given book depended chiefly on its ability to elicit a militant response from the reader. Hence a novel or play was judged in terms of how effectively it advanced the socialist cause rather than how accurately it portrayed the lives of human beings under capitalism. Any work that seemed insufficiently radical was automatically labeled "defeatist." The only acceptable theme was one in which the central character eventually perceived that his salvation lay in revolutionary activism. Hopefully, his example would move the audience to a similar conclusion.

Not surprisingly, the aesthetic and psychological consequences of these edicts were far from satisfying, even to those on the left. By 1935, the *New Masses* conceded that proletarian literature was not fulfilling its promise. In the opinion of Alan Calmer, one of the magazine's more perceptive reviewers, the main weakness of the new art was its reliance on political formulas and melodramatic plots. This was especially true of the obligatory conversion experience which surfaced at the conclusion of most novels, short stories, and plays. By making the hero travel from passivity to commitment, Calmer contended, many writers were forcing their characters to behave as they wished all people would act. They attached a conversion ending to their tales because they believed it their "duty" to insert a revolutionary message. Not only did this lead to ideological abstractions and party slogans in place of real human relationships, but it ultimately failed to convince the reader. Calmer suggested that the schematic framework of proletarian art exposed the authors' middle-class origins, together with their failure to understand the workers' true experiences and motivations. For intellectuals, revolution remained an act of moral will rather than a product of economic necessity; they had voluntarily "converted," whereas the working class enjoyed no such freedom of choice. In effect, he charged, they were still writing about themselves instead of fully absorbing the perspective of the proletariat. They had not yet severed all their ties with the bourgeoisie.[60]

Perhaps this had always been too much to expect. Because intellectuals often feared that they were not producing anything socially useful, and since they suspected that neither their comparatively privileged position nor their traditional concern for art and ideas entitled them to speak for the working class, they had seized on the theory of proletarian literature as a method of allaying their inner doubts. But they could never be certain for whom they actually wrote. Occasionally there were disconcerting signs that the "masses" had not been reached by all these efforts in their behalf. Radical books sold poorly, and the circulation of magazines like the *New Masses* or *Modern Quarterly* seemed limited to teachers, lawyers, doctors, writers, and those already persuaded by the arguments of the Left.[61] If the people did not read novels or attend plays designed for their edification and addressed to their needs, then revolutionary art could only serve as a ceremonial catharsis for a middle-class audience unable to participate directly in the daily struggles of the workers. Thus the obsession with proletarian culture might be in reality a device by which bourgeois intellectuals discharged their feeling of guilt and achieved a vicarious sense of militancy.

4. *Voices in Opposition*

Even if the new genre had met with greater success, there were some who questioned its implications both for art and the role of the intellectual. They were not at all persuaded that the writer should become a political activist, nor that the quality of American culture would be enhanced by forcing literature to focus only on certain preconceived problems. Where men like Cowley and Calmer sometimes acknowledged the weaknesses of revolutionary fiction and the petulant dogmatism of Marxist critics, their reservations sounded tame in comparison with those who steadily opposed the proletarian aesthetic whatever form it took. Throughout the early 1930s a number of writers resisted the call of literary radicalism, seeking instead to preserve the autonomy of art and ideas despite the presence of a social crisis.

Because their number included men of widely divergent beliefs and backgrounds, ranging from conservative "new critics" through practicing novelists and poets to left-wing anti-Stalinists, they never constituted an organized group of dissenters. Nevertheless, they did hold certain attitudes in common, among the most important of which was a hostility to the mystique of collectivism.

Hound and Horn, a central organ of the dissidents, persistently objected to the assumption that an artist's personal and professional problems would be solved if he joined a movement of some kind. On the contrary, one contributor remarked, the radicals' insistence on "conformity [to] class consciousness, mass consciousness, race consciousness, every form of consciousness . . . but the individual" merely encouraged a preoccupation with "types" rather than people, slogans rather than life. Thus both the author and his work suffered immeasurably.[62] Moreover, Conrad Aiken pointed out in the *New Republic,* the country itself received no benefit from this interference with the intellectual's privacy. By submerging the individual's identity in the mores of the group, by distrusting any writer who appeared unique or exceptional, one's "value to society precisely *as* a non-conformist was being lost." Aiken concluded that he needed isolation and anonymity for the very purpose of discharging his artistic and social obligations.[63]

To another *Hound and Horn* reviewer, Lawrence Leighton, the crowning irony of the Communist position was that it intensified the writer's estrangement from his native land by burdening him with an ideology most Americans continued to reject. As long as he was a radical, he would remain an outsider. In addition, the missionary role of "converting the heathen [was] hardly compatible with the more difficult task of being a good critic or a good artist." For Leighton, the only road out of exile lay through a "rapprochement . . . with men and women, not with an economic class."[64] If the intellectual were to find his way home, it must be without the aid of proletariat or party.

Occasionally the voices of dissent were heard in unexpected places. No novelist had garnered more praise from the Left than John Dos Passos; his *U.S.A* was generally considered the finest example of proletarian fiction yet published. Nonetheless, he sent in a paper to the Congress of American Writers which appeared to challenge the assumptions of all the other participants and to question whether writers should even be attending such a conclave.

Invoking Veblen rather than Marx, Dos Passos saw some uncomfortable similarities between the artist's relationship to the Communist party and the technician's position under capitalism. Just as the aims of business thwarted those of the engineer, he suggested, so the growing number of bureaucrats and managers in the revolutionary movement were preventing writers from producing their best work. Extending the analogy, Dos Passos offered a most heretical definition of the intellectual's role: "A writer . . . must never, no matter how much he is carried away by even the noblest political partisanship in the fight for social justice, allow himself to forget that his real political aim, for himself and for his fellows, is liberty." For Dos Passos this meant a situation in which the technican could give his curiosity and experimental impulses full rein, uninhibited by political or group pressures that threatened to sabotage his performance. When intellectuals began to care more about appearing socially "responsible" than about remaining faithful to their cultural skills, he intimated, they betrayed their primary calling as craftsmen of ideas. Dos Passos conceded that writers were obliged to participate in struggles against oppression, but he insisted that one's role as a citizen should be distinguished from one's concerns as an artist. Intellectuals must realize that organizations necessarily meant discipline; they limited not only the individual's freedom of action (which was understandable) but also his freedom of thought (which could be intolerable). Somehow the writer had to strike a balance between his political duties and his personal integrity. "The dilemma that faces all honest technicians . . . today," Dos Passos concluded, "is how to combat the imperial and bureaucratic tendencies of the groups whose aims they believe in without giving aid and comfort to the enemy." Perhaps the writer, like Veblen's engineers, might have to declare his independence from all ideologies and organizational commitments in order to reconcile this inner conflict.[65]

If Dos Passos still felt uneasy about cutting himself off entirely from the

Communists, Archibald MacLeish had no such qualms. Though his opinions were to change dramatically in the later years of the decade, MacLeish spent the early 1930s accusing his fellow writers of becoming whores in the service of the revolution, embracing causes that invariably compromised their talent, trying to turn literature into a vehicle of mass expression at the expense of personal creativity. As far as he was concerned, the authors of the Left had completely misinterpreted their role. The true artist was not an instrument but an "enemy" of society in the sense that he refused to follow the "social and intellectual fashions of his day."[66] MacLeish's blunt indictment reflected the basic outlook of those who remained skeptical about the virtue of merging poetry and politics. In their estimation, the intellectual and the revolutionary had functions which were fundamentally antithetical; they could help one another only by remaining forever apart.

Furthermore, those who shared MacLeish's sentiments were intensely critical of the Communist attitude toward literature itself. Max Eastman, who found himself defending the bohemian "rebels" of the Progressive era against the humorless and pedantic "revolutionists" of the 1930s, considered the proletarian aesthetic neither radical nor creative. Instead, he charged Stalinism with having reduced literature in the Soviet Union to the level of "mechanical engineering or any kind of commodity production." If these tendencies took hold in the United States, Eastman feared, the Left would only be abdicating its cultural leadership to "individualists" like E. E. Cummings, who cared nothing for society but at least respected the integrity of art.[67]

Others, less inclined to blame Moscow alone for the deficiencies of proletarian literature, disputed the general idea that novels and poems must serve as guideposts along the road to revolution. When radicals asserted that any writer who avoided the major issues of his time was indulging in selfish escapism, critics like Henry Hazlitt and William Troy replied that the Marxists had an intolerably narrow conception of what those "major issues" involved. The *New Masses* continually denounced books that did not deal explicitly with class conflict and end with a stirring socialist message, but this merely revealed the Communists' lack of sympathy for experimentation and originality. They could not recognize the varieties of social experience in America, nor admit that literature might justifiably portray life in many different ways. Both Hazlitt and Troy argued that political concerns were only "a small part of the total hierarchy of human values" and that an exclusive preoccupation with economic issues obscured all the other influences affecting people's behavior. In their view, the failure to present man in all his moral and psychological complexity threatened to undermine those qualities that made art unique. If the Marxists insisted on transforming fiction and poetry into propaganda, then one might as well write essays or tracts and forget literature entirely. In order to prevent such a cultural calamity, Hazlitt and Troy maintained that even in the depression a work must be evaluated on its own terms, that the critic had no right to introduce extraneous criteria like politics and ideology into his assessment, that the artist should always feel free to write about any subject in any manner he wished.[68] Only then could the novelist or poet be true to his craft and to life.

However, the most vigorous opposition to proletarian literature came from those who worried not only about the role of the intellectual or the survival of culture but about the very conception of human experience on which Marxism was founded. The *Nation*'s drama editor, Joseph Wood Krutch, shared Max Eastman's distaste for the demand (made by middle-class Babbitts as well as Stalinist commissars) that art be immediately "useful," that it promote specific forms of social action in the present. Yet Krutch went even further. He denied that change of any sort was possible either through literature or politics. For him, the supreme responsibility of art was to make life a bit more tolerable by accepting the world as inherently imperfect and by describing it accurately without extending the hope of some utopian improvement in the future.[69]

Similarly, Allen Tate believed the Communists were deliberately distorting the basic truths about human nature in the interest of extra-literary goals. One of the original Southern Agrarians, Tate was also the most philosophical of the "new critics"—a group whose importance rivaled that of the Proletarians and whose very existence demonstrated that the Left had no monopoly over literary theory in the 1930s. Where others merely attacked the radicals, Tate was fully prepared to offer an alternative definition of art and life.

Writing in the *New Republic* during 1933 and 1934, Tate assailed the Marxists' faith in secular progress and the perfectibility of man which infected their novels and poems. Instead, he maintained that literature should always repudiate the "easy solutions to the human predicament that arise in every age." He went on to remind his contemporaries of art's traditional function as the "instinctive counter-attack of the intelligence against the dogma of future perfection for nations, states, and societies; it is in this sense that poetry is most profoundly the criticism of life." By demanding that literature ignore the intrinsic limitations of human nature, by forcing it to conform to the "latest programs of social improvement," the Communists deprived art of its essential strength. To Tate's Augustinian mind, only literature could restore man's knowledge of eternal sin and human frailty. The Proletarians were therefore asking writers to partici- pate in a monumental deception of mankind.[70]

Tate elaborated on these ideas by distinguishing between three types of poetry. The first he called "positive platonism" because of its "naïve confi- dence in the limitless power of man to impose practical abstractions upon the world." This genre emerged periodically throughout the history of art, and its spirit dominated thought at the present time. Its central characteris- tic, Tate declared, was to elevate the will over the imagination. Under its influence the poet neglected "the whole vision of experience" in favor of a didactic effort to move people toward some definite doctrine or policy. In this sort of allegorical or consciously propagandistic art, the writer subor- dinated insight to exhortation, objectivity to special interest, understanding to activism. Thus literature became an inferior form of science and politics, endowed with a false mission to change the world.[71]

Yet, Tate continued, when the artist realized that life was too ambiguous and contradictory to follow any preconceived plan, when the world refused to correspond to his vision of the millennium, then he often abandoned all designs for external order—including the poetry of social action. Instead he turned to "negative platonism" or Romanticism, a category Tate also dis- liked because it only substituted one kind of utopianism for another. By revolting against science and society, by trying to impose his ego on the chaos of nature, the writer was merely fostering a second illusion—this time centering on the omnipotence of the individual rather than on that of politics or mass movements. Both positive and negative platonism were similar in Tate's judgment because they promised to solve problems and usher in a state of perfection through a simple act of will. Both violated the true purposes of literature by assuming that writers should deal exclusively with those aspects of reality that could be put either to public or private "use." Finally, neither type of poetry acknowledged "the realm of immitiga- ble evil." At the moment, one might find examples of all these notions underlying proletarian art; for this reason Tate dismissed Marxism as a poor theory of aesthetics and an overly simplistic interpretation of human life.[72]

In essence, Tate was pleading for a form of art that would seek to "prove nothing," whose function would simply be to mirror the "totality of experi- ence" rather than incite men to more futile programs of action. Literature could not force the world to move in a single direction, he pointed out, nor should it become an instrument of social or personal regeneration. Tate therefore urged all artists and critics to remember that "poetry finds its true usefulness in its perfect inutility," its supreme value as a "focus of repose for the will-driven intellect." The third type of poetry, which represented Tate's ideal, would reunite the will and the imagination, thus relieving society of "partial formulas" and restoring to individuals their sense of inner "equilibrium." For Tate, the proper calling of the writer was to record objectively the universal and unchanging truths of man and nature. Art needed no other justification beyond the desire and capacity to see life whole.[73]

At various points in the early 1930s the opponents of proletarian culture all agreed that the intellectual should remain independent, that the subject matter of art transcended particular social or historical crises, and that literature was neither a handmaiden of politics nor a weapon in the class struggle. Although they arrived at these conclusions by entirely different paths—MacLeish and Dos Passos rejected any limitations on one's creativity; Eastman traced all the failures of the revolution directly to Stalin; Krutch and Tate seriously questioned whether the impulse to reform society was not itself fundamentally at odds with human nature—they were convinced that the proletarian aesthetic inflicted great harm both on art and on the American writer.

Yet ironically, the Marxists and their detractors shared the same messianic ambition. Both wished to salvage the values of Western culture in the midst of worldwide collapse. They differed only over the means, though this was enough to provoke a fierce and bloody war between the two camps. Unfortunately, neither the Left nor its opposition seemed in the mood for compromise solutions; the mind of the 1930s habitually favored either-or propositions. Thus if one side refused to see any virtue in the literature of social protest, the other proved equally unwilling to grant the writer some detachment from the problems of the day. If *Hound and Horn* advocated an extreme separation between art and society, the *New Masses* insisted that they be irrevocably fused. While Krutch and Tate argued that fiction and poetry were timeless, apolitical, and beyond the claims of any nation or group, Hicks and Gold demanded that art serve only the needs of the working class. In effect, the Formalists and the Communists were each seeking orthodoxy in a time of doubt and disorder. For the "new critics," literature became an end in itself with no social consequences whatsoever; for the radicals, literature was important precisely because it could affect human activities. But in either case the particular view of life was what counted; whether one wanted a perfect work of art or a perfect revolutionary message, culture was regarded as a suitable battleground on which to settle the issues of philosophy, politics, sociology, and morality. Ultimately, none of the combatants could really accept poetry, fiction, and drama on their own terms; instead, these became part of an aesthetic or ideological crusade to save mankind.

In the early 1930s, however, those who rejected proletarian literature were usually on the defensive. No matter how eloquently they celebrated the universality of art or the writer's dedication to his craft, they seemed unable to grasp that these ideals were simply less appealing to intellectuals at present than the desire to play a more direct role in American life. For most writers during the depression, the problem was not how to remain free but how to become committed. Power was not something to be feared but to be sought eagerly in the interest of transforming the world—even if this meant a temporary sacrifice of artistic excellence.

5. *The Radical as Critic*

While the positions of the Formalists and the Marxists seemed increasingly polarized and dogmatic, there was a third group of writers who tried to find a middle ground between the two extremes. Centering largely around the *New Republic,* they included liberals, radicals, and those without any ideological affiliation. To them, the issue was never art for art's sake versus art for humanity's sake; rather, they wished to determine exactly what services literature, as a unique form of communication, could render to man. In effect, they wanted to preserve the autonomy of culture while insisting on its relevance to politics and society.

Despite his flirtation with the Communist party and his occasional willingness to subordinate everything to the class struggle, Newton Arvin cared too much about the country's literary past to abandon artistic expression in the present. The business of the critic, as Arvin saw it, was not to argue about whether literature had a social role to play but rather to define that role more clearly in an age of revolution. Arvin agreed with Calverton and Freeman that every novel and poem had ideological consequences; the point was to discover which form of art most effectively advanced the cause of reform. Because he felt that intellectuals should concentrate on certain key issues uppermost in their own time (at the moment, class conflict) and because he insisted that their present attitude toward these questions must be shaped by a socialist perspective, Arvin remained a partisan of the proletarian aesthetic in the opening years of the decade. But he did not suppose that these ideas restricted the writer's freedom or that they would necessarily turn art into propaganda. On the contrary, he asserted, the proletarian novelist and poet were still interested in the most basic cultural and moral problems: the understanding of nature and man, the exposure of folly and injustice, the elimination of inhumanity, and the cultivation of communal ideals. In Arvin's judgment, the task of the revolutionary intellectual was to discredit the assumptions behind liberal capitalism as a means of improving the quality of life in America. In sum, the writer should engage in political action precisely in order to preserve the values of art and philosophy.[74] Beauty, rather than power, remained the ultimate end.

Where Arvin justified proletarian literature as a continuation of the artist's traditional concerns, others believed that the specific genre was less important than its general impact on the audience. They admitted that art could never be "useful" in the sense of converting men to a particular political program, but this did not mean that it had no utility at all. In their view, it was literature's function neither to respond in an ideologically stereotyped way to every passing crisis nor to document passively those imperfections in human life that seemed true for all time. "If a novel is to have a social effect," suggested a young Marxist critic named William Phillips, "it will come necessarily through its tracing of a shift in values from a position which is in some way identifiable with that of the reader's to one which is more humanly desirable and psychologically credible."[75] Similarly, John Dewey, in sharing the decade's passion to reintegrate art with the daily experiences of ordinary people (thereby overcoming the barriers between men and creating a new sense of community for everyone), rejected the notion that literature should teach man to accept his fate. For Dewey, culture was a "criticism of life" not because it resisted the pressures of social reform (as Allen Tate had claimed) but because it offered a different set of ideals from those that now prevailed; it gave mankind a glimpse of "possibilities that contrast with actual conditions."[76] To both Phillips and Dewey the duty of a novel or poem was to alter the emotional allegiances of the reader by comparing the present limitations of society with its future potential. Art was eternal precisely because it held out the hope of change.

There were some among this middle group who saw in Marxism a way of uniting the goals of both the Proletarians and their opponents. As the novelist Robert Cantwell pointed out, the American working class had not yet shown itself interested in serious art, but this did not imply that the writer should retreat into Bohemia or regard his labors as socially meaningless. The success of a work, he declared, had little to do with the size or nature of its audience in any case; its real value lay in the degree to which it advanced a particular reader's understanding of life as a whole.[77] As a result, argued Edmund Wilson, art must be judged on the basis of its craftsmanship as well as its social significance. Form could not be dissociated from content, as both the Left and the "new critics" seemed to

assume; a revolutionary consciousness depended as much on technical innovation and stylistic originality as on "correct" ideas. Furthermore, Wilson
went on, though no writer could divorce himself fully from society, neither
could he surrender completely to its demands. Instead he had to fulfill his
political obligations while at the same time adopting a critical stance toward
all existing values and institutions. The true vision of Marx and Engels,
Wilson reminded his contemporaries, absorbed and transcended the perspectives of nation and class. Marxism sought to create a culture which was
neither bourgeois nor proletarian but *human*.[78] Hence it drew on the best
traditions of both the capitalist and socialist worlds; it could be at once
"American" and avant-garde.

Arvin, Phillips, Dewey, Cantwell, and Wilson were all convinced that
thought preceded action, that progress depended on prior knowledge and
insight, that a revolution in values rather than a defense of established
doctrines (whether radical or conservative) was the principal task of art. In
their view, literature was indeed an instrument of change because it enabled
the individual to comprehend the chasm between current social arrangements and the ultimate possibilities of human life. By challenging and
hopefully transforming his deepest beliefs, art (however indirectly) could
indeed move man to act.

This conception of literature had obvious implications for the role of the
intellectual in other fields as well. Some writers in the early 1930s attempted
to show that they could maintain a dual commitment to radical politics and
to the life of the mind, that they could be both good citizens and good men.
Thus Matthew Josephson, citing the example of Emile Zola, contended that
the writer often owned two hats: one as a participant in mass movements,
the other as a man of letters. Each had its own criteria for excellence, each
carried separate responsibilities, and one should never try to wear both at
the same time. Josephson assumed that the intellectual could oscillate between the two positions without losing either his effectiveness or his sense
of identity.[79]

In a similar vein, the magazine *Symposium* sought to reconcile its interest
in cultural matters with a growing attraction to the Communist party.
James Burnham and Philip Wheelwright launched the journal in 1930 as
a forum for philosophy, logic, and the arts; its early articles were extremely
abstract and apolitical. But by 1932 the editors had become increasingly
defensive about their detachment from contemporary issues, so they began
to print more and more essays on Marxism. Finally in 1933, just before the
magazine ceased publication altogether and its contributors graduated to

more pressing matters, the editors presented a formal statement of where they now stood in relation to communism.

Like Josephson, Burnham and Wheelwright wished to distinguish between ideas and action, writers and workers. They were certain that the intellectual must commit himself to the revolution. But once having done so his main obligation was to deal with the "moral and spiritual" problems of America, while leaving social and economic policy to the politicians and activists. Apart from their conviction that the realms of theory and practice represented "genuinely different levels of being," they had a very practical reason for making this distinction. Given the sectarianism and vulgarity of Communist doctrine, Wheelwright observed, the radical intellectual could prevent other writers from being unneccessarily offended by translating the party's pronouncements into a persuasive and sophisticated ideology.[80] In this way he could serve the movement while remaining loyal to the special skills and concerns of the intelligentsia.

There were a few who felt that even this sort of commitment—however tenuous and qualified—did not correspond to the true interests of socialism or the intellectual. Both Sidney Hook and Kenneth Burke considered themselves Marxists; for a brief period they were strongly sympathetic to the Communist party. But they really valued their own independence above all else. Like Dos Passos, Hook warned that all political organizations were by their very nature a menace to unrestricted thought. In his opinion it was the function of parties either to justify the status quo or to campaign for reforms, but neither activity seemed conducive to the atmosphere of reason and logic in which writers naturally flourished. He therefore decided that a "passionate pursuit of disinterested truth" would lead to more genuine social enlightenment than an emotional involvement in a cause.[81]

Kenneth Burke went further. He suspected that the depression exposed the inadequacy of all doctrines and long-range programs. To him, the fundamental dilemma of the 1930s was not a lack of stable values and ordered planning but an almost religious need to believe in something regardless of its truth. Thus the hunger for faith, the emphasis on commitment, the longing for "certainty." The basic task of the intellectual, Burke suggested, might be to challenge whatever new truths arose. "If there is ever a millennium," he predicted, "it will be in the reign of doubt." In the meantime, it became the writer's duty to undermine propaganda of every sort by "fostering intellectual distrust."[82] In effect, Hook and Burke were advising the writer to withhold his allegiance from all political and social ideologies, as well as to stay clear of organizational ties. They did not advocate withdrawal from nor apathy toward the issues of the day, but both held that the intellectual could best hasten the victory of socialism by remaining skeptical of any party or belief that insisted on a single solution to all problems.

Perhaps the most detailed effort to locate a position midway between total isolation and total commitment was undertaken by the philosopher Benjamin Ginzburg in the *New Republic* during 1931 and 1932. Ginzburg was friendly to radicalism, but he did not want to surrender the intellectual's traditional prerogatives nor transform himself into an unthinking spokesman for the working class. At the same time, he understood the intense desire among writers to overcome their feeling of marginality by sharing in the daily lives of ordinary people.

Neither alternative seemed attractive to him. In comparing the position of the intellectual in America and in the Soviet Union, Ginzburg contended that "it is . . . the philosopher, the free critic and interpreter of human experience, who has the real grievance in both cases." Writers enjoyed great liberty in the United States, but they had no roots in the society and few means by which they could translate their ideas into effective action. The price of liberty was impotence. In Russia, on the other hand, they were directly engaged in building new institutions, but at the cost of the "intellectual freedom which the philosopher has regarded as the only end that makes socialism worthwhile."[83] Hence the writer found himself confronted with two unpleasant choices: Either he must limit his talents to the aim of influencing public policy or he could preserve his independence while sacrificing any opportunity to put his ideals into practice.

Ginzburg suggested a way out of this dilemma which involved the recognition that the concerns of the intellect and the demands of power were forever in conflict. Like Reinhold Niebuhr, Ginzburg believed the relationship between culture and politics, private morality and collective goals was inevitably paradoxical and full of tension. In his view, writers consistently misinterpreted their own unique function by assuming that programs of reform were "logically prior to everything else," that even personal salvation depended entirely on proper economic policies. Ginzburg characterized this tendency to subordinate art and ideas to the pressures of social change as a form of "messianism" among intellectuals; it led to a subjective analysis of contemporary problems in terms of some future myth, and it made a religion of politics at the expense of one's "crucial consciousness."[84]

Ginzburg held both liberalism and communism accountable for this "depreciation" of intelligence in favor of activism. Where socialists sought to judge all moral and cultural questions in reference to the class struggle and the coming revolution, the Progressives had attempted to ingratiate themselves with the American people to such an extent that they lost sight of the larger issues altogether. But both Marxism and Pragmatism seemed to Ginzburg the ultimate "anti-intellectualism of the American intellectual" overawed by the "practical sweep of American life." Ginzburg argued that the historical obsession of writers with public affairs reflected a pathological fear of being isolated from their fellow citizens. "In no [other] country of the world," he pointed out, "is there such a tremendous gap between the values recognized by intellectuals and the values that actually govern political and economic realities. And yet in no country is the intellectual so preoccupied with affecting the course of politics to the exclusion of his intellectual interests. The less power he has of determining conditions, the more passionate . . . is his will-o'-the-wisp quest for political influence."[85]

For therapy, Ginzburg recommended a return to the intellectual's primary duty of clarifying cultural values as distinct from pursuing doctrines and movements that promised immediate social relevance. This did not mean a retreat to the other extreme of complete indifference to the present crisis. Quite the contrary, he asserted, it was only through a careful cultivation of moral and philosophical ideals that intelligent political and social policies could emerge. Thus writers should protect their autonomy, keeping in mind that the connections between theory and practice were analogous to those between pure science and applied technology. By performing the role of nay-sayer, by exploring and debating issues whatever the consequences, by measuring the aims of all parties and programs against the vision of a truly human civilization, the writer could maintain both his freedom and his effectiveness in society. Above all, Ginzburg declared, the intellectual should remember that his fundamental responsibility was to act like an intellectual—not like a politician, an administrator, a labor leader, or a propagandist.[86]

In essence, Dewey, Wilson, Hook, and Ginzburg all believed that the intelligentsia had its own distinctive place which was as important to the socialist movement as the activities of a professional revolutionary or the militancy of the working class. In their judgment, the writer's special task was to be the custodian of ultimate values, the cultural conscience of the larger society. Through the ideal of the intellectual-as-critic they hoped to maintain their independence while fulfilling their responsibilities to America. Their solution to the problem of the writer's role was subtle and occasionally ambiguous. Its success required time and patience, neither of which the depression permitted. Instead the demands on the intellectual grew more intense as the decade wore on, until it became increasingly difficult to function either as a radical or a writer. But for the moment, at least, this represented the most sophisticated answer to the dilemma of how a man of thought could also be a man of action.

CHAPTER V

DOCUMENTARIES, FICTION, AND THE DEPRESSION

For all the theories about how literature might most effectively promote social change, for all the pronouncements about the proper relation of the writer to society, the art of the 1930s rarely conformed to the standards prescribed by critics in either the Formalist or the Proletarian camps. Although many would later claim that the general quality of American literature suffered during the decade because of an excessive reliance on ideological formulas, pointing specifically to the way in which authors dutifully reduced their novels to political tracts at the behest of cultural commissars in the Communist party, the more memorable works seem easily to have escaped this blight.

If anything, the party's influence was probably beneficial in some cases and irrelevant in others. Those with limited talent, like Jack Conroy and Robert Cantwell, wrote moderately interesting novels when they were closest to the Communists but ceased to produce any significant fiction at all after they broke with the party. Similarly, James Farrell, John Steinbeck, John Dos Passos, and Richard Wright enjoyed their greatest success while temporarily sympathetic to Marxism and never regained this level of excellence in the years of their disillusion. In contrast, the achievements of William Saroyan, Thomas Wolfe, Daniel Fuchs, and Nathanael West were in no way dependent on radical ideas of any kind. In any case, far from being a period of literary decline, the decade could boast in the efforts of William Faulkner and James Agee works which ranked among the finest of the twentieth century.

Ultimately the creative artists of the 1930s were responding to issues and values that had little to do with parties, politics, or ideology. Pessimistic about revolution, suspicious of collectivism, introspective in mood and approach, often nostalgic for the past, and instinctively conservative in outlook, they followed a different path from the rest of the intellectual community. Only one of their number, James Agee, was ever able to fuse the demands of radicalism with the concerns of art into a unified statement of the decade's social, cultural, and moral ideals.

1. *The Quest for the Social Fact*

Faced with the enormity of the crisis, some found it advisable to abandon literature altogether. As long as people remained jobless and hungry, the very occupation of writing seemed ineffectual, pointless, and even parasitical—an irrelevant luxury in an age of crushing necessities. Moreover, at a time of intolerable confusion and disorder, when men could neither explain the present nor anticipate the future, fiction appeared powerless to cope with reality. Since the depression resembled a sort of natural disaster whose causes were ambiguous and whose course was unpredictable, many Americans felt they had lost control over their institutions, their environment, and their lives. Unable to deal rationally with the world around them, uncertain about their relation to other men, they feared that their sense of personal identity and competence had been buried beneath the wreckage of the economy. In these circumstances, more than a few writers suspected that no form of art could impose order on chaos.

Instead they turned to journalism and documentaries, hoping merely to record the experience of a nation in upheaval. An extraordinary number of artists and critics (among them Edmund Wilson, Sherwood Anderson, Theodore Dreiser, John Dos Passos, Gilbert Seldes, Louis Adamic, Nathan Asch, and James Rorty) interrupted their other work to travel around America in search of the thoughts and aspirations of ordinary people— almost as though they might find solace in the discovery that writers shared with the average man a common feeling of bewilderment and despair. Inside the compulsively "proper" homes of the frightened middle class, down the dark alleys and dismal slums of a hundred cities, passing by the stagnant villages and farms of the South and Midwest, along the endless highways and county roads that led to nowhere, pausing briefly at the lonely gas stations and restaurants that served an entire society on the move, they watched and interviewed and listened to their fellow citizens. They picked up hitchhikers and heard the sad stories of failure that soon began to sound the same from state to state: factories shut down, jobs lost, mortgages foreclosed, the small store gone bankrupt, no more credit to till the soil. They attended local meetings and learned about the problems of erosion, drought, dust storms, exhausted land, and exhausted men. They wandered through union halls and assembly lines, becoming expert in matters of pay cuts, scabs, vigilantes, and strikes. Most of all they saw on every street corner and in every flophouse, down every mine shaft and in every family, the look of pain, amazement, and resignation on the faces of men and women trying desperately to survive.

Through it all they cherished the pure, unadorned "facts" of daily life. Before the simple human drama of the depression experience there was no need to embroider, to speculate, to theorize, to indulge in the conventions of "art." Talking to living people and observing their actual behavior seemed more important, and more honest, than creating fictional characters or issues. "With real events looming larger than any imagined happenings," one writer remarked, "documentary films and still photographs, reportage and the like have taken the place once held by the grand invention."[1] Indeed, the very imposition of political formulas or artistic devices would interfere with and distort the author's understanding of his world. Thus a rigorous objectivity became the norm. Rather than adopt the ideological or cultural preoccupations of their colleagues in the intellectual community, many writers chose to let the facts speak for themselves. In *The American Jitters* (1932) and *Travels in Two Democracies* (1936), Edmund Wilson rarely commented on what he saw or heard; he relied instead on direct narration and description, hoping this might evoke the appropriate feelings of horror and anger in his readers. Similarly, James Rorty explicitly disclaimed any intention to teach, moralize, or perhaps even think about his journey. "My trip," he asserted at the outset of *Where Life Is Better* (1936), "was an attempt to substitute physical motion for motions of the mind."[2] Wilson and Rorty wanted their words to correspond to specific events, not act as a gloss on experience. To go further, to employ complex ideas and sophisticated doctrines, was to violate reality.

This passionate urge to face and tell the absolute truth was not simply a reaction to the depression itself but also a way for the writer to solve some of his own personal and career problems. In the first place, the documentary form offered artists a chance to do something useful with their talents and hence relieve their feeling of guilt and marginality. By plunging headlong into American life, by faithfully recording the plight of their countrymen, they were providing the necessary information with which others might act.

At the same time, their exploration of the cities and the land represented a road out of loneliness and isolation. For a man like Edmund Wilson, who always "felt so little at home" in the modern world of machines and monopoly capitalism, who continually thought of himself as an "outsider," who longed for the more "dignified" customs and values of his nineteenth-century ancestors, documentaries were a means of adjusting to and becoming a part of contemporary society.[3] To travel across the continent was literally to duplicate the pioneer adventure and thereby to reassert one's identity and heritage as an American—a crucial goal for intellectuals in the 1930s.

Furthermore, their hunger for facts and their absorption in the details of social behavior appeared an effective antidote to the discord and uncertainty that plagued the entire nation. Journalism tried to deal with whatever was concrete, specific, and essential. Unlike art, it valued substance over images, experience over ideas, situations over symbols. Consequently it gave writers an opportunity to anchor their ideals and ambitions in definite places, people, and events; it permitted them to re-establish communication with their society; it helped them understand their relationship to the "facts" they discovered; and it held out at least a limited sense of order and security in a time when little else seemed real or clear.

Finally, the very advantages of the documentary technique—its emphasis on observation, narration, and unembellished prose—promised to alleviate private as well as public anxieties. In trying to describe the external world, writers sought also to restructure their own lives. The accumulation of facts and the sharing of experience were a means of coping with ambiguity on both the social and personal levels. By asking questions and gathering data, through travel and conversation, the writer might gain a greater knowledge of the country and himself. Ultimately, by portraying what he saw as truthfully and completely as possible, the artist could feel that he was engaged in a purposeful enterprise, that he had regained control over some portion of his life, that he had recovered his competence and self-respect. To this extent, the documentary became for many writers a natural response to social chaos and inner turmoil.

The commitment to truth, honesty, and objectivity forced them to confront America as it really was, not as liberal planners or socialist revolutionaries wished it to be. In their journey through the cities and the countryside, men like Wilson, Anderson, and Rorty had hoped to find support for their own radical convictions. Instead they discovered a nation full of variety and paradox, reacting to the crisis in wholly unexpected ways.

On the one hand, the depression revealed what everyone should have known before—that a civilization based exclusively on the desire for wealth and success was enormously wasteful in terms of economic resources and human lives. Thus Edmund Wilson was shocked and disgusted by the destruction of the land, the polluted air and rivers, the "primal, dismal, undifferentiated city grayness," the disintegration of families and the loss of personal dignity, all of which seemed endemic to capitalism in its death throes.[4] The stories of people he met turned into a litany of decay, defeat, and desolation. In the same vein, James Rorty was dismayed by the contradictions he saw in American society: twentieth-century technical productivity coexisting uneasily with nineteenty-century economic and social prejudices, the financial and organizational adventurousness of the country's entrepreneurs together with their rigid political conservatism, the obstinate persistence of the democratic dogma despite the realities of class stratification and centralized power.[5] And Sherwood Anderson, in *Puzzled America* (1935), found himself appalled by the degree to which the Protestant Ethic had warped the nation's psyche. Having been "taught from childhood that it is a sort of moral obligation for each of us to rise, to get up in the world," to "make two blades of grass grow where but one grew before," to avoid poverty and accumulate money as an "outward sign of inner merit," Americans were now learning that to be poor or unemployed was to suffer not only failure but personal disgrace. In Anderson's somber view, "the breaking down of the moral fiber of the American man, through being out of a job, losing that sense of being some part of the moving world of activity, so essential to an American man's sense of his manhood—the loss of this essential something in the joblessness can never be measured in dollars."[6] To Anderson, this obsession with national progress and individual achievement had always seemed perverse; by the 1930s, it was not only irrelevant but insane.

Yet the average American appeared unable to shake off his inherited attitudes and assumptions. The depression may have radicalized important segments of the intelligentsia, but it was having exactly the opposite effect on the rest of society. While writers searched for signs of revolt, the middle class lowered its standard of living, the workers prowled the hiring halls, and the farmers prayed for rain to end the drought and nourish next year's crop. "The amazing thing to be observed," Anderson mused, "is that there is so very little bitterness."[7] Failure encouraged not anger or militancy but shame; the unemployed blamed not the system but themselves.[8] Throughout the land, noted Wilson, "the people seemed dreary" and "curiously apathetic"; if they could not succeed, they felt somehow incompetent and worthless.[9] The longer the crisis lasted, James Rorty suspected, the more passive men became. In his opinion, the victims of the depression "did not even know the name of the disease from which they were suffering; did not know its causes let alone its treatment and cure. The word 'despair' did not describe their condition. Despair implies consciousness and they were too far gone for that." Instead, 95 percent of the population was living in a world of "make-believe," refusing to face the facts of their predicament, with no access to or interest in a radical critique of capitalism, dependent for their ideas and values on advertising and the Hearst press, addicted to Hollywood and the mass media as the only "unifying bonds" in American culture, unable to think or to act on their own. All of this left Rorty with a feeling of self-hatred and impotence, miserable because he could not make his countrymen aware of what was happening to them and half afraid that such knowledge would only cause them further pain.[10] What emerged most clearly from their travels through the hinterland was the recognition that the people were "wholly unprepared to make a revolution," that the Left had missed its opportunity to "enlighten" the masses and build a movement capable of seizing power, that time was running out even to rehabilitate democracy, that the nation was slowly drifting toward fascism and war.[11]

Nevertheless, their reports were neither entirely negative nor pessimistic. If the reality of American life did not correspond to their radical dreams, it had certain assets they learned to admire and prize. Indeed, what began as an effort to find out where the country had gone wrong frequently ended as a celebration of all that seemed right. The technique of exposure and criticism gradually gave way to a song of affirmation. In essence, most of the documentaries were rarely models of political or ideological analysis, nor were they indictments of the national character; rather, they read like road maps for the exploration of America. Their real subject was not failure but hope, not outrage but patience, not bewilderment but faith, not death but survival. Despite his cynicism and gloomy pronouncements about the coming of fascism, James Rorty was actually consoled by his trip; "I had rediscovered for myself a most beautiful land, and a most vital, creative, and spiritually unsubdued people."[12] The central experience of the depression years, as Rorty and others recorded it, was neither social change nor economic collapse but simple human endurance.

This theme was underscored in curious ways. Ironically, in the midst of an urban-industrial depression, when intellectuals were eagerly awaiting the emergence of working-class consciousness and a strong labor movement, the documentaries often concentrated on and romanticized the *agrarian* victims of capitalism. It was as though the crisis had inspired in many writers a renewed reverence for America's past, for its frontier heritage, for its nineteenth-century small towns and farms rather than for its socialist future. Where once Sherwood Anderson had excoriated rural life as harsh and repressive in *Winesburg, Ohio,* he now admitted that his travels through the South and Midwest had generated "a kind of nostalgia for the land." Somehow, he recalled, the clearing of forests and the struggle with the soil produced a feeling of accomplishment and self-respect "that factory work and clerkship haven't as yet been able to bring into men's lives."[13]

Thus it was not surprising that Anderson, Rorty, and Wilson should continually compare the militancy of the farmers, miners, and lumberjacks with the passivity of the urban proletariat. Without special skills or craft discipline, Rorty declared, with no understanding of the technological processes to which it was enslaved, the working class for whom radicals had so much hope was made up of little more than discouraged and beaten individuals. In contrast, those who labored alone or in groups of two seemed to possess more initiative and a greater sense of responsibility than those who were merely appendages to the assembly line. By the very "nature of their work," Wilson commented, the farmers and coal miners had never been "broken in to the abject life of the industrial cities"; they still enjoyed "a tradition of independence and joint action."[14] Consequently, the impetus for change would come from the men who battled the most elemental forces of nature rather than from those who tended machines.

Behind this rediscovery of rural virtue lay an assertion of faith in a simpler, innocent, uncomplicated America. It had become desperately important for writers to find something alive and good in the United States despite the breakdown of its modern, complex political and economic system. If they could locate a fundamental stability and resilience in the American people, they might again feel at home in their native land. This search for roots led them to praise not only the past but also the democratic instincts of the common man.

Americans, Anderson reported, had not given up on their government, nor were they skeptical about the motivations of their leaders. Throughout the country, he proclaimed, "there is a willingness to believe, a hunger for belief, a determination to believe." Far from moving toward radical solutions, "the minds of the people are fixed upon Roosevelt. Their hopes are in him." And it was this traditional faith in democracy that Anderson found both novel and exhilarating.[15] Similarly, when Edmund Wilson traveled to that other "democracy," the Soviet Union, he began to appreciate the uniqueness of American attitudes and ideals. He disliked the Bolsheviks' insistence on centralized control and the glorification of Stalin into an icon. As the Russian masses became better educated and more accustomed to socialism, he hoped they would grow more critical of the dictatorship and the official press, more capable of thinking for themselves, less docile and timid, more self-reliant—in effect, true democrats. In the meantime, despite the ugliness and brutality of capitalism, Wilson was ready to admit that America's republican institutions had "some permanent and absolute value."[16] Indeed, Anderson concluded his book on a note of supreme optimism. America might be "puzzled," but in contrast to the tyranny and fear that was spreading through Europe, she remained the hope of the world.[17] Thus their journeys were a form of homecoming; they resulted not in a reinforcement of their radical convictions but in a commitment to the land, to the people, to democracy, and to the entire national experience.

In Wilson's case, this act of rededication involved a return to the individualism of his ancestors. Wilson's radicalism had always seemed closer to Thoreau than to Marx, and he looked on socialism primarily as a method of liberating Emersonian values. He admired not the bureaucrats of the revolution but a civil libertarian like Roger Baldwin, who displayed a "truculent independence" and great personal integrity in defending the "non-conformity of others." Even when Wilson discussed the success of the Russian leaders, it was in terms of their "superior brains" triumphing over the "ignorance, the stupidity, and the shortsighted selfishness of the mass. . . ." Hence, he managed to praise Lenin not for carrying off a revolution and establishing a collectivist society but for compelling the world to "extend its conception of what man, *as man alone,* can accomplish." To Wilson, Lenin became a transcendental symbol of the refusal to defer to extra-human authorities (whether God or the dialectic); he represented the victory of the individual genius over external conditions. Like Reinhold Niebuhr, Wilson felt thoroughly ambivalent about communal ideals. Returning from Russia, he was overjoyed to assert his individuality "against those weeks of collective living." And in the spirit of Sidney Hook, he ended his report with an eloquent peroration on the centrality of personal action: "He who said, 'In His will is our peace,'—it was with his own will that he was reconciled; he who said 'Lord, forgive them!' it was he himself who had forgiven. And so . . . he who spoke in the name of the masses— it was he who gave them their soul."[18] For Wilson, as for other writers in the 1930s, the documentary yielded not only a sensitivity to the "facts" of daily life and a notion of one's place in America, not only a plunge into "reality" and an affirmation of national values, but also a recovery of personal control in an absurd and chaotic world. By discovering society they had discovered themselves—and thus the experience was as much existential as ideological.

2. *Novels of Protest, Politics, and the Proletariat*

If some writers found it necessary to abandon fiction for journalism, there were others who tried to adapt the methods of the documentary to the traditional concerns of art. This was especially true of the "proletarian" novel, which, whether or not it was written from a truly revolutionary perspective, exhibited many of the techniques of reportage: a preoccupation with the factual details of modern life, an emphasis on the function and relationship of groups and classes, an interest in social types and external events. Where it differed from conventional journalism was in the effort to invest contemporary issues with poetic (as well as political) significance and thereby to raise brute facts and naturalistic description to the level of art.

In many respects the proletarian novelist, like the proletarian critic, was revolting against the dominant literary values of the 1920s; in writing about the poor, the marginal, and the oppressed, he had much more in common with the social realists of the Progressive era than with Eliot or Fitzgerald. Moreover, his class origins and experiences were strikingly different from those of his immediate predecessors. Growing up in the shadow of urban ghettos, impoverished farms, and dying coal mines, he wanted to make modern literature address itself to *his* America.

Yet despite this desire to write in new ways about new subjects, the typical novelist of the 1930s owed an unconscious debt to the preceding decade. Like those who turned to documentaries during the depression years, the "radical" artist seemed ultimately less interested in investigating social problems than illuminating his own experience and feelings. Indeed the crisis inspired an outpouring of essentially autobiographical works: Malcolm Cowley's *Exile's Return,* Louis Adamic's *My America,* Michael Gold's *Jews Without Money,* Joseph Freeman's *An American Testament,* Woody Guthrie's *Bound for Glory,* Edward Dahlberg's *Bottom Dogs,* Jack Conroy's *The Disinherited,* James Farrell's *Studs Lonigan* trilogy, Henry Roth's *Call It Sleep,* Nelson Algren's *Somebody in Boots,* Henry Miller's *Tropic of Cancer,* William Saroyan's short stories, all the novels of Thomas Wolfe. In most of these cases the primary focus was private and introspective; the central event was not so much a conversion to revolutionary politics as an assertion of personal identity. In such works the author or character who could not understand himself would never understand society; his was a failure not of doctrine but of sensibility.

Ironically, these themes were most often sounded in novels explicitly concerned with politics and the working class. Though Jack Conroy's *The*

Disinherited (1933) was presumably written to illustrate a Marxist vision of the world, it more closely resembled an expatriate memoir in its emphasis on personal flight and search and in its treatment of young men symbolically exiled from their native land.

Narrated in the first person, the work was picaresque and episodic. Conroy's hero, Larry Donovan, wanders through middle America in pursuit of a permanent psychological and political home. Torn between the desire to rise above the workers and make a success of himself on the one hand and his lingering sense of class solidarity on the other, Larry undergoes a series of adventures designed to show that the ideals of Horatio Alger have become dangerous illusions in the modern world.

Yet a constant debate runs through the novel over whether the proletariat is genuinely revolutionary or hopelessly apathetic and defeated. Larry is continually warned by his friends that the workers can always be satisfied if given a "full gut," that they will be forever "gouged" by the bosses, that they are neither brave nor intelligent but docile and "perfectly content" with their lot, that they themselves dream of becoming capitalists some day.[19] Moreover, Larry's own experience validates these claims. Curiously, the most memorable portions of the novel are his cheerless descriptions of working-class life. A mine tipple reminds him of the "gallows," and he compares the mine itself to a "tomb"; the miners are invariably pictured as asthmatic and "deathlike"; factory labor is not only tedious and monotonous, but it transforms the men into "snarling ogres" for whom sex and sleep are merely temporary diversions; the assembly line extracts the "last ounce of energy" from its human "automatons" who continue to toil frantically with "dark shadows under their eyes" and "blackened lips" that resemble those of a "cadaver."[20] Given this confrontation with horror, decay, and death, the admonitions of Larry's friends seem not cynical but eminently realistic.

Nevertheless, he remains unconvinced. Though nearly every argument and episode in the novel points to the opposite conclusion, Larry decides to stick with his class. Renouncing his ambition to escape the factory, he declares himself a member of the "outcasts" and the "disinherited."[21] Since this decision is inexplicable and even irrational in terms of what happens as the story progresses, Larry's conversion becomes an act of personal will transcending society, politics, or ideology. And this is the ultimate irony. Starting out to compose a work of social consciousness, Conroy ended on a note of purely Romantic hope; the ego had triumphed over the world.

In Robert Cantwell's *The Land of Plenty* (1934), another work whose message was ostensibly radical, these contradictions were somewhat less disconcerting. In many ways *The Land of Plenty* was the decade's best novel about factory life—a noteworthy achievement since Cantwell was not a worker himself but a rather sophisticated essayist and literary critic who admired Henry James more than any socialist artist Granville Hicks could recommend. Moreover, his analysis of the class struggle owed more to Thorstein Veblen than to Karl Marx. But despite these doctrinal eccentricities, Cantwell set out to portray the education of a young worker and his conversion to the cause of socialism in terms that would please even the most dogmatic *New Masses* subscriber.

Cantwell's novel opened with a power failure in a lumber factory in the Northwest, which was itself a metaphor for the sudden collapse of the entire economic system. "There was no warning fading or flickering of the bulbs; there was only a swift blotting out of the visible world."[22] The resulting chaos symbolized the terror, uncertainty, and helplessness of the depression years. It also afforded Cantwell the opportunity to suggest that the proletariat was better equipped to run the nation's industrial plant than the incompetent and parasitical middle class. While the managers and the foremen could not accustom themselves to the new environment, groping blindly in the blackness and unable to find their way out of the crisis, the workers "moved casually through the dark, sure of their footing, knowing the floor around their machines as they knew their own houses. . . ." Like Veblenian technicians, they seemed intuitively sensitive to their surroundings and perfectly integrated with the processes of production. Thus "a hundred men moved without orders," instinctively "checking the thousand dangers . . . no foreman could ever see, had ever heard of, could not even imagine." The capitalists and their agents were "strangers" to the factory; no longer playing a functional role, they were literally sabotaging the country's technological potential through their sheer superfluity. Only the workers—themselves incipient engineers—were now capable of taking charge.[23]

Unlike most proletarian novelists, Cantwell did not depict the owners as particularly evil or oppressive; their conduct was far too inefficient and ludicrous to be considered deliberately exploitative. If anything, he characterized them as bloated with "age and weariness," soon to become "rotting" corpses over whom no one would mourn.[24] But their gravest crime, in Cantwell's eyes, was an irrational destruction of men and machines—an interference with the normal tempo of work. They were "wrecking something that had been built up out of years of practice and labor." The workers' task was therefore fundamentally conservative. They must expose and purge the corruption of the bourgeoisie and bring back that happy age when the factory "had run smoothly," humming "like a single, intricate machine . . . perfectly coordinated, perfectly timed." In so doing, they might restore to all men a sense of "pride at the way they worked, each man in his place, each tiny act fitting in perfect time with the swing and drive of the factory."[25]

At any rate, these were the lessons that Cantwell's hero was supposed to learn. The second half of the novel centered on a spontaneous sit-down strike in which a bewildered adolescent is initiated into manhood, sexually and politically. Just as a girl in the factory teaches him how to make love, so the strike gives him a feeling of fraternity and comradeship with his fellow workers. On the surface, Cantwell had rather neatly tied together the personal and social strands of his narrative.

But in the novel's closing pages, the formula disintegrated and the reality of the depression took over. For the most important fact about the strike was not that it heralded the coming of socialism but that it failed. The sit-down falls apart, organization disintegrates, the fledgling union is destroyed, and the workers are clubbed and driven from the factory. In this context of violence and catastrophe, the young man's conversion experience seems a noble but meaningless act. After the final defeat there is nothing left to do but "hit the road."[26] And so the novel concluded not with a vision of community but with the specter of a lonely individual drifting through the countryside in search of something he could never name. Like Conroy, Cantwell had written a radical novel which inadvertently demonstrated the irrelevance of radicalism, a novel about politics whose resolution was apolitical, a study of working-class life which relied in the end on personal commitment rather than collective action. Thus, beneath the proletarian façade of the 1930s lay the individualist foundations of the 1920s.

In trying to make art mirror the plight of the working class, writers like Conroy and Cantwell were constantly torn between the facts of the depression experience and their desire to conclude on a note of revolutionary optimism. Consequently their novels often appeared contrived and melodramatic. They were most effective in evoking the brutality and dehumanization of proletarian life but least successful in suggesting plausible alternatives to the existing order, or in inventing new techniques with which to express their anger at the status quo. As a result, their work was not truly "social" in form or content; rather, they utilized conventional prose, and they resorted to the classic theme of the solitary hero who responds to a crisis on the basis of his own inner strength and conviction.

Yet these traits were by no means unique to the "proletarian" artist. Indeed most of the novels written from a radical perspective were not concerned with the workers at all. Nor did they deal specifically with the problems of politics or social philosophy. In his massive trilogy *Studs Lonigan,* James Farrell concentrated not on the proletariat but on the Irish Catholic lower middle class. Moreover, he saw the turmoil in which the Lonigans found themselves as essentially cultural and psychological rather than economic. Farrell wanted to reveal the "concrete effects of spiritual poverty" on a section of the American bourgeoisie—the meagerness of their moral resources, the banality of their aspirations, the narrow range of their emotions.[27] Thus he studied the deterioration of the home, the family, the church, and the schools, not only as formal institutions but as guides to life. In his view, the Lonigans suffered as much from a general collapse of values as from the social dislocations of the depression years. Their personalities seemed more vulnerable than their pocketbooks to the depredations of the larger society, and they were left with only the street and the poolroom to supply the necessary rituals and sense of community no longer available in the official culture. In effect, they were victimized not by the failure of American capitalism but by the bankruptcy of the American Dream.

Like his journalistic counterparts, Farrell had a limitless capacity for observation and detail. Having himself grown up in the slums of Chicago, he remembered everything—the incessant chatter that passed for family conversation, the hollow pretentiousness of parish priests, the vacuity of parochial schools, the sexual repression in the name of religious morality, the need to prove oneself against the local bully, the blustering camaraderie of the saloon and the brothel, the loss of youth and the monotony of middle age, the scramble for position and the tawdry symbols of self-esteem, the dependence on the radio and the motion picture to provide a vicarious feeling of love and success, the growing number of wakes for friends and the haunting fear of one's own imminent demise.

But Farrell's supreme achievement was to compress this raw data into the character of Studs Lonigan. Far from becoming a prisoner of his facts and his memories, Farrell was always in control of his material, always certain of the point he wished to illustrate, always able to subordinate the incidents of his narrative to a single purpose. For in coming to terms with his past, Farrell was making a bid for freedom; he needed to know precisely what he thought about Studs in order to mark the distance he himself had traveled. And so the novel was as much a diary of Farrell's private pilgrimage as an epic of social protest.

Farrell refused to take the easy road. From the beginning, his attitude toward Studs was marked by ambivalence and even respect. He never allowed his central character to become a one-dimensional cipher or a target for satire and ridicule. Studs's life may have been stunted, but he remained human; his hopes may have been pathetically ordinary, but they were never ignoble.

For the most part Studs is a creature of his time and place. He desires all the things the society teaches him are valuable and necessary: money, power, recognition, status. Hence he continually thinks of himself as in a race for some illusive reward; he is constantly measuring his progress in the eyes of others; he wants desperately to be "noticed," as though his success can only be certified by the crowd; his fights—real and imaginary—become symbols of the competitive world in which he is trapped.[28] Moreover, with the decline of the family and the church as models of moral virtue, his personality and ideals are shaped by the newspapers, the radio, and the movies. Studs is painfully inarticulate; he does not know how to communicate what he feels; the appropriate words "never came to him when he wanted them to"; his true thoughts and emotions are "completely padlocked in his mind."[29] As a result he is forced to rely on the received opinions and language of the media. He carries in his head snatches of popular songs and images from the screen which translate his private aspirations into socially acceptable forms of behavior. Absorbed into mass society, his imagination and identity are tied inextricably to public "events."

Yet Studs is not totally a product of his environment. There are parts of his personality which seem somehow pure and untouched by the pressures of his culture, his friends, and his ambitions. Beneath the desire to fit in there is the yearning to be different. In his most secret moments Studs admits to being a "stranger" among people who "really did not know what went on inside of him, and how he felt about many, many things."[30] Faced with the bleak routine of his daily life, he feels vaguely restless and dissatisfied: "There were lots of things in life he'd been missing. . . . He wanted more and [believed] that somewhere there was something else for him in life." But he has no way of giving a name to his "destiny," no idea of how to be genuinely happy, no words to express what is really "bothering" him beyond the conventional desire to "be" someone important. At most, he can only try to emulate the successful men whom "everyone knew and respected" while holding on desperately to the Algerist faith that "a man could have anything in this life . . . he wanted if he had the guts to go after it."[31] In essence, Studs treasures his whims and fantasies, but the society provides no channels for their realization. Thus he remains stifled and incomplete, his inner values thwarted by the mediocrity and shallowness of the only world he knows.

There is, however, one moment when Studs feels whole and "at peace" with the world. In the summer following his graduation from high school

he is able to throw off the artificial standards and inhibitions of the surrounding culture. Temporarily unashamed of his body and his "goofy"
thoughts, "he felt that the things he saw were part of himself, and he felt
as good as if he were warm sunlight; he was all glad to be living, and to
be Studs Lonigan."[32] The high point of this interlude is an idyllic afternoon
with "Lucy," a girl who represents for Studs what Daisy Buchanan became
for Gatsby: a "saint or a beautiful queen, or a goddess," symbolizing all his
hopes and dreams, however distorted and unreal. Thereafter she fades into
the past, a nostalgic reminder of everything Studs has lost and can never
recover.[33]

Indeed most of the trilogy is concerned with the passage of time and the
process of decay. Studs is growing up and growing old; more and more his
thoughts turn to the past as a refuge from a dismal present and frightening
future. Immobilized by physical infirmities and spiritual ennui, by bad lungs
and a purposeless life, he begins to think increasingly of his own death. He
becomes obsessed with his health, with the condition of his heart and his
stomach, with the fear of dying, with the sense of riding an "express train
. . . carrying him nearer and nearer" to a "waiting grave."[34] And it is
through these preoccupations that Studs comes to function as a model for
the disintegration of the old world, the gradual decline of the middle class,
and the ultimate collapse of the capitalist ethic. For with the onset of the
depression, Farrell brought his story full circle. Just as the first two novels
had connected Studs's youth with the early years of the twentieth century,
emphasizing the turbulence and hysteria beneath their surface optimism, so
the concluding novel (appropriately entitled *Judgment Day*) illuminated
the despair and desperation of the 1930s. The time for confession and
repentance was at hand, and here Farrell blended Marxism with an old-
fashioned Catholic sense of sin and retribution.

As Studs wanders aimlessly through the cold, wet streets of Chicago,
"killing" time, searching for nonexistent jobs, hoping to solve his problems
with one last flyer on the stock market, baffled and terrified by a world he
no longer understands, he begins to recognize the futility of his efforts to
"get anywhere." He is indistinguishable from millions of others in the same
predicament, but for him there is no consolation and no escape except
through death. Unable to imagine any course of action, "trapped" and
"beaten" by the very values he had always cherished and never questioned,
Studs falls into a coma in which the institutions and ideals that shaped his
life appear as lunatic and absurd: the inanities of school captured by the
"twisted face of a maniac" wailing in "toothless idiocy," the hypocritical
church represented by a Pope "dropped unceremoniously on his buttocks,"

the nation itself materializing in the figure of George Washington clothed "in moth-eaten rags . . . and a bartender's towel wrapped around his gray wig," the dreariness of family life summarized by his sister "with a pregnant belly" prattling mindlessly that "Cleanliness is next to Godliness."[35] With this macabre procession, Studs's final illness becomes a metaphor for the passing of a decadent and senile America.

Yet amid these scenes of stagnation and decay, Farrell pointed apocalyptically to revolution as an act of life and purification. At the very moment Studs expires, a Communist demonstration suggests the birth of proletarian power and the hope of a new world. Moreover, Farrell briefly introduced the character of Danny O'Neill, who, alone among the Irish of Chicago, seems capable of breaking the chains that bind him to the ghetto, who can miraculously triumph over his "rotten" and "stupefying" environment, who will dedicate himself to "truth and honesty" by becoming a writer. Like Farrell, Danny would "purge himself completely of the world he knew," destroy the past "with a pen," drive the terrible memories "out of his consciousness with a book."[36]

Thus in the transcendent symbols of a mass movement and the artist-as-hero, Farrell had ended his pilgrimage and discovered the means of his own salvation. If neither of these episodes flowed logically from the narrative, if indeed the reader was more likely to recall the pervasive images of horror and death as negations of every human deed and aspiration, if the victims of the American Dream seemed more real and appealing than the priests of the revolution, this only revealed once again that novelists like Farrell were better equipped to describe the present than to imagine the future. For beneath his urgent need to believe that things might be different lay a profoundly pessimistic notion of what man could actually accomplish. And so Studs, struggling to articulate his deepest feelings, dimly aware that there was something more in life than drinking and dying, but imprisoned forever by his culture and society, was ultimately truer to Farrell's vision than the mythic Danny O'Neill.

Given the difficulties which many radicals encountered in building a socialist movement during the 1930s, the effort among novelists to be totally factual and accurate in their portraits of American life was bound to suffer; when Conroy, Cantwell, and Farrell spoke of the revolution, their language necessarily became allegorical. In part this was because few artists had much familiarity with formal social concepts, nor did it seem the business of a novel to propose a plan of action. Moreover, writers might use journalistic techniques to disclose and clarify the experience of a nation in crisis, but to be consistent they could not invent solutions that had no basis in reality. Yet beyond the natural limitations of their material, a surprising number of novelists—including those whose sympathies lay with the Left —drew back instinctively from the issues of the day. In their eyes the social conflicts of the decade receded before the symbols and metaphors of America's past, contemporary economic problems took on epic connotations, and the daily headlines became a timeless commentary on the state of the national soul.

Nowhere did these tendencies appear more powerful than in Ernest Hemingway's treatment of the Spanish Civil War. Here was an event rich in social texture, diplomatic intrigue, and ideological complexity. At stake were not only the survival of a Republican Spain and the future of Europe but also the strategy and tactics of the Left. In the works of European writers (Malraux's *Man's Hope,* Orwell's *Homage to Catalonia,* Koestler's *Spanish Testament*), the struggle was presented in all its dimensions— political, economic, and human. But for Hemingway, the war was not so much a test of revolutionary ideas as a challenge to one's conscience and integrity—a measure of the individual's capacity to think and act as a moral man.

For Whom the Bell Tolls was published in 1941, long after the Spanish suffering had ended and the world was facing its own great agony, but Hemingway deliberately set his novel in the summer of 1937 when a Loyalist victory still seemed possible even as the signs of defeat were spreading. At this point both the political and psychological pressures were most intense. Hemingway's characters swayed feverishly between the extremes of utopianism and hopelessness, faith and cynicism, euphoria and despair. And it was the very inconsistency of the Spanish people as he presented them—their nobility as well as their treacherousness, their camaraderie as well as their suspicion of foreigners and "outsiders," their ingenuity as well as their lack of cohension and aversion to discipline, their courage as well as their inefficiency and insubordination, their endurance as well as their instability—that presaged their ultimate tragedy. In the sad but sinister figure of Pablo, the guerrilla leader who has lost the taste for fighting, who understands immediately that Robert Jordan's orders to blow up a bridge to facilitate the Republican offensive are suicidal, whose only commitment is to himself and his band, who is at once more cowardly and more practical than anyone else in the novel, these contradictions are inescapable. "There is no people like them when they are good," Jordan observes in the voice of Hemingway, "and when they go bad there is no people that is worse."[37]

For Jordan, the problems of the war and the incidents of his life are compressed into four days. But under the supreme pressures of the present, with no "yesterday" and no "tomorrow," the classic Hemingway preoccupations take precedence over Spain itself; in the short time allotted to him, Jordan must find out how to live and how to die.[38] As the moral center of the novel, he is an unusual hero for an age presumably dedicated to groups and classes, organizations and movements. Jordan wears no uniform and is a member of no army; instead he is an "irregular," always operating behind enemy lines, a man with "orders" but essentially a guerrilla fighting on his own.[39] In effect, the Spanish war offers Jordan a last opportunity to assert himself as an individual against the world's chaos, injustice, and absurdity.

Significantly, Jordan is neither an intellectual nor an ideologue. He keeps reminding himself that he is a "bridge-blower . . . not a thinker." He refuses to permit the official theories behind the conflict to "interfere" with his "work"; instead he takes pride in his ability to concentrate on a given task and to do the job well.[40] He is committed not to a "cause" but to his craft. Whenever he is questioned about his politics, Jordan becomes either inarticulate or embarrassingly platitudinous, and these intervals are usually the weakest part of the novel. Far from accepting the dialectic or Marxism or the concept of a planned society, he will admit only to being an "antifascist." Yet at bottom Jordan is an old-fashioned democrat, a hater of authority who feels that "all people should be left alone and [that] you should interfere with no one," a simple Jeffersonian who believes in "Life, Liberty, and the Pursuit of Happiness." Ultimately, he fights for the Republic because it symbolizes the "dignity and the rights of all men to work and not be hungry" and because it may possibly free the individual from a rigid church and bureaucratic government, but this is the extent of his political and economic vision. After the war he hopes to "discard" the rest of the slogans and let others tend to the details of social reconstruction.[41]

Moreover, the war itself raises issues that cannot be explained or justified in ideological terms. The very violence of the struggle, the need to kill people in the interest of some higher cause, the tragic confusion between means and ends, these become more important than the principles for which the war is officially waged. In Hemingway's eyes the central problems of the conflict are primarily moral. Jordan is continually confronted with the necessity of carrying out military commands which expose the Spanish people to intolerable dangers and which violate his own ethical responsibilities. He learns that armies dehumanize men and release in individuals a capacity for evil that transcends all philosophies. Neither the Republicans nor the Fascists are immune from the temptation to slaughter one another, and in this they are morally—if not politically—indistinguishable. "It is only [the] orders that come between us," Jordan reflects. His opponents are not "fascists. I call them so but they are not. They are poor men as we are. They should never be fighting against us and I do not like to think of the killing." Yet Jordan recognizes that, in order to win, the Loyalists must consciously adopt the tactics of the enemy. By holding to their original ideals they court defeat, so they will have to surrender those ideals even if this leads to a hollow victory. Thus he comes to regard the war, whatever its announced objectives, as basically irrational with everyone a victim of its insane demands.[42]

In these circumstances the individual's survival depends on his ability to suppress his private qualms before the pressures of the moment. To Jordan, this means that one should accept "Communist discipline for the duration of the war," not because their social programs are correct but because they have the soundest military strategy and most efficient organization. Temporarily, he decides to "follow orders" and "try not to think beyond them," for this is the only way the struggle can end. But though he grants the priority of collective action over personal conscience, though his "mind is in suspension until we win," Jordan insists that "nobody owned his . . . faculties for seeing and hearing, and if he were going to form judgments he would form them afterwards."[43] For Hemingway, the best Jordan can do in a morally impossible situation is perform his duty, protect his integrity, and avoid the lofty rationalizations of the bureaucrats and theoreticians— the true madmen of the modern world.

Throughout the novel Hemingway refused to take seriously the doctrinal controversies and factional debates which pervaded the Loyalist cause. He dismissed Communists, Trotskyites, and Anarchists alike as "crazies," preferring instead the more cynical journalists and apolitical generals to the visionaries of the Left. Insofar as he was willing to shift his focus from the personal behavior of his characters to the larger issues of the war, Hemingway portrayed Spain through a series of metaphors only an American could really understand.

Within the framework of *For Whom the Bell Tolls* the war became a struggle between men and machines, nature and industrialization, the past and modernity, culture and civilization. On one side was the natural simplicity and primitive heroism of the peasants: Anselmo's instinctive wisdom, Pablo's love of horses, Pilar's image as an archetypal earth mother, the freedom and spontaneity of the guerrillas together with their hostility to large organizations and regimented armies, Spain itself as a symbol of man's closeness to the soil and his need for an organic community. On the other side were the Fascist planes, blotting out the sky, "moving over the land as the shadows of sharks pass over a sandy floor of the ocean," bringing a routine and impersonal death to El Sordo's band, an advance guard for the tyranny and repression of the twentieth century, harbingers of a "mechanized doom" from which the peasants could have no deliverance. The bombers that terrify Pilar, the artillery shell that fatally wounds Jordan, the sophisticated weaponry that Anselmo never comprehends, these are the instruments of men who had turned from the earth to the machine, who had rejected the values of an agrarian past for the glories of a technological future. Anselmo wants desperately to "take away [the Fascists'] planes, their automatic weapons, their tanks, their artillery, and teach them dignity," but this is plainly impossible. Paradoxically, the Loyalists themselves would have to modernize, accept the demands of authority and discipline, exchange their arcadian dreams for the mechanical nightmare of the present. But this could destroy the very qualities of Spain which Hemingway found so appealing. Where European radicals anticipated a reconciliation between men and machinery, Hemingway left the dilemma unresolved. He continued to fear the dehumanization that was bound to come with "progress."[44]

In effect, Hemingway was looking at Spain through typically American eyes. His emphasis on the conflict between nature and civilization lay firmly within the tradition of nineteenth-century Romanticism; it had little to do with contemporary social or economic issues. Though *For Whom the Bell Tolls* was supposed to mark Hemingway's conversion to collectivism, though Robert Jordan (unlike his famous predecessors, Jake Barnes and Frederick Henry) finds a cause worth fighting and dying for, though he proclaims his feeling of "absolute brotherhood" for "all of the oppressed of the world," though death is no longer an irrational accident but an experience with purpose and meaning, these discoveries bear no relation to organized society. Instead, the comradeship Jordan finds among the peasants transcends ideology and institutions; his ability to merge with other people and conquer his sense of loneliness becomes believable only in his love for Maria.[45] This was as far as Hemingway could go in embracing the values of the 1930s. And ironically, at the conclusion of a novel about the major political event of the decade, Robert Jordan is left alone, "completely integrated" not with people but with the landscape (where at the beginning he was forced to "study" the countryside from a map), struggling in classic Hemingway fashion to meet his end without fear and with dignity, a solitary guerrilla dying a separate death as the fictional heroes of the 1920s had made a separate peace.[46] While Hemingway clearly wished to demonstrate that the bell tolled for all mankind, he could never quite lose his sympathy for the isolated individual, making the revolution on his own terms and for his own reasons, matching his personal skill and courage against the men in ranks, protecting himself against the annihilating forces of the twentieth century.

In trying to cope artistically with the complex and unprecedented social problems of the 1930s, Hemingway seemed always more at ease with traditional images and values than with the radical ideas of his counterparts in the intellectual community. And among novelists on the left, he was not alone. Indeed a surprising number of works, despite their being set in the present time, did not have very much to do with the difficulties of modern life—at least as they were experienced in cities, offices, factories, and department stores. The real heroes of the "radical" novel, as of the documentaries, were neither the industrial proletariat nor the white-collar middle class but tenant farmers, sharecroppers, migrant workers, rural and small-town folk —literally, the descendants of the pioneers. These were the ultimate outsiders—not the working class with its secret bourgeois aspirations, its willingness to ally with the New Deal, and its unbreakable enslavement to machinery and assembly lines. Given the assumption that farmers were the greatest victims of the depression, it seemed logical that they would be the ones most likely to revolt. More important, by concentrating on the men who sprang from the land, artists could subscribe to the ideals of the revolution at the same time they preserved the oldest of American myths.

Yet this dual allegiance had ambiguous implications. In Erskine Caldwell's *Tobacco Road* (1932), the plight of the sharecroppers received a treatment that was both sympathetic and satirical. Jeeter Lester and his family are at once ironic and incredibly sad, larger than life but fundamentally pathetic in their passions and fantasies. Occasionally, Caldwell interrupted his story to "explain" their predicament: the century-long depletion of the soil, the inability to adopt more scientific methods of tilling the fields, the cycle of poverty the Lesters could never escape. And he suggested "co-operative" farming as an antidote to the individualism of the past.[47] But these economic lessons always seem superfluous to the main theme of the novel: Jeeter's inherited love of the land and his refusal to change or to leave. "I can't move off to the cotton mills like the rest of them do," he broods. "The land has got a powerful hold on me." Farming "is the one thing in his life he tried to do with all the strength in his mind and body." Jeeter would "rather die of starvation," agonizing over his unplowed fields, failing year after year to raise credit for seed and fertilizer, than flee to the city. For Caldwell, the supreme indignity of the depression is that it prevents men like Jeeter from "growing things in the ground"; instead it drives them off the soil, forces them to "stand on planks in buildings all the time, and walk around on hard streets" where they lose interest in their work and in themselves, condemns them in effect to a slow death.[48]

Nevertheless, the experience of being uprooted from the land and the impossibility of functioning any longer in traditional ways leads not to social action in *Tobacco Road* but to a mood of uselessness and futility. Jeeter is a victim of processes beyond his comprehension. "He still could not understand why he had nothing, and would never have anything, and there was no one who knew and who could tell him. It was the unsolved mystery of his life."[49] Despite the allusion to cooperatives, there is little expectation that the sharecroppers might join together to deal with their common problems. So Jeeter remains passive, waiting for something to turn up, hoping God will "take notice" and "make the rich give back all they've took from us poor folks."[50] In the meantime, he sleeps away his final days, dreaming of revenge but helpless to save his farm or his family from total disintegration. Ironically, the Lesters are so far "outside" society that they are unable to act at all. Thus the most Caldwell could ask of his readers in the end was not anger but empathy, not outrage but laughter, not optimism but pity.

If Caldwell sounded curiously ambivalent about his agrarian protagonists, treating them with a mixture of grief and ridicule, John Steinbeck felt no such reservations. In the decade's most celebrated novel, *The Grapes of Wrath* (1939), he managed to combine many of the attitudes his generation held dear: a respect for the nation's enormous economic potential together with a feeling of horror at its misuse, a renewed interest in political questions together with a concern for human survival, an insistence on social change together with a reverence for cultural tradition. Unlike other protest novels, *The Grapes of Wrath* was an instant best-seller, appealing equally to radicals, intellectuals, literary critics, and the general public. No other work seemed to capture more effectively the essence of the depression experience. By 1940 it had been made into an immensely popular and beautiful film, with nothing apparently lost in the transition from John Steinbeck to John Ford. Yet the very ease with which the novel was accepted meant that it had struck some familiar chord in the national consciousness, some deep yearning for the world as it had been rather than as it might become. Paradoxically, in a period when radicals were obsessed with the future, when literature was being asked to serve the revolution, *The Grapes of Wrath* called on men to remember their roots and protect what they had. But in a decade characterized as much by a crisis of values as a failure of institutions, this was precisely what people wanted to hear.

Part of the reason for the novel's success was its style and organization. Steinbeck indulged in a good deal of biological symbolism, emphasizing the similarities between human and animal life when conditions were most difficult, underlining the distinctions between men and beasts when the hardships momentarily abated. In addition, he was extraordinarily sensitive to the techniques of the film and the documentary. The interchapters revealed a journalist's appreciation of road signs, place names, facts and figures, conversations in restaurants and gas stations, the sounds and smells of America in the 1930s. Moreover, the images of exhausted farms and menacing tractors, the procession of jalopies along Highway 66, the lyrical portrait of the California valley were all reminiscent of Pare Lorentz. Finally, Steinbeck's characters rarely seemed introspective. Since they were supposed to be products of a distorted environment, he was more interested in their external behavior than in their subjective emotions. Thus he relied heavily on spoken dialogue and physical action—both of which were easily adaptable to the screen. These devices—biological as well as cinematic—helped Steinbeck invest the story of the Joads with universal significance.

Like Caldwell, Steinbeck was preoccupied with the impact of the depression on agrarian ideals. In many ways *The Grapes of Wrath* was a nostalgic hymn to the nation's past. Steinbeck's heroes displayed all the values of an earlier time—an intimate relationship to and love for the land, a firm conviction that "if a man owns a little property, that property is . . . part of him," an unshakable belief that the greatest evil of capitalism was its dependence on mechanization (symbolized by the "machine man, driving a dead tractor," taking the "wonder" out of work, turning the farmers into migrants), an intuitive awareness that men like Muley and Grandpa Joad would surely die when they were forced to abandon their native homesteads.[51]

Steinbeck thought he saw in the historic suffering of the Okies a metaphor for all the problems of the 1930s. But he was never quite able to locate the underlying cause of the crisis, nor to say clearly who was responsible for the crime of want amid plenty. For Steinbeck, the ultimate blame rested not so much with capitalism but with the whole tenor of modern life—its complexity and interdependence, its worship of profit and efficiency at the expense of any direct contact with the earth, its creation of impersonal institutions that gradually became "monsters" no one could possibly control. Yet if the culprit was modernity itself, it made no difference whether or not the social system might be changed. Thus when one dispossessed farmer demanded to know "who can we shoot," Steinbeck had no answer.[52] At most he could only suggest that once men had lost their roots in the soil they were in danger of losing everything else as well.

Indeed the novel was largely an elaboration of this insight. Though Steinbeck provided a smattering of rural sociology and contemporary economics, he was principally concerned with the human consequences of soil erosion, dust storms, and foreclosures. The story of the Okies had epic connotations because it dealt with the most elementary questions of man's fortitude and endurance. For the Joads the basic issue is not whether they may find jobs in California but whether the men will remain unbroken and whether the family can stay intact. Those with the natural instincts for survival are best equipped to accept the pain and tragedy of their situation, yet keep on going. And it is Ma Joad who recognizes more clearly than anyone else that, with the destruction of the land, there is nothing worth saving except the integrity of the clan.[53] As the Joads journey westward, with the truck having become the center of their lives and the highway their new home, no longer pioneers or farmers but "refugees" from machinery and industrialization, symbols of an entire nation "in flight" along Route 66, Ma alone is able to instill in her brood a sense of common purpose and thereby prevent the family from falling apart. Hence the Joads reach California as migrants but not as "shif'less" bums, searching for work and offended by affronts to their dignity, economically unstable but spiritually whole.[54]

Nevertheless, their odyssey does not end once they glimpse the promised land. It is not enough that the Joads survive their trek across the continent; they are still propertyless, and so they must discover some further reason for continuing to exist as a family unit. At this point the quest takes on vague political and social overtones. As they wander through the fertile orchards of the Salinas Valley, sharing their food and shelter and dreams with other families equally oppressed, it is the preacher Casy who illuminates the meaning of their experience. Unable to believe any longer in conventional religion, Casy is looking for a new faith rooted in ordinary human needs. "I'm gonna be near to folks," he proclaims. "I ain't gonna try to teach 'em nothing. I'm gonna try to learn." The love between man and wife, the raising of children, the impulse to help one another, the simple "poetry of folks talkin'"—these are the values that he comes to cherish, and they are echoed throughout the novel. Before his death Casy has a vision of the human community—the idea that "all men got one big soul ever'-body's a part of," the belief that true holiness depends on men "workin' together, not one fella for another fella"—which in his martyrdom he passes on to the Joads.[55] They in turn begin to realize that their misery and loss are somehow universal. "Use' ta be the fambly was fust," Ma observes. "It ain't so now. It's anybody. Worse off we get, the more we got to do."[56]

Consequently the principle of cooperation extends beyond the single family to embrace everyone they meet.

It is in the government camp—the political and moral center of the novel —that Steinbeck's basic philosophy comes into focus. Here the Joads find a temporary haven from poverty and powerlessness. The camp is an almost utopian model of a planned economy, a natural community built on shared responsibilities and collective effort, an experiment in self-government with implications for the entire society. Moreover, in the camp people are no longer selfish or "mean"; they "are getting used to being treated like humans."[57] And through the twin symbols of Casy and the camp, the novel offers its most explicit political message. The experience of men cooperating in work and pleasure, recognizing the necessity of moving from " 'I' to 'we,' " learning that the "hunger" of a single person for "joy and some security" can be "multiplied a million times," understanding that fear and failure may be turned to wrath and retribution, these suggest to Steinbeck that some form of revolution is indeed possible in America.[58] Thus the novel ostensibly concludes with Tom Joad's eloquent declaration of commitment to his fellow man: "I'll be ever'where—wherever you look. Wherever they's a fight so hungry people can eat, I'll be there. Wherever they's a cop beatin' up a guy, I'll be there. . . . I'll be in the way guys yell when they're mad an'—I'll be in the way kids laugh when they're hungry an' they know supper's ready. An' when our folks eat the stuff they raise an' live in the houses they build—why, I'll be there."[59]

Yet for all its bitterness toward the system of private profit, its references to the rising anger of the masses, and its defense of communal ideals, *The Grapes of Wrath* was not really a political novel at all. In the end it is not Tom's conversion to action that lingers in the mind but Ma Joad's innate capacity to confront every misfortune with courage and honor. "We keep a-comin,' " she comforts Tom. "We're the people that live. They ain't gonna wipe us out. Why, we're the people—we go on."[60] What Steinbeck had portrayed in the heroic figure of Ma, as well as in the novel's final image of Rose of Sharon giving the milk meant for her dead baby to a starving stranger, was not the need to act but the will to survive. And what made the novel so moving and so popular was its fervent belief in the natural goodness and inevitable triumph of the "people," quite apart from their adherence to any specific program or ideology. It was therefore fitting that Casy and Tom should seem to be motivated more by their love for the ordinary folk than by a conversion to political consciousness. In effect, the Joads were mythic creations; they spoke for no particular class or economic doctrine but for all humanity. Their victory was assured not because of anything they or their readers might do but simply because they represented the indestructibility of mankind.

If such optimism was unwarranted either in the structure of the novel (the Joads, after all, are forced to leave the government camp and continue their unhappy journey through California, encountering more and more hardships along the way), or in the actual experience of the depression itself, this did not detract from the essential appeal of *The Grapes of Wrath.* On the contrary, in celebrating the inner strength and endurance of the common man, the novel offered its readers what they appeared to want and need —hope rather than analysis, faith rather than ideology, affirmation rather than militance. Thus it was neither surprising nor inappropriate that an Irish Catholic conservative like John Ford could transfer *The Grapes of Wrath* to the screen without violating the "radical" sentiments of John Steinbeck. For both men were saying the same thing—that in a crisis like the depression patience was ultimately more important than revolution, a respect for tradition more compelling than the hunger for social change.

3. *Visions of the Apocalypse*

If works like *For Whom the Bell Tolls, Tobacco Road,* and *The Grapes of Wrath* seemed unconsciously conservative despite the radical intentions of their authors, there were other novelists in the 1930s whose social attitudes were neither revolutionary nor traditionalist but apocalyptic. For writers like Henry Roth, Dalton Trumbo, Horace McCoy, Nelson Algren, and Nathanael West, the depression was not an opportunity to uncover facts and explore America; instead, it drove them beyond the reality of people and places into a world of dreams, hallucinations, and fantasy. The characters in their novels were not heroic specimens of human courage and endurance; rather, they were often mad, grotesque, mystical, and surreal. To these artists the 1930s was a time of unbearable cruelty and terror, an age that demanded not the eye of a journalist or the sympathies of a radical but the imagination of a Symbolist and the outlook of an Old Testament prophet.

Thus Henry Roth's *Call It Sleep* (1934), ostensibly a study of the immigrant experience, was told through the eyes of a highly sensitive, almost neurotic, child for whom assimilation meant a vision of God and liberation from private guilt as much as an adjustment to the realities of American life. Here the battle of social classes gave way to an oedipal struggle between father and son, and the theories of Marx seemed less relevant than the insights of Freud. In addition, Roth's reliance on stream of consciousness owed more to the achievements of James Joyce than to the pronouncements of Michael Gold or Granville Hicks. Though he was a graduate of the John Reed Club, Roth ultimately displayed a greater interest in the problems of personal psychopathology than in the demands of any collective movement.

Sometimes a novelist's desire to make a political statement would conflict dramatically with his instinctive suspicion of all "messages" as singularly unsuitable for a crisis like the depression. One of the best examples of this was Dalton Trumbo's *Johnny Got His Gun* (1939). A member of the Communist party during the late 1930s and early 1940s, Trumbo wanted to write a novel that would stand as the ultimate condemnation of war. He therefore offered as his central character and spokesman the incredibly mutilated figure of Joe Bonham—a soldier returning from battle with no legs, arms, eyes, ears, nose, tongue, or mouth. Joe is so helpless he cannot even kill himself; unable to live or to die, he lies entombed in silence. All that is left to him is his mind and the compulsion to "figure things out all over again."[61] Slowly, painstakingly, he learns to distinguish between night and day, sleep and wakefulness, past and present. Finally, by tapping his head in Morse Code on his pillow, he manages to communicate with the "outside" world. Thus he is prepared to force himself into the consciousness of those who wish to forget or ignore what has happened to him.[62] Having escaped from his eternal prison, Joe wants desperately to rejoin mankind and, more important, to "make an exhibit of himself to show all the little guys what would happen to them" if they permitted themselves to be used as cannon fodder for another war. Through his suffering and martyrdom Joe becomes a "new kind of Christ . . . who carries within himself all the seeds of a new order of things," who will teach the workers and farmers and average citizens to overthrow their rulers and take control of their own destiny.[63] And here the novel ends with a rhetorical celebration of the masses and revolution.

Yet there is little in the book which supports this kind of conclusion. On the contrary, the novel's real power comes not in its propaganda against war or its anticipation of revolt but in Joe's agonizing discovery of his dismemberment, his struggle to cope with the terrible irrationality of his situation, his mute outrage when the doctors finally respond to his tapping by asking him "What do you want?", his poignant desire for all "the things nobody could ever give him," his refusal to be buried alive.[64] Moreover, Joe's very experience stands as a repudiation of every political abstraction, slogan, and cause. To his mind, "the guys who say life isn't worth living without some principle so important you're willing to die for it, they are all nuts." The young men who believed they were trying to make the world safe for democracy died in fact to "make the world safe for words without meaning." Running through the novel is Joe's assertion that "there's no word worth your life. . . . I would trade democracy for life. I would trade independence and honor and freedom and decency for life. I know what death is and all you people who talk about dying for words don't even know what life is. There's nothing noble about dying. . . . The most important thing is your life. . . . Don't let them kid you any more."[65] Given this point of view, those who called for revolution were as dangerous and dishonest as those who called for war; in both cases it was the "little guys" who would be maimed or slaughtered for nothing. Ultimately *Johnny Got His Gun* was a novel in which the horror of Joe's condition outweighed Trumbo's ideology and in which the preservation of human life transcended the rhetoric of social change.

A similar sort of contradiction appeared in Horace McCoy's *They Shoot Horses, Don't They?* (1935), only here the issues were presented with even greater pessimism. The action of the novel took place on the outskirts of Los Angeles at one of those events peculiar to the 1930s—a marathon dance. McCoy's characters lived on the margins of society, supremely disillusioned and cynical about their future, "extras" in a world made up of Hollywood and Central Casting. To them, the West Coast was the end of the line, a last chance to succeed at something and be noticed before they perished.

In their tawdry aspirations, as in the spectacle of the dance itself, McCoy created a metaphor for the way life was organized under capitalism. On the surface the marathon is a "contest" run according to strict rules and regulations, holding out the promise of "free food and a free bed as long as you last and a thousand dollars if you win." Underneath, however, the dancers are gladiators surrounded by "circus seats" for the audience, exploited by promoters who see them as nothing but instruments for profit and sponsors who want to advertise their "names or products on your backs." The point of the dance is to exhaust and eliminate as many contestants as possible; only the strongest or most insensitive can withstand the competition. "I used every ounce of my strength," admits McCoy's narrator, "to move up, to get just one step ahead, to remove that threat from behind." Soon the participants internalize the values of the struggle—cheating, fighting with one another, learning to eat and sleep and breathe in time with the music. Toward the end, survival becomes more important than winning; the dancers are too frightened and tired to care "where we finished so long as it wasn't last."[66]

Yet the novel was more than a sardonic commentary on capitalism's brutality and indifference. In the physical punishment and moral pain it inflicts on the contestants, in its hypnotic command that everyone "keep moving," the marathon comes to stand for a world grown pointless and absurd. "This whole business is a merry-go-round," complains one partici-pant. "When we get out of here we're right back where we started."[67] Since no one can change the rules or stop the dance, there is no way to break out of the existential circle. At one point Robert, McCoy's otherwise passive hero, dreams of sitting in the sun by the Pacific Ocean as a symbolic alternative to the dreary and fraudulent "civilization" inside the dance hall. But if he continues to look at the door leading to the beach, he will be "disqualified" from the one life he knows, and so he resumes his perpetual motion.[68] It is only Gloria, the bitter and defeated heroine of the novel, who knows how to escape. "I think it's a lousy world and I'm finished," she declares. Hence she asks Robert to "pinch-hit for God" by killing her. And in the single act of which he is capable, Robert fires a pistol shot into Gloria's brain, ending her misery as one would slay an injured horse for whom the race is no longer possible.[69]

Like Trumbo, McCoy imagined a universe permeated with violence and death. But because the ultimate source of evil was not so much the social system as the meaningless of life itself, McCoy had little faith in the capacity of the "little guys" to change the world. At most he could only offer a hint of the approaching cataclysm, hovering like a "red, vaporish glow" over exploiters and victims alike.[70] From his somber perspective the entire so-ciety was on a marathon, going around and around, dancing to oblivion.

Perhaps no artist was more faithful to this vision of doom than Nathanael West. On various occasions during the 1930s West acknowledged his fond-ness for the Left, but his novels were generally devoid of "social" content (at least as the New Masses would have defined it) and his characters rarely existed in relation to identifiable institutions or movements. Miss Lonely-hearts (1932), his most celebrated work, was an allegory on the search for belief and the death of feeling in the modern world. "Reality" intruded only in the form of the tragic letters to Miss Lonelyhearts, and these—like everything else in the novel—were transformed by West's Gothic imagina-tion into an essentially symbolic evocation of suffering and horror.

Similarly in The Day of the Locust (1939), Hollywood became not a specific locale or a cultural phenomenon or a set of social relationships but a cosmic metaphor for the falsity, corruption, and decadence of contempo-rary civilization. Here what really interested West was not so much the experience of ordinary people as the surrealistic images and macabre per-sonalities that haunted Southern California. As a writer fearful of having subordinated his own talent to the commercialism of the film factories, West was obsessed with the sham and pretension of Hollywood: its reduction of life to the level of cardboard and papier-mâché, its function as a massive "junkyard" for discarded dreams, its power to make men compromise their integrity and sell out their craft.[71] More important, California seemed to West an enormous stage on which human beings cavorted in a continuous masquerade. *The Day of the Locust* was filled with bad actors and actresses who behaved as though they were participating in a "minstrel show"— flaunting artificial mannerisms, playing roles, giving performances, keeping up appearances, and entertaining the masses with elaborate gestures and impersonations, all as a way of suppressing honest emotion and evading reality.[72]

Each episode in the novel was intensely theatrical, with every character having deliberately transformed himself into a product for the consumption of an insatiable audience. Indeed, West was fascinated most of all with the spectators themselves—a "monstrous," disfigured, harrowing collection of lost souls who "had come to California to die." *The Day of the Locust* was populated with dwarfs, transvestites, and misfits whose anguish and hope-lessness were irremediable. At best, they alternated between suicidal resig-nation and half-deranged fury. In their "vicious, acrid boredom," in their "savage and bitter" disappointment with the tedium of their lives, in their inconsolable feelings of resentment and betrayal, they displayed a propen-sity for mindless violence which no political or ideological doctrine could satisfactorily explain.[73]

West was describing a society composed not of heroic workers and op-pressive capitalists, nor of courageous individuals battling against the pres-sures of modern technology. Instead he saw in California a mob of enraged, hysterical barbarians, full of "anarchic power," whose only collective im-pulse was to sack civilization, who looked forward to a "terrible holocaust" where, "no longer bored," they could sing and dance "joyously in the red light of the flames."[74] Thus in its almost too eager anticipation of the apocalypse, in its careful and detailed portrait of a monumental disaster, in its secret admiration for the sheer destructive power of the mob, *The Day of the Locust* pierced beneath the formal social categories of the decade's intellectuals to express their unconscious fears and unspoken fantasies. West had delivered a funeral oration over the remains of the old society, but there was to be no redemption, no rebirth, no renewal. What he saw in the convulsions of the 1930s was quite simply the end of the world.

If Roth, Trumbo, McCoy, and West made little effort to write about conventional subjects, if their work consistently transcended the bounds of social realism, this did not mean that they constituted an idiosyncratic school of Symbolist artists in a period otherwise devoted to the Naturalist reproduction of daily life. Quite the contrary, even a confirmed "radical" novelist like Nelson Algren could transform the experience of the impoverished and dispossessed into a gloomy parable on the collapse of organized society. In *Somebody in Boots* (1935), Algren prophesied not the coming of revolution but the coming of fascism; he treated the common man with a mixture of awe and disgust that was closer to West than to Conroy or Cantwell.

Like other "proletarian" novels in the 1930s (for example Edward Dahlberg's *Bottom Dogs* and Tom Kromer's *Waiting for Nothing*), *Somebody in Boots* was not really concerned with the working class at all but with the rootless, transient hoboes who lacked both steady employment and permanent homes. The central figure in Algren's novel, Cass McKay, is an archetypal tramp—a descendant of the "pioneer woodsmen" who had once conquered the continent but who now felt completely out of place in the modern world.[75] Yet there is no attempt to endow Cass's plight with the epic heroism of the Joads, nor are his picaresque adventures glorified in the tradition of Natty Bumpo or Huck Finn. Cass is not a romantic outcast from civilization, wandering freely through the countryside with a highly developed set of moral principles, defying all forms of authority, preserving his independence against the intrusions of organized society, reveling in the natural camaraderie of the open road. Instead he is totally isolated and displaced, a marginal man with no sense of community and no genuine allegiance to other people. For Cass, hobo life means thirst, hunger, shame, fear, and fatigue. He lives in a "jungle" full of haggard, broken men in perpetual motion but with "no place to go, and no place to rest. No time to be idling and nothing to do." Beyond a vague sensation of having been somehow tricked and cheated, they are absolutely without social awareness; unable to understand the causes of their humiliation, they cannot possibly imagine a "better or happier world." Consequently, they remain passive victims—each man groping for his own survival, "no two" acting "together."[76]

At several points in the novel Algren clearly hoped to indicate a way out of this degradation. Cass longs for some form of companionship and security that will put an end to his unstable existence. Occasionally he wonders whether there is "anything else" in life besides "killing and cursing, sleeping and eating, drinking and fighting and working and cheating, day after day."[77] For a brief moment, through his love for a prostitute who is equally lost and beaten, Cass achieves a certain feeling of wholeness and humanity beyond anything he had previously experienced.[78] Moreover, he is capable of seeing for the first time an economic system that permitted "the plundering of the millions by the few," that hid its corruption behind patriotic slogans and created unspeakable misery in the name of "private ownership."[79]

But these are peripheral insights in a novel of unrelieved pessimism. Cass's affair is as transitory as his life on the road; once it has faded, he is forced to move on. For him "there was no escape from brutality . . . no asylum from evil or pain or long loneliness. . . . The world was a cruel place, all men went alone in it. . . . Those who were strong beat those who were weak." This was the only immutable fact in a universe without the possibility of permanent love or shelter.[80] In the long run Algren could conceive of no movement that might alleviate the suffering of his characters, nor any ideology that promised to heal their physical and psychic wounds. Instead, he sensed their latent capacity for unrestrained violence—their urge to "kill for the simple pleasure of killing," to "strike out at something, to hurt . . . as [they] had been hurt," to relieve their bitterness through the "sight of another man's blood."[81] Like West, Algren suspected that the "people" were not incipient socialists but potential brownshirts who might come together solely for an orgy of looting and arson. Otherwise they would remain fragmentary individuals, drifting helplessly down the road to nowhere.

Ultimately this suspicion of the masses carried over into an attack on the very ideal of collectivism itself, and the expectation of revolt gave way—at least in the literature of the 1930s—to a growing dread of men in groups. Again, this was true not only of apolitical artists like Nathanael West but also of those more directly concerned with social and economic problems. Thus John Steinbeck, who composed an eloquent hymn to the values of community and cooperation in *The Grapes of Wrath,* could at the same time illuminate the darker aspects of the "people's" fight against injustice in *In Dubious Battle* (1936).

Here Steinbeck revealed his distrust of and ambivalence toward the revolutionary movement, particularly as it was embodied in the Communist party. The novel centered on a strike by migrant workers in the California valley, out of which no one emerges a hero. The party organizers are presented as manipulative and Machiavellian, interested not so much in bringing immediate relief to the poor or even in winning the strike as in radicalizing their constituents for some future if illusive victory, willing to use whatever means are available to accomplish these objectives. When anyone is either hurt or killed, he is quickly converted through marches and public funerals into a device for boosting morale. Indeed the needs and desires of each participant are constantly subordinated to the demands of the struggle. The Communists have no time "to think about the feelings of one man," nor can they waste their energies "liking people." Personal relationships seem a necessary casualty of political warfare, with the result that noble radicals frequently become inhuman fanatics.[82]

Nevertheless, Steinbeck's revolutionaries are simply being realistic. The workers themselves are described throughout the novel as "apathetic" and "listless," able to respond only to the "voice of authority." Hence the Communists provide the required direction, leadership, and discipline without which the proletariat would presumably remain "bedraggled" and inert.[83] Yet once the masses are mobilized, their behavior is as frightening as anything imagined by Algren or West. Through the figure of Doc, an impartial observer and moralist with considerable skepticism for all "causes," Steinbeck pondered the new phenomenon of "group-men"—their irrationality, their immunity to abstractions and ideals, their resemblance to "sleep-walkers" marching silently and mechanically toward unseen and unknown goals, their similarity to "animals" aroused not by ideological conviction but by the "smell of blood."[84] However reluctantly, Steinbeck appeared to suggest in *In Dubious Battle* that the collectivist dream might bring neither social change nor an end to loneliness; instead, it threatened to reduce every man to a mindless beast tearing at the bones and tissues of civilization in a burst of hysterical rage.

4. *The Voice of the Self*

Throughout the 1930s John Steinbeck vacillated betweeen the optimistic and affirmative tone of *The Grapes of Wrath* and a sensitivity to the human capacity for evil which pervaded *In Dubious Battle.* Like other novelists in the decade—Farrell, Trumbo, McCoy, Algren, West—he could never reconcile his longing for fundamental changes in the structure of society with his fear of man's potential for cataclysmic violence. Thus the work of all these writers contained equal amounts of journalistic detail, social criticism, and surreal prophecy. Unable to assimilate such contradictory influences, their novels in the end were more disturbing than radical, more psychologically complex than politically coherent, more effective in the use of symbols than in the description of reality. Curiously, in a period dominated by the issues of economics and ideology, the fiction of the 1930s seemed strongest when it dealt not with the outer world but with inner emotions and states of mind. But given the difficulties which radical intellectuals and activists encountered in transforming America's cultural and political life, it was not surprising that their call for social significance in art should lead instead to a literature of private sensibility.

For some novelists, this meant a quite conscious denial of the Left's most characteristic attitudes—the desire for revolution, the search for community, the anticipation of apocalypse—and a return to the older, more traditional values of individualism. Although one could find strains of this in Edmund Wilson's travelogues, in Hemingway's *For Whom the Bell Tolls,* and in the acts of personal commitment undertaken by Conroy's and Cantwell's "proletarian" heroes, self-liberation and self-expression were seen by these writers as the final product of some cooperative enterprise—a strike, a defense of democratic liberties, a future socialist victory however remote and ill-defined. Even novels like *Johnny Got His Gun, The Day of the Locust, Somebody in Boots,* and *In Dubious Battle,* all of which criticized collectivist assumptions, did so in order to present a more accurate portrait of mob psychology and to convey a greater sense of anger at the ignorance and oppression of mankind. But in the work of certain artists—those like William Saroyan and Dashiell Hammett, whose radicalism was largely intuitive and temperamental, and those like Richard Wright and John Dos Passos, whose social beliefs were clearer and more conceptualized—the solitary individual became the ultimate ideal, existing outside and often in opposition to political parties, organized institutions, economic programs, and modern ideologies.

In the case of William Saroyan, a hostility to groups and an appreciation of private eccentricity seemed as much a part of his life as his art. Indeed the reader was never certain where one ended and the other began, for Saroyan's prose was not only introspective but almost obsessively self-centered. He burst on the literary scene in 1934 with a selection of short stories called *The Daring Young Man on the Flying Trapeze*—the very title of which was a superb commentary on his own carefully nurtured image as a fearless, unconventional artist battling against the odds for fame and fortune. Written largely in the first person from a deliberately autobiographical perspective (Saroyan constantly reminded his audience that he was not "fabricating a fancy plot," "creating memorable characters," or "making up anything," but merely recording the "truth" of his life and adventures), these were the stories of a young man making his debut, establishing his identity, announcing his "presence on earth."[85] Saroyan himself was the central figure of the work, forever interrupting the narrative to deliver personal opinions on art, philosophy, and the state of the world. But the effectiveness of the stories depended not on a journalist's ability to describe events nor on an essayist's clarity and logic but on Saroyan's own reserves of charm, wit, and eloquence. Ultimately the reader was carried along by the force of Saroyan's personality rather than by the persuasiveness of his political and social observations.

Moreover, the stories themselves contained a number of ideas unfamiliar to the collectivist rhetoric of the 1930s. Saroyan instinctively recoiled from the specter of the masses in motion. "One man at a time," he contended, "is capable of the monstrosities performed by mobs." He wished instead to "lift [man] from the nightmare of history to the calm dream of his own soul," to liberate the individual from the prison of social responsibility. "It is proper to herd only cattle," Saroyan exclaimed. "When the spirit of a single man is taken from him and he is made a member of a mob, the body of God suffers a ghastly pain, and therefore the act is a blasphemy."[86] In reasserting the dignity of each person, Saroyan renounced all slogans and causes. One of his stories, "Fight Your Own War," was a declaration against joining national crusades, against being mobilized to destroy one's "enemies," against using art for purposes of propaganda, against becoming "involved" in organized movements which invariably asked people to die for abstractions. Elsewhere he admitted that he was "not at all enthusiastic about progress" nor interested in the "destiny of nations." And "as for the economic and political upheavals . . . reverberating deeply through the bowels of the several continents . . . it would be sheer folly to speak seriously of anything in this connection." At best, Saroyan could only "stick pins in . . . the inflated bags of moralists, cowards, and wise men," while attending to his craft as a writer "because there is nothing more civilized or decent for me to do."[87]

But if Saroyan did not believe in the promise of a glorious socialist future, neither did he share the prophetic vision of writers like Algren and West. Though he acknowledged the "existence of hatred and ugliness in the heart of man," though he conceded the presence of pain and cruelty in the world, he foresaw no catastrophic explosion on the part of the frenzied masses nor any day of judgment for rulers and victims alike—"only slow death, emerging from life."[88] Furthermore, where some writers were both frightened by and fascinated with the destructive impulses of men in groups, Saroyan was more concerned with the tragedy of man in solitude. Many of his stories focused on the terrors of silence and secrecy, the inability to communicate one's inner feelings and desires to another, the plight of "each person hidden within himself." In his view, the individual was condemned to live a "private life," lonely and "alien," a "stranger" to everyone else.[89] And this condition could never be ameliorated by any movement, whether its objectives were evil or benign.

Yet despite Saroyan's attack on the intellectual premises and aesthetic conventions of the 1930s, his underlying sentiments were not entirely at odds with those of his generation. On the contrary, at certain key points Saroyan displayed an inbred sympathy for the "natural dignity and gentleness" of the people that transcended politics and institutions. Like the John Steinbeck of *The Grapes of Wrath,* Saroyan appreciated mankind's elementary survival in the face of war, exploitation, and suffering. If he refused to convert his prose into a sermon on revolution or a jeremiad on the coming of fascism, if he would not permit himself or his characters to "perform some heroic or monstrous deed" in order to illustrate a message, this was because he preferred to write "lovingly" of the "single person," seeking to "understand the miracle of his being," cherishing the "truth of his existence," celebrating "the splendor of the mere fact of his being alive."[90] For all his willingness to satirize and ridicule the decade's reliance on ideological formulas, Saroyan could not resist its tendency to invest the average citizen with epic virtues. While he repudiated the doctrine of collectivism, he retained the myth of the common man. While he scorned the effort to change society, he glorified the individual's will to live. In essence, Saroyan had internalized the emotional loyalties of the depression years even as he consciously rejected their more explicit social values.

Saroyan's ambivalence toward his subject matter and his readiness to dismiss the ideal of community at the very moment he embraced all the "little people" stemmed in part from his desire to protect his own ideological innocence. He refused to think or write in social terms because this might interfere with his understanding of "life" as it was experienced by each individual with whom he came in contact. For him, as for many other artists in the 1930s, the ordinary concerns of home and family seemed ultimately more "real" and more compelling than the elusive call of revolution.

Ironically it was often those with firmer political allegiances than Saroyan who most dramatically rejected the preconceptions of their time. Richard Wright, for example, had become by the late 1930s one of the Communist party's leading literary celebrities. As part of the great Negro migration northward after World War I, Wright emigrated from Mississippi to Chicago, joined the John Reed Club in the early years of the depression, contributed numerous articles to the left-wing press on life in the ghetto, and won an award from no less an authority than the *New Masses* for *Uncle Tom's Children*—a collection of four fairly orthodox novellas, published in 1938. At this point Wright was simply adapting the techniques of Naturalism and the idea of the individual as entirely a social product to the problems of black people in America. The behavior of his characters was conditioned by an oppressive racial code and an economic system over which they had no influence; their very identities were shaped by external events, and their only escape was through collective action. Yet by the end of the decade Wright had begun to question the efficacy of these notions, as well as the intentions of his fellow Communists. His reservations were most clearly illuminated in *Native Son* (1940), a work that was at once powerful, compassionate, and contradictory.

On one level *Native Son* seemed a fairly standard but nonetheless effective novel of social protest. Through the frightening figure of Bigger Thomas, Wright created the supreme prototype of a helpless, disinherited black man, choking on his rage and frustration. Forced to live at the extremes of fear and ignorance, Bigger is a classic victim of economic deprivation and psychological emasculation. In a society which accepts no responsibility for his plight, he cannot feel responsible to anyone; in a country which daily denies his humanity, he is incapable of "normal" human emotions. Instead he deliberately suppresses his true personality and desires. He bears toward his family an attitude of "iron reserve." In the presence of whites he becomes totally subservient, with "his knees slightly bent, his lips partly open, his shoulders stooped, and his eyes [holding] a look that went only to the surface of things." In every situation he gropes "for neutral worlds . . . that would convey information but not indicate any shade of his own feelings." Indeed Bigger's powerlessness goes deeper than the issues of race, poverty, and class relations. He has no freedom of action, no choices to make, no possibility of asserting himself. For Bigger, the whole world is a "jail," in which he must forever submit to the commands of "others." Seventy-five years after emancipation, he is still the "property" of white men, "heart and soul, body and blood; what they did claimed every atom of him, sleeping and waking; it colored life and dictated the terms of death."[91]

Treated like an animal, Bigger responds in kind. In his jungle, hatred becomes the dominant emotion, and violence is the only method of survival. Thus Bigger goes out into society armed with knife and gun to give himself a sense of equality and "completeness." Unable to bear the "strain of living" according to rules laid down by whites, he yearns instinctively to "strike out," to "commit rape every time he looked into a white face," to "clench his fist and swing his arm and . . . kill."[92]

Ultimately, driven by confusion and panic, he strangles a white girl. Yet it is through this very act that he ceases to be an animal, that he raises himself out of the anonymous mass and forces the white community to acknowledge his existence as a unique human being. Bigger is literally reborn. "He had murdered and had created a new life for himself. It was something that was all his own, and it was the first time in his life he had anything that others could not take from him." Moreover, in achieving a measure of individuality, in perceiving the "hidden meaning of his life," he is able to challenge the entire structure of a deterministic universe. Bigger can now seize control of his own destiny. No longer a passive victim of his environment, "he could run away; he could remain; he could even go down and confess what he had done. The mere thought that these avenues of action were open to him made him feel free, that his life was his, that he held his future in his hands." Henceforth, he is thrown back on his inner wit and courage; "the feeling of being always enclosed in the stifling embrace of an invisible force had gone. . . ." Through violence, Bigger has found not only power and liberation but "a sense of wholeness"—a mystical reconciliation between the two worlds of "thought and feeling, will and mind, aspiration and satisfaction."[93]

But Bigger's freedom depends on his willingness and ability to accept responsibility for his deed, to say publicly that he alone had committed murder. And to Wright, this was precisely what the ideology of the 1930s would not permit. The last third of the novel subjects the conventional wisdom of the decade to a severe test. During his trial Bigger is again reduced to a spectator while others decide his fate. Once more he must rely on white men, and they argue over his life in language he does not fathom. In effect, they deny him the right either to save himself or to admit his guilt; he can never explain in his own words why he has killed.[94]

Even his Communist lawyer, Mr. Max, remains oblivious to the true implications of what Bigger had done. In his eloquent summation to the jury, Max seeks to invest Bigger's raw revolt with political and economic significance. Since Bigger is a child of circumstance, Max argues, he cannot be held accountable for his actions. In fact it is not Bigger but society which should be judged. For Max, Bigger represents a deprived class and distinctive culture—a way of life with its "own laws and claims," with its own sense of "right and wrong," with needs and predilections that differ fundamentally from white standards of morality. Thus Bigger stands as a "test symbol" for all the oppression and injustice that America has heaped on its black population:

> Multiply Bigger Thomas twelve million times . . . and you have the psychology of the Negro people. But once you see them as a whole, once your eyes leave the individual and encompass the mass, a new quality comes into the picture. Taken collectively, they are not simply twelve million people; in reality they constitute a separate nation, stunted, stripped, and held captive *within* this nation, devoid of political, social, economic, and property rights.[95]

Even though this plea fails, Max insists that Bigger see himself in relation to other men—both white and black—who are equally exploited. And there are moments in the novel when Bigger appears convinced that he is not "alone," that his situation is part of a common struggle to change the world.[96]

Yet Wright was ultimately unwilling to shift his vision from the individual to the "mass," unable to treat Bigger solely as a political example or social symbol. Indeed the last word is given not to Max but to Bigger, and it denies some of the decade's most cherished assumptions. In the end Bigger accepts not only his inner freedom but *personal* responsibility for the consequences of his actions. "What I killed for, I *am*," he shouts to Max. "It must've been pretty deep in me to make me kill! I must have felt it awful hard to murder. . . . I didn't know I was really alive in this world until I felt things hard enough to kill for them." And as Max staggers back "like a blind man" from this insight, the novel concludes on what is almost an existential note: Bigger's own acts, not those of society, define his identity.[97]

Wright had offered in *Native Son* not so much a sociological examination of racism as a study of how one individual might claim his manhood. The novel was concerned less with revolutionary alternatives than with the portrayal of private thoughts and feelings. It demonstrated not only Wright's growing ambivalence toward the Communist party but also his increasing preoccupation with the problems of self-discovery and self-realization which went beyond classes and movements. In essence, *Native Son* reflected a disenchantment with radical beliefs and a reassertion of the importance of the individual over the group. If Wright could not always make these distinctions clear, this was probably more a failure of form than content. Relying on a documentary prose style and a naturalistic accumulation of detail, he seemed unable to get inside the head of Bigger Thomas. The reader was therefore forced to accept Wright's own explanations and analyses rather than watch Bigger develop as a distinctive personality. But whatever its internal flaws, *Native Son* managed to keep in focus a single, complex, tragic human being beneath the panoply and noise of a public cause.

Yet of all the so-called "social" novels of the 1930s, none was less committed to the twin doctrines of community and collectivism than John Dos Passos's epic trilogy *U.S.A.* Even more than Wright, Dos Passos had been regarded for some time by the Left as its special literary hero. One of the few artists of his generation to retain an interest in politics and radicalism during the 1920s, co-organizer with Michael Gold and John Howard Lawson of the militant New Playwrights Theatre, Dos Passos was moved by the execution of Sacco and Vanzetti to begin a monumental reinterpretation of American life in the twentieth century. Weaving together historical events, newspaper headlines, popular songs, biographies of famous men, conventional narratives, and lyrical prose-poems, he fashioned a bitter indictment of the national soul. With the appearance of *The 42nd Parallel* (1930) and *1919* (1932), Dos Passos was warmly welcomed as the foremost revolutionary novelist—a model for all those who aspired to create a truly proletarian art.

Nevertheless, Dos Passos was already having misgivings about his Communist allies, as reflected in his defense of the intellectual's independence at the first Congress of American Writers. Moreover, his basic philosophy had never really changed from his earliest work, *One Man's Initiation* (1920), to his final disillusion with Marxism during the Spanish Civil War. But with the publication of *The Big Money* (1937), the concluding volume of the trilogy, the Left found itself in the anomalous position of championing a "radical" artist who rejected all its fundamental values and ideals.

Taken as a whole, *U.S.A.* offered little comfort for any political creed. Indeed Dos Passos was primarily concerned not with the ill effects of a particular economic system but with the loss of youth and the ravages of time. His characters are betrayed not so much by their own greed, by the fraudulence of the American Dream, or by the crimes of American capitalism, as by the very process of growing old. If their childhood often seems hopeful, maturity is invariably dreary and dull. And it is the emptiness and triviality of their adult lives, the petty disappointments and sense of being forever trapped, that Dos Passos records with a vengeance. Where *The 42nd Parallel* evokes the yearning of adolescence and the buoyancy of the new century, *1919* and *The Big Money* are studies in decay. As youthful expectations gradually fade, men and women, rich and poor, the bourgeoisie and the workers, are all forced to adjust to the grim and joyless pressures of middle age.

Thus Janey Williams enjoys one romantic afternoon, fantasizing about love, before her horizons begin to narrow and she finds herself "on the shelf," an old maid in a white-collar world.[98] Her brother Joe becomes increasingly nostalgic about his high-school exploits as he drifts from continent to continent, buffeted about by events he barely comprehends, regretting his wasted opportunities, acknowledging finally that "all my future's behind me."[99] For most of the members of the middle class in *U.S.A.*, adulthood is a lonely, unhappy, and frustrating experience. Sex frightens the women and bores the men, human relationships remain fleeting and superficial, and no one is able to sustain a serious interest in social or cultural affairs. Instead they travel constantly, their rootless and transient existence underscored by one character's admission that she leads "such a silly life." They worship power, wealth, and fame, but in the end "everything you've wanted crumbles in your fingers as you grasp it."[100]

With the passage of time comes the corruption of ideals. It is not only that people grow old but that they make compromises, misuse their talents, squander the legacy of their youth. J. Ward Moorehouse employs his native intelligence and charm to manipulate language and people. Entranced by his own voice, he soon sounds as if he is always "rehearsing a speech." Opportunistically, he amasses the "capital and the connections" to set up a public-relations firm that sells patriotism, class collaboration, and the glories of free enterprise. Seeking to become the "key to the key men," Moorehouse winds up as little more than a "megaphone" for the machinations of others.[101]

Similarly Dick Savage, a young man who shows some promise as a poet, eventually surrenders both his artistic aspirations and his radical convictions for the comforts of security and success. Unwilling to "throw a monkeywrench into the industrial machine," he decides instead to help it run more efficiently. By the end of the trilogy he has become merely an aging yes-man for Moorehouse, perverting his skill with words for the sake of advertising campaigns, pompously spouting "phrases that made no sense at all," readily conceding that his "life is a shambles."[102]

But the most pathetic figure in the trilogy is Charley Anderson. To Dos Passos, Charley embodied all the flimsy ambitions and distorted dreams that made America a land not of success but of failure and defeat. Moreover, his career illustrated Dos Passos's central concern: the Veblenian conflict between craftsmanship and profit, engineers and businessmen, work and exploitation. Charley appears initially as an honest "mechanic" who likes "tinkering with motors." Yet he is also a man who wants to escape the "hick towns" of his adolescence, who longs to "get ahead," who hungers for the "big money."[103] Soon he exchanges grease and overalls for a desk and stockbroker; he becomes a "promoter" rather than a producer; his love of engines gives way to his love of dollar bills. And this is the beginning of Charley's tortured decline. Losing touch with the workers in the shop, he remains mystified by the financial intricacies of Wall Street. Growing fat and alcoholic, unable (like all the other characters in U.S.A.) to make a fresh start, Charley wishes that he was "still tinkerin' with that damn motor and didn't have to worry about money all the time." But he is becoming increasingly superfluous both to the world of engineering and high finance. So it is appropriate that he die in an auto crash, a metaphor for the marriage of the machine and capitalism, neither of which Charley any longer understands.[104] In the rise and fall of Charley Anderson, Dos Passos had offered, among other things, an old-fashioned parable of what happened when men sacrificed their birthright for the elusive attractions of modernity.

Yet even the radicals and the working class in U.S.A. are not immune to the devastating effects of age, nor to the accommodations which inevitably accompany maturity. In fact, their lives frequently seem more arid and monotonous than those of the bourgeoisie. Mac, the young Wobbly who fervently admires Eugene Debs and Big Bill Haywood, who learns early that poverty and oppression are intrinsic to the "system," who longs to participate in a revolution against the "bosses" and the "interests," gradually succumbs to the responsibilities of a wife and family. Burdened by children, mortgages, debts, and the demands of respectability, he finds himself as ensnared as his enemies in the middle class.[105]

While Mac ultimately accepts his status as an "onlooker," Mary French yearns to escape from her bourgeois origins, to "get out . . . into the world" and "feel [that] she was doing something real." But this necessarily involves the sacrifice of personal pleasure and the repression of private feeling in the service of a political cause. Mary decides neither to marry nor to have a baby; instead, she dedicates her energies to an increasingly sterile round of meetings, petitions, and the "long grind of officework that took up her days and nights."[106] Moreover, the revolution is itself dehumanizing; it breeds men who are stern, puritanical, and lifeless. The radicals in U.S.A. are either fanatics or hypocrites, either "wellsharpened instruments" with no sensitivity to ordinary human needs or bureaucratic time-servers rising within the Communist hierarchy and playing with words as meaningless as those of Moorehouse and Savage.[107] In all of these instances, speech becomes a means of concealing truth, while self-respect is invariably subordinated to the greater social good.

In essence, most of the figures in U.S.A. were suffering from an incurable disease of the spirit; the extent of their moral disintegration seemed to suggest that the nation itself might be mortally ill. And this was precisely what Dos Passos meant to show. Throughout the trilogy he carefully pointed out the connection between private troubles and public crises, personal duplicity and the violation of national ideals, the loss of youth and the neglect of tradition. Ironically, Dos Passos had indeed written a "social" novel but one which offered no direction for the present or hope for the future. Rather, it represented an elegiac commemoration of his own and America's childhood.

Just as the narrative portions of U.S.A. assessed the impact of time on each fictional character, while the camera eye gradually matured from a curious child to a disillusioned adult, so the biographies and newsreels provided an official "history" of the country's rise and fall. Like Steinbeck and Caldwell, Dos Passos lamented the demise of an earlier, pre-industrial America—a land without fences and highways, without automobiles and assembly lines, without tycoons and efficiency experts, without the evil geniuses of J.P. Morgan and Henry Ford. Where once there had been lakes and forests there were now "summer resorts"; on the sight of the friendly "oldtime shop" there stood the impersonal factory drowning out conversation in the "roar of the motors"; in place of the skilled craftsman there emerged the "Taylorized speedup" which reduced all laborers to "gray shaking husks."[108]

Moreover, the senseless chatter of Moorehouse, Savage, and Charley Anderson had its analogue in the way contemporary political rhetoric degraded the values of the past. If a nation might truly be known by the "speech of the people," then America's decline could be measured through the hollow phrases of its leaders. In this respect the chief villains of U.S.A. were not the usual industrialists and financiers but those who intentionally twisted language to their own ends—men like Bryan ("silver tongue in a big mouth," chanting mindlessly for the approbation of the mob) and Wilson (trumpeting the slogans of liberalism while jailing Debs, calling for self-determination and the 14 Points while protecting the Morgan loans and carving out a new American empire, "talking to save his faith in words" until a stroke left him a "ruined paralyzed man" no longer "able to speak").[109] In their indifference to truth, in their disregard for the meaning of ideas, they went beyond the conventional sins of economic exploitation to tarnish every ideal for which the country stood.

Yet in Dos Passos's view, neither individuals nor countries are given a second chance. Though he admired those like John Reed (who naïvely assumed that "words meant what they said") and Paxton Hibben (the old-fashioned Hoosier radical who heard in the songs of socialist revolutionaries "the measured cadences of the Declaration of Independence"), though he sought some "leverage" which "might pry the owners loose from power and bring back (I too Walt Whitman) our storybook democracy," Dos Passos believed there could be no return to the past nor any retribution in the present.[110] Modern society had grown too strong for ordinary human beings. "Personal feelings" and "private opinions" were being crushed beneath the weight of machines, armies, industrial combines, and government bureaucracies. In a world of groups and organizations, when "they" controlled all the "machineguns" and "printingpresses," it was impossible to fight back with only "songs" and "words."[111] Thus Dos Passos saw in the trial of Sacco and Vanzetti a special symbol of the "two nations"—not a conflict of classes but a struggle between men and institutions, innocence and decadence, the heritage of the pilgrim and pioneer against the "strangers who have turned our language inside out, who have taken the clean words our fathers spoke and made them slimy and foul." Yet it was these very "immigrant haters of oppression," the true defenders of the national faith, who would be "beaten." And at the conclusion of the most passionate prose in *U.S.A.*, Dos Passos felt compelled to acknowledge that "we stand defeated America."[112]

Indeed these references to lost hopes and dead dreams became a recurring litany through most of the trilogy. In *1919* the new society that might be born on "the first day of the first month of the first year" never appears; instead, the reader is bombarded with images of rotting bodies, mutilated "scraps of flesh," and the anonymous casualties of war.[113] Similarly, *The Big Money* ends with the lonely figure of "Vag," a nameless tramp battling hunger and fatigue as he seeks to redeem the promises of American capitalism.[114]

Given this spectacle of defeat and despair, Dos Passos could only hope for the survival of personal honor and integrity despite the intrusions of modern life. For him, the paramount question was not whether to join a social movement but how to preserve the sanctity of the individual. Suspicious of anyone with rank and position, distrusting all those who held economic or political power, he reserved his highest praise for the men who did not fit in, who refused to conform or sell out. These included stubborn rebels like Robert La Follette (fighting always with his "back to the wall," trying to halt "a crazy steamroller with his bare hands," expressing "no opinion but his own") and temperamental outsiders like Thorstein Veblen (whose specific ideas seemed less important to Dos Passos than his roots in rural America, his refusal to bow before any master, his inability to "get his mouth round the essential yes").[115] At heart, Dos Passos opposed capitalists and socialists alike because they represented different but equally constricting forms of collectivism. So he withdrew to the safety of the "camera eye"—the introspective reflections of the honest if impotent artist, the private conscience commenting on a social tragedy, the passive spectator whose inner purity remained unsullied by the corruption and deceit of the twentieth century.

Rejecting the claim of organized society and radical politics, Saroyan,

Wright, and Dos Passos preferred to cast their lot with the lonely individual —however bruised and vulnerable. Yet there was at least one writer in the 1930s who feared that the forces of collectivization had already gone too far to permit either the mobilizing of social classes or the assertion of the self. At first glance Dashiell Hammett seemed a most unlikely novelist to dismiss the activities both of groups and single persons. On the one hand, his sympathy for the Left (particularly the Communist party) remained firm throughout the decade. On the other hand, his special province was the mystery story, a form that normally celebrated the intelligence and resources of the "private" detective. Yet in his masterpiece, *The Maltese Falcon* (1930), Hammett suggested that collectivism and individualism alike were irrelevant philosophies for modern America.

On the surface *The Maltese Falcon* appeared to follow the conventions of its genre, though it did offer a view of society that could be considered vaguely "radical." Sam Spade lives in an environment composed of cynics and liars, hypocrites and frauds, professional thieves and amateur killers. As long as "profitable business relations" govern the behavior of people and institutions at each level of the social order, it is not surprising that "most things . . . can be bought or taken," nor that everyone is for sale.[116] But greed is only a minor annoyance in a world of shifting identities and perpetual intrigue, where nothing is ever what it seems. Spade must never allow himself to be taken in by the "performances" of others; since friends and enemies alike are constantly concealing their true purposes, it becomes impossible for him to function except in a climate of dishonesty and insincerity.[117] Indeed, because the line between appearance and reality continues to be obscure, it is appropriate that all the characters in the novel should be searching for a prize whose actual value none can estimate. The "falcon" remains a mysterious Holy Grail, enveloped in disguises and a maze of historical legends, forever eluding the grasp of ordinary mortals.[118]

Yet the greatest danger confronting Spade is a universe dominated by the unexpected, the irrational, and the absurd. At one point he tells his client and lover, Brigid O'Shaughnessy, the strange story of "Flitcraft," a man whose "sane" and "orderly" existence is nearly obliterated by a "falling beam." Thereafter Flitcraft learns that his very survival depends on his ability to adjust to "blind chance" and random accidents, to the inexplicable terrors of a situation in which beams might or might not fall on one's head at any minute.[119] Through this tale (the meaning of which Brigid, significantly, does not grasp) Spade has revealed his own philosophy of life. As the classic "tough-guy" hero in a decade that presumably admired unsenti-

mental pragmatists both in government and in gangster films, Spade deliberately substitutes action for analysis. He does not try to "understand"
events, nor does he provide elaborate explanations for his behavior. Instead
he concentrates on the few objects that seem concrete and real: cigarettes,
liquor, food, money, and guns. Dispensing with all abstractions, he uses
language that corresponds solely to the immediate pressures of the moment.
The novel itself was written almost entirely in terse dialogue (a style so
readily adaptable to the screen that it later became impossible to read the
words of Spade, Cairo, and Gutman without hearing the voices of Humphrey Bogart, Peter Lorre, and Sidney Greenstreet). Moreover, unlike the
"proletarian" hero who eventually identifies with his class and accepts its
ideology, Spade remains a supreme individualist adhering to his private
conceptions of morality, keeping his emotions and opinions to himself,
carrying out distasteful assignments while preserving his innate sense of
honor.[120] In short, Hammett had created a protagonist who combined a
revolutionary's scorn for modern society with an existential concern for
personal integrity.

Nevertheless, this ethic of the hard-boiled craftsman disappears toward
the end of the novel. For Spade is really neither a free nor a radical man;
rather, he must obey a rigid code of values which restricts his behavior as
completely as any movement or doctrine. In surrendering Brigid to the
police, Spade is finally compelled to justify his decision. His reasons are
varied: a detective is supposed to protect his organization and avenge his
partner's murder, he should not release criminals, he could be arrested
himself if he frees Brigid, he cannot trust her and he does not wish to be
played for a "sucker." But above all he refuses to give in to his own desires
and feelings; he will not let Brigid go *precisely because* "all of me wants to
—wants to say to hell with the consequences and do it. . . ."[121] In effect,
Spade declines to be a rebel or to indulge his natural appetites. Instead he
is forced to curb the demands of his ego, acceding stoically to the rigors of
self-control and self-discipline, subordinating his individuality to professional standards of conduct. This was a remarkably conservative rationale,
one which denied the possibilities of either personal or social liberation. At
the conclusion of *The Maltese Falcon* the reader was left with the image of
Spade as an isolated, detached, almost inhuman figure beyond the normal
temptations of wealth and power, unable to satisfy his inner needs or
transform the outer world, alone and impassive—a curiously restrained and
fatalistic hero for a generation that believed in the redemptive value of
personal commitment and collective action.[122]

5. The Conservative Ethic

Since much of the journalism and fiction of the 1930s diverged so sharply from what critics and artists alike had anticipated—as writers answered the call for documentary realism and radical protest with a literature devoted to the remembrance of the past, the coming of the apocalypse, and the survival of the self—it was not surprising that some works projected a view of the world that implicity reinforced the status quo. Yet it did seem at least ironic that the true "social" novels of the decade—those which portrayed their characters and themes in relation to particular places, events, groups, classes, and institutions—were often the most conservative in general outlook. Nevertheless, one could find in the efforts of writers as different as Daniel Fuchs and William Faulkner a common emphasis on acceptance rather than action, tolerance rather than anger, resignation rather than revolution. In effect, they translated the decade's preoccupation with politics, culture, and community into a defense of established values and patterns of behavior.

Daniel Fuchs was a poet of the Jewish ghetto. From 1934 to 1937 he published three novels—*Summer in Williamsburg, Homage to Blenholt,* and *Low Company*—all of which were rooted in the distinctively ethnic environment of Brooklyn. In each of these works Fuchs displayed an extraordinary sensitivity to the sounds and smells of the ghetto, to the unconscious ceremonies and rituals of Jewish life, to the inflections and nuances of street-corner conversation, to the overriding importance of family and neighborhood relationships that created a special kind of community within the larger American society. Fuchs's characters were at once noble and petty, naïve and sardonic, idealistic and full of self-pity. Yet their ability to suffer disappointment and pain with an earthy humor made them seem both more human and more realistic than their counterparts in the literature of social significance. But these remained the only novels he was to write; they sold poorly, and Fuchs—whose trilogy often centered on the torturous conflict between money and morality—apparently chose the former, fleeing to Hollywood, where he spent the rest of his career grinding out forgettable film scripts for mediocre movies.

Like their author, the people in Fuchs's novels were usually obsessed with the desire to escape their native surroundings, to alter their otherwise commonplace lives, to rise above the mundane burdens and frustrations of the lower middle class. His heroes continually proclaim their hatred of the hysterical crowds that flock to Neptune Beach, the street noise and human odors of Williamsburg, the dreary tenements and fetid candy shops, the trivial concerns of their fellow Jews.[123] For their own part, they frequently take refuge in a world of fantasy. Some admire the "grace and elegance" of their favorite film stars, or the "ease and smoothness" with which problems are solved on the screen.[124] Others dream of the joys to be found in the peaceful countryside, far away from the oppressive heat of city pavements (though one vacationer discovers that he feels lonely and uneasy amid the grass and trees, ultimately "homesick" for the food and gossip of the ghetto).[125] Still others hope to "shut out" the "sordidness and cruelty" of life in Brooklyn by burying themselves in arcane scholarly pursuits, or by imagining that they can become great writers and revolutionaries and lovers all at the same time. Rebelling against reality, unwilling to adapt to their "suffocating" environment, they long for a "share of truth, poetry, beauty."[126]

These extravagant cravings formed the dominant theme of *Homage to Blenholt.* Max Balcan yearns desperately to "lift himself out of Williamsburg and its deadness," to live with "grandeur and significance," to emulate the mythic heroes of the past, to enjoy the power and respect that comes from being somehow "different." But despite Max's romanticism, his notion of an alternative life-style remains painfully conventional. His private dream is the American Dream; he is convinced that one can "get ahead by making money," and so he aspires to be "the richest man in the world."[127] For Max, wealth will surely put an end to the humiliation and indignity of being a mere nobody.

Yet the point of the novel is not that Max holds a set of distorted ideals but that—no matter what the nature of his ambitions—he is fundamentally "impractical." Throughout *Homage to Blenholt* he is reproached by family and friends for behaving like an "adolescent," for refusing to assume the responsibilities of adulthood, for wanting something more out of life than a routine job and the prospects of a slow death. Finally the pressures "to do what everybody else does, to act like a normal human being" become overwhelming, and Max chooses to adjust rather than rebel. "Reality hit him in the face until he knew . . . that his struggle was hopeless." In essence, the very process of "growing up" necessarily involves for Max an acceptance of the world as it is. Maturity means not only the shedding of youthful illusions (as in *Studs Lonigan)* or the inevitability of compromise (as in *U.S.A.)* but also a recognition that there is no escape from the drabness of daily life.[128]

Indeed all of Fuchs's novels concluded on this note of passivity and surrender. To the young protagonist at the end of *Summer in Williamsburg,* man's existence has no other meaning beyond the simple fact that "people were born, grew tired and calloused, struggled and died." The central figure in *Low Company* eventually shows his pity and compassion for the other inhabitants of the ghetto by deciding not to flee Neptune Beach; instead he will remain as a witness to their pathos, wretchedness, and misery.[129] In each instance Fuchs seemed to suggest that those who wished to change the world were unrealistic, immature, and ineffectual. The dreamers in his novels always failed, the young were consistently defeated by age, and the dissident loner eventually reconciled himself to the values of his peers. But Fuchs was not so much outraged by these developments as resigned to their eternal truth. Though his characters might rail against the ugly and distressing conditions in which they were confined, Fuchs himself could still find elements of humor and beauty in the humdrum affairs of ordinary men. He entertained no vision of a legendary past nor any hope for a utopian future; he was preoccupied solely with the present, and he wanted merely to preserve the familiar landmarks and collective spirit of the Brooklyn Jews. Like Saroyan, Fuchs had raised the commonplace to an ideal, but he was far more willing than most of his fellow artists to acquiesce in the way things were.

Of all the novelists in the 1930s, however, William Faulkner was perhaps the most attentive to matters of time and place, history and geography, class gradations and the nuances of race, men and the institutions through which they functioned. His stories took place within clearly defined communities, his readers were often supplied with elaborate maps and genealogical charts, and his characters wrestled with their private problems in an essentially public setting.

The structure of Faulkner's work was almost always circular. He disdained a single point of view or direct narration but instead portrayed events from a variety of perspectives—withholding information and repeating episodes in order to heighten the complexity of a given experience, using townspeople much like a Greek chorus to recount and comment on the activities of his central figures, emphasizing the continuous interconnection between past and present by shifting unexpectedly from one period of time to another, weaving together regional speech patterns and straightforward prose passages with flights of surreal rhetoric and portentous philosophizing, investing the most concrete incidents with historical and even mythic significance, insisting that the identity and position of each individual be fixed in relation to the entire society.

Yet despite their rich social texture, Faulkner's novels remained profoundly conservative. In trying to fuse the Symbolist's faith in the resources of the imagination with the Realist's respect for ordinary men and local detail, he constructed a world at once so eternal and self-enclosed that change of any sort threatened its very existence.

Like Fuchs, Faulkner tended to treat harshly anyone in his novels who valued intellect over feeling, ideas over intuition, moral abstractions over human feeling, the compulsion to act over the need to accept. His most disturbing characters are usually driven by some single purpose, plan, or design. Warped from childhood by their family and environment, obsessed with the desire for recognition or revenge or immortality, they become monomaniacs in the service of a social cause or personal ambition.

Thus the three major protagonists of *Light in August* (1932) are either self-righteous fanatics who put principles above life, or lonely exiles cut off from normal relationships among men: Joanna Burden, the descendant of Puritans and Abolitionists, reducing her religious and political heritage to stern dogma and "bloodless logic," unfeminine and implacably cerebral, seeking one final burst of pleasure and passion before surrendering to the austerity and barrenness of old age; the Reverend Hightower, an intellectual haunted by the past and frightened by the present, a man who has "bought immunity" from the people around him, remote from the world and "sheltered from the harsh gale of living," finding serenity only in his books and inner thoughts; Joe Christmas, isolated and "rootless," alienated from both blacks and whites but with no assured identity of his own, using pride and ruthlessness as a mask for his private emotions, imprisoned by circumstances and powerless to break the repetitive pattern of his life, moved ultimately by a sense of fatalism and self-hatred to seek death as the sole sign of his humanity.[130] Similarly, in *The Sound and the Fury* (1929), Quentin Compson is a tragic victim of his own faith in the rigid "concept" of family honor and sexual purity; his mind seems eminently rational but "he himself [is] incapable of love." Hence Quentin, like Joe Christmas, worships death as a way of achieving certainty in a world of unreason and human weakness.[131]

But of all the Faustian figures Faulkner created in the 1930s, the most terrifying was Thomas Sutpen in *Absalom, Absalom!* (1936). Rejected in his youth by those with greater wealth and power, he dedicates the rest of his life to acquiring the status and respectability that will force men to recognize (and fear) his existence. To achieve this "fixed goal" in a society based on the ownership of property, he sets out to accumulate "land and niggers and a fine house," as well as a "stainless" wife with "unimpeachable" family connections and a son to insure that his name will survive in future generations. For Sutpen, human relationships are merely business transactions. He proceeds with strict rationality, calculating his opportunities, weighing all the implications of his actions, "choosing and discarding" people as if they were livestock or slaves, "putting aside" anyone who cannot help fulfill his consuming ambition. Moreover, Sutpen longs to attain a form of immortality through his children; beyond the material artifacts of his design, he wishes to defy the effects of time and history—to make his mark on an indifferent universe. He is acutely sensitive to the "need for haste" and the possibility that he will not accomplish his plans before he dies; in his old age he tries desperately to turn back the years and halt the tide of change. Yet Sutpen's dream is doomed from the beginning precisely because he is unaware that others have a similar craving to be recognized. Thus in refusing to acknowledge his mulatto son, in dismissing the feelings of family and community, he is ultimately destroyed by those pursuing their own retribution for past injuries. Everyone in *Absalom, Absalom!* is eventually transformed into an "instrument" seeking revenge for the traumatic experience of having been rejected. Each character hungers for vindication and justice at the expense of pity and understanding. By the end of the novel, Sutpen's house, position, and posterity have vanished, and only an idiot Negro boy—the last descendant of Sutpen's dynasty—remains to underscore the dimensions of Sutpen's defeat.[132]

In Faulkner's world the sin of hubris is surpassed only by the illusion that one can conquer time or escape from history. If it is a moral crime to lack compassion or to disregard another man's existence, it is supreme folly to disrupt the natural order of things. If the South is guilty of denying the black man's humanity, the North stands condemned for trying to alter the social customs and cultural values of an entire region. In either case, the children will suffer for the errors of their fathers.

It seems the special burden of the South, however, to internalize the legends and tragedies of the past. The destiny of Faulkner's characters invariably mirrors the fate of Southern society after the Civil War. As the fortunes of the agrarian aristocracy decline, as the plantations crumble and the land is parceled into progressively smaller segments, as the images of ruined fields and rotting families abound, the Sartorises and Compsons give way to the Snopeses—an entirely new breed of men, aspiring bankers and capitalists, harder and more efficient, less concerned with the ceremonies of small-town life, hating the soil and interested solely in profit, "never [making] mistakes in any matter pertaining to money."[133] But the Snopeses themselves carry on the inexorable process of decay; with their stiff bodies, stagnant eyes, and dead voices, they represent the final collapse of the old South.

And amid the wreckage, the survivors must determine how to come to terms with time. Faulkner's people are hypnotized and trapped by history. They memorize the folk tales and listen guiltily to the whispers of ghosts; they inherit the curse of slavery for which the presence of the blacks serves as a persistent reminder; they are molded from infancy by the deeds of their ancestors; they are forever plagued by the "old spilled blood and the old horror and anger and fear." Nothing is forgotten, the past and present merge, time is indivisible, and the living exchange roles with the dead as if the passage of years had not mattered or even occurred.[134] Everyone shares responsibility for the events of history; each individual is therefore part of a human continuum as minutes and hours are units of time. The glories and outrages of the past constitute a permanent legacy to the present and future which can never be renounced, only accepted.

Given Faulkner's extreme sense of historic and social organicism, those of his characters who possess a facility for stoic patience and "static serenity" are able to cope more effectively with the consequences of time. For every Quentin Compson hoping to silence the ticking of his watch through suicide there is a Eula Varner or a Lena Grove capable of ignoring the demand for rationality and purposeful activity, relying instead on natural intuition and feminine simplicity, favoring pure sexuality over consciousness and power, acquiescing in life as it is rather than as the fanatics think it should be. For every Thomas Sutpen who seeks wealth and immortality there is the Negro servant Dilsey who retains her sanity by passively enduring the world's injustice and cruelty. In most of Faulkner's novels during the 1930s, the aesthetic and instinctive personality seems superior to the intellectual and the activist. Those who can remain tranquil in the face of disaster achieve a quality of timelessness precisely by integrating themselves with the landscape, with history, and with the surrounding community. They appear courageous and indomitable because they are "fatalistic" and unconcerned with the need to assert man's significance in the universe.[135]

In the end it is the Joanna Burdens, attempting to impose their private conception of morality on society, needing to direct and transform the way men behave, who are the true violators of human nature and social continuity. They are oblivious to the ambiguities of life; they want to interfere and manipulate, tinker and control, find some sense of permanent order and meaning in the stream of time. In contrast Ratliff, the public conscience of *The Hamlet* (1940), recognizes that the Snopeses represent a new kind of disaster for the South, but he steadfastly refuses to intervene. To him, the town's ceremonies and traditions are more precious than his own theories of right and wrong; therefore, he resists the impulse to "improve and remake" the world according to some higher (if inhuman) ideal.[136] And this reverence for existing institutions and mores, for the culture and beliefs of long-established communities, for the historic values and customs which any society must cherish and preserve, formed the basis of Faulkner's outlook in the 1930s. Like Fuchs, he had converted the social insights of his contemporaries into a conservative—even mystical—plea for the acceptance of reality, the tolerance of man's vices, and the awareness of evil as intrinsic to life on earth.

6. Radicalism and Art: The Achievement of James Agee

If the documentaries and "social" novels of the depression decade had turned out to be introspective, pessimistic, traditionalist, and apolitical, there was at least one work that seemed genuinely radical both in form and content. In 1936 James Agee and Walker Evans were commissioned by *Fortune* magazine to collaborate on a series of articles about tenant farmers in the deep South. Evans was to supply the photographs, Agee the text. Their assignment, as *Fortune* defined it, was to explore in journalistic fashion the problems of rural poverty, soil erosion, and agricultural recovery. In this effort they were supposed to rely primarily on statistics, interviews, direct observation, and "human interest" stories. But Evans and Agee were neither professional reporters nor expatriate artists engaged in renewing their acquaintance with America. What Agee in particular discovered among the sharecroppers of Alabama was not the source material for a novel of social protest, nor another opportunity to celebrate the American past, nor an occasion to indulge in visions of an imminent cataclysm. Instead he began to mold the experience into a lyrical, angry, evocative prose poem on the nature of human suffering and the need for personal commitment. When *Fortune* found this unacceptable, Agee spent the remainder of the decade organizing his thoughts and feelings into a "book" without precedent in the history of American literature. The result was *Let Us Now Praise Famous Men*—a work which, though it sold only six hundred copies when finally published in 1941, managed to summarize and transcend the attitudes and values of an entire generation. In the process, *Let Us Now Praise Famous Men* contained the most sensitive and compassionate writing of which the 1930s was capable. However neglected at the time, it represented the decade's greatest literary achievement.

Essentially, Agee's strength lay in his ability to overcome the aesthetic and intellectual tensions that ran through the work of his contemporaries.

In *Let Us Now Praise Famous Men* he attempted to combine reportage and art, politics and morality, social consciousness and private integrity, a respect for tradition and the necessity for revolt.

To a considerable degree the book was as much a triumph of style as of ideas. In the first place, Agee refused to compose an "objective" travelogue; rather, he conceived of the work as an "effort in human actuality, in which the reader is no less centrally involved than the authors and those of whom they tell."[137] This was meant to be an intensely personal encounter, wherein the writer and reader were active participants, learning more about themselves than about the ostensible subject under discussion. In effect, *Let Us Now Praise Famous Men* seemed as much a quest for identity as a documentation of social disorder. Thus the text included extensive autobiographical passages and continual asides to the audience—all as a way of trying to redefine the relationship between observer and observed, analysis and empathy, internal emotions and the external world.

Secondly, like Faulkner, Agee employed a variety of techniques to transcribe his experience: realistic descriptions of people and places, colloquial dialogue, sophisticated discussions of social and economic issues, philosophical ruminations, polemics on the nature of art and the role of the intellectual, poetry, occasional excursions into Elizabethan rhetoric and religious symbolism, all of which were designed to reproduce a given event from as many vantage points as possible. Agee shared Faulkner's conviction that each moment of an individual's life should be seen in relation to the flow of time and the processes of change, that men were surrounded by objects and institutions which irrevocably conditioned their existence, that a person's identity could be understood only within the context of his house and family and patterns of work. Therefore, since "reality" was pluralistic, the writer needed to be aware of multiple perspectives, using several different forms of perception simultaneously in an effort to arrive at the "truth."

In addition Agee would not adhere to any "chronological progression," and he deliberately dispensed with ordinary narration.[138] The book had no visible beginning, middle, or end; instead its structure was circular, scenes were repeated, arguments were interrupted, themes and characters abruptly disappeared only to re-emerge in another setting, memories of the past were juxtaposed with conversations in the present. The result was an expressionist tour de force in which the reader—no longer a passive recipient of information but a partner in a dialogue with the author—was compelled to see and think about the world in radically new ways.

Moreover, Agee continually shifted back and forth between concrete details and their universal implications, private problems and their historic causes, the uniqueness of each individual and his function as a representative social type. His chief ambition throughout was to remain faithful to "particulars" while illuminating their general significance for politics, for society, for man, and for God. Though Agee's nominal subject was "North American cotton tenantry as examined in the daily living of three . . . white tenant families," at bottom he was inquiring into the "normal predicaments of human divinity."[139]

Ultimately, this aspiration forced him to move beyond the constricting boundaries of journalism and fiction, social criticism and artistic sensibility. In general, Agee abhorred the tendency of the reporter or ideologue to discuss human beings in terms of abstract categories and political slogans. The tenant farmers were more than simply victims of economic deprivation or members of an oppressed class; they were distinctive individuals whose inner feelings seemed as crucial to Agee as their external behavior. But neither was he particularly entranced by the "superior" insights of the literary mind. Indeed he considered the traditional tools of fiction—language, metaphors, allusions, symbols—even more dishonest and harmful than the inflexible preconceptions of the sociologist and humanitarian. The written word often distorted and falsified reality by offering imitations of experience and by destroying the immediacy of sense impressions. Thus he preferred the camera to artistic "invention" because it promised to capture the actual, unrevised, living presence of a man or thing. Nevertheless, Agee never deluded himself that pictures alone were sufficient to the apprehension of truth, nor did he believe that the neutral presentation of "facts" might provide a more objective account of human life. He recognized that the "illusion of embodiment" depended on the author's willingness to shape and control his material, to raise the value of a given subject "at least [to the level] of music and poetry," to describe and reflect on the meaning of what one had seen and heard. In the end, Agee wished to combine the advantages of photography and language, the eye and the imagination, observation and ideas, scientific investigation and artistic license, the documentary and the novel, the traditions of Naturalism and Symbolism.[140]

These stylistic imperatives were best revealed in Agee's special attitude toward the tenant families. He and Evans came to regard themselves as "spies" prying intimately "into the lives of an undefended and appallingly damaged group of human beings. . . ." They were constantly tortured by the problem of how to record the plight of the sharecroppers without intruding on their privacy, converting them into social symbols, or debasing their natural dignity and self-respect. Moreover, Agee was intensely aware of the injury he could inflict on the tenants by treating them with pity or condescension. Hence he spent many pages describing in detail their houses, furniture, utensils, food, clothing, and work habits in the hope that he might shed light on their economic hardships without violating their trust. Yet even as he marveled at the primitive "beauty" of the objects and materials on which their lives depended, he considered it a disgrace and an "abomination" that men should have to endure such misery. For Agee, the tenant hovels were both a holy "tabernacle" and an unspeakable tragedy. Given this dual vision, the most one could do was to insist on correct forms of behavior between otherwise dissimilar people. Agee could neither exchange places with the farmers nor "make expatiation" for their pain. At best, he might preserve his own autonomy while writing of the tenants with honesty, clarity, understanding, and love.[141]

Beyond the moral and psychological tensions involved in his relationship with the sharecroppers, Agee wished to protect their individuality at the same time he recalled their common humanity. On the one hand, he believed with Saroyan that every creature on earth was eternally condemned to loneliness and isolation, each family separate and "remote," each person absorbed with his own troubles and unable to care about or even imagine the difficulties of others. Furthermore, like Dos Passos he detested the fashionable collectivism that threatened to destroy a man's uniqueness and integrity. But on the other hand Agee found it impossible to ignore the social ties and regional loyalties which helped determine the personality and values of the tenant farmers. To overlook their claims on society or their affinities with the entire human race, to overemphasize the extent to which they might never be "duplicated" or "replaced" was equally romantic and misleading. Thus Agee sought to transcend the decade-long conflict between private concerns and public issues by portraying each sharecropper as a "single, unrepeatable, holy individual" who was simultaneously an integral thread in the "fabric" of American life.[142]

Similarly, he wished to reconcile the ideals of "culture" and "civilization." In his view, the tenants' natural innocence and their lack of formal education did not mean that they were ignorant or naïve. Indeed their sense of intuition was highly developed; they possessed an instinctive facility for wonder and joy; they could grow and change with new experiences; they were immune to the hypocrisies and cruelties of the middle class. They rarely suffered from the neuroses that came with a docile adjustment to irrational laws and "insane" institutions. Yet Agee rejected the conclusion that spontaneous understanding was always preferable to acquired knowledge. On the contrary, he considered the sharecroppers at an "immeasurable disadvantage" in a society dependent on advanced ideas, skills, and techniques. Nor did the tenants embody for him the essential goodness of the common man. There were no patient Okies or heroic peasants in Agee's universe, just terribly limited men whose capacity for evil was as great as their more "civilized" counterparts. The people of whom Agee wrote knew so little about how to cope with the modern world that they had become "profoundly anesthetized" to the possibilities of a truly human life. "Helpless cripples," forced to "use themselves as the simplest savages do," they could neither improve their lot nor long survive; they might look forward only to rapid aging and an early death. Therefore, Agee placed his faith in a union of innocence and consciousness, intuition and intelligence, simplicity and sophistication. The resulting balance would be difficult to sustain, but it offered man the one way out of poverty and deprivation. Considered separately, the values associated with culture and civilization were deceptive and dangerous; together they represented the "source and guide of all hope and cure."[143]

Finally, Agee insisted that the connections between ethics and politics, means and ends, human compassion and social justice were always tenuous and paradoxical. For the most part he distrusted the activists and "reformers" who spoke of the sharecroppers as a "problem" to be solved, who were willing to manipulate individuals in the interest of some greater public good, who failed to discern the ways in which a political movement might dehumanize and betray the very people it was supposed to help. Moreover, like West and Faulkner, Agee remained deeply pessimistic about the beneficial effects of social change; he believed that men were forever "trapped" by obligations, rituals, and circumstances over which they had little control and from which there was no escape. In a world where suffering was a permanent part of life, he warned that no organized crusade would "make much difference."[144]

Yet despite his skepticism toward political programs and social causes, Agee still granted the need for some form of revolution. He did not surrender to the conservatism of a Dos Passos or Fuchs, nor to the nihilism of an Algren or McCoy. Instead he demanded of his countrymen both understanding and action, consciousness and commitment, a respect for the sanctity of each man and a willingness to transform the entire society. Given an appreciation of how difficult it would be to alter the conditions of tenantry, given the high risk of disappointment and failure, men must nevertheless strive for a sense of "freedom, joy, health, [and] knowledge."[145] Like Reinhold Niebuhr, Agee was more concerned with the way individuals discharged their moral responsibilities toward one another than with the movements or ideologies they occasionally endorsed. Ultimately, he held out to men an existential vision of the world that emphasized doubt rather than certainty, struggle rather than acceptance, engagement rather than withdrawal.

Following the pattern of Lewis Mumford, John Dewey, Robert Lynd, and Sidney Hook, Agee was asking his readers to believe simultaneously in a series of conflicting ideas. He had suggested in *Let Us Now Praise Famous Men* the possibility of fusing journalism and art, language and visual images, economic analysis and personal insight, the desire for change and the need to preserve cultural values, a commitment to political activity and a tolerance of human limitations. Precisely because he was acutely sensitive to all the social, moral, and aesthetic implications of a particular experience, precisely because he wanted to alter the way his readers saw reality, precisely because he believed that the total understanding of a problem would not immobilize but liberate mankind, Agee had fashioned the most radical work of the 1930s. It was supremely ironic, therefore, that his achievement should come at a moment when his contemporaries seemed increasingly indisposed toward artistic or intellectual innovation of any kind.

CHAPTER VI

THE RADICAL STAGE AND THE
HOLLYWOOD FILM IN THE 1930s

1. *The Rise and Fall of the Workers' Theater*

Even if most of the decade's novels and documentaries had been genuinely radical in style as well as content, there was no assurance that they could have actually helped to transform America's values and institutions. Indeed it was becoming obvious to the more perceptive observers that literature as such lacked the appeal or effectiveness it had once enjoyed. Where the Progressive generation and its successors in the 1920s rarely doubted the regenerative power of the written word, where they tended to invest fiction and poetry with an almost missionary role in creating a new kind of society, their fellow citizens were turning increasingly to other forms of art and communication. By the 1930s the age of the book was giving way to the age of sight and sound. Henceforth, those who sought a cultural revolution in the United States might have to rely less on the arguments of the printed page and more on the impact of the stage, the radio, the picture magazine, the newsreel, and the film. In the process, the traditional problems of political strategy and social philosophy were supplanted by a growing fascination with the mass media and popular taste.

At first, however, many intellectuals believed that these new instruments could be used for radical purposes. They professed a special faith in the capacity of the theater to alter American life—perhaps because they assumed that plays were only a more potent extension of the ordinary prose with which they felt most familiar and comfortable. In any case, during the early 1930s writers like Dwight Macdonald, Edmund Wilson, and Stark Young persistently complained that the commercial theater in the United States was impossibly competitive, banal, and frivolous. Given the general "disorganization of society" and the absence of any revolutionary tradition on the stage, the typical Broadway product had no "passionate matter to express," no "pressing ideas to retail," no "battles of theory to be fought," and no "consistent point of view" with which to analyze American civilization.[1] These weaknesses appeared particularly egregious since, as one radical dramatist pointed out, plays were often more accessible and attractive to people than novels and could therefore affect a greater segment of the population.[2] Thus a number of intellectuals shared John Dos Passos's longing for a "theater that will be a social force," that would "be able to mold the audience . . . instead of everlastingly flattering it," that might serve as the pre-eminent "mass art" in what was hopefully developing into a new "world of collectives."[3]

From the beginning it seemed evident that the sort of plays radicals had in mind would differ fundamentally from earlier attempts to revise the formulas of the commercial stage. During the 1920s organizations such as the Theatre Guild, the Provincetown Players, and the New Playwrights Theater had all experimented with new subjects and techniques, but these enterprises were composed largely of professionals whose primary commitment was aesthetic rather than political. They hoped to enliven Broadway by putting on more modern and sophisticated plays for an audience presumably tired of creaky melodramas and mindless musicals. With the onset of the depression, however, a new movement emerged whose ambition, according to Hallie Flanagan, was nothing less than the creation of a "national culture by and for the working class of America."[4] Like the yearning for a proletarian literature, the spirit behind the "Workers' Theater" could be traced to a disgust with the "irresponsibility" and "escapism" of the 1920s, a hostility to bourgeois individualism, and a desire to reunite the artist with society. Very soon after the stock-market crash, the theatrical manifestations of these ideas began to appear in the blue-collar neighborhoods and outside the factory gates of several major American cities: mobile stages, agit-prop skits, mimeographed broadsides dedicated to propagating the cause of revolutionary drama.

If the initial efforts of the Workers' Theater often seemed primitive and crude, they were not without a certain tactical justification. Originally, the use of agit-prop was never intended as anything more than a placard to promote political organization among the poor and the unemployed. To accomplish this goal many considered it imperative to bring the stage to the masses rather than wait for the masses to come to the stage. Even more important, the workers themselves were supposed to participate in their own productions as writers, actors, and directors; in this scheme, the barriers between performer and audience would vanish forever. Hence radical magazines such as *New Theatre and Film* stressed the virtues of mobility, clarity, and simplicity. Its contributors called for skits that would require only a minimum amount of preparation, for dialogue and situations which the oppressed could easily understand, and for characters with whom they might readily identify.[5]

Though it was not obvious at the time, this emphasis on the most elementary dramatic forms had a good deal in common with the premises of the mass media. Ironically, both the Workers' Theater and the movie industry seemed to assume that the average person possessed a twelve-year-old mind incapable of grasping complex problems and ideas. Thus at the very outset the road was being paved for a relatively smooth journey from Union Square to Hollywood.

Indeed it was not long before a number of radicals began to acknowledge that they could not rely on the simplistic techniques of guerrilla theater if they hoped to compete with radio and films for the attention of the masses. "In order to get the best political results," one theoretician argued, "it must always be our aim to achieve the best performances possible." This meant that the new movement would have to raise the artistic level of its productions, improve the quality of its acting and direction, secure professional advice, reward good craftsmanship, establish permanent companies, and put on full-length plays.[6] Since the typical worker had neither the time nor the training to realize these objectives, the revolutionary stage found it necessary to invite the aid of the bourgeois refugees from Broadway who could serve both as teachers and performers. Within a short time dramatic ability became a more important criterion than class consciousness or doctrinal purity, and the aesthetic of agit-prop gave way to the relative polish of the Theater Union. Gradually, the masses were seen not as active participants but as a passive audience attending plays designed for their betterment. By the mid-1930s the separation of playwrights, actors, designers, and directors from the surrounding proletarian community was complete. In the interest of broadening its impact and appeal, the mobile "Workers' " Theater had become a stationary "People's" Theater, speaking in the idioms with which most Americans were intimate, addressing itself to the customs and preconceptions of "popular life."[7]

At least one writer tried to overcome the growing contradiction between good plays and effective propaganda, between those who cared about the theater and those who hungered for revolution. Throughout the 1930s Mordecai Gorelik, a stage designer who worked for the Yiddish and Group Theaters as well as for Hollywood, was seeking to develop a theory of the drama which might satisfy the demands both of art and politics. He firmly believed that the production of plays was neither an end in itself nor a "weapon" in the class struggle; instead, its principal function was "to influence life by theatrical means." This involved a recognition that the stage existed not for "topical propaganda" nor for "abstract art" but for an "inquiry" into the nature of social institutions and human relationships.[8] In order to define precisely what kinds of scripts, settings, and performances were essential to attain this ideal, Gorelik felt compelled to explore the history of dramatic forms and techniques as they had evolved from antiquity to the present. Only then could he outline his alternatives for the modern theater. His decade-long effort culminated in 1940 with the publication of *New Theatres for Old,* perhaps the most coherent and systematic statement of how a revolution on the stage might contribute to a revolution in society.

The book was an attack on all those devices which had converted the theater into a "magic world of illusion." On the one hand, Gorelik deplored the nineteenth-century Naturalistic attempts to reproduce the details of social behavior on the stage, to design sets as if they could serve as exact replicas of the environment, to train actors to imitate perfectly the people whom they were portraying, to persuade the audience that it was witnessing not a play but life itself.[9] On the other hand, he was equally disparaging of the twentieth-century Symbolist tradition, with its tendency to reduce society to a series of visual metaphors, its overemphasis on individual psychology and subjective feelings, and its general lack of interest in contemporary affairs. In his view, the stylized "atmosphere" of Symbolist drama was merely a more sophisticated means of turning the theater into an instrument for the perpetuation of images and myths.[10]

But most of all Gorelik objected to the effect of these conventions on the mind and attitudes of the playgoer: the appeal to his unconscious emotions, the urge to make him a "passive" and "introspective" spectator, the desire to have him identify instinctively with the characters on the stage. In the bourgeois theater, Gorelik argued, the audience must be "snared, charmed, entranced" and seduced into suspending its "critical judgment."[11] Even the more recent left-wing drama of the 1930s, he complained, had not really broken with the techniques of illusion. The radicals "disagreed only with the 'message' of the Symbolist playwrights"; they challenged neither the "general mode of production" nor "the accepted form of the script."[12]

Hence Gorelik asserted that the revolutionary theater would have to change not just the content of its plays but the total setting in which they were presented.

For his own part, Gorelik championed what he called the "epic" theater of Brecht and Piscator. He wished to restore in the audience a sense that it was attending a "play," not looking at "life." To this end, he insisted that the close rapport between actors and spectators be broken, that the stage become a "platform" for the advancement of new ideas, that the drama function as a "laboratory" or a "lecture-demonstration" for the analysis of "facts" and "objective events," that each of the elements in a given production be granted "autonomy" in order to keep the playgoers constantly alert and thoughtful throughout the performance. For Gorelik, the true goal of the radical stage was to encourage "practical knowledge" rather than an "emotional catharsis," intelligent participation rather than passive entertainment, collective action rather than personal enjoyment.[13] Ultimately, he envisaged a theater that would emphasize "social obligation, communal effort, and a [feeling] of fellowship with one's neighbors" beyond anything the traditions of Naturalism and Symbolism had imagined.[14]

In sum, Gorelik had gone beyond the simplicities of agit-prop and the stereotypes of proletarian melodrama; he was calling for a basic transformation in language, acting, direction, stage design, and the very architecture of the theater hall itself. Yet few radicals seemed willing to follow his prescriptions. Rather than confound the masses with new and unfamiliar techniques, they appeared content to adapt the classic forms of bourgeois drama—complicated plots, realistic or symbolic sets, conventional dialogue —to the current demands of social protest. Where Gorelik had hoped to bombard the audience with extraordinary theatrical effects that might eventually alter its perception of the world, his colleagues on the left preferred to offer revolutionary sentiments in terms with which the average playgoer could always feel at ease.

The one point on which they all agreed, however, was the need for a genuinely "social" theater in keeping with the collectivist impulses of the 1930s. This implied not only scripts dealing with contemporary problems but an intangible spirit of community and cooperation on the part of performers and spectators alike. It was therefore fitting that the depression should give birth to a large number of repertory companies and theatrical "groups"—the Theater Union, the Federal Theater, the Mercury Theater, the Theater Collective, Artef, the Labor Stage. But perhaps the organization that best emobodied these values (and which boasted the most appropriate name) was the Group Theater. Alone among the various dramatic experiments of the period, it managed to function throughout the entire decade. On several occasions it achieved a level of success that was at once political, commercial, and artistic. Moreover, it included some of the finest talents to work on the American stage (and later in films): Lee Strasberg, Cheryl Crawford, Elia Kazan, Sanford Meisner, Boris Aronson, Morris Carnovsky, Lee J. Cobb, Franchot Tone, John Garfield, Luther and Stella Adler, Karl Malden, and Howard Da Silva. Most of all, in its strengths as well as its deficiencies, the Group became a compelling symbol for much of what radicals meant when they spoke of a new culture to accompany the new society.

The guiding force behind the Group was undoubtedly Harold Clurman. Together with Lee Strasberg, he planned and launched the enterprise, articulated its ideals, defended its dreams, and brooded over its triumphs and failures in his memoir *The Fervent Years*—a book that revealed as much about the mind of the 1930s as its more formal doctrines and manifestoes.

Like Gorelik (who designed many of the sets for the Group's productions), Clurman conceived of his theater not merely as a vehicle to put on radical plays but as a house of "communion" in which the otherwise solitary writer, actor, director, and technician might find "companionship," "security," and a "common faith." To Clurman, the drama was "by its very nature . . . an art of collaboration and teamwork"; it therefore demanded that the participant subordinate his urge for "self-assertion" to the higher goals of "harmony" and "collective discipline." There should be a continuous "interchange between society and the individual," he argued in a voice that sounded much like John Dewey and Robert Lynd. "We must get to know ourselves by getting to know one another." Thus when Clurman and Strasberg began to select their colleagues, they were not "hiring a company" but "making a group." Given their longing for a "closer embrace" and a "more rooted togetherness" among men, they felt called on to move from an "experiment in the theater" to an "experiment in living." In essence, they were seeking from the stage not only a cultural renaissance but a surrogate home and family which could overcome the traditional sense of isolation and "loneliness" associated both with American art and American life.[15]

This emphasis on community had certain practical consequences for the structure and ambitions of Clurman's organization. In theory, at least, the Group was to be a theater without "stars." Instead it proclaimed the merits of ensemble acting, "joint creativity," and shared responsibility for the choice of scripts and the kind of treatment they received. Moreover, Clurman wanted to develop a permanent audience which would not only provide a source of steady income and support for the Group but whose relationship with the company was to be reciprocal and mutually beneficial. Presumably, the playgoers would be directly involved in the dramatic process, offering suggestions and criticism, laying the basis for common values and aspirations, giving the artist a feeling that he was genuinely serving society.[16]

The Group was not alone in desiring an intimate bond between the performers and the audience. When Hallie Flanagan took charge of the Federal Theater Project in the mid-1930s, she saw the subsidized spectacles and Living Newspapers not merely as another form of economic relief but as an opportunity for the stage to become an integral part of people's daily lives. By addressing itself to the needs and attitudes of a particular region, city, or neighborhood, by drawing on the resources of the local community, by utilizing all types of media to confront the issues of the time, the Federal Theater could function as an indispensable meeting place for every section of the population.[17] In the long run, both Clurman and Flanagan regarded their theaters as models for a collectivist life-style which the entire country might eventually emulate.

Yet in neither case did they insist on plays which set forth a "message" or advanced a specific "ideology." Clurman, especially, seemed more interested in establishing a "spiritual union" between actors and spectators than in awakening their revolutionary consciousness.[18] As with many other movements in the decade, the "collectivism" of the Group Theater was more a matter of rhetoric, sentiment, and posture than an effort to fashion a coherent social or aesthetic theory. Basically, the Group reflected the yearning of the 1930s to overcome what it considered the puerility and individualism of the 1920s. In their search for comradeship and a sense of belonging, in their desire for "moral guidance" and emotional stability, Clurman and his colleagues were hoping to escape the world's anarchy and "chaos." They longed for something in which to believe, some commitment beyond the limitations of the private conscience, some indication of order and unity in their society and in themselves—even if this meant that they might ultimately exchange their radical impulses for the gratifications of mass acceptance.[19]

Thus it was not surprising that the Group should be concerned less with the promulgation of socialist ideals than with the creation of a "truly representative *American* theater."[20] Throughout the decade its basic orientation was national rather than proletarian. Moreover, since the Group's typical audience was largely Jewish and middle class, most of its actual productions dealt with distinctively bourgeois problems. Its plays tended to attack capitalism on moral and cultural rather than economic grounds—focusing on the myth of success, the dehumanization of work, and the corruption of values under a system of private profit. For the most part the Group was rarely political or propagandistic in the sense that either the Workers' Theater or Gorelik would have approved; instead its style was frequently allegorical, and its main preoccupation was the spiritual poverty of life in the United States.

During the early 1930s the Group experimented with a number of different subjects and techniques. By 1935, however, it had discovered among its own members a writer who was to serve as its truest and most eloquent voice. With the plays of Clifford Odets, both the Group and the radical theater movement as a whole was able to come of age.

Odets made his debut in 1935 with a one-act skit that rapidly became the most celebrated (if somewhat unrepresentative) example of political theater in the 1930s—*Waiting for Lefty*. Essentially, *Lefty*'s remarkable triumph with both the radical and commercial press stemmed from Odets's ability to translate the conventions of agit-prop—choral recitation, episodic structure, satiric caricature, declamatory performances—into fully human terms.[21] Though *Lefty*'s ostensible purpose was to explain and assist a New York taxi strike, its underlying concerns appeared more personal than economic. Most of *Lefty*'s vignettes illustrated not so much the need to organize a union as the distortion of human relationships in a time of poverty and unemployment—the assault on one's manhood, the disintegration of the family, the stifling of emotion, the priority of money over love. The basic issue was not only wages and working conditions but the survival of individual honor in the face of bribes, threats, and coercion. Thus when the predominantly bourgeois audience joined the actors in shouting *"Strike!"* at the end of the play, they were experiencing more than a vicarious sense of participation in the class struggle, more than a rhetorical commitment to the workers' cause. Ultimately, they leaped from their seats in response to their own feeling of social and psychological dislocation and their own yearning for a more humane and satisfying life than seemed presently possible in the United States.

Within a short time Odets found himself being hailed as "the leading revolutionary playwright in America."[22] But his real artistic temperament was best revealed not in the militancy of *Waiting For Lefty* but in the moody lyricism of *Awake and Sing* (1935) and the bitter ambiguity of *Golden Boy* (1937).

On the surface many of Odets's plots appeared contrived and overwrought. To a large extent they were designed to show that the traditional dreams and aspirations of the middle class had collapsed, that the old society was giving way to something new and unprecedented, that to escape from the decay of the present one must undergo an almost mystical process of conversion and rebirth. His plays reached their climactic point when the central character began to recognize that "heartbreak and terror are not the heritage of mankind! The world is beautiful." Henceforth, "men will sing at their work, men will love."[23] With this, the curtain came down on a note of hope and affirmation for which there was hardly any preparation in the script or performances. Like John Steinbeck, Odets believed in man's ability to build a better future, but he offered no political philosophy or plausible course of action beyond the earnest insistence that "life should have some dignity."[24] As a result, the concluding optimism was often forced and ritualistic; the spirit of resurrection and redemption seemed little more than a gesture of faith in the essential goodness and rationality of human nature; the radical message sounded uncomfortably similar to the typical happy ending of a Hollywood film.[25]

Yet if his ideas were hortatory and vague, his dialogue was pungent and precise. The great strength of Odets's plays lay not in their logical structure or intellectual sophistication but in the passionate conversations of his characters—the way they spoke, the words they used, the psychological implications of their apparently aimless and irrelevant chatter. Their stage language combined a hard-boiled urban cynicism with a poetic fervor that conveyed brilliantly the tensions and paradoxes of life among those who were desperately seeking a foothold in American society. For Odets was writing not about the middle class in general but about the second-generation Italians and Jews for whom the daily battle between parents and children, integrity and success, moral idealism and worldly compromise was more pressing than any vision of a socialist utopia. And in his ability to capture the humor and pain of their predicament, Odets was writing about himself as well.[26]

In both *Awake and Sing* and *Golden Boy* Odets examined a culture which worshipped economic security and social prestige at the expense of human feeling and self-respect. But for him the issue was never simple or easily solved. On the one hand were the men of conscience and principle—Jacob, the philosophical grandfather in *Awake and Sing,* an aging admirer of Caruso and Marx, searching for paradise among his musty records and books, a "sentimental idealist with no power to turn ideal into action," an impractical "failure" who once had "golden opportunities but drank instead a glass tea," an ineffectual romantic with "crazy ideas" about communism who cannot hold a job and never grasps the essential point that "charity starts at home"; Mr. Bonaparte, the disappointed father of the "golden boy" who asks his son to choose between music and boxing, who values abstract intellectual discussions over wealth and status, who assumes that "a good life'sa possible" even if art cannot "put bread and butter on the table," whose sense of moral authority seems to his son only a preference for living in the past and "blowing off steam." Their outlook is best summarized in Jacob's moving and poignant appeal to his own grandson Ralph: "Boychick, wake up. Be something. Make your life something good. For the love of an old man who sees in your young days his new life, for such love take the world in your two hands and make it like new. Go out and fight so life shouldn't be printed on dollar bills."[27]

On the other hand were those who perceived and embraced the established values of American society—Bessie Berger, the eminently realistic (and classically Jewish) mother of *Awake and Sing* who accepts the fact that she is living in a "jungle," who considers "food in the house" more important than speeches on street corners, who makes innumerable (and highly vocal) sacrifices so that some day her son should "ride up to the door in a big car with a chauffeur and a radio," who understands that in America "money talks" and therefore "without a dollar you don't look the world in the eye"; Joe Bonaparte who detests the "feeling of no possessions," who yearns for "fame and fortune, not to be different or artistic," who longs to go to the "top of the world" where respect is automatic and "nobody laughs," who refuses to believe "that bull the meek'll inherit the earth," who is willing to turn himself into a commodity and submit to commercial exploitation because culture and morality have absolutely no meaning in modern life.[28]

In this conflict of values it was not always clear where Odets stood. His own attitude toward Broadway and Hollywood was extraordinarily ambivalent; he could never reconcile his strong desire for public recognition and approval with his lingering commitment to radical ideals. In a profound sense, Odets himself was both a revolutionary dreamer and the proverbial golden boy, and everything he wrote from his depression dramas to his later film scripts (especially *The Big Knife* and *The Sweet Smell of Success)* mirrored this double vision with striking consistency.

Indeed the entire Group shared Odets's dilemma. And their plight suggested how difficult it was for artists and radicals to function in America without surrendering to the temptations of the market place or the urge for social respectability. Despite their belief in community and cooperation, the members of the Group were not immune to secret ambitions, inflated egos, and the craving for "personal reward." The moment they achieved even a modicum of success, Harold Clurman observed, they seemed vulnerable to the blandishments of Broadway and Hollywood—partly because, in the absence of a genuine social revolution, these meccas "possessed the only power and glory the world could [presently] offer."[29]

At times they rejected the appeal of glamour, wealth, and success, scorning the commercial theater and movie colony as arch-symbols of "sin," vulgarity, and "money-making unrelated to any other ideal."[30] During these moments they sought in the Group a haven from the corrupting pressures of the larger society, a refuge from the profit motive that would somehow provide a sense of safety and security unavailable in the outside world. But as Clurman recognized, these impulses could have quite conservative consequences. Feeling constantly threatened by the very forces it had tried to combat, the Group during the late 1930s became increasingly inbred and provincial, increasingly isolated from those people it most hoped to inspire and change. Instead of helping to fashion a new set of social and cultural institutions, the company seemed to fear contact with the rest of America, and it began to exhibit what Clurman called a "peculiar spirit of retreat." Thus the Group had more of a protective and inhibiting effect on its own members than a radicalizing influence on its audience. Caught between the effort to rebel and the passion to belong, between the yearning for "anonymity" in a collective enterprise and the subconscious urge for "personal aggrandizement," between the desire for artistic liberation and the need for psychological order and discipline, the Group was being torn apart by a variety of internal conflicts it could never resolve.[31]

Yet the Group's predicament was by no means unique; rather, it reflected perfectly the agony of the radical theater in the decade's closing years. The central problem for all the dramatic experiments—the Federal and Mercury theaters, the Theater Union, the Labor Stage—was their inability to develop a permanent audience, either proletarian or middle class, for whom they could confidently speak. Without stable and consistent support, without the capacity to plan on a long-term or even seasonal basis, they were compelled to rely on irregular subsidies from friends, alumni, Broadway "angels," and Hollywood producers. More often, however, they were totally dependent on the vagaries of the box office. Forced to compete for scripts, performers, theater halls, favorable reviews, and booming ticket sales, they became increasingly a commercial operation, indistinguishable from their show-business counterparts uptown and out west.[32]

As such, the entire movement fell victim to the less adventurous mood of the late 1930s, when the drama of social significance no longer seemed appropriate to a country more concerned with consolidating its gains than engaging in further reforms. Moreover, the failure of the radical theater to invent new styles and techniques for the presentation of its ideas (as Mordecai Gorelik had demanded), its preference for conventional realism over avant-garde experimentation made its identification with the values of Broadway and Hollywood appear natural and inevitable. By the end of the decade the New York stage had been given over to the sentimentalities of Thornton Wilder's *Our Town* and William Saroyan's *The Time of Your Life* —enormously popular plays which celebrated the charm and innocence of the "little people," glorified the simple "beauty" of raising a family and visiting with one's neighbors, preached the virtue of "taking things easy," and praised the "art" of living as more important and less harmful than the impulse to change the world.[33]

In the end, the radical theater could not succeed as long as the surrounding institutions remained unaltered. As an experiment with collective forms of organization in a largely competitive economy, as an effort to create a counter-culture in a mass society, the movement found its growth restricted and its ambitions thwarted.[34] In order to survive in what was essentially a non-revolutionary environment, it would have to discover new forms of expression, new ways of reaching its audience, new powers of communication beyond anything the stage could provide. And for most playwrights, actors, directors, designers, and critics, there was really only one place to turn.

2. *The Appeal of the Mass Media*

Throughout the 1930s few forces were more potent in shaping the way men saw the world than the newsreel, the picture magazine, the radio program, and the Hollywood film. For both the intellectual community and the general public, the influence of the mass media was pervasive and inescapable. It was not only that millions listened to radio every night or attended movies twice a week as a matter of habit, regardless of what the networks broadcasted and the distributors booked. It was not even that one's attitude toward social issues grew increasingly dependent on the Lucean perspective of *Life* and *The March of Time,* or that one's conception of how to talk and act properly could be modeled on the stars of the airwaves and silver screen. Beyond these obvious manifestations of the media's power there were its more subtle effects—the Presidential use of radio to make the government seem a friendly presence by the fireside (and, incidentally, to generate support for the policies of the New Deal), the intrusion of documentary techniques and movie dialogue into literature as if the novelist was unconsciously admitting that his craft could not survive unless it accommodated itself to the fashions of popular culture, the largely justified fear of theater people that (with the advent of sound and the exodus of playwrights and performers from Broadway to Hollywood) their discipline would become obsolete, the willingness of many to abandon the older genres altogether and concentrate instead on converting the movies into a genuine folk art.

From the beginning of the decade a number of radicals were especially captivated by the social possibilities of the cinema. In Dwight Macdonald's view, films had supplanted drama, music, and literature not only as the supreme aesthetic experience of the twentieth century but also as the paramount form of public entertainment. Precisely because "movies are created for the enjoyment of the people, not the delectation of the connoisseur or dilettante," he believed that—properly handled—they could bring the artist and the intellectual into contact with the masses on a scale unprecedented in the nation's history.[35] Moreover, since the neighborhood movie house was attracting Americans in far greater numbers than the theater or the libraries, it seemed advisable to explore the full dimensions of popular taste. Thus, as one Marxist critic argued, "all revolutionary artists aiming to undermine the ideological structure of the middle class and consolidate the working class must, in order to be at this time effectively heard, consider seriously the question of working through Hollywood."[36]

But for radicals, the potential virtues of the cinema were not limited to the size of the audience. To some, the basic elements of film-making—its mass-production techniques, its insistence on the cooperation of everyone on the set, its ability to capture visually the relationships between individuals and their environment, its sensitivity to social background and political events, its realistic reproduction of particular locales and the behavior of crowds—all fulfilled the requirements of a truly collective art.[37]

More important, in the early 1930s many Marxists were quite enthralled with the implications of selective camera work, careful editing, and the principles of montage as inherited from the Russian cinema. They praised at great length the capacity of an Eisenstein to subject his audience "to an emotional shock with mathematically calculated certainty, and direct it from this emotional state to a definite intellectual idea." With such devices, presumably, the public's outlook and allegiances could be radically transformed. But beneath this fascination with the revolutionary consequences of montage there lay an uncomfortably conservative bias—a tendency to celebrate the director's power to "mold" and manipulate the sentiments of the common man, to "dictate to the spectator what to see and how to see it."[38] Thus, depending on who was planning the shots, focusing the camera, and cutting the film, movies could be an instrument either of extraordinary intellectual liberation or rigid social control.

Even among non-Marxists there was considerable discussion about the ways in which society might benefit from radio and films. Many writers assumed that the mass media could strengthen the bonds between people and thereby contribute to the development of an authentic spirit of community in the United States. In analyzing the psychological impact of the radio as of 1935, Hadley Cantril and Gordon Allport were struck by its ability to provide listeners with "an imaginative sense of participation in a common activity." In their judgment, network radio had the power to erase artificial distinctions between men and women, age and youth, social classes and ethnic groups, rural and urban America. Moreover, it stood in opposition to the disintegrative forces of modern life, serving as an antidote to the fragmentation and chaos of the depression years, welcoming the voice of political leaders directly into the home, buttressing the role of the family as a source of shared values and beliefs, giving the "lonely" individual the impression that he was a member of some "vast social unity." Hence they concluded that "when a million or more people hear the same subject matter, the same arguments and appeals, the same music and humor, when their attention is held in the same way and at the same time to the same stimuli, it is psychologically inevitable that they should acquire . . . common interests, common tastes, and common attitudes. In short, it seems to be the nature of radio to encourage people to think and feel alike."[39]

Films appeared to be having a similar effect. According to Lewis Mumford, the camera conveyed to ordinary citizens an intimate sense of the "public world," permitting them to join in the tribulations of those who were otherwise powerful and remote.[40] In addition, another writer observed, "the movies are furnishing the nation with a common body of knowledge. . . . Here are stories, names, phrases, points of view which are common national property." Henceforth, Hollywood's capacity to "span geographical frontiers" and "crumble the barriers between people of different educations and different economic backgrounds" meant that no one in America need be a stranger to anyone else.[41] Thus through the beneficence of mass communications, the entire country could speak the same language, understand the same allusions and references, enjoy the same experiences, indulge in the same expectations, and cherish the same dreams.

In the end, intellectuals of every political persuasion believed that radio and films could be a positive force in the creation of collectivist goals and ideals. Yet in their enthusiasm for the media as a unifying influence they sometimes overlooked its potential for frustrating cultural innovation and social change. To begin with, the intelligentsia's growing interest in the popular arts could lead to a decline in the range and quality of serious thought without necessarily raising the level of public taste. During the 1930s writers were attracted to mass culture as part of a general fascination with the customs and attitudes of the average man. At the same time, they were motivated by a strong desire to play some direct role in reshaping the nation's institutions and beliefs. But as a result, they appeared increasingly reluctant to discriminate between the various forms of artistic expression, assuming instead the relative equality of philosophy and folklore, romanticizing the natural wisdom of the "people," pointing out the superiority of action over ideas, applauding the movies for concentrating on "pure" movement and physical energy in contrast to the "static" talk of novels and plays, arguing even that the conventional "happy ending" might suit a populace which could never conceive of American life as fundamentally tragic and grim.[42] In this way, the intellectuals themselves began to adopt a "middlebrow" mentality, preferring kitsch to art and uplifting pieties to critical inquiry.

But regardless of its effect on writers, the media's impact on the society at large was often quite the opposite from what they anticipated or hoped. While many intellectuals presumed that the radio and newsreel would restore a sense of direct contact between the politicians and the people, only a few recognized that such devices could heighten the possibility of "mass regimentation" by making everyone more susceptible to the molders of public opinion.[43] Indeed the very magnitude and importance of the communications apparatus meant that in the future radicals would have to revise their analysis of the capitalist system, taking into account the fact that whoever controlled its *cultural* machinery might ultimately wield greater power than those who owned its banks and factories.

Moreover, instead of encouraging a change in the way men saw their world, the mass media frequently seemed little more than a mechanism for diversion, entertainment, and escape. Throughout the 1930s a number of commentators charged that the typical radio program and motion picture served largely as an instrument of pacification for people too tired to read or think or act. Forced to live in a "drab, monotonous, unsatisfying environment," unable to rely on their own imaginative resources, many Americans were apparently being consoled by packaged dreams and fantasies, "surrogate" heroes and lovers, illusions of wealth and happiness—all of which "carried the perfume of unreality" into their otherwise "impoverished lives."[44] The decade's radical potential was further weakened by the proneness of the popular arts to avoid controversy at all costs. Despite their faith in the social benefits of radio, Cantril and Allport admitted that the medium was being pressured by advertisers, censors, and the very diversity of its audience to aim at the lowest common denominators of taste and interest, to use words and phrases that would never give offense, to steer a "middle course and appeal to the middle class."[45] And this resulted in a reinforcement of existing values and beliefs through an emphasis on small-town neighborliness and ordinary common sense, a celebration of the maxim that "riches and luxuries cannot buy peace of mind," a constant reiteration of the notion that men should be content with what they had rather than nourish unattainable ambitions, a general suspicion of restlessness and self-assertion, and a discomfort with any sort of person who appeared unstable or rebellious.[46]

Thus the media was indeed functioning as a "socializing" influence, but its daily consequences were more conservative than revolutionary. By educating people to the accepted fashions and forms of behavior, by giving them lessons "in manners and etiquette," by teaching them to appreciate national traditions and ideals, by making their lives more organized and punctual through an adherence to the strict segments of network time and the emotional rhythms of the ninety-minute movie, by standardizing diction and discouraging dialects (except as comic or villainous affectations), by increasing the homogeneity of the population while ignoring its regional or ethnic differences, by stressing the attitudes and assumptions that united Americans rather than the local peculiarities and economic conflicts that drove them apart, the communications industry was inspiring not community but conformity, not anger at but adjustment to the status quo.[47]

Finally, beyond those problems of subject matter and techniques that appeared obvious even to many of the decade's intellectuals, there were the media's hidden dangers of which they rarely seemed aware. The very nature (and appeal) of popular culture often centered on its ability to translate the difficulties of human life into false patterns and easy stereotypes. Indeed, as Robert Warshow has contended, its chief purpose was to interfere with and supersede reality, to offer language and opinions that relieved people of the necessity for coping directly with their environment. Consequently, the networks and the film industry had the capacity to "distort and eventually to destroy the emotional and moral content of experience, putting in its place a system of conventionalized 'responses'" that reduced politics to a form of mass entertainment and knotty social problems to a symbolic contest in which everyone could take a "position" and choose up sides.[48] Furthermore, the phenomenal impact of cartoons and comic strips, pictorial journalism and condensed prose, *Life* magazine and the *Reader's Digest,* regularly scheduled news broadcasts and the monthly *March of Time,* soap operas and movie serials, the omnipresent sound of radio and the enormously persuasive images on the screen, were all contributing to what Lewis Mumford considered a deterioration of "reflective thought."[49] Now, as one historian of the period pointed out, a single photograph "could . . . communicate an area of experience which formerly required a whole essay." As a result, the popular arts were supplying the public with "a tremendous number of shortcuts" that would "save time" and simplify a universe grown "too complicated in meaning and accelerated in pace to be studied at leisure."[50]

In sum, the cultural climate of the 1930s was shifting inexorably from a dependence on words and sentences to a preference for catch phrases and visual metaphors, from systematic social analyses to spot announcements and previews of coming attractions, from the traditional concerns of politics and ideology to the unprecedented magnetism of slogans and myths. Thus if radical writers and activists seriously expected to change American society, they would have to compete not merely with the corporations and the New Deal but also with the expanding power of the networks, Hollywood, and Henry Luce. Accordingly, they had to engage the eyes and ears of the public as well as its mind. In the meantime they needed to consider carefully just what their fellow citizens were really hearing and seeing, not only in the privacy of their living rooms but more significantly in the thousands of darkened movie theaters across the land.

3. *From* Little Caesar *to* Citizen Kane

Just as the literary criticism of the 1930s had little influence on the type of novel that was being written during these years, so the various theories about the good or bad effects of popular culture did not always bear much relation to its actual forms and preoccupations. This was particularly true of the film. With the introduction of the microphone and the consolidation of the studios, Hollywood seemed ready to shape the public's outlook and values as never before. But quite frequently what happened on the screen was far different from the expectations of the producers or the demands of the media critics. In essence, the standard genres of the depression cinema (horror, crime, romance, political melodrama, comedy—whether sophisticated or surreal), its peculiarly anarchic personalities (Edward G. Robinson, James Cagney, Humphrey Bogart, Paul Muni, Spencer Tracy, Gary Cooper, Clark Gable, James Stewart, Cary Grant, Jean Harlow, Jean Arthur, Bette Davis, Katherine Hepburn), its most talented writers (Ben Hecht, Dudley Nichols, Robert Riskin, Preston Sturges, Herman Mankiewicz), and its greatest directors (Ernst Lubitsch, Howard Hawks, John Ford, William Wellman, Fritz Lang, Frank Capra, Leo McCarey) could all on occasion escape the limitations both of commercialism and social "responsibility." In their finest moments they were able to transform movies into genuine works of art—though not in the sense that literary esthetes, theater loyalists, or radical intellectuals would have willingly acknowledged. Moreover, while much of the motion-picture industry did indeed help to inhibit the development of revolutionary ideas and points of view, while many movies did indeed contribute (either intentionally or inadvertently) to the decade's increasingly conservative mood, there was at least one film-maker who succeeded in using the screen as a truly creative and liberating force. Where James Agee had managed to synthesize the novel and the documentary into a new instrument for *seeing* reality, Orson Welles would prove equally adept at fusing the motion picture's basic elements of sight and sound into a new way of *thinking* about the modern world.

Ironically, the very genres which were thought to have the greatest potential for challenging the preconceptions of the public—horror stories, gangster epics, movies with a clear social message—frequently turned out to be the least concerned with upsetting established beliefs. In contrast, the comedies and so-called "escapist" films of the 1930s were often much more effective in exposing and satirizing the status quo. But in either case the ultimate test of a motion picture's value was not its ability to inspire social action but rather its imaginative power and artistic integrity. Given this criterion, many movies which won high praise during the depression for their serious and topical discussion of public issues appeared increasingly ponderous and sentimental in retrospect. Conversely, a number of films which were either ignored or dismissed when first shown continued to seem both refreshing and provocative long after the decade had ended. As the years wore on, it was inevitable that the timely would give way to the timeless.

Of all the kinds of movies made in the 1930s, the horror film should have been the most unsettling. At first glance, it featured eerie lighting and treacherous shadows, lifeless forests and fog-bound swamps, crumbling castles and frightened townspeople, demented scientists and alien monsters. Occasionally its pervasive atmosphere of violence, terror, and death did serve to shock and disturb the audience. In Tod Browning's *Freaks* (1932), a film populated almost entirely by the most hideously deformed creatures ever photographed on the screen, it is the "normals" who eventually become monstrous while the "abnormals" remain thoroughly human if not humane. But the rest of the decade's horror movies rarely assaulted the spectators' assumptions and sense of reality in quite this way. Instead they offered comfort and reassurance in the presence of the grotesque and the unknown.

Universal was the principal studio that specialized in tales of fear, often under the direction of Browning or James Whale and usually starring Boris Karloff or Bela Lugosi. At one point or another they all worked on the classic horror films of the 1930s: *Dracula, The Invisible Man,* the *Frankenstein* series. In each of these movies certain themes and situations reappeared so that, taken together, they expressed a definite attitude toward the possibilities and perils of human creativity.

To some extent the monster's very ugliness and cruelty helped to underscore man's distrust and dread of anything different or strange. If the creature refused to conform, either physically or psychologically, to whatever was considered familiar and acceptable, he had to remain an archetypal outcast—shunned, persecuted, and eventually destroyed.[51]

Yet the true villain of these films was not so much the vampire, the phantom, or the walking dead but rather those who wished to tamper with the natural order of things. Therefore, the symbolic incarnation of evil was generally a solitary scientist who, whether motivated by innocence or megalomania, dedicated his career to the unfettered pursuit of knowledge regardless of its consequences *(The Werewolf of London, Dr. Jekyll and Mr. Hyde),* to the discovery of buried secrets and forgotten myths *(The Mummy),* to the disruption of the past and the imposition of modern civilization on prehistoric forms *(King Kong),* to the re-creation of life and the triumph over death *(Frankenstein),* to the search for unlimited power and control over all the world *(The Invisible Man).* At bottom the scientist threatened society not because he was deranged but because he presumed to put himself in the place of God or fate, because he was too ambitious and inquisitive in his quest for truth and light, because he was willing to ignore the ordinary restrictions of law and morality.[52] Thus the horror movies warned their audience that some mysteries were better left unsolved, that to pass beyond the boundaries of human custom and social tradition was to invite madness and desolation. In this view of the universe, the old and the safe seemed always preferable to the new and uncertain; the men who lived by habits and rules were palpably superior to those who longed for innovation and change.

If in horror films the scientist was usually more sinister and terrifying than the monster, in the gangster melodramas of the 1930s (most of which were made at Warner Brothers) the respectable citizen was sometimes more vicious and menacing than the criminal. Indeed both genres tended to confuse the normal concepts of good and evil, though not necessarily for the purpose of awakening people to alternative values and codes of behavior. On the contrary, they each in their own way wound up defending the very institutions and dogmas they had started out to attack.

In the case of the gangster movie, the reluctance to pursue an uncomfortable idea to its logical conclusion was evident not only as the early fascination with pure sensation and violence was supplanted in the late 1930s by a more didactic concentration on the social causes of crime, but also in the way all of these films drew back from their potentially radical premises. Ostensibly, the sympathetic treatment of rebels and outlaws could be an immensely liberating experience, both emotionally and politically. Thus it was hardly surprising that motion pictures about bootleggers, racketeers, and gunmen should have enjoyed enormous popularity during the opening years of the depression. Moreover, the special look and sound of the gangster movie made it seem indelibly a product of the present time. It firmly dispensed with the contrived pathos and facile moralizing of the silent cinema; it took its stories directly from the headlines and radio bulletins; its central characters were unmistakably urban (in contrast to the agrarian heroes of the documentary and the novel); it conveyed a feeling of intense modernity in its images of touring cars and beer trucks careening down city streets, in its lavish clothes and crackling dialogue, in its sensitivity to the gloom of pool halls and saloons, in its visual appreciation of power and status; it spoke a language that was always terse and understated, cynical and fast-paced, flippant and hard-boiled, tough-minded and worldly-wise; it seemed, in short, thoroughly a *contemporary* phenomenon.[53]

Above all, the gangster film was an adventure in style. The typical criminal rarely indulged in statements of romantic affection or philosophical belief; instead he remained primarily a man of action rather than words, impulses rather than ideals. The elegance and skill with which he conducted himself under extraordinary pressure seemed clearly more important than the quality of his ideas.

For these reasons the gangster film often functioned as a parody of the American Dream. In his longing to escape from the anonymous urban mass and impose his personality on events, in his ambition to eliminate the opposition and rise to the top, in his willingness to use any means no matter how aggressive or ruthless, in his disdain for the timid and conventional, in his insistence that he was merely a "businessman" giving the public what it wanted, the criminal became a kind of psychopathic Horatio Alger embodying in himself the classic capitalist urge for wealth and success. But because he was a thief and murderer as well as a traditional entrepreneur, his very arrogance and inhumanity could stand as a reproach both to the principles of the market place and the reigning values of American life.

Yet the gangster movie did not play this role in the 1930s largely because the criminal was hardly ever what he seemed. Ironically, the hero of these films appeared angry and violent only on the surface; underneath he displayed a peculiar (if often inarticulate) capacity for tenderness and idealism. Indeed this was usually the source of his downfall. The outlaw was rarely defeated by society; rather, he succumbed to his own inner weaknesses and illusions.

Thus in Mervyn Le Roy's *Little Caesar* (1930), Edward G. Robinson hungers not for power and possessions but for immortality. When the audience first encounters him, he is setting back the hands of a clock, partly to conceal his responsibility for a robbery but also to signify his fear of time. Thereafter, clocks are a pervasive presence throughout the film, marking the ebb and flow of Rico's life, mocking his desire to "be" someone, calling him to an early grave. Moreover, with the passage of time and the attainment of position, Rico grows "soft"; like those he originally replaced, he can still "dish it out," but he is no longer able to "take it." And amid these signs of misplaced dreams and internal decay, Little Rico meets his "end" —a victim, like Thomas Sutpen, of the myth that one can make a lasting mark on an indifferent world.

Similarly, in Howard Hawks's *Scarface* (1932)—perhaps the most psychologically complex and visually imaginative of the era's gangster films— Paul Muni ultimately fails not because the law is stronger but because he cannot tolerate loneliness. If in the beginning Scarface seems fully committed to the capitalist ethic ("Do it first, do it yourself, do it often. . . ."), he is eventually incapable of living up to these tenets. Instead his consuming (and vaguely incestuous) love for his sister drives him to destroy both his closest allies and finally himself. By the end of the film Scarface reveals in his own plight the awesome price of individualism; terrified, without friends or family, on the verge of insanity, the gangster dies alone.

During the later years of the depression the movie criminal became somewhat more introspective and conscience-striken. Frequently he was motivated less by the urge for acquisition than by the need for love and the search for exoneration. In the movie version of Robert Sherwood's *Petrified Forest* (1936), Humphrey Bogart as the notorious Duke Mantee is vanquished not only because he (like the film's poet-intellectual) is the "last of the rugged individualists" and therefore increasingly obsolete, but also because he waits too long for the arrival of his girl friend. Both the poet and the gangster turn out to be sensitive romantics who cannot survive in a callous and hard-bitten world; they too are fossils in the forest of stone. Along the same lines, in William Wyler's *Dead End* (1937), Bogart is again gunned down because he makes one last nostalgic visit to his old neighborhood, hoping to win some form of forgiveness from his aging mother. And in William Keighley's *Each Dawn I Die* (1939), George Raft voluntarily re-enters prison and gives up his life solely to prove the innocence and reward the good faith of his friend James Cagney. Throughout all of these movies the criminal is neither an outlaw nor an outcast. Instead his reasons for acting as he does are not very different from the ordinary emotions of the audience; in his fidelity to colleagues, parents, and lovers, he is really just like us.

Even when the gangster film set out to criticize the social system, it often retreated from the radical implications of its message. In keeping with the decade's conviction that men were entirely products of their environment, some movies argued that because slums bred crime the public was as much to blame as the criminal. But in Michael Curtiz's *Angels with Dirty Faces* (a movie written in 1938 by an émigré from the Workers' Theater, John Wexley), it is the gangster who not only pays for his sins, but must also subordinate his understanding of social injustice to the official voice of religion, morality, and law. At the start of the film James Cagney is a hero to the "dead-end kids" because he recognizes the hypocrisy of a society which justifies greed and corruption in the guise of self-improvement and getting ahead. Cagney is at least an authentic gangster, practicing his craft out in the open, in contrast to the hidden connivances of the banker and businessman. Nevertheless Pat O'Brien, an old friend who has since become a priest, persuades Cagney not to struggle further but to accept his fate—indeed to pretend cowardice so that he will no longer serve as an example to the children of the slums. Thus the "honest" criminal is converted into a "dishonest" upholder of social convention, and what begins as a bitter and realistic indictment of the class structure ends as a glorification of the status quo.

Perhaps the underlying conservatism of these movies was best revealed in William Wellman's *Public Enemy* (1931), a film frequently shown on a double bill with *Little Caesar*. Once again James Cagney is the elemental tough guy, a victim of social deprivation and urban cruelty. Yet unlike Little Rico, Scarface, and Duke Mantee, Cagney is not an individualist yearning to be number one. Instead he remains only an average member of the gang, never aspiring to leadership or the symbols of personal power.

Indeed he is moved primarily by a sense of loyalty to his fellow mobsters and his family; the men he most vigorously detests are those who betray their promises or violate the peculiar code of honor among thieves. Therefore, when a rival gang murders his childhood friend, Cagney seeks retribution—invading their hideout alone with guns blazing, mortally wounding himself in the process. As he staggers back through the rain-drenched streets, gasping for breath, he mumbles his famous epitaph: "I ain't so tough." And this of course was the basic point of all the gangster melodramas of the 1930s. The depression criminal failed precisely because he was insufficiently selfish and cynical. At bottom he was not a tough guy at all but a profound sentimentalist whose idea of duty and obligation invariably triumphed over his urge to rebel, who surrendered his sense of alienation and rage for the more acceptable notions of love and comradeship. Ironically, it was society that seemed ruthless and unforgiving while the gangster remained perpetually hopeful and naïve.

Ultimately, the criminal and the monster may have served a similar purpose for depression audiences. In permitting the spectator to indulge in fantasies of anti-social behavior, they appeared to act as a safety valve for the latent feelings of violence and hostility to which men were ordinarily inclined. Moreover, in the story of his rise and fall, the criminal provided both a vicarious symbol of unlimited success and a necessary rationalization for eventual failure. In effect, the obligatory defeat of the gangster emphasized the danger and futility of trying to rise above one's station and class, of seeking wealth and power in an increasingly closed society, of attempting to deviate from (much less modify) the existing laws and customs of the community. Precisely because he wished to live as an outsider, the gangster was forever doomed. So in his demise he offered an object lesson for those who believed that they too might aspire and strive, reject and revolt, attack and transform. If the criminal could never win, then neither could the audience. And in the end it was not his energy and freedom but his loneliness and impotence that might well have offered consolation to Americans for their own misfortunes, while at the same time relieving them of the desire or need to act.[54]

For the most part, however, neither the horror nor the gangster cycles were taken seriously by film critics or radical intellectuals during the 1930s. Instead they were looked on merely as escapist trifles in an age that required more adult fare. It did not matter, therefore, what kinds of social or psychological consequences these movies contained as far as the majority of commentators were concerned. Like their counterparts in the quest for a proletarian novel, they chose to concentrate on those motion pictures which dealt directly and "realistically" with contemporary facts, issues, and ideas. For film historians like Lewis Jacobs and aficionados of the documentary like John Grierson, the main criterion for judging the worth of a movie was not its technical facility, its visual excitement, its moral complexity, or its insight into human relationships, but rather its immediate relevance and "progressive" political sympathies. They could not tolerate a film which threatened to "divert" its audience from the problems of the depression, which offered romance and comedy as a relief from daily injustice, which encouraged the spectator to forget his anxieties and unhappiness in a world of dreams. They were harshly critical of directors like D. W. Griffith, Ernst Lubitsch, and Josef von Sternberg for withdrawing into "cinematic ivory towers" in order to refine their craftsmanship at the expense of "vitality and timeliness." By contrast, they applauded any film-maker who repudiated the "irresponsibility" and "self-indulgence" of the 1920s, who shifted his attention from the individual to the "group," who displayed a willingness to confront questions "of paramount interest to the common man," who saw motion pictures as a device for providing new "codes" and "norms" of behavior in an otherwise disintegrating society.[55] And so, in their decade-long desire to recruit the cinema for the class struggle or the defense of democracy, many writers pleaded with Hollywood to forgo its obsession with the box office and adopt a truly social conscience.

Yet the demand for realism frequently resulted in a dilution of critical taste and a failure to see clearly what was being shown on the screen. Occasionally a film like Mervyn Le Roy's *I Am a Fugitive from a Chain Gang* (1932) would focus on a particular social dilemma—in this case the brutality of American jails and the blindness of American law—with uncompromising force. In its documentary style, its brilliant use of sound to convey the mechanical terror of prison life, its readiness to arraign the society rather than the criminal, and its refusal to resolve all the issues in the final reel, *Fugitive* was an unusually straightforward motion picture in a decade searching for political and ethical absolutes. More often, however, Hollywood was able to discharge its social obligations and satisfy its intellectual detractors by making movies that combined conventional melodrama with currently fashionable ideas. Especially in the late 1930s, when studios like Warner Brothers abandoned their preoccupation with crime and adventure in favor of a more "constructive" approach to the crisis, the film industry became self-consciously serious and sometimes pretentious. Nevertheless, beneath the increasingly topical subjects and the inflated rhetoric there was always a hint of complacency which neither Hollywood nor the intellectual community cared to acknowledge.

Ironically, few of these films dealt with the life-styles or daily problems of the average American, much less with those of the working class. Despite the existence of the depression and their newfound sense of social responsibility, the studios refrained from turning out movies about poverty, politics, labor unions, or white-collar frustration in anything like the number that was to characterize the postwar European cinema. Instead Hollywood was fascinated, even in its treatment of contemporary events, by the exceptional and the bizarre—using factories as a backdrop for the exposure of right-wing terrorism *(Black Legion)*, portraying fascism itself largely as a matter of espionage and an occasion for the passionate reaffirmation of American ideals *(Confessions of a Nazi Spy)*, converting the Spanish Civil War into a suspense thriller in which it seemed unnecessary to mention who was fighting for what *(Blockade)*.

At other points the movies deserted the present altogether, taking refuge in historical allegories set in nineteenth-century Europe or Mexico or the American West. Most of these films offered special views of the past which contained obvious lessons for modern times. In refighting the battles of science and progress versus bigotry and ignorance *(The Story of Louis Pasteur)*, art and personal honesty versus anti-Semitism and censorship *(The Life of Emile Zola)*, democracy versus dictatorship *(Juarez*—though here the issue was slightly confused since the emperor Maximilian emerged as considerably more gracious, attractive, and humane than the Lincoln-esque but painfully stolid Mexican reformer), plain-spoken yeoman farmers versus haughty bankers and rapacious railroad barons *(Jesse James)*, the hatred of violence versus the need to defend the law against all aggressors and criminals *(Destry Rides Again)*, such movies were clearly intended to improve America's morale in the face of domestic difficulties and foreign enemies. Nevertheless, in their eagerness to preach the virtues of traditional Americanism, in their wish to unify the country around a set of common attitudes and presuppositions, they frequently appeared patronizing, simple-minded, and much more removed from "reality" than a film like King Vidor's *Stella Dallas,* which in its romantic portrait of one mother's efforts to help her daughter escape the working class probably reflected more accurately the true sentiments and ambitions of the typical moviegoer.

Indeed the drive toward realism, even in the form of a parable, might contain implications exactly the reverse from those the Left had contemplated. Throughout the 1930s few film-makers were more popular with the general public as well as with intellectuals than Walt Disney. Yet his cartoon shorts and full-length extravaganzas were neither harmless entertainments nor satiric commentaries on modern society. Instead, as Richard

Schickel has pointed out, they expressed a profoundly conservative view of the world. By seeking always to render fantasy and myth in the "most realistic possible style," Disney presented his animated humans and animals in terms that were familiar and easily grasped; at no point would his audience be shocked by the "esthetically daring." Thus *Fantasia* (1940) was an attempt to illustrate music more with prosaic pictures than with the moods and colors of the artist's imagination. Similarly, Disney tended to purge nature of its dangers and mysteries, substituting a fictitious cuteness and cleanliness for its inherent violence and discord. Moreover, through his most famous cartoon heroes, Mickey Mouse and the three little pigs, he emphasized the old-fashioned pioneer values of hard work, self-reliance, quick wit, and eternal persistence. At bottom, Disney's movies reflected a nostalgic longing for rural scenes and small-town amenities, for the fairy tales and folklore of childhood, for the "innocence and playfulness of life in the forests and fields where every prospect pleased and only man was vile." In this way the bewilderments of modernity were made intelligible through jokes and musical cues; the strains of an urban-industrial present were relieved by the cultural traditions and political simplicities of the past; in Disney's cinema of optimism and memory a people afflicted by depression and war could "go to sleep, as Snow White does, and then awaken to find the world unchanged."[56]

If much of the "social" cinema seemed either pedantic or sentimental, there were at least a few directors who managed to portray the problems of political and economic life with considerable sophistication. Their perspective, however, was rarely radical or ideological. On the contrary, despite their sensitivity to the role of groups, classes, and institutions, they were primarily interested in the question of how individuals might comport themselves within a highly structured social order. And their conclusions were not particularly pleasing to those who earnestly awaited the revolution.

In the American movies of Fritz Lang, especially *Fury* (1936) and *You Only Live Once* (1937), society was usually depicted as hostile and confining. Lang's heroes were often trapped and manipulated by environmental forces over which they had no control—fate, chance, heredity, inexplicable accidents, social laws, human intolerance, private compulsions. The pervasive determinism of his films found their visual correlative in innumerable images of jail cells, railroad tracks, geometric shadows on immovable walls, actors rushing toward the camera only to be stopped short at the last moment by some invisible but omnipotent barrier they could never elude. Moreover, like Nathanael West and Nelson Algren, Lang seemed to regard collections of people as a potentially irrational mob ready to destroy the solitary individual in a paroxysm of ignorance and rage.

Yet he was as much concerned with the problem of personal accountability as with the psychology of men in groups. In *Fury,* ostensibly an exposé of lynching, Lang transformed his protagonist from an innocent victim of social injustice to a fanatic seeker of vengeance. Having survived the efforts of a frenzied crowd to murder him, Spencer Tracy vehemently rejects the decade's conviction that men are wholly conditioned by the communities in which they live and demands instead that specific members of the town be held liable for their acts. In the process, he becomes increasingly vicious and cruel, taking on the very attributes of the mob he loathes. Though MGM compelled Lang to attach a happy ending to an otherwise somber tale, *Fury* remained a morally complex film in which the relationship between social responsibility and individual guilt, fatalism and free will, environmental pressures and inner passions were forever tangled and obscure.[57]

Similarly, the movies of Frank Capra were considerably more complicated and ambiguous than they first appeared. On the surface, Capra expressed better than any other Hollywood director the values and assumptions of the depression years. In his social triology—*Mr. Deeds Goes to Town* (1936), *Mr. Smith Goes to Washington* (1939), and *Meet John Doe* (1941) —he seemed to commemorate the natural wisdom and benevolence of the common man. Through the classically "American" faces and distinctively small-town voices of Gary Cooper and James Stewart (who were perpetually battling against the Machiavellian intrigues and swollen greed of big-city capitalism in the corpulent person of Edward Arnold), Capra created a world in which the gullible and the naïve inevitably triumphed over the cunning and the powerful.

But like Lang, Capra was not content to worship at the altar of the "little people," nor did he contend that social groups were intrinsically virtuous and democratic. Underneath the liberal pieties his films tended to lay bare the stupidities of the average citizen and the perils of mass conformity. In the spectacle of Mr. Smith standing alone on the floor of Congress, hoarsely reading from the Constitution and the Declaration of Independence as his erstwhile constituents swallow the propaganda of those who control the radio and the press, or in the figure of John Doe showing his easily duped disciples how populist slogans might serve the cause of fascism, Capra had presented an allegory on the need for personal integrity and independence apart from the herd-instincts of the faceless crowd. Though he still believed in the capacity of good men to prevail over economic inequities and political corruption, though the villains always confessed their sins in the final reel, his was a faith more suited to the individualism of the nineteenth century than to the collectivist dreams of the 1930s.

If Lang and Capra saw society as a set of intolerable constraints from which the individual might or might not escape, Howard Hawks preferred to examine the conditions of human survival within the context of existing institutions. His heroes could neither break their social bonds nor surrender pessimistically to the demands of nature and fate. Instead they were forced to improvise new forms of behavior for an otherwise incomprehensible world.

Thus in *The Dawn Patrol* (1930) and *The Road to Glory* (1936) Hawks weighed the psychic costs of men at war: the willingness of soldiers to follow orders despite the certainty of death, their sense of themselves as interchangeable parts in a military machine, their acceptance of the social roles that armies impose on helpless individuals—the living succeeding the dead in an endless chain of command. Given this view of the universe, only those who dispensed with abstract doctrines and specious moralizing could possibly endure. Accordingly, when a comrade is accidentally killed in *Only Angels Have Wings* (1939), Hawks's people refuse to show horror or remorse. Rather, they engage in an elaborate ceremony of feigned indifference, pretending to go on as if nothing had happened. Like characters in a Hemingway novel, they concentrate on simple skills and observe rigid codes of behavior designed to help them adjust to chaos and uncertainty. Loyal to their friends, committed to their craft, valuing "natural" expertise over "artificial" ideas, they remain stoic professionals in the face of danger and death. In effect, Hawks was responding to the decade's yearning for community with movies devoted largely to the celebration of private honor and existential courage beyond the reach of groups or classes.

Ironically, of all the directors in the 1930s, the one who seemed to possess a genuinely collectivist vision of the world turned out to be the most conservative. Like William Faulkner, John Ford was acutely sensitive to the rituals and customs of social life; his films were filled with public ceremonies, folk songs and dances, clusters of townspeople in whom the spectator could detect all the nuances of status and class. Moreover, his characters were invariably tied to or dependent on large institutional structures—the army, the government, the trade union, the Church. Finally, during the depression Ford appeared more disposed than many of his colleagues in Hollywood to consider the problems of politics and society. It was not surprising, therefore, that in movies like *The Informer* (1935), *The Grapes of Wrath* (1940), and *Tobacco Road* (1941) he should bring to the screen novels that had been normally identified with the Left.

Yet Ford's commitment to the radical cause was always deceptive. For the most part he was less interested in political and ideological questions than in the effort to understand human relationships against the background of public crises. The major preoccupation of *The Informer,* for example, was not the fate of the Irish revolution, nor the internal politics of the IRA, nor even the moral sin of treason and betrayal, but rather the conflict between private feeling and social obligation. Despite their affection for Gypo Nolan, the rebel leaders are compelled to find and execute any traitor whose act endangers the "organization." And as the story proceeds, each man becomes increasingly powerless to alter the course of events. Gypo never comprehends his own motivations, while the revolutionaries reluctantly submit to the decision of their "court."[58] Hence the characters in a Ford film seemed irrevocably bound by duties that must be discharged and roles that must be obeyed whatever the consequences for individuals.

In *Stagecoach* (1939), Ford's classic Western and certainly the most satirical of his depression movies, this theme was developed with significant variations. Here he is deeply sympathetic to those who bend the law or ignore established conventions of taste and propriety. The émigrés from the "East" who try to uphold the artificial standards of high society and who demand that the formalities of "civilized" behavior be imposed on the frontier seem clearly less appealing than the native Westerners with their instinctive sense of right and wrong—the benevolent prostitute, the alcoholic but humane doctor, the compassionate sheriff, the outlaw who is merely trying to avenge the murder of his father and brother. But Ford was not so much defending the merits of non-conformity as paying tribute to a natural community of men who shared the same values, loyalties, and beliefs—and who did not need written rules or self-righteous moralists to teach them the proper codes of social conduct.

Perhaps the motion picture which best reflected Ford's philosophy was not *The Grapes of Wrath* but *How Green Was My Valley* (1941). Unlike many other "social" films of the period, this was a movie that succeeded in presenting a faithful picture of class stratification as well as an insight into the daily lives of ordinary workers. Nevertheless, its central purpose was neither to illuminate the plight of the Welsh miners nor to champion the cause of the labor movement but instead to commend the virtues of family solidarity and social tradition at the expense of personal desire. Moreover, even as the verdant valley gradually succumbed to a colorless industrialism, Ford had his characters pass in review at the close of the film, thereby insisting that the past would live on in the present in the form of legends, memories, nostalgic reminders of youth, and the continuing spiritual legacy of those who had gone before. Thus in movies such as these, he was translating the political and economic concerns of the depression years into a sermon on the preservation of visual symbols and human myths. For Ford, society was a repository of cultural precedents, historic monuments, and inherited responsibilities—all of which could better sustain mankind in the midst of disorder than a reliance on elaborate doctrines or the impulse to change the way things were.

In the end, the movies of Lang, Capra, Hawks, and Ford did not really satisfy the demand for a cinema of social consciousness any more than the Warner Brothers melodramas, historical epics, or Disney fables. Too often most of these films responded to the craving for comradeship with a portrait of the individual struggling against the mass. Too often they answered the call for realism and relevance by taking refuge in the images and values of the past. Too often they approached the difficulties of modern life with a curious blend of fatalism and innocence. Paradoxically, the motion pictures that attempted to deal directly with political or economic issues seemed less critical of established institutions and ideals than those which were scornfully labeled escapist. If the backstage musicals and "screwball" comedies of the 1930s were not particularly radical in content or technique, neither were they trivial diversions from the problems of depression America. Instead, in their own fashion, they offered a running commentary on the social crisis which was at once sardonic and captivating.

Many of these movies were made in the late 1930s, and they vigorously satirized the race for possessions and power, though their indictments were usually based more on cultural than on economic considerations. From the perspective of comedy, the rich were dangerous or unattractive not because they exploited the poor but because they were intolerably smug and insensitive to the possibilities of a truly human life. Conversely, the quick-witted and vaguely rebellious heroes of Leo McCarey's The Awful Truth, George Cukor's Holiday, and Howard Hawks's Bringing Up Baby (played in each instance by Cary Grant), or the wildly eccentric family presided over by Lionel Barrymore in Frank Capra's adaptation of the George S. Kaufman–Moss Hart play, You Can't Take It With You, all seemed comparatively "free" because they recognized the futility of status and position and because they ultimately refused to surrender to the pressures of compulsive money-making or the drudgeries of dead-end jobs.

To some extent, the attack on privilege and the disdain for success could serve as a consolation for whatever disappointments the audience had suffered. If one's ambitions could never be achieved, it might be best not to aspire at all. If the very wealthy remained forever alone and unhappy, it seemed better to seek comfort in the familiar pleasures of home and family. At any rate, this appeared to be the moral of Frank Capra's *It Happened One Night* (1934—the most famous and most imitated of the depression comedies. In the gradual transformation of Claudette Colbert from a spoiled heiress to a conventional bourgeois wife (fleeing her aristocratic wedding for an ordinary honeymoon in a nondescript motel), in the conversion of Clark Gable from a disreputable and self-centered newspaper reporter to a man moved by the claims of love and principle, in the taming of the capitalist father from a blustering tyrant to a benign marriage broker, in the domestication of tramp life from a potentially subversive and cataclysmic experience to a respectable activity for the middle class, *It Happened One Night* tended to reassure the average man that his plain style of living was generally superior to the affectations of the rich and well-born.

Occasionally this lesson was reversed, and the joys of acquisition—whether accidental or deliberate—were celebrated as ends in themselves. In *Easy Living* (1937), a movie directed by Mitchell Leisen from a script by Preston Sturges, the prevailing mood was one of cynicism and fraud. In a capitalist society, the film suggested, people are what they wear and whom they seem to know. Thus one might take advantage of fortune and chance, mistaken identities and unexplained gifts, without the obligatory feelings of guilt or provincial complacency that infected the movies of Disney and Capra. If this was hardly a revolutionary message, if indeed the heroine at the conclusion of *Easy Living* willingly acquiesced in the rewards of the system, the spectator could at least gain a clear understanding of the rules of the game and choose for himself whether or not to play.

In the same vein, the distinctive world of Busby Berkeley was populated by schemers and cheats, manipulators and con artists, the greedy and the ambitious. Though his intricate dance pageants appeared like monuments to collectivism—with their hundreds of anonymous boys and girls, their utilization of massive choruses and gigantic orchestras rather than soloists and small combos, their faultlessly mechanical precision, and their abstract designs—the accompanying plots were usually devoted to the search for commercial triumph and personal vindication. Yet beneath the surface glitter and gaiety of these movies there lay a sober prophecy of social collapse. At the close of the "Lullaby of Broadway" sequence in *Gold Diggers of 1935,* when a regiment of dancers hypnotized by an evening on the town causes a nameless playgirl to tumble to her death, Berkeley offered a surreal vision of civilization's decay and disintegration. In this startling and apocalyptic image, he had momentarily stripped away the banality and shrill humor of the typical depression musical in order to expose the underlying malevolence and corruption of American life.

In these circumstances, what the comedies and musicals of the 1930s really seemed to endorse was the capacity to behave with charm, grace, and savoir-faire in the face of human folly and social absurdity. Thus the films of Ernst Lubtisch—especially *Design for Living* (1933), *The Merry Widow* (1934), *Ninotchka* (1939), *The Shop Around the Corner* (1940), and *To Be or Not to Be* (1942)—were testimonials to the meaninglessness of ideological abstractions and moral absolutes in a universe of shifting values, complex illusions, and impenetrable disguises. Lubitsch's characters maintain their sanity by wearing masks, playing roles, and keeping up appearances despite the continuing presence of sadness and even horror. For them, good manners and clever conversation are more important than political commitment and dogmatic philosophies.[59] And yet the ability to conduct oneself properly no matter how tragic the situation required a strong appreciation of social milieu and a willingness to observe the strict conventions of public discourse. Ultimately, the heroes of a Lubitsch movie were prepared to accept the world as it was, bowing to its forms and limitations, hoping merely to alleviate its more painful wounds through natural wit and a peculiar sense of personal decorum.

Of all the types of farce made in the 1930s, however, the funniest and most penetrating commentaries on the irrationalities of American life were proffered by those without traditional plots or (at least on the surface) explicit moral attitudes. Nevertheless, in the movies of Charles Chaplin, the Marx Brothers, and W. C. Fields, one could detect a gradual transformation in character, situation, and mood that may have revealed more about what happened to the United States during the depression than most of the films of self-conscious social significance.

Although Chaplin, the Marx Brothers, and Fields had enjoyed substantial artistic and commercial fame long before the stock-market crash, either on stage or in the silent cinema, they each had to adjust in some way to the demands of sound and the new concerns of a society in crisis. But where the Marxes' anarchic brand of humor seemed uniquely suited to the depression years, while Fields adopted talk as a perfect instrument of withdrawal into his own private world, Chaplin was forced to undergo the greatest alterations in outlook and style. Whether by chance or intent, his metamorphosis from a solitary tramp to a representative spokesman for all the "little fellows" coincided with the decade's repudiation of individualism and its embrace of corporate ideals.

At the outset, in *City Lights* (1931), Chaplin remained an archetypal outsider with only marginal connections to the social order. Insofar as society acknowledged his presence at all, it was neither deliberately antagonistic nor purposefully repressive; indeed it did not really care about the tramp one way or the other. Hence the cops chase Charlie almost absent-mindedly, as if he were less a genuine danger than a minor annoyance. Conversely, if the tramp fails once again to achieve position or love, he is still relatively independent and free. In effect, the men in power consider Charlie irrelevant, and he in turn responds with indifference to them. All the while he manages to preserve the sentiments of the prewar world—innocence, romance, pathos, the idealization of women, the capacity to communicate through silence rather than speech.

By *Modern Times* (1936), these relationships had significantly changed. Now the factory and the machines have taken the place of pompous butlers and bumbling cops. And Charlie, no longer an unemployed hobo but a certified member of the working class, is increasingly victimized by institutions and movements which seem to possess a conscious design. More and more he becomes a helpless extension of mechanized processes—his arms twisting imaginary bolts even after the assembly line has stopped, swept up in political parades whose programs he finds incomprehensible, literally entrapped by a new and omnipotent technology gone berserk. Though he is still able to extricate himself from the clutches of society and wander down the open road, though the individual is still not so much at odds with as tangential to an impersonal economic system, though the film itself begins as social satire and ends as a picaresque adventure typical of Chaplin's early comedies, the world has grown too regimented and complicated for the free spirit to survive much longer.

Consequently, in *The Great Dictator* (1940), Chaplin was compelled to abandon the refuge of silence and solitude. Confronted by a social structure that pursues the individual not by accident but as a matter of policy, Charlie permanently sheds his disguise as a tramp and becomes instead a symbolic Jew—persecuted by and opposed to the most diabolical devices of exploitation and tyranny. Moreover, it is appropriate that the movie's humor should depend more on dialogue and sound effects than on sight gags and visual tricks. Although there are moments of brilliant pantomime—especially the dictator's dance with the global balloon—slapstick has largely given way to talk. The times clearly call for less spontaneity and more calculation. In the presence of fascism—the ultimate form of collective discipline—escape is physically and morally impossible. And so Charlie must finally "speak," addressing the audience directly at the close of the film, hurling words against organized power, delivering an impassioned statement of political belief, exchanging the consolations of laughter for the rigors of philosophy. Thus in the act of taking a conscious position on questions of public concern, in the decision to surrender the advantages of personal freedom and assume a posture of social "responsibility," the little fellow was at last accommodating himself to the modern world.[60]

If Chaplin had to make a transition from outcast to respectable citizen in the 1930s, the Marx Brothers seemed already at home amid the pressures and constraints of the contemporary scene. Far from fleeing or fighting the established order, they usually succeeded in bending society to their own purposes. Though they engaged in the standard forms of satire—assaulting the pretentions of the wealthy and powerful, lampooning the platitudes of education and politics, exposing the vanities of petty bureaucrats and cabinet ministers—the Marxes operated largely from within, manipulating the system's imbecilities but leaving the basic structure intact.

From the beginning theirs was a highly verbal comedy befitting an age of sound. Aided by Morrie Ryskind, S. J. Perelman, and George S. Kaufman, their scripts were surfeited with puns, *bon mots, non-sequiturs,* and one-liners. Even the silent Harpo relied on horns, whistles, shrieking girls, Chico's translations, and a willful misunderstanding of what other people said. Indeed much of the Marxian humor derived from an attack on various kinds of formal language—law, medicine, business, government—and an insistence on following the logical meaning of words to their illogical conclusions.[61] Moreover, their best films—especially *Duck Soup* (1933) and *A Night at the Opera* (1935)—were less sentimental and more worldly than those of Chaplin. In contrast to the benevolent tramp, Harpo could be a surprisingly violent and lecherous figure bordering sometimes on outright madness, while Groucho remained the ultimate (and not particularly good-natured) con man always looking out for himself. In essence, the Marx Brothers seemed to thrive in an atmosphere of cynicism, unreason, and occasional ruthlessness; if nothing else, they were thoroughly modern men.

Yet in a curious way they were also unalterably middle class. Where Chaplin might be a lonely hobo, a factory worker, or a nameless Jew, Groucho generally held a position of authority. As a doctor, hotel owner, manager of an opera company, president of a university, or head of state, he had not only entered society but actually exercised some form of power —however temporary his station or chaotic his reign. And for his otherwise disreputable brothers, Groucho was a friend on the inside whom they could either swindle or assist without fear of being jailed or exiled. But most of all, his status meant that none of them would ever be alone; instead they were inevitably surrounded by bellhops, secretaries, gangsters, professors, chorus girls, aspiring playwrights, villains, lovers, and Margaret Dumont. Toward the end of the decade, under the influence of Irving Thalberg and MGM, the Marxes grew gentler and more sympathetic to the misfortunes of the rest of the cast. They also began to subordinate their surreal talents to the demands of what had once been extraneous plots; in effect, they lost their anarchistic impulses and became increasingly predictable.[62] But throughout the 1930s their relationship to society was fixed and well defined. Depending on wit and craftiness to get out of tight spots, skillfully maneuvering among the rich and the imperious, protecting their distinctive honor in a world of sham, they were nevertheless intricately involved in the institutional patterns and social customs of American life.

It remained for an odd-looking, acidulous, inveterate mumbler to expose the full consequences of this absorption into the bourgeoisie. If Chaplin seemed eternally young and the Marx Brothers vaguely middle-aged, W. C. Fields was an old man clearly past his prime. Normally weighted down with wives, children, dogs, and in-laws (unlike the tramp or the Marxes, Fields always appeared to be the head of a household), trapped by all the accoutrements of middle-class rectitude, too realistic and too tired to rail against the world or run away, the best he might do was talk to himself and make a dash for the nearest saloon. In a Fields movie, speech was not a means of rebuffing dictators or manipulating heiresses; rather, it was largely a series of inarticulate whines and half-swallowed asides to communicate one's inner sense of bitterness and frustration. Fields was beyond caring about freedom, love, or power. In rare moments of self-appraisal he would acknowledge his destiny as a second-rate con artist merely going through the motions; he expected little and was seldom amazed by disappointment or defeat. Throughout his own films and those of others, he remained a picture of physical and psychological exhaustion.

In the end, despite the fact that he was often gainfully employed and permanently tied to a visible family, Fields seemed lonelier than Chaplin and more cyncial than the Marxes. Indeed he was at once the angriest and saddest of the screen comics in the 1930s. At the conclusion of *The Bank Dick* (1940)—his finest and most integrated movie—Fields has finally triumphed at something, however fortuitously. A hero for having thwarted an attempted robbery, rewarded with a promotion by the president of the bank, elegantly attired in top hat and formal clothes, on unusually good terms with his relatives (if not with the new butler), he wanders out of his house with nothing to do and nowhere to go. Suddenly he spies a strange man on the road and hurries off to catch him, as if the companionship of another solitary human being can relieve the pain not so much of failure but of success. In this last poignant image, the average American was offered a glimpse of his own fate. For Fields, the strategies of Chaplin (escape and revolt) or the Marx Brothers (insults and artifice) were no longer feasible. In an increasingly interdependent and strait-jacketed society, one could find solace only in private rage and public resignation.

Thus by the time the decade closed, many of the Left's expectations about the motion-picture industry had not been realized. On the contrary, the "serious" melodramas of the 1930s often turned out to be less insightful than the comedies; the cinema of social protest was frequently more unrealistic than the "escapist" films of crime or horror or romance. Meanwhile, the best of the depression movies seemed interested not in promoting revolution but in helping their audiences adjust to and endure a period of unprecedented disaster. Yet at the very moment when the problems of the economy were giving way to those of war, one director managed to transform the themes and techniques of the era's films into a genuinely "radical" work of art—if not in the sense of politics or ideology, then in the way one's customary perceptions of the world might be shaken and revised.

In the summer of 1940, after a meteoric career in radio and on stage, Orson Welles brought his Mercury Theater company to Hollywood, where they were joined by Herman Mankiewicz as screenwriter and Gregg Toland as cameraman in making a mysterious movie about a mysterious man. When the finished product was finally released in the spring of 1941 (after weeks of litigation, persistent threats of suppression, and repeated denials that the central character in any way resembled a certain William Randolph Hearst), *Citizen Kane* was immediately hailed as one of the most original, creative, and confusing efforts in the history of film. Though most critics were overwhelmingly impressed with its stylistic expertise, few really felt comfortable with its jumbled story line and ambivalent attitude toward the imposing figure of Charles Foster Kane. Moreover, because the country was on the brink of war, the film suffered a fate somewhat similar to that of *Let Us Now Praise Famous Men*: within several years it was rarely being shown, and its influence on the general population was therefore severely limited. Orson Welles, like James Agee, went on to other things (when either could get the financial support), and their early triumphs survived more by means of underground reputation than through public acclaim. Nevertheless, both works were able to sum up and move beyond the values and ideals of the 1930s, paying homage to the old while simultaneously looking forward to the new.

As with *Let Us Now Praise Famous Men,* much of *Citizen Kane*'s power could be traced to its style. This involved more than the celebrated technical innovations—the dramatic camera angles and heightened performances, the theatrical lighting and portentous shadows, the long takes and rapid cuts, the alteration of pace between slow scenes and brief vignettes, the reliance on deep focus to show individuals in terms of their environment as well as in their relationship to other men. Perhaps of even greater significance was its imaginative use of sound. A veteran of radio, Welles understood the potency of music, disembodied voices, overlapping dialogue, the ability to edit aurally rather than visually by having one person begin a sentence to be completed by someone else in another place at another time. Here words were utilized not simply to convey information, establish character, or lecture the audience but to create a special world filled with extraordinary people in extraordinary situations. All of these devices tended to make the sound track of *Citizen Kane* just as memorable as the images on the screen.

But over and above the experiments with sight and sound, Welles was rebelling against the constraints of formal plot and narrative. Like Agee, he declined to proceed chronologically. Instead he circled around his subject, recounting events exclusively through flashbacks, repeating episodes from different perspectives, juxtaposing scenes of youth and age, shifting abruptly from still photographs to men in motion, leaping from one historical period to another without regard to traditional notions of cause and effect, starting the movie with the death of Kane and then re-exploring his life, mixing up the normal sequences of time as a means of forcing the spectator to see and hear in entirely new ways. In short, Welles was not telling a story or filming a play but raising issues and examining themes. Unconsciously, but nonetheless effectively, he was responding to Mordecai Gorelik's call for a theater of inquiry by converting his film into a portrait of ideas.

Finally, *Citizen Kane* succeeded in dealing both with the real and the symbolic. By blending "objective" newsreels with subjective memories, by oscillating between the mythic qualities of Kane's castle and the historical outlines of Kane's life, by joining the fantastic and the baroque to the familiar and the mundane, by contrasting the visual impressions of material wealth with the verbal recognition of personal emptiness, Welles had drawn on the full resources of the depression cinema in an effort to map the social and psychological dimensions of one man's experience in modern America.[63]

But the film was more than a stylistic tour de force. The technical fireworks served not only to awaken the audience to new conceptions of reality but also to illuminate the moral difficulties in passing judgment both on the character of Charles Foster Kane and the society out of which he sprang. Welles deliberately refrained from the simplistic presentation of good and evil that often passed for social criticism in the plays and movies of the 1930s. His approach to Kane was neither sanctimonious nor "responsible," neither sentimental nor propagandistic. Insofar as he shared the attitudes of the Left, he seemed more attuned to the questioning spirit of the early 1930s than to the pious certitudes of the Popular Front.[64]

Since Welles wished not so much to reconstruct a career as to reveal its underlying significance, he discussed the details of Kane's life from several different points of view. From the opening newsreel, through the enterprising discoveries of the anonymous reporter and the conflicting recollections of the various people he interviews, to the final omniscient camera eye, the movie was a testimonial to the ambiguity of truth. No one knows the whole story about Kane; each bit of information is biased, selective, and incomplete. Hence the spectator is forced both to participate in and reflect on the mystery with which he is confronted, searching like the reporter-detective for clues to the meaning of events, coming to his own conclusions on the basis of whatever he sees and hears and remembers.

This task is made doubly perplexing by the fact that Kane himself emerges as a strange and enigmatic personality. The film makes little effort to condone or condemn, nor to elicit a predictable series of reactions from the audience. Instead it continually shifts in mood from pity and sympathy to satire and mockery. Throughout the movie Kane is pictured both as a dreamer and a cynic, a creative genius and an awesome threat, a man of noble ideals and a selfish hypocrite. Thus at the outset he appears as the symbol of a classic American type—the audacious entrepreneur who thinks it would be "fun to run a newspaper," who values personal independence over the mere acquisition of wealth, who believes that one lone man can affect the destiny of the entire nation. Yet as others offer their commentary on his illusions, it becomes clear that, like Little Caesar and Duke Mantee, he has grown increasingly obsolete in a tightly organized, highly structured society—the last of the rugged individualists in a world of corporate control.

Moreover, his loftiest projects seem somehow shoddy and disturbing, at least in the eyes of his eulogists and critics. For the bitter and disenchanted Jed Leland, Kane is an incipient fascist who appears more interested in power and public applause than in the defense of the common man, whose "declaration of principles" turns out to be as much a relic of the past as the inanimate objects of culture he stores in the basement of Xanadu. For his second wife, Susan Alexander, he is a figure both egocentric and pathetic, an obsessive collector of people and things, an aging emperor surrounded by stone monuments to faded ambitions, but also someone about whom it is possible to "feel sorry." For the loyal Mr. Bernstein, Kane is a person "who lost everything he had," who pokes among the ruins of his childhood for the family, the love, the convictions, and the innocence that can never be retrieved. Taken together, these disparate memories and observations seem to describe a man who yearns both for the ordinary pleasures of daily life available to the average citizen and the extraordinary sense of greatness and magnificence available only to a few. In effect, Kane is at once the product of modern society and a fossil from another time, a fervent champion of his country's values and a melancholy victim of its myths.

But in the end perhaps he is none of these. Indeed the truly liberating and innovative attribute of *Citizen Kane* was its refusal to answer questions, make a statement, deliver a message, or take a stand. Where many intellectuals in the 1930s believed that to be radical a work of art must say this man is wicked, this institution is wrong, this system should be changed, Welles preferred simply to set forth a problem that could not so much be solved as thought about. He seemed to understand that the true function of a revolutionary film—as of revolutionary novels, documentaries, and plays— was to alter men's view of life, to offer new ways of seeing the world, to disrupt the normal patterns of feeling and behavior.

Thus in order to keep the audience alert to what it was experiencing, he maintained a constant tension between the script and the camera, between words and images, between the lessons of print and the insights of film. The entire production was designed as an elaborate spectacle, with each element calling attention to itself. Moreover, the disdain for chronology and conventional narrative meant that the moviegoer would be continually interrupted and never permitted to become too emotionally engrossed in the performances. Like Agee, Welles was forever talking to his audience, commenting on the action through repetitions and multiple perspectives, allowing the camera to contradict the sound track (and vice versa), indulging in a display of "magical" tricks that were often unrelated to the tale, all as a way of reminding the spectator that he was looking not at life but at art.

Above all, Welles was bidding farewell to an age that had relied on rational theories and logical arguments. In their place he seemed to suggest that the new forms of media could more effectively inspire the human imagination and point it in revolutionary directions. Hence it was appropriate that the solitary reporter (the representative of an older, Hearstian style of journalism, armed only with a pencil and depending solely on written or verbal communication, trying to piece together the "history" of Kane's career, concluding finally that no single "word can explain a man's life") should fail, where the camera (the powerful instrument of Luce's newsreels and picture magazines, conveying information through visual impressions, disregarding sequential plots for immediate images, subordinating conscious ideologies to subconscious myths) should succeed in unraveling the mystery of "Rosebud"—itself a symbolic rather than a literal epitaph to the memory of Charles Foster Kane.[65]

Ultimately, Orson Welles had managed to fuse all the components of popular culture in the 1930s, using the mass media for creative instead of conservative purposes. By combining the advantages of theater, radio, and film, by focusing on the psychological sources of social behavior, by attempting to understand the individual against the background of his environment, by comparing the values of the past with the possibilities of the present, by utilizing the traditional forms of realism and the more contemporary techniques of Expressionism, *Citizen Kane* was both an aesthetic and a radical masterpiece. Yet like George Soule, Lewis Mumford, Edmund Wilson, John Dewey, Robert Lynd, Sidney Hook, Reinhold Niebuhr, and James Agee, Welles was offering Americans an unfamiliar and uncomfortable view of their world at precisely a time when they hungered for whatever seemed tranquil and routine. And it was this latter sentiment, not the experimental work of a few artists and intellectuals, that would become increasingly important in the waning years of the depression.

CHAPTER VII

THE DECLINE OF RADICALISM,
1935–1939

1. *The Politics of the Popular Front*

By the fall of 1935 the intellectual community was in a fairly optimistic mood. The worst days of the depression were passing and with them the sense of bewilderment and hopelessness that earlier paralyzed the country. Despite the shortcomings of the New Deal, the first signs of recovery had begun to appear. Whatever the failures of the NRA and the limitations of Social Security, the Wagner Act offered new opportunities to the labor movement, while the TVA was already transforming the lives of millions in the South. Moreover, if the Roosevelt Administration remained unwilling to introduce a truly planned economy, its emergency relief measures and WPA programs at least helped many to survive from day to day. Finally, the Left itself was trying out new strategies and forms of organization, flirting with Floyd Olson in Minnesota, Upton Sinclair's EPIC crusade in California, the American Labor party in New York. Thus it seemed a propitious moment for the realization of radical ideas and programs, for the construction of a broadly based political coalition dedicated to socialist goals, and for the further elaboration of a value system which sought to reconcile the needs of the individual with those of the group. As the decade reached mid-point, many writers serenely assumed that their country possessed both the time and emotional resources to alter its existing social and cultural institutions.

Yet within several years these ambitions had faded. The plans for a new party fell victim to a gradual decline in political energy and vision. The dream of an American-style socialism became more elusive, and the notion of what constituted meaningful reform grew more prosaic. A series of disappointments at home and disasters abroad served to dampen everyone's ardor for intellectual experimentation and social criticism. In short, the period after 1935 was not a fulfillment of but a retreat from the creative ferment and radical possibilities of the early 1930s.

Of all the forces bearing down on America in the later years of the decade, none was more intense than the pressure of international events. From the moment of Adolf Hitler's rise to power in 1933, the specter of fascism and war haunted men's minds and intruded on their political discussions. Where Mussolini had remained something of a joke to intellectuals and policy-makers, when they were not occasionally attracted to his singular form of economic planning, the Nazis clearly posed a more serious threat to mankind. The rapidity with which they crushed the opposition inside Germany, their remarkably effective use of the mass media in the service of racism and cultural reaction, the mindless brutality of their secret police and the rumors of even worse horrors in the concentration camps, the continuing support they received from the German people despite predictions of the regime's imminent collapse, all transformed fascism from an abstract idea to a concrete and inescapable presence. No longer could its economic and military aims be dismissed as irrational or propagandistic. By the mid-1930s, having created the Third Reich in his own special image, Hitler was ready (with the help of Italy and Japan) to remodel the world. Thus, inexorably, the crisis in Europe and the Far East supplanted the depression as the decade's major concern. As writers and politicians grew more and more preoccupied with the task of devising a suitable response to the fascist menace, interest in domestic issues correspondingly waned.

Perhaps the most dramatic example of this shift in attention took place among the Communists. Following the defeat and suppression of the German Communist party in 1933, the Soviet Union began to reappraise its hostile stance toward capitalism and the Western democracies. As the country most endangered by Nazi Germany and therefore most in need of allies, Russia appeared increasingly eager to strike a bargain with the bourgeois states against the day when Hitler should decide to launch his anti-Bolshevik crusade. Gradually, Moscow moderated its rhetoric and revised its policies so that they would seem more palatable to liberal tastes. In 1934 Russia entered the League of Nations and signed a mutual-security pact with France. And in 1935 the Seventh World Congress of the Communist

International issued an official call for a Popular Front to combat fascism throughout the world.

At first no one knew what the consequences of this reorientation might be. The initial explanations of the new tactics often sounded confused and contradictory, especially in America. On the one hand, the Communists tried desperately to preserve the pose, if not the substance, of socialist militancy. Hence they sometimes argued that the Popular Front was merely a temporary expedient to avoid war, since each day of peace presumably strengthened Russia and the forces of revolution everywhere. If the Left was not yet sufficiently powerful to bring about the victory of the proletariat, if the present emergency dictated a policy of compromise and cooperation with the bourgeoisie, if it was now necessary for radicals to distinguish between free enterprise and fascist oligarchy, these developments meant only that the class struggle was being postponed. But according to this line of reasoning, once the danger of German imperialism had abated, the basic conflict between capitalism and socialism would certainly resume.[1]

On the other hand, by emphasizing the degree to which everyone— democrats and Marxists, reformers and revolutionaries, the middle class and the workers—had a stake in fighting fascism, the Communists saw an opportunity to end their political isolation in the United States, bury their ideological differences with other groups, and become respectable members in a friendly coalition of "progressives." Thus they earnestly preached the virtues of collective security in international affairs, while on domestic matters they slowly adapted the old socialist ideals to the more conciliatory language of the Popular Front. Increasingly, the principal issue for them was not the ultimate form society should take but the maintenance of peace, social progress, and democratic values.[2] To avoid frightening their potential bourgeois allies, the Communists began to subordinate their revolutionary goals to the task of preserving whatever gains had already been made.

Since this new posture was primarily defensive, it resulted in a state of mind concerned less with radical innovation than with bolstering the status quo. Given the stormy atmosphere in which the Communists found themselves after 1935, their tendency to abandon the quest for social alternatives was at least understandable. Moreover, the idea that liberals and radicals were locked in mortal combat with the forces of reaction was not an invention of Moscow's foreign office; such a perspective seemed to coincide perfectly with the invasion of Ethiopia, the Japanese assault on China, the agony of Spain, and Hitler's insatiable hunger for Czechoslovakia. When faced with the omnipresent threat of war, it would have been difficult for most men to respond in any other way. Nevertheless, the Communists went to extremes; frequently they appeared all too eager to neglect sustained political analysis in the interest of anti-fascist unity. Because they believed that the firmest solidarity was needed to resist fascism, because they feared that uninhibited debate and criticism might lead to discord in the camp of the progressives, because they came to regard any systematic exploration of ideas as somehow disruptive, the Communists exerted an increasingly conservative influence on the politics of the Left.

Yet the transition from a policy of aggressive radicalism to an acceptance of liberal reform was not particularly rapid or abrupt; it took a long time for the full implications of the Popular Front to emerge. Throughout 1935 and 1936 the Communists kept up their attack on the New Deal, asserting that the Democrats were as much the agents of business, fascism, and war as the Republicans. Though they acknowledged their preference for Roosevelt over Landon in the election of 1936, they continued to call for the formation of an independent Farmer-Labor party that would gather together all the "scattered forces of real democracy," make a respectable showing at the polls in November, maintain pressure on the New Deal from the Left, and build up its strength to the point where it could take power in 1940.[3] In their estimation, the Popular Front could take up where the prewar Marxists had left off, fulfilling the traditional desire of the Left for a political movement that was both broadly based and impeccably militant. If the Communists were now prepared to engage seriously in electoral activity, their official goal remained the creation of socialist America.

For a while the Communists displayed a fairly sophisticated understanding of the tenuous relationship between reform and revolution. Discarding the apocalyptic presumption that men would revolt only in the worst of times, they emphasized the value of organizing groups of people around concrete issues as well as the need to give them an occasional taste of victory in the ongoing struggle for social change. Hence as dedicated participants in the construction of the CIO and the American Labor party, and as uncompromising but realistic critics of the contemporary scene, the Communists raised a series of immediate demands—amendment of the neutrality laws to make them inapplicable to civil wars, extension of Social Security to those not presently covered, the establishment of a thirty-hour work week and a higher minimum-wage rate, restriction of the Supreme Court's capacity to nullify social legislation, full civil rights for Negroes, public housing for low-income families, an increase in mass purchasing power through greater government spending and economic planning—all of which might make capitalism more tolerable while demonstrating the necessity for its eventual overthrow.[4] The expectation of a violent proletarian uprising had been replaced by an approach that was gradualist and evolutionary but ostensibly no less radical.

Yet as the years wore on and the Nazi threat to the Soviet Union grew more ominous, the Communists began to lose sight of their ultimate objectives. Instead they tended to focus on short-range tactics as ends in themselves. The desire to fashion a new party gave way to a rapprochement with the New Deal. Increasingly, the Communists appeared content to work within existing political institutions, dreaming vaguely of converting the Democratic party into a facsimile of the Popular Front but more often willing to adopt Roosevelt as their champion for the duration of the crisis. While the *New Masses* could admit that the President's main ambition was to save the capitalist system by eliminating some of its most blatant injustices, the conservative opposition provoked by even his limited measures persuaded the magazine that the New Deal represented a "forward step requiring the support of the people."[5] The danger from the Right made the Center seem more and more attractive.

In the late 1930s, therefore, whatever Republicans or businessmen disliked the Communists enthusiastically approved. They endorsed Roosevelt's crusade against the Court, his campaign to purge conservative Democrats in the Congressional election of 1938, and his efforts to prevent a general dismantling of the New Deal as the decade closed. But beneath this amiable approach to the White House lay a crucial concession to liberalism as a philosophy as well as a political strategy. The Communists were beginning to embrace the heretical notion that the state was not necessarily an instrument of capitalism, that government could be relatively impartial and thereby serve the people as effectively as it protected corporate profits. By flirting with the idea of government-as-broker, they inadvertently confessed their acceptance of more conventional attitudes about American institutions. And by 1938 the Communists had publicly surrendered the ideal of independent political movement. Despite the inadequacies of Roosevelt's tenure, they argued, the attempt at this time to form a new party to the left would only weaken the Popular Front and aid reaction.[6] Thus the Communists' experiment with coalition politics led them not only to support the New Deal as the first line of defense against fascism but also to mistake a formal unity among the disparate groups on the left with a meaningful social program.

There were occasional efforts during these years to invest the Popular Front with a sense of drama and conflict. Granted that the classic Marxist antagonism between revolutionary socialists and oppressive capitalists no longer seemed appropriate, one might still feel caught up in a titanic contest between "progressives" and "reactionaries." The *New Masses* fervently insisted that "the dominant finance-capitalist groups on one side and the overwhelming majority of workers, farmers, and small business and professional people on the other" were engaged in what amounted to a modern version of class war.[7] Such a "struggle" might be emotionally satisfying even if the contending forces were rather indistinct.

In this battle, however, the Communists displayed a marked solicitude for the well-being of the bourgeoisie. Where radicals had earlier asserted that social change in the United States was hindered by middle-class assumptions and values, the *New Masses* could now criticize other left-wing writers for overemphasizing the moral and economic disintegration of white-collar America at the very moment when the workers needed allies. In its best Rotarian manner, the magazine heatedly denied that "our middle class" was decaying or "withering into oblivion." Quite the contrary, the bourgeoisie should be considered a "vigorous" partner in the movement against fascism and war.[8] Given this perspective, the Communists urged the Roosevelt Administration to strengthen the economic position of the middle class by extending more credit and capital to small businessmen, by subsidizing impoverished landowners, and by breaking up the gigantic monopolies.[9] At the same time, the Communists declared that they themselves were "as devoted as any other group in the camp of progress to the principles and institutions of democracy."[10] If all of this sounded closer to the rhetoric of Woodrow Wilson than to the ideas of Karl Marx, it reflected the Communists' growing eagerness to float placidly in the "main currents" of American life.[11]

At bottom, the Popular Front's retreat from radicalism came as a logical consequence of the fact that it was never really strong enough to put pressure on or wring concessions from the New Deal. In the absence of a national Farmer-Labor party or strong socialist trade unions, the Left had little with which to bargain. Where in France or Spain the Communists played a positive role in shaping government policy, in the United States they could only respond passively to the initiatives of the Roosevelt Administration. Thus it seemed easier to preach consensus, to search for areas of agreement and common purpose, to focus exclusively on the fascist peril as a means of wielding some influence with those in power. Imperceptibly, the urge to enlist as many groups as possible in the Popular Front took precedence over the effort to build a movement whose nature and aims were clearly defined. By the late 1930s the Communists were operating on the principle that the vaguer their program, the less risk of alienating possible sympathizers. The attempt to discuss economic issues in terms of progressives and reactionaries, Wall Street and the "people" was entirely too schematic to serve as anything more than a convenient slogan rather than as the starting point for a thoroughgoing analysis of modern American society. The style and language of the Popular Front emphasized the need for radicals to harmonize with, instead of challenge, the nation's dominant ideals. As a result, the Communists preferred to pose as sane and steady commentators, "responsibly" contributing to the dialogue over the country's future while avoiding their earlier sectarian dogmatism, even if this meant that henceforth they would be less sensitive to sharp social divisions and less willing to engage in political combat with their liberal colleagues.

Yet in a curious way the Communists appeared more comfortable when they could regard themselves as integral members of the larger society rather than when they were forced to act as its critical conscience. As Murray Kempton has observed, the remarkable thing about many radicals in the 1930s was not "how much they demanded but . . . how little it took them to be satisfied. The Communists . . . were happiest when they thought of President Roosevelt as their ally rather than their enemy."[12] It might well have been perfectly justifiable to slow down the movement for social change until fascism was destroyed; the call for collective security and the agitation to lift the blockade against the Spanish Loyalists may quite properly have consumed all the available energy of the Left. Nevertheless, for their part the Communists surrendered too much for too little.

Perhaps this was because, as George Charney recalled, the Popular Front reflected what most radicals "really believed but could not articulate." Its reformist policies and democratic imagery sounded more "natural" and realistic in the American setting. The Popular Front permitted its followers to assume that they were part of a revolutionary vanguard at the same time they shared the "traditions, loyalties, prejudices," and "aspirations of the common man." As a distinctively "American spirit" began to pervade the movement in the late 1930s, it was hardly surprising that the Communists should make their greatest inroads not among workers and immigrants but among the middle class: students, professionals, entertainers, writers and artists, the native-born. The liveliest feature of the *Daily Worker* during these years was the sports page, with its knowledgeable evaluations of Joe Louis and the Brooklyn Dodgers. And appropriately, "the proletarian garb favored by functionaries was replaced by the business suit"; now the typical organizer appeared indistinguishable from a respectable "office executive." The Communists obviously enjoyed the feeling that they were "no longer outsiders, that [they] belonged," that they were marching in lock step with the "masses." In effect, they had ceased to be rebels, alienated by and in resistance to American society; instead, they behaved like men anxious to fit in and conform.[13]

Yet ironically, by submerging their political differences in a common front against reaction, by stressing the need for unity and cooperation above all else, by affirming their solidarity with the average American, the Communists had lost the opportunity to realize even their modest objectives. For in the end, despite all their compromises and accommodations, they could not prevent what they most feared: they were unable to halt the slide toward war. Ultimately, the passionate anti-fascism of the Popular Front succeeded only in paralyzing the Left long before the real guns shattered what remained of the decade's radical dreams.

2. *The Liberal Mind in the Late 1930s*

The Communists were by no means alone in believing that the danger from the Right demanded a readjustment of goals and priorities. By the mid-1930s many liberals had also concluded that the Nazis represented a supreme threat both to Russia and the West. Consequently, journals such as the *Nation* and *Social Frontier* welcomed the Popular Front because they shared its conviction that the primary conflict was not between capitalism and socialism but between fascism and democracy. Furthermore, they had been arguing for some time that it would be mutually advantageous for Midwestern progressives, Eastern intellectuals, Communists, Socialists, and enlightened Democrats to forget their ideological disagreements and unite. Indeed if men who held divergent political ambitions could really cooperate, this might be seen as another reproach to America's traditional competitiveness and individualism. But most of all the Popular Front attracted liberals because it treated social change as an evolutionary process.[14] Thus if the Communists felt more at home speaking to their fellow Americans in the familiar language of the middle class, it proved even easier for non-Marxists to adopt the phrases and thought patterns of gradualism and reform.

But during 1935 and 1936 the liberal magazines were as determined as the *New Masses* to prevent the Popular Front from becoming purely defensive. They too hoped for a nationwide Farmer-Labor party that would offer a practical alternative to the New Deal. Prior to the Presidential election the *New Republic*, the *Nation,* and *Common Sense* remained severely critical of the Roosevelt Administration, continuing to hold the positions they had developed in the early years of the decade. While they applauded the government's efforts to alleviate hunger and unemployment through emergency spending programs, they contended that these "pump-priming" techniques could never increase purchasing power, restore prosperity, or solve the problem of want amid plenty. Even the New Deal's most impressive measures—the Wagner Act, Social Security, and TVA—seemed "sadly deficient" in light of what was really necessary to end the depression. At heart, Roosevelt was wedded irrevocably to the profit system, and this the liberals found unfortunate but unforgivable. So in the absence of full-scale economic recovery, possible only through comprehensive economic planning, they foresaw the gradual disintegration of the Democratic party and the emergence of a robust socialist movement capable of taking power in the near future.[15]

Yet by the summer of 1936 the magazines were forced to admit that the Farmer-Labor party might well postpone its debut until the conservative counterattack had subsided. Given the presumed strength of Alf Landon, Father Coughlin, and the Liberty League, it began to appear that Roosevelt's re-election was a prerequisite for further progress. Moreover, the Supreme Court's nullification of the NRA and AAA removed the onus of failure from the President. Thus as Roosevelt's esteem began to climb with liberals and labor, as the CIO threw its support to the Democrats, and as no radical leader emerged to challenge the New Deal at the polls, the *Nation* suggested that the Left must temporarily "curb itself" at least through November.[16]

This decision was rendered considerably less painful by the kind of campaign the President conducted. His crusade against "economic royalists," his allusions to the "forgotten man," his anger at one-third of a nation "ill-housed, ill-clothed, and ill-fed" gave the New Deal a social-democratic flavor which made it seem as if Roosevelt himself were moving toward the left. More important, however, the election returns revealed not only that the President had been handed a massive popular mandate with which to transform the country if he chose but also that he had put together the very coalition for which the Popular Front ardently yearned. The New Deal was winning the allegiance of all those groups on whom a radical movement depended—workers, farmers, lawyers, teachers, engineers, civil servants, Negroes, Jews, Catholics, old-stock reformers, everyone who had suffered the depression's cruelties and now wished for some changes in the social order. Though a number of liberals, like their Communist counterparts, warned against the temptation to accept the Democrats as a satisfactory substitute for a new party, though they urged the labor unions to preserve their independence, though they declared that any endorsement of Roosevelt should be "withdrawn the day after election," it was to prove increasingly difficult for them to distinguish their own goals from those of the White House.[17] If the radical vision among many journalists and intellectuals was still relatively clear, this did not make them any more immune to the pressure of external events, nor any less susceptible to the allure of the New Deal.

There were some who realized that the greatest weakness of the Left in America was its historic tendency to vacillate between militancy and opportunism, socialist programs and an urge to be close to the masses, revolutionary idealism and a longing for power. Consequently, in the late 1930s writers as different as Max Lerner, Archibald MacLeish, Frederick Schuman, Theodore Brameld, and Corliss Lamont tried to devise a coherent ideology for the Popular Front that would avoid each of these extremes. Following the example of their predecessors in the early years of the decade, they called for a movement both indigenous to the United States and genuinely radical, both effective in fighting fascism and strong enough to reorganize American life.[18]

To this end they stressed the apparent compatibility between liberalism and socialism, dwelling on their shared respect for cultural diversity and the dignity of the individual, their unshakable faith in "Reason and . . . the Common Man," their sincere dedication to the virtues of tolerance and open discussion, their undying commitment to experimentation and the scientific method, their steadfast reliance on human intelligence and parliamentary procedures to direct social change. Brameld was particularly ingenious in contending that the class struggle did not really mean coercion or violence; on the contrary, force was merely a "synonym for action," a more energetic form of "persuasion" and education in the face of resistance from the Right. For at bottom, he asserted, "democracy" remained the "ultimate goal of Marxism." Thus in view of how much the two traditions held in common, Max Lerner found it comparatively easy to dispense with the classical categories of proletariat and bourgeoisie; instead he looked forward to the peaceful transfer of power from a "ruling oligarchy to a democratic majority," whereupon class differences would entirely disappear. And Frederick Schuman suggested optimistically that the "liberal-communist alliance to prevent war" might produce a new philosophical synthesis, combining the best strains of Marxism and Pragmatism, social equality and political freedom.[19]

But despite all this enthusiasm for the "massed power of the people" and the gradual introduction of democratic socialism, men like Lerner and Schuman had already internalized many of the values of the New Deal. As a result, they talked at length about the need for "disciplined leadership" in the task of economic reconstruction; they argued that planning must be carried out by "disinterested experts" whose specific objectives were set by "bodies representative of the majority"; they were willing to tolerate the creation of a "general staff" for the "technical coordination" of social reforms; and they acknowledged that the present crisis demanded a concentration of authority "in the hands of the executive in the interests of efficiency and survival."[20]

During the early 1930s George Soule and Stuart Chase had invoked similar strategies as a solution to the chaos of capitalism. At the same time Lewis Corey and Alfred Bingham had pointed out the necessity for political cooperation between the workers and the middle class. Finally, Edmund Wilson and V.F. Calverton had emphasized the desirability of translating Marxism into terms most Americans would understand. But now these very ideas were being adapted to the special requirements of the Popular Front. In the process, their conservative implications—the reduction of social concepts to expedient slogans which might more effectively appeal to the ordinary citizen, the ease with which collectivist ideals could be used to justify the welfare state and the further consolidation of bureaucratic power in Washington—were all becoming more pronounced. Ironically, the efforts of intellectuals like Lerner, Schuman, and Brameld to prevent the Popular Front from being absorbed within the liberal consensus was leading to an ideology that transcended both radicalism and the New Deal—one that celebrated the advantages of a tightly organized, mass society beyond anything the 1930s had previously envisioned.

3. Crises at Home and Abroad

Even if the Popular Front had succeeded in maintaining a consistent attitude toward the New Deal, even if it had managed to strike a balance between the immediate tactics of reform and the ultimate goal of revolution, it might still have been overwhelmed by the continuing series of crises that plagued the years after 1935. For liberals and radicals alike, the late 1930s was a period in which one emergency followed another almost without interruption, leaving men little time for intellectual subtlety or political creativity. Whatever the strategic and ideological confusions of the Popular Front, these paled beside the daily bombardments of the headline, the newsreel, and the radio bulletin.

Domestically, the Left began to devote most of its post-election attention and energy to the monumental struggles of the CIO. The desire to organize the vast majority of American workers into industrial unions had been smoldering throughout the decade, but now under the leadership of John L. Lewis it erupted into a blaze of sit-down strikes against General Motors and U.S. Steel. To intellectuals in particular, the emergence of the CIO heralded the rise of a politically conscious proletariat committed to overhauling the profit system, imbued with a passion for community and social control, devoted to the principles of planning and production-for-use.[21] This was a grandiose but not entirely distorted vision; by 1937 the unions themselves were seeking more than recognition by the giant corporations. In addition to various economic benefits, the CIO tried to offer its members a feeling of group solidarity, a sense of mission, even a concern for cultural innovation through theatrical experiments like *Pins and Needles* and *The Cradle Will Rock.*

Nevertheless, for the average worker, the union most often meant protection, higher wages, shorter hours, and better conditions inside the plant. Though at times he appeared genuinely willing to risk his life on the picket line, it was not so much for the sake of revolution as for a fairer share of capitalism's rewards. The sit-downs did not portend a seizure of but a respect for private property; the strikers were always careful to keep the factories clean and the machines in good repair. In sum, they sought not power but influence, not mastery but equality.[22]

Moreover, even if the labor movement had been less ready to accept its status as just another interest group within pluralist America, the recession of 1937 and the conservative resurgence in Congress during 1938 were both slowing the momentum of the CIO. So despite the warnings of a few that the Left should want not merely "unionized workers" but "radical workers," the Popular Front seemed increasingly content to stress the need for organization as an end in itself—concentrating on the victorious campaigns in the auto, rubber, and steel industries without worrying too much about what would happen after the barricades came down.[23] The Left continued to declare that the labor movement was the most progressive force in the nation, that the workers possessed truly radical aspirations, and that the current wave of strikes presaged a fundamental shift in power. But the limited objectives of the CIO and the inhospitable political climate of the late 1930s made these pronouncements sound dangerously ritualistic and self-deceptive.

Yet the difficulties which the Popular Front encountered at home were overshadowed by the news from abroad. If the pulse of reform seemed to be faltering in America, it had almost ceased beating completely in Europe —the victim not only of gradual fascist strangulation but also of the mysterious convulsions shaking the Soviet Union. In many ways the latter shocks proved more injurious; while most observers were able to diagnose Nazism as a terrifying but potentially curable disease, they did not know how to treat the Russian illness, nor could they even agree that the patient was actually sick.

Their uncertainty was an inheritance from the early 1930s, when much of the interest in discovering a radical alternative to liberal capitalism had been inspired by the apparent success of socialism in the Soviet Union. The intellectual community was especially encouraged by Russia's economic progress and cultural ferment. A number of social scientists were impressed by the promise of a fully planned society, more than one political theorist thought he saw in the U.S.S.R. an effort to fuse democracy and socialism, artists and literary critics envied the importance of the writer in Russian life, and many were simply invigorated by the Communists' emphasis on human commitment and action in subduing the environment. At the center of these perceptions lay the idea that the Soviet Union was fundamentally different from other lands: its leaders seemed more in touch with the aspirations of the common people; its programs were presumably addressed to the needs of the international working class; with tensions rising in Europe and the Far East, its foreign policy displayed a steadiness of purpose, a consistent anti-fascism, and a dedication to peace that the West evidently lacked. Russia's behavior and goals were therefore to be judged by a unique set of standards, inapplicable to ordinary nation-states. To American writers— whether liberal or radical, whether critical or enthusiastic—the Soviet Union was ultimately not a country but a state of mind.

Nevertheless, by the mid-1930s, as Stalin consolidated his power within Russia and began to seek bourgeois allies, it became increasingly clear that the future of socialism depended in large measure on the fate of the present regime. Although few regarded the Soviet model as relevant to American conditions, and while most disapproved of the dictatorship's obvious "excesses," many writers still looked to Russia for emotional if not ideological guidance. Consequently, it was not surprising that they should be intensely preoccupied with Russian politics, often at the expense of events closer to home. Some intellectuals, particularly those who had either scorned Marxist theory from the beginning or who now believed that Stalin was insufficiently militant in pursuing a world revolution, passed into permanent opposition with the formation of the Popular Front. Others welcomed this change in policy as a sign of Russia's growing political maturity. To them, Soviet society was entering a transitional period in which socialism remained an interesting "experiment." If the Russians enjoyed neither a workers' commonwealth nor the ordinary democratic amenities, this was because the country had known nothing but civil war and international hostility since the revolution.[24] But whichever position one took on the Popular Front or the current quality of Soviet life, the issue of Stalinism was gradually obscuring everything else; with the opening of the Moscow trials, it would turn into an obsession.

Institutionalized terror had been a traditional government weapon in Russia for centuries, yet the majority of American writers were confused and tormented by the sophisticated uses to which it was put by Stalin. In 1934 the regime began to focus its machinery of show trials and judicial executions not on the usual NEP men and kulaks but on the most illustrious party officials together with thousands of lesser Communist functionaries. From 1935 to 1938, as one revolutionary hero after another confessed to incredible crimes for which he faced certain death, as the upheavals within Russia obviously posed a mortal threat both to socialism and to peace, liberals and radicals alike felt compelled to choose sides.

For their part, the Communists defended the trials as a vindication of Stalinist programs. According to the *New Masses,* the internal opponents of the Soviet regime—Zinoviev, Kamenev, Bukharin, the ever-villainous Trotskyites—had resorted to sabotage and assassination because they lacked popular support for a political coup. Confronted with the overwhelming evidence of their guilt, they had no option but to confess.[25] This was a marvelously simplistic argument, but its logic apparently persuaded a number of well-known novelists, literary critics and performers—among them Mark Blitzstein, Morris Carnovsky, Harold Clurman, Jack Conroy, Malcolm Cowley, John Garfield, Dashiell Hammett, Lillian Hellman, Langston Hughes, Dorothy Parker, Henry Roth, and Irwin Shaw—none of whom had qualms about publicly endorsing the official Communist interpretation as late as 1938.[26]

Yet those who accepted the trials as genuine did not always take the confessions or verdicts at face value. They were moved by other, more basic considerations. A man like Granville Hicks might have his private misgivings about the dictatorship, but in the end he "could not denounce Russia and break with the Communist Party. The U.S.S.R. . . . was the only bulwark against Fascism, and the Communist Party in this country was leading the fight against every kind of reaction. Particularly in its new policy [the Popular Front], its emphasis on American radical traditions, its willingness to cooperate with all anti-Fascists, the Party seemed to me more than ever the great hope for the United States, and I would not abandon it because of something that was happening in Russia."[27] Should these motives still seem inadequate, the Communists could always accuse the hesitant of sowing confusion and panic in the face of the fascist enemy. To criticize the trials was to aid the forces of reaction throughout the world. Therefore as an antidote to "doubt," the *New Masses* prescribed "faith—faith in the Soviet Union and in the people's front movement in all countries —if mankind is to be saved from catastrophe."[28] Thus the inclination to value unity on the left over clarity on political issues, and the desire to believe in the essential goodness of Soviet intentions despite the nagging pressures of reason and morality, helped explain why many American intellectuals preferred to acquiesce in the Moscow trials rather than question both their own fundamental assumptions and those of the Popular Front.

If the Communists regarded the trials as a test of one's political orthodoxy, their most vehement opponents saw the purges as a sign that the anti-Christ had taken over the Church. Non-Stalinist radicals excoriated the proceedings as a charade, a frame-up, and a betrayal of the October revolution.[29] Even for those who did not think that Stalin had deliberately sacrificed the cause of international socialism to Russian national interests, the purges were profoundly disillusioning. The government-sanctioned bloodletting reduced the Soviet leadership, in the eyes of Oswald Garrison Villard, "to the level of Adolf Hitler." In his opinion, these killings were not merely a "passing phase"; they had become an integral facet of the Soviet experience, and their persistence mocked the humanitarian aims of Marxism. Villard found the trials "execrable and indefensible"; to him, murder was immoral no matter what the political exigencies or ideological excuses. He still held to certain ethical absolutes, among them the belief that the end never justified the means and the conviction that any regime which relied on oppression and terror to govern its people no longer deserved the support of the Left.[30] Yet for the most part the opposition was as shrill in its indictment of the Soviet Union as the Communists were ecstatic in their approval. Both camps seemed incapable of evaluating the socialist experiment with any objectivity; both were transfixed by the awesome presence of Stalinism.

Many liberals were caught in the middle, wanting neither to surrender their faith in the basic virtues of Soviet society nor to applaud a dictatorship whose tactics appeared increasingly fascist. At the outset they found it hard to believe that the defendants were framed or tortured into admitting nonexistent crimes. But even if the specific charges had been fabricated, even if the trials defied rational analysis, magazines like the *Nation* and the *New Republic* feared that the mounting debate over events in Russia would only shatter the already fragile coalition among American "progressives."

Thus they warned their fellow writers not to become involved in what was essentially an internal Communist quarrel. Instead they recommended a "suspension of judgment until all the facts are available." As long as "we do not know enough to be sure of our ground," they counseled, "we should . . . be content to let opinions differ and turn our attention to the matters nearer home."[31]

But this posture of nonpartisanship was increasingly difficult to maintain as the decade wore on. In refusing either to condemn or to endorse the Moscow trials, the liberal journals left themselves open to the charge that they tolerated political suppressions in Russia while automatically denouncing any abridgments of freedom in the United States. In response, the *New Republic* tried to justify its apparent double standard on the ground that civil liberties were never absolute, that free thought and judicial safeguards were always relative to the nature and aims of a particular social order. Given this perspective, the editors found it possible to distinguish between the Soviet Union and Nazi Germany despite the superficial similarities of party structure and one-man rule. In their view, the U.S.S.R. deserved support because its ultimate objective was the creation of a classless society in which industrial crises and massive unemployment would be permanently abolished. The Nazis, on the other hand, meant to set up a capitalist autocracy based on economic scarcity, belligerent nationalism, and racial mythology. As for their own country, the editors pointed out that America's "undemocratic economic system" undercut whatever personal and political freedoms the people presently enjoyed. Therefore, if liberty was merely a procedural matter even in a nation not threatened by internal subversion or foreign enemies, the *New Republic* could hardly criticize the Russians for forbidding certain activities when their national security was truly at stake.[32]

In each of these instances the editors regarded the social purposes for which a regime stood as the decisive factor in determining one's attitude toward the question of civil liberties. Yet ironically they had learned all too well the lessons of the revolt against liberalism. In the early 1930s many intellectuals had sought to redefine freedom in social terms, arguing that the rights of the individual were dependent on the kind of community in which he lived. Moreover, in the midst of a depression, social and economic issues naturally seemed more important than legal formalities. But by concentrating on the environmental context in which political acts occurred, by insisting that the quest for social justice and security take precedence over the fulfillment of private ambitions, by emphasizing the primacy of class and group needs over all abstract ideals, writers tended to overlook the extent to which these notions might serve the state more effectively than the revolution. In any case, by the late 1930s such assumptions could prevent men from seeing clearly that liberal and socialist values alike were being destroyed in the Soviet Union.

There were some observers who rejected the *New Republic*'s brand of relativism, preferring instead to apologize for Stalinism on the basis of unadulterated *Realpolitik*. Louis Fischer, for example, claimed that judicial pressure and political coercion were perfectly permissible methods for a government to use in protecting itself. "Every state," he explained, "is an organ of violence and suppression. Indeed, social peace is normally maintained by the threat of both." Thus the purges could be understood as a peculiarly Russian application of the general principle that force was essential in preserving order. Furthermore, if the government hesitated to put down its opponents, it ran the risk of losing power and opening the door to a restoration of capitalism.[33]

Frederick Schuman went even further. He believed that it was "pointless" to make *moral* judgments on the validity of the trials. "Both Stalinism and Trotskyism, along with fascism, stand outside of the ethics of liberalism," he contended. Nevertheless, one could decide for *political* reasons to support Stalin, largely because his domestic and foreign policies were closer to those of anti-fascists everywhere. But more significantly, Schuman dismissed Trotsky as a congenital "failure," a man of words rather than action, an "intellectual" rather than an administrator. In contrast, he praised Stalin as a "steeled organizer and activist" who could deal with practical problems quickly and efficiently. For Schuman, the crucial test was "political success," and on these grounds Stalin seemed clearly superior.[34]

Yet in their worship of order and power, in their disdain for principles and ideas, in their discomfort before ethical and ideological issues, both Fischer and Schuman had simply taken the decade's latent anti-intellectualism to its logical extreme. In the process they were being neither radical nor realistic; rather, their defense of Stalinism revealed, however unconsciously, a commitment to the status quo—to a world of shifting alliances, bureaucratic intrigue, and sheer political might.

In the end, however, none of these arguments sounded convincing. No matter how often they attempted to rationalize the dictatorship by recalling the harsh tradition of the Czars and the world-wide animosity toward Bolshevism, no matter how eagerly they fell back on a Hobbesian interpretation of power, no matter how carefully they searched for evidence that Stalin was beginning to relax his grip on Soviet society, most analysts eventually concluded that even if the trials were authentic they had irreparably damaged the radical cause. Both the *Nation* and the *New Republic* came to regard as a glaring weakness "inherent" in the Soviet system the lack of institutional outlets for dissent. If there were no legitimate political channels through which otherwise loyal Marxists might offer alternatives to the policies of their government, then they must inevitably resort to conspiracy and sabotage. As long as the regime made disagreement illegal, the magazines declared, as long as it had to rely on security checks and the secret police, the Russian people would continue to live in a climate of suspicion and fear. In these circumstances no real social progress was possible. Thus as a result of the trials, a growing number of American writers began to discover a "new respect and affection" for the "old-fashioned" virtues of liberalism—"the value," in the *New Republic*'s words, "of free political expression for opposition under the forms of political democracy."[35] Meanwhile, they agreed that the macabre proceedings in Moscow constituted a supreme tragedy for the Soviet Union, for socialism, and for mankind.

Yet despite the terrible spectacle of the purges, Russia managed to retain a measure of its prestige and moral authority among intellectuals because she was the only country (besides Mexico) to aid the Republican government in Spain. And this was no minor consideration. Indeed the Spanish Civil War came as a welcome relief from the controversies and disappointments that afflicted the Left in the late 1930s. Not only did the plight of the Loyalists divert attention from the turmoil in Russia and the rebirth of conservatism in America, but it also permitted men to hope that regardless of every other setback they could still halt the spread of fascism if the issue was clear and their tactics were sound.

The roots of the Spanish conflict lay deep in the country's rigid class structure and fierce regional pride, but the war quickly became a compelling symbol for all the values and aspirations to which the Left had given its allegiance in the 1930s. In America, no group followed the news from Spain with greater intensity than the intellectual community. "People of my sort," observed Malcolm Cowley, "were more deeply stirred by the Spanish Civil War than by any other international event since the World War and the Russian Revolution." To writers like Cowley, Spain seemed the ultimate test of the Popular Front; here the struggle between democracy and fascism, progress and reaction was not an ideological abstraction but a daily reality. On one side stood the landlords, the generals, the bishops, and the banks —all the "old traditions of class intolerance." On the other were the peasants, artisans, small tradesmen, painters, poets, and workers—those who fought for "more knowledge, more freedom, more of everything."[36] Significantly, Cowley portrayed the Republicans as defenders of liberty, reason, and representative government, battling valiantly against the forces of feudalism, clerical superstition, and military regimentation. Though there were some who wanted the war transformed into a proletarian struggle for control of the factories and the land, most American writers saw the conflict not as a social revolution but as a classic liberal crusade.[37] And when these concepts sounded too artificial or pretentious, Spain remained the one place where individuals might conceivably translate their lofty ideals into concrete action.[38] At its most elementary level, the war demanded from men a highly personal sense of commitment; its ultimate importance, as Hemingway had recognized, was not political but moral.

In essence, Spain provided the last occasion in the 1930s when liberals and radicals could unite in defense of their most precious ideals, when it did seem possible that democracy might finally triumph, when the individual could still believe that his efforts made a difference in shaping the course of public events. Thus the defeat of the Loyalists in 1939 came as a crushing blow to the hopes of an entire generation. If in Spain truth, virtue, and morality could not conquer fascism, if the values of the Popular Front proved pitifully unequal to the power of tanks and bombs, if the struggle eventually degenerated into an ugly vendetta between Communists and Trotskyites while the Western governments passively watched as democracy died, then there was little reason to suppose that the Left might succeed anywhere else. And so the movement for social change became another of the war's many casualties—the victim of a world that would no longer respond to ideals or ideologies of any kind.

4. *The Rediscovery of America*

By the late 1930s, the Left had reached an impasse from which there seemed no way out. In America the economic recession of 1937 and Roosevelt's failure to liberalize the Democratic party in the elections of 1938 had resulted in a political stalemate with the New Deal itself under increasingly heavy attack from the Right. The formidable opposition to further social legislation within the House and Senate, as well as the average citizen's apparent desire for a respite from the turbulence of the depression years, forced the Popular Front to abandon its halting efforts to replace the capitalist system with a new set of economic institutions based on the concepts of planning and production-for use. At the same time the spread of fascism in Europe and the purge of all the old Bolsheviks in Russia induced many American writers and activists to reconsider the virtues of their native land. Given the growing menace of totalitarianism, a fervent apologist for the Moscow trials like Louis Fischer could admit by 1939 that he had learned "to treasure freedom above all else. Without civil rights there is no economic security even when unemployment has disappeared. The dictatorships have taught us to love democracy more."[39] And moved by similar fears, the editors of *Common Sense* decided to give up their decade-long search for a new party, declaring instead that "it was never more important than today for the independent progressive and labor forces . . . to cement their ties to the New Deal."[40] Thus the accumulated impact of domestic frustrations and foreign crises had propelled most liberals and radicals into a desperate defense of conventional politics and piecemeal reform.

Yet the pressure of external events was not the only—or even the most significant—reason for the general failure to fulfill the promise of the decade's early years. In many respects the Popular Front was more important as a cultural phenomenon than as a political strategy; it exerted a greater influence on the intellectual community than on the labor movement or the organized parties of the Left. The Popular Front represented not only a tactical response to the resurrection of conservatism at home and the spectacular victories of fascism abroad but also a set of deeply cherished values and a distinctive state of mind. In the period from 1935 to 1939, the attitude of most writers toward literature, social thought, and the role of the intellectual in American life were profoundly shaped by its perspective.

But ironically, what made all of this possible was the extent to which the Popular Front drew on the ideas and assumptions of the early 1930s. For behind the desire to transform the nation's economic system there lurked a number of propositions about the relationship between culture and society whose conservative consequences were to become much more visible after 1935. If the second half of the decade was marked by a gradual diminution of radical energy, the causes of this decline could ultimately be traced to the very political and intellectual ferment with which the depression began.

Nowhere was the cultural mood of the late 1930s better illustrated than in the Communists' willingness to tolerate the heresies and quirks of those liberal intellectuals they had previously despised. But now with the party making friendly overtures to the middle class, its essayists and book reviewers were becoming scrupulously courteous toward the leading poets, journalists, and philosophers of bourgeois America. The polemical tones of the early 1930s were subsiding; there was simply no room in the Popular Front for the spirited vivisection Michael Gold had once performed on the novels of Thornton Wilder. Thus the *New Masses* critic, Stanley Burnshaw, admonished his fellow Marxists to treat men like Wilder and Archibald MacLeish with greater sympathy, analyzing their "mistakes" constructively rather than condemning their work to a political purgatory. Similarly, Corliss Lamont was eager to enroll John Dewey in the Popular Front because, in view of the "large following" that made Dewey such a "singularly significant and influential figure," his drawing power might attract other converts. And even Michael Gold was prepared to smooth the rough edges of his controversial temperament by warmly praising the liberal newspaperman Heywood Broun as an "old-fashioned American patriot."[41] In all of these cases the Communists seemed less interested in carrying on an extended ideological debate than in embracing any writer who announced his dislike for the Nazis. As a result, the typical *New Masses* commentator functioned in the late 1930s as both a travel agent and a welcoming committee to the growing number of intellectual tourists who could be persuaded to spend some time on the left.

Given the continuing penchant for adding famous names to the marquee, there was always a hint of entertainment and showmanship about the party's cultural activities. Perhaps the best example of the Popular Front as a public performance came at the second Congress of American Writers held in New York during June 1937. This event featured such literary celebrities as Archibald MacLeish and Ernest Hemingway, while Earl Browder was on hand to offer political direction. But the contributions of the headliners seemed less revealing than the rhetoric and imagery of the Congress as a whole. For the proceedings, as Matthew Josephson later recalled, were really a "festival in honor of Spain," in which each participant ceremoniously affirmed his commitment to the struggle against fascism and war.[42]

As a consequence, most of the papers sounded rather different from those delivered at the first Congress two years earlier. By 1937 there were few references to the creation of a "proletarian" culture; instead, speakers like Joseph Freeman, Newton Arvin, Granville Hicks, and Malcolm Cowley called for a "democratic" literature more in keeping with the need to protect America's traditional values against attacks from the Right. No longer must the writer expose and criticize the hypocrisies of the bourgeoisie or champion the cause of the workers. The major problem at present, they asserted, was how intellectuals could most effectively utilize their talents in the international contest between "Progress" and "Reaction." Indeed the entire Congress tended to regard the world as a cosmic battlefield. And in such a war, as Earl Browder pointed out, the highest priorities were unity and discipline; neutrality and detachment remained the luxuries of peacetime.

Hence the contributors to the Congress urged their fellow writers to behave like dedicated soldiers in an unending campaign against the enemies of democracy.[43]

The martial spirit of the second Congress was by no means unique to the Communists or their sympathizers. Throughout this period Max Lerner persistently berated his colleagues for not joining the ranks of the "progressive" army. The trouble with most writers, he complained, was that they considered the fight for power beneath their dignity. The typical intellectual preferred to remain aloof from popular movements, concentrating on his esoteric ideologies and and his moral purity but declining to face "reality" however sordid or harsh. Lerner believed that the intellectual would continue to be a marginal and indecisive figure until he discarded his fear of the "mass mind" and became instead an "organic part of the life, the thinking, the striving of the common people."[44]

Though Lerner was unwilling to specify which class deserved the intellectual's allegiance, his passion to share the values and aspirations of the "man in the street" did not differ so very much from the earlier notion that bourgeois writers might best fulfill their radical obligations by taking on a totally new identity. One of the decade's principal characteristics had been the strong desire on the part of many intellectuals to overcome their sense of loneliness and isolation, to establish some enduring ties with a group or community larger and more satisfying than the fleeting relationships between individuals. The artist had been told throughout the 1930s that he could never depend on his "inner resources," that he must "step out of his private world" in order to discover "a subject and an audience," that his interests were really "identical" with those of the workers. Now the Popular Front enlarged on these ambitions, inviting the writer to embrace not only the proletariat but all the "people," promising him not merely the vicarious excitement of a radical movement but the much more durable feeling of "belonging to America."[45]

If the writer's discomfort with solitude led him first to the working class and then to the Popular Front, it also accounted for the ease with which his literary radicalism could be converted into a defense of existing cultural standards. Where novelists, poets, and playwrights had been exhorted to create revolutionary works of art in the early 1930s, they were now encouraged to immerse themselves in the mores and customs of the common man. The author must avoid all ideologies and formulas "not inherent in the American mind," warned one critic. Indeed he should think of his work as an instrument through which the nation might hear "its own voice speaking."[46] Similarly, the *New Masses* argued that the bond between literature and society was perfectly "reciprocal and mutual," with the public participating as actively in the creative process as the writer himself.[47] And in the *Modern Quarterly,* still a bastion of proletarian culture, Thomas Hart Benton suggested that painting be firmly rooted in the "direct experience" of specific locales; it ought to function as a "mirror held up to life" rather than as a purveyor of unfamiliar ideas and doctrines.[48]

What all of this meant was best summed up by the poet laureate of the Popular Front, Archibald MacLeish. On numerous occasions during the late 1930s he castigated his intellectual associates for having "irresponsibly" undermined the nation's historic principles and ideals, for having failed as aspiring revolutionaries to take into account the "tradition of the people and the land," and for having refused to abandon their critical stance despite the need for positive "action" in the face of the fascist peril. Repudiating his earlier defense of the artist as an independent critic affiliated with no causes or crusades, MacLeish now insisted on the absolute inseparability of poetry and politics, and he demanded the creation of a new, more "constructive" literature based not on the images of "revolt" but on the language of "acceptance and belief."[49]

In short, the present role of the intellectual was not to transform the values and consciousness of the larger society but to reinforce what people already knew and felt. The aesthetic of social protest was to be supplanted by a literature of "democratic affirmation" which would allow the "progressive" artist to express his "sense of solidarity" with the American citizenry.[50] The major difference between these axioms and those of the early 1930s was that the writer might now speak for the entire country rather than for a particular class. But the central proposition remained the same: the intellectual could discharge his political and moral responsibilities only by absorbing the outlook and attitudes of a group other than his own.

One of the most important results of this romance between the intellectuals and the "people" was a growing fascination on both sides with the American past. In the case of many writers on the left, the search for an alternative social philosophy gave way in the late 1930s to a renewed appreciation for the habits and precedents that had sustained the country through previous crises. The Communists in particular were quick to recognize that the "reinterpretation of our history is not a matter of academic interest but an immediate political need."[51] Accordingly, the *New Masses* continually alerted its readers to the similarities between past and present, eagerly aligning itself with the heritage of Jefferson and Lincoln against all the twentieth-century "tories" and "confederates" who still infested American life.[52]

But the Communists were not alone in their sensitivity to the contemporary uses of history. The urge to expose and debunk the past, once so fashionable in the Progressive period and the 1920s, had faded in the era of depression and war. With the whole of Western civilization in upheaval, with the guns firing daily over Addis Ababa and Madrid, a number of professional historians sought refuge in multivolume biographies designed to refurbish the reputation of America's legendary heroes, while others began to portray the much-maligned Puritans in a considerably more favorable light. Where men like Beard and Parrington had hoped to disclose the injustices and inequities at the heart of the nation's leadership, their successors in the 1930s preferred to document the average American's ability to endure and triumph over any calamity. Thus the WPA projects—the local chronicles and detailed guidebooks, the compulsive accumulation of raw statistics and the countless murals on post-office walls—amounted to a special form of folk history. In the rivers, roads, and towns, in the country's forgotten failures as well as its unrecorded triumphs, in the millions of discrete facts about a continent and its people, writers were seeking somehow to uncover the hidden meaning of the American experience.

To Max Lerner, this affectionate reassessment of the nation's development was a thoroughly welcome phenomenon. When radicals had been entranced by the "future" in Russia, he argued, they succeeded only in making people feel insecure. Now, as the Left rediscovered the value of patriotism and as intellectuals displayed a newfound respect for the underlying vigor of the national character, the past was being transformed into precisely the sort of compelling "political myth" that could comfort the populace in an age of chaos and uncertainty.[53] For as Malcolm Cowley observed in his sympathetic review of Van Wyck Brooks's *The Flowering of New England*—itself a nostalgic ode to simpler times by a writer who had spent his youth deploring the meager cultural legacy of the nineteenth century—many men were "turning back to the great past in order to see the real nature of the traditions that we are trying to save, and in order to gain new strength for the struggles ahead."[54] Thus in the lyrical epics of poets like Carl Sandburg and Archibald MacLeish, in best-selling historical novels like *Gone with the Wind,* in the carefully preserved folklore which often passed for serious scholarship, in books like Constance Rourke's *American Humor* where nineteenth-century artists and philosophers were recast into homespun storytellers and cracker-barrel sages, in Harold Stearns's new anthology—*America Now*—whose contributors displayed a considerably more "tolerant" attitude toward life in their native land than they had earlier shown in the mocking and bitter *Civilization in the United*

States, in the capacity of a hundred cities to organize symphony orchestras and build art galleries and launch universities—learning to do in a depression what they could never accomplish during prosperity—the entire country seemed ready to cope with the very real terrors of the present by rejoicing in the apparent serenity of the past.[55]

Perhaps the revival of nationalism—in culture as well as in politics—was best expressed by Gilbert Seldes's *Mainland,* published during 1936. As a normally unsentimental film critic and book reviewer, as a journalist who produced a particularly biting account of the nation's social and economic disintegration in his documentary of 1932, *The Year of the Locust,* Seldes had not been known for his veneration of American customs and traditions. But now he chose to turn his talents to history, searching for the values that made the United States unique, hoping to illuminate the reasons for the country's greatness, trying to defend the virtues of the old against the invasion of the new.

Like Lerner and MacLeish, Seldes regarded the intelligentsia as the main enemy—the supreme agent of contemporary confusion and decay. Its cardinal crime was the effort to impose "an alien system of ideals upon America, or to attach America to the intellectual system of Europe." To Seldes, the typical writer was far more dangerous than the predatory industrialist or financier who had merely ravaged the country's environment and resources. For in their morbid assault on the nation's political institutions, in their willful ignorance of the excellence and variety of American life, in their naïve enthusiasm for foreign ideologies at the expense of any "feeling for their own history," the intellectuals had committed the gravest sin of all—they had "prevented us from understanding ourselves."[56] Hence, Seldes confessed his predilection for the "common man against the intellectual," the "average against the exception," the ordinary against the unusual, the popular against the dissident.[57]

In his own interpretation of America's past, Seldes appeared content to follow the path of Turner and Beard. He focused at length on the epic struggle between the radical West and the conservative East, between the egalitarian hinterland and the elitist shoreline, between agriculture and industry, between prairie democrats and plantation aristocrats, between populism and plutocracy.[58] But Seldes was less interested in exploring class conflicts and sectional antagonisms than in finding out what traits united his countrymen. At bottom, he was attracted to the West not because it stood for political freedom and openness to social change but because in its practicality and classlessness, in its disdain for formal intellect and rigid theory, the plains states seemed to him most thoroughly "American."[59]

Here Seldes's basic allegiances became clear. Significantly, he approved of precisely those qualities in American life, past and present, that earlier critics had angrily denounced. For him, the United States was morally superior to Europe because it had always rejected social philosophies and fixed programs, because it remained pluralistic and pragmatic, because its class lines were mobile and fluid, because its institutions were marvelously chaotic and unplanned and haphazard and experimental.[60] Where others longed for community and social control, Seldes admired the instinctive individualism and competitiveness of his fellow citizens. And so his special view of history led him naturally to a celebration of Franklin Roosevelt as the archetypal American—flexible, optimistic, preferring to act rather than think, willing to modify the system of capitalism while keeping intact its spirit of entrepreneurship and opportunity, seeking ultimately to lift every person into the ranks of the middle class.[61] Thus in its passionate anti-intellectualism, in its aversion to anything ideological or abstract, in its love affair with the past, in its affirmation of bourgeois democracy, *Mainland* was a perfect embodiment of the assumptions and attitudes that characterized the years after 1935.

In effect, the social and cultural mood of the Popular Front was shaped by a peculiar combination of realism and innocence, seriousness and sentimentality, fervor and passivity. Ironically, the various crises of the 1930s were beginning to inhibit rather than stimulate the desire for radical innovation. Though many writers had started out to re-examine themselves and their society, they ended by rediscovering their national heritage. Under the impact of world events they were driven ineluctably from disenchantment to faith, criticism to praise, rebellion to reconciliation. What mattered now was not despair but confidence, not anger but belief, not alienation but acceptance. And the Popular Front offered intellectuals a means by which they were able to satisfy these political and psychological demands. Through its auspices, the writer could commit himself to the cause of the "people," help raise America's morale in the face of international disaster, and trace his revolutionary impulses to the nation's democratic past. With its aid, he no longer had to feel isolated and estranged, observing but never participating in the country's social life. Even if he could not directly influence or alter the course of history, he might at least know what it was like to be on the "inside"—actively involved in the paramount problems of his age and intimately affected by experiences common to everyone. In the sense of "unity" and shared purpose provided by the Popular Front, the intellectual could finally belong to a mass movement that was also indigenously American.

Yet this emphasis on collective action and social responsibility had unfortunate consequences for the life of the mind. In rejecting the image of the independent intellectual who maintained only a tenuous connection with society at best, too many writers swung to the opposite extreme. Unable to sustain the delicate balance between cultural analysis and political engagement which men like Edmund Wilson and Benjamin Ginzburg had earlier recommended, a large number of intellectuals eagerly assumed the role of spokesmen for a particular group, organization, or doctrine (whether of the Communist party or the New Deal). The desire for autonomy gave way to an obsession with power; the capacity to ask new questions was replaced by a willingness to defend already fixed positions; the quest for a coherent social theory became confused with the act of signing petitions and "taking a stand." In the late 1930s many writers considered any sort of neutrality or detachment immoral because these could lead to an unconscious acquiescence in the spread of fascism. Instead the continuing emergency at home and abroad was seen as a further opportunity for intellectuals to reaffirm their democratic allegiances rather than as a chance to propose long-range alternatives for existing programs and policies. Hence the act of commitment grew more important than rational debate, and a feeling of solidarity with other "progressives" absolved the writer of the need to think clearly about the problems of the day.

Ultimately, the insistence on cooperation among all good anti-fascists resulted in the decline of the intellectual as a critic of American culture and society. When writers began to worry about being "responsible," about whether or not their statements might weaken the united front and thereby encourage the class enemy, they were engaging in a subtle form of self-censorship. When they refused to scrutinize the Moscow trials too closely, or challenge the schematic division of the world into Right and Left, they were acknowledging that they craved emotional assurance over ideological uncertainty.In a perverse way, the Popular Front suspected that Stalin had been justified in purging his opponents, not because they were saboteurs but because they were behaving like traditional intellectuals at a time when sustained controversy and open disagreement were regarded as dangerous and disruptive. In essence, the majority of American writers had chosen to commit themselves to a social *movement* rather than to social *issues,* thus exalting action over thought and loyalty over dissent. Given the understandable desire to maintain an appearance of unity on the left in the face of the fascist onslaught, the Popular Front had contributed nonetheless to the corruption of the very values and ideas for which it was supposedly fighting. In the process, the social and cultural ferment of the decade's early years was dissipated not only by the experience of living in a state of perpetual crisis but also by the tendency of writers themselves to surrender their critical faculties at precisely the moment when these were most urgently needed.

5. *The End of Ideology*

The interrelationship between external events and an internal failure of nerve, each set of pressures feeding on the other, accounted in large measure for the decline of radicalism in the late 1930s. But the particular tactics and attitudes of the Popular Front were only partially responsible for what happened after 1935. In the end, the political, social, and cultural life of America was shaped by the very nature of the depression itself—the peculiar problems it presented, the way the issues were defined, the kinds of responses they seemed to require. Behind the weaknesses of the Left and the labor movement, behind the tolerance for Russia and the sympathy for Spain, behind the acceptance of the New Deal and liberal reform, behind the intellectual's appeal to the people and the past, there was an inescapable feeling that things had literally fallen apart. In a time of dislocation and disorder, many men yearned not for revolt but recovery, not for change but stability, not for conflict but community. Ultimately, in their politics as well as their philosophy, they sought to conserve rather than transform, to unify rather than divide, to adjust rather than rebel. The American intellectual and the American public found themselves dealing with a crisis whose dimensions were as much psychological as economic. Given these special difficulties, the depression was proving to be a most inauspicious occasion for the development of alternative values and ideas.

Instead the 1930s was pre-eminently a period in which new symbols and myths were used to defend old forms of behavior. No observers were more sensitive to this phenomenon than Robert and Helen Lynd. In 1935 they returned to Middletown to study the changes the depression had brought. But what they found was considerably different from what they expected. Admittedly Muncie, Indiana, was not an especially typical American metropolis. Dominated by the Ball family, outside the orbit of the large industrial centers, wedded to the open shop, traditionally Republican, much of Middletown had resisted both the CIO and the New Deal. Its working class was largely native-born; the average laborer had deserted the farm for the city, but he lived in his own house, tended his own garden, and followed his own instincts. At the same time, the economy of Muncie was primarily dependent on its salesmen, small businessmen, and white-collar professionals. Nevertheless, there was enough about Middletown's experience during the 1930s to give the Lynds an insight into how the rest of America coped with the worst depression in its history.

Among the most illuminating of their discoveries was Middletown's reluctance even to admit the existence of hard times. Because of the city's official optimism and its congenital faith in the future, the residents of Muncie tended to regard the depression as a momentary interruption in the normal flow of progress and prosperity, an inexplicable accident which had to be "endured as cheerfully as possible." Business failures, plant closings, and rising unemployment were considered little more than temporary setbacks, not the symptoms of a possibly incurable economic and social disease. Middletown simply did not believe that anything "permanently bad [could] happen to America." Therefore the effects of the depression were deliberately minimized in public statements and private comments, forcing the Lynds to conclude that the people of Middletown would rather grasp at any "straw of hope" than face the reality of their situation.[62]

These sentiments were particularly evident among the workers. If "radicalism was in the wind," the Lynds mused, "it never attained any large proportions locally." At no point did the laboring class display any propensity for violence, or any fondness for socialism. Instead the Lynds were impressed by the tenacious grip of the two-party system on the loyalities of Middletown's poor and by the substantial amount of blue-collar antagonism toward left-wing movements or ideas. Even the programs of the New Deal and the advantages to be gained from joining trade unions were looked upon more as a "personal life line . . . than [as] a commitment to social change." Essentially, the typical worker seemed to confront the problems of the depression on individual rather than cooperative terms. He was moved more by considerations of immediate security and survival than by the long-range benefits of collective action. Unfamiliar with the traditions of proletarian militancy, suspicious of appeals to class solidarity, lacking any coherent theory which might explain his role in a capitalist economy, he shared the same symbols and assumptions as the businessman. In the Lynds' sober view, what the workers of Middletown wanted above all else was the opportunity to pay off their mortgages, purchase a car, go to the movies, and "get ahead under [their] own steam and ingenuity." In the end, they remained "individualists in an individualistic culture."[63]

There were, however, some signs that Middletown had not entirely ignored the collapse of the economy or the cause of reform. Ironically, the Lynds noticed that Muncie's upper class was often more innovative and susceptible to new ideas than those on smaller income. While the workers, both white-collar and blue, seemed to fear the unusual, many wealthier residents welcomed "alternatives to Middletown's traditional values" at least in matters of culture and life-style.[64] More important, the Lynds believed that certain precedents were being established during the crisis which might well alter Muncie's behavior and attitudes in the future. The depression had forced Middletown to assume some "corporate responsibility" for a quarter of its population; to deal with the problems of unemployment and relief, the private citizen found himself increasingly dependent on the services of the city, which was itself turning eagerly to Washington for help. Thus as Middletown gave up some of its faith in the competence of local government and personal initiative, its people were being drawn closer together, and the connections between the city and the larger society were becoming more clear.[65]

Nevertheless, Middletown's willingness to take on these social and national obligations did not necessarily have a transforming effect on its cultural and mental life. Indeed in the Lynds' judgment, the need for cooperation and mutual aid, so ardently preached by the Left, was having quite the opposite result. The inhabitants of Middletown reported that they had assuredly done more socializing during the depression—spending time with family and neighbors, renewing acquaintances, relying on organized yet inexpensive group activities like block parties and folk dances, playing games like Monopoly and bridge as an escape from and substitute for the thrill of competition no longer available in the "real" world.[66] But in their use of leisure time they displayed an overwhelming desire to fit in, to be just "like other people," to accept and conform to the existing patterns of social conduct. For the most part, they deliberately refrained from speaking out on controversial issues, and they appeared uncomfortable behaving differently from their peers.[67] Such traits, according to the Lynds, hardly encouraged "new designs for living." On the contrary, they revealed that the people of Middletown preferred the feeling of security to the possibilities of adventure and risk. In the midst of crisis they longed for whatever was certain and familiar; they rejected whatever seemed threatening or alien.[68] The emphasis on accommodation and adjustment, on improving the individual's character and personality rather than his ideas, on encouraging sociability rather than originality, all suggested that the 1930s was a period for the manageable and the middle-aged—in spirit if not in fact.

Thus the experience of Middletown demonstrated for the Lynds that most men—at least in America—were inherently conservative and resistant to change. The city was not very different now from what it had been like during their first visit in 1925. The depression might have altered some of its institutions and policies, but the people's habits and beliefs—whether economically individualistic or socially conformist—remained largely the same. "No major new . . . ideologies of a positive sort have developed as conspicuous rallying points," they declared. Instead the residents of Muncie appeared increasingly vulnerable to "gross emotional symbols" which shaped their view of the world and prevented them from becoming fully conscious of their plight.[69] And this disturbed the Lynds more than anything else they found. Rather than searching for more effective ways of dealing with the crisis, Middletown responded to the depression by invoking popular slogans and images which gave the citizenry a spurious sense of unity and common purpose. To the Lynds this dependence on symbolism as a substitute for ideology accounted in large measure for the ultimate failure of radicalism in the 1930s—not only in Muncie but throughout the United States.

Yet at the very moment when they were worrying about the dangerous consequences of misleading words and phrases, others were beginning to investigate the positive uses of mythology and rhetoric. It was hardly surprising that intellectuals should be interested in the role of propaganda during the late 1930s; they had witnessed the remarkable success of the torchlight parades in Germany, the spectacular "show" trials in Russia, and the awesome capacity of the mass media in every country to mobilize people behind a particular leader or doctrine. But far from objecting to these new techniques for molding public opinion, a number of writers were increasingly enraptured by their beneficial effects. And their enthusiasm contributed to the further retreat from social theory that characterized the decade's closing years.

In part, many were simply responding to the apparent lessons of modern social science. When Malcolm Cowley and Bernard Smith came to edit a series of essays on the intellectuals who had transformed Western thought in the twentieth century, they selected only those who emphasized the importance of environment, instinct, custom, prejudice, and power in human affairs—Freud, Lenin, Sumner, Veblen, Boas, Spengler, Turner, and Beard. Together, these figures were responsible for what Cowley called the "attack on the Reasoning Man."[70] Elsewhere, Bruce Bliven observed that his contemporaries had learned "how profound is the role of the emotions and . . . subconscious impulse in determining men's actions, how little 'rational' intellectual processes really matter."[71] To some extent such attitudes were the legacy of the revolt against liberalism and the resulting tendency to see the individual as merely a product of economic forces, historical pressures, and class influences.

But not everyone was simply rejecting Dewey in favor of Marx. If the liberals placed too much trust in science and intelligence, the radicals seemed equally naïve in depending on the inexorable laws of social development. In Frederick Schuman's view, "the masses of men are moved not by Reason, nor even by economic self-interest, but by emotions, mysticism, and mythology. . . . Societies are held together never by cold intellect but always by nonlogical symbols of warmly felt collective experience." In an age when the "human soul cries out for something to believe in," Schuman proclaimed, no revolution was possible unless its leaders inspired "awe, reverence, and fanatical devotion" and unless its programs were invested with the "psychological equivalents of religious supernaturalism." What the Left needed most was neither theory nor organization but "faith."[72]

In the same vein, Kenneth Burke had delivered a highly controversial paper at the first Congress of American Writers in which he argued that the effective use of propaganda was as crucial to the success of the radical movement as the workers' ability to seize control over the means of production. He therefore urged his listeners to adopt the symbol of the "people" as a way of unifying the masses and gaining their support—a position for which he was roundly criticized in the summer of 1935, only to be vindicated soon after by the formation of the Popular Front.[73] For both Schuman and Burke, the significance of rhetoric, folklore, and myth lay in the capacity of these devices to create an intuitive sense of community among all Americans; in this sense, they might satisfy the collectivist dreams of the 1930s far better than the concepts of planning or socialism.

Divorced from their radical premises, however, the fascination with symbolism and propaganda could have quite conservative implications. It was a sign of the times that the most sophisticated and influential studies of political behavior in the late 1930s were written from a deliberately non-radical and anti-ideological perspective. Where a Herbert Croly during the Progressive era or a George Soule in the early years of the depression had confidently assumed that the coherent presentation of an alternative theory might persuade men to change their society, writers like Harold Lasswell and Thurman Arnold were more inclined to analyze the psychological effects of ideology in strengthening already established values and attitudes. They preferred to deal with the *function* rather than the formal content of ideas; they were less concerned with the substance of principles and creeds than with the impact of rituals and ceremonies. Thus it seemed appropriate that the titles of their books should reflect this preoccupation with the mythic and the manipulative—Lasswell's *Politics: Who Gets What, When, How* (1936), which followed his earlier *Psychopathology and Politics* (1930), and Arnold's *The Folklore of Capitalism* (1937), which was a more elaborate sequel to *The Symbols of Government* (1935).

For Arnold in particular, social and political beliefs had "no meaning whatever" apart from the organizations and movements to which they were "attached." To his mind, all systems of thought served similar purposes: they raised morale, ministered to the "emotional needs" of a given population, made "each individual feel [that he was] an integral part of [a] group," inspired unconscious cooperation among regions and classes, rationalized the habits and behavior patterns of mankind through the invocation of "magic words." From this point of view, public debate and philosophies of government were merely "a series of parables through which men see the world before them"; they served as "argumentative tools by which priests and scholars condemn heresy or else attack the established Church"; they were designed primarily to "create enthusiasm, increase faith, and quiet doubt." But they had "nothing to do with the actual practical analysis of facts." Accordingly, Arnold directed his attention to the "psychology of social institutions" as the only way of finding out how societies really operated; his method was consistently reductionist, and he interpreted every doctrine as a semantic instrument for the regulation of human activity.[74]

Yet unlike Marx, neither Lasswell nor Arnold wished to "unmask" reactionary ideas in the interest of objective laws or revolutionary truths. They conceived of political struggle not as the rise to power of new classes with new ideologies but rather as the ability of one group to substitute its own "mythology" for that of another. In Lasswell's case, politics was largely the "study of influence and the influential." It involved issues of deference, prestige, and security. In his judgment, the history of the nineteenth and twentieth centuries had "pivoted on the rivalry of elites for the control of all the symbols capable of arousing submissive responses from the masses." Social change therefore depended on the facility with which an aspiring elite could elicit "loyalty, blood, and taxes from the populace with new combinations of vowels and consonants." The principal objective, he insisted, was not to create an alternative society but to acquire the trappings of authority. To achieve this goal, different kinds of talent might now be necessary. Where dexterity in fighting, organizing, or bargaining had been a "major avenue to power" in the past, more recently the effective leader was one who demonstrated "skill in propaganda." Thus Arnold argued that the American Revolution was successful primarily because its perpetrators had invented "democracy" as a "useful slogan" to hurl against the outmoded clichés of the English aristocracy. And when the myth of individualism no longer corresponded to an era of depression and war, Lasswell observed, men would naturally turn to the "collective symbols" of social-ism, fascism, or the welfare state.[75] In all of these instances, Arnold and Lasswell deliberately shifted their readers' attention from economic and political questions to those of rhetoric and personality—a transition neither radicals nor liberals would normally welcome.

Moreover, to stay in power any new elite must know precisely how to function. Like Reinhold Niebuhr, Arnold and Lasswell based their analyses of contemporary social life on the assumption that "men in groups" were rarely "rational." Therefore the modern head of state had to perform much like a "trained psychiatrist," understanding that the management of people was more important than the "management of things," recognizing that the problems of "love, destructiveness, guilt, and weakness" were as central to the domain of government as matters of food and shelter. Public rituals and ceremonies were psychologically necessary in order to comply with the "taboos and customs of the tribe." Hence Lasswell concentrated on the emotional significance of speeches, news stories, radio programs, motion pictures, and novels with a message in "manipulating symbols" and "han-dling persons." At the same time, Arnold pointed out the need to treat social policy not as a logical plan but as a "dramatic spectacle." For him, the art of government involved the "technique of achieving willing popular acceptance" by giving people not what they "*ought* to want" but what they "*do* want."[76] If the masses were properly satisfied, the leadership should enjoy a long and comfortable reign.

But Arnold was not content merely to recommend that politicians fit their programs to whatever orthodoxies currently prevailed. Though cer-tain forms of myth and symbolism could reinforce the status quo, they might also serve the cause of reform—at least as he defined it. The true task of government, Arnold declared, was both "to put on a public show" and "to be exceedingly practical behind the scenes." In this respect he was quite specific about what he considered effective political conduct. Like many other writers in the 1930s, Arnold distrusted an excessive reliance on ab-stract theory not only because it seemed to him romantic and naïve but also because it obscured institutional needs and prevented men from experi-menting freely with new types of organization. The devotion to principle and the obsession with moral rectitude only interfered with Arnold's su-preme criterion: the ability of a nation to "produce and distribute goods to the maximum of its technical capacity." Consequently he favored those leaders who were "unencumbered by doctrine," who could resolve the "conflicting interests" of society through compromise and "horse trading," who would deal with "facts" rather than philosophy, who might take advantage of present opportunities rather than search for future utopias, who remembered to put their "ideals" and their "practices into different compartments." This celebration of pragmatism and expertise, of organization and technique, of anything that seemed tough-minded and hard-boiled, led Arnold in the end to embrace Franklin Roosevelt as the only political "personality" who could reshape America's institutions while paying heed to its "national mythology."[77] And so, soon after the publication of *The Folklore of Capitalism*, Arnold left for Washington to participate in one of the country's most venerable rituals—the flailing of monopoly and the busting of the trusts, both of which might distract the people from their domestic difficulties while the leadership prepared for war.

In sum, the works of Arnold and Lasswell confirmed the Lynds' complaint that the depression had failed to generate an alternative ideology to those of the pioneer and the businessman. Indeed many writers in the late 1930s were attracted to the New Deal precisely because it seemed to utilize the traditional rhetoric, images, and slogans of American culture far more effectively than any of the parties farther to the left, thereby uniting people around the lowest common denominators of belief and action. They applauded the Roosevelt Administration's success in modifying capitalism without challenging the nation's historic values and habits or appearing to be too radical—even if this meant that poverty had merely been driven out of sight while the profit system remained intact.[78] But the inability of either the intelligentsia or the politicans to educate the people to the revolutionary needs of a collectivist era, the glorification of practical programs and the worship of power at the expense of systematic social theory, the fascination with folklore and the strain of anti-intellectualism that ran through much of American thought during these years resulted in a mood of acquiescence and complacency.

As the decade drew to a close, most writers were no longer interested in mounting a radical critique of American society or in laying the foundations for a social revolution. Slowly, they had given up the quest for a new politics and a new culture, preferring instead to concentrate on the menace of Germany and Japan as an issue on which everyone could agree—socialists and liberals, the poor and the affluent, the intellectual and the common man. Increasingly hostile to the ideological (or even utopian) concerns of the early 1930s, mentally exhausted by the continuing crises at home and abroad, they displayed neither the power nor the disposition for sustained analysis.

To many, the period after 1935 was not a time for talk but for choices. As the *New Republic* declared, the only important question left to ask was

"Are you for fascism . . . or against it?"[79] Given this climate, it seemed easier to seek refuge in negative slogans, catch phrases, and *ad hoc* demands—collective security, Progressives versus Reactionaries, anti-fascism, defense of democracy, unity on the left. Here the Popular Front, with its affinity for political symbols and national myths, played a crucial role; its distinctive rhetoric took the place of social thought. On the whole, the Popular Front provided very little in the way of substantive programs or cultural innovation; its schematic view of the world tended to blur rather than to clarify the issues at stake.[80] But it did offer a set of attitudes, a sense of commitment, and a feeling of moral certainty at precisely the moment when the tension and turmoil of the depression years had grown intolerable. In the late 1930s intellectuals as well as ordinary people were attracted to either-or propositions, yes-or-no answers. They could not live with ambiguity, paradox, and contradiction, as men like Soule and Mumford, Dewey and Lynd, Hook and Niebuhr, Wilson and Ginzburg, Agee and Welles all had urged. Hence they turned to the Popular Front and the New Deal as an escape from the necessity of thinking further about the problems of morality and politics, democracy and socialism, culture and civilization, art and revolution, self and society.

Furthermore, some of the very concepts writers had hoped would produce a different social structure and value system—the search for community and the theory of collectivism, the view of society as an organic unit, the attraction to planning and efficiency, the image of the intellectual as activist—appeared in the end to retard the development of a radical movement and the acceptance of socialist ideas. The assumption that the United States was no longer a land of infinite progress and opportunity, that the country had left its youth behind and passed into middle age, that its people were living in an increasingly closed and limited world, prompted men not so much to denounce the race for wealth and success as to stress the virtues of consolidation and stability. It seemed more appropriate to make the best of what one presently had than to rail against the past or expend one's energy in shaping the future. Similarly, the tendency to interpret the causes of the depression in terms of the chaos of capitalism, the anarchy of the market place, and the breakdown of institutions induced both the Left and the New Deal to insist on the need for order, security, and social control. This in turn led not to the reorganization of industry and agriculture along socialist lines but to an emphasis on economic recovery, an inclination to approve the centralization of power in the executive branch of government, a faith in the beneficence of an ever-expanding bureaucracy, and a too eager reliance on administrative authority. And if, in such an unprecedented

emergency, writers and politicians talked more about the necessity of cooperation and sacrifice than about class conflict and revolution, it was hardly
surprising that they should eventually call for a truce between business and
labor in the interest of national unity.[81]

At the same time, the widespread belief that American life was entirely
too fragmented, competitive, and individualistic resulted not in the creation
of an alternative ethic but in the reinforcement of existing values. Writers
in the late 1930s were unable to maintain a balance between personal
freedom and collective goals, self-expression and social priorities. Instead
they grew increasingly hostile to any manifestation of private eccentricity
or intellectual "irresponsibility." What began as an effort to reconcile the
individual to society ended with an indiscriminate celebration of the family,
the group, the region, and the nation. In the process, the intellectual's desire
to participate in the affairs of his country drove him to treat ideas not as
tools of inquiry and analysis but as weapons or myths in the contest for
popular approval. Indeed throughout the decade the sharp edge of social
criticism had been tempered by a compulsion to reassure the people that
things would doubtlessly improve; one might concede America's failures
without shattering public confidence or hope. Thus the attack on the capitalist misuse of science and technology led not to a more humane industrialism but to a rediscovery of tradition and folklore, national identity and the
common man. Moreover, the repudiation of individualism and the hunger
to belong inspired neither a spirit of rebellion nor a commitment to some
more satisfying form of community but rather a fascination with power and
a willingness to conform. Ultimately, the subordination of a person's secret
dreams and ambitions to the demands of a cause or doctrine became a
means of translating the ideal of collectivism into a defense of the American
Way.

Yet even had the intellectuals been more successful in preserving their
sense of equilibrium during the 1930s, they could not depend on the crisis
itself to generate a socialist upheaval. The depression might have functioned
as a catalyst for revolutionary changes only if the country had undergone
several decades of continuous political and ideological ferment preceding
the stock-market crash. But despite the Populist and Progressive interludes,
most writers had little experience with ongoing mass movements for whom
they could speak, nor did they exhibit much taste for long-term social
commitments. Consequently, they could not easily sustain their faith in
radical programs and ideas when the people themselves seemed increasingly
conservative as the decade wore on.

Instead it was simpler to surrender to the press of events, to acknowledge that the opportunity for creative social thought and action had passed. By 1939 the depression no longer seemed an important issue for many writers; they began to think of themselves as a prewar generation for whom time was swiftly running out. Surveying the mood of his contemporaries, George Soule observed that "the mental season has changed." The hopes for a better world, the enthusiasm for new philosophies, the appetite for cultural experimentation, all these had vanished. Intellectuals "who had for so long been struggling with impersonal and complicated difficulties like unemployment and depression, suddenly were confronted by an external enemy against whom we could easily canalize our aggression." Indeed Soule suspected that the international crisis came as a relief from the formidable social and economic problems which neither the intelligentsia nor the government could solve. "It is always far easier," he pointed out, "to use one's energy in hating a foreign devil than in adjusting [to] complex internal realities. And the bitterness of disputes within our national boundaries became subdued as the factions were drawn together by a common fear and a common enmity. . . . The in-group had an out-group whom it could prepare to punish for its own frustrations and deprivations."[82]

To Soule, this situation presented a mirror image of the moral climate under fascism. Just as the German economy had been mobilized around a huge armaments program which absorbed the country's unemployed and provided a new market for business, so the United States began to talk of constructing a great military machine both for defense and industrial recovery. Just as the fascist nations evaded their internal difficulties by concentrating on the external foe, so Americans conveniently forgot their domestic strains and "prepared to fight the foreigner."[83] In Soule's judgment there was nothing left to do but pray that the final catastrophe might somehow be averted.

Thus a period that began with the effort to redefine and extend democracy ended with the likelihood of crushing it altogether under the weight of militarism and war. Conceived in the shadow of the stock-market crash, nurtured on one disaster after another, the decade was now anticipating its death in some final calamity. This sense of imminent doom haunted the intellectual community, and it shaped the outlook not only of those who took solace in the Popular Front but also of those who were groping frantically for an alternative response to the crises of the late 1930s.

CHAPTER VIII

FROM DEPRESSION TO WAR

Not everyone was avid to climb aboard the Popular Front. Throughout the closing years of the depression a small but exceedingly articulate and increasingly influential band of writers stood in vigorous opposition to the official policies of the Left and the New Deal. Disenchanted with the Soviet brand of socialism, unimpressed by the persistent calls for unity in the face of the fascist menace, hostile to the passionate adoration of national traditions, antagonized by the renewed embrace of bourgeois life-styles, and uneasy in the role of spokesmen for the "people," they were profoundly disturbed by the implications of the Popular Front both for culture as well as for politics. Forming a brigade of dissident intellectuals around the banners of V. F. Calverton's *Modern Quarterly* and the fledgling *Partisan Review,* they proceeded to mount a full-scale assault on the ideological fortifications of Communists and liberals alike.

Eventually, they began to attack the central assumptions of the entire decade: the belief that moral and psychological problems could be effectively solved through a transformation of social and economic institutions, the notion that a planned society dedicated to the ideals of community and cooperation would lead to a more orderly world at the same time it expanded the boundaries of individual freedom and human creativity. No longer certain that the collectivist strain in Marxism could be reconciled with the libertarian bias of liberalism, suspicious of the decade-long desire to marry the concerns of art with the demands of the revolution, they entered battle on behalf of a highly personal radicalism shaped by the image

of the writer as an independent critic of all political and literary orthodoxies.

The result was precisely what the Popular Front most feared: a bitter and
fratricidal quarrel within the intellectual community over short-run tactics
and long-range goals. The generous temper of the decade's early years—
when "we" briefly replaced "I" as the dominant symbol and writers sought
to participate somehow in the daily struggles of mankind—was drowned in
the clamor of public controversy and private denunciation. At issue was the
very integrity and direction of the radical movement. Divisiveness and
polarization were therefore inevitable. Where the Popular Front celebrated
the virtue of patriotism, the efficacy of mass action, and the nobility of the
common man, the dissenters retaliated with a new glorification of individualism, a revival of the idea that the intellectual had no business in politics,
and a heightened appreciation of the tragic aspects of human life. In these
circumstances, the attempt to merge the heritage of liberalism and socialism, to redefine the possibilities of self-fulfillment within the context of a
complex and interdependent society were gradually forgotten amid the din
of doctrinal combat.

Only in the period between 1939 and 1941, when the clash of ideas gave
way to a clash of arms, did it become clear how much the two camps really
shared, how committed both sides were to American values and American
power. Thus beneath the thunderous polemics of the late 1930s lay the basis
for an alliance that would permit the opposing intellectual armies to compose their differences, enlist in the crusade against Adolf Hitler, and extend
their services after 1945 to the defense of the United States in the Cold War.

1. *The Politics of Anti-Stalinism*

To the men who spoke for the Socialist party, to the American representatives of the Trotskyite wing of Marxism, to the growing number of
writers who had departed the Bolshevik locomotive at various points on its
tortured journey from the Finland Station to the Moscow trials, the formation of the Popular Front signaled the Soviet Union's unequivocal desertion
of the radical cause. In their eyes, the objectives of the revolution—whether
proletarian or democratic—were being deliberately sacrificed to the needs
of Russian foreign policy. And the supreme architect of this betrayal was
Josef Stalin. Throughout the late 1930s, therefore, they sought to separate
themselves from the domestic and international consequences of the Popular Front, hoping to stake out a position that would be both genuinely
Marxist and impeccably anti-Stalinist.

For the most part, however, their stance was negative. To a considerable extent the attention and ideas of a Norman Thomas, a V. F. Calverton, or a Dwight Macdonald were directed to the task of maintaining their own radical purity—which after 1935 often involved a single-minded attack on whatever the majority of Americans seemed to believe. Moreover, the necessity of having to resist the Popular Front in all its manifestations meant that the thrust of the anti-Stalinist argument was largely determined by the programs of the Communist party or the New Deal. Hence even in opposition the dissident intellectuals were inordinately dependent on the vagaries of the Kremlin and the White House.

Accordingly, they spent most of their time accusing the Communist party of surrendering to expediency in its willingness to enter a coalition with any middle-class group or government that would join Russia in an anti-fascist entente, they insisted that both Republicans and Democrats were equally devoted to the preservation of capitalism, and they warned against cooperating with liberals who remained loyal either to nineteenth-century individualism or the twentieth-century corporate state. To concentrate exclusively on immediate reforms, to give unqualified support to the New Deal was in their judgment to relinquish the opportunities for meaningful social change. Thus the anti-Stalinists reaffirmed their commitment to the class struggle, proclaiming socialism rather than the defense of an anachronistic bourgeois democracy as their ultimate aim. Furthermore, they firmly rejected the concept of collective security in international matters, charging that such a strategy was merely an overture to another imperialist war. No matter how barbaric Hitler appeared, they were convinced that a bloody crusade against Germany would simply result in repression at home in the form of universal conscription, anti-strike legislation, the merger of Wall Street and Washington, and the smothering of dissent. That the Soviet Union should be seeking alliances in this situation seemed to them only additional evidence of the decay of Marxist ethics under Stalin; that most American intellectuals should have become apologists for the Roosevelt Administration and apostles of war underscored the Left's retreat from the revolution. In sum, the opponents of the Popular Front dismissed the notion of a titanic contest between dictatorship and democracy, calling instead for a socialist upheaval within every country (including Russia) as the single alternative to fascist might.[1]

Though the ultra-militance of the anti-Stalinist intellectuals on domestic issues failed to win many converts, their critique of foreign entanglements was not unpersuasive to some in the opposite camp. During much of the decade the *New Republic* steadfastly condemned the idea of American participation in a European conflict, not only because of its chilling effect on social progress within the United States but also because the magazine was loath to repeat the experiences of 1917. For most writers, liberal as well as radical, World War I had come to symbolize more than a greedy struggle for markets and empire, more than the inability of Wilsonian idealism to understand the world it sought to remake. At bottom, the war stood as a reminder of how easily the intelligentsia had forgotten its socialism or pacifism while ardently applauding America's intervention. If capitalism emerged triumphant from the wreckage of nations and parties, if social democracy and Progressive reform were among the war's chief casualties, writers blamed themselves as much as the bankers and munitions makers. The memory of compromise and complicity haunted their imagination in the following decades and accounted for their reluctance to champion a new adventure overseas.

When commentators like Bruce Bliven or Oswald Villard attempted to salvage something from the ruins of Versailles, they frequently fell back on a pervasive sense of history and a compelling need to "learn" from past mistakes. Since he agreed with the anti-Stalinists that contemporary wars were caused by imperialist ambitions, Bliven asked his fellow intellectuals in 1938 whether the United States must fight to preserve the status quo of 1919 "which many of us have spent much of our time . . . in denouncing as unjust and unworkable." Should American radicals, he wondered, now forsake their lifelong principles and "support one type of exploitative international capitalism against another for temporary and opportunistic reasons?"[2] Bliven's question was motivated not by the sentiments of an isolationist but by the habit of explaining events in the present on the basis of precedents in the past. And he was not unique.[3] Just as writers in the early 1930s often compared America to the Russia of 1917 (with Roosevelt conveniently playing the role of Kerensky), so in the late 1930s they tended to confuse Hitler's designs with those of the Kaiser. Yet this passionate dedication to history did not take into account the possibility that a crisis might be completely unprecedented. By relying on analogies with the past, the intellectual community found it difficult to conceive of Nazism as a phenomenon entirely new in human affairs. Committed to the axioms of process and development handed down by Marx, presuming that national behavior conformed to certain historical patterns and laws, hoping that the rule of the brownshirts was only a momentary phase in the inevitable transition from capitalism to socialism, neither liberals, Communists, nor anti-Stalinists were mentally equipped to deal cogently with the horror of fascism.

But beyond the areas of agreement or disagreement on specific political issues, the Popular Front and its most vehement critics displayed a strikingly similar state of mind. Both sides went to extremes in defense of their particular creed. If the Communists indulged in the language of reformism, the anti-Stalinists were not above resorting to their own revolutionary incantations. If most writers on the left were prepared to overlook the authoritarian nature of the Soviet regime in the interest of anti-fascist solidarity, the dissidents became obsessed with the task of documenting Stalin's treachery in minute detail. If the *Nation* appeared content to invoke the slogan of collective security in order to exorcise the specter of war, *Partisan Review* naïvely declared that a proletarian uprising was a practical alternative for a nation under Nazi assault. If the *New Masses* ritualistically swore its allegiance to democracy and the New Deal, the *Modern Quarterly* ceaselessly reiterated its fidelity to Marx and the working class. If the liberals abandoned the dream of comprehensive economic planning in favor of piecemeal experimentation, the militants scorned every short-range proposal from the White House as a distraction from the socialist agenda.

In the process, the necessary connection between interim measures and ultimate goals remained obscure. More important, neither camp could develop a coherent program that might stem the rising tide of fascism in Europe while continuing to inspire social change at home. Instead they each took refuge in rhetoric, catch phrases, and ideological absolutes as a substitute for creative thought. Unable to escape the Marxist tradition of factional strife, the battlefield psychology which condemned political neutrality as immoral, the conviction that radical intellectuals had a special responsibility to articulate the needs of groups and classes other than their own, both the Popular Front and the anti-Stalinists ended by reducing ideas to attitudes, rational debate to religious exhortation, systematic analysis to symbolic gestures.

2. *The Pilgrimage of* Partisan Review

Within the camp of the militants, however, there was a distinctive cluster of writers whose temperament and interests differed sharply from those on either side of the left-wing civil war. Whatever the doctrinal conflicts between the typical member of the Popular Front and his anti-Stalinist opponent, each had inherited certain key assumptions from the Progressive era and the 1920s: a belief in the capacity to reform men by altering their social and economic environment, a faith in the superior wisdom of engineers and administrators, an admiration for managerial expertise and organizational efficiency, a yearning to harmonize the values of individual liberty and cultural uplift with a sense of communal participation and technological progress, a desire to influence both the mind of the masses and the course of political power. To a newer generation of intellectuals conditioned almost entirely by the catastrophic effects of the depression, these aspirations seemed increasingly suspect. By the late 1930s they had begun to doubt the automatic benefits of social innovation, they had grown skeptical of bureaucratic elites and ideological soothsayers, they had become ambivalent about the economic and psychological implications of "collectivism," and they now distrusted all efforts to make literature a handmaiden of politics (whether in the name of the proletariat or the "people"). In their view, the ultimate source of human suffering and alienation lay not in the system of private profit or in the temporary privileges of the capitalist class but in the violence and irrationality that appeared endemic to modern life. Consequently, they chose to concentrate on the problems of artistic expression and personal morality as the central concerns of the radical intellectual in a totalitarian age.

From the outset, their characteristic form of communication was the intricately argued, flamboyantly allusive, intensely critical, twenty-page essay in little magazines like the *Menorah Journal, Miscellany,* and *Symposium.* But by the middle of the decade they were finding a spiritual home at *Partisan Review.* Launched in 1934 as a vehicle of the John Reed Club in New York City, initially committed to combating the spread of a "debilitating liberalism" in social as well as cultural affairs, yet equally averse to the "narrow-minded, sectarian theories and practices" that passed for literary analysis among the cruder disciples of proletarian art, *Partisan*'s original editorial board included such reliable figures as Joseph Freeman and Edwin Seaver together with two younger, less orthodox minds—Philip Rahv and William Phillips.[4] Within a short time this tenuous coalition fell apart. Rahv and Phillips emerged as the dominant voices in the magazine; both grew disillusioned with the attempt to transform fiction and poetry into a social medium, and both were appalled by the deterioration of radicalism under the benign aegis of the Popular Front. By 1937 they had reorganized the magazine on an independent basis with the help of Dwight Macdonald, F. W. Dupee, George L. K. Morris, and Mary McCarthy. Henceforth *Partisan* would serve as a platform for writers like Lionel Trilling, Sidney Hook, Meyer Shapiro, Clement Greenberg, Harold Rosenberg, Paul Goodman, and Lionel Abel—all of whom felt bitterly estranged from the prevailing opinions and attitudes of the official Left.

Yet their objections to the Popular Front were as much aesthetic and stylistic as philosophical. They often seemed to regard Philistinism as a greater danger to America than fascism. Thus they repudiated the liberal faith in industrial development and pragmatic reform not only because these threatened to retard the revolution but also because they believed that such utilitarian preoccupations contributed to the banal artistic tastes of the middle class. Similarly, they detested Stalinism not only because it led to the erection of a police state and a permanent reign of terror but also because its encouragement of "realistic" novels and plays amounted to an attack on the whole modern sensibility. In response, the men who edited and wrote for *Partisan Review* sought to point out the positive uses of avant-garde culture for the radical movement, insisting that the values of artistic experimentation and intellectual freedom were absolute prerequisites for the construction of a truly humane socialist society.

This defense of anything modernist and avant-garde contained a psychological dimension as well. At heart, the distaste of many anti-Stalinists for the Popular Front reflected their own sense of isolation from bourgeois America. The founders of *Partisan Review* considered themselves outsiders, unassimilated products of the New York Jewish ghetto, much more at ease with the literary traditions and intellectual ambiance of the old world than with the folkways and popular culture of the new. As Norman Podhoretz later observed, "they did not feel that they belonged to America or that America belonged to them."[5] Consequently, they could not conceal their discomfort when the Left began to become enthusiastic over regional customs and national myths, populist politics and middle-brow art, the incipient social conscience of Broadway playwrights and Hollywood moguls.

Unable to share or to sympathize with the insular symbols of the Popular Front, they frequently turned in desperation to the icons of internationalism. Rejecting the nativist policies of a Stalin or Roosevelt, they briefly endorsed the cause of Leon Trotsky—not so much on ideological grounds but because he represented to them the aloof brilliance and alienated perspective of the cosmopolitan Jew.[6] Unlike the liberal celebrants of activism and practicality or the Communist devotees of force and resolve, *Partisan* admired Trotsky precisely because he was something of a failure—a man of ideas rather than power, of culture rather than politics. Similarly, though they wrote a great deal about American fiction and poetry, their favorite authors were clearly European (and often philosophically conservative despite their willingness to improvise with language and form)—Proust, Joyce, Eliot, Kafka, the very Symbolists over whom Edmund Wilson had delivered an obituary at the beginning of the decade. Finally, despising the American worship of material growth, they conceived their role as primarily *moral;* they would speak for literary standards and intellectual ideals in a time of commercial vulgarity, shoddy thinking, and political manipulation.[7]

Perhaps their attitude toward the aesthetic predilections of the Popular Front were best summarized in two essays by Clement Greenberg and Dwight Macdonald which appeared in *Partisan Review* during 1939 and 1941. In the first, Greenberg identified the reigning cultural tradition of both Russia and the West as "kitsch"—a product of the urban-industrial revolution when the emerging proletariat and petit-bourgeoisie, having lost touch with the more "authentic" folk art of the countryside and hungry for some new diversion from the boredom of the assembly line and the white-collar factory, were fed a steady diet of dime novels, comic strips, tabloid journalism, the songs of Tin Pan Alley, vaudeville, picture magazines, radio programs, and movies. To Greenberg, kitsch "looted," "watered down," and "debased" the richness of "genuine" culture—serving up in its place "mechanical" formulas, "spurious" dreams, "vicarious" experiences, and "faked sensations." It demanded of its customers neither their time nor attention, only their money. But its most sinister attribute, in Greenberg's estimation, was not that governments deliberately conditioned their subjects to appreciate kitsch, or that writers intentionally throttled their talent in order to win the fame and wealth it could bestow. Rather, the masses themselves preferred "ersatz" art to the real thing. In this respect, the Popular Front was truly democratic; it was simply responding to the prosaic appetites of the common man.[8]

Given this analysis, an apologist for cultural nationalism like Van Wyck Brooks might seem nearly as great a villain as Josef Stalin. Where the latter presided over the destruction of the experimental cinema in the Soviet Union, Dwight Macdonald complained, the former kept calling for a literature of social optimism and patriotic fervor. In each case they were encouraging the creation of a derivative culture for the middlebrow and the middle class.[9] Thus what had begun for Brooks as a search for "organic" works of art that would reunite the writer and society, and what had begun for Russia as an effort to transform men's minds as well as their institutions, were ending in an ignominious surrender to the dictates of mass taste.

Ironically, the learned contributors to *Partisan Review* were not themselves invulnerable to periodic flirtations with popular culture. Macdonald had made his debut in 1930 as an astute critic of American and European film directors; his disaffection with the Soviet Union seemed motivated as much by the suppression of Sergei Eisenstein as by the political consequences of Stalinism. Moreover, throughout the late 1930s *Partisan* was filled with extended discussions of contemporary movies and plays, as though the magazine's public protestations against the mass media could never completely hide a private fascination with its wares. Indeed, what writers like Greenberg and Macdonald really objected to in kitsch was not so much its cultivation of trivia as its passion for social significance, its yearning for intellectual respectability, its pathetic ambition to be taken seriously. In their judgment, both the proletarian aesthetic of the early 1930s and the more recent literature of democratic affirmation were less imaginative and less revolutionary than either the "high" culture of the capitalist era or the "escapist" entertainment on the airwaves and silver screen. Hence in the years following the depression, the offspring of *Partisan Review*'s founding family would frequently vent their wrath on the descendants of the Popular Front by elevating the lowbrow at the expense of the middlebrow—preferring cartoons to didactic novels, "action" movies to plodding moral epics, Samuel Fuller to Stanley Kramer.[10]

In the meantime, Greenberg and Macdonald exhorted their fellow intellectuals to resist the implications of kitsch. Yet their stance was as conservative in its own way as that of the Popular Front. Though they praised the works of the avant-garde for having historically rejected the *"specific* and *immediate* values of society" in favor of "those *general* and *eternal* human values . . . on which culture depends," though they asserted that modern literature must always be "negativistic, cynical, skeptical," and "destructive" of official assumptions and prejudices, they no longer believed in the possibility of further artistic "advance." In a period of reaction it was necessary to fight all the old battles again, to defend the triumphs of the past against the mediocrity of the present, to expect from socialism not a "new culture" but "simply . . . the preservation of whatever living culture we have right now."[11] Thus the sense of diminished hopes and declining opportunities that afflicted the rest of the intellectual community in the late 1930s had penetrated the radical sanctuary of *Partisan Review* as well.

If Greenberg and Macdonald were returning to the artistic wars of the 1920s, Philip Rahv and William Phillips had begun to reconnoiter the whole of American fiction in search of some passageway through which the avant-garde might escape its contemporary predicament. They concluded that the central weakness of the nation's literature was not its refusal to deal with daily issues or build a permanent audience but its persistent failure to integrate the realms of "consciousness" and "experience," the inner world of intelligence and the outer world of social behavior, the interpretative and the descriptive. In particular, Rahv and Phillips charged that the tradition of naturalism in American literature—of which the typical protest novel of the 1930s was only the latest example—had prevented the writer from portraying reality on the level of "values, ideas, and judgments." Instead he seemed content to report the facts of oppression and survival, to document the external manifestations of economic disaster, to keep abreast of the headlines without any sense of their "imaginative" meaning or moral consequences. Seeking to be a citizen as well as a novelist, hypnotized by the possibilities of action, he remained indifferent to the power of thought.[12]

Yet like Greenberg and Macdonald, Rahv and Phillips were retreating to the battleground on which the Progressives and expatriates had earlier fought. Indeed, they were simply restating the original arguments of their current arch-enemy, Van Wyck Brooks. From their perspective, the most dangerous foe of modern art was neither kitsch nor the Popular Front but rather the "pragmatic patterns" and "anti-intellectual bias" that made up the "national heritage." If most American writers shunned artistic discipline, if they immersed themselves mindlessly in the "sights and sounds" of social life, this was because the United States had never recognized the need for theory and speculation. Hence the Left in the late 1930s, by idolizing the "folkways of the masses," was only reinforcing the "provincial smugness" of American culture against which Brooks had railed in 1915.[13]

Where Rahv and Phillips differed from Brooks, however, was in their skepticism about the creative potential of a national aesthetic or the worth of the writer's direct engagement in public affairs. On the contrary, they hoped for a future "Europeanization of American literature" in which the native artist and critic, recognizing that the problems of human existence involved the issue of individual consciousness as well as material well-being, would lead his country finally into the "mainstream of world culture." For them the most relevant model of artistic excellence and personal commitment was neither Walt Whitman (the hero of the Proletarians) nor Henry James (the darling of the Formalists) but instead André Malraux and Ignazio Silone—men who comprehended both the social and the aesthetic importance of action and ideas.[14]

Ultimately, *Partisan Review*'s attack on naturalism, pragmatism, kitsch, and the bourgeois mentality of the Popular Front implied a special role for the intellectual who wished to preserve his radical impulses in a time of political and cultural stagnation. For to the editors of the magazine, the tension between consciousness and experience in American literature was merely a symptom of the writer's larger inability to understand both his own fragile relation to society and the paradoxical ways in which art might serve the revolution. Hence Rahv and Phillips tried at the end of the decade to remind the intelligentsia of its proper calling—though in terms that seemed far more limited than the instructions of a Benjamin Ginzburg or an Edmund Wilson during the opening years of the depression.

The trouble with the intellectual community, Phillips complained, was precisely that it had never seen itself as a *community,* never achieved "a detached and self-sufficient group existence," never possessed the moral and professional resources of "esthetic and social subversion that are normally provided by an organized bohemia." Lacking a sense of generational continuity, constantly having to start from a "clean slate," the American writer had no cultural or ideological "traditions" of the sort that sustained his European counterpart in periods of crisis. Consequently, Phillips contended, the intellectuals had always been torn between the extremes of "dissidence and conformity," between the impulse to rebel and the craving to adapt, between the "urge toward some degree of autonomy and an equally strong tendency to self-effacement."[15] This explained both the erratic quality of the nation's fiction and poetry and the historic failure of an indigenous radical movement to take root in the United States.

Here again the Popular Front only exacerbated a disease whose origins lay deep in the "ambivalent psyche" of the intellectual community. When the writer had attempted in the 1920s to differentiate himself from the mass, practicing his craft in exile and solitude, he was dismissed as a charming eccentric. Now, in pursuit of social influence and public acceptance, anxious to "appease" the "official voice of society," he was being engulfed by the "tides of prevailing opinion." To Rahv and Phillips, the Left's most serious error had been its decade-long presumption that the artist would improve both his mind and his work by entering the political world. In the end, this axiom not only inspired a commitment to reformism rather than revolution but it also prevented the birth of a healthy American avant-garde. Thus instead of the withering away of capitalism, the 1930s had witnessed the "withering away of literature," at least insofar as *Partisan Review* was concerned.[16]

Yet despite their displeasure with the writer's present submissiveness to social convention, Rahv and Phillips were advocating neither a complete withdrawal from contemporary problems nor a compulsive search for sectarian purity. In Rahv's opinion, the depression-scarred artist could never return to "pre-political modes of expression," but neither could he bind himself to "some closed and definitive political doctrine" already clogged with innumerable cultural prohibitions. Once the writer became a "mouthpiece" for a particular dogma, aesthetic or ideological, he inevitably sacrificed both his independence and his effectiveness.[17] Thus the editors called on the intellectual to behave not as an isolated individual nor as an eager participant in mass movements but as a member of a unique social group (if not a full-fledged class) with its own distinctive needs, allegiances, and responsibilities.

In their eyes, this group—the intelligentsia—was a classic creature of capitalism's division of labor; restricted solely to the sphere of art and ideas, it earned its livelihood "by preserving the old and by producing the new forms of consciousness."[18] At the moment it had a dual function. On the one hand, Phillips pointed out, the "special properties of modern literature" sprang directly from the "characteristic moods and interests of the intellectuals."[19] Hence as the source of all stylistic experimentation and cultural inquiry, as protectors of everything avant-garde, the intellectual community could challenge the deepest assumptions of any social order through the creation of great works of art. In this sense, the finest literature of the western world, whether aristocratic or bourgeois or proletarian, was inherently radical and subversive—continually questioning, analyzing, and exposing the hypocrisies and deceptions of human life.

On the other hand, with the surrender of the Popular Front and the labor unions to the politics of expediency, the intelligentsia became for Phillips and Rahv the only revolutionary class left in the United States. It was the intellectuals' task, therefore, to rise in "permanent mutiny" against the "petty regime of utility and conformity" that continually plagued American thought, to adopt the role of critic within the context of bourgeois civilization, to encourage "individual and group secession from, and protest against, the dominant values of our time." What *Partisan Review* desperately wanted was a coterie of writers who knew how "to swim against the current"—who could rely on nothing more than personal integrity, a "probing conscience," and the "will to repulse and to assail the forces released by a corrupt society."[20]

In effect, the editors had transformed their own feelings of alienation into a positive virtue. For them, detachment was a superior form of political, artistic, and moral commitment. Given their perspective, the man who remained aloof from all factions, doctrines, preconceived formulas, and organized movements, the man who clarified issues while disdaining the incessant demands of power and respectability, the man who cultivated his private sense of estrangement as a way of enriching both modern culture and socialist ideals became the perfect radical. Thus *Partisan Review* could still maintain a tenuous connection between its literary passions and its waning interest in the revolution, between its pride in being different and its fear of being ignored, between its sympathy for the oppressed and its endorsement of an artistic elite.

Yet it seemed a sign of the times that the magazine was reduced to redefining the intellectual's role rather than the content of his beliefs. By the late 1930s the radicalism of even the anti-Stalinists had grown more existential than ideological. Moreover, there were few in the camp of the dissidents who shared *Partisan*'s desire to keep the bonds between cultural criticism and social activism relatively intact. On the contrary, an increasing number of writers who had once looked favorably on the proletarian aesthetic—among them V. F. Calverton, James Farrell, and Edmund Wilson—now began to call for a total separation of literature from society beyond anything Rahv and Phillips had recommended.

In several cases, disenchantment with the political tactics of the Popular Front led to a general reappraisal of Marxism's usefulness for literary theory. The radical appreciation of class bias and environmental conditioning seemed only to have confused the social origins of art with its permanent worth and moral significance, according to Wilson and Farrell. Equipped with a Marxist outlook, a writer might understand the historical background of a given novel or poem, but he could never judge whether the work was good or bad.[21] Consequently, the Left had been mistaken in believing that the concerns of culture and politics were mutually reciprocal and interdependent. The business of the Marxist agitator and organizer, Calverton insisted, was to promote the "social revolution"; the business of the creative artist and literary critic was to forward "the esthetic values of literature." And here the fundamental conflict between thought and action was most apparent, because "the esthetic values of literature do not stand in any intimate relationship with revolutionary values."[22]

For some, this dilemma was resolved through the forthright declaration that the domain of culture was completely independent of "economic interests and the struggle of classes," that the contributions of art and philosophy persisted long after the particular society in which they were born had entirely disappeared, that indeed the intellectual functioned best not in periods of stress and revolution but in eras of comparative leisure and stability.[23] As a result, Lionel Trilling argued in *Partisan Review,* the writer should be relieved once and for all of the "messianic responsibility" to rescue America by converting his work into an instrument of national salvation.[24] In the future, Farrell and Wilson predicted, literature would deal not with the contemporary needs of a specific party or class but with all the problems of the modern world. And it would do so on its own terms —as a separate "department of activity which has its own aims, techniques, and rights."[25] What this position ultimately meant was a repudiation of the effort—launched by the Progressives and sustained throughout the 1920s and 1930s—to establish some kind of rapport between the artist and the public. Henceforth, novelists and poets would write only for one another, and the dream of finding a place in an organic American community gave way to a celebration of the homeless intellectual, forever alienated and uprooted, the eternal exile without hope of return.[26]

For others, the apparent incompatibility between cultural preoccupations and political engagement led not only to an insistence on the autonomy of the arts but also to a renunciation of any social ambitions whatsoever. To William Saroyan, never an apostle of the collectivist faith at any time, the late 1930s had taught the writer an invaluable lesson: that he must elude every attempt at external coercion, that he was "inescapably a dweller in an ivory tower" for whom "historical action" was "out of the question."[27] This militant reassertion of a creed long in disfavor during the depression (except in such rectories of New Criticism as *Hound and Horn* and the *Southern Review*) seemed an indication of how far certain intellectuals were prepared to go in abandoning the orthodoxies of the Left.

Perhaps the artist who best embodied this new mood of withdrawal was Henry Miller, and it was not accidental that he should emerge as a major culture hero by 1940. One of the few expatriates who did not re-enter America in the 1930s, Miller was a stranger to its literary and ideological wars. Moreover, his novels and essays were largely unavailable until the close of the decade. But when they were "discovered," he became the subject of enormous critical interest.

Essentially, Miller stood for everything the Popular Front disapproved. Unlike those writers who tried to share the plight of the workers or speak in the idiom of the "folk," Miller had thoroughly dissociated himself from organized society. In a series of essays published during 1939 under the symbolic title *The Cosmological Eye,* he proclaimed his absolute indifference to worldly affairs, to the "life of the masses," and to the "intentions of existing governments." In his mind, "the whole social-political scheme of existence is crazy—because it is based on vicarious living." Laws, moral codes, religious myths, philosophies of history, economic theories of every kind merely interfered with direct human experience. Even worse, these "abstract ideas" deceived men into believing that freedom and justice could be achieved through the construction of some new social order, some new form of industrial production, some new "system of ideal rights." In response, Miller announced that for him society was made up entirely of individuals, not groups or classes. Consequently, each single man should try desperately to rise "above the crowd," declining to "lay down his life for his country, or for a cause or principle," repudiating all gods and "leaders," recognizing instead that the solitary individual must "work with his own hands to save himself. . . . " In sum, Miller favored whatever was "active, immediate, and personal." And so he decided to "turn his gaze inward," contemplating his "private fate" with "awe and wonder, mystery and reverence," inventing his own realities, wreaking his "own havoc," making his "own miracles," the perfect narcissist in a universe bereft of revolutionary visions and utopian dreams.[28]

To Philip Rahv, Miller's exquisite lack of interest in "belonging" to a close-knit community or participating in a broad-based social movement was a refreshing departure from the portentous sermons of a Van Wyck Brooks or an Archibald MacLeish on the intellectual's myriad "responsibilities" to America. By 1941, Rahv was enchanted with Miller's glorious *irresponsibility*, his anarchistic impulses, his posture as an "utterly declassed and alienated man." Far from seeking to recover his lost relation to society, Miller seemed in Rahv's eyes a fearless nay-sayer who could dismiss the political and cultural convictions of his contemporaries as so many delusions, while accepting the world's imminent collapse with sublime equanimity. "Released not only from any allegiance to the past but also from all commitments to the future," Miller was an authentic "desperado" preoccupied solely with the immediate problem of physical survival. For Rahv, Miller's existential courage in the face of madness and disaster made him both more realistic and more revolutionary than most of the decade's self-appointed radicals; he was therefore better qualified than anyone else to pronounce judgment on the official beliefs of the 1930s.[29]

Yet in several respects this extreme disillusion with all conventional institutions and ideals, the retreat from Joseph Freeman's Marxist "We" to Henry Miller's cosmic "I," was neither liberating nor original. As Malcolm Cowley observed in 1941, the current denial that literature possessed any overt social purpose, or that intellectuals possessed any special political obligations, was both familiar and ironic. Despite having bade a permanent farewell in the early 1930s to the cult of self-analysis and the ideal of "pure" art, many writers were now eagerly resurrecting the values of the 1920s. By returning to a view of the social order as composed of atomistic individuals rather than as an organic unit, by reviving the classic conflict between private integrity and public duty, by insisting that the intellectual function as an unaffiliated critic of culture and politics, they had come full circle. But Cowley noticed one crucial difference between the mental climate of 1941 and that of the past twenty years. A growing number of writers were not trying to alter the American's imagination and style of life as in the 1920s, or his ideological presuppositions and property relationships as in the

1930s; indeed they were "not bent on changing anything." On the eve of war, the anti-Stalinist intellectuals had lost faith in the capacity of all revolutions—whether psychological or economic—to transform attitudes, create a new society, or solve human problems. As a result, they appeared to Cowley increasingly passive and resigned.[30]

What Cowley neglected to add was that these traits might lead not only to a recovery of previously abandoned doctrines but also to an unconscious acquiescence in the status quo. Paradoxically, the renewed concern for artistic autonomy and intellectual independence helped prepare the way for a postwar alliance between the intelligentsia and the state. By deliberately limiting themselves to the task of commenting on modern literature and the popular arts, the anti-Stalinists in general and the group around *Partisan Review* in particular were acknowledging their political impotence and their willingness to leave the larger social issues in the hands of the administrators and bureaucrats. Thus while they cultivated their role as cultural radicals, government policy could go largely unchallenged, and the capitalist system—against which they had originally revolted—would remain firmly intact.

Indeed, the gradual metamorphosis of *Partisan Review* from a position of militant Marxism to a virtual acceptance of established social arrangements was neither surprising nor altogether unintentional. Once the journal's editors and contributors began to question the value of revolutionary activities in the wake of the Stalinist experience, and once they began to re-emphasize the traditional liberal belief that ideas and individuals should be totally free, it seemed natural for them to transfer their loyalties to America as the main defense against the totalitarian menace both of Germany and the Soviet Union.[31]

Even more important, however, the intellectuals at *Partisan Review* were never quite as alienated as they liked to appear. In their lives and in their work, Alfred Kazin later remembered, there was always a sense of conflict between the ghetto and America, a feeling of duplicity at having deserted the Brownsvilles of their Jewish forebears together with an overpowering ambition to conquer the mythical city of the "gentiles," a fidelity to ethnic roots and radical instincts existing side by side with a secret urge to make what Norman Podhoretz called one of sthe "longest journey in the world" —the pilgrimage from Brooklyn to Manhattan. These psychic and cultural strains were further intensified by the fact that the Jews, of all the immigrant groups, had most internalized the American version of the Protestant Ethic: the postponement of immediate rewards in the interest of "getting ahead," the belief in hard work and competitive striving, the respect for achievement and the dread of being "kept back" in poverty or the working class, the pressure to succeed and the terrible fear of failure. In many cases, therefore, the yearning to escape the ghetto was interwoven with an intuitive and enduring respect for the American Dream.[32]

Thus for a number of *Partisan Review* alumni, the occupation of writing became not so much a way of keeping faith with one's radical origins as a means of finding a "path to the outside world."[33] It was hardly accidental that the one full-length book to emerge from *Partisan*'s stable—an extensive and basically sympathetic treatment of twentieth-century American literature—was entitled *On Native Grounds*. When Alfred Kazin started the work in the late 1930s, it seemed an illustration of *Partisan*'s favorite themes —the inability of American artists to deal with social experience at the level of conscious ideas, the innate conformism of the Popular Front, the emphasis on a moral and cultural critique of national institutions. But by the time it was published in 1942, Kazin had infused the book with a lyrical sensitivity to the American past and an eloquent appreciation of the writer's inviolable (if sometimes ambiguous) ties to the larger society worthy of a Van Wyck Brooks or Lewis Mumford. In effect, *On Native Grounds* represented an act of assimilation, a symbolic rite of passage over the Brooklyn Bridge into the "great world" beyond, a spiritual transformation from "outsider" to "insider"—from alienation to adjustment.[34] And in the process of accommodating himself to his native land, Kazin revealed how much the anti-Stalinist writer shared in common with the rest of the intellectual community, how eagerly he wished to make himself a part of America's values and traditions, how rapidly the ideological and aesthetic battles of the 1930s were giving way to a mood of consensus with the approach of World War II.

3. *The New Mandarins*

Throughout the spring and summer of 1939, vague rumors of an imminent shift in Russian foreign policy began to circulate in various newspapers and magazines. Ever since the surrender of Czech democracy at Munich and the final collapse of the Loyalists in Spain, relations between the West and the Soviet Union were increasingly marked by mutual vacillation and mistrust. During the same period Europe was alive with frantic diplomatic maneuvers, each country jockeying for position before the outbreak of a war no one seemed able any longer to prevent. While the governments of Britain and France were officially engaged in elaborate negotiations with Russia over border guarantees in

Eastern Europe, some Western politicians still entertained the hope that Hitler could be turned against the U.S.S.R. The Russians, exceedingly fearful of just such a possibility, were themselves exploring the prospects of a rapprochement with the Third Reich. All of this intrigue took place against the background of yet another crisis carefully orchestrated by Germany but building toward a far different climax: if Hitler could convert one of his potential foes to a temporary neutrality, thereby removing the danger of military encirclement, he could then launch the war of revenge for which the Naxis had long prepared. Amid the growing tension over German demands on Poland, Hitler appeared as determined as everyone else that there be no more Munichs.

Yet despite the periodic warnings that Stalin might eventually decide to withdraw from the coming European conflict, the majority of American commentators—Communist as well as liberal—appeared initially dumbfounded by the event which destroyed the remaining moral and ideological foundations of their world. Although the decade's social and cultural ambitions had been severely blunted during the late 1930s, although the radical inclinations of many writers had led to some unexpectedly conservative consequences, few anticipated that the beliefs of a generation could be so casually cast aside in a single act. But a sense of political and personal betrayal instantly swept through the entire intellectual community with the announcement on August 23, 1939, of a treaty between the Soviet Union and Nazi Germany. While the full ramifications of the agreement were not immediately known, it was clear that the last barrier to war had crumbled —and with it whatever was left of the radical conscience. It seemed painfully ironic that, having survived the shock of an impersonal stock-market crash and having dedicated themselves to the notion that Americans might regain control of their environment if given the power and the proper intellectual guidance, writers should be facing an even greater catastrophe induced by two European dictators for whom men and ideas possessed no value whatever. Nevertheless, the intelligentsia was now confronted by a new crisis whose violence and terror would stand as a mockery to the fragile hopes and assumptions of the 1930s.

It was perhaps appropriate that the group most shaken by the Nazi–Soviet pact should be the Communists themselves. For the party, the years between 1939 and 1941 would be difficult indeed. At first reacting to the news from Europe with an incoherent stammer, the Communists swiftly discarded the rhetoric of the Popular Front and began to refurbish the revolutionary slogans of the early 1930s. Soon the columns of the *New*

Masses and the *Daily Worker* were replete with ingenious explanations of Russia's refusal to participate in a war for profits and empire.

Behind the façade of collective security, the argument ran, the Western "democracies" had worked feverishly to promote their own selfish interests and overcome their weaknesses at the Soviet Union's expense. Now the socialist world was shrewdly extricating itself from these shabby deceptions, reminding everyone in the process that there could be no "non-aggression" pact between communism and capitalism. Moreover, the party declared, American diplomacy was every bit as cynical and rapacious as that of the Allies or Germany. As long as the battle raged, the United States would try to improve its position in the overseas market, create a war economy at home to stimulate industrial recovery, and make the combatants totally dependent on American resources. Ultimately, the United States wanted to manipulate the conflict so that it might emerge as the dominant imperialist power both in Europe and the Far East at the war's end—even if this meant an extended military presence on foreign soil to insure "stability" and protect American investments.[35]

In the meantime, the Communists conceded that the return to a militant posture would probably cause some "difficulties with the intellectuals" who had naïvely mistaken the Popular Front for a permanent policy. But they expected the "painful Hamlet-like period of indecision" to be mercifully brief. And whatever antagonism the party might encounter in the immediate future, the Communists seemed relieved that "the time [had] come to add up some accounts and settle others."[36]

On the surface, the party's interpretation of events was not altogether unpersuasive or unprophetic. Indeed, many liberals and anti-Stalinist radicals held a similar view at least until the fall of France. The memory of World War I, the assumption that modern wars were always fought for imperialist reasons, the suspicion of an economic revival generated solely by military spending, the hostility to a further consolidation of monopoly capital, the fear of giving any President unlimited power in foreign affairs, and the rising martial spirit in the United States, all disturbed those intellectuals who were not yet completely converted to the cause of intervention against fascism. But the Communists had lost their credibility. No matter how effectively they presented their case for American neutrality, their motives and sincerity were constantly in question. For the past five years the party had championed collective security and condemned isolationism; now it had abruptly switched sides. The ease with which its spokesmen could exhort the United States to resist Nazism on one day and on the next argue just as plausibly that there was no moral distinction between Great

Britain and the Third Reich rendered all its statements suspect. At bottom, the party seemed to be suggesting simply that whatever benefited the Soviet Union must also aid world socialism. When neither the liberals nor the anti-Stalinists would accept this tautology, the Communists wound up talking only to themselves.

Moreover, the party was confronted not only with political isolation and increasing legal harassment, but also with a series of noisy and embarrassing resignations from the ranks of its own intellectual entourage.[37] For the most part, the Communists attempted to rationalize this well-publicized exodus by minimizing the impact of European events while concentrating instead on the behavior of the defectors themselves. Thus the *New Masses* performed a sociological and psychological autopsy on what it considered the deserters, characterizing them as essentially petit-bourgeois, emotionally unstable, unable to understand the true needs of the working class, and ultimately incapable of withstanding the pressures of a long-term ideological struggle. The intellectual faced a crucial test of "personal manhood and social faith," exclaimed Michael Gold, in which only the strong and the resolute could emerge unscathed. The rest, the *New Masses* concluded sadly, would inevitably succumb to hysteria and demoralization.[38]

Among other advantages, this sort of reductionist interpretation permitted the Communists to avoid troublesome questions about their own apostasy. But at heart, they were less interested in answering their critics than in buttressing the faith of their followers. By dwelling on the motives of the "renegades" and by reaffirming his commitment in the midst of crisis, the loyal Communist could feel both courageous and morally superior at having remained steadfast while weaker souls were selling out. Accordingly, the *New Masses* consoled its readers by telling them that, like the early Christians, their religion was being challenged by the temptation to choose an easier path and that they could demonstrate their indomitability only by rebuffing every effort to subvert their belief. And in such a trial the power and prestige of the Soviet Union could still provide them with a vicarious sense of strength and righteousness. It was this state of mind, more than the particular positions they adopted, that sustained the Communists during 1940 and 1941.

Nevertheless, no amount of intellectual legerdemain or psychological reinforcement could hide the fact that the party in America had suffered an enormous setback as a result of the Nazi–Soviet pact, the partition of Poland, and the invasion of Finland. While the Communists were busy "settling accounts," others were launching a bitter and sustained attack on

Russia, the present socialist movement, and the ultimate validity of Marx-ism.

If the dissidents at *Partisan Review* and the *Modern Quarterly* had been vociferous in their denunciation of Soviet policies since the birth of the Popular Front, many liberals had refrained from public criticism so as not to divide the Left at precisely the moment when it needed a unified stand against the danger of reaction at home and fascism abroad. But throughout the 1930s their private doubts gradually swelled in the face of the Moscow trials, the venomous factional warfare behind the Loyalist lines in Spain, and the solidification of the dictatorship through police terror and thought control. The pact came as the final blow; with the collapse of the Popular Front, the justifications for self-censorship had become obsolete, and the majority of American intellectuals felt free to join their anti-Stalinist col-leagues in reappraising the convictions of a decade.

To the *Nation* and *New Republic,* the spectacle of the Red Army march-ing into Eastern Europe and Finland signaled the end of Russia's special status as a workers' commonwealth and its moral claims to the leadership of a world-wide "progressive" movement. Men like Bruce Bliven, George Soule, and Oswald Villard—all of whom had once seen the Soviet "experi-ment" as a genuine alternative to capitalist inefficiency and decay—could not now accept the argument that the U.S.S.R. was merely engaging in traditional balance-of-power politics motivated by an understandable desire for military security. Having presumed that the land of socialism would never behave like an ordinary nation-state, that Russia "constituted a bul-wark of honesty and humanity in a treacherous world," they were appalled to discover that Stalin had no qualms about "playing the imperialistic game" if it suited his own nationalist purposes. In the process, the best ideals of the Popular Front—the defense of democratic values, the concern for the welfare of the ordinary citizen, the continuing battle against fascism in all its manifestations—seemed little more than a temporary invention of Moscow's foreign office. In these circumstances, the *New Republic* charged, *Realpolitik* was simply an inadequate rationale because "people like to have something to believe in that is not raw power." Thus the Soviet Union's willingness to "break her word when it was to her advantage," her cynical resort to intimidation and armed might made her appear no different from and a natural ally of Nazi Germany. "Henceforth," the magazine con-cluded, "the [strength] of the Russian state abroad must rest on fear rather than trust."[39]

For a number of other observers, some of whom had too easily identified the cause of radicalism with the success or failure of the Stalinist regime, the pact inspired not only a condemnation of Russian diplomacy but also a critical inquiry into the nature of Soviet life. Increasingly preoccupied at the close of the decade with the issue of freedom versus dictatorship, they began to challenge the very character of the Bolshevik revolution—and with it the traditional Communist reliance on centralized power, the dominance of a single party over the direction of social change, the emergence of an elite bureaucracy entirely separate from the masses, and the authoritarian implications of the Marxist prophecy.

This reassessment induced many intellectuals—regardless of their previous political loyalties—to question whether the collectivization of a nation's economic institutions necessarily resulted in a truly socialist society. If the events in the U.S.S.R. since 1917 were any test, Sidney Hook declared, "all that has been achieved [is] the industrialization of the country following the pattern of capitalist development in the West."[40] Even worse, the Soviet example seemed merely to prove that "proletarian" government could be just as oppressive and hierarchical as a traditional bourgeois state. As Edmund Wilson observed in *To the Finland Station*—an initially sympathetic study of European radical thought that took him the decade to write, during which time the book inadvertently became a record of his own creeping disillusion with Marxism—the Bolsheviks had not erected a "classless society out of the old illiterate feudal Russia." Rather, "they encouraged the rise and the domination of a new controlling and privileged class, who were soon exploiting the workers almost as callously as the Tsarist industrialists had done. . . ."[41] Thus in the opinion of ex-Communists like Granville Hicks and Lewis Corey, as well as in the views of veteran anti-Stalinists like Sidney Hook and Norman Thomas, the socialization of property alone made absolutely no difference as far as the problems of political freedom and economic justice were concerned. Given the absence of democratic safeguards, a revolution officially dedicated to the abolition of private enterprise in the name of the working class would merely lead to a dangerous "increase in the bureaucratic powers of the state," the enthronement of a "monolithic party" which "in effect [owned] the instruments of production" while regulating every other aspect of political and cultural life, and the creation of a society which was neither socialist nor capitalist but rigidly "totalitarian."[42]

For the most part, these judgments represented not so much a re-evaluation or rejection of Marxist theory as a catalogue of its weaknesses based on the Soviet experience. By the end of the 1930s, however, numerous writers were beginning to argue that the sort of society Stalin had built was not merely peculiar to the U.S.S.R. but intrinsic both to socialism and the modern world. Hence Max Lerner, a former pillar of the Popular Front, conceded that Marxism was rapidly becoming irrelevant to an understanding of contemporary issues. Under its spell, he asserted, the Left had managed only to underestimate the strength and endurance of capitalism, overestimate the revolutionary impulses of the proletariat, minimize the emergence of a new middle class of technicians and administrators whose instincts and interests were less ideological than professional, misinterpret the extent to which political power transcended property relationships, and miscalculate man's capacity to withstand the irrational appeal of nationalism and dictatorship.[43] Along the same lines, Sidney Hook finally agreed with Max Eastman that the dialectic interfered with "clear thinking" and could no longer provide "reliable knowledge about ourselves and the world we live in"; therefore, it should be irrevocably "dropped."[44] And in the face of these indictments, Lewis Corey morosely acknowledged that "Marxism as a progressive social force is dead"—at least for those intellectuals who had reached maturity in the period between the Wilsonian era and the depression.[45]

But of all the last rites delivered over the grave of Marxism, perhaps the most somber was James Burnham's *The Managerial Revolution.* Published first as a speculative essay in *Partisan Review* before appearing as a book in 1941, the work drew on an impressive variety of sources unique to twentieth-century thought: Trotsky, Pareto, Croly, Veblen, Berle and Means, even the Anarchist tradition. Burnham hoped not merely to demonstrate the shortcomings of Marxist philosophy or to summarize the arguments for and against a highly centralized and interdependent economy but rather to offer an altogether different kind of analysis that would both explain the failure to carry through a socialist revolution on an international scale and point out the path over which every advanced nation seemed now to be moving.

Burnham began by rejecting the universal assumption of the 1930s that "capitalism and socialism are 'the only alternatives' for modern society; either capitalism will continue or socialism will replace it." In his estimation, the unquestioned acceptance of this idea made it virtually impossible to comprehend the true purposes of the Stalinist regime, the underlying objectives of Nazism, the ambiguous impact of the New Deal, or the complicated nature of the present European war. A generation of writers had almost religiously believed that "the elimination of property rights in the instruments of production is a guarantee, a sufficient guarantee, of socialism." But the example of the Soviet Union, whose collectivist institutions were neither "economically classless" nor "politically democratic," proved that such predictions had no basis in reality. Indeed since fascism also struck at private industry and corporate finance, most radicals were compelled to distort "terminology, sense, and facts" beyond recognition in order to contend that the Nazi state was only a final stage of monopoly capitalism. But when trying to evaluate the New Deal, Burnham observed, the Left really found itself intellectually helpless—unable to decide whether it was witnessing a disguised form of socialism, a Machiavellian effort to save the market economy, or something vaguely in between.[46] In effect, Burnham was suggesting that the writers of the 1930s, like their predecessors in the Progressive period, were relying on outmoded concepts and sheer utopian fervor in seeking to cope with the upheavals of twentieth-century life.

To fill this ideological vacuum, Burnham submitted a new theory of social revolution which he was certain would illuminate the actual changes taking place in economic and political arrangements, class relations, and public attitudes. Essentially, he asserted that modern society was evolving from its historic dependence on capitalist methods (characterized by private ownership and control of a country's technological and agricultural resources, production for personal profit, regulation of the economy by the laws of the market place, parliamentary procedures, an abiding faith in the beneficence of competition, and a liberal emphasis on individual freedom as the paramount ideal) to "a type of society that I call 'managerial.' " The stigmata of this new social structure included state ownership of the major industries, the transfer of sovereignty from legislative institutions to central planning boards, the abolition of the profit motive in favor of organizational efficiency and economic rationalization, the development of a new ruling class composed of "production executives, administrative engineers, supervisory technicians, plant coordinators, government bureau heads and commissioners," and the emergence of a few "super-states" contesting among themselves for world domination. According to Burnham, the leaders of the managerial revolution would ultimately invoke all the slogans and values associated with "collectivism"—the search for community, the celebration of the "people," the urge for order and discipline, the need for national unity —in order to obtain philosophical and moral legitimacy. Meanwhile, given the sophisticated techniques of political propaganda, the hypnotic spell of the mass media, and the customary passivity of the common man, it was becoming impossible for the workers or their potential middle-class allies to prevent what for Burnham was the inevitable triumph and consolidation of bureaucratic and executive power throughout the world.[47]

Though he admitted that the managerial society assumed many different shapes, Burnham still saw Stalinist Russia, the Third Reich, and New Deal

America as variants of the same fundamental pattern. Hence he considered the Nazi–Soviet pact a most appropriate symbol of the new era. As the last remnants of European capitalism were destroyed in the war, as the surviving super-powers converted themselves into outright dictatorships or benevolent welfare states, Burnham concluded that the distinctive social transformations of the twentieth century promised an intolerably bleak future for radicals and liberals alike.

Ironically, Burnham's description of the managerial revolution corresponded perfectly to what the Left in the 1930s had confidently endorsed. When Marxists as well as some New Dealers talked about collectivism, planning, or simply a greater sense of economic stability and social control, they often had in mind precisely those qualities of organizational complexity, technological sophistication, and administrative skill whose authoritarian implications Burnham feared and deplored. Thus because this concept of the good society contained such conservative—even autocratic—possibilities, a growing number of writers came to feel by the close of the 1930s that the decade's most cherished beliefs must not be merely revised but repudiated, that a more comprehensive attempt to regulate or nationalize property might only perpetuate the worst features of corporate capitalism, that the emphasis on community and cooperation had obscured the value of personal liberty, and that revolution was neither practicable nor desirable in the modern world. Though they differed over how far to go in jettisoning the ideological and cultural baggage of the depression years, their newfound skepticism about Russia, Marxism, and the specialized talents associated with a rising managerial class amounted in most cases to a complete abandonment of the radical perspective.

This was expressed in a variety of ways. In the eyes of some intellectuals, among them Sidney Hook, private enterprise began to appear increasingly preferable to any socialist society that lacked the ordinary channels of "political democracy." Similarly, George Counts contended that the Left had been preoccupied for too long with the iniquities of capitalist exploitation, while overlooking the far more repressive effects of military arrogance and dictatorial rule. What radicals failed to perceive, Lewis Corey added, was that "political power may bring more woe than economic power. A Stalin and a Hitler are responsible for infinitely more oppression, degradation, and misery than a Krupp or a J. P. Morgan." Consequently, as many writers shifted their attention from economic injustice to governmental coercion, they were accepting the notion not only that a successful revolt in the face of "tanks, airplanes, poison gases, and the radio" was now virtually "impossible" but that the maldistribution of wealth might be considerably more tolerable than the curtailment of freedom.[48]

No one was more adamant about these propositions than Max Eastman. In the fall of 1939 he officially severed his last ties with the socialist movement. Having always regarded Marxism as a hypothesis that deserved to be tested, he had finally determined that the "experiment" was a total disaster. Transfixed by the danger of centralized power, philosophically hostile to all forms of bureaucratic elitism, temperamentally sympathetic to every sign of individualism and non-conformity, Eastman offered an eloquent explanation for this decision which revealed his own enduring commitment to libertarian ideals.

In the halcyon days of the early 1930s, he recalled, socialism had promised to satisfy the often incompatible aspirations of three distinct groups on the American left. The first were the natural rebels against all types of tyranny (men like John Dos Passos and Edmund Wilson) "in whose motivation the concept of human freedom formed the axis." They were attracted to the Marxist creed because it offered to "put an end to wage-slavery and make all men genuinely free-and-equal." The second group saw in the principles of socialism a modern version of Christian brotherhood; at heart, a Granville Hicks or a Waldo Frank wished to replace competition with comradeship, egocentric ambition with an altruistic concern for the public welfare, loneliness and isolation with a sense of communal solidarity. The third group, composed largely of liberal economists and political theorists horrified by the chaos of the depression, turned to socialism in an effort to find relief from the "anarchy of capitalist production, and make possible a planned and scientific efficiency in the important business of keeping alive."[49]

But given what Eastman now considered the totalitarian potential of Marxism, this uneasy coalition had inevitably disintegrated. For his part, Eastman did not hesitate to ally himself unequivocally with the position of Wilson and Dos Passos. Neither the fraternal impulse nor the need for a rational system of production and distribution, he pointed out, could ever justify arbitrary limitations on self-expression and personal creativity. In short Eastman was contradicting the basic premise of the 1930s:

> Those who want to see men really free, each to enjoy the values of his own life in his own fashion, will have to abandon the religion of the collective will. They will have to decide whether by socialism they meant individualism generalized and made accessible to all, or whether they meant a general surrender to some authoritarian concept of the collective good. The decision is easy in my case, for I have not the glimmer of a desire to lose my identity in a collection, nor would I wish this loss upon a single working man. The essential meaning of the revolution to me was the liberation of individuality, the extension of my privilege of individuality to the masses of mankind.[50]

Thus in rejecting the collectivist rhetoric of the 1930s, in refusing to subordinate his inner desires to the demands of social responsibility, in reminding his contemporaries about the eternal merits of individualism, he was also reviving the classic nineteenth-century idea that liberty depended on the "absence of governmental restraint"—an old-fashioned maxim which might be realizable only in a market place economy.[51] Unlike Burnham, Eastman could not resign himself to the managerial revolution; in his judgment, the historic battle for individual freedom should still be waged —and from the Right if necessary. Accordingly, he took his leave from the still doctrinaire *Modern Quarterly,* finding in the belligerent traditionalism of the *Reader's Digest* a more suitable platform from which to lecture Americans on the evils of the omnipotent state.

Others were less ready, at least for the moment, to share Eastman's enthusiasm for such conspicuously conservative axioms. While writers as diverse as John Dewey, Sidney Hook, James Burnham, Lewis Corey, and John Chamberlain all agreed that the Left had been wrong to encourage the further centralization of political and economic power in American life, while they appreciated the need to distinguish clearly between democratic and totalitarian attitudes (even if this meant that the larger conflict between capitalist and socialist institutions might henceforth be neglected), while they called for the strengthening of those groups and forces in contemporary society that could remain relatively independent of governmental or bureaucratic manipulation, they were still trying to locate some point midway between collectivism and laissez faire on which to make their stand.[52] But whatever their intentions, they too—like their counterparts among the anti-Stalinists and the survivors of the Popular Front—found it difficult to avoid the rightward drift in the period following the Nazi–Soviet pact.

It was especially ironic that John Chamberlain, having welcomed liberalism's impending demise in 1932, should now be praying for the rebirth of reform in 1940. Nevertheless, together with Burnham, Dewey, Corey, and Hook, he was part of an intellectual movement that had rediscovered the virtues of decentralization, pluralism, the "democratic process," and a system of checks and balances in which the state acted as a "broker's office" for rival interest groups none of whom would ever become ascendant over the others. At this juncture, Chamberlain believed that the only way a society could survive was through the diffusion of power and the resolution of conflict. Thus long before such arguments grew fashionable in the 1950s, he was insisting that America's greatness stemmed from its willingness to rely on compromise rather than class struggle, concessions rather than victories, the bargaining table rather than the barricades, political consensus rather than ideological combat.[53]

Moreover, since the abolition of private property did not necessarily contribute either to social justice or human freedom, Chamberlain and his colleagues began to re-emphasize the importance of parliamentary methods and civil liberties, both of which now seemed to deserve priority over the elimination of poverty and unemployment. Thus they proceeded to extol the benefits of the two-party tradition, frequent elections, open discussion, and majority rule. At the same time they stressed the need to remain constantly critical of all political leaders while maximizing the opportunities for cultural variety and personal development. To implement these worthy if familiar ideals, they invested much hope in the voluntary association, praising it rather extravagantly as an indispensable component of modern democracy, the intermediate unit between self and society, "the corporate age's analogue to the individual freedom of Jeffersonian times." In their estimation, the labor unions, the professional organizations, the churches, the schools, the local clubs and national foundations could all act as a meaningful counterweight to the policies of the government, the bureaucrats, the military, and the managerial elite. Through these mechanisms, each man might preserve his sense of "uniqueness" apart from the "dull, dead uniformity" of mass society.[54]

But above all, they were convinced that the chief prerequisite for a democratic nation was a "mixed economy" in which the "socialization of industry" was limited to a "strategic minimum." Under this scheme, small businesses and giant corporations would persist indefinitely, coexisting easily with publicly owned utilities and transportation networks, experiments in regional planning such as TVA and federal agencies like the Post Office, marketing combines and consumer cooperatives, each with its own privileges and functions, each making sure that the average citizen exercised some control over the direction in which his country was headed.[55]

Yet despite the passion with which the case for pluralism was presented, none of these ideas was either imaginative or radical. Though writers like Chamberlain talked at length about enjoying the advantages both of socialism and private enterprise, though they optimistically assured their readers that a social order containing such widely different kinds of economic activity would leave "plenty of interstices in which personal freedom may flourish," what they really envisioned was a merger of welfare capitalism and village democracy, enlightened administration and grass-roots initiative, the New Deal and *Our Town*.[56] In effect, they were merely espousing theories and programs identical to those already in operation in the United States. And it was this curious blend of pragmatism and national glorification, the tendency to mistake the commonplaces of American liberalism for a new and sophisticated ideology that not only marked the deterioration of left-wing thought at the end of the decade but also prepared the way for the complacent mood of the postwar years.

If many former members of the Popular Front together with the scarred veterans of the anti-Stalinist crusade were finding Marxism inapplicable to American culture and society, if they no longer believed in the efficacy of central planning or large-scale expropriation, if they now considered it more "realistic" to celebrate the virtues of evolutionary reform and interest-group democracy, there were some who regarded even these prosaic sentiments as romantic and naïve. Faced with a record of deception and disaster in international affairs, appalled by the steady growth of collectivist institutions which threatened to silence the individual conscience through overt terror or bureaucratic rigidity, resigned to a calamitous war from which the United States could not remain aloof, this latter group of writers was drawn increasingly to a more tragic view of man's experience than either liberalism or Marxism had ever imagined.

Culturally, these attitudes often involved a renewed respect for the insights of religion. Thus where Philip Rahv and William Phillips had always tried to justify their admiration for writers like James Joyce and Marcel Proust on the ground that—whatever the politics of a given author—all great literature was inherently subversive, Lionel Trilling found himself attracted to T. S. Elliot in 1940 because of the poet's perceptive grasp of human sinfulness. According to Trilling, Eliot's work was extremely pertinent at present because it questioned the optimistic anticipation of material progress, scorned both the liberal and Marxist faith in social innovation, and recognized that economic explanations of man's behavior were obviously insufficient in a world of irrational violence and mystery.[57] Similarly, V. F. Calverton, having grown skeptical about the value of revolution and the feasibility of a socialist millennium, began to call for a new kind of literature based on principles that sounded remarkably like those of Allen Tate and Joseph Wood Krutch. Whether in fiction or reality, he brooded, "tragedy still remains . . . the most inspiring form of art" because "as sensitive human beings, we can never, under any regime, escape the tragic sense of life."[58] The flight from radicalism, in Calverton's case, was leading to the sort of Augustinian pessimism that would become increasingly stylish among ex-socialists in the next few years.

Politically, however, this journey from Mill and Marx to Tillich and Freud did not necessarily invite a withdrawal from public affairs; rather, it frequently led to a strong emphasis on instinct over ideas, organized force over rational persuasion, existential doubt over ideological certainty. These attitudes had surfaced at various points throughout the 1930s, but during the closing years of the decade—especially in the essays and books of Reinhold Niebuhr and Lewis Mumford—they tended to assume the dimensions of a full-fledged philosophy.

Niebuhr in particular had exchanged much of his Marxist rhetoric for the language of Christian neo-orthodoxy by 1939. To some extent this was a logical culmination of his earlier insistence on the perpetual need for struggle and on self-interest as a primary ingredient in social behavior. If in *Moral Man and Immoral Society* Niebuhr had criticized liberalism for relying exclusively on intelligence and the "essential goodness" of mankind to surmount all problems, he now attacked socialism for being too reasonable and utopian in its own right. In his judgment, radicals had blindly ascribed every injustice to capitalism without seeing that the eradication of economic suffering would not change human nature or banish evil from the world.[59] As a result, Niebuhr firmly rejected all doctrines that promised an improvement in man's inner condition through an alteration of his external environment. Social engagement was still necessary, but true salvation lay outside the boundaries of time and place.

Lewis Mumford was more precise about what this meant. In *Faith for Living,* a compilation of articles published in 1940, he accused both liberals and Marxists of being frighteningly innocent and impractical. By assuming that only "faulty economic and political institutions" were to blame for obstructing progress, by disregarding that side of man's personality which was intuitive and capricious, by minimizing the historical role of prejudice and emotion, by underestimating the "dark forces of the unconscious" in shaping human activity, these erstwhile reformers and revolutionaries had become the new mythologists of Western civilization.[60] But what really bothered Mumford was their "childish" trust in the perfectibility of mankind, their willful ignorance of human limitations, and their consequent inability to comprehend or deal effectively with the problem of evil. In his jaundiced opinion, "the most old-fashioned theologian, with a sense of human guilt and sin and error, was by far the better realist." Though its understanding of science and society might be technically weak, the Christian perspective at least recognized that wickedness, corruption, and tragedy were the "constant" and universal hallmarks of life on earth.[61]

At bottom, Niebuhr and Mumford were seeking to dismantle the entire structure of American social thought as it had existed from the Progressive era through the Great Depression. But in this enterprise they were motivated as much by the fear of fascism as by the apparent shallowness of the Left. The barbarism of the Third Reich confirmed their belief that the ultimate causes of man's wretchedness and deprivation had little to do with the "surface" phenomena of class relationships or political policy. To Mumford, the Nazi propensity for violence and destruction was fundamentally "irrational" and could therefore never be analyzed in traditional social or ideological terms. "It is not in Ricardo or Marx or Lenin," he observed, "but in Dante and Shakespeare and Dostoyevsky, that an understanding of the true sources of fascism are to be found. These sources are in the human soul, not in economics."[62] Thus Germany had become, in Mumford's mind, the arch-symbol of man's insatiable thirst for power and innate capacity for evil.

To meet this extraordinary challenge, both Niebuhr and Mumford began to urge certain measures—the denial of civil liberties to subversive elements within the United States, the readiness to use "any necessary amount of coercion" on "recalcitrant minorities" who refused to play by democratic rules, the acceptance of "force" as a legitimate weapon in quelling domestic and international disturbances—some of which seemed potentially as totalitarian as the Nazi menace they were supposed to combat.[63] But during this period, Niebuhr and Mumford were hardly alone. Even Sidney Hook, who later characterized the quasi-religious preoccupation with tragedy and original sin as symptomatic of a profound "failure of nerve" among intellectuals, did not hesitate in 1940 to charge the "enemies of democracy"—Left as well as Right—with "treason," nor to demand that such criminals "be swiftly dealt with" if America should survive.[64] Though these tactics were usually seen as a temporary response to an unprecedented emergency, the fact that some writers could advocate repression in the name of "freedom" was an ominous sign whose full implications became clearer when the hot war with Germany gave way to a cold war with Russia.

In the long run, however, men like Mumford were calling for something much broader (and perhaps more dangerous) than the selective suspension of the Bill of Rights for the duration of the crisis. In Mumford's opinion, neither a renovation of Marxism nor the creation of a mixed economy "with a few socialistic planks added or taken away," neither an "extension of the New Deal" nor a retreat to laissez faire would succeed in halting the Nazi juggernaut. "One cannot counter the religious faith of fascism," he asserted, "unless one possesses a faith equally strong, equally capable of fostering devotion and loyalty, and commanding sacrifice."[65] For his part, Mumford felt that the American people could not triumph over Germany until they had developed their own version of nationalism based on the mystical values of the land, the region, the local community, and the family. Only then would their sense of common purpose be strong and enduring enough to withstand the evil in the world and in themselves.

Mumford's sentimental embrace of the nation's *spirit,* as distinct from his pessimism about its institutions, was only the most extreme example of how chastened the intellectual community had grown in the late 1930s and early 1940s. The disaffection with Russia and the dismay at the Nazi–Soviet pact, the dread of totalitarianism and the attack on collectivist ideals, the suspicion of social revolution and the sanctification of the American Way, all suggested that writers—whether liberal or radical, ex-Communist or anti-Stalinist—were at last becoming reconciled to and thoroughly integrated with their native land. What really mattered here was not so much the content of their beliefs as their implicit state of mind. In their willingness to subordinate the larger concerns of literature and ideology to the immediate task of supporting the allied war effort, in their tendency to invest their trust in charismatic leaders like Roosevelt and Churchill rather than in economic programs and political strategies, in their eagerness to adopt the role of official spokesmen for a national cause, many writers were confusing rational argument with patriotic exhortation, the ideals of democracy with the dogmas of Americanism.[66]

Ironically, this stance was entirely consistent with their longing since the turn of the century to influence policy and affect the course of history. Because most intellectuals disliked the sense of being isolated and socially irrelevant, they had always been fatally attracted to the trappings of power —either as advisers to the New Freedom or to the New Deal, as radical emissaries to the working class on behalf of the Socialist or Communist parties, or simply as independent artists and critics with a special mission to preside over America's cultural rebirth. But when the workers failed to revolt against capitalism and the populace refused to be saved from the mass media, it was neither difficult nor surprising for writers ultimately to identify with the power and destiny of the nation as a whole. Thus after 1939 much of the intellectual community saw the United States—whatever its faults—as the final repository for their hopes and ambitions. In essence, they were transferring their loyalties from one set of symbols to another: from socialism to democracy, from economic justice to political pluralism, from collective action to personal mobility, from the Internationale to the American Dream.

Yet if their basic motivations remained the same, their position in the country was about to change. By committing themselves to America, they were laying the foundations for their own postwar emergence as a privileged elite, the tough-minded tacticians of anti-Communist diplomacy, the indispensable experts in a managerial society, no longer marginal to the social system but increasingly the arbiters of its programs, values, and style of life.

Henceforth, many members of the intelligentsia would function neither as bohemian rebels nor as the voice of the people but rather as the well-adjusted servants of the modern state.

4. The Spirit of Pearl Harbor

Despite the animosity of most American intellectuals toward Stalin following his rapprochement with the Third Reich, there were scattered signs that the Soviet Union was not considered completely beyond redemption. With prophetic insight, the New Republic conceded that, although Russia's moral stature had been severely compromised, its prestige might be somewhat restored if the present European struggle expanded into a "world war in which the Soviet peoples themselves became victims of armed conquest."[67] At the same time, many Communists throughout this period longed to escape from the political wilderness to which they were consigned by the necessity of having to defend the Kremlin's erratic diplomacy. Thus when the Germans launched their invasion of Russia along a thousand-mile front in June 1941, both these impulses came into play.

Overnight the Communists were compelled to liquidate all the organizations and programs they had laboriously constructed during the past two years. Saddled with an imposing array of slogans which regularly denounced the European conflict as "imperialist" and exhorted the United States to remain aloof, the party nimbly adapted to the altered circumstances with a brand new "orientation." To keep pace with events, Corliss Lamont exclaimed in the New Masses, the Soviet Union needed mobile armies and her American supporters needed "mobile minds."[68] Accordingly, the Communists stopped criticizing Roosevelt's domestic and foreign policies, endorsed his lend-lease and rearmament measures, encouraged the development of hemispheric solidarity (even if this meant that Latin America must bow to the economic hegemony of the United States), opposed any efforts to appease Japan, ceased equating Nazi brutality with British colonialism, and unreservedly praised every anti-fascist novel or film. In their journals and newspapers, the war was now interpreted as a simple battle between good and evil in which each nation and class had a vital stake.[69] Essentially, the party demanded that all controversy about the nature of Stalinism or the character of the postwar world be suspended. "It is far too early to worry about the kind of peace we will have when the war is won," the New Masses counseled. "It is never too soon, however, to emphasize winning the war. That is really the first and foremost issue. Considerations of the far future will only tend to divide the anti-fascist forces. Considerations of present tasks will unite them."[70] By the fall of 1941, with Russian armies reeling under the Nazi blitzkrieg, the Communists were reduced to hysterical cries for American intervention, the opening of a second front in Western Europe, and "action" at all costs. Everything else had to wait.

If the military advantages of this abrupt conversion to the allied cause seemed momentarily unclear, the psychological rewards were obviously immense. The resurgence of anti-fascist sentiment among the Communists permitted them once again to experience the "flush of patriotism" and to enjoy the sense of being in fundamental harmony with their fellow Americans.[71] Indeed, the war years would find the party even less concerned with political or ideological questions than during their most conciliatory days in the Popular Front.

But ultimately, the Communists were able to feel at home in the United States because many Americans agreed with their estimate of what the war required. This was especially true for the intelligentsia. If some anti-Stalinists like Dwight Macdonald continued to resist the arguments for intervention on Trotskyite and later pacifist grounds, the *Nation* and the *New Republic* echoed the attitude of most writers when they urged the Roosevelt Administration to aid the Soviet Union as well as Britain (because any enemy of Hitler was a friend of the United States), undertake a massive mobilization of the economy for war (relying on the instrument of executive order if necessary), and prepare the American people to join the battle against the Axis. The traditional fear of subordinating democratic institutions and values to the exigencies of military production, as well as the lingering memories of 1917, had all faded before the greater horror of a fascist triumph. In the *New Republic*'s opinion, the reasons for going to war were neither economic nor moral. The United States must intervene, the editors argued, not to protect its investments or to liberate the world from tyranny but simply to save its way of life from extinction. And in the interest of self-defense and national survival, "our determination should be canalized less to speech, and more to action." From now on, the journal proclaimed, the central problems would be "technical and practical. . . . "[72] The time for thought and debate had passed.

In the end, most of the intellectual community seemed ready to postpone all political activity and cultural criticism until Nazi Germany and imperial Japan were destroyed. The surprise raid on Pearl Harbor only intensified their commitment to the primary business of winning the war. Indeed, liberals and Communists alike responded to the Japanese attack with marked relief—as though America's entrance into combat would cleanse the atmosphere of all the ideological disputes and social disappointments that had characterized the waning years of the depression. Pearl Harbor, the *Nation* declared, "has made America one. Today we love each other and our country. We feel a happy sense of union swelling in our hearts. . . . "[73] And moved by this lyrical feeling of national solidarity, the American intellectual graduated from the crises of the 1930s into the far greater holocaust of World War II and its aftermath.

EPILOGUE

Despite the enormous suffering and insecurity caused by the depression, the 1930s was a time of extraordinary ferment and hope not only for the intellectual community but for the entire American people. Not since the Civil War had the United States been confronted with as serious a political and social crisis nor as great an opportunity for altering the country's institutional arrangements and class relationships. Indeed while writers had been searching since the days of Reconstruction for an effective social theory and value system which might provide the technical resources and moral vision to transform American life, the need for such an alternative ideology appeared even more dramatic during the 1930s when the nation's economic foundations had crumbled and the familiar assumptions of democratic capitalism seemed no longer relevant to the increasingly corporate structure of the modern world. Though there were numerous efforts in the Progressive era and the 1920s to transcend the liberal perspective and to explore the possibilities of a cultural revolution, the startling collapse of America's economic machinery after 1929, the sense of a society rapidly dissolving into its component parts, and the rising threat of fascism overseas, all demanded new solutions in politics, philosophy, and art beyond anything earlier generations had proposed.

Throughout the early and mid-1930s, therefore, intellectuals wrestled with a series of problems arising not merely from the depression itself but from the very nature of American life as it had developed over the past half century. The concept of a competitive society composed of separate in-

dividuals whose ties to one another revolved around the impersonal pressures of the market place was already being challenged during the Progressive era, but at no point was there such a distaste for this idea as in the
opening years of the depression. Disturbed not only by the specter of
poverty and joblessness but also by the pervasive atmosphere of breakdown,
dislocation, and chaos for which capitalism seemed ultimately to blame,
many writers tried to imagine a different kind of social organization based
on the principles of planning and production-for-use. In effect, they were
making a series of authentically radical suggestions: that the nationalization
of America's agricultural and industrial plant could finally eradicate the
historic crime of want amid plenty, that the liberal respect for free intelligence and individual fulfillment could be combined with the Marxist emphasis on class consciousness and collective action, that the power of the
machine could be harnessed to truly human ends, that a socialist movement
could enjoy mass support and still remain faithful to revolutionary goals.
In each of these instances the intelligentsia wanted not only to stimulate
recovery and to restore stability but also to liberate the American people
from the bondage of economic anxiety—to shift their attention from
material to moral and existential concerns.

Hence it was not surprising that many writers regarded the crisis of
capitalism as only a reflection of some larger spiritual and psychological
affliction. In their view, the depression exposed for all time the fundamental
unreality of the American Dream— especially the fact that the quality of
human life in a system dedicated to private profit offered people no feeling
of community or common vision. For this reason the criticisms they leveled
and the programs they recommended were as much cultural as political or
economic. What they hoped for was not only a new party but also a new
relationship between the intellectual and society, not only a radical ideology
but also radical works of art—in literature, on stage, and in films—which
would change the way men saw their world, not only the construction of
an American-style socialism but also the expansion of opportunities for
self-expression within a cooperative enterprise, not only a change in the
country's institutions but also a transformation of personal identity. In
essence, they wished to build a new society as a first step in the creation of
a new man.

These were large and noble aspirations. Given the course of American
history in the twentieth century, the ideas advanced by intellectuals during
the 1930s were genuinely innovative without being outrageously impractical. Yet within the special context of the depression, they did contain
implications the exact opposite from those most writers had intended.

Ironically, the very existence of such a monumental crisis made the 1930s an unpropitious time for radical change. In the face of massive confusion and uncertainty, the far-off benefits of a socialist commonwealth seemed less compelling than immediate improvements in one's daily life. Moreover, many writers exaggerated the revolutionary inclinations of the American people—particularly the working class—while underrating the resilience and durability of capitalism. Thus at the very moment they were waiting —in some cases apocalyptically—for the masses to revolt, the stock-market crash was ushering in a period which witnessed not the death of the old world but the rejuvenation of liberal reform.

Furthermore, as the despair of the Hoover years was supplanted by the relative optimism of the New Deal, and as the concentration on domestic affairs faded before the peril of fascism and war, the conservative impulses of the intelligentsia grew more pronounced. Now the values associated with collectivism took on a less radical cast. The preoccupation with the anarchy of the market place gave way to a compulsive urge for order and security. The ideal of planning tended increasingly to stand for administrative exper-tise and managerial efficiency in the interest not of social revolution but of social control. Under the inhibiting influence of the Popular Front, the search for community slowly became a celebration of conformity, the long-ing to be different became a hunger to fit in, the feeling of alienation became an excuse for adjustment, and the demand for a conflict of classes became an appeal for national unity.

At the same time, the notion of fashioning a "proletarian" culture as an alternative to the outlook and life-style of the middle class seemed more and more chimerical as long as the surrounding institutions remained unaltered. Meanwhile, the finest documentaries, novels, plays, and films of the 1930s were often contemplative rather than militant, comic rather than angry, surrealistic rather than factual, nostalgic rather than millennial, introspec-tive rather than activist.

Finally, the intellectual's century-long missionary zeal to serve society and shape the course of history led him gradually to suspend his critical faculties. Inexorably, he moved from rebellion to "responsibility," from dissent to affirmation, from an interest in the avant-garde to a fascination with the mass media, from a concern for ideology to an obsession with symbols and myths, from an unlimited investigation of social issues to a ritual glorification of America. In the process, the necessary and creative tension between thought and action, art and revolution, culture and civiliza-tion, men and machines, morality and politics, self and society was irrevoca-bly shattered. Thus by the close of the decade, as the country forgot the depression and girded for war, as writers began to abandon completely their faith in the collectivist ideal, as they emphasized instead the need for personal survival in an absurd and tragic world, the pressure of external events coincided with an internal sense of defeat to bring an end to the radical dreams of the 1930s.

If time ran out on those intellectuals who had grown up during the Progressive era, the 1920s, and the Great Depression, if they had lost the energy and imagination to commit themselves further to the continuing struggle for radical change, they left behind an awesome legacy of unsolved social, cultural, and moral dilemmas which postwar America would some- day have to confront. Long after the crises of depression and war had passed, the question of how to preserve a sense of personal freedom and independence in a technological society still required an answer. Long after the New Deal had introduced the mixed economy and the welfare state to the nation, the problem of how to eliminate hunger and poverty still en- dured. Long after the concept of proletarian literature was discarded, the consequences of mass culture and the proper place of the intellectual in American life was still largely unclear. Long after the most savage forms of totalitarianism in Nazi Germany and Stalinist Russia had disappeared, the menace of bureaucratic coercion and centralized power still disturbed an ostensibly democratic society whose citizens could not halt the decay of their cities, the pollution of their environment, the misuse of their resources, the misallocation of their priorities, or the imperial ambitions of their government. And long after the more obsolete features of a competitive economy had vanished, the feeling of private isolation, the lack of shared values and common ideals, the absence of human responsibility for other classes and other races still challenged those who wished to transform the social order.

The fundamental tragedy of the 1930s was not that men raised the wrong issues or failed to supply satisfactory answers but that the political and psychic wounds of the decade's final years virtually paralyzed an entire generation of intellectuals. Though their capacity for artistic experimenta- tion remained undiminished, they were as a result of these experiences unable (and perhaps unwilling) to break with political and doctrinal rigidity which permeated America following World War II. Thus it seemed possible that only when a new generation of writers emerged who were unscarred by the disappointments and disasters of the late 1930s could the search for an alternative culture and society be resumed and the promise of the decade be redeemed.

NOTES

I. Prologue—Progressivism and the 1920s

1. The best elucidation of this strain in Progressivism is Richard Hofstadter's *The Age of Reform* (New York, 1955).
2. Robert Wiebe, *The Search for Order, 1877–1920* (New York, 1967). See also Gabriel Kolko, *The Triumph of Conservatism* (Glencoe, Illinois, 1963).
3. For a detailed discussion of the new trends in philosophy, history, social science, and the law, see Morton White, *Social Thought in America* (New York, 1949).
4. Herbert Croly, *The Promise of American Life* (New York, 1909), 23.
5. *Ibid.,* 22.
6. *Ibid.,* 209.
7. *Ibid.,* 62.
8. *Ibid.,* 414.
9. Van Wyck Brooks, "America's Coming-of-Age," in Claire Sprague, ed., *Van Wyck Brooks: The Early Years* (New York, 1968), 83.
10. *Ibid.,* 91.
11. *Ibid.,* 128.
12. Van Wyck Brooks, "Toward a National Culture," in Sprague, *loc. cit.,* 185.
13. *Ibid.,* 189.
14. Brooks, "America's Coming-Of-Age," in Sprague, *loc. cit.,* 95.
15. *Ibid.,* 120.
16. Christopher Lasch, *The New Radicalism in America, 1889–1963* (New York, 1965), 163.
17. Brooks, "America's Coming-Of-Age," in Sprague, *loc. cit.,* 132.
18. T. S. Matthews, "Review of *All Quiet on the Western Front,*" *New Republic,* LIX (June 19, 1929), 130.
19. For an extended analysis of both the economic and social structure of the 1920s, see George Soule, *Prosperity Decade* (New York, 1947).
20. See James Weinstein, *The Decline of Socialism in America, 1912–1925* (New York, 1967).
21. V. F. Calverton, "The American Scene," *Modern Quarterly,* V (November 1928–February 1929), 1.

22. For a representative example of this kind of critique, see A. D. Emmart (pseud., Richel North), "The Limitations of American Magazines," *Modern Quarterly,* I (March 1923), 2–12.

23. Michael Gold, "Hemingway—White Collar Poet," *New Masses,* III (March 1928), 21.

24. Michael Gold, "John Reed and the Real Thing," *New Masses,* III (November 1927), 7.

25. "An Economic Program," *New Republic,* LIX (July 10, 1929), 191–92.

26. *Ibid.,* 193.

27. "Agitation Through Action," *New Republic,* LVI (September 12, 1928), 84–86.

28. "Hoover: Conservative," *New Republic,* LVI (October 31, 1928), 287–89.

29. "Progressives and Socialists," *New Republic,* LVI (November 7, 1928), 316.

30. "This Week," *New Republic,* LVI (November 14, 1928), 336.

31. George Soule, "Hoover's Task at Home," *New Republic,* LVIII (February 27, 1929), 34–36.

32. *Ibid.,* 35.

33. "Unemployment and National Planning," *New Republic,* LVII (December 5, 1928), 56.

34. "Liberal Business and Politics," *New Republic,* LVI (November 14, 1928), 340.

35. "Trade Unions as Social Technique," *New Republic,* LVIII (April 10, 1929), 214.

36. *Ibid.,* 215. For an eloquent summary of liberal attitudes in the 1920s, see Frederic Howe, *The Confessions of a Reformer* (New York, 1925).

37. Van Wyck Brooks, "Our Awakeners," in Sprague, *loc. cit.,* 210.

38. Waldo Frank, "The Treason of the Intellectuals," *Modern Quarterly,* V (Spring 1929), 161–64.

39. Lewis Mumford, "The City," in Harold Stearns, ed., *Civilization in the United States* (New York, 1922), 9–10.

40. Harold Stearns, "The Intellectual Life," in Stearns, *loc. cit.,* 145.

41. *Ibid.,* 136. Italics his.

42. Robert and Helen Lynd, *Middletown* (New York, 1929), 498.

43. *Ibid.,* 500.

44. Stuart Chase, "Skilled Work and No Work," *New Republic,* LVIII (March 20, 1929), 121.

45. *Ibid.,* 123.

46. *Ibid.,* 122.

47. Stuart Chase, "Leaning Towers," *New Republic,* LVIII (March 27, 1929), 171.

48. Babette Deutsch, "The Tradition of Poetry," *New Republic,* LX (August 21, 1929), 12–15.

49. Joseph Wood Krutch, *The Modern Temper* (New York, 1956, c. 1929), 164. Hereafter a publication date given in this fashion means "copyright 1929," but that the pagination and quotations are from the 1956 edition.

50. *Ibid.,* 167–68.

51. *Ibid.,* 168–69.

52. Lewis Mumford, "Toward Civilization?" *New Republic,* LXIII (May 28, 1930), 50.

53. Lewis Mumford, "The Voice of Despair," *New Republic,* LIX (May 22, 1929), 36–38.

54. John Dewey, "Middletown: A House Divided Against Itself," *New Republic,* LVIII (April 24, 1929), 271. See also John Dewey, " 'America' By Formula," *New Republic,* LX (September 18, 1929), 119.

55. Charles Beard, ed., *Whither Mankind* (New York, 1928), 403–4.

56. William Troy, "Literature or History," *New Republic,* LIX (June 19, 1929), 132. Italics his.

57. "Comment," *Hound and Horn,* III (October–December 1929), 5.

58. Gilbert Seldes, "Letter on Russian and American Movies," *New Republic,* LIX (August 7, 1929), 317.

59. Kenneth Fearing, "Hoboken Blues," *New Masses,* III (April 1928), 27.

60. Alfred Kazin, *On Native Grounds* (New York, 1956, c. 1942), 253.
61. Malcolm Cowley, *Exile's Return* (New York, Viking Press edition, 1951), 149.
62. Frederick Hoffman, *The Twenties* (New York, 1965, c. 1955), 434–35.
63. For a detailed elaboration of these ideas, see William Wasserstrom, *The Time of the Dial* (Syracuse, New York, 1963).
64. Frank, "The Treason of the Intellectuals," *loc. cit.*, 166.
65. Edmund Wilson, "Dostoyevsky Abroad," *New Republic*, LVII (January 30, 1929), 302.
66. Edmund Wilson, "T. S. Eliot and the Church of England," *New Republic*, LVIII (April 24, 1929), 283.
67. Matthew Josephson, *Portrait of the Artist as American* (New York, 1930), xviii.
68. *Ibid.*, 292–93.
69. *Ibid.*, 306–7.
70. For an excellent description of the cultural mood at the close of the decade, see Matthew Josephson, *Infidel in the Temple* (New York, 1967), 4–16.
71. Edmund Wilson, "John Jay Chapman," *New Republic*, LIX (May 22, 1929), 29, 31–32.
72. *Ibid.*, 30–31.
73. Cowley, *Exile's Return*, 221.

II. Political and Economic Thought, 1929–1935

1. "Wall Street's Crisis," *Nation*, CXXIX (November 6, 1929), 511.
2. "After the Whirlwind," *Nation*, CXXIX (November 27, 1929), 614.
3. "This Week," *New Republic*, LX (October 30, 1929), 283.
4. "Hoover's First Year," *New Republic*, LXII (March 5, 1930), 58–59.
5. Matthew Josephson, *Infidel in the Temple* (New York, 1967), 50. The circulation of *New Republic* during these years was usually put at 35,000.
6. "Will Prosperity Return?" *New Republic*, LXIII (May 21, 1930), 4–5; George Soule, "Gold and the Industrial Depression," *New Republic*, LXIV (November 12, 1930), 343.
7. "Bankrupt Business Leadership," *New Republic*, LXV (November 19, 1930), 4–5; "A Progressive Program," *Nation*, CXXXI (December 3, 1930), 598. A year later, they were still calling for the same reforms. See "What Congress Might Do," *New Republic*, LXIX (December 16, 1931), 120–22.
8. "Hoover Plays His Part," *New Republic*, LXI (December 11, 1929), 56.
9. *Ibid.*, 56.
10. "The Need for a New Party," *New Republic*, LXV (January 7, 1931), 204–5.
11. "A Party for the People," *Nation*, CXXXII (January 28, 1931), 88.
12. "Just Before the Battle," *New Republic*, LXIV (November 5, 1930), 311.
13. John Dewey, "Who Might Make a New Party," *New Republic*, LXVI (April 1, 1931), 177–78.
14. *Ibid.*, 178–79.
15. John Dewey, "Policies for a New Party," *New Republic*, LXVI (April 8, 1931), 202.
16. *Ibid.*, 203.
17. James Rorty, "Revolution Made Respectable," *New Republic*, LXVI (April 29, 1931), 308.
18. Michael Gold, "The Intellectual Road to Fascism," *New Masses*, VII (November 1931), 10.
19. Michael Gold, "Notes of the Month," *New Masses*, V (April 1930), 3.
20. Lincoln Steffens, "Bankrupt Liberalism," *New Republic*, LXX (February 17, 1932), 15.
21. John Chamberlain, *Farewell to Reform* (New York, 1932), 310.
22. *Ibid.*, 282.
23. *Ibid.*, 220.
24. *Ibid.*, 315–16.
25. Lincoln Steffens, *The Autobiography of Lincoln Steffens* (New York, 1931), 47, 250.

26. *Ibid.*, 165.
27. *Ibid.*, 567.
28. *Ibid.*, 238, 417–18.
29. *Ibid.*, 837.
30. Edmund Wilson, "An Appeal to Progressives," *New Republic,* LXV (January 14, 1931), 235.
31. *Ibid.*, 236.
32. *Ibid.*, 237.
33. *Ibid.*, 238.
34. *Ibid.*, 238.
35. George Soule, "Hard-Boiled Radicalism," *New Republic,* LXV (January 21, 1931), 261.
36. *Ibid.*, 263.
37. George Soule, "What We Hope For," *New Republic,* LXIX (February 10, 1932), 337.
38. Soule, "Hard-Boiled Radicalism," *loc. cit.*, 262.
39. *Ibid.*, 264.
40. Soule, "What We Hope For," *loc. cit.*, 337.
41. Stuart Chase, "The Engineer as Poet," *New Republic,* LXVII (May 20, 1931), 24.
42. Soule, "Hard-Boiled Radicalism," *loc. cit.*, 265.
43. For an excellent discussion of changing American attitudes toward Russia, see Peter Filene, *Americans and the Soviet Experiment, 1917–1933* (Cambridge, Massachusetts, 1967).
44. See "The Last War—and the Next," *New Masses,* VII (August 1931), 3–4; "Fourteen Years," *New Masses,* VII (November 1931), 3–5; "Toward a Classless Society," *New Masses,* VIII (November 1932), 3–4; and Joshua Kunitz, "The Second Five-Year Plan," *New Republic,* LXXVII (January 17, 1934), 275–77.
45. See Frank Warren, *Liberals and Communism* (Bloomington, Indiana, 1966), 86.
46. *Ibid.*, 87.
47. Frederick Schuman, "The Soviets," *New Republic,* LXIII (May 28, 1930), 51.
48. Louis Fischer, "Will the Five-Year Plan Succeed?" *Nation,* CXXXII (February 4, 1931), 119–20.
49. John Dewey, "Impressions of Soviet Russia—III," *New Republic,* LVII (November 28, 1928), 38.
50. *Ibid.*, 40.
51. John Dewey, "Impressions of Soviet Russia—I," *New Republic,* LVII (November 14, 1928), 344; John Dewey, "Surpassing America," *New Republic,* LXVI (April 15, 1931), 242.
52. John Dewey, "Impressions of Soviet Russia—IV," *New Republic,* LVII (December 5, 1928), 64–67.
53. John Dewey, "Impressions of Soviet Russia—VI," *New Republic* LVII (December 19, 1928), 136.
54. *Ibid.*, 135.
55. Max Eastman, "Discrimination About Russia," *Modern Quarterly,* VIII (September 1934), 479.
56. Edmund Wilson, *Travels in Two Democracies* (New York, 1936), 245.
57. *Ibid.*, 226.
58. Adolph Berle and Gardiner Means, *The Modern Corporation and Private Property* (New York, 1932), 1–9.
59. *Ibid.*, 125.
60. *Ibid.*, 356.
61. George Soule, *A Planned Society* (New York, 1932), 20, 39–57, 182; Stuart Chase, *A New Deal* (New York, 1932), 21, 187.

62. Soule, *A Planned Society*, 129, 232–34; Chase, *A New Deal*, 1, 23, 78, 96.
63. Soule, *A Planned Society*, 161, 171–72, 203, 277; Chase, *A New Deal*, 47–59, 153–54, 185.
64. Soule, *A Planned Society*, 87–91.
65. Chase, *A New Deal*, 213, 219.
66. Soule, *A Planned Society*, 111–19, 152; Chase, *A New Deal*, 152, 161, 173, 178–79, 191.
67. Soule, *A Planned Society*, 128–33.
68. *Ibid.*, 283.
69. Alfred Bingham, "Looking Forward," *Common Sense*, I (March 30, 1933), 4.
70. *Ibid.*, 5.
71. *Ibid.*, 3–4.
72. See Josephson, *Infidel in the Temple*, 144, 155, 173.
73. Edmund Wilson, "Foster and Fish," *New Republic*, LXV (December 14, 1930), 162.
74. *Culture and The Crisis* (League of Professional Groups for Foster and Ford, New York, 1932). Other signers included Em Jo Basshe, Slater Brown, Kyle Crichton, Countee Cullen, Horace Gregory, Sidney Howard, Orrick Johns, Alfred Kreymborg, Louis Lozowick, Felix Morrow, Samuel Ornitz, Isidor Schneider, Edwin Seaver, and Ella Winter.
75. George Soule, "William Z. Foster," *New Republic*, LXXII (October 5, 1932), 199.
76. "Roosevelt's Revolution," *New Republic*, LXXII (November 9, 1932), 340.
77. "Roosevelt Wins!" *Nation*, CXXXV (July 13, 1932), 22; "How Shall We Vote?" *New Republic*, LXXII (August 17, 1932), 5; "Voting for a Party," *New Republic*, LXXII (October 26, 1932), 274.
78. "This Week," *New Republic*, LXXIII (November 16, 1932), 1.
79. "Mr. Roosevelt Must Lead," *Nation*, CXXXVI (February 8, 1933), 137.
80. *Ibid.;* "Mr. Roosevelt's Task," *New Republic*, LXXIV (March 8, 1933), 89; "Twenty-One Demands on President Roosevelt," *Common Sense*, I (March 16, 1933), 3–5.
81. "Mr. Roosevelt's Task," *loc. cit.*, 88–89.
82. For a more detailed account of the ideological and class differences between Progressivism and the New Deal, see Otis Graham, *An Encore for Reform* (New York, 1967).
83. See Arthur Ekirch, *Ideologies and Utopias: The Impact of the New Deal on American Thought* (Chicago, 1969), 94, 101.
84. See William Leuchtenburg, *Franklin D. Roosevelt and the New Deal* (New York, 1963), 35, 84; also Ekirch, *Ideologies and Utopias*, 100.
85. Henry Wallace, *New Frontiers* (New York, 1934), 200.
86. *Ibid.*, 21.
87. *Ibid.*, 47.
88. *Ibid.*, 283–84.
89. *Ibid.*, 254.
90. *Ibid.*, 274.
91. Leuchtenburg, *Franklin D. Roosevelt and the New Deal*, 61.
92. "Can Controlled Capitalism Save Us?" *Nation*, CXXVI (June 7, 1933), 629–30; "Lenin's Proposal—and Roosevelt's," *New Republic*, LXXV (May 17, 1933), 4; "The Industrial Recovery Bill," *New Republic*, LXXV (May 31, 1933), 58; "Capitalism Enters the Operating Room," *New Republic*, LXXV (July 12, 1933), 221–22; "News Behind the News," *Common Sense*, I (June 8, 1933), 4.
93. George Soule, "Roosevelt Confronts Capitalism," *New Republic*, LXXVI (October 18, 1933), 270–71. See also "Public Works to the Rescue," *New Republic*, LXXVI (September 6, 1933), 87–89.
94. "Mr. Roosevelt—So Far," *Nation*, CXXXVI (June 28, 1933), 711–12.
95. "The Crisis of the N.R.A.," *New Republic*, LXXVI (November 8, 1933), 350.

96. "Roosevelt in Review," *Nation*, CXXXVII (December 20, 1933), 696.
97. Lewis Mumford, "Pragmatism Gone Bankrupt," *New Republic*, LXXX (October 3, 1934), 223. For other examples of this kind of criticism, see "This Week," *New Republic*, LXXIV (May 10, 1933), 347; T.R.B., "Washington Notes," *New Republic*, LXXIX (June 20, 1934), 153–54; and Henry Pratt Fairchild, "A Sociologist Views the New Deal," *Social Frontier*, I (October 1934), 15–18.
98. James Burnham, "Comment," *Symposium*, IV (July 1933), 277. See also C. Hartley Grattan. "What Is Liberalism?" *Common Sense*, II (September 1933), 15–17.
99. For a typical Communist appraisal of the New Deal, see David Ramsey, "A New Deal in Trusts," *New Masses*, X (January 9, 1934), 17–18.
100. Earl Browder, "What Is Communism: I?" *New Masses*, XV (May 7, 1935), 9–10.
101. See "The 'Security' Bill," *New Masses*, XV (April 30, 1935), 8; and "Two Kinds of Social Security," *New Masses*, XVI (July 9, 1935), 7.
102. See "Is Roosevelt Slipping?" *New Republic*, LXXXIV (August 14, 1935), 6; "This Week," *New Republic*, LXXXIV (September 4, 1935), 87; and "The President Completes the Record," *Nation*, CXLI (September 18, 1935), 313.
103. Bruce Bliven, "A Century of Treadmill" and "New England is Waiting," *New Republic*, LXXVII (November 15 and December 20, 1933), 12, 159.
104. Roger Baldwin, "The Coming Struggle for Liberty." *Common Sense*, IV (January 1935), 7.
105. C. Hartley Grattan, "The Problem of Stabilization," *New Republic*, LXXI (June 15, 1932), 133.
106. V. F. Calverton, "The Farmer Cocks His Rifle," *Modern Quarterly*, VII (January 1934), 727–31; V. F. Calverton, "Father Coughlin—The Silver Messiah," *Modern Quarterly*, IX (March 1935), 8–11.
107. Malcolm Cowley, "The Art of Insurrection," *New Republic*, LXXIV (April 12, 1933), 250. For another analysis of the persistence of bourgeois attitudes, see "What Makes Men Act," *Common Sense*, IV (March 1935), 2–3.
108. George Soule, *The Coming American Revolution* (New York, 1934), 8–10.
109. *Ibid.*, 12–21, 66–71.
110. *Ibid.*, 146–47, 298–99.
111. *Ibid.*, 275–76.
112. *Ibid.*, 69, 207.
113. *Ibid.*, 198–200.
114. *Ibid.*, 302.
115. *Ibid.*, 283–85.
116. Lewis Corey, *The Crisis of the Middle Class* (New York, 1935), 139–47.
117. *Ibid.*, 260.
118. *Ibid.*, 223–27.
119. *Ibid.*, 249–55.
120. *Ibid.*, 170.
121. *Ibid.*, 15.
122. *Ibid.*, 243.
123. *Ibid.*, 353.
124. The quotations are from, respectively, "Unity on the Left," *Common Sense*, IV (February 1935), 2; and V. F. Calverton, "Will Fascism Come to America?" *Modern Quarterly*, VIII (September 1934), 478. For other examples of these ideas, see "For a Farmer-Labor Party," *Common Sense* II (August 1933), 3; John Dewey, "The Imperative Need for a New Radical Party," *Common Sense*, II (September 1933), 6–7; "The L.I.P.A. and the Chicago Conference," *Common Sense*, II (September 1933), 27–28; "Tear Gas and Rainbows," *Common Sense*, III (August 1934), 3; "Crucial Strategy," *Common Sense*,

IV (September 1935), 2–3; "Will It Happen Here?" *Common Sense,* V (July 1936), 4; "In Defense of the Democratic Tradition," *Modern Quarterly,* VII (March 1933), 69–70; Benjamin Gitlow, "A Labor Party for America," *Modern Quarterly,* VII (September, 1933), 492–95; V. F. Calverton, "The Pulse of Modernity," *Modern Quarterly,* VII (October 1933), 518; V. F. Calverton, "The Pulse of Modernity," *Modern Quarterly,* VII (December 1933), 645–47; Ludwig Lore, "The Death of Social Democracy," *Modern Quarterly,* VII (December 1933), 687; V. F. Calverton, "An Editorial," *Modern Quarterly,* VII (January 1934), 707; Herbert Solow, "After Madison Square Garden," *Modern Quarterly,* VIII (April 1934), 177–82; V. F. Calverton, "The Pulse of Modernity," *Modern Quarterly,* VIII (May 1934), 197; V. F. Calverton, "Socialism Leans Left," *Modern Quarterly,* VIII (January 1935), 647–49; Charles Beard, "The Promise of American Life," *New Republic,* LXXXI (February 6, 1935), 351–52; "Toward a New Party," *New Republic,* LXXXIII (May 22, 1935), 33–34; and "A New Party—The Program," *New Republic,* LXXXIII (May 29, 1935), 60–61.

125. "An Opportunity for Action," *Common Sense,* II (September 1933), 3.

III. The Search for Community

1. For a sensitive description of this apocalyptic mood, see Saul Maloff, "The Mythic Thirties," *Texas Quarterly,* XI (Winter 1968), 109–118.
2. Edmund Wilson, "Marxist History," *New Republic,* LXXII (October 12, 1932), 226–28.
3. Stuart Chase, *A New Deal* (New York, 1932), 156, 164.
4. *Ibid.,* 252.
5. James Rorty, "The Great Wall Facing America," *Symposium,* III (October 1932), 455.
6. Sherwood Anderson, "Danville, Virginia," *New Republic,* LXV (January 21, 1931), 268.
7. Henry Wallace, *New Frontiers* (New York, 1934), 275; Chase, *A New Deal,* 163; George Soule, *A Planned Society* (New York, 1932), 283.
8. Rorty, "The Great Wall Facing America," *loc. cit.,* 454–75.
9. Waldo Frank, "Socialism and Value," *Modern Quarterly,* V (Winter 1929–1930), 448–50; Waldo Frank, "Marx and David Markand," *New Republic,* LXXXI (November 21, 1934), 48.
10. Samuel Schmalhausen, "Psychoanalysis and Communism," *Modern Quarterly,* VI (Summer 1932), 63–69; Samuel Schmalhausen, "Psychological Portrait of Modern Civilization," *Modern Quarterly,* VI (Autumn 1932), 85–95.
11. Lionel Trilling, "D. H. Lawrence: A Neglected Aspect," *Symposium,* I (July 1930), 363–64.
12. Waldo Frank, "Pilgrimage to Mexico," *New Republic,* I (July 1, 1931), 183–84.
13. Stuart Chase, "Men Without Machines—I, II, and V," *New Republic,* LXVII (June 17, June 24, and July 15, 1931), 114–17, 143–44, 232–33.
14. Waldo Frank, "How I Came to Communism," *New Masses,* VIII (September 1932), 7.
15. Howard Odum, "Of New Social Frontiers in Contemporary Society," *Social Frontier,* VI (October 1939), 16.
16. Herbert Agar, "Culture Versus Colonialism in America," *Southern Review,* I (July 1935), 1–19.
17. Lewis Mumford, "Survey and Plan as Communal Education," *Social Frontier,* IV (January 1938), 110.
18. Lyle Lanier, "A Critique of the Philosophy of Progress," *I'll Take My Stand* (New York, 1962, c. 1930), 148–50.
19. Donald Davidson, "A Mirror for Artists," *I'll Take My Stand, loc. cit.,* 34.
20. Lanier, "A Critique of the Philosophy of Progress," *loc. cit.,* 131, 145–46; Stark Young, "Not in Memorium, But in Defense," *I'll Take My Stand, loc. cit.,* 350.
21. Edmund Wilson, "Tennessee Agrarians," *New Republic,* LXVII (July 29, 1931), 281.

22. Odum, "Of New Social Frontiers in Contempory Society," *loc. cit.*, 16.

23. Lewis Mumford, *Technics and Civilization* (New York, 1934), 12–13, 20, 197.

24. *Ibid.*, 34, 46–47, 49–51, 132–33.

25. *Ibid.*, 25.

26. *Ibid.*, 41–42, 92.

27. *Ibid.*, 112, 123, 139, 142–50.

28. *Ibid.*, 104, 153–56, 162, 168, 176, 210.

29. *Ibid.*, 99, 129–30, 392.

30. *Ibid.*, 301–3, 311.

31. *Ibid.*, 6, 214, 227, 239.

32. *Ibid.*, 323, 350, 356, 363.

33. *Ibid.*, 27, 280, 324, 353–55, 366–67.

34. *Ibid.*, 422.

35. *Ibid.*, 372, 383–85, 418.

36. *Ibid.*, 429–32.

37. *Ibid.*, 414, 425–27.

38. Edmund Wilson, "Brokers and Pioneers," *New Republic,* LXX (March 23, 1932), 142–45. For another example of this argument, see Matthew Josephson, "The Frontier and Literature," *New Republic,* LXVIII (September 2, 1931), 77.

39. Lewis Mumford, "Foreword," in Findlay MacKenzie, ed., *Planned Society: Yesterday, Today, Tomorrow* (New York, 1937), vii.

40. "Liberalism Twenty Years After," *New Republic,* LXXXI (January 23, 1935), 290–92.

41. John Dewey, "Liberty and Social Control," *Social Frontier,* II (November 1935), 41–42.

42. John Dewey, "Liberalism and Civil Liberties," *Social Frontier,* II (February 1936), 138. For additional expressions of this point of view, see "Champions of Freedom," *Social Frontier,* I (December 1934), 9; and "Freedom in a Collectivist Society," *Social Frontier,* I (April 1935), 9–10.

43. Soule, *A Planned Society,* 89–91, 265–66; George Soule, "The Real Basis of Freedom," *Modern Quarterly,* VII (January 1935), 659.

44. Ruth Benedict, *Patterns of Culture* (Boston, 1934), 2–3, 55, 248, 251.

45. For a summary statement of these ideas, see Karen Horney, *The Neurotic Personality of Our Times* (New York, 1937). A shrewd analysis of the implications of the neo-Freudian position can be found in John Burnham's "The New Psychology: From Narcissism to Social Control," in John Braeman, Robert Bremner, and David Brody, eds., *Change and Continuity in Twentieth-Century America: The 1920s* (Columbus, Ohio, 1968), 351–98.

46. George Counts, "Education and the Social Problem," *Southern Review,* I (Autumn 1935), 303–6.

47. Charles Beard, "The Educator in the Quest for National Security," *Social Frontier,* I (April 1935), 14.

48. V. F. Calverton, "Book of the Month," *Modern Quarterly,* IX (September 1935), 320.

49. V. F. Calverton, "The Mind's Coming of Age," *Modern Quarterly,* VIII (June 1934), 275–84.

50. Newton Arvin, "Individualism and American Writers," *Nation,* CXXXIII (October 14, 1931), 391–93.

51. Rebecca Pitts, "Something to Believe In," *New Masses,* X (March 13, 1934), 14.

52. *Ibid.*, 15–16.

53. *Ibid.*, 15. Italics hers.

54. *Ibid.*, 16. For a similar expression of these ideas, see Meridel Le Sueur, "I Was Marching," *New Masses,* XII (September 18, 1934), 16–18.

55. John Dewey, *Individualism Old and New* (New York, 1930), 14, 56, 68, 70, 93; John

Dewey, *Liberalism and Social Action* (New York, 1935), 75–77.

56. Dewey, *Individualism Old and New,* 31, 36, 58–59, 74; Dewey, *Liberalism and Social Action,* 5, 11, 34, 36, 61.

57. Dewey, *Individualism Old and New,* 32–34, 49–50, 65; Dewey, *Liberalism and Social Action,* 25.

58. Dewey, *Individualism Old and New,* 81–83, 143; Dewey, *Liberalism and Social Action,* 32, 53–54, 56, 90.

59. Dewey, *Individualism Old and New,* 124–25.

60. Robert Lynd, *Knowledge for What?* (Princeton, 1939), 15, 18–19, 152.

61. *Ibid.,* 19, 50, 162.

62. *Ibid.,* 22, 24, 41–42, 53, 153–54. Italics his.

63. *Ibid.,* 189–92, 205. Italics his.

64. *Ibid.,* 43, 63, 100, 105, 208.

65. *Ibid.,* 45, 197.

66. *Ibid.,* 234.

67. *Ibid.,* 70–71, 79–80, 196, 238–39.

68. *Ibid.,* 215, 220.

69. *Ibid.,* 209, 211.

70. Max Eastman, "The State Philosophy of Soviet Russia," *Modern Quarterly,* IV (January–April 1927), 19–23; Max Eastman, "Lenin Was an Engineer," *New Masses,* III (November 1927), 14–16.

71. Max Eastman, "Against the Marxian Dialectic," *New Republic,* LXXXVIII (February 21, 1934), 36–38.

72. *Ibid.,* 39.

73. See, for example, the contributions of John Dewey and Morris Cohen to a symposium on Marxism, both entitled "Why I Am Not a Communist," in the *Modern Quarterly,* VIII (April 1934), 135–42.

74. Max Eastman, "Excommunication and Exorcism as Critical Methods," *Modern Quarterly,* VII (May 1933), 210–13; Max Eastman, "A Master Magician," *Modern Quarterly,* VII (June 1933), 291–307.

75. Max Eastman, "The Doctrinal Crisis in Socialism," *Modern Quarterly,* V (Winter 1929–1930), 426–28. Italics his.

76. Theodore Brameld, "John Strachey Was Wrong," *Modern Quarterly,* IX (May 1935), 140–41.

77. See Norman Podhoretz, *Making It* (New York, 1969, c. 1967), 84.

78. Sidney Hook, *Towards the Understanding of Karl Marx* (New York, 1933), 210.

79. *Ibid.,* 89.

80. Sidney Hook, *From Hegel to Marx* (New York, 1936), 38.

81. Hook, *Towards the Understanding of Karl Marx,* 58, 114; Hook, *From Hegel to Marx,* 19.

82. Hook, *Towards the Understanding of Karl Marx,* 59, 172.

83. Hook, *From Hegel to Marx,* 275, 284.

84. Hook, *Towards the Understanding of Karl Marx,* 31; Hook, *From Hegel to Marx,* 125, 157.

85. Hook, *From Hegel to Marx,* 58. Italics his. See also Sidney Hook, "The Meaning of Marxism," *Modern Quarterly,* V (Winter 1929–1930), 434.

86. Hook, *Towards the Understanding of Karl Marx,* 84; Hook, *From Hegel to Marx,* 71, 278.

87. Hook, *Towards the Understanding of Karl Marx,* 7–8.

88. Hook, *From Hegel to Marx,* 277. Italics his.

89. *Ibid.*, 48–49, 53. For the origins of these ideas in the Progressive era, see Morton White, *Social Thought in America* (Boston, 1949).

90. Hook, *From Hegel to Marx*, 25, 281, 284–85.

91. Sidney Hook, "John Dewey and His Critics," *New Republic*, LXVII (June 3, 1931), 74. Italics his.

92. Hook, *From Hegel to Marx*, 60; Sidney Hook, "Why I Am a Communist: Communism Without Dogmas," *Modern Quarterly*, VIII (April 1934), 145.

93. Hook, *From Hegel to Marx*, 39, 46, 161, 302.

94. *Ibid.*, 42–43, 45, 162.

95. *Ibid.*, 303; Hook, "Why I Am a Communist," *loc. cit.*, 148, 164.

96. Hook, *Towards the Understanding of Karl Marx*, 92; Hook, *From Hegel to Marx*, 289.

97. Hook, *Towards the Understanding of Karl Marx*, 98.

98. *Ibid.*, 99–101. Italics his.

99. Donald Meyer, *The Protestant Search for Political Realism, 1919–1941* (Berkeley and Los Angeles, 1961), 3, 29, 58, 109–10, 113, 117, 218, 225.

100. Reinhold Niebuhr, *Moral Man and Immoral Society* (New York, 1932), 78–79.

101. *Ibid.*, xxiv, 35, 40, 116, 213–15; Reinhold Niebuhr, "The Pathos of Liberalism," *Nation*, CXLI (September 10, 1935), 303.

102. Niebuhr, *Moral Man and Immoral Society*, xvi, 3, 209.

103. *Ibid.*, 146.

104. *Ibid.*, 61–62, 155–56, 160–61; Reinhold Niebuhr, "Religion and Marxism," *Modern Quarterly*, VIII (February 1935), 712–13.

105. Niebuhr, *Moral Man and Immoral Society*, 167, 192, 194, 199; Niebuhr, "Religion and Marxism," *loc. cit.*, 714; Meyer, *The Protestant Search for Political Realism*, 253–256.

106. Niebuhr, *Moral Man and Immoral Society*, xi, 48–49, 75, 85, 89, 91, 248, 262.

107. *Ibid.*, xxiii, 9, 31, 57, 73–74, 85, 172–73, 257–59, 263; Meyer, *The Protestant Search for Political Realism*, 32–34, 104–6, 229–230, 260, 312–13.

108. Niebuhr, *Moral Man and Immoral Society*, 4, 171, 271–73; Meyer, *The Protestant Search for Political Realism*, 284.

109. Niebuhr, *Moral Man and Immoral Society*, 16, 90, 164.

110. *Ibid.*, xv, xx, 196–97.

111. *Ibid.*, 231–34.

112. *Ibid.*, 236–38.

113. *Ibid.*, 81–82.

114. *Ibid.*, 69–70.

115. *Ibid.*, 37–38.

116. *Ibid.*, 21–22, 256.

IV. Literary Theory and the Role of the Intellectual

1. Joseph Freeman, "The Wilsonian Era in American Literature," *Modern Quarterly*, IV (June–September 1927), 130–36.

2. Dwight Macdonald, "Robinson Jeffers," *Miscellany*, I (July 1930), 1.

3. Edmund Wilson, *Axel's Castle* (New York, 1931), 265, 268–69.

4. *Ibid.*, 20–22.

5. *Ibid.*, 59, 89, 92, 248, 286.

6. *Ibid.*, 283, 287.

7. *Ibid.*, 292–94, 296–98.

8. Malcolm Cowley, *Exile's Return* (New York, Viking Press edition, 1951), 9, 27, 80, 206, 213–14.

9. *Ibid.*, 236, 240. See also Malcolm Cowley, "Ivory Towers to Let," *New Republic*, LXXVIII (April 18, 1934), 261–62.

10. Cowley, *Exile's Return,* 113–31.
11. *Ibid.,* 284.
12. *Ibid.,* 244–45, 285, 291.
13. *Ibid.,* 286–87, 305.
14. F. O. Matthiessen, "The Isolation of Hawthorne," *New Republic,* LXI (January 22, 1930), 281–82.
15. Newton Arvin, "Quebec, Nebraska, and Pittsburg," *New Republic,* LXVII (August 12, 1931), 345–46.
16. Donald Davidson, "A Mirror for Artists," *I'll Take My Stand* (New York, 1930), 44, 47–48, 50–51, 60.
17. Michael Gold, "American Jungle Notes," *New Masses,* V (December 5, 1929), 10.
18. Edwin Seaver, "American Writers and Kentucky," *New Masses,* VII (June 1932), 9–10.
19. Bernard Smith, "The Lost Generation," *New Masses,* XII (July 3, 1934), 40.
20. See, for example, *Culture and the Crisis* (League of Professional Groups for Foster and Ford, New York, 1932), 3, 29–30.
21. "Teachers and Labor," *Social Frontier,* II (October 1935), 7–8.
22. Michael Gold, "John Reed and the Real Thing," *New Masses,* III (November 1927), 7.
23. Robert Gorham Davis (pseud. Obed Brooks), "The Problem of the Social Novel," *Modern Quarterly,* VI (Autumn 1932), 78.
24. Meridel Le Sueur, "The Fetish of Being Outside," *New Masses,* XIV (February 26, 1935), 22–23.
25. Joseph Freeman, *An American Testament* (New York, 1936), 67.
26. *Ibid.,* 100, 112.
27. *Ibid.,* 99, 186, 198, 238, 284.
28. *Ibid.,* 117, 285, 287.
29. *Ibid.,* 56, 148, 168.
30. *Ibid.,* 113.
31. *Ibid.,* 49, 53, 224, 252, 312, 453, 631, 648, 657.
32. *Ibid.,* 292, 455, 524, 658.
33. *Ibid.* 595, 667. Italics his.
34. Sherwood Anderson, "At Amsterdam," *New Masses,* VIII (November 1932), 11.
35. Sherwood Anderson, "A Writer's Note," *New Masses,* VIII (August 1932), 10.
36. See Christopher Lasch, *The New Radicalism in America, 1889–1963* (New York, 1965), xv, 64.
37. Granville Hicks, *Part of the Truth* (New York, 1965), 96.
38. *Ibid.,* 100–1. Italics his.
39. For a good description of what attracted men to the Communist party in the early 1930s, see George Charney, *A Long Journey* (Chicago, 1968), 23–24.
40. See Alfred Kazin, *A Walker in the City* (New York, 1951), 60–61, 143–45; and Alfred Kazin, *Starting Out in the Thirties* (Boston, 1965), 83, 86, 102–3. For a contemporary expression of these views, see Malcolm Cowley, "Art Tomorrow," *New Republic,* LXXIX (May 23, 1934), 36.
41. For a typical expression of this argument, see V. F. Calverton, "Art and Social Change: The Radical Approach," *Modern Quarterly,* VI (Winter 1931), 16–27.
42. Granville Hicks, "Revolution and the Novel—VI," *New Masses,* XI (May 15, 1934), 25; Granville Hicks, "H. L. Mencken and Robert Herrick," *New Masses,* XIII (October 30, 1934), 21.
43. Joseph Freeman, "Introduction," *Proletarian Literature in the United States* (New York, 1935), 10, 17.
44. "Authors' Field Day: A Symposium on Marxist Criticism," *New Masses,* XII (July 3, 1934), 32.

45. Michael Gold, "A Letter to the Author of a First Book," *New Masses*, X (January 9, 1934), 25.
46. Granville Hicks, *The Great Tradition* (New York, 1933 and 1935), x.
47. *Ibid.*, ix.
48. *Ibid.*, 45, 227, 259, 266.
49. *Ibid.*, 156.
50. *Ibid.*, 3, 72, 95, 188, 206, 231.
51. *Ibid.*, 290; Granville Hicks, "American Fiction: The Major Trend," *New Republic*, LXXIV (April 12, 1933), 241.
52. Malcolm Cowley, "To a Revolutionary Critic," *New Republic*, LXXVI (November 8, 1933), 368–69. For a similar evaluation, see Ernest Sutherland Bates, "Review of *The Great Tradition*," *Modern Quarterly*, VIII (February 1934), 57.
53. Kyle Crichton (pseud. Robert Forsythe), "Speaking of the Dance," *New Masses*, XII (July 24, 1934), 29.
54. Michael Gold, "Wilder: Prophet of the Genteel Christ," *New Republic*, LXIV (October 22, 1930), 266–67.
55. Michael Gold, "A Letter from a Clam-Digger," *New Masses*, V (November 1929), 11; Michael Gold, "Notes of the Month," *New Masses*, V (January 1930), 7; Michael Gold, "Notes of the Month," *New Masses*, VI (September 1930), 5.
56. V. F. Calverton, "Can We Have a Proletarian Literature?" *Modern Quarterly*, VI (Autumn 1932), 40–50; Joseph Freeman, "You Can't Fight Here," *New Masses*, XIII (December 11, 1934), 25.
57. Malcolm Cowley, "What the Revolution Can Do for a Writer," in Henry Hart, ed., *American Writers' Congress* (New York, 1935), 59–64.
58. Matthew Josephson, "The Role of the Writer in the Soviet Union," in Hart, *loc. cit.*, 38–45.
59. Michael Gold, "Toward an American Revolutionary Culture," *New Masses*, VII (July 1931), 12–13.
60. Alan Calmer, "The Proletarian Short Story," *New Masses*, XVI (July 2, 1935), 17–18.
61. See "Between Ourselves," *New Masses*, XI (April 3, 1934), 46; "Between Ourselves," *New Masses*, XVI (July 2, 1935), 46.
62. Martha Gruening, "The Vanishing Individual," *Hound and Horn*, VII (January–March 1934), 318–19.
63. Conrad Aiken, "A Plea for Anonymity," *New Republic*, LXXXIV (September 18, 1935), 155–57. Italics his.
64. Lawrence Leighton, "The Ax Grinds," *Hound and Horn*, VI (January–March 1933), 325–27.
65. John Dos Passos, "The Writer as Technician," in Hart, *loc. cit.*, 79–82.
66. Archibald MacLeish, "Invocation to the Social Muse," *New Republic*, LXXII (October 26, 1932), 296; Archibald MacLeish, "Lines for an Interment," *New Republic*, LXXVI (September 20, 1933), 160.
67. Max Eastman, "Artists in Uniform," *Modern Quarterly*, VII (August 1933), 397–404.
68. Henry Hazlitt, "Communist Criticism," *Nation*, CXXXI (November 26, 1930), 583–84; William Troy, "Economics and Fiction," *Nation*, CXXXV (October 5, 1932), 314.
69. Joseph Wood Krutch, "Literature and Utopia," *Nation*, CXXXVII (October 18, 1933), 441–43.
70. Allen Tate, "A Note on Elizabethan Satire," *New Republic*, LXXIV (March 15, 1933), 130. See also Allen Tate, "Poetry and Politics," *New Republic*, LXXV (August 2, 1933), 310.
71. Allen Tate, "Three Types of Poetry—I," *New Republic*, LXXVIII (March 14, 1934), 126–28.

72. Allen Tate, "Three Types of Poetry—II," *New Republic*, LXXVIII (March 28, 1934), 180–82.
73. Allen Tate, "Three Types of Poetry—III," *New Republic*, LXXVIII (April 11, 1934), 238–39.
74. Newton Arvin, "Literature and Social Change," *Modern Quarterly*, VI (Summer 1932), 20–25.
75. William Phillips, "The Humanism of André Malraux," *Partisan Review*, III (June 1936), 18.
76. John Dewey, *Art as Experience* (New York, 1934), 346.
77. Robert Cantwell, "What the Working Class Reads," *New Republic*, LXXXIII (July 17, 1935), 274.
78. Edmund Wilson, "The Literary Class War—I & II," *New Republic*, LXX (May 4 and May 11, 1932), 320–23, 347–49; Edmund Wilson, "Art, the Proletariat, and Marx," *New Republic*, LXXVI (August 23, 1933), 41–45.
79. Matthew Josephson, "Citizen Zola," *New Republic*, LXXIII (February 8, 1933), 355. See also Matthew Josephson, *Infidel in the Temple* (New York, 1967), 361.
80. James Burnham and Philip Wheelwright, "Thirteen Propositions," *Symposium*, IV (April 1933), 127–34; James Burnham and Philip Wheelwright, "Comment," *Symposium*, IV (October, 1933), 409–19.
81. Sidney Hook, "The Philosophy of Morris R. Cohen," *New Republic*, LXIII (July 23, 1930), 279.
82. Kenneth Burke, "Boring from Within," *New Republic*, LXV (February 4, 1931), 329.
83. Benjamin Ginzburg, "Science Under Communism," *New Republic*, LXIX (January 6, 1932), 209.
84. Benjamin Ginzburg, "Against Messianism," *New Republic*, LXVI (February 18, 1931), 16.
85. *Ibid.*, 17.
86. *Ibid.*, 16–17.

V. Documentaries, Fiction, and the Depression

1. Elizabeth Noble, "The Fine Arts," *New Masses*, XXV (November 30, 1937), 27.
2. James Rorty, *Where Life Is Better* (New York, 1936), 33.
3. Edmund Wilson, *The American Jitters* (New York, 1932), 305, 308; Edmund Wilson, *Travels in Two Democracies* (New York, 1936), 79.
4. Wilson, *The American Jitters*, 137; Wilson, *Travels in Two Democracies*, 27.
5. Rorty, *Where Life Is Better*, 10.
6. Sherwood Anderson, *Puzzled America* (New York, 1935), 25, 46, 161–62.
7. *Ibid.*, ix.
8. *Ibid.*, 158, 164.
9. Wilson, *Travels in Two Democracies*, 43.
10. Rorty, *Where Life Is Better*, 13, 23, 27, 30, 107–8, 117.
11. *Ibid.*, 11, 380–81; Wilson, *The American Jitters*, 295, 298; Anderson, *Puzzled America*, 11.
12. Rorty, *Where Life Is Better*, 50.
13. Anderson, *Puzzled America*, 76, 244.
14. *Ibid.*, 18, 189, 207; Wilson, *The American Jitters*, 169; Rorty, *Where Life Is Better*, 106.
15. Anderson, *Puzzled America*, xv–xvi, 99, 241, 260.
16. Wilson, *Travels in Two Democracies*, 225, 250, 320.
17. Anderson, *Puzzled America*, 287.
18. Wilson, *The American Jitters*, 26, 311; Wilson, *Travels in Two Democracies*, 314, 322, 325. Italics mine.

19. Jack Conroy, *The Disinherited* (New York, 1963, c. 1933), 91, 114–15, 196, 202, 209, 215, 250.

20. *Ibid.*, 10, 12, 43, 60, 81, 160, 165, 197, 216.

21. *Ibid.*, 175, 195, 286, 292.

22. Robert Cantwell, *The Land of Plenty* (New York, 1934), 3.

23. *Ibid.*, 8, 14, 49, 148.

24. *Ibid.*, 304, 334, 344.

25. *Ibid.*, 279–80.

26. *Ibid.*, 369.

27. James Farrell, "Introduction," *Studs Lonigan Trilogy* (New York, Modern Library edition, 1938), xii.

28. James Farrell, *Judgment Day* (New York, 1935), 11, 267.

29. James Farrell, *Young Lonigan* (New York, 1932), 79, 102, 166, 168–69; James Farrell, *The Young Manhood of Studs Lonigan* (New York, 1934), 277; Farrell, *Judgment Day*, 334–35.

30. Farrell, *Judgment Day*, 26.

31. Farrell, *Young Lonigan*, 87; Farrell, *The Young Manhood of Studs Lonigan*, 49–50, 132, 146–47, 211; Farrell, *Judgment Day*, 20–21, 45.

32. Farrell, *Young Lonigan*, 67, 144, 146–47.

33. *Ibid.*, 139, 197; Farrell, *Judgment Day*, 31, 378.

34. Farrell, *Young Lonigan*, 18, 152; Farrell, *The Young Manhood of Studs Lonigan*, 34, 40, 109, 228; Farrell, *Judgment Day*, 5–6, 345.

35. Farrell, *Judgment Day*, 194–95, 317–18, 330, 386, 394–95.

36. Farrell, *The Young Manhood of Studs Lonigan*, 369–72.

37. Ernest Hemingway, *For Whom the Bell Tolls* (London, 1955, c. 1940), 18–19. For a further elaboration of these ideas, see Frederick Benson, *Writers in Arms; the Literary Impact of the Spanish Civil War* (New York, 1967), 128.

38. Hemingway, *For Whom the Bell Tolls*, 160–61.

39. *Ibid.*, 11.

40. *Ibid.*, 20, 37, 87.

41. *Ibid.*, 64, 155, 282, 321.

42. *Ibid.*, 153, 182, 280–81; Benson, *Writers in Arms*, 277.

43. Hemingway, *For Whom the Bell Tolls*, 129, 155, 230, 271, 308.

44. *Ibid.*, 74, 83, 86, 303; Benson, *Writers in Arms*, 261, 266. See also Allen Guttmann, *The Wound in the Heart* (New York, 1962), 175, 190–93.

45. Hemingway, *For Whom the Bell Tolls*, 220–22, 245–46, 425–28.

46. *Ibid.*, 5, 288, 424, 429–32. See also Alfred Kazin, *On Native Grounds* (New York, 1956, c. 1942), 264.

47. Erskine Caldwell, *Tobacco Road* (New York, 1959, c. 1932), 60–62.

48. *Ibid.*, 20, 59, 63–64, 104, 158–59.

49. *Ibid.*, 153.

50. *Ibid.*, 14, 20, 102, 157.

51. John Steinbeck, *The Grapes of Wrath* (New York, 1939), 50, 152, 157–58, 199, 205.

52. *Ibid.*, 42–49, 52, 316–17, 319, 476–77.

53. *Ibid.*, 6, 100, 231, 294, 311, 479, 536, 572. See also George Bluestone, *Novels into Film* (Baltimore, 1957), 155.

54. Steinbeck, *The Grapes of Wrath*, 135–36, 160, 222, 256, 267, 333, 381, 385.

55. *Ibid.*, 33, 77, 110, 127–28; Bluestone, *Novels into Film*, 153.

56. Steinbeck, *The Grapes of Wrath*, 264–65, 606.

57. *Ibid.*, 404, 406, 550.

58. *Ibid.*, 119, 204, 206, 324–26, 477, 488, 591–92.

59. *Ibid.,* 572.

60. *Ibid.,* 383.

61. Dalton Trumbo, *Johnny Got His Gun* (New York, 1939), 13, 55, 69, 83.

62. *Ibid.,* 130, 133, 147, 170.

63. *Ibid.,* 175, 177, 189–91.

64. *Ibid.,* 172, 174.

65. *Ibid.,* 96, 98.

66. Horace McCoy, *They Shoot Horses, Don't They?* (New York, 1935), 21, 25–26, 28, 81, 118.

67. *Ibid.,* 21, 82, 111.

68. *Ibid.,* 26, 48, 51–52, 110.

69. *Ibid.,* 21, 141–43.

70. *Ibid.,* 19.

71. Nathanael West, *The Day of the Locust* (New York, 1939), 3, 13–14, 82–84.

72. *Ibid.,* 4, 19, 34, 36, 40, 45–49, 57, 61–62, 67, 113–14.

73. *Ibid.,* 2–3, 5, 21, 30–31, 45, 69–70, 85, 88, 102, 119–20.

74. *Ibid.,* 60, 84, 118, 123–26.

75. Nelson Algren, *Somebody in Boots* (New York, 1965, c. 1935), 16.

76. *Ibid.,* 12, 53, 80–82, 90, 103–5, 230, 242–45.

77. *Ibid.,* 33, 147, 240.

78. *Ibid.,* 190–92, 209–10, 228.

79. *Ibid.,* 219–20.

80. *Ibid.,* 55, 77, 206, 253–54.

81. *Ibid.,* 20, 30, 189.

82. John Steinbeck, *In Dubious Battle* (New York, 1961, c. 1936), 22, 42, 72, 82, 111–12, 118–19, 122, 146–50, 165, 184, 199, 206–7, 234, 244, 250.

83. *Ibid.,* 40, 48, 126, 143.

84. *Ibid.,* 104–5, 118, 163, 221, 229–31.

85. William Saroyan, *The Daring Young Man on the Flying Trapeze* (London, 1958, c. 1934), 12, 47, 85, 103, 206.

86. *Ibid.,* 19, 208–9.

87. *Ibid.,* 126, 194, 197–98, 207, 212–13.

88. *Ibid.,* 107, 177, 179, 181–82, 185.

89. *Ibid.,* 74, 79–80, 94, 96, 155.

90. *Ibid.,* 141.

91. Richard Wright, *Native Son* (New York, 1966, c. 1940), 14, 16, 22–23, 50, 73, 307.

92. *Ibid.,* 31, 44, 133, 214.

93. *Ibid.,* 100–102, 106, 141–42, 179, 216, 224–26.

94. *Ibid.,* 286, 337, 350, 380.

95. *Ibid.,* 354, 358–60, 364, 366–67. Italics his.

96. *Ibid.,* 277, 334–35, 390–91.

97. *Ibid.,* 392. Italics his.

98. John Dos Passos, *The 42nd Parallel* (New York, 1961, c. 1930), 156–61, 329, 380.

99. *Ibid.,* 388; John Dos Passos, *1919* (New York, 1961, c. 1932), 2, 37, 51.

100. Dos Passos, *The 42nd Parallel,* 394; Dos Passos, *1919,* 119, 136–38, 321, 348, 355; Dos Passos, *The Big Money* (New York, 1961, c. 1937), 159.

101. Dos Passos, *The 42nd Parallel,* 195–97, 200, 219, 293, 301, 304–5, 307, 311, 320; Dos Passos, *1919,* 244, 320, 327.

102. Dos Passos, *1919,* 79, 90, 102, 216, 226, 228, 412, 420, 423; Dos Passos, *The Big Money,* 538, 540, 544, 572.

103. Dos Passos, *The 42nd Parallel,* 421, 424, 428, 439, 442, 446.

104. Dos Passos, *The Big Money*, 6–7, 81–82, 97–98, 219, 240, 248–49, 327, 337, 344–46, 355, 361, 380, 398, 409.
105. Dos Passos, *The 42nd Parallel*, 14, 39, 65–67, 83–84, 115–17, 128, 134–37, 350.
106. Dos Passos, *The Big Money*, 125, 128, 132, 163, 504.
107. Dos Passos, *1919*, 467–70, 479; Dos Passos, *The Big Money*, 594, 599.
108. Dos Passos, *1919*, 273, 460, 495; Dos Passos, *The Big Money*, 57–58, 350.
109. Dos Passos, *The 42nd Parallel*, xii, 192–94; Dos Passos, *1919*, 259–67.
110. Dos Passos, *1919*, 11, 192–97; Dos Passos, *The Big Money*, 165.
111. Dos Passos, *1919*, 224–25, 303, 453–54, 509–10; Dos Passos, *The Big Money*, 584–85.
112. Dos Passos, *The Big Money*, 490–92, 520–21.
113. Dos Passos, *1919*, 9–10, 14, 109, 271, 369.
114. Dos Passos, *The Big Money*, 620–23.
115. Dos Passos, *The 42nd Parallel*, 411–14; Dos Passos, *The Big Money*, 101–12.
116. Dashiell Hammett, *The Maltese Falcon* (New York, 1930), 60, 66.
117. *Ibid.*, 43, 64, 67.
118. *Ibid.*, 153–54.
119. *Ibid.*, 77–79.
120. See David Madden, ed., *Tough Guy Writers of the Thirties* (Carbondale and Edwardsville, Illinois, 1968), xviii, xix, xxxii, 55–56.
121. Hammett, *The Maltese Falcon*, 261–65.
122. *Ibid.*, 223, 266.
123. Daniel Fuchs, *Low Company* (New York, 1965, c. 1937), 36, 52, 137, 220, 222.
124. Daniel Fuchs, *Summer in Williamsburg* (New York, 1965, c. 1934), 125; Fuchs, *Homage to Blenholt* (New York, 1965, c. 1936), 106; Fuchs, *Low Company*, 206.
125. Fuchs, *Summer in Williamsburg*, 97, 100, 103, 109, 137, 140, 143; Fuchs, *Low Company*, 166.
126. Fuchs, *Summer in Williamsburg*, 114, 126–27, 165–66, 208–9, 213, 252; Fuchs, *Homage to Blenholt*, 67, 69.
127. Fuchs, *Homage to Blenholt*, 10, 39, 68, 120, 126–27, 136, 156, 177.
128. *Ibid.*, 50–54, 141–42, 158–60, 182, 202, 207–8.
129. Fuchs, *Summer in Williamsburg*, 300; Fuchs, *Low Company*, 283–84.
130. William Faulkner, *Light in August* (New York, 1959, c. 1932), 27, 52, 98–99, 205, 212, 225–26, 241–45, 270–71, 296, 317, 321–22, 419–21.
131. William Faulkner, *The Sound and the Fury* (New York, 1956, c. 1929), 9–10.
132. William Faulkner, *Absalom, Absalom!* (New York, 1936), 42–43, 51, 53, 155, 160, 165, 179, 233–34, 238, 240, 263–65, 267, 299, 327, 356, 376.
133. Faulkner, *The Sound and the Fury*, 7, 17; Faulkner, *Absalom, Absalom!*, 325; Faulkner, *The Hamlet* (New York, 1959, c. 1940), 3, 23, 57.
134. Faulkner, *Light in August*, 41, 55, 221–23, 392–93; Faulkner, *Absalom, Absalom!*, 9–12, 31, 207, 212–13, 261–62, 334, 336, 361; Faulkner, *The Hamlet*, 214, 221.
135. Faulkner, *The Sound and the Fury*, 22, 102, 106, 282; Faulkner, *Light in August*, 16, 24–25, 356, 364; Faulkner, *Absalom, Absalom!*, 127; Faulkner, *The Hamlet*, 95, 114–15.
136. Faulkner, *The Hamlet*, 72, 201, 210, 326.
137. James Agee, *Let Us Now Praise Famous Men* (New York, 1966, c. 1941), xv.
138. *Ibid.*, 220.
139. *Ibid.*, xiv, 220.
140. *Ibid.*, xv, 11, 165, 203, 209–18.
141. *Ibid.*, 7, 40, 125, 182, 291, 331, 337.
142. *Ibid.*, 51–54, 92, 291.
143. *Ibid.*, 96, 99, 188–89, 203, 264, 275–82, 286.
144. *Ibid.*, 74, 94, 185–86, 193–94, 292.
145. *Ibid.*, 263, 356, 399.

VI. The Radical Stage and the Hollywood Film in the 1930s

1. See Stark Young, "H——'s Predicament," *New Republic,* LVIII (March 20, 1929), 128–29; Young, "To Wait and See," *New Republic,* LXI (January 8, 1930), 197; Dwight Macdonald, "The Modern Theatre: An Inquest," *Miscellany,* I (March 1930), 7; and Edmund Wilson, "Painting, Opera, and Theatre," *New Republic,* LXV (February 4, 1931), 323.

2. Albert Maltz, "The Left-Wing Theatre in America," *New Republic,* LXXXIII (July 24, 1935), 304.

3. John Dos Passos, "The American Theatre: 1930–1931," *New Republic,* LXVI (April 1, 1931), 174.

4. Hallie Flanagan, "A Theatre Is Born," *Theatre Arts,* XV (November 1931), 908.

5. See Albert Prentis, "Basic Principles," *New Theatre and Film,* I (May 1931), 1–2; and Jack Shapiro, "On Breaking Thro' the Proscenium," *New Theatre and Film,* I (June 1931), 7–8.

6. See John Bonn, "Problems of Play-Directing," *New Theatre and Film,* I (October 1931), 4; Nathaniel Buchwald, "Narrowing the Field of the Workers' Theatre," *New Theatre and Film,* I (October 1931), 6–9; Albert Prentis, "Techniques in the Workers' Theatre," *New Theatre and Film,* I (February 1932), 14; John Bonn, "Situation and Tasks of Workers' Theatres in the U.S.A.," *New Theatre and Film,* II (August 1932), 11; Bernard Reines, "Our Widening Front," *New Theatre and Film,* II (September–October 1932), 4; Arthur Doar, "Broadway and the Group Theatre," *New Theatre and Film,* II (September–October 1932), 6; Harry Elion, "The Problem of Repertory," *New Theatre and Film,* III (April 1933), 5; "Workers Theatre to Become New Theatre," *New Theatre and Film,* III (July–August 1933), 2; Emery Northrup, "Meet the Theatre Union," *New Theatre and Film,* I (February 1934), 8–9; and Mordecai Gorelik, "Theatre Is a Weapon," *Theatre Arts,* XVIII (June 1934), 421–28.

7. Mark Marvin, "An American Peoples Theatre," *New Theatre and Film,* II (December 1935), 24–25.

8. Mordecai Gorelik, *New Theatres for Old* (New York, 1940), 5, 11, 409, 466.

9. *Ibid.,* 142, 148.

10. *Ibid.,* 107, 196–97, 200, 209, 221, 266, 283–84.

11. *Ibid.,* 261–63, 271, 287–88.

12. *Ibid.,* 210.

13. *Ibid.,* 323, 411, 413, 415, 423, 436, 440. For a similar view, see Louis Lozowick, "V. E. Meyerhold and His Theatre," *Hound and Horn,* IV (October–December 1930), 99.

14. Mordecai Gorelik, "The Conquest of Stage Space," *Common Sense,* XVIII (March 1934), 217.

15. Harold Clurman, *The Fervent Years* (New York, 1957, c. 1945), 11, 26, 38–39, 41, 47, 170, 269, 288–89. See also Gerald Weales, "The Group Theatre and Its Plays," in John Brown and Bernard Harris, eds., *American Theatre* (London, 1967), 70.

16. Clurman, *The Fervent Years,* 58, 67; Clurman, "Real Theatre," *New Republic,* LXXXVII (July 8, 1936), 275; Gorelik, *New Theatres for Old,* 36, 41.

17. Hallie Flanagan, "Federal Theatre Project," *Theatre Arts,* XIX (November 1935), 867–68. See also Gerald Rabkin, *Drama and Commitment* (Bloomington, Indiana, 1964), 99.

18. Clurman, *The Fervent Years,* 283.

19. *Ibid.,* 267.

20. *Ibid.,* 127. Italics mine.

21. See Rabkin, *Drama and Commitment,* 171.

22. See, for example, Mary Virginia Farmer, "Awake and Sing," *New Theatre and Film,* II (March 1935), 20.

23. Clifford Odets, *Paradise Lost*, in *Six Plays of Clifford Odets* (New York, 1939), 230.

24. Clifford Odets, *Awake and Sing*, *loc. cit.*, 70.

25. See Weales, "The Group Theatre and Its Plays," *loc. cit.*, 72–73, 75.

26. *Ibid.*, 80–82. For a more detailed and extremely perceptive discussion of these ideas, see Robert Warshow, "Clifford Odets: Poet of the Jewish Middle Class," in *The Immediate Experience* (New York, 1962), 55–67.

27. Odets, *Awake and Sing*, *loc. cit.*, 38, 48, 55–56, 72–73, 77–78, 84; Odets, *Golden Boy*, *loc. cit.*, 249, 271, 297.

28. Odets, *Awake and Sing*, *loc. cit.*, 37, 41, 66, 83, 95; Odets, *Golden Boy*, *loc. cit.*, 252, 264, 265, 282, 288, 298, 305, 309, 316.

29. Clurman, *The Fervent Years*, 84, 158, 166, 198.

30. *Ibid.*, 159.

31. *Ibid.*, 197, 225, 249, 255, 266, 268.

32. *Ibid.*, 59, 170–71, 263, 265. See also Rabkin, *Drama and Commitment*, 51; and Weales, "The Group Theatre and Its Plays," *loc. cit.*, 68.

33. See William Saroyan, *The Time of Your Life*, in Harold Clurman, ed., *Famous American Plays of the 1930s* (New York, 1959), 410, 413, 417–418, 422, 438, 451–452, 456.

34. Clurman, *The Fervent Years*, 265.

35. Dwight Macdonald, "Our Elizabethan Movies," *Miscellany*, I (December 1929), 27–28.

36. Robert Gessner, "Massacre in Hollywood," *New Theatre and Film*, I (March 1934), 17. For a similar view from a non-radical, see Ashley Dukes, "The Theatre and the Talkies," *Theatre Arts*, XIV (June 1930), 468–69.

37. For a typical expression of these attitudes, see V. F. Calverton, "Can We Have a Proletarian Literature?" *Modern Quarterly*, VI (Autumn 1932), 45; and Lewis Jacobs, *The Rise of the American Film* (New York, 1968, c. 1939), 312–13.

38. Louis Lozowick, "The Soviet Cinema: Eisenstein and Pudovkin," *Theatre Arts*, XII (September 1929), 669–75. See also Dwight Macdonald, "Eisenstein, Pudovkin, and Others," *Miscellany*, I (March 1931), 19–20.

39. Hadley Cantril and Gordon Allport, *The Psychology of Radio* (New York, 1935), 8, 18, 20, 24, 260. See also Robert and Helen Lynd, *Middletown in Transition* (New York, 1937), 263.

40. Lewis Mumford, *Technics and Civilization* (New York, 1934), 243.

41. Margaret Thorp, *America at the Movies* (New Haven, 1939), 271.

42. See Macdonald, "Our Elizabethan Movies," *loc. cit.*, 32; and Gilbert Seldes, *Mainland* (New York, 1936), 95–96, 98–99. For a more recent discussion of these ideas, see Reuel Denney, "The Discovery of Popular Culture," in Robert Spiller and Eric Larrabee, eds., *American Perspectives* (Cambridge, Massachusetts, 1961), 154–77; and Warshow, "The Legacy of the 1930s," *loc. cit.*, 34.

43. Mumford, *Technics and Civilization*, 241.

44. *Ibid.*, 315; Louis Reid, "Amusement: Radio and Movies," in Harold Stearns, ed., *America Now* (New York, 1938), 3; Thorp, *America at the Movies*, 5.

45. Cantril and Allport, *The Psychology of Radio*, 21.

46. See Jacobs, *The Rise of the American Film*, 264; and James Thurber, "Soapland," in *The Beast in Me* (New York, 1948), 189–260.

47. See William Ogburn, "Social Effects of Radio," in *Recent Social Trends in the United States* (New York, 1933), 152–57; Cantril and Allport, *The Psychology of Radio*, 24; Lynd, *Middletown in Transition*, 264, 378–79; and Jacobs, *The Rise of the American Film*, 12, 338.

48. Warshow, "The Legacy of the 1930s," *loc. cit.*, 38–40. See also Pauline Kael, "Raising Kane—I," *The New Yorker*, XLVII (February 20, 1971), 71.

49. Mumford, *Technics and Civilization*, 240.

50. Leo Gurko, *The Angry Decade* (New York, 1947), 1–3, 177.
51. Drake Douglas, pseud., *Horror!* (New York, 1966), 101.
52. *Ibid.,* 78, 80, 83, 92–93, 98.
53. See Thomas Wiseman, *Cinema* (London, 1964), 67, 69; and Kael, "Raising Kane—I," *loc. cit.,* 50.
54. For a further elaboration of these ideas, see Warshow, "The Gangster as Tragic Hero," and "The Westerner," *loc. cit.,* 133, 137.
55. See Jacobs, *The Rise of the American Film,* 277–78, 360–61, 385, 397, 402–3, 415, 466, 468, 506–7.
56. Richard Schickel, *The Disney Version* (New York, 1968), 51–53, 154–55, 157, 194–95, 210–13, 361. See also Parker Tyler, *The Hollwood Hallucination* (New York, 1944), 153.
57. For a perceptive analysis of Lang's films, see Paul Jensen, *The Cinema of Fritz Lang* (New York, 1969), 9, 14, 116–23.
58. See George Bluestone, *Novels into Film* (Baltimore, 1957), 72, 88.
59. See Andrew Sarris, *The American Cinema* (New York, 1968), 66–67.
60. For a sensitive discussion of the change in Chaplin's image, see Warshow, "Monsieur Verdoux," *loc. cit.,* 207–10. See also Theodore Huff, *Charlie Chaplin* (New York, 1951), 253, 256, 263.
61. See Paul Zimmerman and Burt Goldblatt, *The Marx Brothers at the Movies* (New York, 1968), 37.
62. See Allen Eyles, *The Marx Brothers: Their World of Comedy* (London, 1966), 174, 214.
63. See Andrew Sarris, "Citizen Kane: The American Baroque," in Ronald Gottesman, ed., *Focus on Citizen Kane* (Englewood Cliffs, New Jersey, 1971), 103, 106.
64. See Kael, "Raising Kane—I," *loc. cit.,* 66–67.
65. See Pauline Kael, "Raising Kane—II," *The New Yorker,* XLVII (February 27, 1971), 50; and Tyler, *The Hollywood Hallucination,* 199–205.

VII. The Decline of Radicalism, 1935–1939

1. For an illustration of this position, see Liston Oak, "Dialectics of Diplomacy," *New Masses,* XII (September 11, 1934), 28–29.
2. See Joseph Freeman, "Issues False and True," *New Masses,* XXI (October 27, 1936), 3–4; and R. Palme Dutt, "Outlook for 1937," *New Masses,* XXII (January 19, 1937), 11–14.
3. Michael Gold, "No Blank Check for Roosevelt," *New Masses,* XVIII (January 21, 1936), 6. See also A. B. Magil, "Roosevelt's Record," *New Masses,* XIX (June 9, 1936), 14–15; Joseph Freeman, "The Middle Class and the Election," *New Masses,* XX (August 11, 1936), 28; and "The Meaning of the Elections," *New Masses,* XXI (November 17, 1936), 11–12.
4. See "As Congress Opens," *New Masses,* XXII (January 12, 1937), 22; and "I Will Not Let You Down," *New Masses,* XXVI (January 11, 1938), 11.
5. "The Coming Test of Strength," *New Masses,* XXV (October 26, 1937), 14. See also "Roosevelt and His Party," *New Masses* XXIV (August 31, 1937), 14; and "A People's Front in the Making," *New Masses,* XXV (November 16, 1937), 15.
6. For an example of these views, see A. B. Magil, "Still Time to Unite," *New Masses,* XXVII (May 10, 1938), 5–6.
7. A. B. Magil, "Box Score on the Primaries," *New Masses,* XXIX (October 11, 1938), 12.
8. Stanley Burnshaw, " 'Paradise Lost': An Obituary," *New Masses,* XVIII (February 11, 1936), 28.
9. See, for example, "Help Little Business," *New Masses,* XXXI (June 13, 1939), 19–20.
10. "New York Elections," *New Masses,* XXIX (October 25, 1938), 11.
11. "The Challenge and the Answer," *New Masses,* XX (September 15, 1936), 20.

12. Murray Kempton, *Part of Our Time* (New York, 1967, c. 1955), 337.

13. George Charney, *A Long Journey* (Chicago, 1968), 33, 59–61, 64, 71, 74, 78, 82. See also Kempton, *Part of Our Time,* 336–37.

14. See "Moscow Offers an Olive Branch," *Nation,* CXLI (August 7, 1935), 145; "A Plea for Unity," *Social Frontier,* II (October 1935), 3–4; and "Toward a United Front," *Social Frontier,* II (January 1936), 104. Frank Warren has analyzed these attitudes in *Liberals and Communism* (Bloomington, Indiana, 1966), 114–15.

15. For an excellent summary of these views, see "Balance Sheet of the New Deal," *New Republic,* LXXXVII (June 10, 1936), 141–57.

16. "Mr. Roosevelt Holds Fast," *Nation,* CXLIII (July 4, 1936), 5. See also "New Party Prospects," *New Republic,* LXXXVI (April 1, 1936), 208.

17. "Roosevelt: Radicals' Nemesis," *Common Sense,* V (June 1936), 3–4; "How Shall I Vote?" *Common Sense,* V (October 1936), 3, 33; "Will Roosevelt Go Left?" *Nation,* CXLIII (November 7, 1936), 536; Max Lerner, "The Task for Progressives," *Nation,* CXLIII (November 14, 1936), 569–70; Stuart Chase, "Elegy for the Elite," *Nation,* CXLIII (November 21, 1936), 600.

18. Max Lerner, *It Is Later Than You Think* (New York, 1938), 196; Archibald MacLeish, *A Time to Speak* (Cambridge, Massachusetts, 1940), 9–10, 14.

19. Lerner, *It Is Later Than You Think,* 20–22, 197, 210; Corliss Lamont, "John Dewey, Marxism, and the United Front," *New Masses,* XVIII (March 3, 1936), 22–23; Theodore Brameld, "American Education and the Class Struggle," *Science and Society,* I (Fall 1936), 2, 4–5, 11–12; Frederick Schuman, "Liberalism and Communism Reconsidered," *Southern Review,* II (Autumn 1936), 327–28, 338.

20. Lerner, *It Is Later Than You Think,* 139, 188, 190; Schuman, "Liberalism and Communism Reconsidered," *loc. cit.,* 333.

21. See, for example, Matthew Josephson, "The Symbolism of the Sit-Down," *New Masses,* XXIII (April 20, 1937), 15–16.

22. Kempton, *Part of Our Time,* 290.

23. "Striking for a New America," *Modern Quarterly,* X (April 1937), 2.

24. See "Russia's New Constitution," *New Republic,* LXXXIX (December 9, 1936), 160.

25. See Joshua Kunitz, "The Moscow Trial," *New Masses,* XXVI (March 15, 1938), 6.

26. "The Moscow Trials: A Statement by American Progressives," *New Masses,* XXVII (May 3, 1938), 19.

27. Granville Hicks, *Part of the Truth* (New York, 1965), 145. For a contemporary argument along similar lines, see Upton Sinclair, "A Letter to Eugene Lyons," *New Masses,* XXVI (March 8, 1938), 6.

28. "The Editorial Jitters," *New Masses,* XXVI (March 22, 1938), 10.

29. See "Stalin on Trial," *Modern Quarterly,* X (October 1936), 3; "Is Leon Trotsky Guilty?" *Modern Quarterly,* X (March 1937), 4–6; and Max Eastman, "An Open Letter to the *Nation,*" *Modern Quarterly,* X (April 1937), 5.

30. Oswald Villard, "The Russian 'Purging,'" *Nation,* CXXXIX (December 26, 1934), 729. See also "Russia's 'Purge,'" *Common Sense,* IV (January 1935), 5.

31. "The Russian Executions," *New Republic,* LXXXI (January 23, 1935), 293; "Russian Politics in America," *New Republic,* LXXXX (February 17, 1937), 33–34. See also Warren, *Liberals and Communism,* 178–79, 186.

32. "The Conditions of Civil Liberty," *New Republic,* LXXXI (February 6, 1935), 60–62.

33. Louis Fischer, "Behind the Kirov Executions," *Nation,* CXL (May 15, 1935), 567–68.

34. Frederick Schuman, "Leon Trotsky: Martyr or Renegade," *Southern Review,* III (Summer 1937), 64–74.

35. "Behind the Soviet Trials," *Nation,* CXLIV (February 6, 1937), 145; "Another Russian Trial," *New Republic,* LXXXIX (February 3, 1937), 400; "Soviet Chills and Fever," *New*

Republic, LXXXXI (June 23, 1937), 174; Malcolm Cowley, "Moscow Trials: II," *New Republic,* LXXXXV (May 25, 1938), 80. See also "Bolshevism and Fascism," *Common Sense,* V (November 1936), 6.

36. Malcolm Cowley, "To Madrid, V: International Brigade," *New Republic,* LXXXXII (October 6, 1937), 237.

37. For examples of the more militant position, see "Bolshevism in Spain," *Modern Quarterly,* X (May 1937), 2; and V. F. Calverton, "Will England Give Spain to Franco?" *Modern Quarterly,* X (August 1937), 5–7. For a defense of the Popular Front strategy in Spain, see "The Meaning of Spain," *New Masses,* XX (August 4, 1936), 6; "World War in Spain," *New Republic,* LXXXVIII (August 12, 1936), 5; Ludwig Lore, "The Challenge of Catalonia," *Modern Quarterly,* X (May 1937), 7; and "Spain Is Not Russia," *New Republic,* LXXXXIII (November 10, 1937), 5. See also Allen Guttmann, *The Wound in the Heart* (New York, 1962), 3–4, 82, 114.

38. Cowley, "To Madrid, V: International Brigade," *loc. cit.,* 237. See also Josephine Herbst, "The Starched Blue Sky of Spain," *Noble Savage,* I (1960), 76–117.

39. Louis Fischer, "America and Europe," *Nation,* CXLIX (July 22, 1939), 98.

40. "New Deal or New Party," *Common Sense,* VI (September 1937), 3.

41. Stanley Burnshaw, " 'Middle-Ground' Writers," *New Masses,* XV (April 30, 1935), 19–21; Lamont, "John Dewey, Marxism, and the United Front," *loc. cit.,* 22; Michael Gold, "It Seems to More of Us," *New Republic,* LXXXIV (October 23, 1935), 303. See also Bruce Minton, "A Program for Democracy," *New Masses,* XXIX (October 11, 1938), 27; and V. J. McGill, "An Evaluation of Logical Positivism," *Science and Society,* I (Fall 1936), 77–78.

42. Matthew Josephson, *Infidel in the Temple* (New York, 1967), 434.

43. The papers and speeches of the second Congress are contained in Henry Hart, ed., *The Writer in a Changing World* (New York, 1937).

44. Max Lerner, "The Liberalism of O. G. Villard," *New Republic* (April 26, 1939), 343–44; Lerner, "Hamlet and the Presidency," *New Republic,* CIV (January 27, 1941), 114; Lerner, "I Thought of Lincoln," *New Republic,* CIV (February 10, 1941), 177; Lerner, "The War as Revolution, II: The Attitude of the Intellectuals," *Nation,* CLI (August 3, 1940), 88–92.

45. Malcolm Cowley, "Poet in Politics," *New Republic,* LXXXXVI (September 21, 1938), 191–92; "A National Congress of American Writers," *New Republic,* LXXXX (May 5, 1937), 390; Granville Hicks, "The American Writer Faces the Future," in Hart, *loc. cit.,* 193.

46. Meyer Levin, "Playwriting and Protest," *Theatre Arts,* XVII (May 1933), 354–59.

47. Elizabeth Noble, "The Federal Arts Bill," *New Masses,* XXVI, (February 8, 1938), 17.

48. Thomas Hart Benton, "Art and Nationalism," *Modern Quarterly,* VIII (May 1934), 233–36.

49. Archibald MacLeish, "The Irresponsibles," *Nation,* CL (May 18, 1940), 619–23; MacLeish, "Postwar Writers and Prewar Readers," *New Republic,* CII (June 10, 1940), 789–90; MacLeish, "The Tradition of the People," *New Masses,* XX (August 11, 1936), 25–27; MacLeish, *A Time to Speak,* 81–96.

50. Samuel Sillen, "The People, Yes," *New Masses,* XXXI (June 6, 1939), 22.

51. David Ramsey, "Front Men for Wall Street," *New Masses,* XXVIII (May 17, 1938), 24. See also Newton Arvin, "The Democratic Tradition in American Letters," in Hart, *loc. cit.,* 36.

52. See, for example, "Thomas Jefferson," *New Masses,* XIX (April 21, 1936), 8; and Samuel Sillen, "History and Fiction," *New Masses,* XXVII (June 14, 1938), 22–23.

53. Lerner, *It Is Later Than You Think,* 78–81.

54. Malcolm Cowley, "The Puritan Legacy," *New Republic,* LXXXVIII (August 26, 1936), 80.

55. Harold Stearns, ed., *America Now* (New York, 1938), viii. See also Lewis Mumford, "Writers Project," *New Republic,* LXXXXII (October 20, 1937), 306–7. In 1933 Kansas City managed to initiate all of these projects, though with the return of prosperity after World War II public support began to decline. See Richard Rhodes, *The Inland Ground* (New York, 1970), 166–67.

56. Gilbert Seldes, *Mainland* (New York, 1936), 6, 10, 12.

57. *Ibid.,* 7.

58. *Ibid.,* 7, 11, 174.

59. *Ibid.,* 176.

60. *Ibid.,* 242, 249–50.

61. *Ibid.,* 379–404.

62. Robert and Helen Lynd, *Middletown in Transition* (New York, 1937), 7, 13, 15, 20, 147, 487.

63. *Ibid.,* 20, 26, 41, 110, 356, 429, 447, 449, 453–55.

64. *Ibid.,* 448, 455.

65. *Ibid.,* 125–26, 134, 366, 369.

66. *Ibid.,* 146, 252, 271.

67. *Ibid.,* 404–5, 492.

68. *Ibid.,* 25, 97, 217, 292–94, 315–16, 427, 492.

69. *Ibid.,* 468, 489.

70. Malcom Cowley and Bernard Smith, eds., *Books That Changed Our Minds* (New York, 1939), 250–51.

71. Bruce Bliven, "Public Opinion," in Stearns, *loc. cit.,* 252.

72. Schuman, "Liberalism and Communism Reconsidered," *loc. cit.,* 335–36.

73. Kenneth Burke, "Revolutionary Symbolism in America," in Henry Hart, ed., *American Writer's Congress* (New York, 1935), 87–90.

74. Thurman Arnold, *The Folklore of Capitalism* (New Haven, 1937), 13–14, 21–23, 25, 41, 119, 333, 379.

75. *Ibid.,* 12, 37–38, 42; Harold Lasswell, *Politics: Who Gets What, When, How* (Cleveland, 1958, c. 1936), 13, 42, 103, 112–13, 115, 161.

76. Arnold, *The Folklore of Capitalism,* 45, 83, 138, 141, 162, 205, 331, 343–45; Lasswell, *Politics: Who Gets What, When, How,* 16, 100, 169. The italics are Arnold's.

77. Arnold, *The Folklore of Capitalism,* 34, 100, 111, 120, 178, 220, 384, 390, 393.

78. See William Leuchtenburg, *Franklin D. Roosevelt and the New Deal* (New York, 1963), 165, 195, 273; and Rexford Tugwell, "The New Deal: The Progressive Tradition," *Western Political Quarterly,* III (September 1950), 390–427.

79. "A People's Front for America," *New Republic,* LXXXV (January 8, 1936), 241.

80. See Warren, *Liberals and Communism,* 106–8, 142.

81. See William Leuchtenburg, "The New Deal and the Analogue of War," in John Braeman, Robert Bremner, and Everett Walters, eds., *Change and Continuity in Twentieth-Century America* (Columbus, Ohio, 1964), 81–143.

82. George Soule, "After the New Deal—I: The New Political Landscape," *New Republic,* LXXXXIX (May 17, 1939), 35–36.

83. *Ibid.,* 37.

VIII. From Depression to War

1. For specific examples of the anti-Stalinist position, see Norman Thomas, "The Communists' New Line," *New Republic,* LXXXVI (May 6, 1936), 373–74; V. F. Calverton, "The Farmer-Labor Party: Who Shall Lead It?" *Modern Quarterly,* IX (March 1936),

463–68; "Will Landon Bring Fascism to America?" *Modern Quarterly*, IX (August 1936), 3–4; "Declaration for Thomas and Nelson," *Modern Quarterly*, X (October 1936), 13–14; "The Second World War," *Modern Quarterly*, XI (Summer 1939), 3–7; "Munich and the Intellectuals," *Partisan Review*, VI (Fall 1938), 8–10; Dwight Macdonald, "War and the Intellectuals: Act Two," *Partisan Review*, VI (Spring 1939), 3–20; "The War of the Neutrals," *Partisan Review*, VI (Fall 1939), 3–15.

2. Bruce Bliven, "What Next?" *New Republic*, LXXXXIV (March 16, 1938), 159.

3. See "When America Goes to War—A Symposium," *Modern Quarterly*, IX (June 1935), 198; Malcolm Cowley, "Lines for an Interment," *New Republic*, LXXVI (September 10, 1933), 161; "Withdraw from Europe," *New Republic*, LXXVI (October 25, 1933), 294; Walter Millis, "Will We Stay Out of the Next War?" *New Republic*, LXXXII (July 31, 1935), 325; "Another War for Democracy," *New Republic*, LXXXV (February 5, 1936), 354; "England Shows Her Colors," *New Republic*, LXXXXIV (March 2, 1938), 88; and Oswald Villard, "Valedictory," *Nation*, CL (June 29, 1940), 782.

4. "Editorial Statement," *Partisan Review*, I (February–March 1934), 2. See also Philip Rahv and William Phillips, "Problems and Perspectives in Proletarian Literature," *Partisan Review*, I (June–July 1934), 5–6.

5. Norman Podhoretz, *Making It* (New York, 1969, c. 1967), 88.

6. For an eloquent expression of this attitude by a writer who was not officially a member of but intellectually close to the group around *Partisan Review*, see Edmund Wilson, "Trotsky: II," *New Republic*, LXXIII (January 11, 1933), 238.

7. See William Phillips, "Thomas Mann: Humanism in Exile," *Partisan Review*, IV (May 1938), 3–10.

8. Clement Greenberg, "Avant-Garde and Kitsch," *Partisan Review*, VI (Fall, 1939), 39–42, 47.

9. Dwight Macdonald, "Kulturbolschewismus Is Here," *Partisan Review*, VIII (November–December 1941), 446. See also Dwight Macdonald, "Soviet Cinema, 1930–1938," *Partisan Review*, V (July and August–September 1938), 35–60; Dwight Macdonald, "Soviet Society and Its Cinema," *Partisan Review*, VI (Winter 1939), 80–94; and F. W. Dupee, "The Americanism of Van Wyck Brooks," *Partisan Review*, VI (Summer 1939), 69–85.

10. For two excellent examples of this tendency, see Robert Warshow, *The Immediate Experience* (New York, 1962); and Andrew Sarris, *The American Cinema* (New York, 1968).

11. Greenberg, "Avant-Garde and Kitsch," *loc. cit.*, 40, 49; Macdonald, "Kulturbolschewismus Is Here," *loc. cit.*, 448–51. The italics are Macdonald's.

12. Philip Rahv and William Phillips, "Literature in a Political Decade," in Horace Gregory, ed., *New Letters in America* (New York, 1937), 174–76; Philip Rahv, "The Cult of Experience in American Writing," *Partisan Review*, VII (November–December, 1940), 413–14, 417–20, 423. For an elaboration of these ideas, see Alfred Kazin, *On Native Grounds* (New York, 1956, c. 1942), 24, 382.

13. Rahv and Phillips, "Literature in a Political Decade," in Gregory, *loc. cit.*, 176–78; Rahv, "The Cult of Experience in American Writing," *loc. cit.*, 422.

14. Rahv and Phillips, "Literature in a Political Decade," in Gregory, *loc. cit.*, 178–79; Rahv, "The Cult of Experience in American Writing," *loc. cit.*, 419.

15. William Phillips, "The Intellectuals' Tradition," *Partisan Review*, VIII (November–December 1941), 485, 487, 489–90.

16. *Ibid.*, 490; Philip Rahv, "Twilight of the Thirties," *Partisan Review*, VI (Summer 1939), 5–7, 9–10, 14.

17. Rahv, "Twilight of the Thirties," *loc. cit.*, 15.

18. *Ibid.*, 10–11.

19. Phillips, "The Intellectuals' Tradition," *loc. cit.,* 482.
20. *Ibid.,* 483; Rahv, "Twilight of the Thirties," *loc. cit.,* 14–15.
21. James Farrell, *A Note on Literary Criticism* (New York, 1936), 88; Edmund Wilson, "Marxism and Literature," in *The Triple Thinkers* (New York, 1938), 277. See also Kazin, *On Native Grounds,* 321–22.
22. V. F. Calverton, "Criticism on the Barricades," *Modern Quarterly,* IX (August 1936), 17–18.
23. Benjamin Ginzburg, "Science and Socialism," *Marxist Quarterly,* I (January–March 1937), 5; Farrell, *A Note on Literary Criticism,* 46, 61, 77; Wilson, "Marxism and Literature," *loc. cit.,* 287–89.
24. Lionel Trilling, "Hemingway and His Critics," *Partisan Review,* VI (Winter 1939), 60.
25. Farrell, *A Note on Literary Criticism,* 73, 162; Edmund Wilson, ed., "American Writing: 1941," *New Republic,* CIV (April 21, 1941), 545.
26. See William Wasserstrom, *The Time of the Dial* (Syracuse, New York, 1963), 137–39.
27. William Saroyan, "American Bureau to Aid Saroyan," *New Republic,* LXXXXV (July 13, 1938), 282.
28. Henry Miller, *The Cosmological Eye* (Norfolk, Connecticut, 1939), 3–4, 155–56, 158, 160, 162, 174–75, 184, 371.
29. Philip Rahv, "The Artist as Desperado," *New Republic,* CIV (April 21, 1941), 557–59.
30. Malcolm Cowley, "What New Directions?" *New Republic,* CIV (February 17, 1941), 218–20.
31. Podhoretz, *Making It,* 94.
32. *Ibid.,* 3; Alfred Kazin, *A Walker in the City* (New York, 1951), 11–12, 17, 21–22, 56.
33. Alfred Kazin, *Starting Out in the Thirties* (Boston, 1965), 10.
34. Kazin, *A Walker in the City,* 170–73.
35. For examples of this analysis, see Alter Brody, "Hitler Loses the Baltic," *New Masses,* XXXIII (October 10, 1939), 3–4; Joseph Starobin, "F.D.R.'s Road to War," *New Masses,* XXXV (April 9, 1940), 7–10; "Why Vote for War?" *New Masses,* XXXVII (October 1, 1940), 13–14; and "Not a Speech–A Harangue," *New Masses,* XXXIX (March 25, 1941), 11.
36. Theodore Draper, "The Case of the Stupid Statesmen," *New Masses,* XXXII (September 5, 1939), 3–4.
37. See, for example, Granville Hicks, "On Leaving the Communist Party," *New Republic,* LXXXXX (October 4, 1939), 244–45; and Louis Fischer, "Soviet Russia Today—III: Death of a Revolution," *Nation,* CL (January 13, 1940), 40–41.
38. Michael Gold, "John Reed: He Loved the People," *New Masses,* XXXVII (October 22, 1940), 11. See also "Granville Hicks Resigns," *New Masses,* XXXIII (October 3, 1939), 21; Joseph North, "Vincent Sheean, the Summer Soldier," *New Masses,* XXXIII (December 19, 1939), 21; and George Charney, *A Long Journey* (Chicago, 1968), 125.
39. See Oswald Villard, "Issues and Men," *Nation,* CXLIX (November 4, 1939), 499; "What Stalin Has Lost," *New Republic,* LXXXXX (September 27, 1939), 197–98; "Communist Imperialism," *New Republic,* LXXXXX (October 11, 1939), 257–58; "Common Sense About Russia," *New Republic,* CI (November 15, 1939), 98–100; "Power Politics and People," *New Republic,* CI (November 29, 1939), 155; and "The Soviet–Nazi Partnership," *New Republic,* CIV (May 26, 1941), 716. For a defense of the Nazi–Soviet pact on the basis of *Realpolitik,* see Frederick Schuman, "Machiavelli in Moscow," *New Republic,* CI (November 29, 1939), 158–60.
40. Sidney Hook, *Reason, Social Myths, and Democracy* (New York, 1940), 145. See also Bertram Wolfe, "The U.S. and the U.S.S.R.," in Irving Talmadge, ed., *Whose Revolution?* (New York, 1941), 225.
41. Edmund Wilson, *To the Finland Station* (New York, 1953, c. 1940), 481. For a similar

analysis, see Max Nomad, "The Tragedy of the Underdog," *Modern Quarterly*, X (December 1936), 21–25.

42. Granville Hicks, "Communism and the American Intellectuals," in Talmadge, *loc. cit.*, 110; Lewis Corey, "A Liberal Looks at Life," *Social Frontier*, VII (May 15, 1941), 233; Hook, *Reason, Social Myths, and Democracy*, 138, 160, 164, 180; Norman Thomas, "The Moscow Trials," *Modern Quarterly*, X (March 1938), 4.

43. Max Lerner, "Six Errors of Marxism," *New Republic*, LXXXXVIII (November 16, 1938), 37–38. See also Lewis Corey, "The Need Still Is: A New Social Order," in Talmadge, *loc. cit.*, 251.

44. Hook, *Reason, Social Myths, and Democracy*, 223–24, 266.

45. Corey, "The Need Still Is: A New Social Order," in Talmadge, *loc. cit.*, 249.

46. James Burnham, "The Theory of the Managerial Revolution," *Partisan Review*, VIII (May–June 1941), 182–86.

47. *Ibid.*, 187–90, 196.

48. Hook, *Reason, Social Myths, and Democracy*, 138; George Counts, "A Liberal Looks at Life," *Social Frontier*, VII (May 15, 1941), 232; Corey, "The Need Still Is: A New Social Order," in Talmadge, *loc. cit.*, 267.

49. Max Eastman, "Motive-Patterns of Socialism," *Modern Quarterly*, XI (Fall 1939), 45.

50. *Ibid.*, 54.

51. *Ibid.*, 52.

52. See Sidney Hook, "Ethereal Politics," *Nation*, CXLII (May 20, 1936), 654; James Burnham, "Is Democracy Possible?" in Talmadge, *loc. cit.*, 214; Corey, "The Need Still Is: A New Social Order," in Talmadge, *loc. cit.*, 253; and John Chamberlain, *The American Stakes* (New York, 1940), 281.

53. Chamberlain, *The American Stakes*, 12, 22, 31; Chamberlain, "Mr. Strachey and the State," *New Republic*, LXXXXVI (August 10, 1938), 25. See also Burnham, "Is Democracy Possible?" in Talmadge, *loc. cit.*, 195; and Corey, "A Liberal Looks at Life," *loc. cit.*, 233–34.

54. Chamberlain, *The American Stakes*, 28; Burnham, "Is Democracy Possible?" in Talmadge, *loc. cit.*, 196, 199; Corey, "The Need Still Is: A New Social Order," in Talmadge, *loc. cit.*, 255; Hook, *Reason, Social Myths, and Democracy*, 124–25, 287, 290, 294–95; John Dewey, *Freedom and Culture* (New York, 1939), 94.

55. Chamberlain, *The American Stakes*, 287; Lewis Corey, "Marxism Reconsidered," *Nation*, CL (March 2, 1940), 305–7; Corey, "The Need Still Is: A New Social Order," in Talmadge, *loc. cit.*, 263–66; Corey, "A Liberal Looks at Life," *loc. cit.*, 233; Hook, *Reason, Social Myths, and Democracy*," 286–87, 290.

56. John Chamberlain, "Mathematics of Domination," *New Republic*, LXXXXVI (October 12, 1938), 276.

57. Lionel Trilling, "Elements That Are Wanted," *Partisan Review*, VII (September–October 1940), 367–79.

58. V. F. Calverton, "A Plea for Proletarian Tragedy," *Modern Quarterly*, X (March 1937), 14.

59. For an illustration of these ideas, see Reinhold Niebuhr, "Peace and the Liberal Illusion," *Nation*, CXLIII (January 28, 1939), 117, 119.

60. Lewis Mumford, *Faith for Living* (New York, 1940), 66, 72, 94, 108, 111.

61. *Ibid.*, 75, 86, 89–91, 221–22. For a similar view, see Malcolm Cowley, "Faith and the Future," in Talmadge, *loc. cit.*, 154.

62. Mumford, *Faith For Living*, 11, 117–18.

63. *Ibid.*, 95, 100, 105–6; Niebuhr, "Peace and the Liberal Illusion," *loc. cit.*, 118.

64. Hook, *Reason, Social Myths, and Democracy*, 296.

65. Mumford, *Faith for Living*, 46–47, 192.

66. See Sidney Hook, "The Failure of the Left," *Partisan Review,* X (March–April 1943), 171–72; and Arthur Ekirch, *Ideologies and Utopias: The Impact of the New Deal on American Thought* (Chicago, 1969), 264.

67. "Mobilizing Against Russia," *New Republic,* CI (December 20, 1939), 247.

68. Corliss Lamont, "Why We Must Aid the Soviet Union," *New Masses,* XL (July 15, 1941), 12.

69. See "The Soviet-Nazi War: How It Happened," *New Masses,* XL (July 1, 1941), 3–7; "Angles for Americans," *New Masses,* XL (July 1, 1941), 8; "Why This Is Our War: I," *New Masses,* XL (July 8, 1941), 3–6; "Why This Is Our War: II," *New Masses,* XL (July 15, 1941), 5–6; and "The Anglo-Soviet Pact," *New Masses,* XL (July 22, 1941), 3.

70. "Three Speeches," *New Masses,* XLI (October 14, 1941), 20.

71. See Charney, *A Long Journey,* 126, 129, 133.

72. See "Keeping Out of the Next War," *New Republic,* CII (June 3, 1940), 745; "The Way to Help the Allies," *New Republic,* CII (June 17, 1940), 813–14; "Let's Get Down to Business," *New Republic,* CII (June 24, 1940), 839; "One Day That Shook the World," *New Republic,* CIV (June 30, 1941), 871–72; and Freda Kirchwey, "Order of the Year," *Nation,* CLII (January 4, 1941), 6.

73. Freda Kirchwey, "Fruits of Appeasement," *Nation,* CLIII (December 13, 1941), 599. See also "And We Will Win!" *New Masses,* XLI (December 16, 1941), 3.

BIBLIOGRAPHY

What follows is an evaluation of selected journals, books, and articles on which a study of this kind depends. It is not intended to be a complete listing of the source materials, nor has every entry cited in the notes been duplicated in the bibliography. Rather, a review of some of the more important primary and secondary literature may serve as an introductory guide for those readers who wish to pursue further the issues and ideas that shaped depression America.

I. PERIODICALS

To a considerable degree, the mind of twentieth-century America is best revealed in the nation's magazines, for these supply the most immediate record of the debates and tensions that have swept the intellectual community. This was particularly true in the 1930s, where many of the books and novels published during the decade appeared first as journal articles. More important, the magazines provided a forum for collective experimentation, dialogue, and criticism at a time when events often threatened to overwhelm the solitary writer. Thus the journals became a crucial channel through which intellectuals could raise issues, test ideas, refine their arguments, and comment directly on the problems of the day.

Of all the periodicals, the *New Republic* was the most influential during the 1930s. It published the broadest range of intellectuals from orthodox Communists through liberal reformers to apolitical (and frequently conservative) literary critics. Whenever a writer wished to make a major statement, more often than not he presented his case in the *New Republic*. The journal enjoyed a larger circulation than any of the other magazines, but its most attractive features were its tradition of political independence and its customary tolerance for differing points of view. Throughout the 1930s, Bruce Bliven and George Soule were responsible for the journal's editorial policy on domestic and international affairs. Edmund Wilson presided over the literary department until 1932, when he broke with the magazine because it did not at that point seem to him sufficiently radical. He was succeeded by Malcolm Cowley. Stark Young remained the drama editor during the entire decade. In addition, the *New Republic* always boasted on its masthead a number of glittering names as associate editors; these included John Dewey, Stuart Chase, Rexford Tugwell, and Lewis Mumford, among others.

The *Nation* had a longer and more celebrated history than the *New Republic,* but it was never able to play as significant a role in the 1930s. Until 1933, the magazine largely reflected the sometimes idiosyncratic interests and opinions of Oswald Garrison Villard. Once he relinquished direct editorial control, the *Nation* began to participate more actively in the decade's intellectual dialogue. During the middle and late 1930s, Freda Kirchwey and Max Lerner set forth the journal's position on political and social issues, while Joseph Wood Krutch served both as drama and literary editor. But throughout the period the *Nation* lacked the passion or immediacy which frequently animated the *New Republic.*

Two other magazines shared the generally liberal orientation of the *Nation* and *New Republic* during these years. From 1932 on Alfred Bingham and Selden Rodman edited *Common Sense,* a magazine more explicitly concerned with the political problems of reform, more sensitive to the strategic needs of the middle class, and less interested in cultural affairs or radical ideologies. *Social Frontier* made its appearance in 1934 as a journal of educational innovation, but under the editorship of George Counts and given the frequent contributions of writers like Dewey and Charles Beard, it also concentrated on the larger problems of social change.

All four of these journals positioned themselves to the left of the New Deal, at least until the late 1930s, when their sympathy for socialist ideas gave way before the need to defend American democracy in the face of the fascist menace. By the end of the decade, therefore, they had become the most consistent spokesmen for the Roosevelt Administration within the intellectual community.

On the Communist left, the major voice was the *New Masses.* The magazine underwent numerous editorial and stylistic changes during the opening years of the depression. With Michael Gold as editor, the early *New Masses* was devoted largely to publishing proletarian fiction and issuing ecstatic progress reports on the construction of socialism in the Soviet Union. But after 1932, under the more sober editorial control of Joseph Freeman, Granville Hicks, and Joseph North, the magazine's format was altered to resemble that of the *New Republic,* and it began to focus almost exclusively on the problems of American life. Indeed during the height of the Popular Front, the *New Masses* attracted a wide range of contributors and rivaled the *New Republic* as the spokesman for a major segment of the intellectual community. Much of its influence, however, collapsed after the announcement of the Nazi–Soviet pact.

Two other sources are important for understanding the stance of the Communist party during the 1930s. The *Daily Worker,* especially its Sunday edition, is of course indispensable as a record of direct commentary on political and social events. On a more theoretical level *Science and Society,* launched in 1936, attempted to discuss the philosophical implications of Communism, often with considerable sophistication.

Among anti-Stalinists, one of the most interesting journals was V. F. Calverton's

Modern Quarterly. As a radical but highly eclectic editor, Calverton in the early 1930s managed to mediate between liberals, Communists, Trotskyites, and writers of no definite political persuasion. These years were marked by innumerable symposiums, manifestoes, and the angry debate between Max Eastman and Sidney Hook over the best means of synthesizing Pragmatism and Marxism. But after 1935 the magazine grew increasingly shrill and sectarian as it denounced Stalinism, the Popular Front, and collective security. By the close of the decade, both Calverton and his contributors were in the process of re-examining (and abandoning) their commitment to radicalism.

During 1937 the *Marxist Quarterly* emerged as a rival to *Science and Society,* seeking to argue the philosophical case against Stalinism. Though it lasted very briefly, the magazine published important essays and reviews by Hook, Meyer Shapiro, Benjamin Ginzburg, and Lewis Corey, among others.

Along more literary (and also more conservative) lines, *Hound and Horn* in the early 1930s and the *Southern Review* in the later years of the decade defended the position of the "new critics" and the independent intellectual against the onslaught of the proletarian aesthetic. Though both journals accepted the contributions of left-wing writers, their basic antagonism toward radical politics and propagandistic art was reflected in the essays of R. P. Blackmur, Allen Tate, Cleanth Brooks, and Robert Penn Warren.

But the most systematic opposition both to Stalinism and the Popular Front can be found in the pages of *Partisan Review.* Its origins may be traced to two journals that appeared in but did not survive the early 1930s: *The Miscellany* (edited largely by Dwight Macdonald and F. W. Dupee) and *Symposium* (edited by James Burnham and Philip Wheelwright). Both magazines were primarily interested in literature, philosophy, and films rather than in matters of politics or ideology, and these preoccupations carried over into the late 1930s, when *Partisan's* hostility to the Popular Front seemed as much cultural as doctrinaire. In any case, under the direction of Macdonald, William Phillips, and Philip Rahv, publishing the essays of writers like Hook, Burnham, Lionel Trilling, and Edmund Wilson, *Partisan Review* became the central vehicle for those intellectuals who tried to remain both radical and anti-Stalinist, both avant-garde and influential. Thus the magazine brilliantly reflects the painful transition of the American writer from the depression to the postwar world.

II. PROGRESSIVISM AND THE 1920s

The essential studies of Progressive politics are John Morton Blum, *The Republican Roosevelt* (Cambridge, Massachusetts, 1954); George Mowry, *The Era of Theodore Roosevelt* (New York, 1958); and Arthur Link, *Woodrow Wilson and the Progressive Era* (New York, 1954). But for more interpretative accounts of the society out of which the Progressive movement sprang, as well as for the values and objectives of liberal reform in the early years of the twentieth century, one must turn elsewhere. Richard Hofstadter's *The Age of Reform* (New York, 1955) remains a classic discussion of the efforts on the part of both Populists and Progressives to restore nineteenth-century America; his thesis influenced an entire generation of American historians. Two more recent works, however, challenge this view. Gabriel Kolko's

The Triumph of Conservatism (Glencoe, Illinois, 1963) seeks to connect the reform impulse to the desire of businessmen to rationalize the economy and put an end to competition. Robert Wiebe's *The Search for Order, 1877–1920* (New York, 1967) is a more comprehensive analysis of the bureaucratic and organizational forces in American society that gave rise to Progressivism. Of the two, Wiebe provides the more provocative and persuasive argument. On the subject of radical politics during the Progressive era, James Weinstein has made a strong if not altogether convincing case for the existence of an indigenous and broad-based socialist alternative in *The Decline of American Socialism, 1912–1925* (New York, 1967).

The primary sources for the intellectual life of this period are readily accessible either in paperback editions or anthologies. Without listing specific titles here, it should be said that no student of American culture can neglect the works of John Dewey, Thorstein Veblen, Charles Beard, Jane Addams, Herbert Croly, Walter Lippmann, Van Wyck Brooks, or Randolph Bourne during these years. The secondary sources are steadily multiplying, but a few deserve special mention. Morton White's *Social Thought in America: The Revolt Against Formalism* (New York, 1949) is a brilliant synthesis of the ideas of Dewey, Beard, Veblen, and Oliver Wendell Holmes; it is also a major statement about the intellectual revolution that transformed American thought from a concern with timeless abstractions to an interest in social "reality." Some of the moral and psychological consequences of this transformation are explored in Christopher Lasch's *The New Radicalism in America, 1889–1963* (New York, 1965), a series of disjointed but enormously challenging essays on the relationship between ideas and action, intellectuals and power. Charles Forcey's *The Crossroads of Liberalism* (New York, 1961) is a less arresting but still useful account of the early days of the *New Republic.* August Meier's *Negro Thought in America, 1880–1915* (Ann Arbor, Michigan, 1966) provides a detailed analysis of black intellectuals and is particularly good on the ideas of Booker T. Washington and W. E. B. DuBois. Henry May's *The End of American Innocence* (New York, 1959) discusses the transition from Progressivism to the 1920s, but it too often seems little more than a superficial survey of moods and trends. David Noble's *The Progressive Mind, 1890–1917* (Chicago, 1970) is too confusing and eccentric to be of much help as an introduction to the period, though it may be useful when read in conjunction with other accounts.

Like the Progressive era, the 1920s are rich with primary material on intellectual life, much of it conveniently reprinted in paperback. The place to begin is with literature; the poetry and novels of T. S. Eliot, Ezra Pound, E. E. Cummings, Sherwood Anderson, Sinclair Lewis, Theodore Dreiser, F. Scott Fitzgerald, and Ernest Hemingway, as well as the essays of H. L. Mencken, are all essential to any understanding of postwar culture. There are, however, certain works which should be cited for their relevance to the present study. The best example of the kind of social criticism that prevailed during the 1920s is the collection of essays in Harold Stearns, ed., *Civilization in the United States* (New York, 1922). The insights these essays provide can be enlarged by turning to books like William Ogburn, *Social Change* (New York, 1922); Charles Beard, ed., *Whither Mankind* (New York, 1928); and especially Joseph Wood Krutch, *The Modern Temper* (New York, 1929). In addition, Frederic Howe's autobiography, *The Confessions of a Reformer* (New York, 1925), offers an extremely revealing (if sometimes disingenuous) portrayal of what happened to the Progressive mind when it confronted the war and the disillusions of the 1920s. There were many works of literary criticism published during the decade, but one of the best summary statements (particularly because of what it portended for the 1930s) is Matthew Josephson's *Portrait of the Artist as American* (New York, 1930). Finally, Robert and Helen Lynd's *Middletown* (New York, 1929) is not only a pioneering study of middle- and working-class life in the 1920s but also a superb illustration of the cultural and social issues that most disturbed intellectuals during the entire period.

The secondary accounts of the 1920s are neither as numerous nor as interesting. There are several, however, which should be consulted. William Leuchtenburg's *The Perils of Prosperity* (Chicago, 1958) is a brief and often popularized survey of the decade's more legendary political social events. Roderick Nash's *The Nervous Generation: American Thought, 1917–1930* (Chicago, 1970) has a tendentious and uneven argument about the conservatism of the decade's cultural life, but it contains a provocative essay on Henry Ford. The most complete, though laborious, discussion of the boom and its collapse is George Soule's *Prosperity Decade* (New York, 1947). For a livelier if less comprehensive account, see John Kenneth Galbraith, *The Great Crash* (Boston, 1955). There are also a number of important essays on every aspect of life in the 1920s in John Braeman, Robert Bremner, and David Brody, eds., *Change and Continuity in Twentieth-Century America: The 1920s* (Columbus, Ohio, 1968). On literature, Frederick Hoffman's *The Twenties* (New York, 1955) is an imaginative and frequently profound reading of the decade's major works of art—indeed, it is a model intellectual history which has never yet been duplicated. This may be supplemented, however, by William Wasserstrom's *The Time of the Dial* (Syracuse, New York, 1963), an impenetrably written but perceptive evaluation of the millennial impulse among American writers; Malcolm Cowley's *Exile's Return* (New York, Viking Press edition, 1951), which remains the quintessential analysis of expatriation; Matthew Josephson's *Life Among the Surrealists* (New York, 1962), an informative memoir but not nearly as suggestive as Cowley's; and R. P. Blackmur's valuable essay "The American Literary Expatriate" in David Bowers, ed., *Foreign Influences in American Life* (New York, 1952), 126–45. Finally, as a study not only of the *cause célèbre* of the 1920s but also as a harbinger of the commitments that would characterize the 1930s, G. L. Joughlin and E. M. Morgan's *The Legacy of Sacco and Vanzetti* (New York, 1948) is unsurpassed.

III. THE DEPRESSION EXPERIENCE

The New Deal has received more extended treatment than any other facet of the 1930s. The best one-volume history of the Roosevelt Administration is still William Leuchtenburg's *Franklin Delano Roosevelt and the New Deal* (New York, 1963); its value is enhanced by Leuchtenburg's ability not only to narrate the story but also assess the strengths and weaknesses of Roosevelt's tenure. In addition, one should see his suggestive essay "The New Deal and the Analogue of War," in John Braeman, Robert Bremner, and Everett Walters, eds., *Change and Continuity in Twentieth-Century America* (Columbus, Ohio, 1964), 81–143. There are also some worthwhile essays in Alonzo Hamby, ed., *The New Deal: Analysis and Interpretation*

(New York, 1969). Arthur Ekirch's *Ideologies and Utopias: The Impact of the New Deal on American Thought* (Chicago, 1969) is superficial and often disappointing, given the possibilities of the subject. Though his view of Progressivism may be flawed, Otis Graham has skillfully chronicled the response of early twentieth-century liberals to the New Deal in *An Encore for Reform* (New York, 1967). On specific aspects of the Roosevelt Administration one should consult Rexford Tugwell, *The Brains Trust* (New York, 1968), which is excellent on the campaign of 1932; Paul Conkin, *Toward a New World: The New Deal Community Program* (Ithaca, New York, 1959), which evaluates some of the more utopian strains in the New Deal; and James Patterson, *Congressional Conservatism and the New Deal* (Lexington, Kentucky, 1967), which traces the increasingly powerful Republican-Southern Democratic-rural opposition to Roosevelt in the late 1930s. Finally, there are at least three articles that provide important insights into the "ideology" of the New Deal. Rexford Tugwell's "The New Deal: The Progressive Tradition," *Western Political Quarterly*, III (September 1950), 390–427, assesses Roosevelt's failure to offer a new social philosophy and value system for an interdependent society; T. V. Smith's "The New Deal as a Cultural Phenomenon," in F. S. C. Northrup, ed., *Ideological Differences and World Order* (New Haven, Connecticut, 1949), 208–28, analyzes the New Deal's legendary pragmatism as an imaginative (and necessarily non-ideological) solution to the problems of collectivism; while Barton Bernstein's "The New Deal: The Conservative Achievements of Liberal Reform," in Bernstein, ed., *Towards a New Past* (New York, 1967), 263–88, is a forceful but sometimes simplistic indictment of the New Deal's efforts to superimpose a welfare state on the foundations of corporate capitalism.

There are no very good histories of social life in the 1930s. Indeed the best analysis of the depression's impact on ordinary citizens is not a history at all but a contemporary account: Robert and Helen Lynd's *Middletown in Transition* (New York, 1937). In addition, Leo Gurko's *The Angry Decade* (New York, 1947) contains some interesting ideas on popular culture. There are scattered insights on social behavior in Caroline Bird's *The Invisible Scar* (New York, 1966) and Robert Bendiner's *Just Around The Corner* (New York, 1967), but both books are too superficial to be of great value. On the problems of working-class life, however, Irving Bernstein's *The Lean Years* (New York, 1960) and *The Turbulent Years* (Boston, 1971) provide a richly detailed and generally perceptive appraisal of how the average laborer endured the period between the wars. The psychological mood of the depression years, particularly the extent to which people responded to the crisis in personal rather than political terms, is sensitively discussed by Saul Maloff, "The Mythic Thirties," *Texas Quarterly*, XI (Winter, 1968), 109–18, and by Daniel Aaron, "The Treachery of Recollection: The Inner and the Outer History," in Robert Bremner, ed., *Essays on History and Literature* (Columbus, Ohio, 1966), 3–27.

The treatment of radical movements in the 1930s is usually of no higher quality than those on social history. Most attention has been paid to the Communist party. The standard works here are Theodore Draper, *The Roots of American Communism* (New York, 1957) and *American Communism and Soviet Russia* (New York, 1960), as well as Irving Howe and Lewis Coser, *The American Communist Party* (Boston, 1957); each of these accounts, however intelligent, is weakened by the authors' own personal involvement in the subject together with their polemical need to establish a non-Stalinist alternative on the left. For a less ideological (but also less provocative) interpretation of the American fascination with Russia, see Peter Filene, *Americans and the Soviet Experiment, 1917–1933* (Cambridge, Massachusetts, 1967). On other issues and causes, Dan T. Carter's *Scottsboro* (Baton Rouge, Louisiana, 1969) is an indispensable study of one of the decade's headline events; while Donald McCoy's *Angry Voices* (Lawrence, Kansas, 1958) is an incomplete and unimaginative discussion of radical politics both left and right. Murray Kempton's *Part of Our Time* (New York, 1955) remains an extraordinarily sensitive, if often uncharitable, lament for the Left's fundamental lack of rebelliousness in the 1930s. Finally Christopher Lasch has weighed the strengths and weaknesses of American radicalism throughout the twentieth century in *The Agony of the American Left* (New York, 1969); these essays should not be neglected by any reader interested in the subject past or present.

There are no adequate general histories of intellectual life in the 1930s, though Warren Susman's "The Thirties," in Stanley Coben and Lorman Ratner, eds., *The Development of an American Culture* (Englewood Cliffs, New Jersey, 1970), 179–218, is the beginning of a major re-evaluation of the decade's philosophical and cultural commitments; this essay has been extremely important to the present study and should not be missed by anyone interested in all aspects of the depression experience. In addition, trends in specific areas are often treated with insight and intelligence. For example, Donald Meyer's *The Protestant Search for Political Realism, 1919–1941*(Berkeley and Los Angeles, 1961) is not only an impressive study of the transition from the Social Gospel to neo-orthodoxy, but it is also a brilliant intellectual history that ultimately transcends the special concerns of Protestantism and sheds light on some of the basic problems of American culture in the 1930s. Two less valuable analyses of developments in religion are Paul Carter's *The Decline and Revival of the Social Gospel, 1920–1940* (Ithaca, New York, 1954) and Robert Miller's *American Protestantism and Social Issues, 1919–1939* (Chapel Hill, North Carolina, 1958). On the mind of Black America, Harold Cruse's *The Crisis of the Negro Intellectual* (New York, 1967) is a redundant and bitter attack on the relation of black writers to the Communist party, but it also contains some valuable ideas on the general connections between culture and politics that cannot be dismissed. Michael Wrezin's *Oswald Garrison Villard* (Bloomington, Indiana, 1967) is a workmanlike biography of a particularly elusive figure. For an evaluation of the impact of European émigrés on American thought, Donald Fleming and Bernard Bailyn, eds., "The Intellectual Migration: Europe and America, 1930–1960," *Perspectives in American History,* II (Cambridge, Massachusetts, 1968), is first-rate. Other studies of cultural affairs are listed under the appropriate headings in the bibliography.

If the secondary works on social and intellectual history are minimal and generally disappointing, the 1930s has spawned a proliferating number of memoirs and autobiographies that are often quite useful. Perhaps the most perceptive are Alfred Kazin's *A Walker in the City* (New York, 1951) and *Starting Out in the 1930s* (Boston, 1965); these offer an incomparable portrait of what it meant to be young, Jewish, radical, and passionately in love with literature in the years before Pearl Harbor. Irving Howe has recorded similar impressions in "A Memoir of the Thirties," in *Steady Work* (New York, 1966), 349–64. Matthew Josephson's *Infidel in the Temple* (New York, 1967) is extremely informative if not as insightful as Kazin's recollections. Max Eastman's *Love and Revolution* (New York, 1964) is an exhaustive but too egocentric account to be very reliable either on Eastman's own life or the times in which he did his most significant work. Michael Gold's *Jews Without Money* (New York, 1930) is really about the author's adolescence rather than the 1930s, but it does focus on the experiences that shaped Gold's later commitments; it is also the best writing Gold ever achieved. There are two important biographies by ex-Communists: Granville Hicks's *Part of the Truth* (New York, 1965), which makes the author seem peculiarly colorless and detached from the very movements he is describing; and George Charney's *A Long Journey* (Chicago, 1968), which is periodically suggestive but ultimately evades the moral problems of cynicism and manipulation which persistently plagued the party's functionaries. The memories of some other radicals are preserved (perhaps embalmed is a more appropriate word) in Ruth Simon, ed., *As We Saw the Thirties* (Urbana, Illinois, 1967). Louis Fischer's *Men and Politics* (New York, 1941) is less an autobiography than a detailed study of European diplomacy between the wars. One of the most interesting and least predictable memoirs is Woody Guthrie's *Bound for Glory* (New York, 1943); for all his celebration of collective action and the common man, Guthrie's experience often seems bizarre, rootless, and highly personal. Finally, before her death Josephine Herbst was engaged in what promised to be an invaluable reconstruction of the 1920s and 1930s; for her insights into these years, the reader should consult "The Starched Blue Sky of Spain," *The Noble Savage*, I (1960), 76–117; "A Year of Disgrace," *The Noble Savage*, III (1961), 128–60; "Moralist's Progress," *Kenyon Review*, XXVII (Autumn 1965), 772–77; and "Yesterday's Road," *New American Review*, III (1968), 84–104.

Though anthologies are no substitute for direct immersion in the primary sources, there are several that supply helpful introductions to the period. For politics and headline events, see Howard Zinn, ed., *New Deal Thought* (Indianapolis, Indiana, 1967); Daniel Aaron and Robert Bendiner, eds., *The Strenuous Decade* (New York, 1970); and Donald Congdon, ed., *The Thirties: A Time to Remember* (New York, 1962). On cultural and literary matters, see Louis Filler, ed., *The Anxious Years* (New York, 1963); Harvey Swados, ed., *The American Writer and the Great Depression* (Indianapolis, Indiana, 1966); and Jack Salzman and Barry Wallerstein, eds., *Years of Protest* (New York, 1967).

IV. POLITICAL AND ECONOMIC THOUGHT

The most important efforts to discover political and economic alternatives to liberal capitalism are treated extensively in the text. These include John Chamberlain, *Farewell to Reform* (New York, 1932); Lincoln Steffens, *The Autobiography of Lincoln Steffens* (New York, 1931); Adolph Berle and Gardiner Means, *The Modern Corporation and Private Property* (New York, 1932); Stuart Chase, *A New Deal* (New York, 1932); George Soule, *A Planned Society* (New York, 1932) and *The Coming American Revolution* (New York, 1934); and Lewis Corey, *The Crisis of the Middle Class* (New York, 1935). Similar arguments for planning and political reform are advanced in Stuart Chase, *The Economy of Abundance* (New York, 1934) and *The Government in Business* (New York, 1935); Rexford Tugwell, *The Industrial Discipline and the Governmental Arts* (New York, 1933); Lewis Corey,

The Decline of American Capitalism (New York, 1934); Charles Beard, ed., *America Faces the Future* (Boston, 1932) and his own "The Myth of Rugged Individualism," *Harper's,* CLXIV (December 1931) , 13–22; and Findlay MacKenzie, ed., *Planned Society: Yesterday, Today, Tomorrow* (New York, 1937). The politics of the New Deal are formally defended in Henry Wallace, *New Frontiers* (New York, 1934), and Rexford Tugwell, *The Battle for Democracy* (New York, 1935). Charles Beard's *The Open Door at Home* (New York, 1934) is one of the few systematic attempts during the decade to define a radically new foreign policy for America, and Beard's arguments still have relevance for the present. In conjunction with this, one should read David Marcell, "Charles Beard: Civilization and the Revolt Against Empiricism," *American Quarterly,* XXI (Spring 1969), 65–86, for a perceptive appraisal of Beard's shift in the 1930s from a reliance on economic determinism to an interest in ideological forces. The most coherent expression of the conservative position on political and economic problems may be found in Lawrence Dennis, *The Coming of American Fascism* (New York, 1936); and Walter Lippmann, *The Good Society* (New York, 1937).

V. SOCIAL PHILOSOPHY AND CULTURAL CRITICISM

Again, the central works are analyzed in the text. For the conflict between "culture" and "civilization," see 12 Southerners, *I'll Take My Stand* (New York, 1930), as well as its sequel, Herbert Agar and Allen Tate, eds., *Who Owns America?* (Boston, 1936); also Lewis Mumford's *Technics and Civilization* (New York, 1934) and *The Culture of Cities* (New York, 1938). On the relationship between the individual and modern society, see Ruth Benedict, *Patterns of Culture* (Boston, 1934); Karen Horney, *The Neurotic Personality of Our Times* (New York, 1937); John Dewey's *Individualism Old and New* (New York, 1930) and *Liberalism and Social Action* (New York, 1935); and Robert Lynd, *Knowledge for What?* (Princeton, New Jersey, 1939). The most sophisticated efforts to synthesize liberalism and Marxism are Sidney Hook's *Toward the Understanding of Karl Marx* (New York, 1933) and *From Hegel to Marx* (New York, 1936). The existential critique of collectivism is best elaborated in Reinhold Niebuhr, *Moral Man and Immoral Society* (New York, 1932).

In addition, two secondary studies of social philosophy have recently appeared: Robert Crunden's *From Self to Society, 1919–1941* (Englewood Cliffs, New Jersey, 1972), which is a highly suggestive but all-too-brief summary of the main trends in American thought between the wars; and R. Alan Lawson's *The Failure of Independent Liberalism, 1930–1941* (New York, 1971), which is an informative reconstruction of liberal ideas in the 1930s, though it ultimately fails to offer enough in the way of interpretation or analysis.

VI. LITERARY CRITICISM, DOCUMENTARIES, AND NOVELS

Here the primary materials are wide and varied. On the role of the intellectual in American society, the Left's position in the early 1930s is most succinctly presented in Henry Hart, ed., *American Writers' Congress* (New York, 1935), which reproduces the speeches and papers delivered at the first Writers' Congress. But see also *Culture and the Crisis* (League of Professional Groups for Foster and Ford, 1932), which argues the case for the intelligentsia's support of the Communist candidates in the Presidential election; and the introduction to Joseph Freeman, Granville Hicks, and Michael Gold, eds., *Proletarian Literature in the United States* (New York, 1935). This whole volume is an excellent representation of what the Left considered revolutionary literature. Finally, no reader should neglect Joseph Freeman's *An American Testament* (New York, 1936), not only for what it reveals about the relation between poetry and politics in the 1930s but also because it is (especially in its early sections) an enormously sensitive autobiography about cultural (as well as immigrant) life in New York during the Wilsonian era and the early 1920s.

The 1930s is probably better known for the ferocity of its literary arguments than for the quality of its literary criticism, but Edmund Wilson's *Axel's Castle* (New York, 1931) remains a seminal interpretation of modernism in the fiction and poetry of the twentieth century, a movement toward which Wilson was at once skeptical and sympathetic. John Dewey's *Art as Experience* (New York, 1934) is a more theoretical, but no less profound, discussion of the role of art in social affairs. Nevertheless, the more typical attitude toward literature (especially on the part of the Left) is reflected in Granville Hicks, *The Great Tradition* (New York, 1933 and 1935); V. F. Calverton, *The Liberation of American Literature* (New York, 1932); and Bernard Smith, *Forces in American Criticism* (New York, 1939). For the formalist opposition to the proletarian aesthetic, see Allen Tate, *Reactionary Essays on Poetry and Ideas* (New York, 1936). At the same time, Horace Gregory, ed., *New Letters in America* (New York, 1937) contains a variety of opinions on contemporary literature from differing points of view.

Many writers tried their hand at documentaries in the 1930s. For purposes of this study, the most valuable are Edmund Wilson's *The American Jitters* (New York, 1932) and *Travels in Two Democracies* (New York, 1936); James Rorty's *Where Life Is Better* (New York, 1936); and Sherwood Anderson's *Puzzled America* (New York, 1935). These should be supplemented with Nathan Asch's *The Road: In Search of America* (New York, 1936), a highly personal encounter with the depression experience; John Dos Passos's *In All Countries* (New York, 1934) and *Journeys Between Wars* (New York, 1938), both of which record the author's European travels; Theodore Dreiser's *Tragic America* (New York, 1932), a not always coherent account of Dreiser's attempt to comprehend the crisis; Louis Adamic's *My America* (New York, 1938), as much an autobiography as a documentary; Erskine Caldwell's *Some American People* (New York, 1935) and Caldwell and Margaret Bourke-White's *You Have Seen Their Faces* (New York, 1937), a combination of interviews and photographs of the sort James Agee despised; and Gilbert Seldes's *The Year of the Locust* (Boston, 1932), a more conventionally journalistic narrative of the years between 1929 and 1932.

In addition to the novels specifically treated in the text, the reader should consult Edward Dahlberg's *Bottom Dogs* (New York, 1930) and Tom Kromer's *Waiting for Nothing* (New York, 1935) for examples of "protest" fiction about marginal men; Tess Slesinger's *The Unpossessed* (New York, 1934), one of the few depression novels that tries to understand urban radicals, though even here the issues ultimately become more sexual than political; John Dos Passos's *The Adventures of a Young Man* (New York, 1939), a study of the Spanish Civil War which was also the beginning of the author's explicit disenchantment with the Left; F. Scott Fitzgerald's *Tender Is the Night* (New York, 1933) and John O'Hara's *Appointment in Samarra* (New York, 1934), both of which offer superb portraits of the way in which certain values and life-styles associated with the 1920s gradually disintegrated in the depression decade; and above all Thomas Wolfe's *Look Homeward, Angel* (New York, 1929), *The Web and the Rock* (New York, 1939), and *You Can't Go Home Again* (New York, 1940), the private account of an entire world in crisis.

The secondary assessments of American literature in the 1930s are uneven and too often dependent on stereotypes about the decade's "social" consciousness. The standard work on radical intellectuals is Daniel Aaron's *Writers on the Left* (New York, 1961); although it provides a great deal of information, it is more preoccupied with what writers did than with what they wrote. Walter Rideout's *The Radical Novel in the United States, 1900–1954* (Cambridge, Massachusetts, 1956) and Warren French's *The Social Novel at the End of an Era* (Carbondale, Illinois, 1966) are both competent if not terribly imaginative surveys of protest fiction. Maxwell Geismar's *Writers in Crisis* (Boston, 1942) contains some interesting interpretations, particularly of Dos Passos, Steinbeck, and Wolfe. Along the same lines, there are several extremely suggestive essays in David Madden, ed., *Proletarian Writers of the Thirties* (Carbondale and Edwardsville, Illinois, 1968) and *Tough Guy Writers of the Thirties* (Carbondale and Edwardsville, Illinois, 1968). The tough-guy genre is further explored by William Aydellotte, "The Detective Story as a Historical Force," *Yale Review*, XXXIX (September, 1949), 76–95. On the intellectuals' response to the major political event of the decade, see Frederick Benson's *The Literary Impact of the Spanish Civil War* (New York, 1967), which contrasts Hemingway with Orwell, Koestler, and Malraux; and Allen Guttmann's *The Wound in the Heart* (New York, 1962), which is valuably chiefly for a perceptive interpretation of *For Whom the Bell Tolls.* There are a growing number of analyses of specific writers, but two that seem useful for this study are Sherman Paul's *Edmund Wilson* (Urbana, Illinois, 1965) and Richard Chase's *The American Novel and Its Tradition* (New York, 1957), which contains a shrewd reading of Faulkner.

VII. THE MASS MEDIA, THEATER, AND FILMS

Historians, media theorists, drama critics, and film buffs are just beginning to explore the impact of the theater and popular culture on depression America. Nevertheless, there are already some interesting and important studies available for anyone who wants to know what the average citizen was hearing and seeing in the 1930s.

Two magazines published during the decade are central to an understanding of developments on the stage. *Theatre Arts* covered every conceivable facet of the theater from Broadway, regional, and community playhouses, to folk dances and local ceremonies at home and abroad. But the journal's reviews and discussions of contemporary plays, whether radical or commercial, provide an indispensable record of how critics in the 1930s responded to the depression theater. On the other hand, *New Theatre and Film* was concerned from 1931 through 1937 exclusively with the left-wing stage. Here one finds the basic theories behind agit-prop productions, the radical reaction to the Group Theater and the Theater Union, and the increasing interest in the revolutionary possibilities of film. The journal also reveals, however unconsciously, the gradual decline of the proletarian theater as it gave way to the more conventional impulses of the Popular Front and mass culture.

The major plays of the 1930s are all readily available both in print and frequently in revivals. For purposes of this study, the most important were Clifford Odets, *Six Plays of Clifford Odets* (New York, 1939); Thorton Wilder, *Our Town* (New York, 1939); Mark Blitzstein, *The Cradle Will Rock* (New York, 1937) and *Pins and Needles* (New York, 1937); William Kozlenko, ed., *The Best Short Plays of the Social Theatre* (New York, 1939); and Harold Clurman, ed., *Famous American Plays of the 1930s* (New York, 1959), which reprints S. N. Behrman's *End of Summer,* Robert Sherwood's *Idiot's Delight,* and William Saroyan's *The Time of Your Life.* Perhaps the decade's two most sophisticated efforts to define a unique aesthetic for the radical stage were Mordecai Gorelik's *New Theatres for Old* (New York, 1940) and John Howard Lawson's *The Theory and Technique of Playwrighting* (New York, 1936).

Among the secondary discussions of the depression theater, the most perceptive is easily Harold Clurman's *The Fervent Years* (New York, 1945); indeed, this is not only a sensitive history of the Group Theater but also an extraordinarily penetrating commentary on the general problem of cultural rebellion both in the 1930s and thereafter. Along the same lines Gerald Weales, "The Group Theater and its Plays," in John Brown and Bernard Harris, eds., *American Theatre* (London, 1967), 67–86, offers an interesting interpretation of Odets. For a more general survey of theatrical developments in the 1930s, Gerald Rabkin's *Drama and Commitment* (Blooming-ton, Indiana, 1964) analyzes with intelligence the plays of Behrman, Lawson, Odets, and Maxwell Anderson, as well as those of the Federal Theater Project; while Morgan Himmelstein's *Drama Was a Weapon* (New Brunswick, New Jersey, 1963) is little more than a simplistic diatribe against the way in which the Communists presumably destroyed the radical stage. Hallie Flanagan's *Arena* (New York, 1940) is an informative account of the political and economic problems that plagued the Federal Theater Project by its continually embattled director; this should be supple-mented with Jane Matthews, *The Federal Theatre* (New York, 1968). Norris Houghton's *Moscow Rehearsals* (New York, 1936) and *Advance from Broadway* (New York, 1941) both cover theatrical movements beyond the range of Broadway and New York. David Lifson's *The Yiddish Theatre in America* (New York, 1965) is a fascinating analysis of the foreign-language stage where a remarkable number of performers, directors, and stage designers who became important in the 1930s first began. Unfortunately, John Houseman's *Run-Through* (New York, 1972), the memoir of his stormy collaboration with Orson Welles in the Federal and Mercury theaters, which may rival Clurman in its insights into the problems of creating a community on stage, appeared too late for inclusion in this study.

Investigations of the media, especially radio, are less profuse. In the decade itself, Hadley Cantril and Gordon Allport offered a pioneering evaluation of radio's effects on public taste and attitudes in their *Psychology of Radio* (New York, 1935). In a more limited vein, Cantril's *The Invasion from Mars* (Princeton, New Jersey, 1940) explored the nature and consequences of the Mercury Theater's famous broadcast, "War of the Worlds." Along similar lines, one should see William Ogburn, "Social Effects of Radio," in *Recent Social Trends in the United States* (New York, 1933),

152–57; indeed, this whole volume contains invaluable raw material for the social history of the 1920s and early 1930s. More recently, Erik Barnouw's three-volume *History of Broadcasting in the United States* (New York, 1970) is a detailed examination of the radio and television industries from their inception to the present. But one might find more stimulating analyses in James Thurber's "Soapland," in *The Beast in Me* (New York, 1948), 189–260, which discusses the values implicit in the world of soap operas; Bernard Rosenberg and David Manning White, eds., *Mass Culture* (New York, 1957), which contains a variety of essays on every aspect of the popular arts; and Reuel Denney's "The Discovery of Popular Culture," in Robert Spiller and Eric Larrabee, eds., *American Perspectives* (Cambridge, Massachusetts, 1961), 154–77, which is an extremely perceptive evaluation of the transition from print to auditory and visual forms of communication.

Of all the types of popular culture, however, the movies have attracted the widest attention. During the 1930s, several works attempted to weigh the impact of the cinema both as a form of art and as entertainment. Of these, the most elaborate (and also the most knowledgeable) is Lewis Jacobs's *The Rise of the American Film* (New York, 1939); it not only provides a fairly complete history of the motion-picture industry but it is also an excellent example of how and why intellectuals in the 1930s continually insisted that Hollywood adopt a social conscience. For the social and economic consequences of movie-making and movie-viewing, one should see Margaret Thorp's *America at the Movies* (New Haven, 1939) and Leo Rosten's *Hollywood* (New York, 1941). In addition, Edmund Wilson contributed a classic essay on novelists turned screenwriters in *The Boys in the Back Room* (San Francisco, 1941).

The secondary studies are numerous, though of highly uneven quality. Andrew Sarris, *The American Cinema* (New York, 1968), is the place to begin for an understanding of the American sound film; whatever the weaknesses of the *auteur* theory, Sarris's all-too-brief interpretation of major directors like Ford, Hawks, Lubitsch, Sternberg, Capra, Lang, and Welles are sensitive and first rate. Similarly, Robert Warshow's *The Immediate Experience* (New York, 1962) contains three absolutely brilliant investigations of the Western, the gangster film, and the changing screen persona of Charlie Chaplin, as well as more general inquiries into the nature of popular culture (including the best single essay on Clifford Odets as an essentially ethnic rather than political dramatist). On a lesser level, Parker Tyler's *The Hollywood Hallucination* (New York, 1944) has a number of challenging insights into the psychology and mythology of the cinema, but it is marred by an almost incoherent prose style; Daniel Talbot, ed., *Film: An Anthology* (Berkeley and Los Angeles, 1959) reprints some historic essays in film criticism; Arthur Knight's *The Liveliest Art* (New York, 1957) is indeed a lively but also superficial history of motion pictures; George Bluestone's *Novels into Film* (Baltimore, 1957) offers an interesting comparison of specific novels and films (with two excellent studies of John Ford's *The Informer* and *The Grapes of Wrath*), together with a theoretical essay that is turgid and needlessly abstract; while Thomas Wiseman's *Cinema* (London, 1964) adds very little to our comprehension or appreciation of the cinema. One should also see "The Hollywood Screenwriter," *Film Comment,* VI (Winter 1970–1971) for several penetrating essays on those who wrote the words the stars repeated. For specific critiques of the depression cinema, John Baxter's *Hollywood in the 1930s* (London, 1968), Charles Higham and Joel Greenberg's *Hollywood in the 1940s* (London, 1968), and Andrew Bergman's *We're in the Money* (New York, 1971) are all competent and informative if not noticeably original.

There are a growing number of studies of particular producers, directors, and genres. Among the very best is Richard Schickel's *The Disney Version* (New York, 1968), which not only offers a thoughtful analysis of Disney's films but also an exceedingly perceptive evaluation of a special type of American entrepreneur. Robert Thomas has written two occasionally useful but ultimately disappointing biographies of Hollywood's more influential moguls: *King Cohn* (New York, 1967) and *Thalberg, Life and Legend* (New York, 1969). There is a suggestive investigation of famous fictional and screen monsters in Drake Douglas, pseud., *Horror!* (New York, 1966). Paul Jensen has contributed a knowledgeable assessment of one of Hollywood's more complex directors in *The Cinema of Fritz Lang* (New York, 1969). By contrast, Herman Weinberg fails to offer any insights into the films of Ernst Lubitsch in *The Lubitsch Touch* (New York, 1968). Indeed comedy has never been treated as adequately as films of adventure or crime or romance. Thus Theodore Huff's *Charlie Chaplin* (New York, 1951) is a workmanlike biography, but its discussion of Chaplin's films manages to read like little more than a series of plot summaries. Allen Eyles's *The Marx Brothers: Their World of Comedy* (London, 1966) contains some interesting if undeveloped ideas, while Paul Zimmerman and Burt Goldblatt's *The Marx Brothers at the Movies* (New York, 1968) has very little in the way of interest or ideas. Focusing on an entirely different type of motion picture, Robert Snyder's *Pare Lorentz and the Documentary Film* (Norman, Oklahoma, 1968) describes Lorentz's working habits and his endless negotiations with the federal government, but not what he ultimately put on the screen. Finally, some of the literature on *Citizen Kane* has approached the quality of the film itself. Pauline Kael's "Raising Kane: I and II," *The New Yorker*, XLVII (February 20 and 27, 1971), 43–89 and 44–81, is rapidly becoming the most famous essay this enormously intelligent critic has ever written; nevertheless, while the piece is absolutely crucial to an understanding of the whole Hollywood culture in the 1930s (especially the values and motivations of the screenwriters), it reveals very little about the finished movie. For this, one should turn to Ronald Gottesman, ed., *Focus on Citizen Kane* (Englewood Cliffs, New Jersey, 1971), as good a collection of essays on a single motion picture as has ever been compiled.

In the end, however, there is no substitute for seeing the movies themselves.

VIII. THE POPULAR FRONT AND THE DESCENT INTO WAR

The late 1930s is rich in source material on the mentality of the Popular Front. For this study, the most essential books are Gilbert Seldes's *Mainland* (New York, 1936); Max Lerner's *It is Later Than You Think* (New York, 1938), *Ideas Are Weapons* (New York, 1939), and *Ideas for the Ice Age* (New York, 1941); Archibald MacLeish's *A Time to Speak* (Cambridge, Massachusetts, 1940); Harold Stearns, ed., *America Now* (New York, 1938); and Henry Hart, ed., *The Writer in a Changing World* (New York, 1937), which collects the papers and speeches of the Second Writers' Congress. In addition, the reader should consult Carl Sandburg's epic poem *The People, Yes* (New York, 1936); George Counts's endorsement of liberal politics in *The Prospects for Democracy* (New York, 1937); Granville Hicks's patriotic celebration of his native land in *I Like America* (New York, 1938); Michael Gold's militant defense of social commitment and his assault on those who had defected from the Communist party in *The Hollow Men* (New York, 1941); and Constance Rourke's sensitive exploration of America's forgotten past in *The Roots of American Culture* (New York, 1942). For the growing fascination with symbols and myths, see Harold Lasswell's *The Psychopathology of Politics* (Chicago, 1930) and *Politics: Who Gets What, When, How* (New York, 1936); Thurman Arnold's *The Symbols of Government* (New York, 1935) and *The Folklore of Capitalism* (New Haven, Connecticut, 1937); as well as the collection of essays in Malcolm Cowley and Bernard Smith, eds., *Books That Changed Our Minds* (New York, 1939). For examples of the renewed attraction to concepts of tragedy and original sin at the close of the decade, see Lewis Mumford's *Men Must Act* (New York, 1939) and *Faith for Living* (New York, 1940), as well as Reinhold Niebuhr's *Christianity and Power Politics* (New York, 1940).

The opponents of the Popular Front were equally articulate. The attack on its consequences for literature and the intellectual are set forth in James Farrell's *A Note on Literary Criticism* (New York, 1936); Edmund Wilson's series of typically provocative essays on American and European writers (past and present) in *The Triple Thinkers* (New York, 1938) and *The Wound and the Bow* (Boston, 1941); Henry Miller's *The Cosmological Eye* (Norfolk, Connecticut, 1939) and *The Wisdom of the Heart* (Norfolk, Connecticut, 1941); and Alfred Kazin's *On Native Grounds* (New York, 1942), which remains, among other virtues, one of the most sensitive and thoughtful critiques of twentieth-century American literature ever written. The gradual disenchantment with Marxism and the rediscovery of the liberal tradition is best reflected in Edmund Wilson's *To the Finland Station* (New York, 1940); John Dewey's *Freedom and Culture* (New York, 1939); Sidney Hook's *Reason, Social Myths, and Democracy* (New York, 1940); James Burnham's *The Managerial Revolution* (New York, 1941); John Chamberlain's *The American Stakes* (New York, 1940) and *The Broker State* (New York, 1940); and the collection of essays in Irving Talmadge, ed., *Whose Revolution?* (New York, 1941).

Among secondary accounts of intellectual life in the late 1930s, three books are especially important: Frank Warren's *Liberals and Communism* (Bloomington, Indiana, 1966), which, in addition to surveying the decade-long relationships between independent writers and the Communist party, has an excellent chapter on the anti-intellectual values of the Popular Front; James Gilbert's *Writers and Partisans* (New York, 1968), which provides a detailed if not sufficiently interpretative history of *Partisan Review;* and Norman Podhoretz's autobiography, *Making It* (New York, 1967), which, though it concentrates on postwar culture, still reveals brilliantly the moods and aspirations of the Jewish intelligentsia as they moved from alienation to acceptance. For evaluations of more specific developments during the waning years of the depression, the reader should consult Arthur Murphy, "Ideals and Ideologies, 1917–1947," *Philosophical Review,* LVI (July 1947), 374–89, which discusses the transition from a concern for ideas as rational explanations of external events to their use as weapons and myths in manipulating mass emotions; Clement Greenberg, "The Late Thirties in New York," in *Art and Culture: Critical Essays* (Boston, 1961), 230–35, which argues that radical painters were more interested in aesthetic experimentation and abstract art than in political reform and social realism; Norman Holmes Pearson, "The Nazi–Soviet Pact and the End of a Dream," in Daniel Aaron, ed., *America in Crisis* (New York, 1952), 327–48, which recounts the story of the Popular Front's demise; Leslie Fiedler, *"Partisan Review:* Phoenix or Dodo?"in *Perspectives U.S.A.,* XV (Spring 1956), 83–97, which traces the retreat from political (if not cultural) radicalism among the anti-Stalinist intellectuals; and William Phillips, "What Happened in the 1930s," *Commentary,* XXXIV (September 1962), 204–12, a general defense of *Partisan Review*'s continuing insistence that cultural concerns be separated from those of politics and that the intellectual act as a moral critic rather than as a spokesman for the people or their government.

INDEX